S0-ABU-042

Microsoft

PowerPoint 2002

Comprehensive Concepts and Techniques

Gary B. Shelly
Thomas J. Cashman
Susan L. Sebok

THOMSON
COURSE TECHNOLOGY

COURSE TECHNOLOGY
25 THOMSON PLACE
BOSTON MA 02210

SHELLY
CASHMAN
SERIES®

Australia • Canada • Denmark • Japan • Mexico • New Zealand • Philippines • Puerto Rico • Singapore
South Africa • Spain • United Kingdom • United States

THOMSON

COURSE TECHNOLOGY

COPYRIGHT © 2002 Course Technology, a division of Thomson Learning.
Printed in the United States of America

Asia (excluding Japan)
Thomson Learning
5 Shenton Way #01-01
UIC Building
Singapore 068808

Latin America
Thomson Learning
Seneca, 53
Colonia Polanco
11560 Mexico D.F. Mexico

Canada
Nelson/Thomson Learning
1120 Birchmount Road
Scarborough, Ontario
Canada M1K 5G4

Japan
Thomson Learning
Nihonjisyo Brooks Bldg 3-F
1-4-1 Kudankita, Chiyoda-Ku
Tokyo 102-0073 Japan

South Africa
Thomson Learning
15 Brookwood Street
P.O. Box 1722
Soverset West 7120
South Africa

UK/Europe/Middle East
Thomson Learning
Berkshire House
168-173 High Holborn
London, WC1V 7AA United Kingdom

Australia/New Zealand
Nelson/Thomson Learning
102 Dodds Street
South Melbourne, Victoria 3205
Australia

Spain
Thomson Learning
Calle Magallanes, 25
28015-MADRID
ESPANA

Course Technology, the Course Technology logo, the SHELLY CASHMAN SERIES®, and **Custom Edition**® are registered trademarks used under license. All other names used herein are for identification purposes only and are trademarks of their respective owners.

For more information, contact Course Technology, 25 Thomson Place, Boston, MA 02210.

Or visit our Internet site at www.course.com

All rights reserved. No part of this work covered by the copyright hereon may be reproduced or used in any form or by any means without the written permission of the publisher.

For permission to use material from this product, contact us by
• Tel (800) 730-2214
• Fax (800) 730-2215
• www.thomsonrights.com

Course Technology reserves the right to revise this publication and make changes from time to time in its content without notice.

APPROVED COURSEWARE

"Microsoft and the Microsoft Office User Specialist Logo are registered trademarks of Microsoft Corporation in the United States and other countries. Course Technology is an independent entity from Microsoft Corporation, and not affiliated with Microsoft Corporation in any manner. This textbook may be used in assisting students to prepare for a Microsoft Office User Specialist Exam. Neither Microsoft Corporation, its designated review company, nor Course Technology warrants that use of this textbook will ensure passing the relevant Exam.

"Use of the Microsoft Office User Specialist Approved Courseware Logo on this product signifies that it has been independently reviewed and approved in complying with the following standards: 'Acceptable coverage of all content related to the Microsoft Office Exam entitled "Microsoft PowerPoint 2002 Comprehensive Exam," and sufficient performance-based exercises that relate closely to all required content, based on sampling of text.'"

PHOTO CREDITS: Microsoft PowerPoint 2002 *Project 1, pages PP 1.04-05* Business people, cell phone, circuit boards and gears, fiber optic cable, notebook computer, number printout, telephone jack, utility wires and towers, world on computer screen, Courtesy of PhotoDisc, Inc.; *Project 2, pages PP 2.02-03* Conference room meeting, office meeting, three businesspeople, woman in taxi, woman speaking at a meeting, Courtesy of PhotoDisc, Inc.; *Project 3, pages PP 3.02-03* Marble background, film strip, drama masks, Courtesy of ArtToday; Bill Gates, Courtesy of Microsoft; Business meeting, man lecturing, business presentation, row of business people; Courtesy of PhotoDisc; *Project 4, pages pp 4.02-03* background art, mouse, two business meetings, man and woman reviewing documents, Courtesy of PhotoDisc.; *Project 5, pages PP 5.02-03* Hands typing on keyboard, monitor cable image, Courtesy of PhotoDisc, Inc.; background image, business people working, woman talking on telephone, Courtesy of Dynamic Graphics, Inc.; *Project 6, pages PP 6.02-03* Margi Presenter-to-Go™ Courtesy of MARGI SYSTEMS, INC.

ISBN 0-7895-6285-5

4 5 6 7 8 9 10   BC   06 05 04 03

Microsoft
PowerPoint 2002
Comprehensive Concepts and Techniques

Contents

4   PROJECT FOUR

MODIFYING VISUAL ELEMENTS AND PRESENTATION FORMATS

■   WEB FEATURE

DELIVERING PRESENTATIONS TO AND COLLABORATING WITH WORKGROUPS

Preface

The Shelly Cashman Series® offers the finest textbooks in computer education. We are proud of the fact that our series of Microsoft Office 4.3, Microsoft Office 95, Microsoft Office 97, and Microsoft Office 2000 textbooks have been the most widely used books in education. With each new edition of our Office books, we have made improvements based on the software and comments made by the instructors and students who use our textbooks. The *Microsoft Office XP* books continue with the innovation, quality, and reliability that you have come to expect from the Shelly Cashman Series.

Office XP is the most significant upgrade ever to the Office suite. It provides a much smarter work experience for users. Microsoft has enhanced Office XP in the following areas: (1) streamlined user interface; (2) smart tags and task panes to help simplify the way people work; (3) speech and handwriting recognition; (4) an improved Help system; (5) enhanced Web capabilities; and (6) application-specific features. Each one of these enhancements is part of Microsoft PowerPoint 2002 and is discussed in detail.

In this *Microsoft PowerPoint 2002* book, you will find an educationally sound and easy-to-follow pedagogy that combines a step-by-step approach with corresponding screens. All projects and exercises in this book are designed to take full advantage of the PowerPoint 2002 enhancements. The popular Other Ways and More About features offer in-depth knowledge of PowerPoint 2002. The new Learn It Online page presents a wealth of additional exercises to ensure your students have all the reinforcement they need. The project openers provide a fascinating perspective of the subject covered in the project. The project material is developed carefully to ensure that students will see the importance of learning PowerPoint for future coursework.

Objectives of This Textbook

Microsoft PowerPoint 2002: Comprehensive Concepts and Techniques is intended for a two- to three-unit course that presents in-depth coverage of PowerPoint 2002. No experience with a computer is assumed, and no mathematics beyond the high school freshman level is required. The objectives of this book are:

- To teach the fundamentals of PowerPoint 2002
- To expose students to practical examples of the computer as a useful tool
- To acquaint students with the proper procedures to create presentations suitable for coursework, professional purposes, and personal use
- To help students discover the underlying functionality of PowerPoint 2002 so they can become more productive
- To develop an exercise-oriented approach that allows learning by doing
- To introduce students to new input technologies
- To encourage independent study, and help those who are working alone
- To assist students preparing to take the Microsoft Office User Specialist examination for the Microsoft PowerPoint 2002 Comprehensive level.

Approved by Microsoft as Courseware for the Microsoft Office User Specialist Program Comprehensive Level

Microsoft PowerPoint 2002: Comprehensive Concepts and Techniques has been approved by Microsoft as courseware for the Microsoft Office User Specialist (MOUS) program. After completing the first four projects, the first two Web features, and the corresponding exercises in this book, students will be prepared to take the Comprehensive-level Microsoft Office User Specialist Exam for Microsoft PowerPoint 2002. See Appendix E for additional information on the MOUS program and for a Comprehensive-level table that includes the PowerPoint 2002 MOUS skill sets and corresponding page numbers on which a skill is discussed and practiced in the book, or visit the Web site mous.net.

By passing the certification exam for a Microsoft software program, students demonstrate their proficiency in that program to employers. This exam is offered at participating centers, participating corporations, and participating employment agencies. To purchase a Microsoft Office User Specialist certification exam, visit certiport.com.

The Shelly Cashman Series Microsoft Office User Specialist Center Web page (Figure 1) has more than fifteen Web pages you can visit to obtain additional information on the MOUS Certification program. The Web page scsite.com/offxp/cert.htm includes links to general information on certification, choosing an application for certification, preparing for the certification exam, and taking and passing the certification exam.

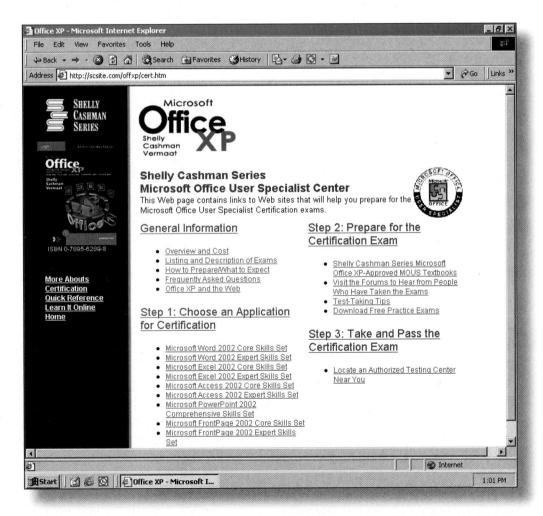

FIGURE 1   The Shelly Cashman Series Microsoft Office User Specialist Center Web Page

Other Ways

1. Right-click AutoShape, Click
   Custom Animation on
   shortcut menu, click Add
   Effect button
2. Press ALT+D, press M
3. In Voice Command mode,
   say "Slide Show, Custom
   Animation, Add Effect,
   Entrance"

More About

Customizing the VBA Appearance

To customize the appearance
of VBA code, click Tools on
the VBA menu bar, click
Options, and then click the
Editor Format tab. You can
specify the foreground and
background colors used for
different types of text, such as
Comments Text and Syntax
Error Text. You also can
change the font and font size.

The Shelly Cashman Approach

Features of the Shelly Cashman Series *Microsoft PowerPoint 2002* books include:

- **Project Orientation:** Each project in the book presents a practical problem and complete solution in an easy-to-understand approach.
- **Step-by-Step, Screen-by-Screen Instructions:** Each of the tasks required to complete a project is identified throughout the development of the project. Full-color screens accompany the steps.
- **Thoroughly Tested Projects:** Every screen in the book is correct because it is produced by the author only after performing a step, resulting in unprecedented quality.
- **Other Ways Boxes and Quick Reference Summary:** PowerPoint 2002 provides a variety of ways to carry out a given task. The Other Ways boxes displayed at the end of most of the step-by-step sequences specify the other ways to do the task completed in the steps. Thus, the steps and the Other Ways box make a comprehensive reference unit. A Quick Reference Summary that summarizes the way specific tasks can be completed can be found at the back of this book and on the Web at scsite.com/offxp/qr.htm.
- **More About Feature:** These marginal annotations provide background information and tips that complement the topics covered, adding depth and perspective.
- **Integration of the World Wide Web:** The World Wide Web is integrated into the PowerPoint 2002 learning experience by (1) More About annotations that send students to Web sites for up-to-date information and alternative approaches to tasks; (2) a MOUS information Web page and a MOUS map Web page so students can better prepare for the Microsoft Office Use Specialist (MOUS) Certification examination; (3) a PowerPoint 2002 Quick Reference Summary Web page that summarizes the ways to complete tasks (mouse, menu, shortcut menu, and keyboard); and (4) the Learn It Online page at the end of each project, which has project reinforcement exercises, learning games, and other types of student activities.

Organization of This Textbook

Microsoft PowerPoint 2002: Comprehensive Concepts and Techniques provides basic instruction on how to use PowerPoint 2002. The material is divided into six projects, three Web Features, five appendices, and a Quick Reference Summary.

Project 1 – Using a Design Template and Text Slide Layout to Create a Presentation
In Project 1, students are introduced to PowerPoint terminology, the PowerPoint window, and the basics of creating a bulleted list presentation. Topics include choosing a design template by using a task pane; creating a title slide and text slides; changing the font size and font style; ending a slide show with a black slide; saving a presentation; viewing the slides in a presentation; checking a presentation for spelling errors; printing copies of the slides; and using the PowerPoint Help system.

Project 2 – Using the Outline Tab and Clip Art to Create a Slide Show In Project 2, students create a presentation from an outline, insert clip art, and add animation effects. Topics include creating a slide presentation by indenting paragraphs on the Outline tab; changing slide layouts; inserting clip art; changing clip art size; adding an animation scheme; animating clip art; running an animated slide show; printing audience handouts from an outline; and e-mailing a slide show from within PowerPoint.

Web Feature – Creating a Presentation on the Web Using PowerPoint In this Web Feature, students are introduced to saving a presentation as a Web page. Topics include saving an existing PowerPoint presentation as an HTML file; viewing the presentation as a Web page; editing a Web page through a browser; and viewing the editing changes.

Project 3 – Using Visuals to Enhance a Slide Show In Project 3, students create a presentation from a Microsoft Word outline and then enhance it with visuals. Topics include modifying clips; customizing bullets using the slide master; inserting and formatting a table; creating and formatting an organization chart; applying a new design template to a single slide; rearranging slides; adding animation schemes to selected slides; and printing slides as handouts.

Project 4 – Modifying Visual Elements and Presentation Formats In Project 4, students create a presentation using the AutoContent Wizard and customize this slide show. Topics include adding a graphical heading using WordArt; modifying the presentation template by changing the color scheme; adding information to the slide master footer; creating a slide background using a picture; adding data from other sources, including an Excel chart and a Word table; adding hyperlinks and sound effects; and printing speaker notes and comments pages.

Web Feature – Delivering Presentations to and Collaborating with Workgroups In this Web Feature, students learn to use the Pack and Go Wizard to condense files. Topics include setting up a review cycle; reviewing presentation comments; and scheduling and delivering presentation broadcasts. A discussion of the PowerPoint Viewer also is included.

Project 5 – Working with Macros and Visual Basic for Applications (VBA) In Project 5, students use VBA to develop an electronic career portfolio designed for viewing during a job interview. The slides are customized for each interview and include a digital picture and a video clip. Topics include creating a new toolbar and adding buttons; using the macro recorder to create a macro that prints a pure black and white handout displaying four slides per page; assigning the macro to a command on the File menu; and creating a user interface.

Project 6 – Creating a Self-Running Presentation Containing Interactive Documents In Project 6, students create a self-running presentation to view at a kiosk. The slides contain action buttons and hyperlinks to a Visual Basic program, an Excel chart, and a Word table. Topics include inserting a slide from another presentation; applying custom animation; using guides to position objects; setting slide timings manually; and inserting, formatting, and animating a diagram and an AutoShape.

Web Feature – Importing Clips and Templates from the Microsoft Web Site In this Web Feature, students are introduced to downloading clips and design templates from a source on the Internet and adding them to a presentation. Topics include connecting to the Microsoft Web site; searching for and downloading clips and templates; and importing clips into a presentation.

Appendices The book includes five appendices. Appendix A presents an introduction to the Microsoft PowerPoint Help system. Appendix B describes how to use the speech and handwriting recognition capabilities of PowerPoint 2002. Appendix C explains how to publish Web pages to a Web server. Appendix D shows how to reset the menus and toolbars. Appendix E introduces students to the Microsoft Office User Specialist (MOUS) Certification program.

Quick Reference Summary This book concludes with a detailed Quick Reference Summary. In Microsoft PowerPoint 2002, you can accomplish a task in a number of ways, such as using the mouse, menu, shortcut menu, and keyboard. The Quick Reference Summary provides a quick reference to each task presented in this book.

End-of-Project Student Activities

A notable strength of the Shelly Cashman Series *Microsoft PowerPoint 2002* books is the extensive student activities at the end of each project. Well-structured student activities can make the difference between students merely participating in a class and students retaining the information they learn. The activities in the Shelly Cashman Series *Microsoft PowerPoint 2002* books include the following.

- ■ **What You Should Know** A listing of the tasks completed within a project together with the pages on which the step-by-step, screen-by-screen explanations appear. This section provides a perfect study review for students.
- ■ **Learn It Online** Every project features a Learn It Online page comprised of ten exercises. These exercises utilize the Web to offer project-related reinforcement activities that will help students gain confidence in their PowerPoint 2002 abilities. These exercises include True/False, Multiple Choice, Short Answer, Flash Cards, Practice Test, Learning Games, Tips and Tricks, Newsgroup usage, Expanding Your Horizons, and Search Sleuth.

- ■ **Apply Your Knowledge** This exercise usually requires students to open and manipulate a file on the Data Disk. To obtain a copy of the Data Disk, follow the instructions on the inside back cover of this textbook.
- ■ **In the Lab** Three in-depth assignments per project require students to apply the knowledge gained in the project to solve problems on a computer.
- ■ **Cases and Places** Up to seven unique case studies that require students to apply their knowledge to real-world situations.

Shelly Cashman Series Teaching Tools

The three basic ancillaries that accompany this textbook are: Teaching Tools (ISBN 0-7895-6323-1), Course Presenter (ISBN 0-7895-6466-1), and MyCourse.com. These ancillaries are available to adopters through your Course Technology representative or by calling one of the following telephone numbers: Colleges and Universities, 1-800-648-7450; High Schools, 1-800-824-5179; Private Career Colleges, 1-800-477-3692; Canada, 1-800-268-2222; and Corporations and Government Agencies, 1-800-340-7450.

Teaching Tools

The Teaching Tools for this textbook include both teaching and testing aids. The contents of the Teaching Tools CD-ROM are listed below.

- ■ **Instructor's Manual** The Instructor's Manual is made up of Microsoft Word files. The files include lecture notes, solutions to laboratory assignments, and a large test bank. The files allow you to modify the lecture notes or generate quizzes and exams from the test bank using your own Word processing software. Where appropriate, solutions to laboratory assignments are embedded as icons in the files. When an icon appears, double-click it and the application will start and the solution will display on the screen. The Instructor's Manual includes the following for each project: project objectives; project overview; detailed lesson plans with page number references; teacher notes and activities; answers to the end-of-project exercises; a test bank of 110 questions for every project (25 multiple-choice, 50 true/false, and 35 fill-in-the-blank) with page number references; and transparency references. The transparencies are available through the Figures in the Book. The test bank questions are the same as in ExamView and Course Test Manager. Thus, you can print a copy of the project test bank and use the printout to select your questions in ExamView or Course Test Manager.

- **Figures in the Book** Illustrations for every screen and table in the textbook are available in electronic form. Use this ancillary to present a slide show in lecture or to print transparencies for use in lecture with an overhead projector. If you have a personal computer and LCD device, this ancillary can be an effective tool for presenting lectures.

- **ExamView** ExamView is a state-of-the-art test builder that is easy to use. ExamView enables you to create quickly printed tests, Internet tests, and computer (LAN-based) tests. You can enter your own test questions or use the test bank that accompanies ExamView. The test bank is the same as the one described in the Instructor's Manual section. Instructors who want to continue to use our earlier generation test builder, Course Test Manager, rather than ExamView, can call Customer Service at 1-800-648-7450 for a copy of the Course Test Manager database for this book.

- **Course Syllabus** Any instructor who has been assigned a course at the last minute knows how difficult it is to come up with a course syllabus. For this reason, sample syllabi are included that can be customized easily to a course.

- **Lecture Success System** Lecture Success System files are for use with the application software, a personal computer, and projection device to explain and illustrate the step-by-step, screen-by-screen development of a project in the textbook without entering large amounts of data.

- **Instructor's Lab Solutions** Solutions and required files for all the In the Lab assignments at the end of each project are available. Solutions also are available for any Cases and Places assignment that supplies data.

- **Lab Tests/Test Outs** Tests that parallel the In the Lab assignments are supplied for the purpose of testing students in the laboratory on the material covered in the project or testing students out of the course.

- **Project Reinforcement** True/false, multiple choice, and short answer questions help students gain confidence.

- **Student Files** All the files that are required by students to complete the Apply Your Knowledge exercises are included.

- **Interactive Labs** Eighteen completely updated, hands-on Interactive Labs that take students from ten to fifteen minutes each to step through help solidify and reinforce mouse and keyboard usage and computer concepts. Student assessment is available.

Course Presenter

Course Presenter is a CD-ROM-based multimedia lecture presentation system that provides PowerPoint slides for each project. Presentations are based on the projects' objectives. Use this presentation system to present well-organized lectures that are both interesting and knowledge-based. Course Presenter provides consistent coverage at schools that use multiple lecturers in their applications courses.

MyCourse 2.0

MyCourse 2.0 offers instructors and students an opportunity to supplement classroom learning with additional course content. You can use MyCourse 2.0 to expand on traditional learning by accessing and completing readings, tests, and other assignments through the customized, comprehensive Web site. For additional information, visit mycourse.com and click the Help button.

SAM XP

SAM XP is a powerful skills-based testing and reporting tool that measures your students' proficiency in Microsoft Office applications through real-world, performance-based questions. SAM XP is available for a minimal cost.

TOM, Training Online Manager for Microsoft Office XP

TOM is Course Technology's MOUS-approved training tool for Microsoft Office XP. Available via the World Wide Web and CD-ROM, TOM allows students to actively learn Office XP concepts and skills by delivering realistic practice through both guided and self-directed simulated instruction.

Acknowledgments

The Shelly Cashman Series would not be the leading computer education series without the contributions of outstanding publishing professionals. First, and foremost, among them is Becky Herrington, director of production and designer. She is the heart and soul of the Shelly Cashman Series, and it is only through her leadership, dedication, and tireless efforts that superior products are made possible.

Under Becky's direction, the following individuals made significant contributions to these books: Doug Cowley, production manager; Ginny Harvey, series specialist and developmental editor; Ken Russo, senior Web and graphic designer; Mike Bodnar, associate production manager; Mark Norton, technical analyst; Betty Hopkins and Richard Herrera, interior design; Michelle French, Christy Otten, Kellee LaVars, Stephanie Nance, Chris Schneider, Sharon Lee Nelson, Sarah Boger, Amanda Lotter, Michael Greco, and Ryan Ung, graphic artists; Jeanne Black and Betty Hopkins, QuarkXPress compositors; Lyn Markowicz, Nancy Lamm, Kim Kosmatka, Pam Baxter, Eva Kandarpa, Ellana Russo, and Marilyn Martin, copy editors/proofreaders; Cristina Haley, proofreader/ indexer; Sarah Evertson of Image Quest, photo researcher; Ginny Harvey, Rich Hansberger, Kim Clark, and Nancy Smith, contributing writers; and Richard Herrera, cover art.

Finally, we would like to thank Richard Keaveny, associate publisher; Cheryl Ouellette, managing editor; Jim Quasney, series consulting editor; Alexandra Arnold, product manager; Erin Runyon, associate product manager; Francis Schurgot and Marc Ouellette, Web product managers; Rachel VanKirk, marketing manager; and Reed Cotter, editorial assistant.

Gary B. Shelly
Thomas J. Cashman
Susan L. Sebok

Shelly Cashman Series – Traditionally Bound Textbooks

The Shelly Cashman Series presents the following computer subjects in a variety of traditionally bound textbooks. For more information, see your Course Technology representative or call 1-800-648-7450. For Shelly Cashman Series information, visit Shelly Cashman Online at **scseries.com**

COMPUTERS	
Computers	Discovering Computers 2002: Concepts for a Digital World, Web Enhanced, Complete Edition
	Discovering Computers 2002: Concepts for a Digital World, Web Enhanced, Introductory Edition
	Discovering Computers 2002: Concepts for a Digital World, Web Enhanced, Brief Edition
	Teachers Discovering Computers: Integrating Technology in the Classroom 2e
	Exploring Computers: A Record of Discovery 4e
	Study Guide for Discovering Computers 2002: Concepts for a Digital World, Web Enhanced
	Essential Introduction to Computers 4e (32-page)

WINDOWS APPLICATIONS	
Microsoft Office	Microsoft Office XP: Essential Concepts and Techniques (5 projects)
	Microsoft Office XP: Brief Concepts and Techniques (9 projects)
	Microsoft Office XP: Introductory Concepts and Techniques (15 projects)
	Microsoft Office XP: Advanced Concepts and Techniques (11 projects)
	Microsoft Office XP: Post Advanced Concepts and Techniques (11 projects)
	Microsoft Office 2000: Essential Concepts and Techniques (5 projects)
	Microsoft Office 2000: Brief Concepts and Techniques (9 projects)
	Microsoft Office 2000: Introductory Concepts and Techniques, Enhanced Edition (15 projects)
	Microsoft Office 2000: Advanced Concepts and Techniques (11 projects)
	Microsoft Office 2000: Post Advanced Concepts and Techniques (11 projects)
Integration	Integrating Microsoft Office XP Applications and the World Wide Web: Essential Concepts and Techniques
PIM	Microsoft Outlook 2002: Essential Concepts and Techniques
Microsoft Works	Microsoft Works 6: Complete Concepts and Techniques[1] • Microsoft Works 2000: Complete Concepts and Techniques[1] • Microsoft Works 4.5[1]
Microsoft Windows	Microsoft Windows 2000: Complete Concepts and Techniques (6 projects)[2]
	Microsoft Windows 2000: Brief Concepts and Techniques (2 projects)
	Microsoft Windows 98: Essential Concepts and Techniques (2 projects)
	Microsoft Windows 98: Complete Concepts and Techniques (6 projects)[2]
	Introduction to Microsoft Windows NT Workstation 4
	Microsoft Windows 95: Complete Concepts and Techniques[1]
Word Processing	Microsoft Word 2002[2] • Microsoft Word 2000[2] • Microsoft Word 97[1] • Microsoft Word 7[1]
Spreadsheets	Microsoft Excel 2002[2] • Microsoft Excel 2000[2] • Microsoft Excel 97[1] • Microsoft Excel 7[1] • Microsoft Excel 5[1]
Database	Microsoft Access 2002[2] • Microsoft Access 2000[2] • Microsoft Access 97[1] • Microsoft Access 7[1]
Presentation Graphics	Microsoft PowerPoint 2002[2] • Microsoft PowerPoint 2000[2] • Microsoft PowerPoint 97[1] • Microsoft PowerPoint 7[1]
Desktop Publishing	Microsoft Publisher 2002[1] • Microsoft Publisher 2000[1]

PROGRAMMING	
Programming	Microsoft Visual Basic 6: Complete Concepts and Techniques[1] • Programming in QBasic
	Java Programming: Complete Concepts and Techniques[1] • Structured COBOL Programming 2e

INTERNET	
Browser	Microsoft Internet Explorer 5: An Introduction • Microsoft Internet Explorer 4: An Introduction
	Netscape Navigator 6: An Introduction • Netscape Navigator 4: An Introduction
Web Page Creation and Design	Web Design: Introductory Concepts and Techniques • HTML: Complete Concepts and Techniques[1]
	Microsoft FrontPage 2002: Essential Concepts and Techniques • Microsoft FrontPage 2002[2]
	Microsoft FrontPage 2000[1] • JavaScript: Complete Concepts and Techniques[1]

SYSTEMS ANALYSIS	
Systems Analysis	Systems Analysis and Design 4e

DATA COMMUNICATIONS	
Data Communications	Business Data Communications: Introductory Concepts and Techniques 3e

[1]Also available as an Introductory Edition, which is a shortened version of the complete book
[2]Also available as an Introductory Edition, which is a shortened version of the complete book and also as a Comprehensive Edition, which is an extended version of the complete book

2002

Microsoft
POWERPOINT

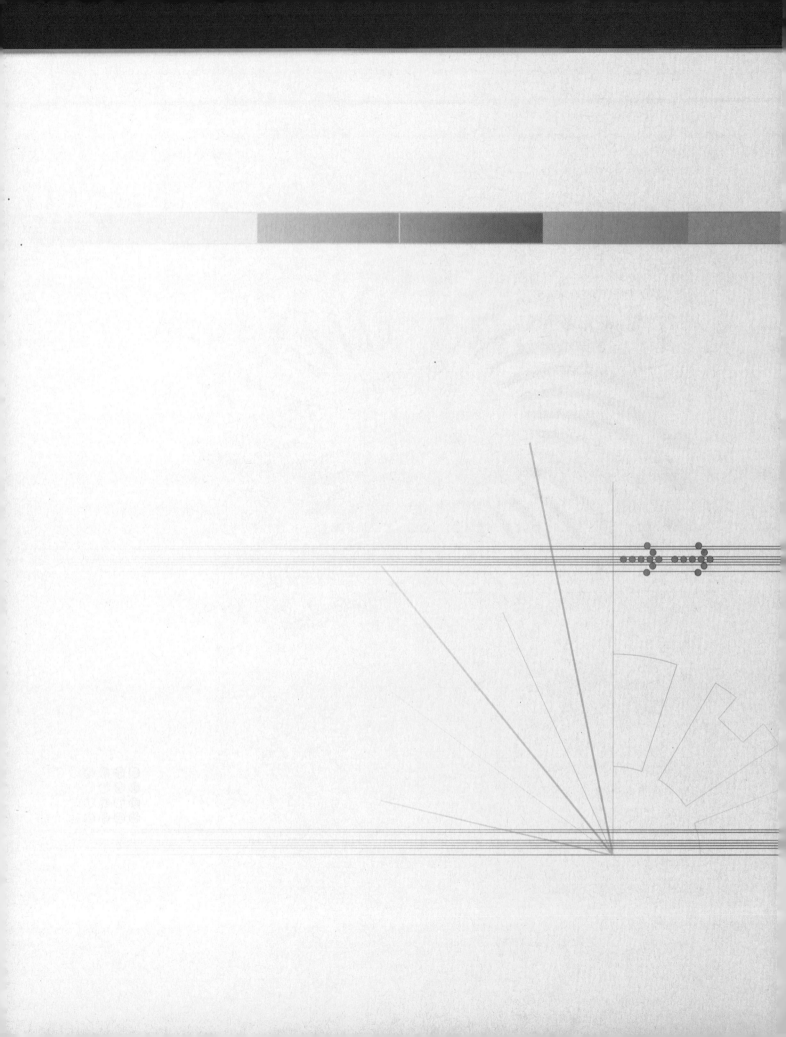

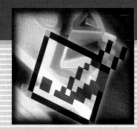

Microsoft PowerPoint 2002

PROJECT

1

Using a Design Template and Text Slide Layout to Create a Presentation

You will have mastered the material in this project when you can:

O B J E C T I V E S

- Start and customize PowerPoint
- Describe the PowerPoint window
- Describe the speech recognition capabilities of PowerPoint
- Select a design template
- Create a title slide
- Change the font size and font style
- Save a presentation
- Add a new slide
- Create a text slide with a single-level bulleted list
- Create a text slide with a multi-level bulleted list
- End a slide show with a black slide
- Move to another slide in normal view
- View a presentation in slide show view
- Quit PowerPoint
- Open a presentation
- Check spelling and consistency, correct errors, and edit a presentation
- Display a presentation in black and white
- Print a presentation in black and white
- Use the PowerPoint Help system to answer your questions

COMDEX Glitz

Presentations Dazzle the Masses

Thousands of the world's computer industry executives attend, including keynote speakers, Bill Gates, Andy Grove, and Michael Dell. They are joined by hundreds of thousands of technology enthusiasts, industry professionals, and curious spectators seeking the latest trends in hardware, software, and the Internet, as well as the hottest new gizmos, gadgets, and games.

They will be attending COMDEX, North America's largest trade show. COMDEX/Fall is held in Las Vegas each November, and COMDEX/Spring is held in Chicago in April. Both shows feature speeches by industry leaders, tutorials on the latest technologies, and thousands of square feet of exhibits showcasing the latest in computer technology.

Information technology (IT) experts headline COMDEX as the premier IT event in the world. Indeed, more than 10,000 new products are unveiled at the Fall show. Since COMDEX's inception in 1979, some of the more notable product launches have been the IBM PC in 1981, COMPAQ's suitcase-sized portable computer, Microsoft's first version of Windows, Apple's original Macintosh computer, and CD-ROM drives, and the promise of wireless technology utilizing the Bluetooth™ standard.

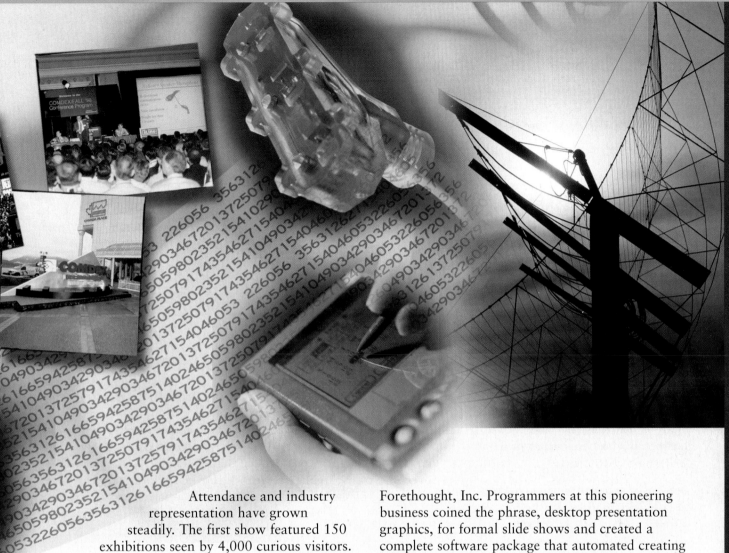

Attendance and industry representation have grown steadily. The first show featured 150 exhibitions seen by 4,000 curious visitors. Six years later, more than 1,000 companies displayed their wares for more than 100,000 techies. Recent shows have produced as many as 2,400 booths visited by 250,000-plus attendees.

Computer companies realize their sales forces need to capture their audiences' attention, so they add sensory cues to their exhibits. They treat the trade show visitors to a multimedia blitz of sound, visuals, and action with the help of presentation software such as Microsoft PowerPoint 2002. This program enhances the presenters' speeches by highlighting keywords in the presentation, displaying graphs, pictures, and diagrams, and playing sound and video clips.

In this project, you will learn to use PowerPoint 2002 to create a presentation (also called a slide show) for a Westview College counselors' orientation using a design template and one of PowerPoint's layouts. Then, you will run the slide show and print audience handouts.

PowerPoint's roots stem from the innovative work performed by a small company called Forethought, Inc. Programmers at this pioneering business coined the phrase, desktop presentation graphics, for formal slide shows and created a complete software package that automated creating slides containing text, charts, and graphics. Microsoft liked the visual appeal of the software and acquired Forethought in 1987. Company executives decided to market the software to Apple Macintosh users because Mac computers were considered clearly superior to IBM-based personal computers for graphics applications.

Microsoft PowerPoint became a favorite among Mac users. Meanwhile, Lotus Freelance Graphics and Software Publishing Harvard Graphics were popular within the PC community. This division ceased, however, when Microsoft released Windows 3.0 in 1990 and subsequently developed a Windows version of PowerPoint to run on PCs.

Since that time, Macintosh and PC users alike have utilized the presentation power of PowerPoint. The package has grown to include animation, audio and video clips, and Internet integration. Certainly the technology gurus at COMDEX have realized PowerPoint's dazzling visual appeal. So will you as you complete the exercises in this textbook.

Microsoft PowerPoint 2002

Using a Design Template and Text Slide Layout to Create a Presentation

PROJECT 1

C A S E   P E R S P E C T I V E

As a receptionist in your college's counseling office, you meet students who are waiting for their scheduled appointments. You have noticed that many of them seem sad. They sit silently and do not make eye contact or speak with their fellow students.

Because of your concern, you mention this observation to Jennifer Williams, the dean of counseling. She tells you that most college students are lonely. In fact, a Carnegie study finds that only 36 percent of college students participate in student activities other than sports. Consequently, they are self-absorbed and miss the joys of college. She says that Intro to Loneliness would be one class that would fill quickly because loneliness is one of college students' worst enemies. Many of these students do not adjust well to the initial move from home, which makes it difficult for them to meet new people and make friends. Therefore, they play it safe and stay by themselves.

You suggest that counselors discuss this loneliness at freshmen orientation, and Jennifer agrees. She knows you are proficient at PowerPoint and asks you to develop a presentation focusing on how to make friends on campus.

What Is Microsoft PowerPoint?

Microsoft PowerPoint is a complete presentation graphics program that allows you to produce professional looking presentations. A PowerPoint **presentation** also is called a **slide show**. PowerPoint gives you the flexibility to make presentations using a projection device attached to a personal computer (Figure 1-1a) and using overhead transparencies (Figure 1-1b). In addition, you can take advantage of the World Wide Web and run virtual presentations on the Internet (Figure 1-1c). PowerPoint also can create paper printouts of the individual slides, outlines, and speaker notes.

PowerPoint contains several features to simplify creating a slide show. For example, you can instruct PowerPoint to create a predesigned presentation, and then you can modify the presentation to fulfill your requirements. You quickly can format a slide show using one of the professionally designed presentation design templates. To make your presentation more impressive, you can add tables, charts, pictures, video, sound, and animation effects. You also can check the spelling or style of your slide show as you type or after you have completed designing the presentation. For example, you can instruct PowerPoint to restrict the number of bulleted items on a slide or limit the number of words in each paragraph. Additional PowerPoint features include the following:

- ▶ **Word processing** — create bulleted lists, combine words and images, find and replace text, and use multiple fonts and type sizes.
- ▶ **Outlining** — develop your presentation using an outline format. You also can import outlines from Microsoft Word or other word processing programs.
- ▶ **Charting** — create and insert charts into your presentations. The two chart types are: standard, which includes bar, line, pie, and xy (scatter) charts; and custom, which displays such objects as floating bars, colored lines, and three-dimensional cones.

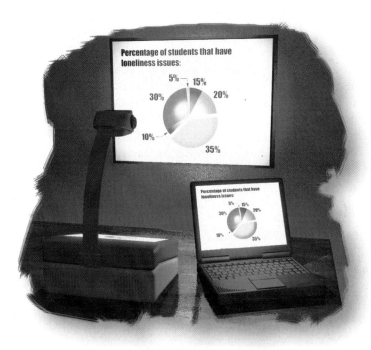

(a) Projection Device Connected to a Personal Computer

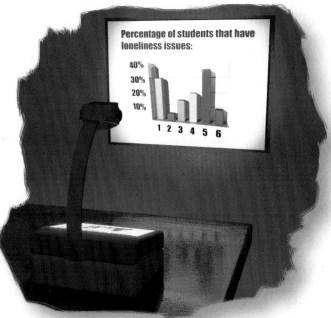

(b) Overhead Transparencies

(c) PowerPoint Presentation on the World Wide Web

FIGURE 1-1

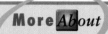

Microportable Projectors

Light, sleek multimedia projectors are extremely popular. The newer devices weigh less than three pounds and can be held in one hand. They offer zooms, contrast controls, and HDTV support. For more information, visit the PowerPoint 2002 More About Web page (scsite.com/pp2002/more.htm) and then click Projectors.

▶ **Drawing** — form and modify diagrams using shapes such as arcs, arrows, cubes, rectangles, stars, and triangles.

▶ **Inserting multimedia** — insert artwork and multimedia effects into your slide show. The Microsoft Media Gallery contains hundreds of clip art images, pictures, photos, sounds, and video clips. You can search for clips by entering words or phrases that describe the subject you want by looking for clips with similar artistic styles, colors, or shapes, or by connecting to a special Web site just for clip art. You also can import art from other applications.

▶ **Web support** — save presentations or parts of a presentation in HTML format so they can be viewed and manipulated using a browser. You can publish your slide show to the Internet or to an intranet. You also can insert action buttons and hyperlinks to create a self-running or interactive Web presentation.

▶ **E-mailing** — send your entire slide show as an attachment to an e-mail message.

▶ **Using Wizards** — create a presentation quickly and efficiently by answering prompts for specific content criteria. For example, the **AutoContent Wizard** gives prompts for the type of slide show you are planning, such as communicating serious news or motivating a team, and the type of output, such as an on-screen presentation or black and white overheads. If you are planning to run your presentation on another computer, the **Pack and Go Wizard** helps you bundle everything you need, including any objects associated with that presentation. If you cannot confirm that this other computer has PowerPoint installed, you also can include the **PowerPoint Viewer**, a program that allows you to run, but not edit, a PowerPoint slide show.

Project One — Time to Start Making Friends

PowerPoint allows you to produce slides similar to those you would develop in an academic or business environment. In Project 1, you create the presentation shown in Figures 1-2a through 1-2d. The objective is to produce a presentation, called Time to Start Making Friends, to display using a projection device. As an introduction to PowerPoint, this project steps you through the most common type of presentation, which is a **text slide** consisting of a bulleted list. A **bulleted list** is a list of paragraphs, each preceded by a bullet. A **bullet** is a symbol such as a heavy dot (•) or other character that precedes text when the text warrants special emphasis.

(a) Slide 1

Meet People

- Develop confidence to introduce yourself to others
- Make eye contact
- Smile and say, "Hi"
- Do not wait; start early in the semester

(b) Slide 2

Find the Right Places

- Go where people congregate
  - Student union, sports events
- Get involved in extracurricular activities
  - Participate in intramurals
  - Join Student Government

(c) Slide 3

Start a Conversation

- Talk about almost anything
  - Comment on what is going on
    - Long lines, class assignments
- Ask questions
  - Get people to discuss their lives
    - Hobbies, classes, and work

(d) Slide 4

FIGURE 1-2

Starting and Customizing PowerPoint

To start PowerPoint, Windows must be running. The quickest way to begin a new presentation is to use the **Start button** on the **Windows taskbar** at the bottom of the screen. Perform these steps to start PowerPoint and a new presentation, or ask your instructor how to start PowerPoint for your system.

Steps **To Start PowerPoint**

1 **Click the Start button on the Windows taskbar, point to Programs on the Start menu, and then point to Microsoft PowerPoint on the Programs submenu.**

The commands on the Start menu display above the Start button and the Programs submenu displays (Figure 1-3). If the Office Speech Recognition software is installed on your computer, then the Language bar may display somewhere on the desktop.

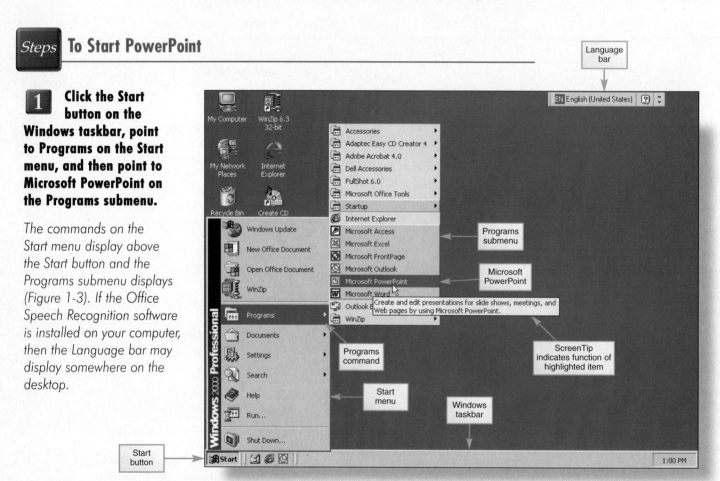

FIGURE 1-3

2 **Click PowerPoint.**

PowerPoint starts. While PowerPoint is starting, the mouse pointer changes to the shape of an hourglass. After a few moments, a blank presentation titled Presentation1 displays in the PowerPoint window (Figure 1-4).

3 **If the PowerPoint window is not maximized, double-click its title bar to maximize it.**

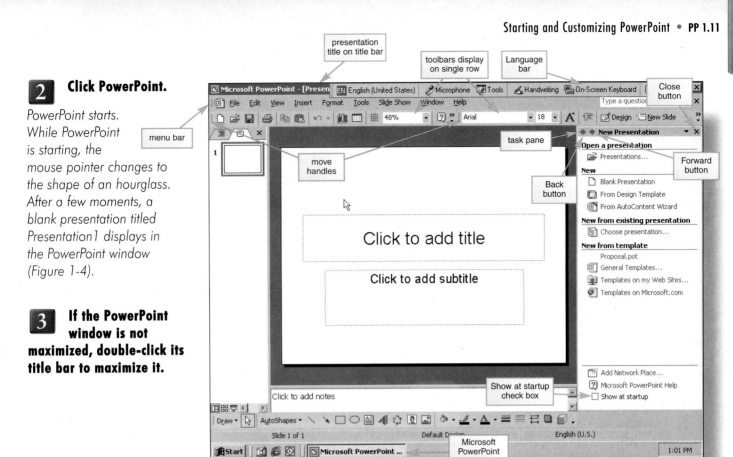

FIGURE 1-4

The screen in Figure 1-4 shows how the PowerPoint window looks the first time you start PowerPoint after installation on most computers. Notice that a task pane displays on the screen and the toolbars display on a single row. A **task pane** is a separate window within the application that provides commonly used commands and enables users to carry out some PowerPoint tasks efficiently. By default, both toolbars display on the same row immediately below the menu bar. Unless the resolution of your display device is greater than 800 × 600, many of the buttons that belong on these toolbars do not display. Hidden buttons display on the **Toolbar Options list**.

In this book, to allow the maximum slide space in the PowerPoint window, the New Presentation task pane that displays at startup is closed. For the most efficient use of the toolbars, the buttons are displayed on two separate rows instead of sharing a single row. You show the toolbar buttons on two rows by clicking the **Show Buttons on Two Rows command** in the Toolbar Options list. You also may display all the buttons on either toolbar by double-clicking the **move handle** on the left side of each toolbar (Figure 1-4). Perform the steps on the next page to customize the PowerPoint window at startup by removing the task pane from the startup instructions and displaying the toolbar buttons on two rows, instead of one.

Other **Ways**

1. Double-click PowerPoint icon on desktop

2. Right-click Start button, click Open All Users, double-click New Office Document, click General tab, double-click Blank Presentation icon

3. On Start menu click New Office Document, click General tab, click New Presentation icon

4. Click New Office Document button on Microsoft Office Shortcut Bar, click General tab, double-click Blank Presentation icon, point to Programs, click Microsoft PowerPoint

Steps **To Customize the PowerPoint Window**

1 **If the New Presentation task pane displays in your PowerPoint window, click the Show at startup check box to remove the check mark, and then click the Close button in the upper-right corner of the task pane title bar (Figure 1-4 on the previous page). If the Language bar displays, point to its Minimize button.**

PowerPoint removes the check mark from the Show at startup check box. PowerPoint will not display the New Presentation task pane the next time PowerPoint starts. The New Presentation task pane closes (Figure 1-5).

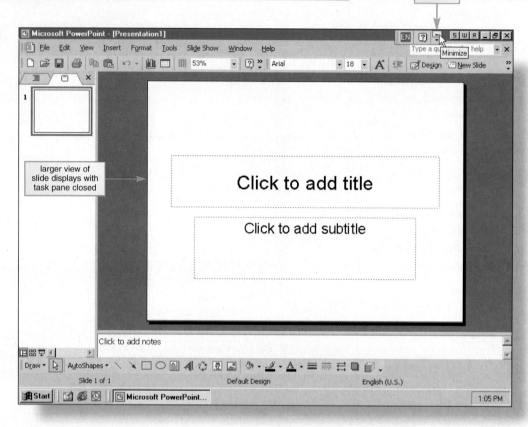

FIGURE 1-5

2 **Click the Minimize button on the Language bar. If the toolbars display positioned on the same row, click the Toolbar Options button on the Standard toolbar and then point to Show Buttons on Two Rows.**

The Toolbar Options list displays showing the buttons that do not fit on the toolbars when the buttons display on one row (Figure 1-6).

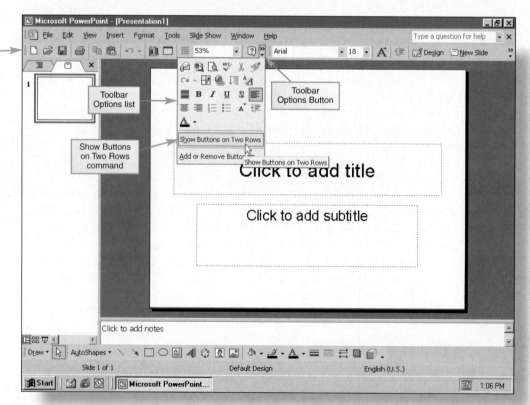

FIGURE 1-6

3 Click Show Buttons on Two Rows.

PowerPoint displays the buttons on the Standard and Formatting toolbars on two separate rows (Figure 1-7). The Toolbar Options list is empty because all the buttons fit on two rows.

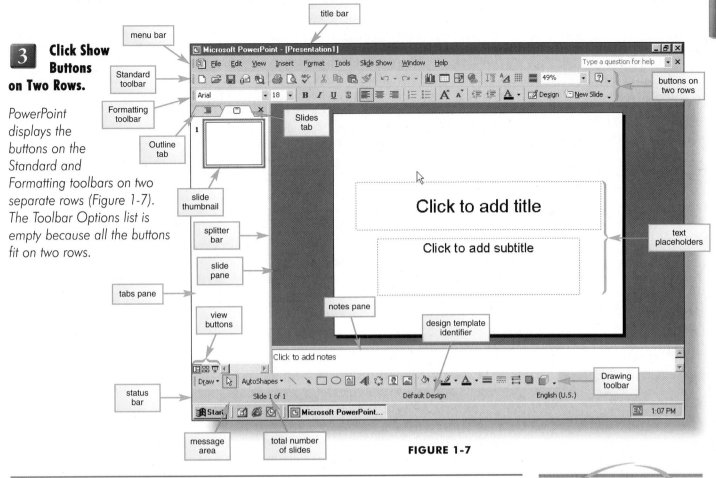

FIGURE 1-7

When you point to a button or other areas on a toolbar, PowerPoint displays a ScreenTip. A **ScreenTip** is a short onscreen note associated with the object to which you are pointing, such as the name of the button. For examples of ScreenTips, see Figure 1-3 on page PP 1.10 and Figure 1-5.

As you work through creating a presentation, you will find that certain PowerPoint operations result in displaying a task pane. Besides the New Presentation task pane shown in Figure 1-4 on page 1.11, PowerPoint provides nine additional task panes: Clipboard, Basic Search, Advanced Search, Slide Layout, Slide Design – Design Templates, Slide Design – Color Schemes, Slide Design – Animation Schemes, Custom Animation, and Slide Transition. These task panes are discussed as they are used. You can display or hide a task pane by clicking the **Task Pane command** on the View menu. You can activate additional task panes by clicking the down arrow to the left of the Close button on the task pane title bar and then selecting a task pane in the list. To switch between task panes, use the Back and Forward buttons on the left side of the task pane title bar.

More About

Task Panes

When you first start PowerPoint, a small window called a task pane may display docked on the right side of the screen. You can drag a task pane title bar to float the pane in your work area or dock it on either the left or right side of a screen, depending on your personal preference.

The PowerPoint Window

The basic unit of a PowerPoint presentation is a **slide**. A slide contains one or many **objects**, such as a title, text, graphics, tables, charts, and drawings. An object is the building block for a PowerPoint slide. PowerPoint assumes the first slide in a new presentation is the **title slide**. The title slide's purpose is to introduce the presentation to the audience.

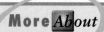

Resolution

Resolution refers to the number of pixels, or dots, that can fit into one square inch. It is measured, consequently, in dots per inch, which is abbreviated, dpi. PowerPoint's default screen resolution is 72 dpi, and it can be set as high as 1,200 dpi. Use a resolution of 150 dpi if you are going to print handouts of your slides. For more information, visit the PowerPoint 2002 More About Web page (scsite.com/pp2002/more.htm) and then click Resolution.

In PowerPoint, you have the option of using the PowerPoint default settings or establishing your own. A **default setting** is a particular value for a variable that PowerPoint assigns initially. It controls the placement of objects, the color scheme, the transition between slides, and other slide attributes, and it remains in effect unless you cancel or override it. **Attributes** are the properties or characteristics of an object. For example, if you underline the title of a slide, the title is the object, and the underline is the attribute. When you start PowerPoint, the default **slide layout** is **landscape orientation**, where the slide width is greater than its height. In landscape orientation, the slide size is preset to 10 inches wide and 7.5 inches high. You can change the slide layout to **portrait orientation**, so the slide height is greater than its width, by clicking Page Setup on the File menu. In portrait orientation, the slide width is 7.5 inches, and the height is 10 inches.

When a PowerPoint window is open, its name displays in an icon on the Windows taskbar. The **active application** is the one displaying in the foreground of the desktop. That application's corresponding icon on the Windows taskbar displays recessed.

PowerPoint Views

PowerPoint has three main views: normal view, slide sorter view, and slide show view. A **view** is the mode in which the presentation displays on the screen. You may use any or all views when creating a presentation, but you can use only one at a time. You also can select one of these views to be the default view. Change views by clicking one of the view buttons located at the lower-left of the PowerPoint window above the Drawing toolbar (Figure 1-7 on the previous page). The PowerPoint window display varies depending on the view. Some views are graphical while others are textual.

You generally will use normal view and slide sorter view when you are creating a presentation. **Normal view** is composed of three working areas that allow you to work on various aspects of a presentation simultaneously (Figure 1-7). The left side of the screen has a tabs pane that consists of an **Outline tab** and a **Slides tab** that alternate between views of the presentation in an outline of the slide text and a thumbnail, or miniature, view of the slides. You can type the text of the presentation on the Outline tab and easily rearrange bulleted lists, paragraphs, and individual slides. As you type, you can view this text in the **slide pane**, which displays a large view of the current slide on the right side of the window. You also can enter text, graphics, animations, and hyperlinks directly in the slide pane. The **notes pane** at the bottom of the window is an area where you can type notes and additional information. This text can consist of notes to yourself or remarks to share with your audience.

Sizing Panes

The three panes in normal view allow you to work on all aspects of your presentation simultaneously. You can drag the splitter bar and the pane borders to make each area larger or smaller.

In normal view, you can adjust the width of the slide pane by dragging the **splitter bar** and the height of the notes pane by dragging the pane borders. After you have created at least two slides, **scroll bars**, **scroll arrows**, and **scroll boxes** will display below and to the right of the windows, and you can use them to view different parts of the panes.

Slide sorter view is helpful when you want to see all the slides in the presentation simultaneously. A thumbnail version of each slide displays, and you can rearrange their order, add transitions and timings to switch from one slide to the next in a presentation, add and delete slides, and preview animations.

Slide show view fills the entire screen and allows you to see the slide show just as your audience will view it. Transition effects, animation, graphics, movies, and timings display as they will during an actual presentation.

Table 1-1 identifies the view buttons and provides an explanation of each view.

Table 1-1 View Buttons and Functions

BUTTON	BUTTON NAME	FUNCTION
	Normal View	Displays three panes: the tabs pane with either the Outline tab or the Slides tab, the slide pane, and the notes pane.
	Slide Sorter View	Displays thumbnail versions of all slides in a presentation. You then can copy, cut, paste, or otherwise change the slide position to modify the presentation. Slide sorter view also is used to add timings, to select animated transitions, and to preview animations.
	Slide Show View	Displays the slides as an electronic presentation on the full screen of your computer's monitor. Looking much like a slide projector display, you can see the effect of transitions, build effects, slide timings, and animations.

Placeholders, Text Areas, Mouse Pointer, and Scroll Bars

The PowerPoint window contains elements similar to the document windows in other Microsoft Office applications. Other features are unique to PowerPoint. The main elements are the text placeholders, the mouse pointer, and scroll bars.

PLACEHOLDERS **Placeholders** are boxes that display when you create a new slide. All layouts except the Blank slide layout contain placeholders. Depending on the particular slide layout selected, placeholders display for the slide title, body text, charts, tables, organization charts, media clips, and clip art. You type titles, body text, and bulleted lists in **text placeholders**; you place graphic elements in chart placeholders, table placeholders, organizational chart placeholders, and clip art placeholders. A placeholder is considered an **object**, which is a single element of a slide.

TEXT AREAS **Text areas** are surrounded by a dotted outline. The title slide in Figure 1-7 has two text areas that contain the text placeholders where you will type the main heading, or title, of a new slide and the subtitle, or other object. Other slides in a presentation may use a layout that contains text areas for a title and bulleted lists.

MOUSE POINTER The **mouse pointer** can become one of several different shapes depending on the task you are performing in PowerPoint and the pointer's location on the screen. The different shapes are discussed when they display.

SCROLL BARS When you add a second slide to a presentation, a **vertical scroll bar** displays on the right side of the slide pane. PowerPoint allows you to use the scroll bar to move forward or backward through the presentation.

The **horizontal scroll bar** may display. It is located on the bottom of the slide pane and allows you to display a portion of the slide when the entire slide does not fit on the screen.

Status Bar, Menu Bar, Standard Toolbar, Formatting Toolbar, and Drawing Toolbar

The status bar displays at the bottom of the screen above the Windows taskbar (Figure 1-7). The menu bar, Standard toolbar, and Formatting toolbar display at the top of the screen just below the title bar. The Drawing toolbar displays above the status bar.

More About

Pointing Devices

The Microsoft IntelliMouse® pointing device can help you build presentations efficiently. For example, you can roll the wheel forward or backward instead of clicking a scroll bar. You also can have your document scroll automatically. For more information, visit the PowerPoint 2002 More About Web page (scsite.com/pp2002/more.htm) and then click IntelliMouse.

More About

The Default Design Template

Some PowerPoint slide show designers create presentations using the Default Design template. This blank design allows them to concentrate on the words being used to convey the message and does not distract them with colors and various text attributes. Once the text is entered, the designers then select an appropriate design template.

STATUS BAR   Immediately above the Windows taskbar at the bottom of the screen is the status bar. The **status bar** consists of a message area and a presentation design template identifier (Figure 1-7 on page PP 1.13). Generally, the message area displays the current slide number and the total number of slides in the slide show. For example, in Figure 1-7 the message area displays Slide 1 of 1. Slide 1 is the current slide, and of 1 indicates the slide show contains only 1 slide. The template identifier displays Default Design, which is the template PowerPoint uses initially.

MENU BAR   The **menu bar** is a special toolbar that includes the PowerPoint menu names (Figure 1-8a). Each **menu name** represents a menu of commands that you can use to perform tasks such as retrieving, storing, printing, and manipulating objects in a presentation. When you point to a menu name on the menu bar, the area of the menu bar containing the name changes to a button. To display a menu, such as the Edit menu, click the Edit menu name on the menu bar. A **menu** is a list of commands. If you point to a command on a menu that has an arrow to its right edge, a **submenu** displays another list of commands.

(a) Menu Bar and Toolbars

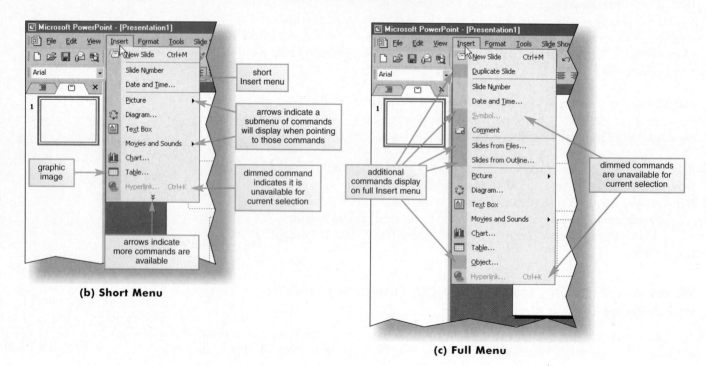

(b) Short Menu

(c) Full Menu

FIGURE 1-8

When you click a menu name on the menu bar, a short menu displays that lists your most recently used commands (Figure 1-8b).

If you wait a few seconds or click the arrows at the bottom of the short menu, it expands into a full menu. A **full menu** lists all the commands associated with a menu (Figure 1-8c). You immediately can display a full menu by double-clicking the menu name on the menu bar. In this book, when you display a menu, always display the full menu using one of these techniques:

1. Click the menu name on the menu bar and then wait a few seconds.
2. Click the menu name on the menu bar and then click the arrows at the bottom of the short menu.
3. Click the menu name on the menu bar and then point to the arrows at the bottom of the short menu.
4. Double-click the menu name on the menu bar.

Both short and full menus display some commands with an image to the left, which associates the command with a graphic image and dimmed commands that appear gray, or dimmed, instead of black, which indicates they are not available for the current selection. A command with a dark gray shading to the left of it on a full menu is called a hidden command because it does not display on a short menu. As you use PowerPoint, it automatically personalizes the short menus for you based on how often you use commands. That is, as you use hidden commands, PowerPoint *unhides* them and places them on the short menu.

The menu bar can change to include other menu names depending on the type of work you are doing in PowerPoint. For example, if you are adding a chart to a slide, Data and Chart menu names are added to the menu bar with commands that reflect charting options.

STANDARD, FORMATTING, AND DRAWING TOOLBARS The Standard toolbar (Figure 1-9a), Formatting toolbar (Figure 1-9b), and Drawing toolbar (Figure 1-9c on the next page) contain buttons and boxes that allow you to perform frequent tasks more quickly than when using the menu bar. For example, to print a slide show, you click the Print button on the Standard toolbar. Each button has an image on the button and a ScreenTip that help you remember the button's function.

Figure 1-9 illustrates the Standard, Formatting, and Drawing toolbars and describes the functions of the buttons. Each of the buttons and boxes are explained in detail when they are used.

More About

Hiding Toolbars

To display more of the PowerPoint window, you can hide a toolbar you no longer need. To hide a toolbar, right-click any toolbar and then click the check mark next to the toolbar you want to hide on the shortcut menu.

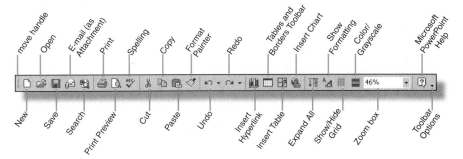

FIGURE 1-9a Standard Toolbar

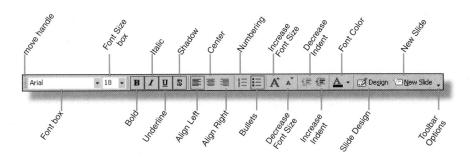

FIGURE 1-9b Formatting Toolbar

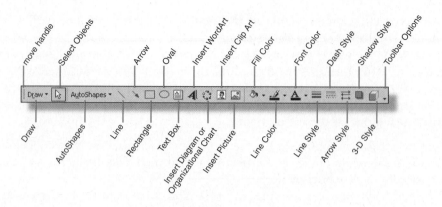

FIGURE 1-9c Drawing Toolbar

Shortcut Menus

When you point to or select an item and right-click, a shortcut menu usually displays. This special menu contains frequently used commands related to that object. In some cases, you also can display the shortcut menu by selecting an object, such as a paragraph, and then pressing SHIFT+F10. To hide a shortcut menu, click outside the shortcut menu or press the ESC key.

PowerPoint has several additional toolbars you can display by pointing to Toolbars on the View menu and then clicking the respective name on the Toolbars submenu. You also may display a toolbar by pointing to a toolbar and right-clicking to display a shortcut menu, which lists the available toolbars. A **shortcut menu** contains a list of commands or items that relate to the item to which you are pointing when you right-click.

Speech Recognition

With the **Office Speech Recognition software** installed and a microphone, you can speak the names of toolbar buttons, menus, menu commands, list items, alerts, and dialog box controls, such as OK and Cancel. You also can dictate cell entries, such as text and numbers. To indicate whether you want to speak commands or dictate cell entries, you use the **Language bar** (Figure 1-10a), which also is used for handwriting recognition and for Input Method Editors (IME) that convert keystrokes to East Asian characters. You can display the Language bar in two ways: (1) click the Language Indicator button in the Windows taskbar tray status area by the clock, and then click Show the Language bar on the Language bar menu (Figure 1-10b); or (2) click the **Speech command** on the **Tools menu**.

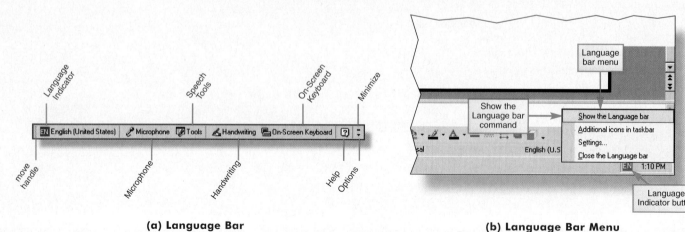

(a) Language Bar

(b) Language Bar Menu

FIGURE 1-10

If the Language Indicator button does not display in the tray status area, and if the Speech command is not displayed or is dimmed on the Tools menu, the Office Speech Recognition software is not installed. To install the software, you first must start Word and then click Speech on the Tools menu.

If you have speakers, you can instruct the computer to read a slide show to you. By selecting the appropriate option, you can have the slides read in a male or female voice.

Additional information on the Office speech and handwriting recognition capabilities is available in Appendix B.

Choosing a Design Template

A **design template** provides consistency in design and color throughout the entire presentation. It determines the color scheme, font and font size, and layout of a presentation. PowerPoint has three Slide Design task panes that allow you to choose and change the appearance of slides in your presentation. The **Slide Design – Design Templates task pane** displays a variety of styles. You can alter the colors used in the design templates by using the **Slide Design – Color Schemes task pane**. In addition, you can animate elements of your presentation by using the **Slide Design – Animation Schemes task pane**.

In this project, you will select a particular design template by using the Slide Design – Design Templates task pane. The top section of the task pane, labeled Used in This Presentation, displays the template currently used in the slide show. PowerPoint uses the **Default Design** template until you select a different style. When you place your mouse over a template, the name of the template displays. The next section of the task pane is the Recently Used templates. This area displays the four templates you have used in your newest slide shows. The Available For Use area shows additional templates. The templates display in alphabetical order in the two columns.

You want to change the template for this presentation from the Default Design to Proposal. Perform the following steps to apply the Proposal design template.

More About

Additional Templates

While the Slide Design task pane displays a wide variety of templates, more are available in the Microsoft Office Template Gallery at the Microsoft Web site. These templates are arranged in various categories according to the type of presentation.

More About

The PowerPoint Help System

Need Help? It is no further than the Ask a Question box in the upper-right corner of the window. Click the box that contains the text, Type a question for help (Figure 1-8a on page PP 1.16), type help, and then press the ENTER key. PowerPoint will respond with a list of items you can click to learn about obtaining help on any PowerPoint-related topic. To find out what is new in PowerPoint 2002, type what's new in PowerPoint in the Ask a Question box.

Steps **To Choose a Design Template**

1 **Point to the Slide Design button on the Formatting toolbar (Figure 1-11).**

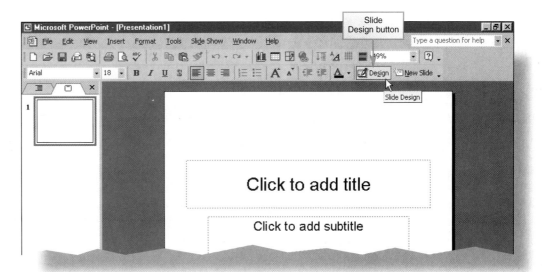

FIGURE 1-11

2 **Click the Slide Design button and then point to the down scroll arrow in the Apply a design template list.**

The Slide Design task pane displays (Figure 1-12). The Apply a design template list displays thumbnail views of numerous design templates. Your list may look different depending on your computer. The Default Design template is highlighted in the Used in This Presentation area. Other templates display in the Available For Use area and possibly in the Recently Used area. The Close button in the Slide Design task pane can be used to close the task pane if you do not want to apply a new template.

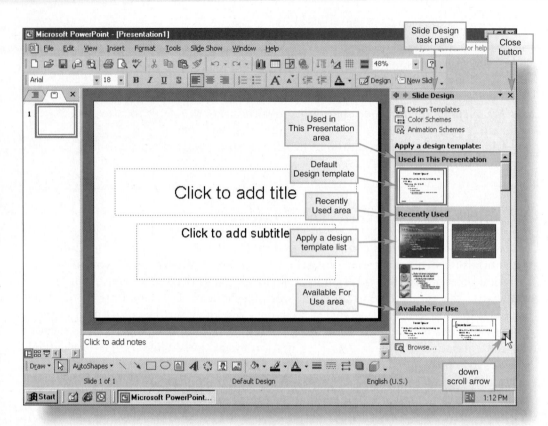

FIGURE 1-12

3 **Click the down scroll arrow to scroll through the list of design templates until Proposal displays (row 17, column 1) in the Available For Use area. Point to the Proposal template.**

The proposal template is selected, as indicated by the blue box around the template and the arrow button on the right side (Figure 1-13). PowerPoint provides 45 templates in the Available For Use area. Their names are listed in alphabetical order. A ScreenTip displays the template's name. Your system may display the ScreenTip, Proposal.pot, which indicates the design template's file extension (.pot).

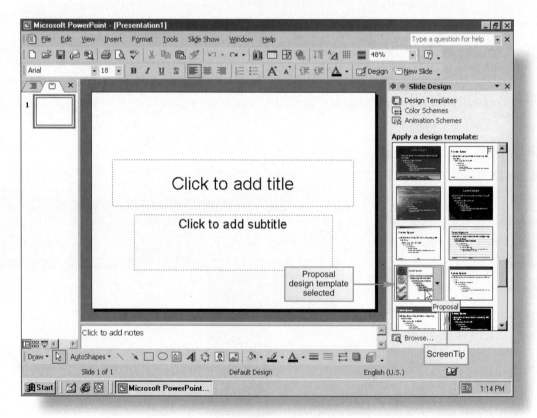

FIGURE 1-13

4 **Click Proposal. Point to the Close button in the Slide Design task pane.**

The template is applied to Slide 1, as shown in the slide pane and Slides tab (Figure 1-14).

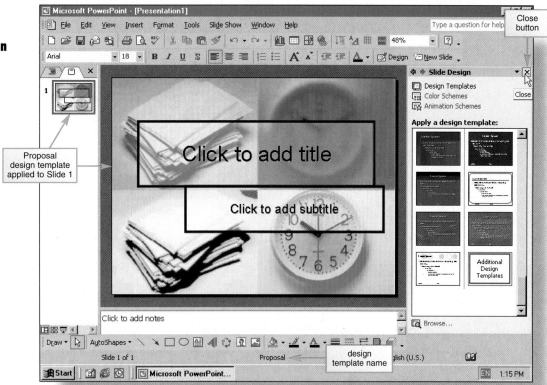

FIGURE 1-14

5 **Click the Close button.**

Slide 1 displays in normal view with the Proposal design template (Figure 1-15).

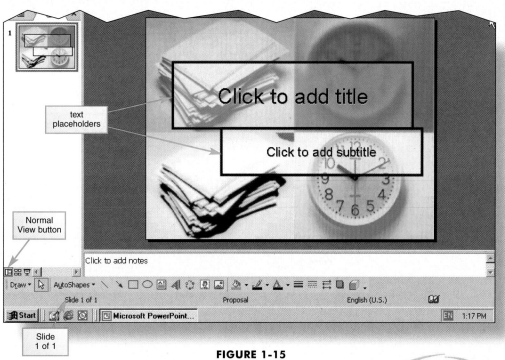

FIGURE 1-15

Other Ways

1. Double-click Proposal in list

Creating a Title Slide

With the exception of a blank slide, PowerPoint assumes every new slide has a title. To make creating a presentation easier, any text you type after a new slide displays becomes title text in the title text placeholder.

Entering the Presentation Title

The presentation title for Project 1 is Time to Start Making Friends. To enter text in your slide, you type on the keyboard or speak into the microphone. As you begin entering text in the title text placeholder, the title text displays immediately in the Slide 1 thumbnail in the Slides tab. Perform the following steps to create the title slide for this presentation.

 To Enter the Presentation Title

1 **Click the label, Click to add title, located inside the title text placeholder.**

The insertion point is in the title text placeholder (Figure 1-16). The insertion point is a blinking vertical line (|), which indicates where the next character will display. The mouse pointer changes to an I-beam. A selection rectangle displays around the title text placeholder. The placeholder is selected as indicated by the border and sizing handles displaying on the edges.

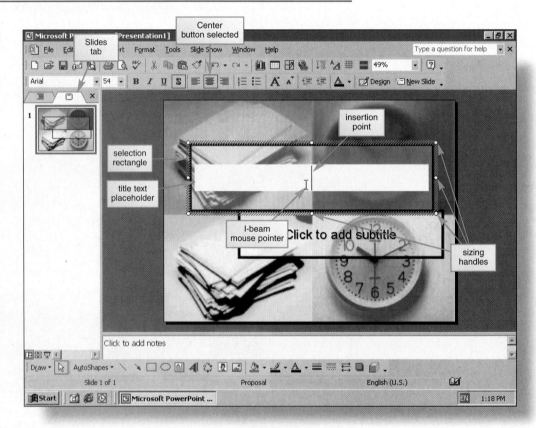

FIGURE 1-16

2 **In the title text placeholder type** Time to Start **and then press the ENTER key. Type** Making Friends **but do not press the ENTER key.**

The title text, Time to Start Making Friends, displays on two lines in the title text placeholder and in the Slides tab (Figure 1-17). The insertion point displays after the letter s in Friends. The title text displays centered in the placeholder with the default text attributes: Arial font, font size 54, and shadow effect.

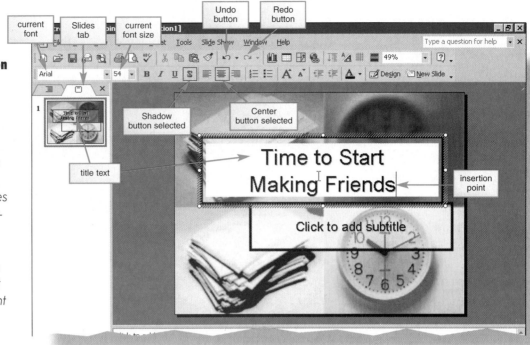

FIGURE 1-17

PowerPoint **line wraps** text that exceeds the width of the placeholder. One of PowerPoint's features is **text AutoFit**. If you are creating a slide and need to squeeze an extra line in the text placeholder, PowerPoint will prompt you to resize the existing text in the placeholder so the spillover text will fit on the slide.

Correcting a Mistake When Typing

If you type the wrong letter, press the BACKSPACE key to erase all the characters back to and including the one that is incorrect. If you mistakenly press the ENTER key after typing the title and the insertion point is on the new line, simply press the BACKSPACE key to return the insertion point to the right of the letter s in the word Friends.

When you install PowerPoint, the default setting allows you to reverse up to the last 20 changes by clicking the **Undo button** on the Standard toolbar. The ScreenTip that displays when you point to the Undo button changes to indicate the type of change just made. For example, if you type text in the title text placeholder and then point to the Undo button, the ScreenTip that displays is Undo Typing. For clarity, when referencing the Undo button in this project, the name displaying in the ScreenTip is referenced. Another way to reverse changes is to click the **Undo command** on the Edit menu. As with the Undo button, the Undo command reflects the last type of change made to the presentation.

You can reapply a change that you reversed with the Undo button by clicking the **Redo button** on the Standard toolbar. Clicking the Redo button reverses the last undo action. The ScreenTip name reflects the type of reversal last preformed.

Entering the Presentation Subtitle

The next step in creating the title slide is to enter the subtitle text into the subtitle text placeholder. Complete the steps on the next page to enter the presentation subtitle.

Other **Ways**

1. In Dictation mode, say "Time to start, New Line, Making friends"

More *About*

The 7 × 7 Rule

All slide shows in the projects and exercises in this book follow the 7 × 7 rule. This guideline states that each slide should have a maximum of seven lines, and each of these lines should have a maximum of seven words. This rule requires PowerPoint designers to choose their words carefully and, in turn, helps viewers read the slides easily.

Steps **To Enter the Presentation Subtitle**

1 **Click the label, Click to add subtitle, located inside the subtitle text placeholder.**

The insertion point displays in the subtitle text placeholder (Figure 1-18). The mouse pointer changes to an I-beam indicating the mouse is in a text placeholder. The selection rectangle indicates the placeholder is selected.

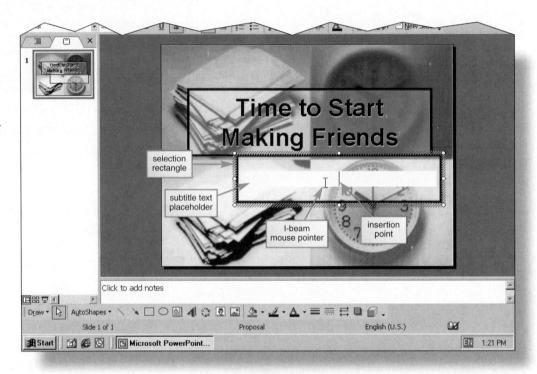

FIGURE 1-18

2 **Type** Presented by **and then press the ENTER key. Type** Westview College Counselors **but do not press the ENTER key.**

The subtitle text displays in the subtitle text placeholder and the Slides tab (Figure 1-19). The insertion point displays after the letter s in Counselors. A red wavy line displays below the word, Westview, to indicate a possible spelling error.

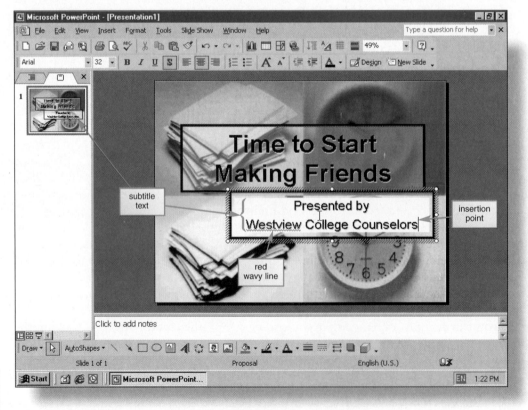

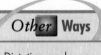

1. In Dictation mode, say "Presented by, New Line, Westview College Counselors"

FIGURE 1-19

After pressing the ENTER key in Step 2, PowerPoint created a new line, which is the second paragraph in the placeholder. A **paragraph** is a segment of text with the same format that begins when you press the ENTER key and ends when you press the ENTER key again.

Text Attributes

This presentation uses the Proposal design template. Each design template has its own text attributes. A **text attribute** is a characteristic of the text, such as font, font size, font style, or text color. You can adjust text attributes any time before, during, or after you type the text. Recall that a design template determines the color scheme, font and font size, and layout of a presentation. Most of the time, you use the design template's text attributes and color scheme. Occasionally, you may want to change the way a presentation looks, however, and still keep a particular design template. PowerPoint gives you that flexibility. You can use the design template and change the font and the font's color, effects, size, and style. Text may have one or more font styles and effects simultaneously. Table 1-2 explains the different text attributes available in PowerPoint.

The next two sections explain how to change the font size and font style attributes.

> **More About**
>
> **Modifying Fonts**
>
> Designers recommend using a maximum of two fonts and two font styles or effects in a slide show. This design philosophy maintains balance and simplicity.

Table 1-2	Design Template Text Attributes
ATTRIBUTE	**DESCRIPTION**
Color	Defines the color of text. Displaying text in color requires a color monitor. Printing text in color requires a color printer or plotter.
Effects	Effects include underline, shadow, emboss, superscript, and subscript. Effects can be applied to most fonts.
Font	Defines the appearance and shape of letters, numbers, and special characters.
Size	Specifies the height of characters on the screen. Character size is gauged by a measurement system called points. A single point is about 1/72 of an inch in height. Thus, a character with a point size of 18 is about 18/72 (or 1/4) of an inch in height.
Style	Font styles include regular, bold, italic, and bold italic.

Changing the Style of Text to Italic

Text font styles include plain, italic, bold, shadowed, and underlined. PowerPoint allows you to use one or more text font styles in a presentation. Perform the steps on the next page to add emphasis to the first line of the subtitle text by changing regular text to italic text.

Steps **To Change the Text Font Style to Italic**

1 **Triple-click the paragraph, Westview College Counselors, in the subtitle text placeholder, and then point to the Italic button on the Formatting toolbar.**

The paragraph, Westview College Counselors, is highlighted (Figure 1-20). The Italic button is surrounded by a blue box. You select an entire paragraph quickly by triple-clicking any text within the paragraph.

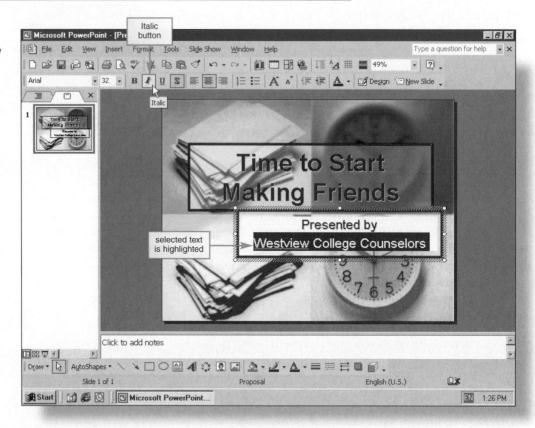

FIGURE 1-20

2 **Click the Italic button.**

The text is italicized on the slide and the slide thumbnail (Figure 1-21).

Other **Ways**

1. Right-click selected text, click Font on shortcut menu, click Italic in Font style list
2. On Format menu click Font, click Italic in Font style list
3. Press CTRL+I
4. In Voice Command mode, say "Italic"

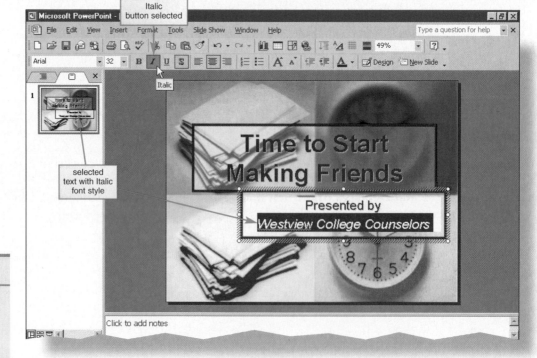

FIGURE 1-21

To remove the italic style from text, select the italicized text and then click the Italic button. As a result, the Italic button is not selected, and the text does not have the italic font style.

Changing the Font Size

The Proposal design template default font size is 54 point for title text and 32 point for body text. A point is 1/72 of an inch in height. Thus, a character with a point size of 54 is 54/72 (or 3/4) of an inch in height. Slide 1 requires you to increase the font size for the paragraph, Presented by. Perform the following steps to increase the font size.

 To Increase Font Size

1 **Position the mouse pointer in the paragraph, Presented by, and then triple-click.**

PowerPoint selects the entire paragraph (Figure 1-22).

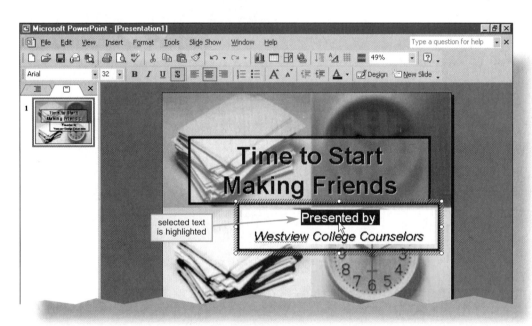

FIGURE 1-22

2 **Point to the Font Size box arrow on the Formatting toolbar.**

The ScreenTip displays the words, Font Size (Figure 1-23). The Font Size box is surrounded by a blue box and indicates that the subtitle text is 32 point.

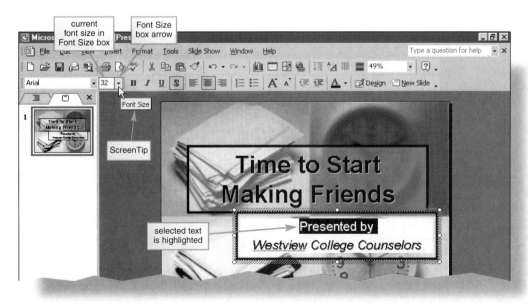

FIGURE 1-23

3 Click the Font Size box arrow, click the Font Size box scroll bar one time, and then point to 40 in the Font Size list.

When you click the *Font Size box arrow*, a list of available font sizes displays in the Font Size list (Figure 1-24). The font sizes displayed depend on the current font, which is Arial. Font size 40 is highlighted.

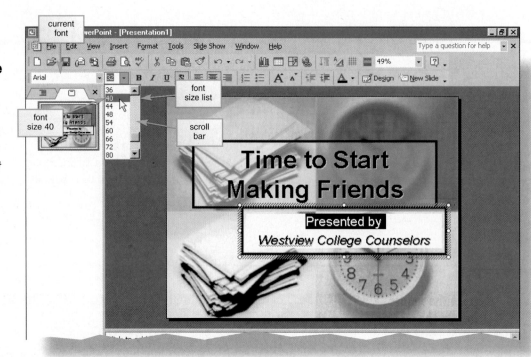

FIGURE 1-24

4 Click 40.

The font size of the subtitle text, Presented by, increases to 40 point (Figure 1-25). The Font Size box on the Formatting toolbar displays 40, indicating the selected text has a font size of 40.

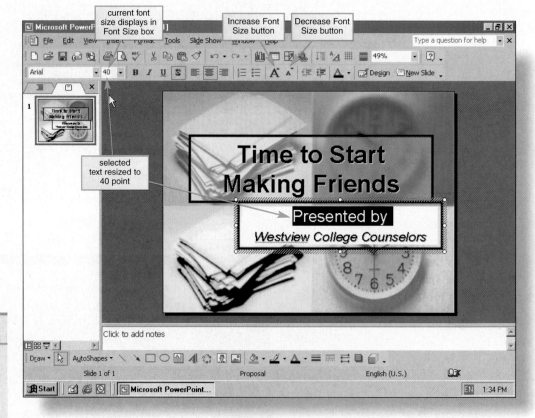

FIGURE 1-25

Other **Ways**

1. Click Increase Font Size button on Formatting toolbar

2. On Format menu click Font, click new font size in Size box, or type font size between 1 and 4000, click OK button

3. Right-click selected text, click Font on shortcut menu, type new font size in Size box, click OK button

4. In Voice Command mode, say "Font Size, [font size]"

The **Increase Font Size button** on the Formatting toolbar (Figure 1-25) increases the font size in preset increments each time you click the button. If you need to decrease the font size, click the Font Size box arrow and then select a size smaller than 32. The **Decrease Font Size button** on the Formatting toolbar (Figure 1-25) also decreases the font size in preset increments each time you click the button.

Saving the Presentation on a Floppy Disk

While you are building a presentation, the computer stores it in memory. It is important to save the presentation frequently because the presentation will be lost if the computer is turned off or you lose electrical power. Another reason to save your work is that if you run out of lab time before completing your project, you may finish the project later without starting over. Therefore, always save any presentation you will use later. Before you continue with Project 1, save the work completed thus far. Perform the following steps to save a presentation on a floppy disk using the Save button on the Standard toolbar.

More About

Text Attributes

The Microsoft Web site contains a comprehensive glossary of typography terms. The information includes a diagram illustrating text attributes. For more information, visit the PowerPoint 2002 More About Web page (scsite.com/pp2002/more.htm) and then click Attributes.

Steps **To Save a Presentation on a Floppy Disk**

1 **Insert a formatted floppy disk in drive A. Click the Save button on the Standard toolbar.**

The Save As dialog box displays (Figure 1-26). The default folder, My Documents, displays in the Save in box. Time to Start Making Friends displays highlighted in the File name text box because PowerPoint uses the words in the title text placeholder as the default file name. Presentation displays in the Save as type box. Clicking the Cancel button closes the Save As dialog box.

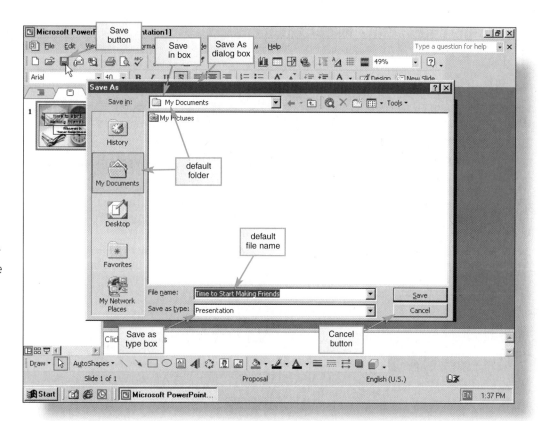

FIGURE 1-26

2 **Type** Make Friends **in the File name text box. Do not press the ENTER key after typing the file name. Point to the Save in box arrow.**

The name, Make Friends, displays in the File name text box (Figure 1-27).

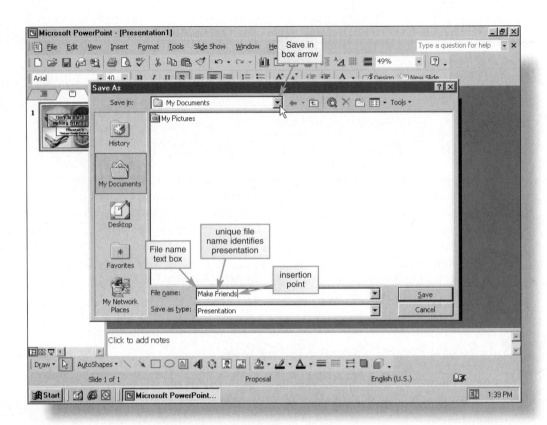

FIGURE 1-27

3 **Click the Save in box arrow. Point to 3½ Floppy (A:) in the Save in list.**

The Save in list displays a list of locations in which to save a presentation; 3½ Floppy (A:) is highlighted (Figure 1-28). Your list may look different depending on the configuration of your system.

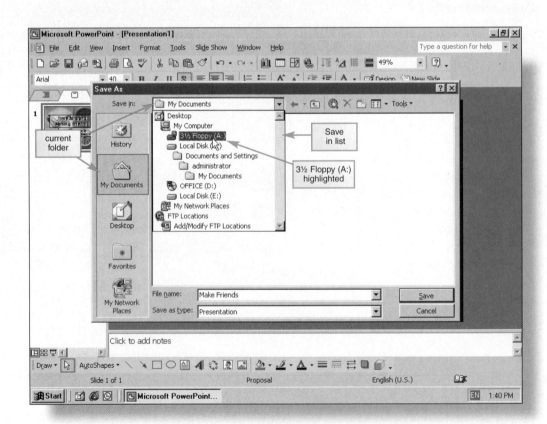

FIGURE 1-28

4 Click 3½ Floppy (A:) and then point to the Save button in the Save As dialog box.

Drive A becomes the current drive (Figure 1-29).

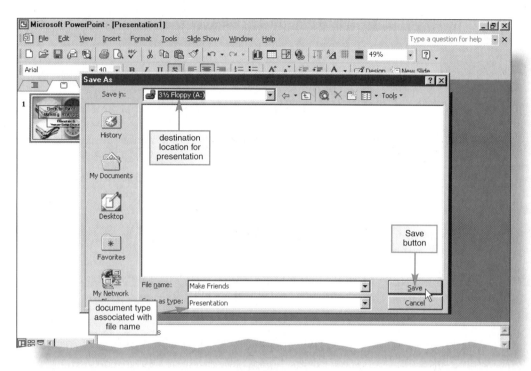

FIGURE 1-29

5 Click the Save button.

PowerPoint saves the presentation on the floppy disk in drive A. The title bar displays the file name used to save the presentation, Make Friends (Figure 1-30).

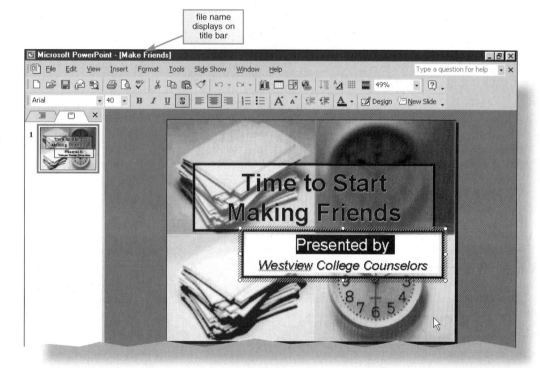

FIGURE 1-30

PowerPoint automatically appends the extension .ppt to the file name, Make Friends. The **.ppt** extension stands for **P**ower**P**oint. Although the slide show, Make Friends, is saved on a floppy disk, it also remains in memory and displays on the screen.

1. On File menu click Save As
2. Press CTRL+S or press SHIFT+F12
3. In Voice Command mode, say "File, Save As, [type file name], Save"

It is a good practice to save periodically while you are working on a project. By doing so, you protect yourself from losing all the work you have done since the last time you saved.

Adding a New Slide to a Presentation

With the title slide for the presentation created, the next step is to add the first text slide immediately after the title slide. Usually, when you create a presentation, you add slides with text, graphics, or charts. When you add a new slide, PowerPoint uses the Title and Text slide layout. Some placeholders allow you to double-click the placeholder and then access other objects, such as media clips, charts, diagrams, and organization charts.

Perform the following steps to add a new Text slide layout with a bulleted list.

 Steps **To Add a New Text Slide with a Bulleted List**

1 **Click to the New Slide button on the Formatting toolbar (Figure 1-31).**

The Slide Layout task pane opens. The Title and Text slide layout is selected. Slide 2 of 2 displays on the status bar.

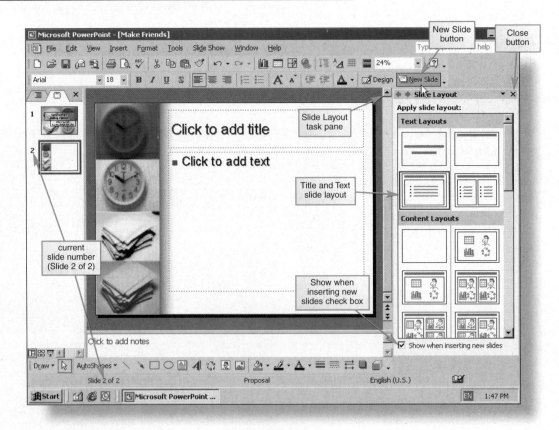

FIGURE 1-31

2   Click the Show when inserting new slides check box to remove the check mark. Click the Close button on the Slide Layout task pane.

Slide 2 displays in both the slide pane and Slides tab retaining the attributes of the Proposal design template (Figure 1-32). The vertical scroll bar displays in the slide pane. The bullet displays as a square.

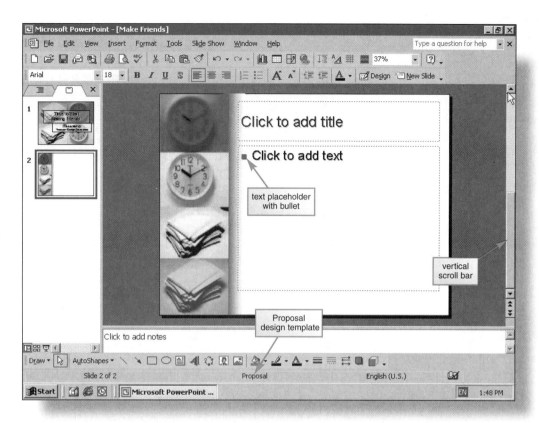

FIGURE 1-32

Slide 2 displays with a title text placeholder and a text placeholder with a bullet. You can change the layout for a slide at any time during the creation of a presentation by clicking Format on the menu bar and then clicking Slide Layout. You also can click View on the menu bar and then click Task Pane. You then can double-click the slide layout of your choice from the Slide Layout task pane.

Other **Ways**

1. On Insert menu click New Slide
2. Press CTRL+M
3. In Voice Command mode, say "New Slide"

Creating a Text Slide with a Single-Level Bulleted List

The information in the Slide 2 text placeholder is presented in a bulleted list. All the bullets display on one level. A **level** is a position within a structure, such as an outline, that indicates the magnitude of importance. PowerPoint allows for five paragraph levels. Each paragraph level has an associated bullet. The bullet font is dependent on the design template.

Entering a Slide Title

PowerPoint assumes every new slide has a title. The title for Slide 2 is Meet People. Perform the step on the next page to enter this title.

Steps **To Enter a Slide Title**

1 **Type** Meet People **in the title text placeholder. Do not press the ENTER key.**

The title, Meet People, displays in the title text placeholder and in the Slides tab (Figure 1-33). The insertion point displays after the e in People. The selection rectangle indicates the title text placeholder is selected.

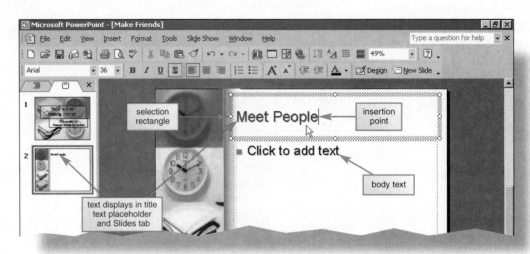

FIGURE 1-33

Other Ways

1. In Dictation mode, say "Meet People"

Selecting a Text Placeholder

Before you can type text into the text placeholder, you first must select it. Perform the following step to select the text placeholder on Slide 2.

Steps **To Select a Text Placeholder**

1 **Click the bulleted paragraph labeled, Click to add text.**

The insertion point displays immediately to the right of the bullet on Slide 2 (Figure 1-34). The mouse pointer may change shape if you move it away from the bullet. The selection rectangle indicates the text placeholder is selected.

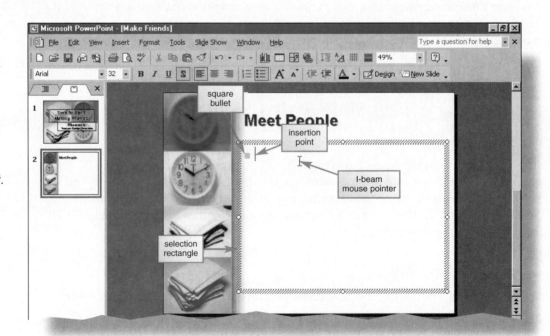

FIGURE 1-34

Other Ways

1. Press CTRL+ENTER

Typing a Single-Level Bulleted List

As discussed previously, a bulleted list is a list of paragraphs, each of which is preceded by a bullet. A paragraph is a segment of text ended by pressing the ENTER key. The next step is to type the single-level bulleted list, which consists of four entries (Figure 1-2b on page PP 1.09). Perform the following steps to type a single-level bulleted list.

Steps **To Type a Single-Level Bulleted List**

1 **Type** Develop confidence to introduce yourself to others **and then press the ENTER key.**

The paragraph, Develop confidence to introduce yourself to others, displays (Figure 1-35). The font size is 32. The insertion point displays after the second bullet. When you press the ENTER key, PowerPoint ends one paragraph and begins a new paragraph. With the Text slide layout, PowerPoint places a pink square bullet in front of the new paragraph.

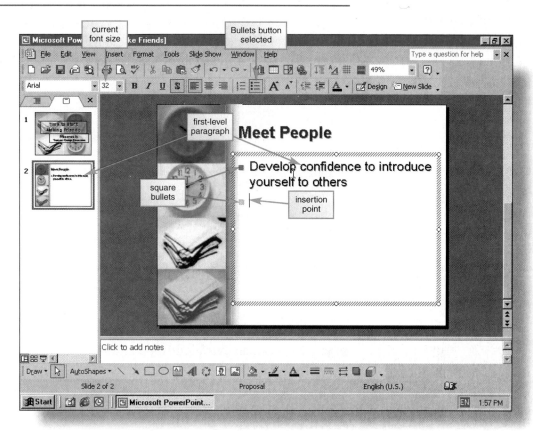

FIGURE 1-35

2 **Type** Make eye contact **and then press the ENTER key. Type** Smile and say, "Hi" **and then press the ENTER key. Type** Do not wait; start early in the semester **but do not press the ENTER key. Point to the New Slide button on the Formatting toolbar.**

The insertion point displays after the r in semester (Figure 1-36). Three new first-level paragraphs display with square bullets in both the text placeholder and the Slides tab. When you press the ENTER key, PowerPoint adds a new paragraph at the same level as the previous paragraph.

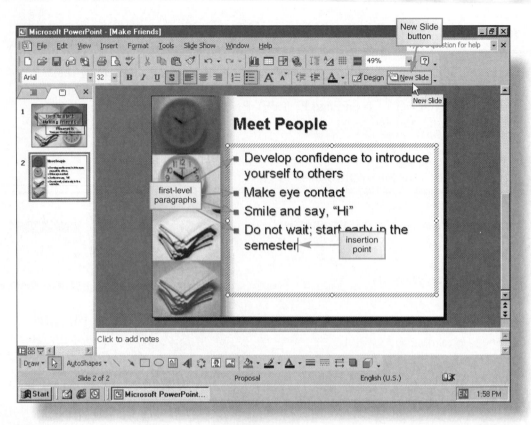

FIGURE 1-36

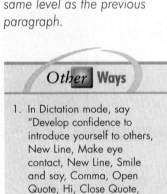

Other Ways

1. In Dictation mode, say "Develop confidence to introduce yourself to others, New Line, Make eye contact, New Line, Smile and say, Comma, Open Quote, Hi, Close Quote, New Line, Do not wait semicolon start early in the semester"

Notice that you did not press the ENTER key after typing the last paragraph in Step 2. If you press the ENTER key, a new bullet displays after the last entry on this slide. To remove an extra bullet, press the BACKSPACE key.

Creating a Text Slide with a Multi-Level Bulleted List

Slides 3 and 4 in Figure 1-2 on page PP 1.09 contain more than one level of bulleted text. A slide that consists of more than one level of bulleted text is called a **multi-level bulleted list slide**. Beginning with the second level, each paragraph indents to the right of the preceding level and is pushed down to a lower level. For example, if you increase the indent of a first-level paragraph, it becomes a second-level paragraph. This lower-level paragraph is a subset of the higher-level paragraph. It usually contains information that supports the topic in the paragraph immediately above it. You increase the indent of a paragraph by clicking the **Increase Indent button** on the Formatting toolbar.

When you want to raise a paragraph from a lower level to a higher level, you click the **Decrease Indent button** on the Formatting toolbar.

Creating a text slide with a multi-level bulleted list requires several steps. Initially, you enter a slide title in the title text placeholder. Next, you select the body text placeholder. Then, you type the text for the multi-level bulleted list, increasing and decreasing the indents as needed. The next several sections explain how to add a slide with a multi-level bulleted list.

Adding New Slides and Entering Slide Titles

When you add a new slide to a presentation, PowerPoint keeps the same layout used on the previous slide. PowerPoint assumes every new slide has a title. The title for Slide 3 is Find the Right Places. Perform the following steps to add a new slide (Slide 3) and enter a title.

Steps To Add a New Slide and Enter a Slide Title

1 **Click the New Slide button.**

Slide 3 of 3 displays in the slide pane and Slides tab (Figure 1-37).

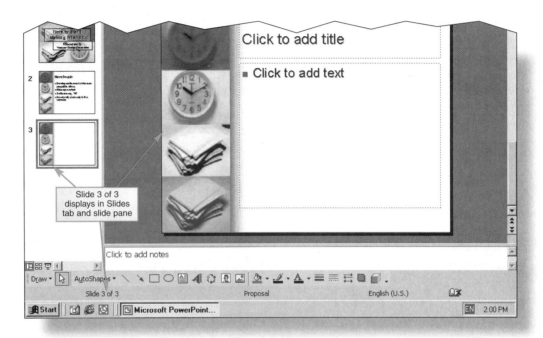

FIGURE 1-37

2 **Type** Find the Right Places **in the title text placeholder. Do not press the ENTER key.**

Slide 3 displays the Text slide layout with the title, Find the Right Places, in the title text placeholder and in the Slides tab (Figure 1-38). The insertion point displays after the s in Places.

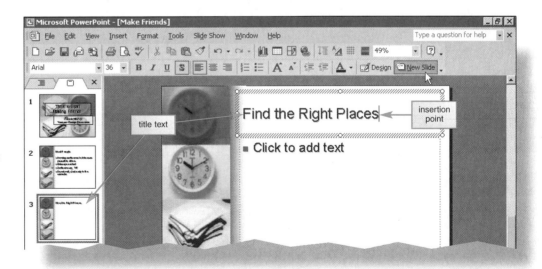

FIGURE 1-38

Slide 3 is added to the presentation with the desired title.

Other Ways

1. Press SHIFT+CTRL+M
2. In Dictation mode, say "New Slide, Find the right places"

Typing a Multi-Level Bulleted List

The next step is to select the body text placeholder and then type the multi-level bulleted list, which consists of five entries (Figure 1-2c on page PP 1.09). Perform the following steps to create a list consisting of three levels.

 To Type a Multi-Level Bulleted List

1 **Click the bulleted paragraph labeled, Click to add text.**

The insertion point displays immediately to the right of the bullet on Slide 3. The mouse pointer may change shape if you move it away from the bullet.

2 **Type** Go where people congregate **and then press the ENTER key. Point to the Increase Indent button on the Formatting toolbar.**

The paragraph, Go where people congregate, displays (Figure 1-39). The font size is 32. The insertion point displays to the right of the second bullet.

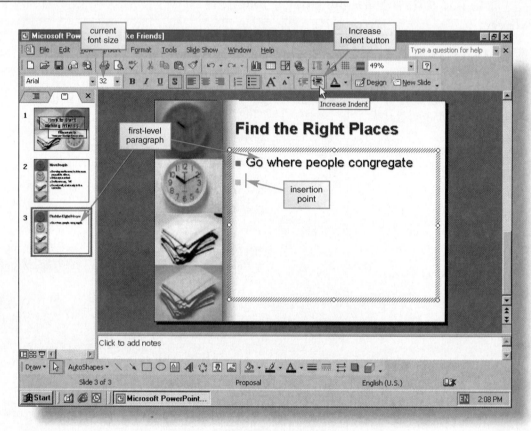

FIGURE 1-39

3 **Click the Increase Indent button.**

The second paragraph indents below the first and becomes a second-level paragraph (Figure 1-40). The bullet to the left of the second paragraph changes from a square to a circle, and the font size for the paragraph now is 28. The insertion point displays to the right of the circle.

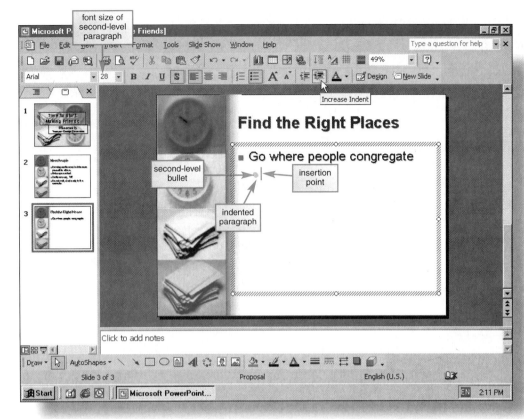

FIGURE 1-40

4 **Type** Student union, sports events **and then press the ENTER key. Point to the Decrease Indent button on the Formatting toolbar.**

The first second-level paragraph displays with a brown circle bullet in both the slide pane and the Slides tab (Figure 1-41). When you press the ENTER key, PowerPoint adds a new paragraph at the same level as the previous paragraph.

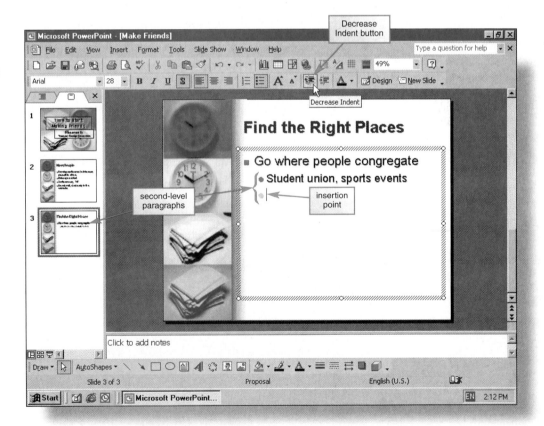

FIGURE 1-41

5 **Click the Decrease Indent button.**

The second-level paragraph becomes a first-level paragraph (Figure 1-42). The bullet of the new paragraph changes from a circle to a square, and the font size for the paragraph is 32. The insertion point displays to the right of the square bullet.

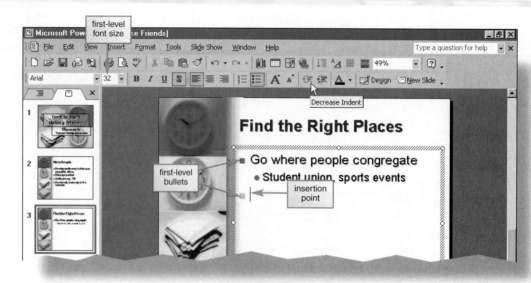

FIGURE 1-42

Other **Ways**

1. In Dictation mode, say, "Go where people congregate, New Line, Tab, Student union comma sports events, New Line, [type Backspace]"

Perform the following steps to complete the text for Slide 3.

TO TYPE THE REMAINING TEXT FOR SLIDE 3

1 Type Get involved in extracurricular activities and then press the ENTER key.

2 Click the Increase Indent button on the Formatting toolbar.

3 Type Participate in intramurals and then press the ENTER key.

4 Type Join Student Government but do not press the ENTER key.

Slide 3 displays as shown in Figure 1-43. The insertion point displays after the t in Government.

Other **Ways**

1. In Dictation mode, say "Get involved in extracurricular activities, New Line, Tab, Participate in intramurals, New Line, Join Student Government"

FIGURE 1-43

In Step 4 above, you did not press the ENTER key after typing the last paragraph. If you press the ENTER key, a new bullet displays after the last entry on this slide. To remove an extra bullet, press the BACKSPACE key.

Slide 4 is the last slide in this presentation. It also is a multi-level bulleted list and has three levels. Perform the following steps to create Slide 4.

TO CREATE SLIDE 4

1 Click the New Slide button on the Formatting toolbar.

2 Type Start a Conversation in the title text placeholder.

3 Press CTRL+ENTER to move the insertion point to the body text placeholder.

4 Type Talk about almost anything and then press the ENTER key.

5 Click the Increase Indent button on the Formatting toolbar. Type Comment on what is going on and then press the ENTER key.

The title and first two levels of bullets are added to Slide 4 (Figure 1-44).

Other Ways

1. In Dictation mode, say "New Slide, Start a conversation, New, Talk about almost anything, New Line, Tab, Comment on what is going on"

Creating a Third-Level Paragraph

The next line in Slide 4 is indented an additional level to the third level. Perform the following steps to create an additional level.

Steps **To Create a Third-Level Paragraph**

1 **Click the Increase Indent button on the Formatting toolbar.**

The second-level paragraph becomes a third-level paragraph (Figure 1-44). The bullet to the left of the new paragraph changes from a circle to a square, and the font size for the paragraph is 24. The insertion point displays after the square bullet.

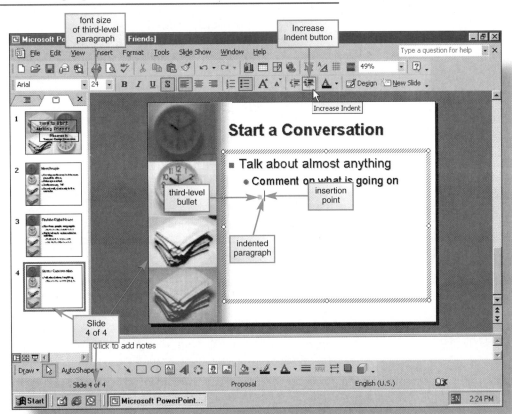

FIGURE 1-44

2 **Type** Long lines, class assignments **and then press the ENTER key. Point to the Decrease Indent button on the Formatting toolbar.**

The first third-level paragraph, Long lines, class assignments, displays with the bullet for a second third-level paragraph (Figure 1-45).

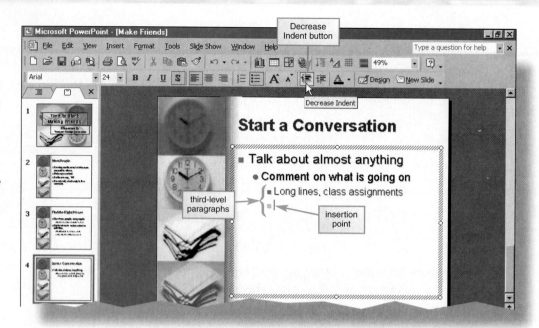

FIGURE 1-45

3 **Click the Decrease Indent button two times.**

The insertion point displays at the first level (Figure 1-46).

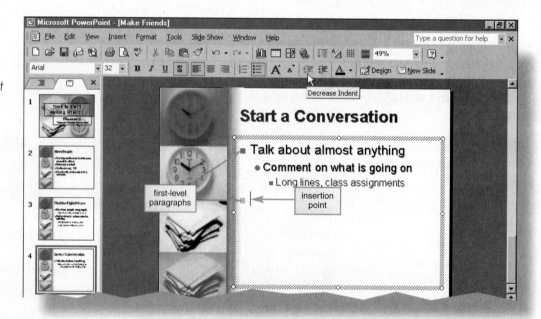

FIGURE 1-46

Other **Ways**

1. In Dictation mode, say "Tab, Long lines comma class assignments, New Line, [type backspace]"

The title text and three levels of paragraphs discussing conversation topics are complete. The next three paragraphs concern the types of questions to ask. As an alternative to clicking the Increase Indent button, you can press the TAB key. Likewise, instead of clicking the Decrease Indent button, you can press the SHIFT+TAB keys. Perform the following steps to type the remaining text for Slide 4.

TO TYPE THE REMAINING TEXT FOR SLIDE 4

1 Type Ask questions and then press the ENTER key.

2 Press the TAB key to increase the indent to the second level.

3 Type Get people to discuss their lives and then press the ENTER key.

4 Press the TAB key to increase the indent to the third level.

5 Type Hobbies, classes, and work but do not press the ENTER key.

Other Ways

1. In Dictation mode, say "Ask questions, New Line, Tab, Get people to discuss their lives, New Line, Tab, Hobbies comma classes comma and work"

The Slide 4 title text and body text display in the slide pane and Slides tabs (Figure 1-47). The insertion point displays after the k in work.

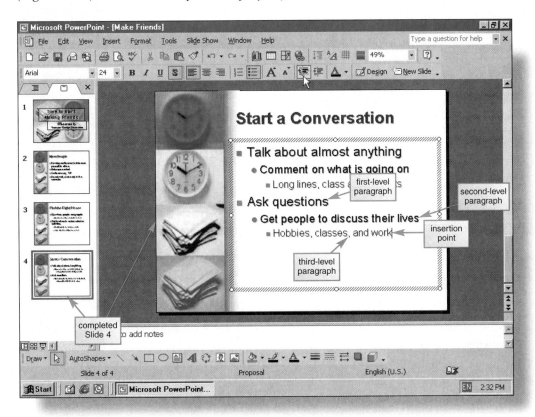

FIGURE 1-47

All the slides are created for the Make Friends slide show. This presentation consists of a title slide and three text slides with a multi-level bulleted list.

Ending a Slide Show with a Black Slide

After the last slide in the slide show displays, the default PowerPoint setting is to end the presentation with a black slide. This black slide displays only when the slide show is running and concludes the slide show gracefully so your audience never sees the PowerPoint window. A **black slide** ends all slide shows unless the option setting is deselected. Perform the steps on the next page to verify the End with black slide option is activated.

More About

More About Black Slides

Black slides can be used effectively to end a presentation, to pause for discussion, or to separate sections of a large presentation. The black slide focuses the audience's attention on you, the speaker, and away from the screen display.

Steps **To End a Slide Show with a Black Slide**

1 Click Tools on the menu bar and then point to Options (Figure 1-48).

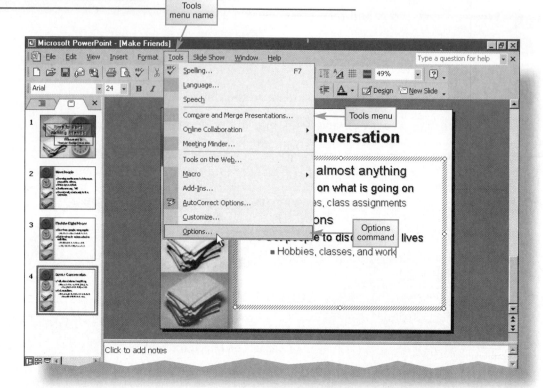

FIGURE 1-48

2 Click Options. If necessary, click the View tab when the Options dialog box displays. Verify that the End with black slide check box is selected. If a check mark does not display, click End with black slide, and then point to the OK button.

The Options dialog box displays (Figure 1-49). The View sheet contains settings for the overall PowerPoint display and for a particular slide show.

3 Click the OK button.

The End with black slide option will cause the slide show to end with a black slide until it is deselected.

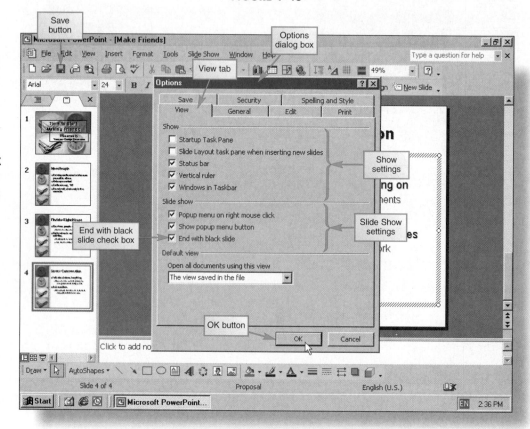

FIGURE 1-49

With all aspects of the presentation complete, it is important to save the additions and changes you have made to the Make Friends presentation.

Saving a Presentation with the Same File Name

Saving frequently cannot be overemphasized. When you first saved the presentation, you clicked the Save button on the Standard toolbar and the Save dialog box displayed. When you want to save the changes made to the presentation after your last save, you again click the Save button. This time, however, the Save dialog box does not display because PowerPoint updates the document called Make Friends.ppt on the floppy disk. Perform the following steps to save the presentation again.

TO SAVE A PRESENTATION WITH THE SAME FILE NAME

1   Be sure your floppy disk is in drive A.

2   Click the Save button on the Standard toolbar.

PowerPoint overwrites the old Make Friends.ppt document on the floppy disk in drive A with the revised presentation document. Slide 4 displays in the PowerPoint window.

Other Ways

1. In Voice Command mode, say "Save"

Moving to Another Slide in Normal View

When creating or editing a presentation in normal view, you often want to display a slide other than the current one. You can move to another slide using several methods. In the Outline tab, you can point to any of the text in a particular slide to display that slide in the slide pane, or you can drag the scroll box on the vertical scroll bar up or down to move through the text in the presentation. In the slide pane, you can click the Previous Slide or Next Slide button on the vertical scroll bar. Clicking the **Next Slide button** advances to the next slide in the presentation. Clicking the **Previous Slide button** backs up to the slide preceding the current slide. You also can drag the scroll box on the vertical scroll bar. When you drag the scroll box, the **slide indicator** displays the number and title of the slide you are about to display. Releasing the mouse button displays the slide.

A slide's **Zoom setting** affects the portion of the slide displaying in the slide pane. PowerPoint defaults to a setting of approximately 50 percent so the entire slide displays. This percentage depends on the size and type of your monitor. If you want to display a small portion of the current slide, you would zoom in by clicking the **Zoom box arrow** and then clicking the desired magnification. You can display the entire slide in the slide pane by clicking **Fit** in the Zoom list. The Zoom setting affects the action of the vertical and horizontal scroll bars. If Zoom is set so the entire slide is not visible in the slide pane, clicking the up scroll arrow on the vertical scroll bar displays the next portion of the slide, not the previous slide.

More About

Zoom Settings

You can increase your Zoom setting as large as 400% when you want to see details on small objects. Likewise, you can decrease your Zoom setting as small as 10%. When you want to redisplay the entire slide, click Fit in the Zoom list.

Using the Scroll Box on the Slide Pane to Move to Another Slide

Before continuing with Project 1, you want to display the title slide. Perform the steps on the next page to move from Slide 4 to Slide 1 using the scroll box on the slide pane vertical scroll bar.

Steps **To Use the Scroll Box on the Slide Pane to Move to Another Slide**

1 **Position the mouse pointer on the scroll box. Press and hold down the mouse button.**

Slide: 4 of 4 Start a Conversation displays in the slide indicator (Figure 1-50). When you click the scroll box, the Slide 4 thumbnail is not shaded in the Slides tab.

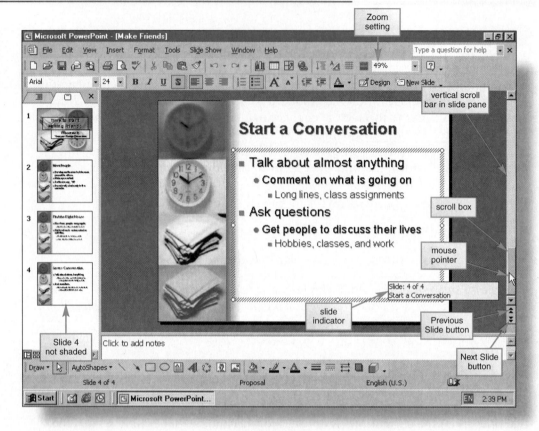

FIGURE 1-50

2 **Drag the scroll box up the vertical scroll bar until Slide: 1 of 4 Time to Start Making Friends displays in the slide indicator.**

Slide: 1 of 4 Time to Start Making Friends displays in the slide indicator (Figure 1-51). Slide 4 still displays in the PowerPoint window.

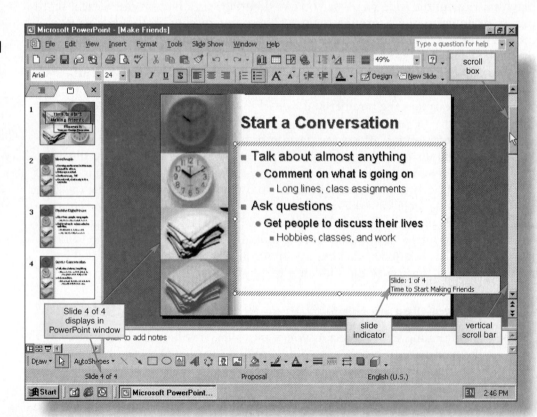

FIGURE 1-51

3 **Release the mouse button.**

Slide 1, titled Time to Start Making Friends, displays in the PowerPoint window (Figure 1-52). The Slide 1 thumbnail is shaded in the Slides tab indicating it is selected.

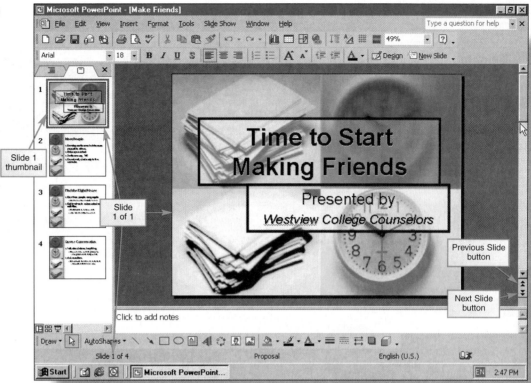

FIGURE 1-52

Other Ways

1. Click Next Slide button or Previous Slide button to move forward or back one slide
2. Press PAGE DOWN or PAGE UP to move forward or back one slide
3. In Voice Command mode, say "Next page" or "Previous page"

Viewing the Presentation in Slide Show View

The **Slide Show button**, located at the lower-left of the PowerPoint window above the status bar, allows you to display a presentation electronically using a computer. The computer acts like a slide projector, displaying each slide on a full screen. The full screen slide hides the toolbars, menus, and other PowerPoint window elements. When making a presentation, you use **slide show view**. You can start slide show view from normal view or slide sorter view.

Starting Slide Show View

Slide show view begins when you click the Slide Show button at the lower-left of the PowerPoint window above the status bar. PowerPoint then displays the current slide on the full screen without any of the PowerPoint window objects, such as the menu bar or toolbars. Perform the steps on the next page to start slide show view.

Steps **To Start Slide Show View**

1 **Point to the Slide Show button in** the lower-left corner of the PowerPoint window above the status bar (Figure 1-53).

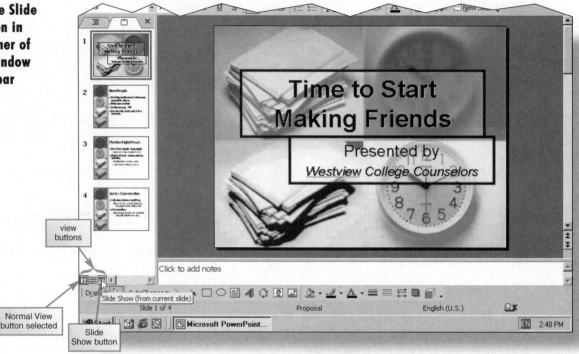

FIGURE 1-53

2 **Click the Slide Show button.**

A starting slide show message displays momentarily and then the title slide fills the screen (Figure 1-54). The PowerPoint window is hidden.

FIGURE 1-54

Other Ways

1. On View menu click Slide Show
2. Press F5
3. In Voice Command mode, say "View show"

Advancing Through a Slide Show Manually

After you begin slide show view, you can move forward or backward through the slides. PowerPoint allows you to advance through the slides manually or automatically. Perform the following steps to move manually through the slides.

 Steps To Move Manually Through Slides in a Slide Show

1 **Click each slide until the Start a Conversation slide (Slide 4) displays.**

Slide 4 displays (Figure 1-55). Each slide in the presentation displays on the screen, one slide at a time. Each time you click the mouse button, the next slide displays.

Slide 4 displays in slide show view

Start a Conversation

- Talk about almost anything
  - Comment on what is going on
    - Long lines, class assignments
- Ask questions
  - Get people to discuss their lives
    - Hobbies, classes, and work

FIGURE 1-55

2 **Click Slide 4.**

The black slide displays (Figure 1-56). The message at the top of the slide announces the end of the slide show. If you wanted to end the presentation at this point and return to normal view, you would click the black slide.

End of slide show, click to exit.

message

FIGURE 1-56

Using the Popup Menu to Go to a Specific Slide

Slide show view has a shortcut menu, called the **Popup menu,** that displays when you right-click a slide in slide show view. This menu contains commands to assist you during a slide show. For example, clicking the **Next command** moves to the next

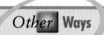

Other Ways

1. Press PAGE DOWN to advance one slide at a time, or press PAGE UP to go backward one slide at a time

2. Press RIGHT ARROW to advance one slide at a time, or press LEFT ARROW key to go back one slide at a time

slide. Clicking the **Previous command** moves to the previous slide. Pointing to the **Go command** and then clicking Slide Navigator allows you to move to any slide in the presentation. The **Slide Navigator dialog box** contains a list of the slides in the presentation. Go to the requested slide by double-clicking the name of that slide. Perform the following steps to go to the title slide (Slide 1) in the Make Friends presentation.

Steps **To Display the Popup Menu and Go to a Specific Slide**

1 **With the black slide displaying in slide show view, right-click the slide. Point to Go on the Popup menu, and then point to Slide Navigator on the Go submenu.**

The Popup menu displays on the black slide, and the Go submenu displays (Figure 1-57). Your screen may look different because the Popup menu displays near the location of the mouse pointer at the time you right-click.

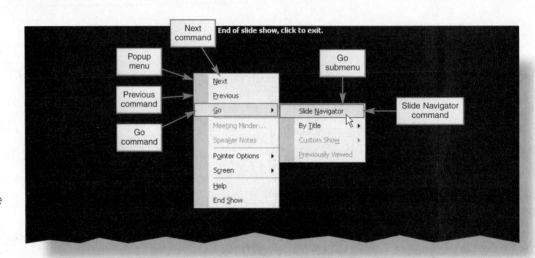

FIGURE 1-57

2 **Click Slide Navigator. When the Slide Navigator dialog box displays, point to 1. Time to Start Making Friends in the Slide titles list.**

The Slide Navigator dialog box contains a list of the slides in the presentation (Figure 1-58).

3 **Double-click 1. Time to Start Making Friends.**

The title slide, Time to Start Making Friends (shown in Figure 1-54 on page PP 1.48), displays.

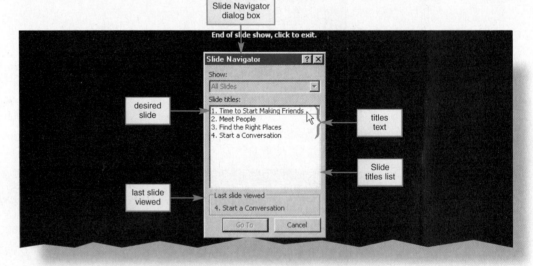

FIGURE 1-58

1. Right-click slide, point to Go on Popup menu, click Slide Navigator, type slide number, press ENTER

Additional Popup menu commands allow you to write meeting minutes or to create a list of action items during a slide show, change the mouse pointer to a pen that draws in various colors, blacken the screen, and end the slide show. Popup menu commands are discussed as they are used.

Using the Popup Menu to End a Slide Show

The **End Show command** on the Popup menu ends slide show view and returns to the same view as when you clicked the Slide Show button. Perform the following steps to end slide show view and return to normal view.

 Steps To Use the Popup Menu to End a Slide Show

1 **Right-click the title slide and then point to End Show on the Popup menu.**

The Popup menu displays on Slide 1 (Figure 1-59).

2 **Click End Show. If the Microsoft PowerPoint dialog box displays, click the Yes button.**

PowerPoint ends slide show view and returns to normal view (shown in Figure 1-60 on the next page). Slide 1 displays because it is the last slide displayed in slide show view.

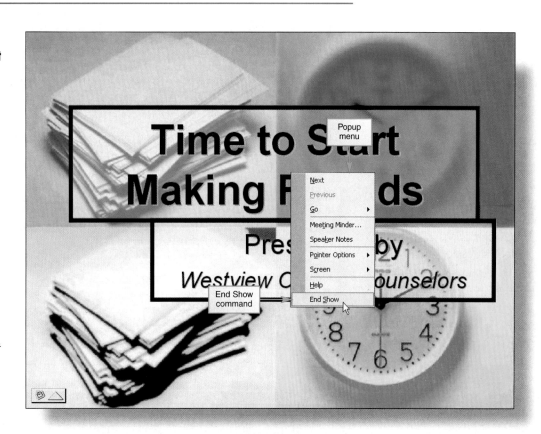

FIGURE 1-59

Quitting PowerPoint

The Make Friends presentation now is complete. When you quit PowerPoint, PowerPoint prompts you to save any changes made to the presentation since the last save, closes all PowerPoint windows, and then quits PowerPoint. Closing PowerPoint returns control to the desktop. Perform the steps on the next page to quit PowerPoint.

Other **Ways**

1. Click last slide in presentation (returns to normal view to slide at which slide show view began)
2. Press ESC (displays slide last viewed in slide show view)
3. In Voice Command mode say "Escape"

Steps **To Quit PowerPoint**

1 **Point to the Close button on the PowerPoint title bar (Figure 1-60).**

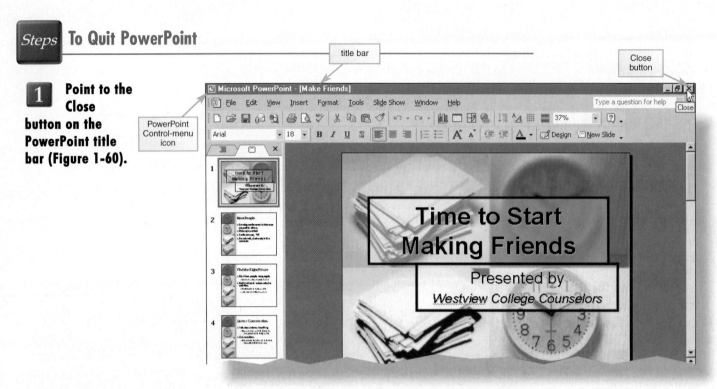

FIGURE 1-60

2 **Click the Close button.**

PowerPoint closes and the Windows desktop displays (Figure 1-61). If you made changes to the presentation since your last save, a Microsoft PowerPoint dialog box displays asking if you want to save changes. Clicking the Yes button saves the changes to the presentation before closing PowerPoint. Clicking the No button quits PowerPoint without saving the changes. Clicking the Cancel button returns to the presentation.

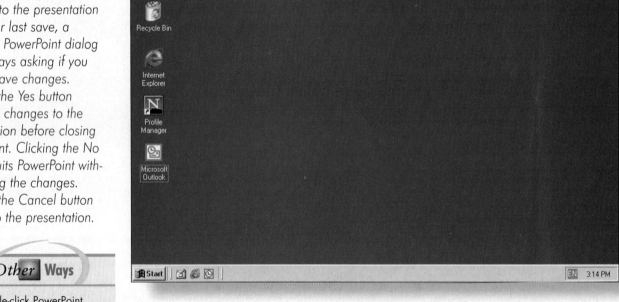

FIGURE 1-61

Other **Ways**

1. Double-click PowerPoint Control-menu icon; or click PowerPoint Control-menu icon, on Control menu click Close
2. On File menu click Exit
3. Press CTRL+Q or press ALT+F4

Opening a Presentation

Earlier, you saved the presentation on a floppy disk using the file name, Make Friends. Once you create and save a presentation, you may need to retrieve it from the floppy disk to make changes. For example, you may want to replace the design template or modify some text. Recall that a presentation is a PowerPoint document. Use the **Open Office Document command** to open an existing presentation.

Opening an Existing Presentation

Be sure that the floppy disk used to save the Make Friends presentation is in drive A. Then, perform the following steps to open the presentation using the Open Office Document command on the Start menu.

More About

Sound Files

Creating slide shows can be exciting if you add sound cues that play sounds when you scroll, open dialog boxes, and zoom in or out. You can download sound files from the Microsoft Web site. For more information, visit the PowerPoint 2002 More About Web page (scsite.com/ pp2002/more.htm) and then click Sound Files.

 To Open an Existing Presentation

1 **Click the Start button on the Windows taskbar and then point to Open Office Document.**

The Windows Start menu displays and Open Office Document is highlighted (Figure 1-62). The ScreenTip displays the function of the command.

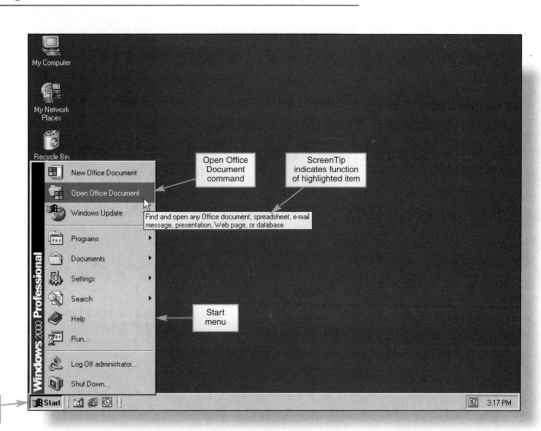

FIGURE 1-62

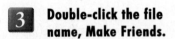

2 **Click Open Office Document. When the Open Office Document dialog box displays, if necessary, click the Look in box arrow and then click 3½ Floppy (A:) in the Look in list.**

The Open Office Document dialog box displays (Figure 1-63). A list of existing files displays on drive A. Notice that Office Files displays in the Files of type box. The file, Make Friends, is highlighted. Your list of existing files may be different depending on the files saved on your floppy disk.

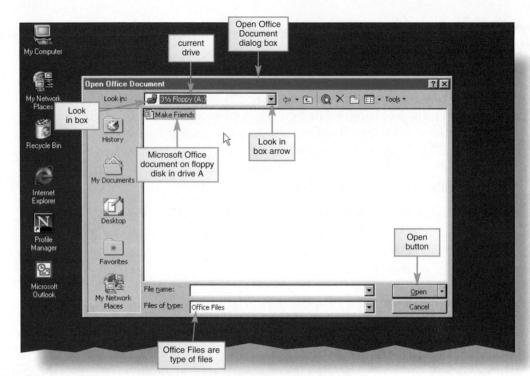

FIGURE 1-63

3 **Double-click the file name, Make Friends.**

PowerPoint starts, opens Make Friends on drive A, and displays the first slide in the PowerPoint window (Figure 1-64). The presentation displays in normal view because PowerPoint opens a presentation in the same view in which it was saved.

Other Ways

1. Click Open button on Standard toolbar, select file name, click Open button in Open Office Document dialog box

2. On File menu click Open, select file name, click Open button in Open dialog box

3. From desktop, right-click Start button, click either Open or Open All Users on shortcut menu, double-click Open Office Document, select file name, click Open button in Open Office Document dialog box

4. In Voice Command mode, say "Open file, [type file name], Open"

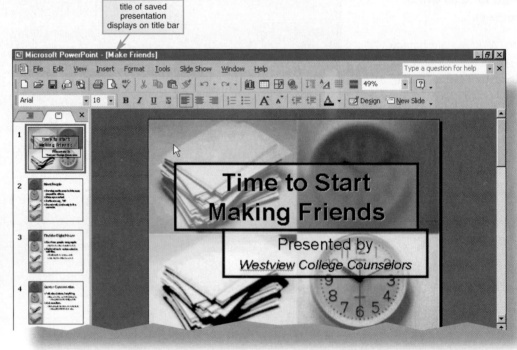

FIGURE 1-64

When you start PowerPoint and open Make Friends, the application name and file name display on a recessed button on the Windows taskbar. When more than one application is open, you can switch between applications by clicking the appropriate application button.

Checking a Presentation for Spelling and Consistency

After you create a presentation, you should check it visually for spelling errors and style consistency. In addition, you can use PowerPoint's Spelling and Style tools to identify possible misspellings and inconsistencies.

Checking a Presentation for Spelling Errors

PowerPoint checks the entire presentation for spelling mistakes using a standard dictionary contained in the Microsoft Office group. This dictionary is shared with the other Microsoft Office applications such as Word and Excel. A **custom dictionary** is available if you want to add special words such as proper names, cities, and acronyms. When checking a presentation for spelling errors, PowerPoint opens the standard dictionary and the custom dictionary file, if one exists. When a word displays in the Spelling dialog box, you perform one of the actions listed in Table 1-3.

> **More About**
>
> ## Spelling Checker
>
> While PowerPoint's Spelling checker is a valuable tool, it is not infallible. You should proofread your presentation carefully by saying each word aloud and pointing to each word as you say it. Be mindful of commonly misused words such as its and it's, their and they're, and you're and your.

Table 1-3	Summary of Spelling Checker Actions
FEATURE	*DESCRIPTION*
Ignore the word	Click the Ignore button when the word is spelled correctly but not found in the dictionaries. PowerPoint continues checking the rest of the presentation.
Ignore all occurrences of the word	Click the Ignore All button when the word is spelled correctly but not found in the dictionaries. PowerPoint ignores all occurrences of the word and continues checking the rest of the presentation.
Select a different spelling	Click the proper spelling of the word from the list in the Suggestions box. Click the Change button. PowerPoint corrects the word and continues checking the rest of the presentation.
Change all occurrences of the misspelling to a different spelling	Click the proper spelling of the word from the list in the Suggestions box. Click the Change All button. PowerPoint changes all occurrences of the misspelled word and continues checking the rest of the presentation.
Add a word to the custom dictionary	Click the Add button. PowerPoint opens the custom dictionary, adds the word, and continues checking the rest of the presentation.
View alternative spellings	Click the Suggest button. PowerPoint lists suggested spellings. Click the correct word from the Suggestions box or type the proper spelling. Then click the Change button. PowerPoint continues checking the rest of the presentation.
Add spelling error to AutoCorrect list	Click the AutoCorrect button. PowerPoint adds the spelling error and its correction to the AutoCorrect list. Any future misspelling of the word is corrected automatically as you type.
Close	Click the Close button to close the Spelling checker and return to the PowerPoint window.

The standard dictionary contains commonly used English words. It does not, however, contain proper names, abbreviations, technical terms, poetic contractions, or antiquated terms. PowerPoint treats words not found in the dictionaries as misspellings.

Starting the Spelling Checker

Perform the steps on the next page to start the Spelling checker and check the entire presentation.

Steps **To Start the Spelling Checker**

1 **Point to the Spelling button on the Standard toolbar (Figure 1-65).**

FIGURE 1-65

2 **Click the Spelling button. When the Spelling dialog box displays, point to the Ignore button.**

PowerPoint starts the Spelling checker and displays the Spelling dialog box (Figure 1-66). The word, Westview, displays in the Not in Dictionary box. Depending on the custom dictionary, Westview may not be recognized as a misspelled word.

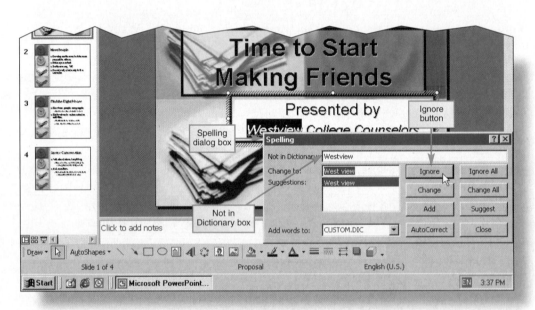

FIGURE 1-66

3 **Click the Ignore button. When the Microsoft PowerPoint dialog box displays, point to the OK button.**

PowerPoint ignores the word, Westview, and continues searching for additional misspelled words. PowerPoint may stop on additional words depending on your typing accuracy. When PowerPoint has checked all slides for misspellings, it displays the Microsoft PowerPoint dialog box informing you that the spelling check is complete (Figure 1-67).

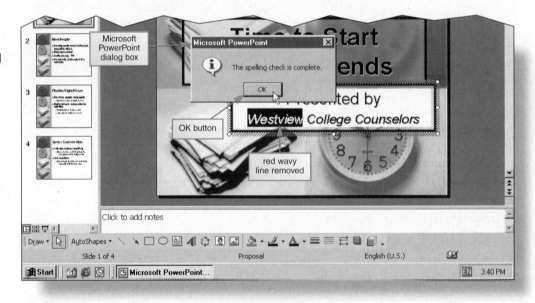

FIGURE 1-67

4 **Click the OK button.**

PowerPoint closes the Spelling checker and returns to the current slide, Slide 1 (Figure 1-68), or to the slide where a possible misspelled word displayed.

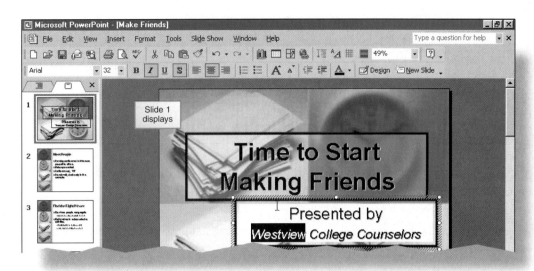

FIGURE 1-68

The red wavy line below the word, Westview, is gone because you instructed PowerPoint to ignore that word, which does not appear in the standard dictionary. You also could have added that word to the dictionary so it would not be flagged as a possible misspelled word in subsequent presentations you create using that word.

Other Ways

1. On Tools menu click Spelling
2. Press ALT+T, press S; when finished, press ENTER
3. In Voice Command mode, say "Tools, Spelling"

Correcting Errors

After creating a presentation and running the Spelling checker, you may find that you must make changes. Changes may be required because a slide contains an error, the scope of the presentation shifts, or the style is inconsistent. This section explains the types of errors that commonly occur when creating a presentation.

Types of Corrections Made to Presentations

You generally make three types of corrections to text in a presentation: additions, deletions, and replacements.

▶ **Additions** are necessary when you omit text from a slide and need to add it later. You may need to insert text in the form of a sentence, word, or single character. For example, you may want to add the rest of the presenter's first name on the title slide.

▶ **Deletions** are required when text on a slide is incorrect or no longer is relevant to the presentation. For example, a slide may look cluttered. Therefore, you may want to remove one of the bulleted paragraphs to add more space.

▶ **Replacements** are needed when you want to revise the text in a presentation. For example, you may want to substitute the word, their, for the word, there.

Editing text in PowerPoint basically is the same as editing text in a word processing package. The following sections illustrate the most common changes made to text in a presentation.

More About

Quick Reference

For a table that lists how to complete tasks covered in this book using the mouse, menu, shortcut menu, and keyboard, see the Quick Reference Summary at the back of this book or visit the Shelly Cashman Series Office XP Web page (scsite.com/offxp/qr.htm) and then click Microsoft PowerPoint 2002.

Deleting Text

You can delete text using one of four methods. One is to use the BACKSPACE key to remove text just typed. The second is to position the insertion point to the left of the text you wish to delete and then press the DELETE key. The third method is to double-click the word you wish to delete and then type the correct text. The fourth method is to drag through the text you wish to delete and then press the DELETE key. (Use the fourth method when deleting large sections of text.)

Table 1-4	Appearance in Black and White View	
OBJECT	**APPEARANCE IN BLACK AND WHITE VIEW**
Bitmaps	Grayscale
Embossing	Hidden
Fills	Grayscale
Frame	Black
Lines	Black
Object shadows	Grayscale
Pattern fills	Grayscale
Slide backgrounds	White
Text	Black
Text shadows	Hidden

Replacing Text in an Existing Slide

When you need to correct a word or phrase, you can replace the text by selecting the text to be replaced and then typing the new text. As soon as you press any key on the keyboard, the highlighted text is deleted and the new text displays.

PowerPoint inserts text to the left of the insertion point. The text to the right of the insertion point moves to the right (and shifts downward if necessary) to accommodate the added text.

Displaying a Presentation in Black and White

Printing handouts of a presentation allows you to use them to make overhead transparencies. The **Color/Grayscale button** on the Standard toolbar displays the presentation in black and white before you print. Table 1-4 identifies how PowerPoint objects display in black and white.

Perform the following steps to display the presentation in black and white.

Steps **To Display a Presentation in Black and White**

1 **Click the Color/ Grayscale button on the Standard toolbar and then point to Pure Black and White in the list.**

The Color/Grayscale list displays (Figure 1-69). Pure Black and White alters the slides' appearance so that only black lines display on a white background. Grayscale displays varying degrees of gray.

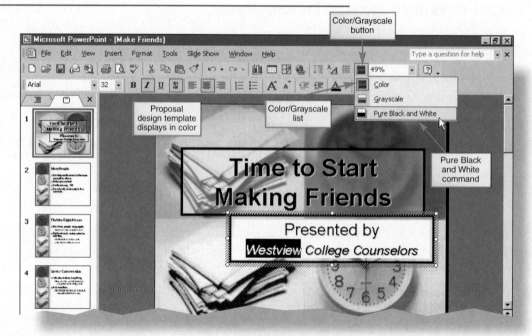

FIGURE 1-69

2 **Click Pure Black and White.**

Slide 1 displays in black and white in the slide pane (Figure 1-70). The four slide thumbnails display in color in the Slides tab. The Grayscale View toolbar displays. The Color/Grayscale button on the Standard toolbar changes from color bars to black and white.

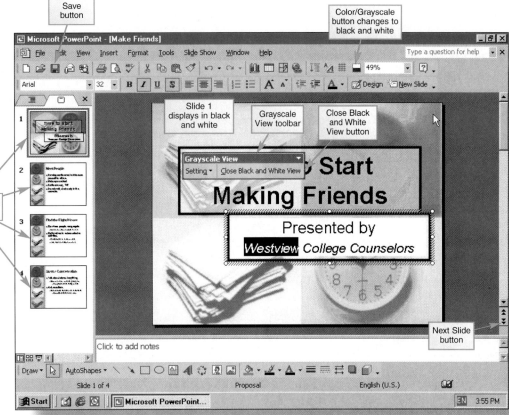

FIGURE 1-70

3 **Click the Next Slide button three times to view all slides in the presentation in black and white. Point to the Close Black and White View button on the Grayscale View toolbar (Figure 1-71).**

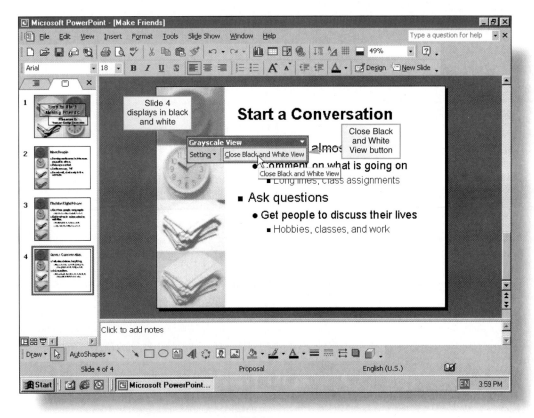

FIGURE 1-71

4 Click the Close Black and White View button.

Slide 4 displays with the default Proposal color scheme (Figure 1-72).

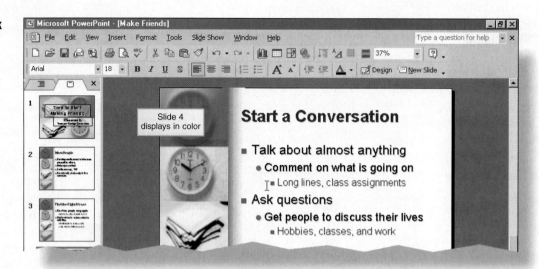

FIGURE 1-72

Other Ways

1. On View menu point to Color/Grayscale and then click Pure Black and White

2. In Voice Command mode, say "View, Color Grayscale, Pure Black and White"

More About

Printing

If you want to save ink, print faster, or decrease printer overrun errors, print a presentation in black and white. Click File on the menu bar and then click Print. When the Print dialog box displays, click the Color/grayscale box arrow, click Pure Black and White in the list, and then click the OK button.

After you view the text objects in the presentation in black and white, you can make any changes that will enhance printouts produced from a black and white printer or photocopier.

Printing a Presentation

After you create a presentation, you often want to print it. A printed version of the presentation is called a **hard copy**, or **printout**. The first printing of the presentation is called a **rough draft**. The rough draft allows you to proofread the presentation to check for errors and readability. After correcting errors, you print the final copy of the presentation.

Saving Before Printing

Before printing a presentation, you should save your work in the event you experience difficulties with the printer. You occasionally may encounter system problems that can be resolved only by restarting the computer. In such an instance, you will need to reopen the presentation. As a precaution, always save the presentation before you print. Perform the following steps to save the presentation before printing.

TO SAVE A PRESENTATION BEFORE PRINTING

1 Verify that the floppy disk is in drive A.

2 Click the Save button on the Standard toolbar.

All changes made after your last save now are saved on a floppy disk.

Printing the Presentation

After saving the presentation, you are ready to print. Clicking the **Print button** on the Standard toolbar causes PowerPoint to print all slides in the presentation. Perform the following steps to print the presentation slides.

PowerPoint Help System • PP 1.61

Steps To Print a Presentation

1 **Ready the printer according to the printer instructions. Then click the Print button on the Standard toolbar.**

The printer icon in the tray status area on the Windows taskbar indicates a print job is processing (Figure 1-73). After several moments, the slide show begins printing on the printer. When the presentation is finished printing, the printer icon in the tray status area on the Windows taskbar no longer displays.

2 **When the printer stops, retrieve the printouts of the slides.**

The presentation, Make Friends, prints on four pages (Figures 1-2a through 1-2d on page PP 1.09).

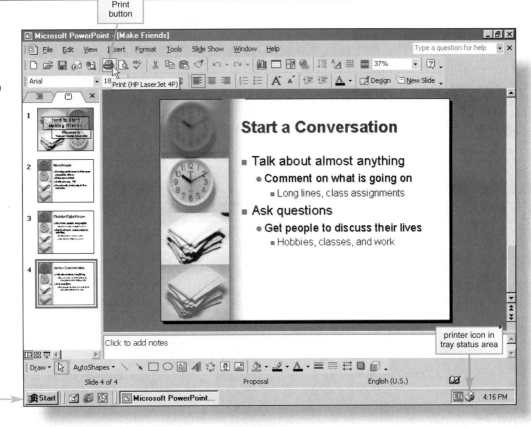

FIGURE 1-73

You can click the printer icon next to the clock in the tray status area on the Windows taskbar to obtain information about the presentations printing on your printer and to delete files in the print queue that are waiting to be printed.

Making a Transparency

With the handouts printed, you now can make overhead transparencies using one of several devices. One device is a printer attached to your computer, such as an ink-jet printer or a laser printer. Transparencies produced on a printer may be in black and white or color, depending on the printer. Another device is a photocopier. Because each of these devices requires a special transparency film, check the user's manual for the film requirement of your specific device, or ask your instructor.

PowerPoint Help System

You can get answers to PowerPoint questions at any time by using the **PowerPoint Help system.** Used properly, this form of assistance can increase your productivity and reduce your frustrations by minimizing the time you spend learning how to use PowerPoint.

Other Ways

1. On File menu click Print
2. Press CTRL+P or press CTRL+SHIFT+F12
3. In Voice Command mode, say "Print"

More *About*

The PowerPoint Help System

The best way to become familiar with the PowerPoint Help system is to use it. Appendix A includes detailed information on the PowerPoint Help system and exercises that will help you gain confidence in using it.

The following section shows how to get answers to your questions using the Ask a Question box on the menu bar. For additional information on using the PowerPoint Help system, see Appendix A and Table 1-5 on page PP 1.65.

Obtaining Help Using the Ask a Question Box on the Menu Bar

The **Ask a Question box** on the right side of the menu bar lets you type free-form questions such as, how do I save or how do I create a Web page, or you can type terms such as, copy, save, or format. PowerPoint responds by displaying a list of topics related to what you typed. The following steps show how to use the Ask a Question box to obtain information on formatting a presentation.

Steps **To Obtain Help Using the Ask a Question Box**

1 **Click the Ask a Question box on the right side of the menu bar and then type** bullet **(Figure 1-74).**

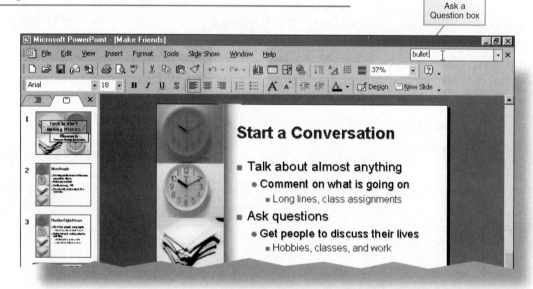

FIGURE 1-74

2 **Press the ENTER key. When the list of topics displays below the Ask a Question box, point to the topic, Change the bullet style in a list.**

A list of topics displays relating to the phrase, change the bullet style in a list (Figure 1-75). The mouse pointer changes to a hand, which indicates it is pointing to a link.

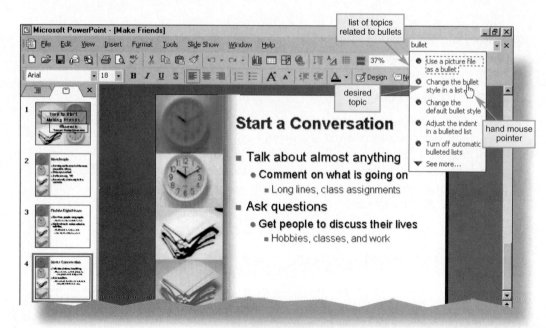

FIGURE 1-75

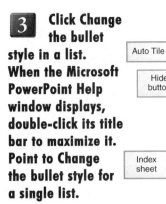

3 **Click Change the bullet style in a list. When the Microsoft PowerPoint Help window displays, double-click its title bar to maximize it. Point to Change the bullet style for a single list.**

A Microsoft PowerPoint Help window displays that provides Help information about changing the bullet style for a slide (Figure 1-76). The mouse pointer changes to a hand. The Index, Answer Wizard, or Content sheet is active on the left side of the Microsoft PowerPoint Help window.

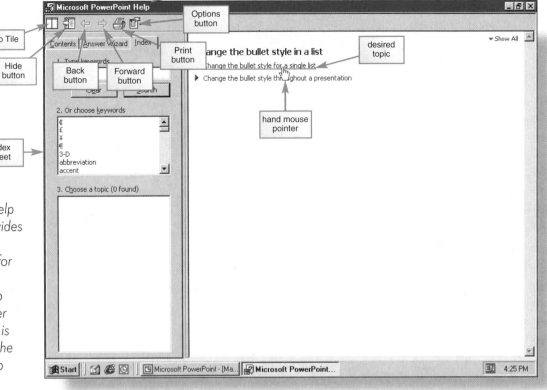

FIGURE 1-76

4 **Click Change the bullet style for a single list. Point to Change the bullet color.**

Directions for changing a bullet style on a single slide display. Options include changing a bullet character, changing a bullet size, and changing a bullet color (Figure 1-77).

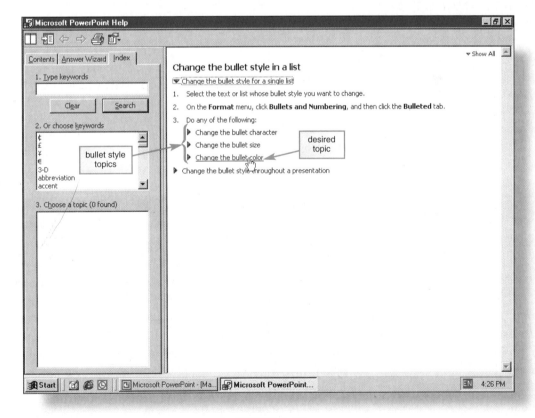

FIGURE 1-77

5 Click Change the bullet color. Point to the Close button on the Microsoft PowerPoint Help window title bar.

Specific details of changing the color of the bullets on a slide display (Figure 1-78).

6 Click the Close button on the Microsoft PowerPoint Help window title bar.

The PowerPoint Help window closes, and the PowerPoint presentation displays.

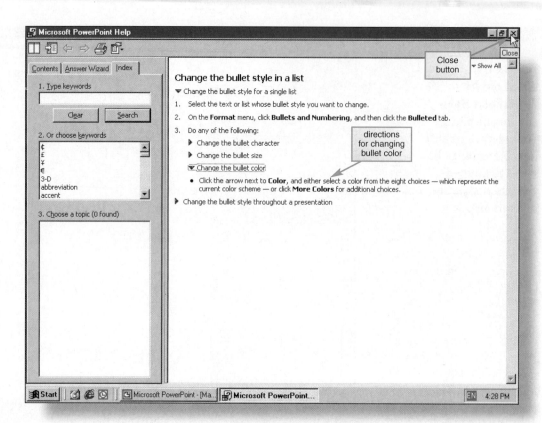

FIGURE 1-78

Other **Ways**

1. Click Microsoft PowerPoint Help button on Standard toolbar; or on Help menu click Microsoft PowerPoint Help
2. Press F1

Use the buttons in the upper-left corner of the Microsoft PowerPoint Help window (Figure 1-76 on page PP 1.63) to navigate through the Help system, change the display, and print the contents of the window.

As you enter questions and terms in the Ask a Question box, PowerPoint adds them to its list. Thus, if you click the Ask a Question box arrow, a list of previously asked questions and terms will display.

Table 1-5 summarizes the 10 categories of Help available to you. Because of the way the PowerPoint Help system works, be certain to review the rightmost column of Table 1-5 if you have difficulties activating the desired category of help. For additional information on using the PowerPoint Help system, see Appendix A.

Quitting PowerPoint

Project 1 is complete. The final task is to close the presentation and quit PowerPoint. Perform the following steps to quit PowerPoint.

TO QUIT POWERPOINT

1 Click the Close button on the title bar.

2 If prompted to save the presentation before quitting PowerPoint, click the Yes button in the Microsoft PowerPoint dialog box.

Table 1-5 PowerPoint Help System

TYPE	DESCRIPTION	HOW TO ACTIVATE
Answer Wizard	Answers questions or searches for terms that you type in your own words.	Click the Microsoft PowerPoint Help button on the Standard toolbar. Click the Answer Wizard tab.
Ask a Question box	Answers questions or searches for terms that you type in your own words.	Type a question or term in the Ask a Question box on the menu bar and then press the ENTER key.
Contents sheet	Groups Help topics by general categories. Use when you know only the general category of the topic in question.	Click the Microsoft PowerPoint Help button on the Standard toolbar. Click the Contents tab.
Detect and Repair	Automatically finds and fixes errors in the application.	Click Detect and Repair on the Help menu.
Hardware and Software Information	Shows Product ID and allows access to system information and technical support information.	Click About Microsoft PowerPoint on the Help menu and then click the appropriate button.
Index sheet	Similar to an index in a book. Use when you know exactly what you want.	Click the Microsoft PowerPoint Help button on the Standard toolbar. If necessary, maximize the Help window by double-clicking its title bar. Click the Index tab.
Office Assistant	Similar to the Ask a Question box in that the Office Assistant answers questions that you type in your own words, offers tips, and provides help for a variety of PowerPoint features.	Click the Office Assistant icon if it is on the screen. If the Office Assistant does not display, click Show the Office Assistant on the Help menu.
Office on the Web	Used to access technical resources and download free product enhancements on the Web.	Click Office on the Web on the Help menu.
Question Mark button	Used to identify unfamiliar items in a dialog box.	Click the Question Mark button on the title bar of a dialog box and then click an item in the dialog box.
What's This? Command	Used to identify unfamiliar items on the screen.	Click What's This? on the Help menu, and then click an item on the screen.

C A S E   P E R S P E C T I V E   S U M M A R Y

Jennifer Williams is pleased with the Time to Start Making Friends PowerPoint slide show. The counseling staff will present methods of facing loneliness to incoming freshmen attending orientation sessions at your school. The four slides display a variety of ways students can make friends on campus. The title slide identifies the topic of the presentation, and the next three slides give key pointers regarding going to appropriate places to meet people and start a conversation. The counselors will use your slides to make overhead transparencies to organize their speeches, and the students will keep handouts of your slides for future reference.

Project Summary

Project 1 introduced you to starting PowerPoint and creating a presentation consisting of a title slide and single- and multi-level bulleted lists. You learned about PowerPoint design templates, objects, and attributes. This project illustrated how to create an interesting introduction to a presentation by changing the text font style to italic and increasing font size on the title slide. Completing these tasks, you saved the presentation. Then, you created three text slides with bulleted lists, two with multi-level bullets, to explain how to meet friends in college. Next, you learned how to view the presentation in slide show view. Then, you learned how to quit PowerPoint and how to open an existing presentation. You used the Spelling checker to search for spelling errors. You learned how to display the presentation in black and white. You learned how to print hard copies of the slides in order to make handouts and overhead transparencies. Finally, you learned how to use the PowerPoint Help system.

What You Should Know

Having completed this project, you now should be able to perform the following tasks:

▶ Add a New Slide and Enter a Slide Title *(PP 1.37)*

▶ Add a New Text Slide with a Bulleted List *(PP 1.32)*

▶ Change the Text Font Style to Italic *(PP 1.26)*

▶ Choose a Design Template *(PP 1.19)*

▶ Create a Third-Level Paragraph *(PP 1.41)*

▶ Create Slide 4 *(PP 1.41)*

▶ Customize the PowerPoint Window *(PP 1.12)*

▶ Display a Presentation in Black and White *(PP 1.58)*

▶ Display the Popup Menu and Go to a Specific Slide *(PP 1.50)*

▶ End a Slide Show with a Black Slide *(PP 1.44)*

▶ Enter a Slide Title *(PP 1.34)*

▶ Enter the Presentation Subtitle *(PP 1.24)*

▶ Enter the Presentation Title *(PP 1.22)*

▶ Increase Font Size *(PP 1.27)*

▶ Move Manually Through Slides in a Slide Show *(PP 1.49)*

▶ Obtain Help Using the Ask a Question Box *(PP 1.62)*

▶ Open an Existing Presentation *(PP 1.53)*

▶ Print a Presentation *(PP 1.61)*

▶ Quit PowerPoint *(PP 1.52, 1.64)*

▶ Save a Presentation Before Printing *(PP 1.60)*

▶ Save a Presentation on a Floppy Disk *(PP 1.29)*

▶ Save a Presentation with the Same File Name *(PP 1.45)*

▶ Select a Text Placeholder *(PP 1.34)*

▶ Start PowerPoint *(PP 1.10)*

▶ Start Slide Show View *(PP 1.48)*

▶ Start the Spelling Checker *(PP 1.56)*

▶ Type a Multi-Level Bulleted List *(PP 1.38)*

▶ Type a Single-Level Bulleted List *(PP 1.35)*

▶ Type the Remaining Text for Slide 3 *(PP 1.40)*

▶ Type the Remaining Text for Slide 4 *(PP 1.43)*

▶ Use the Popup Menu to End a Slide Show *(PP 1.51)*

▶ Use the Scroll Box on the Slide Pane to Move to Another Slide *(PP 1.46)*

More About

Microsoft Certification

The Microsoft Office Specialist Certification program provides an opportunity for you to obtain a valuable industry credential — proof that you have the PowerPoint 2002 skills required by employers. For more information, see Appendix E or visit the Shelly Cashman Series Microsoft Office Specialist Web page at scsite.com/offxp/cert.htm.

Learn It Online

Instructions: To complete the Learn It Online excercises, start your browser, click the Address bar, and then enter scsite.com/offxp/exs.htm. When the Office XP Learn It Online page displays, follow the instructions in the exercises below.

1 Project Reinforcement TF, MC, and SA

Below PowerPoint Project 1, click the Project Reinforcement link. Print the quiz by clicking Print on the File menu. Answer each question. Write your first and last name at the top of each page, and then hand in the printout to your instructor.

2 Flash Cards

Below PowerPoint Project 1, click the Flash Cards link. When Flash Cards displays, read the instructions. Type 20 (or a number specified by your instructor) in the Number of Playing Cards text box, type your name in the Name text box, and then click the Flip Card button. When the flash card displays, read the question and then click the Answer box arrow to select an answer. Flip through Flash Cards. Click Print on the File menu to print the last flash card if your score is 15 (75%) correct or greater and then hand it in to your instructor. If your score is less than 15 (75%) correct, then redo this exercise by clicking the Replay button.

3 Practice Test

Below PowerPoint Project 1, click the Practice Test link. Answer each question, enter your first and last name at the bottom of the page, and then click the Grade Test button. When the graded practice test displays on your screen, click Print on the File menu to print a hard copy. Continue to take practice tests until you score 80% or better. Hand in a printout of the final practice test to your instructor.

4 Who Wants to Be a Computer Genius?

Below PowerPoint Project 1, click the Computer Genius link. Read the instructions, enter your first and last name at the bottom of the page, and then click the Play button. Hand in your score to your instructor.

5 Wheel of Terms

Below PowerPoint Project 1, click the Wheel of Terms link. Read the instructions, and then enter your first and last name and your school name. Click the Play button. Hand in your score.

6 Crossword Puzzle Challenge

Below PowerPoint Project 1, click the Crossword Puzzle Challenge link. Read the instructions, and then enter your first and last name. Click the Play button. Work the crossword puzzle. When you are finished, click the Submit button. When the crossword puzzle redisplays, click the Print button. Hand in the printout.

7 Tips and Tricks

Below PowerPoint Project 1, click the Tips and Tricks link. Click a topic that pertains to Project 1. Right-click the information and then click Print on the shortcut menu. Construct a brief example of what the information relates to in PowerPoint to confirm you understand how to use the tip or trick. Hand in the example and printed information.

8 Newsgroups

Below PowerPoint Project 1, click the Newsgroups link. Click a topic that pertains to Project 1. Print three comments. Hand in the comments.

9 Expanding Your Horizons

Below PowerPoint Project 1, click the Articles for Microsoft PowerPoint link. Click a topic that pertains to Project 1. Print the information. Construct a brief example of what the information relates to in PowerPoint to confirm you understand the contents of the article. Hand in the example and printed information.

10 Search Sleuth

Below PowerPoint Project 1, click the Search Sleuth link. To search for a term that pertains to this project, select a term below the Project 1 title and then use the Google search engine at google.com (or any major search engine) to display and print two Web pages that present information on the term. Hand in the printout.

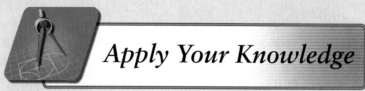

Apply Your Knowledge

1 Trends in Computer Technology

Instructions: Start PowerPoint. Open the presentation Computer Trends from the Data Disk. See the inside back cover of this book for instructions for downloading the Data Disk or see your instructor for information on accessing the files required for this book. This slide lists hardware and software trends in the computer industry. Perform the following tasks to change the slide so it looks like the one in Figure 1-79.

1. Click the Slide Design button on the Formatting toolbar. Scroll down and then choose the Kimono design template (row 12, column 1).
2. Select the title text. Click the Italic button on the Formatting toolbar.
3. Click the Font Size box arrow on the Font Size button on the Formatting toolbar and then click font size 36.
4. Click the paragraph, Microdisplays the size of stamps. Click the Increase Indent button on the Formatting toolbar to change the paragraph to a second-level paragraph. Then change these three paragraphs to second-level paragraphs: Digital books, Speech recognition, and Control of home systems.
5. Click the Appear as large as regular monitors paragraph. Click the Increase Indent button on the Formatting toolbar twice to change this paragraph to a third-level paragraph.
6. Click File on the menu bar and then click Save As. Type Trends in Technology in the File name text box. If drive A is not already displaying in the Save in box, click the Save in box arrow, and then click 3½ Floppy (A:). Click the Save button.
7. Click the Color/Grayscale button on the Standard toolbar, and then click Pure Black and White to display the presentation in black and white.
8. Click the Print button on the Standard toolbar.
9. Click the Close Black and White View button on the Grayscale View toolbar.
10. Click the Close button on the title bar to quit PowerPoint.
11. Write your name on the printout, and hand it in to your instructor.

Trends in Computer Technology

■ Software and hardware advances
   ■ Microdisplays the size of stamps
      ■ Appear as large as regular monitors
   ■ Digital books
   ■ Speech recognition
   ■ Control of home systems

FIGURE 1-79

In the Lab

Note: These labs require you to create presentations based on notes. When you design these slide shows, use the 7 × 7 rule, which states that each line should have a maximum of seven words, and each slide should have a maximum of seven lines.

1 Decades of Nutrition in the Twentieth Century

Problem: You are enrolled in a health class, and one of your assignments is to analyze nutrition and eating habits during the twentieth century. You decide to prepare a presentation for your class discussing food and related health problems during 20-year periods. You first develop the notes shown in Figure 1-80, and then you create the presentation shown in Figures 1-81a through 1-81f on pages PP 1.70 and PP 1.71.

I) Decades of Nutrition
Eating in the Twentieth Century
  A) Presented by
  B) Melissa Ruiz
  C) Health 101
II) 1900 - 1919
  A) Cold breakfast cereals introduced
  B) Ice cream sales soar
      1) First ice cream cone served
  C) Hershey introduces its chocolate bar
  D) Plump is preferred body type
      1) Slim is considered sickly
III) 1920 – 1939
  A) Kraft introduces Macaroni and Cheese
      1) Cooking from scratch begins to decline
  B) Red meat, vegetable intakes increase
  C) Heart disease on the rise
      1) Surpasses TB as leading cause of death
  D) Slim becomes preferred body type
IV) 1940 - 1959
  A) First McDonald's Hamburgers opens
      1) Home cooking begins to decline
  B) Research links heart disease with high saturated fats
  C) Fewer than 25 percent of Americans have healthy diets
V) 1960 - 1979
  A) Whole grains, Vitamin C gain popularity
  B) Soft drink consumption increases
      1) Exceeds milk consumption by 1980
  C) Federal committee finds unhealthy diets
      1) Too high in fats, sugar, salt, and meat
      2) Too low in grains, fruits, and vegetables
VI) 1980 - 1999
  A) Low-fat snacks flood grocery stores
      1) Americans still become more overweight
  B) Omega-3 fats found heart-healthy
      1) Found in fish, flaxseed
  C) Fish consumption increases
  D) Dairy and egg intakes decrease

FIGURE 1-80

In the Lab

Decades of Nutrition in the Twentieth Century *(continued)*

Decades of Nutrition
Eating in the Twentieth Century

Presented by
Melissa Ruiz
Health 101

(a) Slide 1 (Title Slide)

1900 - 1919

➢ Cold breakfast cereals introduced
➢ Ice cream sales soar
  • First ice cream cone served
➢ Hershey introduces its chocolate bar
➢ Plump is preferred body type
  • Slim is considered sickly

(b) Slide 2

1920 – 1939

➢ Kraft introduces Macaroni and Cheese
  • Cooking from scratch begins to decline
➢ Red meat, vegetable intakes increase
➢ Heart disease on the rise
  • Surpasses TB as leading cause of death
➢ Slim becomes preferred body type

(c) Slide 3

1940 - 1959

➢ First McDonald's Hamburgers opens
  • Home cooking begins to decline
➢ Research links heart disease with high saturated fats
  • Fewer than 25 percent of Americans have healthy diets

(d) Slide 4

FIGURE 1-81

In the Lab

1960 - 1979

➢ Whole grains, Vitamin C gain popularity
➢ Soft drink consumption increases
  • Exceeds milk consumption by 1980
➢ Federal committee finds unhealthy diets
  • Too high in fats, sugar, salt, and meat
  • Too low in grains, fruits, and vegetables

(e) Slide 5

1980 - 1999

➢ Low-fat snacks flood grocery stores
  • Americans still become more overweight
➢ Omega-3 fats found heart-healthy
  • Found in fish, flaxseed
    ‧ Fish consumption increases
➢ Dairy and egg intakes decrease

(f) Slide 6

FIGURE 1-81 *(continued)*

Instructions: Perform the following tasks.

1. Create a new presentation using the Ripple design template (row 19, column 1).

2. Using the typed notes illustrated in Figure 1-80, create the title slide shown in Figure 1-81a using your name in place of Melissa Ruiz. Italicize your name. Decrease the font size of the second paragraph of the title text to 36. Decrease the font size of the paragraph, Presented by, to 28. Decrease the font size of the paragraph, Health 101, to 24.

3. Using the typed notes in Figure 1-80 on page PP 1.69, create the five text slides with bulleted lists shown in Figures 1-81b through 1-81f.

4. Click the Spelling button on the Standard toolbar. Correct any errors.

5. Save the presentation using the file name, Nutrition.

6. Display the presentation in black and white.

7. Print the black and white presentation. Quit PowerPoint.

(continued)

In the Lab

2 Select Electric Products Open House

Problem: You work at Select Electric, a local store featuring a variety of electronic products. Your manager has asked you to participate in the semi-annual open house showcasing the latest consumer electronics. You decide to get involved by developing a PowerPoint presentation that helps customers view key features of various devices. You review the products that will be featured and develop the list shown in Figure 1-82. Then, you select a PowerPoint design template and decide to modify it.

> I) Electronics Explosion
>   A) Presented by
>   B) Select Electric
> II) High-Definition TV
>   A) Screens from 34 to 61 inches
>   B) Some models have two tuners
>   1) Picture-in-picture
>   a) Watch two shows at once
>   C) Inputs maximize digital sources
>   1) DVD and satellite
> III) Digital Camcorders
>   A) Razor-sharp recording
>   1) Image stabilization
>   B) Crystal-clear audio
>   C) Digital still photos
>   1) Store on removable memory card
>   a) CompactFlash, Memory Stick
> IV) Digital Cameras
>   A) Megapixels increase clarity
>   1) 4.3, 3.3, 2.1 megapixels
>   B) Optical and digital zoom
>   C) MPEG movie mode
>   1) Up to 60 seconds
>   a) 15 frames per second

FIGURE 1-82

In the Lab

Instructions: Perform the following tasks.

1. Create a new presentation using the Fireworks design template (row 10, column 2).

2. Using the notes in Figure 1-82, create the title slide shown in Figure 1-83a. Increase the font size of the paragraph, Electronics Explosion, to 48 and change the text font style to italic. Decrease the font size of the paragraph, Presented by, to 28.

3. Using the notes in Figure 1-82, create the three text slides with multi-level bulleted lists shown in Figures 1-83b through 1-83d.

(a) Slide 1 (Title Slide)

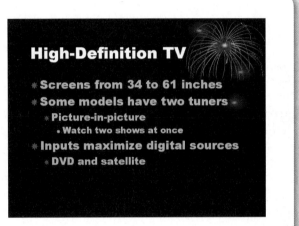

(b) Slide 2

(c) Slide 3

(d) Slide 4

FIGURE 1-83

(continued)

In the Lab

Select Electric Products Open House *(continued)*

4. Click the Spelling button on the Standard toolbar. Correct any errors.

5. Drag the scroll box to display Slide 1. Click the Slide Show button to start slide show view. Then click to display each slide.

6. Save the presentation using the file name, Select Electric. Display and print the presentation in black and white. Quit PowerPoint.

3 West Shore College Job Fair

Problem: Your school, West Shore College, is planning a job fair to occur during the week of midterm exams. The Placement Office has invited 150 companies and local businesses to promote its current and anticipated job openings. The Placement Office director, Bob Thornton, hands you the outline shown in Figure 1-84 and asks you to prepare a presentation and handouts to promote the event.

Instructions: Using the list in Figure 1-84, design and create a presentation. The presentation must include a title slide and three text slides with bulleted lists. Perform the following tasks.

1. Create a new presentation using the Cliff design template (row 4, column 1).

2. Create a title slide titled, West Shore College Career Fair. Include a subtitle, using your name in place of Bob Thornton. Decrease the font size for paragraphs, Presented by, and, West Shore Placement Office, to 28. Italicize your name.

3. Using Figure 1-84 create three text slides with multi-level bulleted lists. On Slide 4, change the color of the diamond bullets from gold to white.

4. View the presentation in slide show view to look for errors. Correct any errors.

5. Check the presentation for spelling errors.

6. Save the presentation with the file name, Career Fair. Print the presentation slides in black and white. Quit PowerPoint.

In the Lab

I) West Shore College Career Fair
  A) Presented by
  B) West Shore Placement Office
  C) Bob Thornton, Director
II) Who Is Coming?
  A) National corporations
        1) Progressive companies looking for high-quality candidates
  B) Local companies
        1) Full-time and part-time
          a) Hundreds of jobs
III) When Is It?
  A) Midterm week
        1) Monday through Friday
  B) West Shore College Cafeteria
  C) Convenient hours
        1) 9:00 a.m. to 8:00 p.m.
IV) How Should I Prepare?
  A) Bring plenty of resumes
        1) More than 150 companies expected
  B) Dress neatly
  C) View the Placement Office Web site
        1) Up-to-date information
        2) Company profiles

FIGURE 1-84

Cases and Places

The difficulty of these case studies varies:
▶ are the least difficult; ▶▶ are more difficult; and ▶▶▶ are the most difficult.

Note: Remember to use the 7 × 7 rule as you design the presentations: a maximum of seven words on a line and a maximum of seven lines on one slide.

1 ▶ Fitness Center employees present many classes on a variety of physical and emotional wellness topics. The coordinator, Carol O'Malley, has contacted you to help her prepare a presentation that will be delivered at community fairs and at the local shopping mall. She has prepared the notes shown in Figure 1-85 and has asked you to use them to develop a title slide and additional text slides that can be used on an overhead projector. Use the concepts and techniques introduced in this project to create the presentation.

> **Enhance Your Physical and Emotional Wellness**
> **At the Mid-City College Fitness Center**
> Carol O'Malley, director
>
> **Mind/Body Programs**
>   Meditation
>   Various techniques
>   Time to practice included
>   Stress Management Workshop
>   Relaxation strategies
>   Four-part series
>
> **Lifestyle Programs**
>   CPR and First Aid
>   Certification and recertification
>   American Red Cross instructors
>   Smoking Cessation
>   Eight-session group program
>   Individual consultations
>
> **Nutrition Programs**
>   Nutrition Connection
>   Semester-long program
>   Change your lifestyle to enhance your health
>   Achieve your weight-management goals
>   Increase your self-esteem
>   Dining Out: Eat and Be Healthy

FIGURE 1-85

Cases and Places

2 ▶ More than 76 million Americans currently carry cellular telephones, and many of these people use their telephones while driving. Although 87 percent of adults believe using a cellular telephone impairs their ability to drive, motorists continue to place and receive calls while driving. Andy Allman, your Lo-Rate Insurance agent, knows you are learning PowerPoint and asks you to help him prepare a presentation that will be delivered at shopping centers and on campus. He has prepared the notes shown in Figure 1-86 and wants you to use them to develop a title slide and additional text slides for a presentation and handouts. Use the concepts and techniques introduced in this project to create the slide show.

Calling All Cars
Using Your Telephone Safely in Your Vehicle
Andy Allman
Lo-Rate Insurance Agency

Cellular telephones distract from driving
   37 percent of drivers say they have had a near miss with someone using a cellular telephone
   2 percent of drivers have had an accident with someone using a cellular telephone
   Some communities have banned cellular telephone use behind the wheel

Your telephone can be a safety tool
   More than 118,000 calls placed daily to 911 from cellular telephones
   Emergency response times have decreased as 911 calls have increased

Use your telephone responsibly
   Place calls before pulling into traffic
   Use your telephone's special features such as speed dial and redial
   Do not call in hazardous weather or heavy traffic
   Do not take notes or look up numbers while driving
   Do not engage in emotional or stressful conversations
   50 percent of drivers seldom or never use a telephone while driving

FIGURE 1-86

Cases and Places

3 ▶▶ Road Warrior is a business near campus that specializes in quick oil changes, headlight and windshield wiper replacement, flat repair, battery recharging, and interior and exterior cleaning. The owners, Homer and Hank Wilson, want to attract new customers, and they have asked you to help design a PowerPoint advertising campaign for them. Having graduated from your college, they are familiar with the vehicles students drive and the students' financial situations. Students can make appointments to bring their vehicles to the shop or to arrange for on-site service 24 hours a day. Road Warrior also carries a complete line of accessories, including lightbulbs, fuses, air fresheners, and air and oil filters. Many students consult with the technicians to plan for future service and to arrange financing for their repairs. The business is located in Highwood Mall, 1580 North Western Street, West Grove, Michigan. The telephone number is 555-2297. Using the techniques presented in this project, prepare a title slide and four text slides with bulleted lists for the presentation and for handouts.

4 ▶▶ Every year people suffer from more than one billion colds. While no remedy cures the runny nose and sore throat that accompany the common cold, students can reduce their chances of catching a cold and feel better when they are sick. Peter Script, the pharmacist at the drug store near campus, would like you to prepare a short PowerPoint presentation and handouts to educate customers about how to thwart the common cold. He tells you that students should get plenty of rest, drink plenty of fluids, and consume chicken soup when they feel cold symptoms. If their throats are sore, they should gargle with warm salt water or let a lozenge with menthol and a mild anesthetic dissolve slowly in their mouths. Decongestants help relieve a stuffy nose by shrinking blood vessels, but these drugs should not be taken for more than three days. Antihistamines relieve a runny nose, itching, and sneezing by having a drying effect. To avoid a cold, students should stay away from other people with colds, wash their hands frequently and keep them away from their mouths and noses, and dispose of tissues promptly. Using the techniques presented in this project, prepare a title slide and several text slides for their presentation and for handouts.

5 ▶▶ Family reunions are popular ways to unite relatives from all parts of the globe. You have successfully planned three reunions for your family, and your friends have asked you for assistance with their plans. You decide to prepare a PowerPoint presentation to share with them and use as a planning outline. As you reflect on your reunion successes, you recall that the first step is to find the right location for the event. You try to choose somewhere centrally located. You consider a city that everyone can reach by plane or by driving in a few hours, that has adequate accommodations, and a variety of tourist attractions for entertainment, sightseeing, and dining. Avoid cities with adverse weather conditions or with poor airline connections. Favorable cities are Dallas; Washington, D.C.; Las Vegas; and Reno/Lake Tahoe. Cruises and all-inclusive resorts are possibilities. Other planning tips are to use e-mail extensively to send plans to family members simultaneously and to use the Internet to find inexpensive airline tickets and explore the destination's Web site. Using the concepts and techniques presented in this project, prepare a title slide and at least three text slides for the presentation and for handouts.

Cases and Places

6 ▶▶▶ As discussed in the beginning of this project, approximately one-third of college students participate in student activities other than sports. Visit your campus student activities or Student Government
offices and discover what activities are among the more popular at school. Find out which events drew
the largest audiences this past semester, how much revenue was generated from these events, and what
the expenses were for the college. Then, learn which activities are planned for the next semester and for
next year. Who plans these events, and how are these individuals appointed or elected to these positions?
Using the concepts and techniques presented in this project, prepare a presentation to inform students
and staff about campus activities. Create a title slide and at least three additional slides that can be used
with an overhead projector and as handouts.

7 ▶▶▶ Dry cleaning expenses can affect a student's budget. Visit two local dry cleaning establishments and
obtain the costs of cleaning and pressing a shirt, a pair of pants, a jacket, and a dress. Discover if dis-
counts are available for students and on certain days of the week. Finally, learn how students may
reduce cleaning expenses by treating spots on their clothing. Then, using the concepts and techniques
presented in this project, prepare a presentation to report your findings. Create a title slide and at least
three additional slides that can be used with an overhead projector and as handouts.

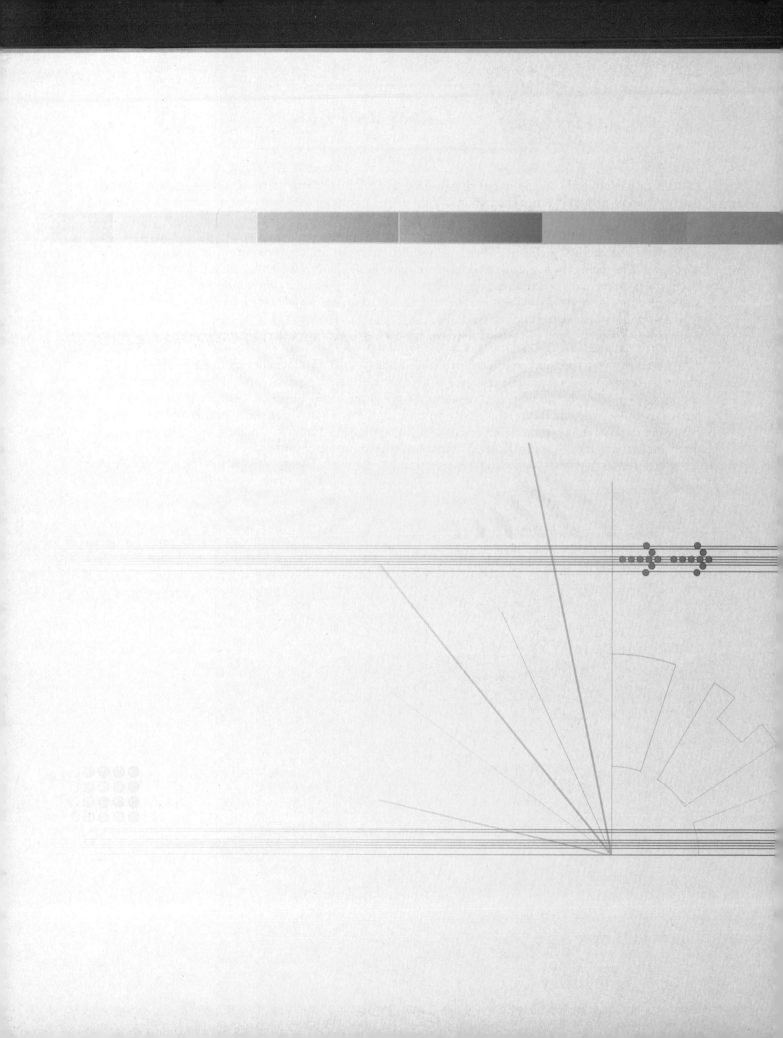

Microsoft PowerPoint 2002

Using the Outline Tab and Clip Art to Create a Slide Show

You will have mastered the material in this project when you can:

O B J E C T I V E S

- ▦ Create a presentation from an outline
- ▦ Start and customize a new slide show
- ▦ Create a presentation using the Outline tab
- ▦ Add a slide on the Outline tab
- ▦ Create text slides with a single-level bulleted list on the Outline tab
- ▦ Create text slides with a multi-level bulleted list on the Outline tab
- ▦ Create a closing slide on the Outline tab
- ▦ Save and review a presentation
- ▦ Change the slide layout
- ▦ Insert clip art from the Microsoft Clip Organizer
- ▦ Use the Automatic Layout Options button
- ▦ Move clip art
- ▦ Change clip art size
- ▦ Add a header and footer to outline pages
- ▦ Add an animation scheme to a slide show
- ▦ Animate clip art
- ▦ Run an animated slide show
- ▦ Print a presentation outline
- ▦ E-mail a slide show from within PowerPoint

Plan, Prepare, and Practice

Formula for a Flawless Presentation

Public speaking are two words that strike panic in the hearts of millions of people the world over. The mere thought of standing in front of an audience and trying to maintain composure and focus to convey a message tops the list of absolute fears for the vast majority of people. When asked to describe their experience of public speaking, many individuals recall dry mouths, sweaty palms, queasy stomachs, and shaky knees.

Business News Now

- Sales have increased by an amazing 34%
- Employee productivity is up by 12%
- You just impressed your boss with a great presentation.

Now, with the powerful presentation graphics capabilities of PowerPoint, the anxiety of speech-making can be somewhat eased. You have learned that this software helps you organize your thoughts and present information in an orderly, attractive manner. In this project, you will add to your current knowledge of PowerPoint by creating a presentation from an outline, changing the slide layout, and inserting and modifying clip art from the Microsoft Clip Organizer. With the abundant tools available in PowerPoint, your slide shows will have visual appeal and ample content.

While the PowerPoint slide shows help you plan your speeches, they also help your audience absorb your message. People learn most effectively when their five senses are involved. Researchers have determined that individuals remember 10 percent of what they read, 20 percent of what they hear, 30 percent of what they see, and an amazing 70 percent when they both see and hear. That is why it is important to attend class instead of copying your classmate's notes. When you see and hear your instructor deliver a lecture and write your own notes, you are apt to interpret the concepts correctly and recall this information at the ever-important final exam.

The synergy of the speech-graphics combo is recognized in a variety of venues. For example, some college administrators and instructors are requiring students to register for their communications and PowerPoint classes concurrently. The theories of structuring effective communication presentations are deep rooted. Dale Carnegie wrote *How to Win Friends and Influence People* in 1936, and the millions of people who have read that book have learned practical advice on achieving success through communication. He formed the Dale Carnegie Institute, which has taught millions of graduates worldwide the techniques of sharing ideas effectively and persuading others. Microsoft has included Carnegie's four-step process — plan, prepare, practice, and present — in the PowerPoint Help system. Dale Carnegie Training® has incorporated Microsoft PowerPoint to provide powerful presentation tips in its courses and seminars.

In the days prior to PowerPoint, slides and overhead transparencies were the domain of artists in a corporation's graphic communications department. With the influx of Microsoft Office on desktops throughout a company, however, employees from all departments now develop the slide shows.

With proper planning, preparation, practice, and the popularity of PowerPoint for organizing ideas into artful presentations, speakers today successfully deliver their messages with poise and confidence.

Microsoft PowerPoint 2002

Using the Outline Tab and Clip Art to Create a Slide Show

PROJECT

2

CASE PERSPECTIVE

Cruising has taken on a new meaning for college students. Instead of driving endlessly with a few friends in an old car down boring neighborhood streets, today's students sail endlessly with friends on spectacular ships to exciting destinations. They experience an adventure they will never forget as they snorkel in crystal clear waters among glimmering tropical fish, explore fascinating cities, and watch the sun set from some of the most scenic locations in the world.

Wanting to capitalize on this vacation trend, the Office of Student Activities (OSA) at your school wants to sponsor a college-wide Spring Break cruise to the Caribbean. The Student Activities director, Maria Lopez, has asked you to help with the marketing efforts. She knows you have extensive computer experience and wants you to develop a PowerPoint presentation that advertises the trip and its highlights. The slide show will give an overview of the ports of call, activities, and cruise details. You decide to add clip art and animation to increase visual interest. Then you e-mail the completed presentation to Maria.

Introduction

At some time during either your academic or business life, you probably will make a presentation. The presentation may be informative by providing detailed information about a specific topic. Other presentations may be persuasive by selling a proposal or a product to a client, convincing management to approve a new project, or influencing the board of directors to accept the new fiscal budget. As an alternative to creating your presentation in the slide pane in normal view, as you did in Project 1, PowerPoint provides an outlining feature to help you organize your thoughts. When the outline is complete, it becomes the foundation for your presentation.

Project Two — Enjoy Spring Break in the Caribbean

Project 2 uses PowerPoint to create the five-slide Spring Break presentation shown in Figures 2-1a through 2-1e. You create the presentation from the outline shown in Figure 2-2 on page 2.06.

You can create your presentation outline using the Outline tab. When you create an outline, you type all the text at one time, as if you were typing an outline on a sheet of paper. This technique differs from creating a presentation in the slide pane in normal view, where you type text as you create each individual slide and the text displays in both the slide pane and on the Outline tab. PowerPoint creates the presentation as you type the outline by evaluating the outline structure and displaying a miniature view of the slide. Regardless of how you build a presentation, PowerPoint automatically creates the three views discussed in Project 1: normal, slide sorter, and slide show.

PP 2.04

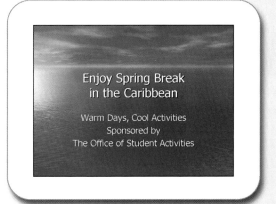

(a) Slide 1

(b) Slide 2

(c) Slide 3

(d) Slide 4

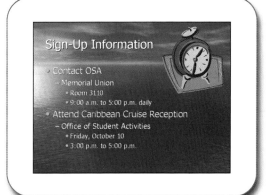

(e) Slide 5

FIGURE 2-1

The first step in creating a presentation on the Outline tab is to type a title for the outline. The **outline title** is the subject of the presentation and later becomes the presentation title text. Then, you type the remainder of the outline, indenting appropriately to establish a structure, or hierarchy. Once the outline is complete, you make your presentation more persuasive by adding **clips**, which are media files of art, animation, sound, and movies. This project uses outlining to create the presentation and clip art to support the text visually.

More *About*

The PowerPoint Help System

Need Help? It is no further than the Ask a Question box in the upper-right corner of the window. Click the box that contains the text, Type a question for help (Figure 2-3), type help, and then press the ENTER key. PowerPoint will respond with a list of items you can click to learn about obtaining help on any PowerPoint-related topic. To find out what is new in PowerPoint 2002, type what's new in PowerPoint in the Ask a Question box.

I. Enjoy Spring Break in the Caribbean
   A. Warm Days, Cool Activities
   B. Sponsored by
   C. The Office of Student Activities
II. Onshore Adventures
   A. Golf, play volleyball, swim, and relax
   B. Experience a submarine tour
   C. Try parasailing
   D. Explore a rainforest
III. Onboard Activities
   A. Theaters, fitness center, and stores
      1. Make new friends
      2. Dance to the hits
   B. Indoor and outdoor pools and whirlpools
IV. Cruise Details
   A. Only $999, including all meals
      1. Seven-day vacation departs from Miami
   B. Unforgettable ports of call
      1. Frederiksted, St. Croix
      2. San Juan, Puerto Rico
      3. Charlotte Amalie, St. Thomas
V. Sign-Up Information
   A. Contact OSA
      1. Memorial Union
      2. Room 3110
      3. 9:00 a.m. to 5:00 p.m. daily
   B. Attend Caribbean Cruise Reception
      1. Office of Student Activities
      2. Friday, October 10
      3. 3:00 p.m. to 5:00 p.m.

FIGURE 2-2

Start a New Presentation

Project 1 introduced you to starting a presentation document, choosing a layout, and applying a design template. The following steps summarize how to start a new presentation, choose a layout, and apply a design template. To reset your toolbars and menus so they display exactly as shown in this book, follow the steps outlined in Appendix D. Perform the following steps to start and customize a new presentation.

TO START AND CUSTOMIZE A NEW PRESENTATION

1 Click the Start button on the Windows taskbar, point to Programs on the Start menu, and then click Microsoft PowerPoint on the Programs submenu.

2 If the New Presentation task pane displays, click the Show at startup check box to remove the check mark and then click the Close button on the task pane title bar.

3 If the Language bar displays, click its Minimize button.

4 Click the Slide Design button on the Formatting toolbar. When the Slide Design task pane displays, click the down scroll arrow in the Apply a design template list, and then click the Ocean template in the Available For Use area.

5 Click the Close button in the Slide Design task pane.

6 If the Standard and Formatting toolbars display on one row, click the Toolbar Options button on the right side of either toolbar and then click Show Buttons on Two Rows on the Toolbar Options menu.

PowerPoint displays the Title Slide layout and the Ocean template on Slide 1 in normal view (Figure 2-3).

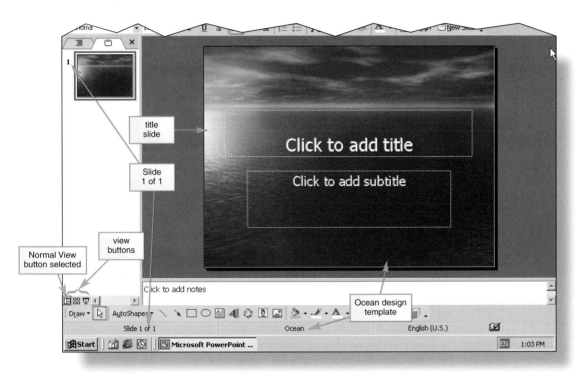

FIGURE 2-3

Using the Outline Tab

The **Outline tab** provides a quick, easy way to create a presentation. **Outlining** allows you to organize your thoughts in a structured format. An outline uses indentation to establish a **hierarchy**, which denotes levels of importance to the main topic. An outline is a summary of thoughts, presented as headings and subheadings, often used as a preliminary draft when you create a presentation.

The three panes — tabs, slide, and notes — shown in normal view also display when you click the Outline tab. The notes pane displays below the slide pane. In the tabs pane, the slide text displays along with a slide number and a slide icon. Body text is indented below the title text. Objects, such as pictures, graphs, or tables, do not display. The slide icon is blank when a slide does not contain objects. The attributes for text on the Outline tab are the same as in normal view except for color and paragraph style.

PowerPoint formats a title style and five levels of body text in an outline. The outline begins with the slide title, which is not indented. The title is the main topic of the slide. Body text supporting the main topic begins on the first level and also is not indented. If desired, additional supporting text can be added on the second through

Text Levels

While PowerPoint gives you five levels of body text to use on each slide, graphic designers suggest you limit your levels to three. The details on all five levels may overwhelm audiences. If you find yourself needing more than three levels, consider combining content in one level or using two different slides.

fifth levels. Each level is indented. Levels four and five generally are used for very detailed scientific and engineering presentations. Business and sales presentations usually focus on summary information and use the first, second, and third levels.

PowerPoint initially displays in normal view when you start a new presentation. To type the outline, click the Outline tab in the tabs pane. Perform the following steps to change to the Outline tab and display the Outlining toolbar.

Steps **To Change to the Outline Tab and Display the Outlining Toolbar**

1 **Point to the Outline tab located in the tabs pane.**

The tabs pane consists of the Outline tab and the Slides tab (Figure 2-4).

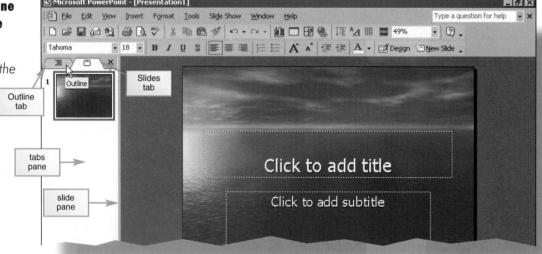

FIGURE 2-4

2 **Click the Outline tab.**

The Outline tab is selected. The tabs pane increases and the slide pane decreases in size.

3 **Click View on the menu bar and then point to Toolbars. Point to Outlining on the Toolbars submenu.**

The View menu and Toolbars submenu display (Figure 2-5).

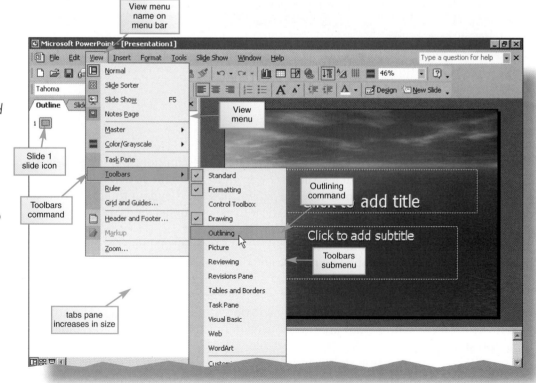

FIGURE 2-5

4 **Click Outlining.**

The Outlining toolbar displays (Figure 2-6).

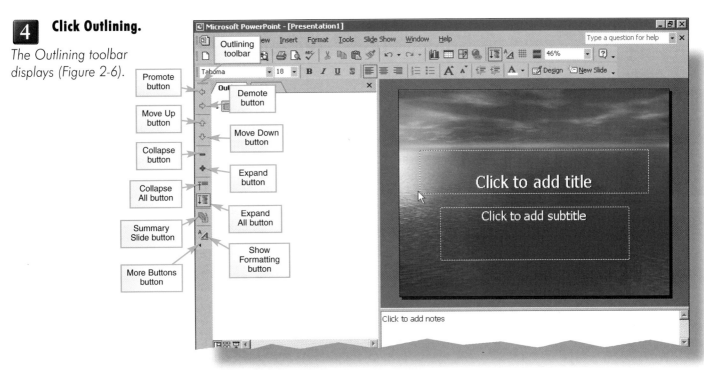

FIGURE 2-6

You can create and edit your presentation on the Outline tab. This tab also makes it easy to sequence slides and to relocate title text and body text from one slide to another. In addition to typing text to create a new presentation on the Outline tab, PowerPoint can produce slides from an outline created in Microsoft Word or another word processing application, if you save the outline as an RTF file or as a plain text file. The file extension **RTF** stands for **R**ich **T**ext **F**ormat.

Table 2-1 describes the buttons on the Outlining toolbar.

Table 2-1	Buttons on the Outlining Toolbar	
BUTTON	**BUTTON NAME**	**DESCRIPTION**
	Promote	Moves the selected paragraph to the next-higher heading level (up one level, to the left).
	Demote	Moves the selected paragraph to the next-lower heading level (down one level, to the right).
	Move Up	Moves a selected paragraph and its collapsed (temporarily hidden) subordinate text above the preceding displayed paragraph.
	Move Down	Moves a selected paragraph and its collapsed (temporarily hidden) subordinate text below the following displayed paragraph.
	Collapse	Hides all but the title of selected slides. Collapsed text is represented by a gray line.
	Expand	Displays the titles and all collapsed text of selected slides.
	Collapse All	Displays only the title of each slide. Text other than the title is represented by a gray line below the title.
	Expand All	Displays the titles and all the body text for each slide.
	Summary Slide	Creates a new slide from the titles of the slides you select in slide sorter or normal view. The summary slide creates a bulleted list from the titles of the selected slides. PowerPoint inserts the summary slide in front of the first selected slide.
	Show Formatting	Shows or hides character formatting (such as bold and italic) in normal view. In slide sorter view, switches between showing all text and graphics on each slide and displaying titles only.
	Toolbar Options	Allows you to select the particular buttons you want to display on the toolbar.

Creating a Presentation on the Outline Tab

The Outline tab enables you to view title and body text, add and delete slides, drag and drop slide text, drag and drop individual slides, promote and demote text, save a presentation, print an outline, print slides, copy and paste slides or text to and from other presentations, apply a design template, and import an outline. When you **drag and drop** slide text or individual slides, you change the order of the text or the slides by selecting the text or slide you want to move or copy and then dragging the text or slide it its new location.

Developing a presentation on the Outline tab is quick because you type the text for all slides on one screen. Once you type the outline, the presentation fundamentally is complete. If you choose, you then can enhance your presentation with objects in the slide pane.

Creating a Title Slide on the Outline Tab

Recall from Project 1 that the title slide introduces the presentation to the audience. In addition to introducing the presentation, Project 2 uses the title slide to capture the attention of the students in your audience by using a design template with an image of water. Perform the following steps to create a title slide on the Outline tab.

Smart Quotes

When you type an apostrophe and quotation marks, PowerPoint automatically converts these symbols to "smart quotes," which also are called curly quotes. These symbols are in the shape of a dot and curved line ("") instead of a straight line (' "). If you want to use straight quotes instead, click Tools on the menu bar and then click AutoCorrect Options. Click the AutoFormat As You Type tab, and then click the "Straight quotes" with "smart quotes" check box.

 To Create a Title Slide on the Outline Tab

1 **Click the Slide 1 slide icon on the Outline tab.**

The Slide 1 slide icon is selected. You also could click anywhere in the tabs pane to select the slide icon (Figure 2-7).

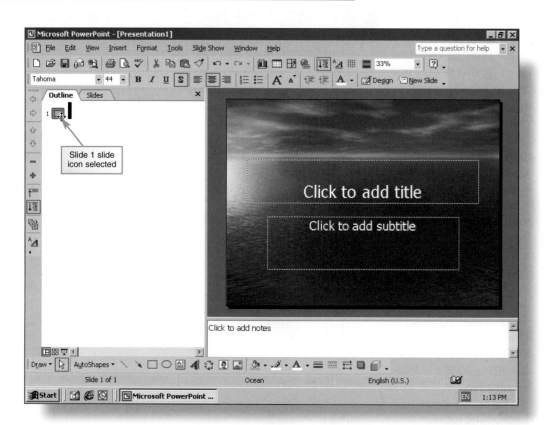

FIGURE 2-7

2 **Type** Enjoy Spring Break **and then press** SHIFT + ENTER. **Type** in the Caribbean **and then press the** ENTER **key. Point to the Demote button on the Outlining toolbar.**

The Demote ScreenTip displays (Figure 2-8). Pressing SHIFT + ENTER *moves the insertion point to the next line and maintains the same first level. The insertion point is in position for typing the title for Slide 2. Pressing the* ENTER *key inserts a new slide.*

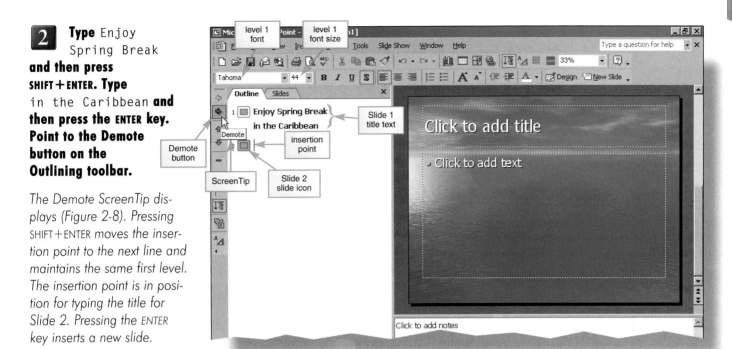

FIGURE 2-8

3 **Click the Demote button on the Outlining toolbar. Type** Warm Days, Cool Activities **and then press the** ENTER **key. Type** Sponsored by **and then press the** ENTER **key. Type** The Office of Student Activities **and then press the** ENTER **key.**

Clicking the Demote button deletes a blank slide. The two paragraphs are subtitles on the title slide (Slide 1) and demote to the second level (Figure 2-9). The second level is indented to the right below the first-level paragraph.

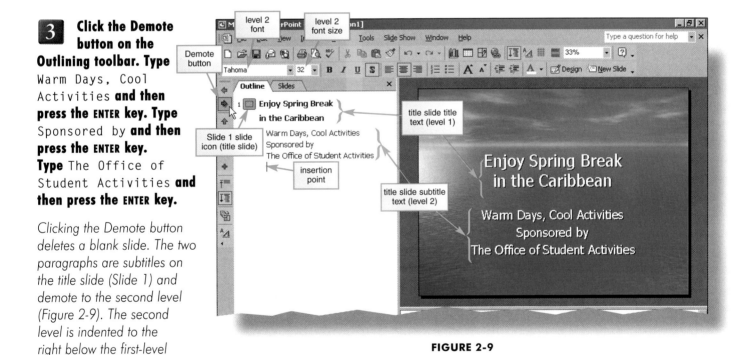

FIGURE 2-9

The title slide text for the Enjoy Spring Break presentation is complete. The next section explains how to add a slide on the Outline tab.

Other Ways

1. Type title text, press ENTER, click Demote button on Formatting toolbar, type subtitle text, press ENTER
2. Type title text, press ENTER, press TAB, type subtitle text, press ENTER

Adding a Slide on the Outline Tab

Recall from Project 1 that when you add a new slide in normal view, PowerPoint defaults to a Text slide layout with a bulleted list. This action occurs on the Outline tab as well. One way to add a new slide on the Outline tab is to promote a paragraph to the first level by clicking the Promote button on the Outlining toolbar until the insertion point or the paragraph displays at the first level. A slide icon displays when the insertion point or paragraph reaches this level. Perform the following step to add a slide on the Outline tab.

Steps **To Add a Slide on the Outline Tab**

1 **Click the Promote button on the Outlining toolbar.**

The Slide 2 slide icon displays indicating a new slide is added to the presentation (Figure 2-10). The insertion point is in position to type the title for Slide 2 at the first level.

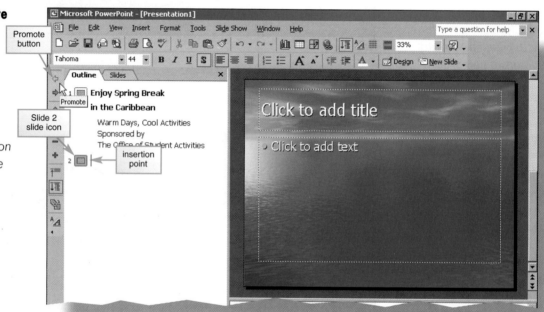

FIGURE 2-10

Other Ways

1. Click New Slide button on Standard toolbar, click OK button
2. On Insert menu click New Slide, click OK button
3. Press CTRL+M
4. Press ALT+I, press N.
5. In Voice Command mode, say "New Slide"

After you add a slide, you are ready to type the slide text. The next section explains how to create a text slide with a single-level bulleted list on the Outline tab.

Creating a Text Slide with a Single-Level Bulleted List on the Outline Tab

To create a text slide with a single-level bulleted list, you demote or promote the insertion point to the appropriate level and then type the paragraph text. Recall from Project 1 that when you demote a paragraph, PowerPoint adds a bullet to the left of each level. Depending on the design template, each level has a different bullet font. Also recall that the design template determines font attributes, including the bullet font.

Slide 2 is the first text slide in Project 2 and describes the activities students can enjoy when the cruise ship docks at various ports. Each of the four major activities displays as second-level paragraphs on the Outline tab and in the slide pane. The following steps explain how to create a text slide with a single-level bulleted list on the Outline tab.

To Create a Text Slide with a Single-Level Bulleted List on the Outline Tab

1 **Type** Onshore Adventures **and then press the ENTER key. Click the Demote button on the Outlining toolbar to demote to the second level.**

The title for Slide 2, Onshore Adventures, displays and the insertion point is in position to type the first bulleted paragraph (Figure 2-11). A bullet displays to the left of the insertion point.

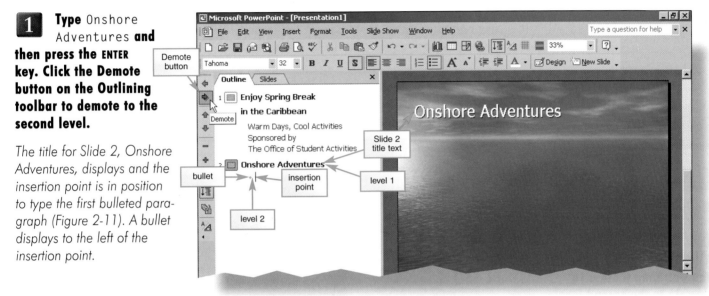

FIGURE 2-11

2 **Type** Golf, play volleyball, swim, and relax **and then press the ENTER key. Type** Experience a submarine tour **and then press the ENTER key. Type** Try parasailing **and then press the ENTER key. Type** Explore a rainforest **and then press the ENTER key.**

Slide 2 displays two levels: the title, Onshore Adventures, on the first level; and four bulleted paragraphs and the insertion point on the second level (Figure 2-12).

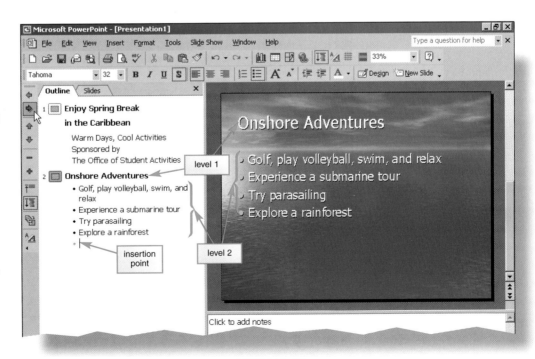

FIGURE 2-12

Slide 2 is complete. The text on this slide abides by the 7 × 7 rule. As you learned in Project 1, this rule recommends that each line should have a maximum of seven words, and each slide should have a maximum of seven lines. All slides in this slide show use the 7 × 7 rule.

Bullets

Besides using bullets, a numbered list can add emphasis to your presentation. When necessary, numbering can show ordered steps or sequences. To make a numbered list, click the Numbering button on the Formatting toolbar

Creating Text Slides with Multi-Level Bulleted Lists on the Outline Tab

The remaining three slides in the presentation contain multi-level bulleted lists. Slide 3 provides information about onboard activities, Slide 4 gives details about the cost and ports of call, and Slide 5 lists information on signing up for the cruise. It is easy and efficient to type the text for these slides on the Outline tab. Perform the following steps to create multi-level bulleted slides on the Outline tab.

Steps: To Create a Text Slide with a Multi-Level Bulleted List on the Outline Tab

1 **Click the Promote button on the Outlining toolbar. Type** Onboard Activities **and then press the ENTER key. Click the Demote button on the Outlining toolbar to demote to the second level.**

The title for Slide 3, Onboard Activities, displays and the insertion point is in position to type the first bulleted paragraph (Figure 2-13). A bullet displays to the left of the insertion point in the second level.

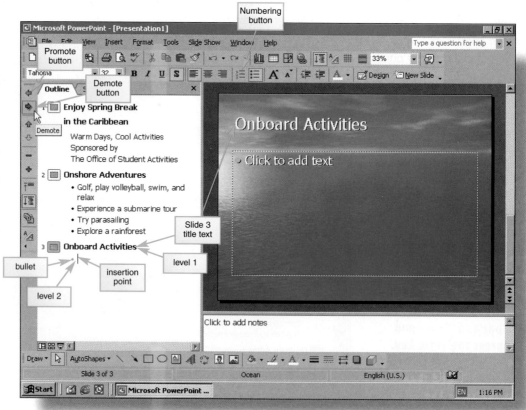

FIGURE 2-13

2 **Type** Theaters, fitness center, and stores **and then press the ENTER key. Click the Demote button on the Outlining toolbar to demote to the third level. Type** Make new friends **and then press the ENTER key. Type** Dance to the hits **and then press the ENTER key. Click the Promote button on the Outlining toolbar to promote to the second level. Type** Indoor and outdoor pools and whirlpools **and then press the ENTER key.**

The text for Slide 3 is complete (Figure 2-14). Pressing the ENTER key begins a new paragraph at the same level as the previous paragraph.

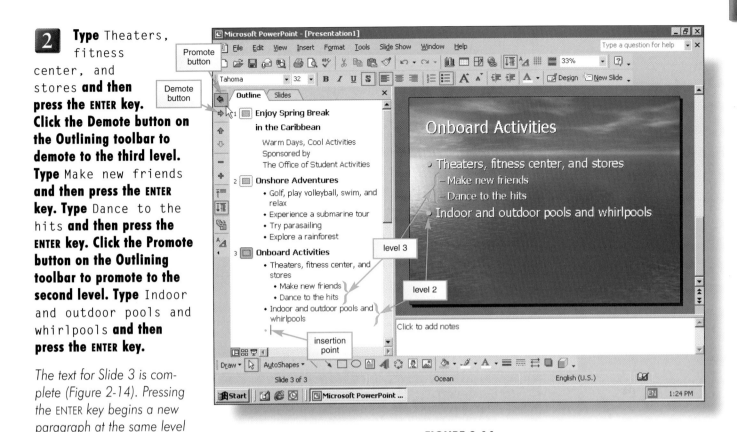

FIGURE 2-14

Entering text on the Outline tab is a quick and efficient process. You can view all the text you type in the outline in the tabs pane to check organization. The last two slides in the presentation give specific information about the cruise itinerary and registration process.

Creating a Second Text Slide with a Multi-Level Bulleted List

The next slide, Slide 4, provides details about the cost, duration, and itinerary for the cruise. Perform the following steps to create this slide.

TO CREATE A SECOND TEXT SLIDE WITH A MULTI-LEVEL BULLETED LIST

1 Click the Promote button on the Outlining toolbar so Slide 4 is added after Slide 3.

2 Type Cruise Details and then press the ENTER key.

3 Click the Demote button on the Outlining toolbar to demote to the second level.

4 Type Only $999, including all meals and then press the ENTER key.

5 Type Seven-day vacation departs from Miami and then press the ENTER key.

6 Type Unforgettable ports of call and then press the ENTER key.

7 Click the Demote button to demote to the third level.

The Pointing Device

You can expand or collapse an outline by pointing to a heading and then holding down the SHIFT key as you rotate the wheel on the Microsoft IntelliMouse® pointing device forward or backward.

8 Type Frederiksted, St. Croix and then press the ENTER key.

9 Type San Juan, Puerto Rico and then press the ENTER key.

10 Type Charlotte Amalie, St. Thomas and then press the ENTER key.

The completed Slide 4 displays (Figure 2-15). Red wavy lines display below the words Frederiksted and Amalie to indicate those words are not found in the Microsoft main dictionary or open custom dictionaries.

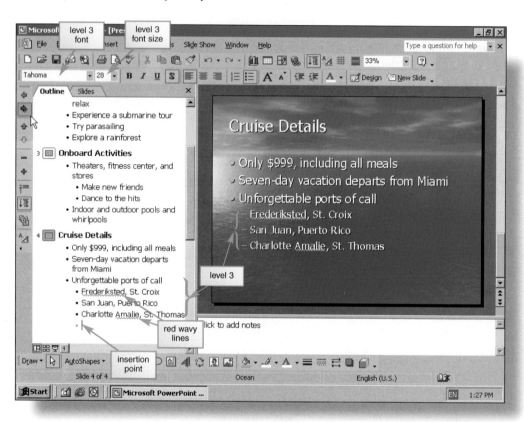

FIGURE 2-15

Creating a Closing Slide on the Outline Tab

The last slide in a presentation is the closing slide. A **closing slide** gracefully ends a presentation. Often used during a question and answer session, the closing slide usually remains on the screen to reinforce the message delivered during the presentation. Professional speakers design the closing slide with one or more of these methods.

1. List important information. Tell the audience what to do next.
2. Provide a memorable illustration or example to make a point.
3. Appeal to emotions. Remind the audience to take action or accept responsibility.
4. Summarize the main point of the presentation.
5. Cite a quotation that directly relates to the main point of the presentation. This technique is most effective if the presentation started with a quotation.

The closing slide in this project uses a multi-level bulleted list to provide contact information for the Office of Student Activities and for a reception held for students desiring additional details. Perform the following steps to create this closing slide.

Closing Slides

When faced with constructing a new slide show, you may find it helpful to start by designing your closing slide first. Knowing how you want the slide show to end helps you focus on reaching this conclusion. You can create each slide in the presentation with this goal in mind.

TO CREATE A CLOSING SLIDE ON THE OUTLINE TAB

1 Click the Promote button on the Outlining toolbar two times to add Slide 5 after Slide 4. Type Sign-Up Information and then press the ENTER key.

2 Click the Demote button on the Outlining toolbar to demote to the second level. Type Contact OSA and then press the ENTER key.

3 Click the Demote button to demote to the third level. Type Memorial Union and then press the ENTER key.

4 Click the Demote button to demote to the fourth level. Type Room 3110 and then press the ENTER key. Type 9:00 a.m. to 5:00 p.m. daily and then press the ENTER key.

5 Click the Promote button two times to promote to the second level. Type Attend Caribbean Cruise Reception then press the ENTER key.

6 Click the Demote button. Type Office of Student Activities and then press the ENTER key. Click the Demote button and then type Friday, October 10 and press the ENTER key. Type 3:00 p.m. to 5:00 p.m. but do not press the ENTER key.

Backgrounds

The most popular background color is blue. Used in more than 90 percent of business presentations, this color connotes serenity, reflection, and proficiency.

The completed Slide 5 displays (Figure 2-16).

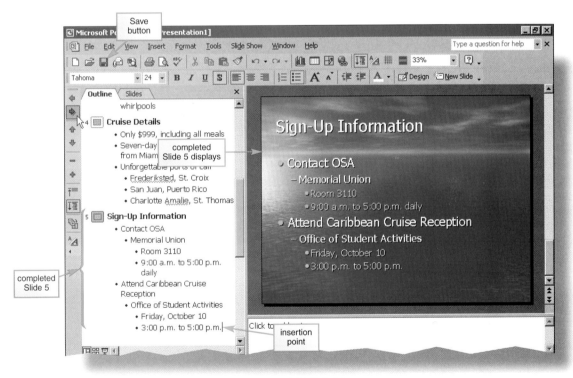

FIGURE 2-16

The outline now is complete and you should save the presentation. The next section explains how to save the presentation.

Saving a Presentation

Recall from Project 1 that it is wise to save your presentation frequently. With all the text for your presentation created, save the presentation using the steps on the next page.

TO SAVE A PRESENTATION

1 Insert a formatted floppy disk in drive A and then click the Save button on the Standard toolbar.

2 Click the Save in box arrow. Click 3½ Floppy (A:) in the Save in list.

3 Click the Save button in the Save As dialog box.

The presentation is saved on the floppy disk in drive A with the file name Enjoy Spring Break. PowerPoint uses the first text line in a presentation as the default file name. The file name displays on the title bar.

More *About*

Quick Reference

For a table that lists how to complete tasks covered in this book using the mouse, menu, shortcut menu, and keyboard, see the Quick Reference summary at the back of this book or visit the Shelly Cashman Series Office XP Web page (scsite.com/offxp/qr.htm) and then click Microsoft PowerPoint 2002.

Reviewing a Presentation in Slide Sorter View

In Project 1, you displayed slides in slide show view to evaluate the presentation. Slide show view, however, restricts your evaluation to one slide at a time. The Outline tab is best for quickly reviewing all the text for a presentation. Recall from Project 1 that slide sorter view allows you to look at several slides at one time, which is why it is the best view to use to evaluate a presentation for content, organization, and overall appearance. Perform the following step to change from the Outline tab to slide sorter view.

Steps **To Change the View to Slide Sorter View**

1 **Click the Slide Sorter View button at the lower left of the PowerPoint window.**

PowerPoint displays the presentation in slide sorter view (Figure 2-17). Slide 5 is selected because it was the current slide on the Outline tab. The Slide Sorter View button is selected.

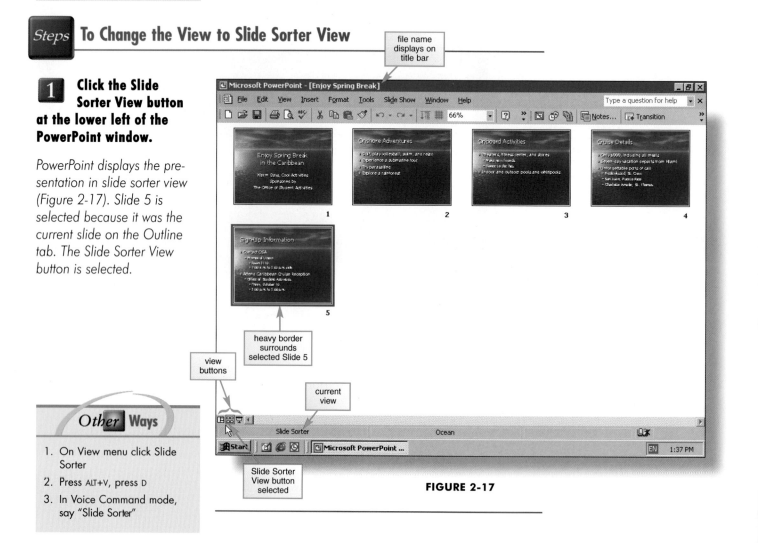

FIGURE 2-17

Other **Ways**

1. On View menu click Slide Sorter
2. Press ALT+V, press D
3. In Voice Command mode, say "Slide Sorter"

You can review the five slides in this presentation all in one window. Notice the slides have a significant amount of space and look plain. These observations indicate a need to add visual interest to the slides by using clips. The next several sections explain how to improve the presentation by changing slide layouts and adding clip art.

You can make changes to text in normal view and on the Outline tab. It is best, however, to change the view to normal view when altering the slide layouts so you can see the result of your changes. Perform the following steps to change the view from slide sorter view to normal view.

More About

Slide Space

Some blank space on a slide can be advantageous. The absence of text, called white space, helps the viewer focus attention on the presenter. Do not be afraid to leave some white space on your slide to give your text and visual elements some breathing room.

 To Change the View to Normal View

1 Click the Slide 2 slide thumbnail. Point to the Normal View button at the lower left of the PowerPoint window.

Slide 2 is selected, as indicated by the thick blue border around that slide (Figure 2-18).

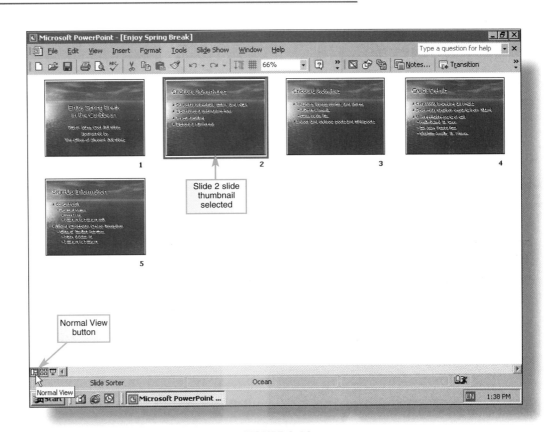

FIGURE 2-18

2 **Click the Normal View button. Point to the Slides tab in the tabs pane.**

The Normal View button is selected at the lower left of the PowerPoint window. The Slide 2 slide icon is selected in the tabs pane, and Slide 2 displays in the slide pane (Figure 2-19).

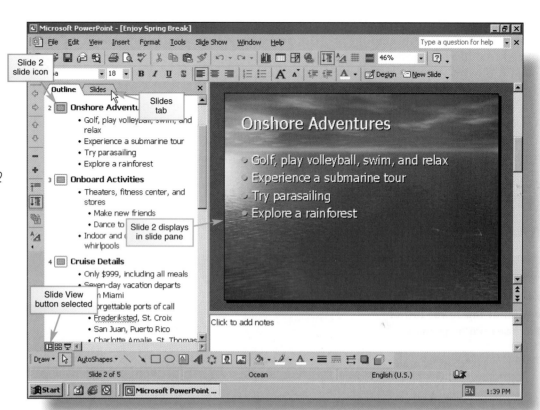

FIGURE 2-19

3 **Click the Slides tab.**

The tabs pane reduces in size. Slide thumbnails of the five slides display (Figure 2-20).

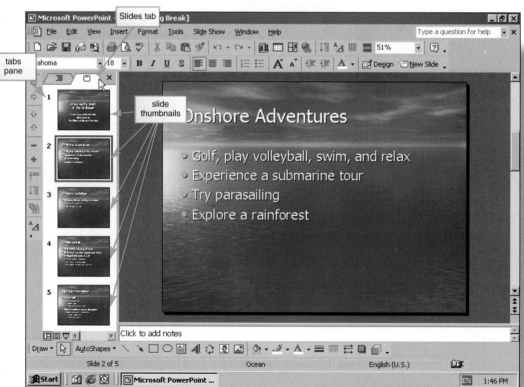

FIGURE 2-20

Switching between slide sorter view and normal view helps you review your presentation and assess whether the slides have an attractive design and adequate content.

Changing Slide Layout

When you developed this presentation, PowerPoint applied the Title Slide layout for Slide 1 and the Title and Text layout for the other four slides in the presentation. These layouts are the default styles. A **layout** specifies the arrangement of placeholders on a slide. These placeholders are arranged in various configurations and can contain text, such as the slide title or a bulleted list, or they can contain content, such as clips, pictures, charts, tables, and shapes. The placement of the text, in relationship to content, depends on the slide layout. The content placeholders may be to the right or left of the text, above the text, or below the text. You can specify a particular slide layout when you add a new slide to a presentation or after you have created the slide.

Using the **Slide Layout task pane**, you can choose a slide layout. The layouts in this task pane are arranged in four areas: Text Layouts, Content Layouts, Text and Content Layouts, and Other Layouts. The two layouts you have used in this project Title Slide and Title and Text — are included in the Text Layouts area along with the Title Only and Title and 2-Column Text layouts. The Content Layouts area contains a blank slide and a variety of placeholder groupings for charts, tables, clip art, pictures, diagrams, and media clips. The Text and Content Layouts have placeholders for a title, a bulleted list, and content. The Other Layouts area has layouts with placeholders for a title and one object, such as clip art, charts, media clips, tables, organization charts, and charts. Some layouts have one, two, three, or four content placeholders.

When you change the layout of a slide, PowerPoint retains the text and objects and repositions them into the appropriate placeholders. Using slide layouts eliminates the need to resize objects and the font size because PowerPoint automatically sizes the objects and text to fit the placeholders. If the objects are in **landscape orientation**, meaning their width is greater than their height, PowerPoint sizes them to the width of the placeholders. If the objects are in **portrait orientation**, meaning their height is greater than their width, PowerPoint sizes them to the height of the placeholder.

Adding clips to Slides 2 and 3 requires two steps. First, change the slide layout to Title, Text, and 2 Content or to Title, Content and Text. Then, insert clip art into each of the two content placeholders. Perform the steps on the next page to change the slide layout on Slide 2 from Title and Text to Title, Text, and 2 Content.

More **About**

Slide Colors

One in twelve males has color perception difficulties, with the most common problem being distinguishing red and green. For more information on this color deficiency, visit the PowerPoint 2002 Project 2 More About Web page (scsite.com/pp2002/more.htm) and then click Slide Colors.

More **About**

Customizing Buttons

Customize your toolbars by using buttons that are larger than the ones normally displayed. To enlarge the buttons, click Tools on the menu bar and then click Customize. Click the Options tab and then click the Large icons check box. This setting will affect all of your Microsoft Office programs.

Steps | **To Change the Slide Layout to Title, Text, and 2 Content**

1 **Click Format on the menu bar and then point to Slide Layout (Figure 2-21).**

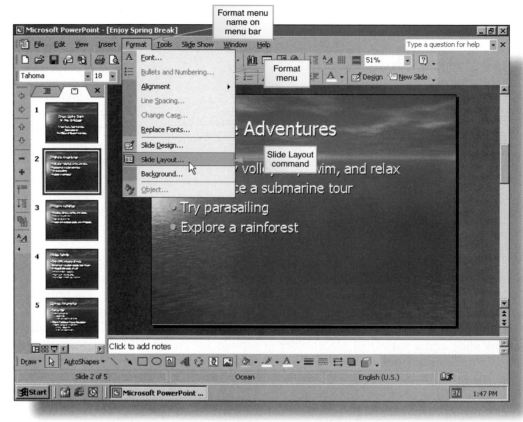

FIGURE 2-21

2 **Click Slide Layout. Point to the Title, Text, and 2 Content layout in the Text and Content Layouts area.**

The Slide Layout task pane displays (Figure 2-22). The Title, Text, and 2 Content layout is selected, as indicated by the blue box around the template, the ScreenTip, and the arrow button on the right side.

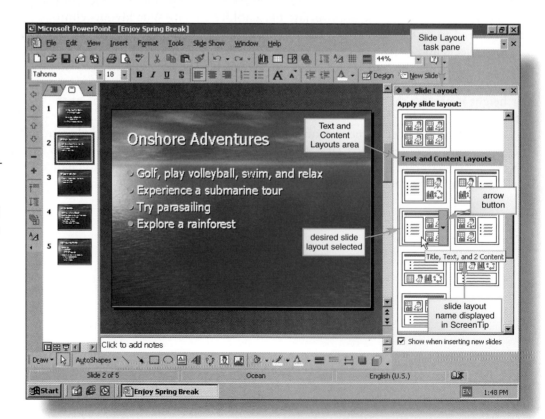

FIGURE 2-22

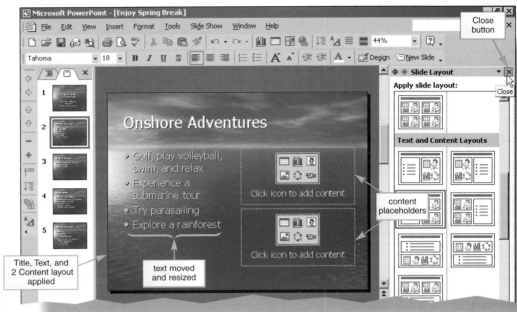

3 Click Title, Text, and 2 Content. Point to the Close button in the Slide Layout task pane.

The layout is applied to Slide 2 (Figure 2-23). PowerPoint moves the text placeholder containing the bulleted list to the left side of the slide and automatically resizes the text. The two content placeholders on the right side of the slide displays the message, Click icon to add content.

FIGURE 2-23

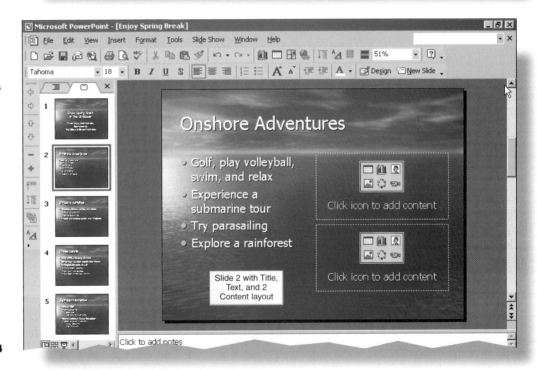

4 Click the Close button.

Slide 2 displays in normal view with the new slide layout applied (Figure 2-24).

FIGURE 2-24

PowerPoint reduced the second-level text in the Slide 2 text placeholder from a font size of 32 point to 18 point so all the words fit into the placeholder.

Other Ways

1. Right-click slide anywhere except text placeholders, click Slide Layout on shortcut menu, double-click desired slide layout

2. Press ALT+O, press L, press ARROW keys to select desired slide layout, press ENTER

3. In Voice Command mode, say "Format, Slide Layout, Title Text and Two Content, Close"

Adding Clip Art to a Slide

More About

Legal Use of Clips

If you use clips in your slide show, be certain you have the legal right to use these files. Read the copyright notices that accompany the clips and are posted on Web sites. The owners of these images and files often ask you to give them credit for using their work, which may be accomplished by stating where you obtained the images.

Clip art helps the visual appeal of the Enjoy Spring Break slide show and offers a quick way to add professional looking graphic images to a presentation without creating the images yourself. This art is contained in the **Microsoft Clip Organizer**, a collection of drawings, photographs, sounds, videos, and other media files shared with Microsoft Office applications.

You can add clip art to your presentation in two ways. One way is by selecting one of the slide layouts that includes a content placeholder with instructions to open the Microsoft Clip Organizer to add content. You will add art to Slides 2 and 3 in this manner. Double-clicking a button in the content placeholder activates the instructions to open the Select Picture dialog box, which allows you to enter key-words to search for clips.

The second method is by clicking the Insert Clip Art button on the Drawing toolbar to open the Insert Clip Art task pane. The **Insert Clip Art task pane** allows you to search for clips by using descriptive keywords, file names, media file formats, and clip collections. Specific file formats could be for clip art, photographs, movies, and sounds. Clips are organized in hierarchical **clip collections**, which combine topic-related clips into categories, such as Academic, Business, and Technology. You also can create your own collections for frequently used clips. You will insert clip art into Slides 4 and 5 using this process. You then will arrange the clips on the slides without using a placeholder for content.

Table 2-2 shows four categories from the Office Collections in the Microsoft Clip Organizer and keywords of various clip art files in those categories. Clip art images have one or more keywords associated with various entities, activities, labels, and emotions. In most instances, the keywords give the name of the clip and related categories. For example, an image of a cow in the Animals category has the key-words animals, cattle, cows, dairies, farms, and Holsteins. You can enter these keywords in the Search text box to find clips when you know one of the words associated with the image. Otherwise, you may find it necessary to scroll through several categories to find an appropriate clip.

Depending on the installation of the Microsoft Clip Organizer on your computer, you may not have the clip art used in this project. Contact your instructor if you are missing clips when you perform the following steps. If you have an open connection to the Internet, clips from the Microsoft Web site will display automatically as the result of your search results.

Table 2-2 Microsoft Clip Organizer Category and Keyword Examples	
CATEGORY	**CLIP ART KEYWORDS**
Academic	Books; knowledge; information; schools; school buses; apple for the teacher; professors
Business	Computers; inspirations; ideas; currencies; board meetings; conferences; teamwork; profits
Nature	Lakes; flowers; plants; seasons; wildlife; weather; trees; sunshine; rivers; leaves
Technology	Computers; diskettes; microchips; cellular telephones; e-commerce; office equipment; data exchanges

Inserting Clip Art into a Content Placeholder

With the Title, Text, and 2 Content layout applied to Slide 2, you insert clip art into the content placeholder. Perform the following steps to insert clip art of a golfer into the content placeholder on Slide 2.

Steps **To Insert Clip Art into a Content Placeholder**

1 **Point to the Insert Clip Art button in the top content placeholder.**

The Insert Clip Art button is selected (Figure 2-25). A ScreenTip describes its function.

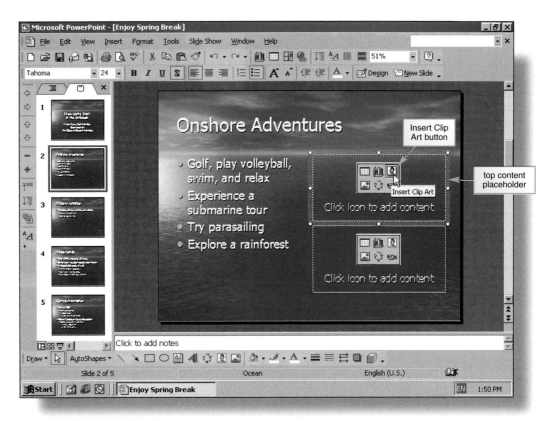

FIGURE 2-25

2 **Click the Insert Clip Art button. Type** golf **in the Search text text box and then point to the Search button.**

The Select Picture dialog box displays (Figure 2-26). The clips displayed on your computer may vary.

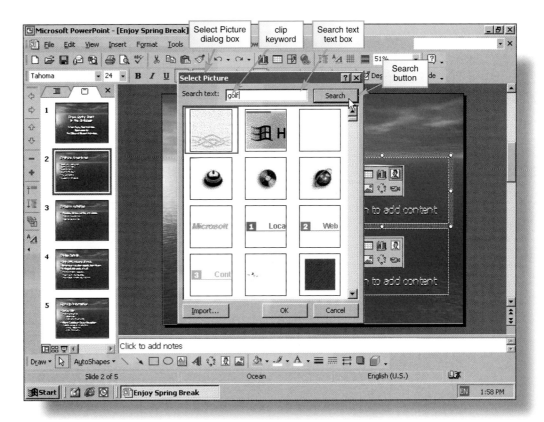

FIGURE 2-26

3 **Click the Search button. If necessary, click an appropriate clip and then point to the OK button.**

The Microsoft Clip Organizer searches for and displays all pictures having the keyword golf (Figure 2-27). The desired clip of a female golfer displays with a blue box around it. Your clips may be different depending on the clips installed on your computer and if you have an open connection to the Internet, in which case you may need to obtain an appropriate clip from the Internet.

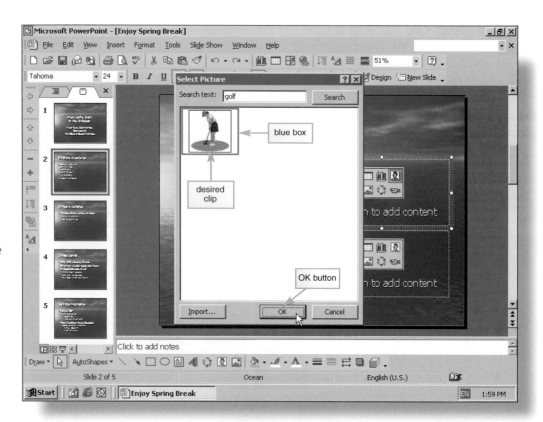

FIGURE 2-27

4 **Click the OK button. If the Picture toolbar displays, click the Close button on the Picture toolbar.**

The selected clip is inserted into the top content placeholder on Slide 2 (Figure 2-28). PowerPoint sizes the clip automatically to fit the placeholder.

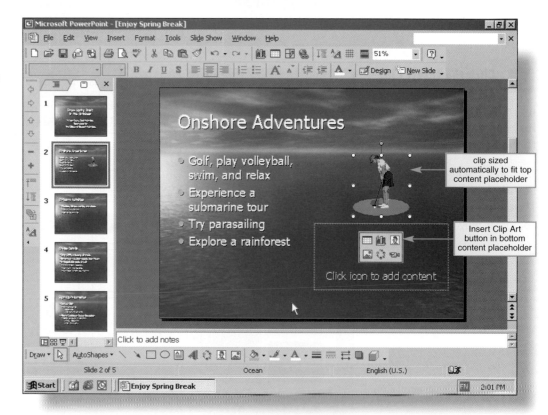

FIGURE 2-28

Inserting a Second Clip into a Slide

Another clip on Slide 2 is required to fill the bottom content placeholder. This clip should be the image of a volleyball. Perform the following steps to insert the volleyball into the bottom placeholder on Slide 2.

TO INSERT A SECOND CLIP INTO A SLIDE

1 Click the Insert Clip Art button in the bottom content placeholder.

2 Type volleyball in the Search text text box and then click the Search button.

3 If necessary, scroll down the list to display the desired clip of a volleyball and net, click the clip to select it, and then click the OK button.

The selected clip is inserted into the bottom content placeholder on Slide 2 (Figure 2-29). PowerPoint automatically sizes the clip to fit the placeholder.

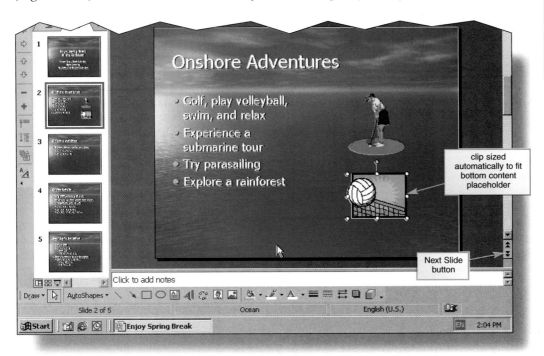

FIGURE 2-29

More *About*

Design

Consider designing a presentation in black and white and then adding color to emphasize particular areas on the slide. Graphic artists suggest starting with black letters on a white background to concentrate on basic design principles, such as balance, contrast, rhythm, and harmony.

Slide 2 is complete. The next step is to add other clip to Slide 3. This slide uses the Title, Content and Text slide layout so the clip displays on the left side of the slide and the bulleted list displays on the right side. Perform the following steps to change the slide layout and then add clip art to Slide 3.

TO CHANGE THE SLIDE LAYOUT TO TITLE, CONTENT AND TEXT AND INSERT CLIP ART

1 Click the Next Slide button on the vertical scroll bar to display Slide 3.

2 Click Format on the menu bar and then click Slide Layout.

3 Scroll to display the Title, Content and Text slide layout located in the Text and Content Layouts area of the Slide Layout task pane.

4 Click the Title, Content and Text slide layout and then click the Close button in the Slide Layout task pane.

5 Click the Insert Clip Art button in the content placeholder. Type party in the Search text text box and then click the Search button.

6 If necessary, scroll down the list to display the desired party clip and then click the clip to select it. Click the OK button.

The selected party clip is inserted into the content placeholder on Slide 3 (Figure 2-30). The slide has the Title, Content and Text slide layout.

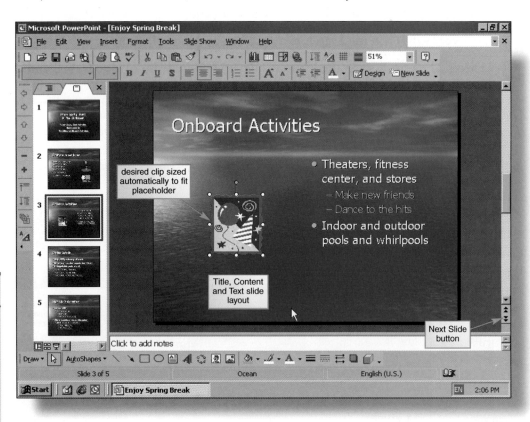

FIGURE 2-30

Changing Clip Art

Be certain you have the legal right to use and modify a clip art image. For example, you cannot use photographs and illustrations to damage people's reputations by representing them falsely, such as inserting a photograph of someone on the FBI's Top Ten Most Wanted list. In addition, corporate logos are designed using specific colors and shapes and often cannot be altered.

Slide 3 is complete. Your next step is to add a clip to Slide 4 without changing the slide layout.

Inserting Clip Art into a Slide without a Content Placeholder

PowerPoint does not require you to use a content placeholder to add clips to a slide. You can insert clips on any slide regardless of its slide layout. On Slides 2 and 3, you added clips that enhanced the message in the text. Recall that the slide layout on Slide 4 is Title and Text. Because this layout does not contain a content place-holder, you can use the Insert Clip Art button on the Drawing toolbar to start the Microsoft Clip Organizer. The clip for which you are searching has a globe and luggage. A few of its keywords are baggage, Earth, global, and globes. Perform the following steps to insert this clip into a slide that does not have a content placeholder.

Steps **To Insert Clip Art into a Slide without a Content Placeholder**

1 **Click the Next Slide button on the vertical scroll bar to display Slide 4. Click Tools on the menu bar and then click AutoCorrect Options. When the AutoCorrect dialog box displays, if necessary, click the AutoFormat As You Type tab. Click Automatic layout for inserted objects in the Apply as you work area if a check mark does not display.**

2 **Click the Insert Clip Art button on the Drawing toolbar. If the Add Clips to Organizer dialog box displays asking if you want to catalog media files, click Don't show this message again, or, if you want to catalog later, click the Later button.**

The Insert Clip Art task pane displays (Figure 2-31).

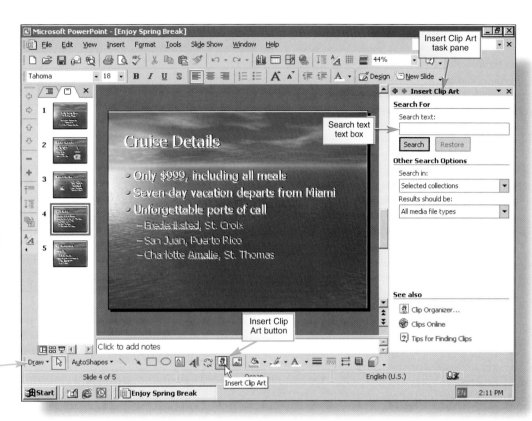

FIGURE 2-31

3 **Click the Search text text box. Type** earth **and then press the ENTER key. If necessary, scroll to display the desired clip of a globe and luggage. Point to this image.**

The clip of a globe and piece of luggage displays with other clips sharing the earth keyword (Figure 2-32). Your clips may be different. The clip's keywords, size in pixels (260 × 247), file size (10 KB), and file type (WMF) display.

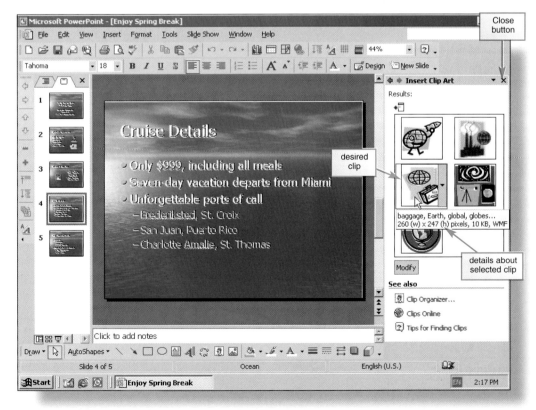

FIGURE 2-32

4 **Click the desired clip. Click the Close button on the Insert Clip Art task pane title bar.**

PowerPoint inserts the clip into Slide 4 (Figure 2-33). The slide layout changes automatically to Title, Text, and Content. The Automatic Layout Options button displays.

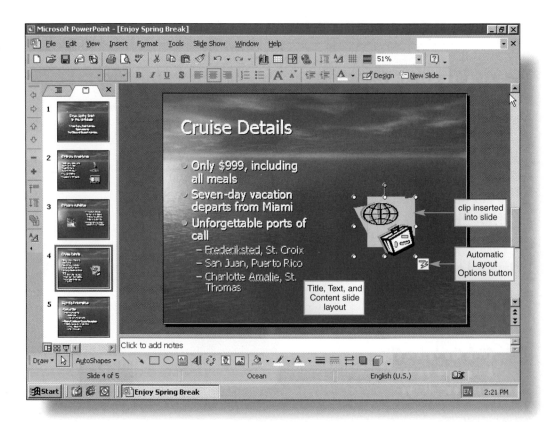

FIGURE 2-33

Table 2-3 Primary File Formats PowerPoint Recognizes	
FORMAT	*FILE EXTENSION*
Computer Graphics Metafile	.cgm
CorelDRAW	.cdr, .cdt, .cmx, and .pat
Encapsulated PostScript	.eps
Enhanced Metafile	.emf
FlashPix	.fpx
Graphics Interchange Format	.gif
Hanako	.jsh, .jah, and .jbh
Joint Photographic Experts Group (JPEG)	.jpg
Kodak PhotoCD	.pcd
Macintosh PICT	.pct
PC Paintbrush	.pcx
Portable Network Graphics	.png
Tagged Image File Format	.tif
Windows Bitmap	.bmp, .rle, .dib
Microsoft Windows Metafile	.wmf
WordPerfect Graphics	.wpg

In addition to clip art, you can insert pictures into a presentation. These may include scanned photographs, line art, and artwork from compact discs. To insert a picture into a presentation, the picture must be saved in a format that PowerPoint can recognize. Table 2-3 identifies some of the formats PowerPoint recognizes.

You can import files saved with the .emf, .gif, .jpg, .png, .bmp, .rle, .dib, and .wmf formats directly into PowerPoint presentations. All other file formats require separate filters that are shipped with the PowerPoint installation software and must be installed. You can download additional filters from the Microsoft Office Update Web site.

Smart Tags

A **smart tag** is a button that automatically appears on the screen when PowerPoint performs a certain action. The Automatic Layout Options button in Figure 2-33 is a smart tag. In addition to the Automatic Layout Options button, PowerPoint provides three other smart tags. Table 2-4 summarizes the smart tags available in PowerPoint.

Table 2-4	Smart Tags in PowerPoint	
BUTTON	*NAME*	*MENU FUNCTION*
	AutoCorrect Options	Undoes an automatic correction, stops future automatic corrections of this type, or displays the AutoCorrect Options dialog box
	Paste Options	Specifies how moved or pasted items should display, e.g., with original formatting, without formatting, or with different formatting
	AutoFit Options	Undoes automatic text resizing to fit the current placeholder or changes single-column layouts to two-column layouts, inserts a new slide, or splits the text between two slides
	Automatic Layout Options	Adjusts the slide layout to accommodate an inserted object

Clicking a smart tag button displays a menu that contains commands relative to the action performed at the location of the smart tag. For example, if you want PowerPoint to undo the layout change when you add a clip to a slide, click the Automatic Layout Options button to display the Smart Tag Actions menu, and then click Undo Automatic Layout on the Smart Tag Actions menu to display the initial layout.

Using the Automatic Layout Options Button to Undo a Layout Change

The Title and Text layout used in Slide 4 did not provide a content placeholder for the clip you inserted, so PowerPoint automatically changed the layout to Title, Text, and Content. Because the text now violates the 7 × 7 rule with this layout and because you want to place the clip in a location other than the areas specified, you should change the layout to the Title and Text layout.

The **Automatic Layout Options button** displays because PowerPoint changed the layout automatically. If you move your mouse pointer near the changed object or text, the Automatic Layout Options button displays as an arrow, indicating that a list of options is available that allow you to undo the new layout, stop the automatic layout of inserted objects, or alter the AutoCorrect Options settings. Perform the steps on the next page to undo the layout change.

Smart Tags

Microsoft PowerPoint automatically formats or corrects text as you type. For example, if you type a fraction, such as 1/4, the characters change to a fraction symbol. When you place your mouse on the symbol, the AutoCorrect Options button displays. Click the button to see the menu of choices.

More About

Layouts

Placement of text and graphics is important to a good persuasive presentation. Using the Internet for resources, tips, and articles on making clear and interesting presentations will increase your productivity. For more information on presentation design resources, visit the PowerPoint 2002 More About Web page (scsite.com/pp2002/more.htm) and then click Resources.

Steps **To Use the Automatic Layout Options Button to Undo a Layout Change**

1 **Click the Automatic Layout Options button. Point to Undo Automatic Layout.**

The Automatic Layout Options list displays (Figure 2-34). Clicking Undo Automatic Layout will reverse the layout change.

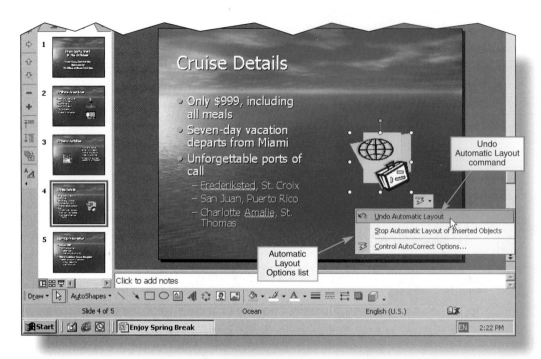

FIGURE 2-34

2 **Click Undo Automatic Layout.**

The layout reverts to Title and Text (Figure 2-35).

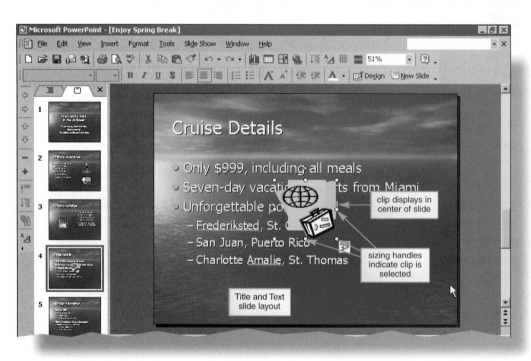

FIGURE 2-35

The desired clip displays in the center of Slide 4, which has the original Title and Text slide layout. The next step is to move the clip to the bottom-right corner of the slide.

Moving Clip Art

After you insert a clip into a slide, you may want to reposition it. The globe and luggage on Slide 4 overlays the bulleted list. You want to move the clip away from the text to the bottom-right corner of the slide. First move the clip and then change its size. Perform the steps below to move the clip to the bottom-right side of the slide.

More *About*

Voice Commands

Moving clip art with the mouse is easy. Using the Voice Command mode requires that you repeat commands several times to position the clip art. For example, after a clip has been placed in the slide, you must keep repeating the "down" command several times to move the clip art down to the place where you want it to display.

Steps To Move Clip Art

1 **With the clip selected, point to the clip and then click.**

2 **Press and hold down the mouse button.** Drag the clip to the bottom-right corner of the slide. Release the mouse button.

When you drag a clip, a dotted box displays. The dotted box indicates the clip's new position. When you release the left mouse button, the clip of the globe and luggage displays in the new location and the dotted line disappears (Figure 2-36). Sizing handles display at the corners and along its edges.

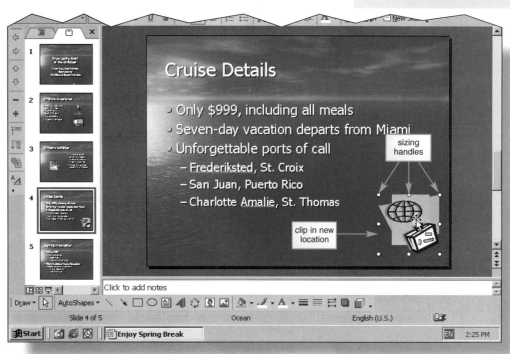

FIGURE 2-36

Other Ways

1. Select clip, press ARROW keys to move to new position

Changing the Size of Clip Art

Sometimes it is necessary to change the size of clip art. For example, on Slide 4 too much space displays around the clip. To make the object fit onto the slide, you increase its size. To change the size of a clip by an exact percentage, use the **Format Picture command** on the shortcut menu. The Format Picture dialog box contains six tabbed sheets with several formatting options. The **Size sheet** contains options for changing a clip's size. You either enter the exact height and width in the Size and rotate area, or enter the height and width as a percentage of the original clip in the Scale area. When the **Lock aspect ratio check box** displays a check mark, the height and width settings change to maintain the original aspect ratio. **Aspect ratio** is the relationship between an object's height and width. For example, a 3-by-5-inch object scaled to 50 percent would become a 1½-by-2½-inch object. Perform the steps on the next page to increase the size of the clip using the Format Picture dialog box.

Steps **To Change the Size of Clip Art**

1 **Right-click the clip. Point to Format Picture on the shortcut menu (Figure 2-37).**

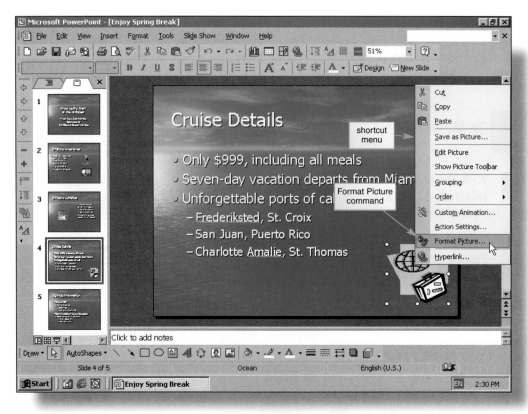

FIGURE 2-37

2 **Click Format Picture. Click the Size tab when the Format Picture dialog box displays.**

The Size sheet in the Format Picture dialog box displays (Figure 2-38). The Height and Width text boxes in the Scale area display the current percentage of the clip, 100 %. Check marks display in the Lock aspect ratio and Relative to original picture size check boxes.

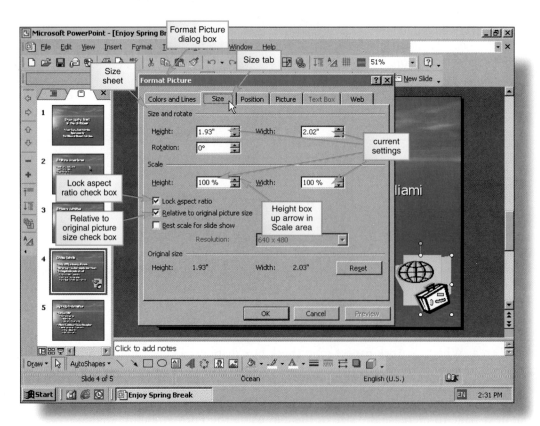

FIGURE 2-38

3 **Click and hold down the mouse button on the Height box up arrow in the Scale area until 125 % displays and then point to the OK button.**

Both the Height and Width text boxes in the Scale area display 125 % (Figure 2-39). PowerPoint automatically changes the Height and Width text boxes in the Size and rotate area to reflect changes in the Scale area.

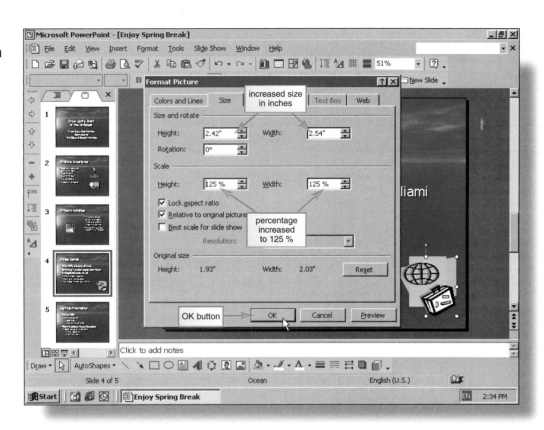

FIGURE 2-39

4 **Click the OK button. Drag the clip to the center of the space in the bottom-right corner of the slide.**

PowerPoint closes the Format Picture dialog box and displays the enlarged clip in the desired location (Figure 2-40).

Other Ways

1. Click clip, on Format menu click Picture, click Size tab, click and hold down mouse button on Height box up or down arrow in Scale area until desired size is reached, click OK button

2. Right-click slide anywhere except the text placeholders, click Slide Layout on shortcut menu, double-click desired slide layout

3. Click clip, drag a sizing handle until clip is desired shape and size

4. Press ALT+O, press I, press CTRL+TAB three times to select Size tab, press TAB to select Height text box in Scale area, press UP or DOWN ARROW keys to increase or decrease size, press ENTER

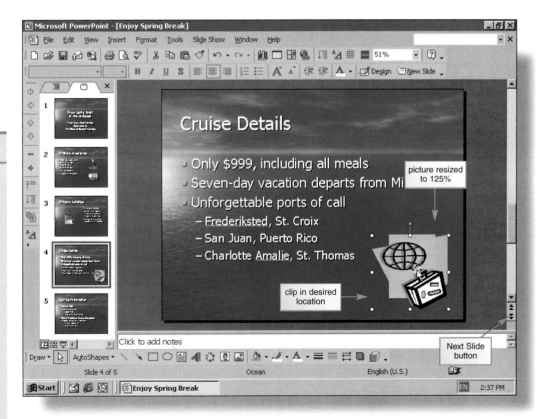

FIGURE 2-40

Inserting, Moving, and Sizing a Clip into a Slide

With Slide 4 complete, the final step is to add the alarm clock clip to the closing slide, Slide 5. Perform the following steps to add an alarm clock to Slide 5 without changing the Title and Text layout, size the clip, and then move it to the upper-right corner of the slide.

TO INSERT, MOVE, AND SIZE A CLIP INTO A SLIDE

1 Click the Next Slide button on the vertical scroll bar to display Slide 5.

2 Click the Insert Clip Art button on the Drawing toolbar. Type clock in the Search text text box and then press the ENTER key. Click the alarm clock or another appropriate clip. Click the Close button on the Insert Clip Art task pane title bar.

3 Click the Automatic Layout Options button and then click Undo Automatic Layout. Drag the clock to the upper-right corner of the slide.

4 Right-click the clock and then click Format Picture on the shortcut menu. Click the Size tab in the Format Picture dialog box, click and hold down the mouse button on the Height box up arrow in the Scale area until 150 % displays, and then click the OK button.

5 Drag the clock to the center of the space in the upper-right corner of the slide.

The alarm clock is inserted, moved, and sized into Slide 5 (Figure 2-41).

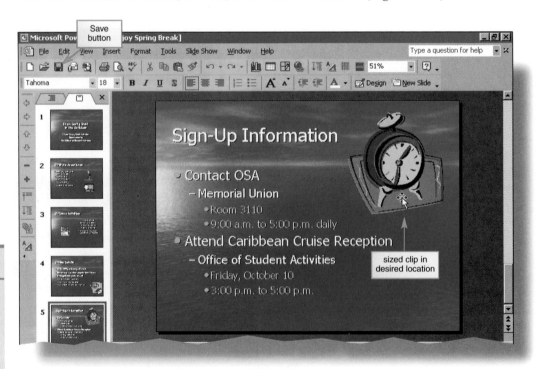

FIGURE 2-41

Choosing Clip Art

When selecting clip art, consider the direction in which the art faces. To focus the viewer's attention on the center of the slide, images should face in rather than out of the slide. For more information, visit the PowerPoint 2002 More About Web page (scsite.com/pp2002/more .htm) and then click Selecting Clip Art.

Saving the Presentation Again

To preserve the work completed, perform the following step to save the presentation again.

TO SAVE A PRESENTATION

1 Click the Save button on the Standard toolbar.

The changes made to the presentation after the previous save are saved on a floppy disk.

A default setting in PowerPoint allows for **fast saves**, which saves only the changes made since the last time you saved. To save a full copy of the complete presentation, click Tools on the menu bar, click Options on the Tools menu, and then click the Save tab. Remove the check mark in the Allow fast saves check box by clicking the check box and then click the OK button.

Adding a Header and Footer to Outline Pages

A printout of the presentation outline often is used as an audience handout. Distributing a copy of the outline provides the audience with paper on which to write notes or comments. Another benefit of distributing a copy of the outline is to help the audience see the text on the slides when lighting is poor or the room is too large. To help identify the source of the printed outline, add a descriptive header and footer. A **header** displays at the top of the sheet of paper or slide, and a **footer** displays at the bottom. Both contain specific information, such as the presenter's name or the company's telephone number. In addition, the current date and time and the slide or page number can display beside the header or footer information.

More About

Using Footers

Nothing can be more frustrating than having overhead transparencies of your slides get out of order when you are giving a presentation. Help keep them organized by using page numbers and the presentation name in the footer.

Using the Notes and Handouts Sheet to Add Headers and Footers

You add headers and footers to outline pages by clicking the Notes and Handouts sheet in the Header and Footer dialog box and entering the information you want to print. Perform the following steps to add the current date, header information, the page number, and footer information to the printed outline.

Steps To Use the Notes and Handouts Sheet to Add Headers and Footers

1 Click View on the menu bar and then point to Header and Footer (Figure 2-42).

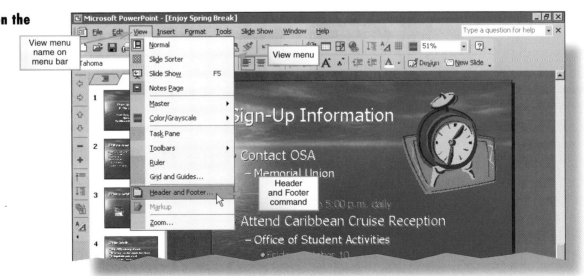

FIGURE 2-42

2 **Click Header and Footer. Click the Notes and Handouts tab when the Header and Footer dialog box displays. Point to the Update automatically option button.**

The Notes and Handouts sheet in the Header and Footer dialog box displays (Figure 2-43). Check marks display in the Date and time, Header, Page number, and Footer check boxes. The Fixed option button is selected.

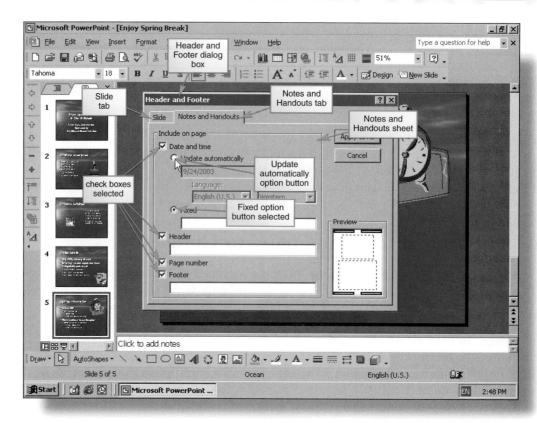

FIGURE 2-43

3 **Click the Update automatically option button and then click the Header text box. Type** Spring Break Cruise **in the Header text box. Click the Footer text box. Type** Office of Student Activities **in the Footer text box and then point to the Apply to All button (Figure 2-44).**

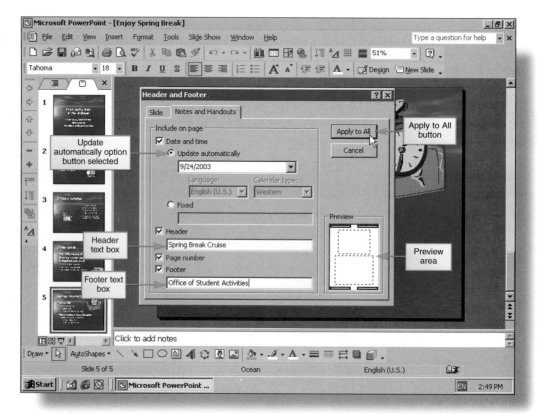

FIGURE 2-44

4 **Click the Apply to All button.**

PowerPoint applies the header and footer text to the outline, closes the Header and Footer dialog box, and displays Slide 5 (Figure 2-45). You cannot see header and footer text until you print the outline (shown in Figure 2-62 on page PP 2.49).

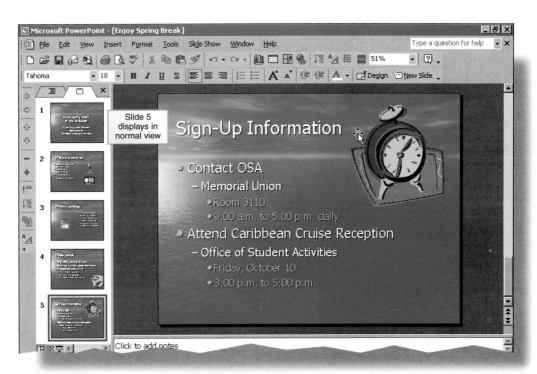

FIGURE 2-45

Applying Animation Schemes

PowerPoint provides many animation effects to add interest and make a slide show presentation look professional. **Animation** includes special visual and sound effects applied to text or content. For example, each line on the slide can swivel as it displays on the screen. Or an object can zoom in from the top of the screen to the bottom. PowerPoint provides a variety of **preset animation schemes** that determine slide transitions and effects for the title and body text. A **slide transition** is a special effect used to progress from one slide to the next in a slide show. PowerPoint also allows you to set your own **Custom animation** effects by defining your own animation types and speeds and sound effects on a slide. The following pages discuss how to add these animation effects to the presentation.

Adding an Animation Scheme to a Slide Show

PowerPoint has preset animation schemes with visual effects that vary the slide transitions and the methods in which the slide title and bullets or paragraphs display on the slides. Not all animation schemes have the slide transition element or effects for both the title and body text. These schemes are grouped in three categories: Subtle, Moderate, and Exciting. The name of the animation scheme characterizes the visual effects that display. For example, the Unfold animation scheme in the Moderate category uses the Push Right slide transition effect, the Fly In effect for the title text, and the Unfold effect for the body text. The Pinwheel scheme in the Exciting category does not use a slide transition effect, but it uses the Pinwheel effect for the title text and the Peek In effect for the body text.

More **About**

Animation Effects

Graphic designers suggest using a maximum of two different animation effects in one presentation. Any more than two can distract your audience from your important ideas by causing them to fixate on the visual effects and not on the slide content or the speaker. These effects should enhance your ideas in the presentation.

In this presentation, you apply the Float animation scheme to all slides. This effect is added easily by using the Slide Design task pane, which you used earlier in this project to select a design template. Perform the following steps to apply the Float animation scheme to the Enjoy Spring Break presentation.

Steps **To Add an Animation Scheme to a Slide Show**

1 **Click Slide Show on the menu bar and then point to Animation Schemes (Figure 2-46).**

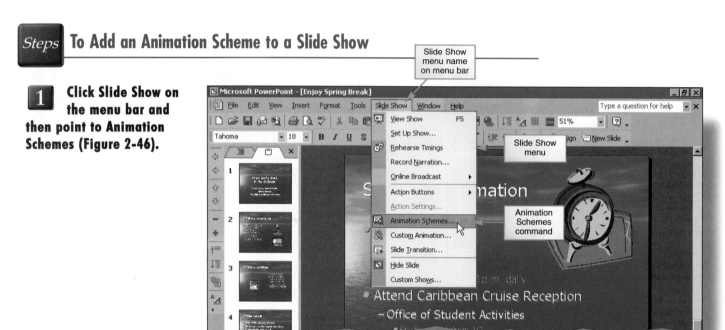

FIGURE 2-46

2 **Click Animation Schemes. Scroll down the Apply to selected slides list and then point to Float in the Exciting category.**

The Slide Design task pane displays (Figure 2-47). The list of possible slide transition effects displays in the Apply to selected slides area. Exciting is one of the animation scheme categories. The Float ScreenTip shows that the Float animation scheme uses the Comb Horizontal slide transition, the Float effect for the title text, and the Descend effect for the body text.

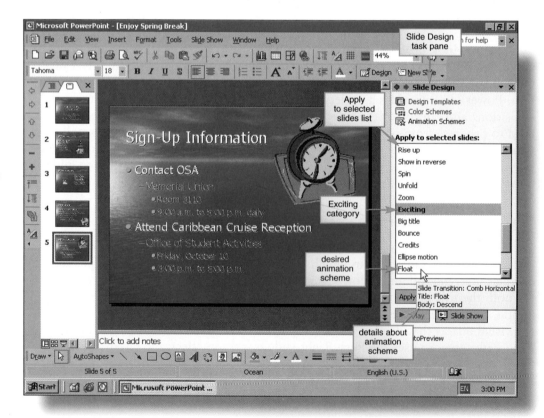

FIGURE 2-47

3 Click Float. Point to the Apply to All Slides button.

PowerPoint applies the Float animation effect to Slide 5, as indicated by the animation icon on the left side of the Slide 5 slide thumbnail on the Slides tab (Figure 2-48). The Float animation effect is previewed because the AutoPreview check box is selected.

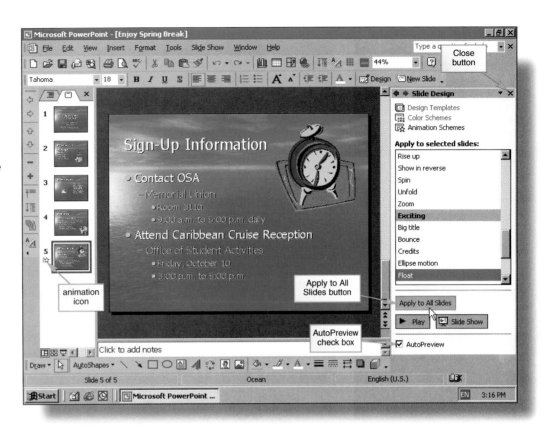

FIGURE 2-48

4 Click Apply to All Slides. Click the Close button in the Slide Design task pane.

The Float animation effect is applied to all slides in the presentation (Figure 2-49).

FIGURE 2-49

Other Ways

1. Right-click slide anywhere other than a placeholder or object, click Slide Design on shortcut menu, click Animation Schemes, select desired animation effect, click Apply to All Slides button

2. Right-click slide anywhere except text placeholders, click Slide Layout on shortcut menu, double-click desired slide layout

3. Press ALT+D, press C

Locating Clip Art

Thousands of public domain clips are available on the Internet. Use a search engine and the keywords, clip art and clip+art, to find these Web sites, which often contain bullets, lines, buttons, and sound files sorted into easy-to-navigate categories. You can import these files directly into your presentations.

Animating Clip Art

To add visual interest to a presentation, you can **animate** certain content. On Slide 5, for example, having the alarm clock rise from the bottom of the screen will provide a pleasing effect. Animating clip art takes several steps as described in the following sections.

Adding Animation Effects

PowerPoint allows you to animate clip art along with animating text. Because Slide 5 lists the times when students can gain additional information about the cruise, you want to emphasize these times by having the clip of the alarm clock move from the bottom of the screen to the top. One way of animating clip art is to select options in the Custom Animation dialog box. Perform the following steps to add the Flying animation effect to the clip on Slide 5.

 To Add Animation Effects

1 **Right-click the clip art image and then point to Custom Animation on the shortcut menu.**

The shortcut menu displays (Figure 2-50). The clip is selected, as indicated by the sizing handles that display at the corners and along its edges.

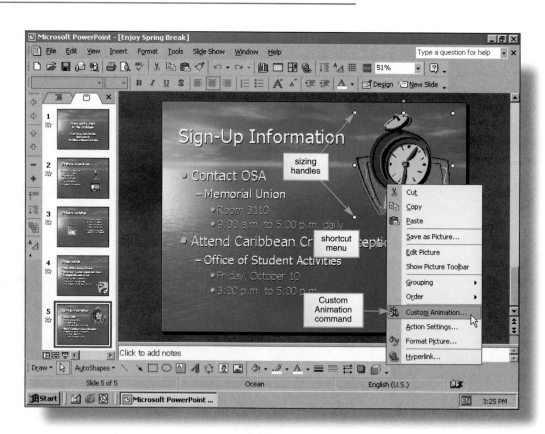

FIGURE 2-50

2   Click Custom Animation. Point to the Add Effect button.

The Custom Animation task pane displays (Figure 2-51). Two animation effects have been applied to the title and body of the slide previously.

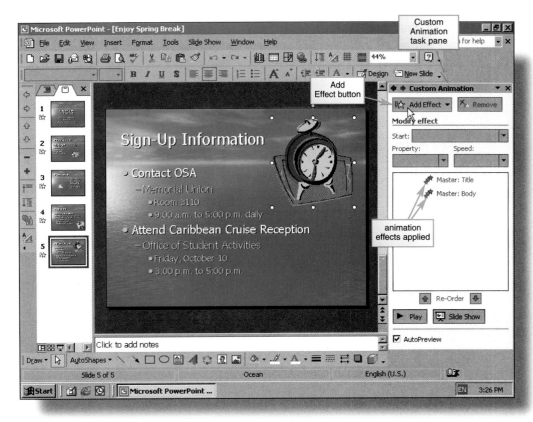

FIGURE 2-51

3   Click the Add Effect button, point to Entrance, and then point to Fly In in the Entrance effects list.

A list of possible effects for the Entrance option displays (Figure 2-52). Your system may display a different list of effects. You can apply a variety of effects to the clip, including how it enters and exits the slide.

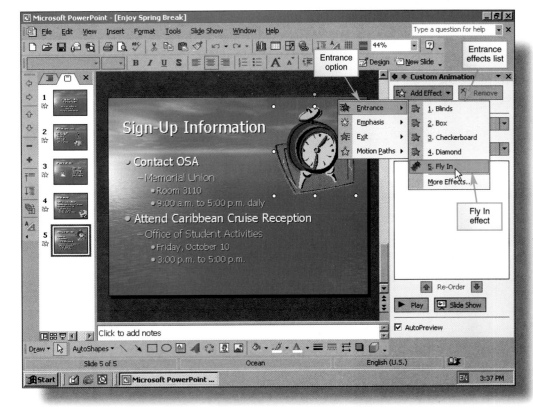

FIGURE 2-52

4 **Click Fly In. Point to the Close button on the Custom Animation task pane title bar.**

The animation effect is applied to the alarm clock, as indicated by the number 1 icon displaying to the left of the clip and the corresponding 1 display-ing in the Custom Animation list (Figure 2-53). You will see this effect when you click the mouse on that slide during your slide show. J0234131 is Microsoft's internal identifier for the alarm clock clip.

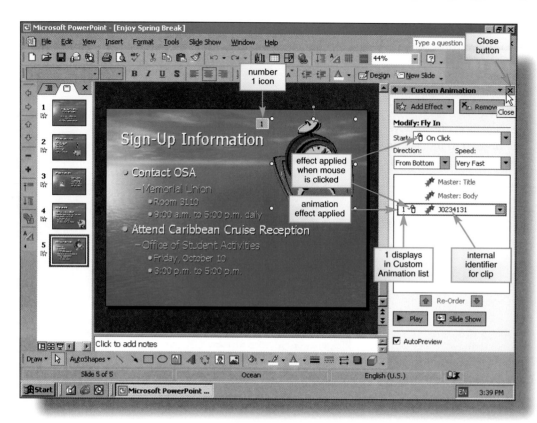

FIGURE 2-53

5 **Click the Close button (Figure 2-54).**

The alarm clock clip will appear in the presentation using the Fly In animation effect during the slide show.

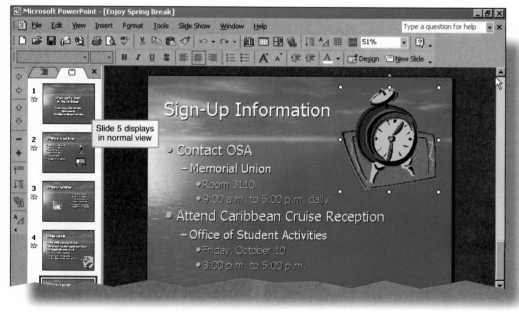

FIGURE 2-54

Other **Ways**

1. Click clip art, on Slide Show menu click Custom Animation, click desired animation effect, click OK button

2. Press TAB until clip art is selected, press ALT+D, press M, press DOWN ARROW key until desired animation effect selected, press ENTER

When you run the slide show, the bulleted list paragraphs will display, and then the clip art will begin moving from the bottom of the slide and stop at the position where you inserted it into Slide 5.

Animation effects are complete for this presentation. You now can review the presentation in slide show view and correct any spelling errors.

Saving the Presentation Again

The presentation is complete. Perform the following step to save the finished presentation on a floppy disk before running the slide show.

TO SAVE A PRESENTATION

1   Click the Save button on the Standard toolbar.

PowerPoint saves the presentation on your floppy disk by saving the changes made to the presentation since the last save.

Running an Animated Slide Show

Project 1 introduced you to using slide show view to look at your presentation one slide at a time. This project introduces you to running a slide show with preset and custom animation effects. When you run a slide show with slide transition effects, PowerPoint displays the slide transition effect when you click the mouse button to advance to the next slide. When a slide has text animation effects, each paragraph level displays in the sequence specified by the animation settings in the Custom Animation dialog box. Perform the following steps to run the animated Enjoy Spring Break presentation.

> ### More About
>
> ### Giving a Slide Show
>
> If you are displaying your slide show on a projection system or external monitor, you need to match the resolutions of your computer and the projector. To do this, open the Display Properties dialog box for your computer and click the Settings tab. In the Screen area box, move the slider to adjust the resolution. If you are uncertain of the resolution, try 800 x 600 pixels. When you are using two monitors, you can display your slide show on one monitor and view your notes, outline, and slides on the second monitor.

Steps   **To Run an Animated Slide Show**

1   **Click the Slide 1 slide thumbnail on the Slides tab. Click the Slide Show button at the lower left of the PowerPoint window. When Slide 1 displays in slide show view, click the slide anywhere.**

PowerPoint applies the Comb Horizontal slide transition effect and displays the title slide title text, Enjoy Spring Break in the Caribbean (Figure 2-55) using the Float animation effect. When you click the slide, the first paragraph in the subtitle text placeholder, Warm Days, Cool Activities, displays using the Descend animation effect.

FIGURE 2-55

Click the slide again.

PowerPoint displays the second paragraph in the subtitle text placeholder, Sponsored by, using the Float animation effect (Figure 2-56). If the Popup Menu buttons display when you move the mouse pointer, do not click them.

FIGURE 2-56

3 **Click the slide again.**

PowerPoint displays the third paragraph in the subtitle text placeholder, The Office of Student Activities, below the second paragraph. PowerPoint again uses the Descend animation effect (Figure 2-57).

FIGURE 2-57

4 **Continue clicking to finish running the slide show and return to normal view.**

Each time a new slide displays, PowerPoint first displays the Comb Horizontal slide transition effect and only the slide title using the Float effect. Then, PowerPoint builds each slide based on the animation settings. When you click the slide after the last paragraph displays on the last slide of the presentation, PowerPoint displays a blank slide. When you click again, PowerPoint exits slide show view and returns to normal view (Figure 2-58).

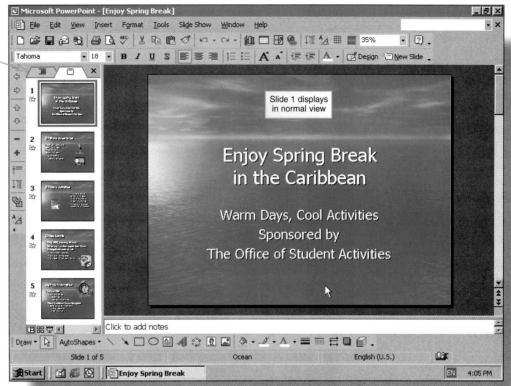

FIGURE 2-58

With the presentation complete and animation effects tested, the last step is to print the presentation outline and slides.

Printing a Presentation Created on the Outline Tab

When you click the Print button on the Standard toolbar, PowerPoint prints a hard copy of the presentation component last selected in the Print what box in the Print dialog box. To be certain to print the component you want, such as the presentation outline, use the Print command on the File menu. When the Print dialog box displays, you can select the appropriate presentation component in the Print what box. The next two sections explain how to use the Print command on the File menu to print the presentation outline and the presentation slides.

Printing an Outline

During the development of a lengthy presentation, it often is easier to review your outline in print instead of on the screen. Printing your outline also is useful for audience handouts or when your supervisor or instructor wants to review your subject matter before you develop your presentation fully.

Recall that the Print dialog box displays print options. When you want to print your outline, select Outline View in the Print what list in the Print dialog box. The outline, however, prints as last viewed on the Outline tab. This means that you must select the Zoom setting to display the outline text as you want it to print. If you are uncertain of the Zoom setting, you should return to the Outline tab and review it before printing. Perform the steps on the next page to print an outline from slide view.

Other **Ways**

1. On Slide Show menu click View Show, click slide until slide show ends
2. Press ALT+D, press V, press ENTER until slide show ends
3. In Voice Command mode, say "Slide Show, View Show"

More **About**

Sending Presentations to Word

You can create handouts and other documents by sending your PowerPoint outline to Microsoft Word and then using that text. To perform this action, click File on the menu bar, point to Send To, click Microsoft Word, and then click Outline only.

Steps **To Print an Outline**

1 **Click the Outline tab. Ready the printer according to the printer manufacturer's instructions. Click File on the menu bar and then point to Print.**

*The File menu displays (Figure 2-59). The Expand All button on the Outlining toolbar is selected, so the entire outline will print. If you want to print only the slide titles, you would click the **Collapse All button** before you click File on the menu bar.*

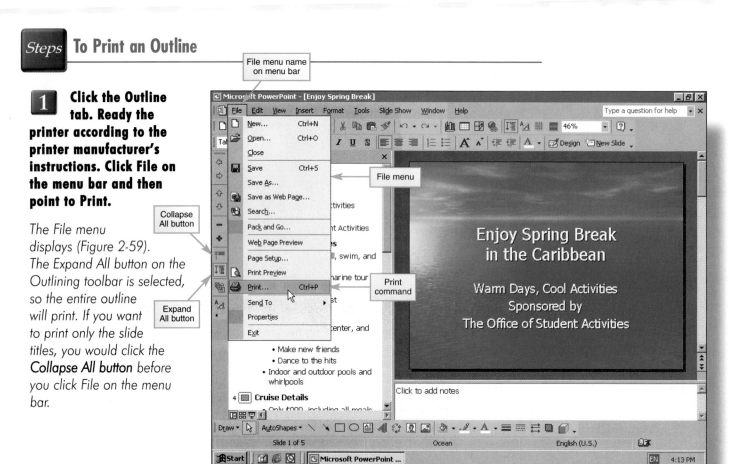

FIGURE 2-59

2 **Click Print on the File menu. When the Print dialog box displays, click the Print what box arrow and then point to Outline View.**

The Print dialog box displays (Figure 2-60). Outline View displays highlighted in the Print what list.

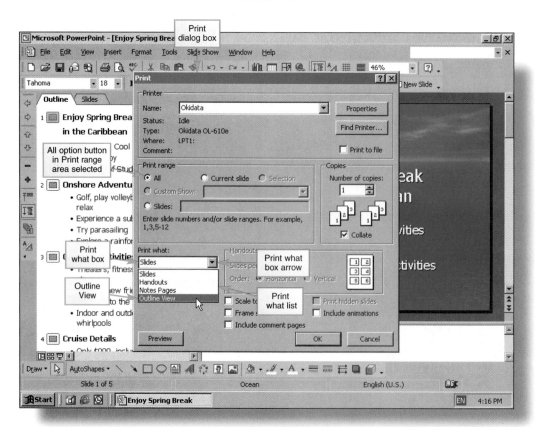

FIGURE 2-60

3 **Click Outline View in the list and then point to the OK button (Figure 2-61).**

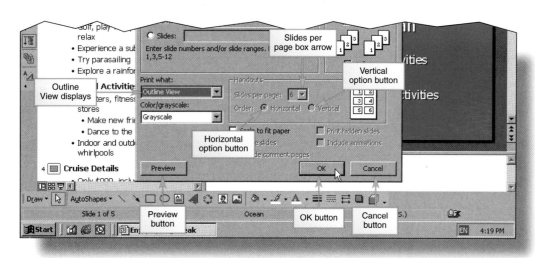

FIGURE 2-61

4 **Click the OK button.**

To cancel the print request, click the Cancel button.

5 **When the printer stops, retrieve the printout of the outline (Figure 2-62).**

The five PowerPoint slides display in outline form. The words, Spring Break Cruise, and the current date display in the header, and the words, Office of Student Activities, and the page number display in the footer.

Other **Ways**

1. On File menu click Print Preview, click Outline View in Print What list, click Print button on Print Preview toolbar

2. Press ALT+F, press P, press TAB, press W, press DOWN ARROW until Outline View is selected, press ENTER, press ENTER

3. In Voice Command mode, say "File, Print, Print What, Outline View, OK"

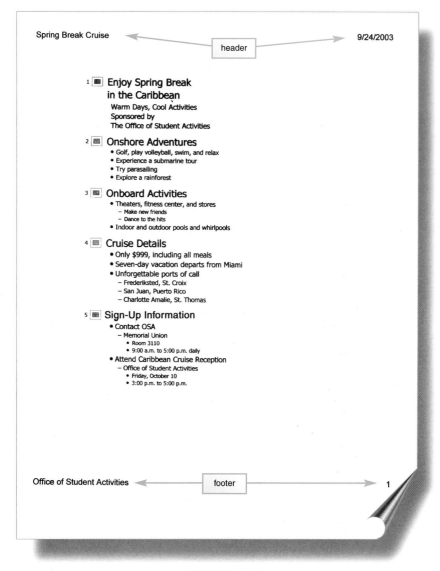

FIGURE 2-62

The **Print what list** in the Print dialog box contains options for printing slides, handouts, notes, and an outline. The Handouts area allows you to specify whether you want one, two, three, four, six, or nine slide images to display on each page. Printing handouts is useful for reviewing a presentation because you can analyze several slides displaying simultaneously on one page. Additionally, many businesses distribute handouts of the slide show before a presentation so the attendees can refer to a copy. To print handouts, click Handouts in the Print what box, click the Slides per page box arrow in the Handouts area, and then click 1, 2, 3, 4, 6, or 9. You can change the order in which the Enjoy Spring Break slides display on a page by clicking the Horizontal option button for Order in the Handouts area, which displays Slides 1 and 2, 3 and 4, and 5 and 6 adjacent to each other, or the Vertical option button for Order, which displays Slides 1 and 4, 2 and 5, and 3 and 6 adjacent to each other.

You also can click the Preview button if you want to see how your printout will look. After viewing the preview, click the Close button on the Preview window toolbar to return to normal view.

Printing Presentation Slides

At this point, you may want to check the spelling in the entire presentation and instruct PowerPoint to ignore any words spelled correctly. After correcting errors, you will want to print a final copy of your presentation. If you made any changes to your presentation since your last save, be certain to save your presentation before you print.

Perform the following steps to print the presentation.

TO PRINT PRESENTATION SLIDES

1. Ready the printer according to the printer manufacturer's instructions.

2. Click File on the menu bar and then click Print.

3. When the Print dialog box displays, click the Print what box arrow.

4. Click Slides in the list.

5. Click the OK button. When the printer stops, retrieve the slide printouts.

The printouts should resemble the slides in Figures 2-63a through 2-63e.

More About

Printing

If your printer seems to print slowly, Microsoft suggests clearing at least two megabytes of space on your hard drive and also closing any unnecessary programs that are running simultaneously.

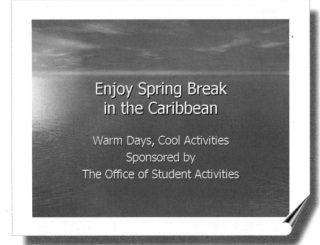

FIGURE 2-63a Slide 1

FIGURE 2-63b Slide 2

FIGURE 2-63c Slide 3

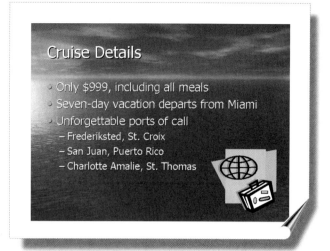

FIGURE 2-63d Slide 4

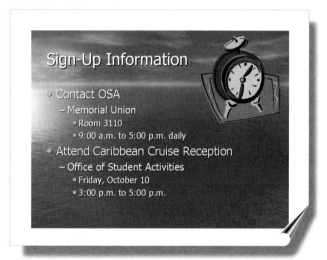

FIGURE 2-63e Slide 5

E-Mailing a Slide Show from within PowerPoint

Billions of e-mail messages are sent throughout the world each year. Computer users use this popular service on the Internet to send and receive plain text e-mail or to send and receive rich e-mail content that includes objects, links to other Web pages, and file attachments. These attachments can include Office files, such as Word documents or PowerPoint slide shows. Using Microsoft Office, you can e-mail the presentation directly from within PowerPoint.

For these steps to work properly, users need an e-mail address and a 32-bit e-mail program compatible with a Messaging Application Programming Interface, such as Outlook, Outlook Express, or Microsoft Exchange Client. Free e-mail accounts are available at hotmail.com. The steps on the next page show how to e-mail the slide show from within PowerPoint to Maria Lopez. Assume her e-mail address is maria_lopez2002@hotmail.com. If you do not have an E-mail button on the Standard toolbar, then this activity is not available to you.

More About

Sending E-Mail

Americans send more than 2.2 billion e-mail messages daily, compared with fewer than 300 million pieces of first-class mail. Professor Leonard Kleinrock sent the first e-mail message in 1969 to a colleague at Stanford University.

Steps **To E-Mail a Slide Show from within PowerPoint**

1 **Click the E-mail button on the Standard toolbar. When the e-mail Message window displays, type** maria_lopez2002@ hotmail.com **in the To text box. Select the text in the Subject text box and then type** Spring Break slide show **in the Subject text box. Click the message body.**

PowerPoint displays the e-mail Message window (Figure 2-64). The insertion point is in the message body so you can type a message to Maria Lopez.

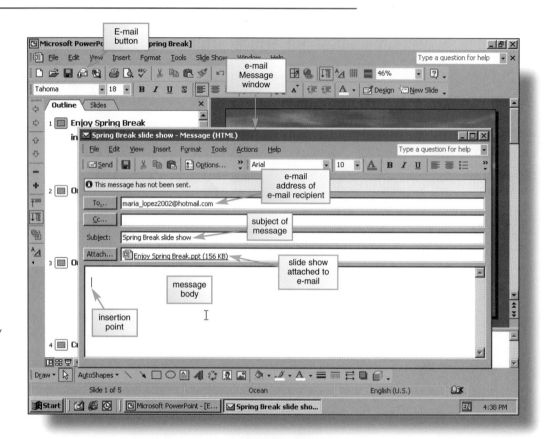

FIGURE 2-64

2 **Type** Attached is the PowerPoint presentation you can use to promote the Spring Break cruise. **in the message body. Point to the Send button.**

The message is indented to help the recipient of the e-mail understand the purpose of your e-mail (Figure 2-65).

3 **Click the Send button on the Standard Buttons toolbar.**

The e-mail with the attached presentation is sent to maria_ lopez2002@hotmail.com.

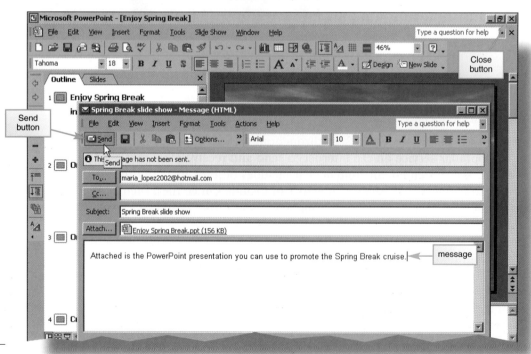

FIGURE 2-65

Because the slide show was sent as an attachment, Maria Lopez can save the attachment and then open the presentation in PowerPoint. You can choose many more options when you send e-mail from within PowerPoint. For example, the **Background command** on the Format menu changes the colors of the message background and lets you add a picture to use as the background. In addition, the **Security button** on the Standard Buttons toolbar allows you to send secure messages that only your intended recipient can read.

Saving and Quitting PowerPoint

If you made any changes to your presentation since your last save, you should save it again before quitting PowerPoint. Perform the following steps to save changes to the presentation and quit PowerPoint.

TO SAVE CHANGES AND QUIT POWERPOINT

1 Click the Close button on the Microsoft PowerPoint window title bar.

2 If prompted, click the Yes button in the Microsoft PowerPoint dialog box.

PowerPoint saves any changes made to the presentation since the last save and then quits PowerPoint.

Microsoft Certification

The Microsoft Office User Specialist (MOUS) Certification program provides an opportunity for you to obtain a valuable industry credential — proof that you have the PowerPoint 2002 skills required by employers. For more information, see Appendix E or visit the Shelly Cashman Series MOUS Web page at scsite.com/offxp/cert.htm.

CASE PERSPECTIVE SUMMARY

The Enjoy Spring Break presentation should help Maria Lopez market the cruise to students at your school. These classmates viewing your presentation will learn about the onshore adventures and onboard activities and discover the details of the trip and how to find more information and register. When Maria runs your slide show, she will describe and expand upon the details you list in your slides. The audience members should have a better understanding of the cruise and the fun they can have during Spring Break this school year.

Project Summary

Project 2 introduced you to the Outline tab, clip art, and animation effects. You created a slide presentation on the Outline tab where you entered all the text in the form of an outline. You arranged the text using the Promote and Demote buttons. Once the outline was complete, you changed slide layouts and added clip art. After adding clip art to slides without using a content placeholder, you moved and sized the clips. You added preset animation effects and applied animation effects to a clip. You learned how to run an animated slide show demonstrating slide transition and animation effects. Finally, you printed the presentation outline and slides using the Print command on the File menu and e-mailed the presentation.

What You Should Know

Having completed this project, you now should be able to perform the following tasks:

▶ Add a Slide on the Outline Tab *(PP 2.12)*

▶ Add an Animation Scheme to a Slide Show *(PP 2.40)*

▶ Add Animation Effects *(PP 2.42)*

▶ Change the Size of Clip Art *(PP 2.34)*

▶ Change the Slide Layout to Title, Content and Text and Insert Clip Art *(PP 2.27)*

▶ Change the Slide Layout to Title, Text, and 2 Content *(PP 2.22)*

▶ Change the View to Normal View *(PP 2.19)*

▶ Change the View to Slide Sorter View *(PP 2.18)*

▶ Change to the Outline Tab and Display the Outlining Toolbar *(PP 2.08)*

▶ Create a Closing Slide on the Outline Tab *(PP 2.17)*

▶ Create a Second Text Slide with a Multi-Level Bulleted List *(PP 2.15)*

▶ Create a Text Slide with a Multi-Level Bulleted List on the Outline Tab *(PP 2.14)*

▶ Create a Text Slide with a Single-Level Bulleted List on the Outline Tab *(PP 2.13)*

▶ Create a Title Slide on the Outline Tab *(PP 2.10)*

▶ E-Mail a Slide Show from within PowerPoint *(PP 2.52)*

▶ Insert a Second Clip into a Slide *(PP 2.27)*

▶ Insert Clip Art into a Content Placeholder *(PP 2.25)*

▶ Insert Clip Art into a Slide without a Content Placeholder *(PP 2.29)*

▶ Insert, Move, and Size a Clip into a Slide *(PP 2.36)*

▶ Move Clip Art *(PP 2.33)*

▶ Print an Outline *(PP 2.48)*

▶ Print Presentation Slides *(PP 2.50)*

▶ Run an Animated Slide Show *(PP 2.45)*

▶ Save a Presentation *(PP 2.18, 2.37, 2.45)*

▶ Save Changes and Quit PowerPoint *(PP 2.53)*

▶ Start and Customize a New Presentation *(PP 2.06)*

▶ Use the Automatic Layout Options Button to Undo a Layout Change *(PP 2.32)*

▶ Use the Notes and Handouts Sheet to Add Headers and Footers *(PP 2.37)*

Learn It Online

Instructions: To complete the Learn It Online exercises, start your browser, click the Address bar, and then enter scsite.com/offxp/exs.htm. When the Office XP Learn It Online page displays, follow the instructions in the exercises below.

1 Project Reinforcement TF, MC, and SA

Below PowerPoint Project 2, click the Project Reinforcement link. Print the quiz by clicking Print on the File menu. Answer each question. Write your first and last name at the top of each page, and then hand in the printout to your instructor.

2 Flash Cards

Below PowerPoint Project 2, click the Flash Cards link. When Flash Cards displays, read the instructions. Type 20 (or a number specified by your instructor) in the Number of Playing Cards text box, type your name in the Name text box, and then click the Flip Card button. When the flash card displays, read the question and then click the Answer box arrow to select an answer. Flip through Flash Cards. Click Print on the File menu to print the last flash card if your score is 15 (75%) correct or greater and then hand it in to your instructor. If your score is less than 15 (75%) correct, then redo this exercise by clicking the Replay button.

3 Practice Test

Below PowerPoint Project 2, click the Practice Test link. Answer each question, enter your first and last name at the bottom of the page, and then click the Grade Test button. When the graded practice test displays on your screen, click Print on the File menu to print a hard copy. Continue to take practice tests until you score 80% or better. Hand in a printout of the final practice test to your instructor.

4 Who Wants to Be a Computer Genius?

Below PowerPoint Project 2, click the Computer Genius link. Read the instructions, enter your first and last name at the bottom of the page, and then click the Play button. Hand in your score to your instructor.

5 Wheel of Terms

Below PowerPoint Project 2, click the Wheel of Terms link. Read the instructions, and then enter your first and last name and your school name. Click the Play button. Hand in your score to your instructor.

6 Crossword Puzzle Challenge

Below PowerPoint Project 2, click the Crossword Puzzle Challenge link. Read the instructions, and then enter your first and last name. Click the Play button. Work the crossword puzzle. When you are finished, click the Submit button. When the crossword puzzle redisplays, click the Print button. Hand in the printout.

7 Tips and Tricks

Below PowerPoint Project 2, click the Tips and Tricks link. Click a topic that pertains to Project 2. Right-click the information and then click Print on the shortcut menu. Construct a brief example of what the information relates to in PowerPoint to confirm you understand how to use the tip or trick. Hand in the example and printed information.

8 Newsgroups

Below PowerPoint Project 2, click the Newsgroups link. Click a topic that pertains to Project 2. Print three comments. Hand in the comments to your instructor.

9 Expanding Your Horizons

Below PowerPoint Project 2, click the Articles for Microsoft Powerpoint link. Click a topic that pertains to Project 2. Print the information. Construct a brief example of what the information relates to in PowerPoint to confirm you understand the contents of the article. Hand in the example and printed information to your instructor.

10 Search Sleuth

Below PowerPoint Project 2, click the Search Sleuth link. To search for a term that pertains to this project, select a term below the Project 2 title and then use the Google search engine at google.com (or any major search engine) to display and print two Web pages that present information on the term. Hand in the printouts to your instructor.

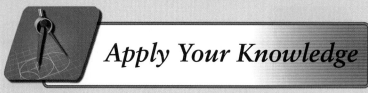

Apply Your Knowledge

1 Intensifying a Presentation by Applying a Design Template, Changing Slide Layout, Inserting Clip Art, and Applying Animation Effects

Instructions: Start PowerPoint. Open the presentation Intramurals from the Data Disk. See the inside back cover of this book for instructions for downloading the Data Disk or see your instructor for information on accessing the files required for this book. Perform the following tasks to change the presentation so it looks like the slides in Figures 2-66a through 2-66d.

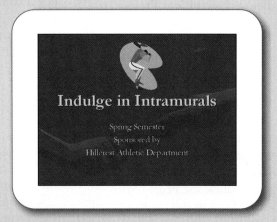

(a) Slide 1

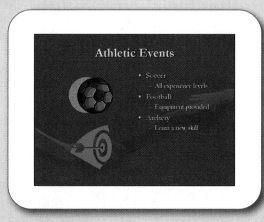

(b) Slide 2

(c) Slide 3

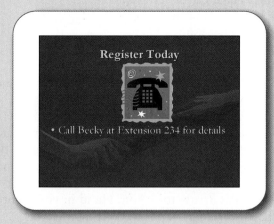

(d) Slide 4

FIGURE 2-66

1. Apply the Teamwork design template. Add the current date and your name to the notes and handouts footer.
2. On Slide 1, increase the font size of the Indulge in Intramurals paragraph to 60 point. Insert the baseball clip shown in Figure 2-66a. Scale the clip art to 130% using the Format Picture command on the shortcut menu. Drag the baseball clip to the top center of the slide, as shown in Figure 2-66a. Apply the Diamond Entrance custom animation effect to the clip.

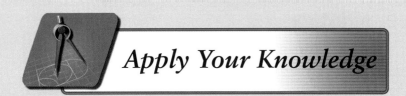

Apply Your Knowledge

3. Go to Slide 2. Change the slide layout to Title, 2 Content and Text. Insert the sports clips shown in Figure 2-66b. Change the size of both clips to 110%.

4. Go to Slide 3. Insert the clip shown in Figure 2-66c. Increase the clip size to 75%. Drag the clip to the bottom-right corner of the slide. Apply the Spin Emphasis custom animation effect to the clip.

5. Go to Slide 4. Change the slide layout to Title and Content over Text. Insert the telephone clip shown in Figure 2-66d and then center it between the title and the body text. Change the size of the clip to 150%. Apply the Grow/Shrink Emphasis custom animation effect to the clip. Increase the font size of the body text to 40 point.

6. Apply the Bounce animation scheme in the Exciting category list to all slides.

7. Save the presentation on a floppy disk using the file name, Intramurals Publicity.

8. Print the presentation and the outline.

9. Quit PowerPoint.

In the Lab

1 Adding Clip Art and Animation Effects to a Presentation Created on the Outline Tab

Problem: One of your assignments in your Health 101 class is to write a research paper and then share your knowledge during a five-minute presentation. You decide to research the topic of keeping your heart healthy. You generate the outline shown in Figure 2-67 to prepare the presentation. You use the outline to create the presentation shown in Figures 2-68a through 2-68d on the next page.

Instructions: Perform the following tasks.

I. Healthy Heart Hints
   A. Presented by Jennifer Korvath
   B. Health 101
II. Healthy Heart Diet
   A. General guidelines
      1) Eat foods that maintain healthy cholesterol levels
      2) Limit saturated fats
         a) In animal products
III. Exercise Benefits
   A. Aerobic activities improve cholesterol levels
      1) Brisk walking, swimming, fencing, and racquet sports
      2) May take year to see significant improvement
   B. Weight training reduces bad cholesterol levels
IV. Decrease Risk Factors
   A. Reduce stress
      1) Mental stress triggers heart disease
   B. Lose weight
      1) Obesity contributes to heart attack risk
   C. Quit smoking
      1) Responsible for 20% of heart disease deaths

FIGURE 2-67

(continued)

In the Lab

Adding Clip Art and Animation Effects to a Presentation Created on the Outline Tab *(continued)*

(a) Slide 1

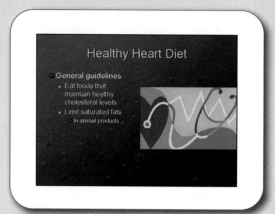

(b) Slide 2

(c) Slide 3

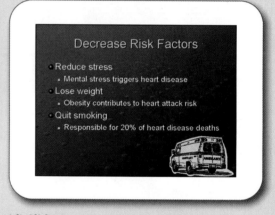

(d) Slide 4

FIGURE 2-68

1. Use the Outline tab to create a new presentation. Apply the Digital Dots design template.

2. Using the outline shown in Figure 2-67, create the title slide shown in Figure 2-68a. Use your name instead of the name Jennifer Korvath. Decrease the font size of the class name to 28 point. Insert the heart clip art. Scale the clip to 75% and then center it at the top of the slide. Add the Box Entrance custom animation effect to the clip.

3. Using the outline in Figure 2-67, create the three text slides with bulleted lists shown in Figures 2-68b through 2-68d.

4. Change the slide layout on Slide 2 to Title, Text, and Content. Insert the heart clip art shown in Figure 2-68b. Scale the clip art to 245% and then move it to the right side of the slide. Add the Checkerboard Entrance custom animation effect to the clip.

5. Change the slide layout on Slide 3 to Title and Text over Content. Insert the clip art shown in Figure 2-68c, scale it to 215%, and then move it to the bottom left of the slide. Add the Right Motion Paths custom animation effect.

6. On Slide 4, insert the ambulance clip art shown in Figure 2-68d. Add the Box Exit custom animation effect.

In the Lab

7. Add your name to the outline header and your school's name to the outline footer.

8. Apply the Rise up animation scheme in the Moderate category to all slides in the presentation.

9. Save the presentation on a floppy disk using the file name, Healthy Heart Hints.

10. Print the presentation outline. Print the presentation.

11. Quit PowerPoint.

2 Inserting Clip Art and Animating a Slide Show

Problem: Many students at your school have asked members of the Campus Computer Club for advice on purchasing and upgrading a personal computer. To help these students best, the Club members have decided to prepare a PowerPoint presentation to show to these students. They have given you the outline shown in Figure 2-69. You create the text for the presentation on the Outline tab, and you decide to add animation effects to the slide show. The completed slides are shown in Figures 2-70a through 2-70d on the next page.

Instructions: Perform the following tasks.

1. Use the Outline tab to create a new presentation from the outline shown in Figure 2-69. Apply the Glass Layers design template.

2. On the title slide, increase the font size of Buyer's Guide to 72 point. Decrease the font size of Campus Computer Club to 28 point. Using Figure 2-70a as a reference, insert the clip art shown, scale it to 180%, and then drag it to the lower-right corner of the slide.

3. On Slide 2, insert the clip art shown in Figure 2-70b, click the AutoCorrect Options button to undo the layout change, and then drag the art to the right edge of the slide. Scale the clip to 185%.

4. On Slide 3, change the slide layout to Title, Content and Text. Insert the clip art shown in Figure 2-70c. Scale the clip to 205% and then move it to the location show in the figure.

5. Do not make any changes to Slide 4. On Slide 5, change the slide layout to Title, Text, and Content. Insert the clip art shown in Figure 2-70e. Scale the clip to 210%.

I. Buyer's Guide
    A. Purchasing and Installing a Personal Computer
    B. Campus Computer Club
II. Determine the Type
    A. Desktop
        1) Low cost, large screen
    B. Notebook
        1) Computing capacity when you travel
    C. Handheld
        1) Handle basic organizer-type applications
III. Do Some Research
    A. Talk to friends and instructors
    B. Visit Web sites and read reviews
    C. Use a worksheet to record comparisons
IV. Make the Purchase
    A. Use a credit card
        1) Gives purchase protection, extended warranty benefits
    B. Consider an onsite service agreement
        1) Available through local dealer or third-party company
        2) Technician will arrive within 24 hours
V. Install the System
    A. Read the manuals before you start
    B. Have a well-designed work area
        1) Use ergonomic chair and keyboard

FIGURE 2-69

(continued)

In the Lab

Inserting Clip Art and Animating a Slide Show *(continued)*

(a) Slide 1

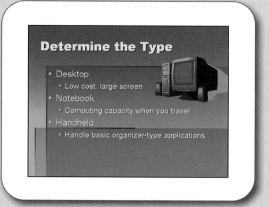

(b) Slide 2

(c) Slide 3

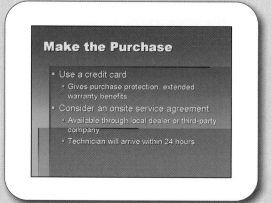

(d) Slide 4

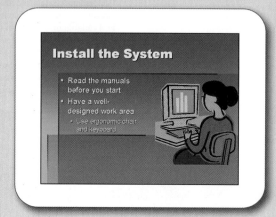

(e) Slide 5

FIGURE 2-70

In the Lab

6. Add the current date and your name to the outline header. Include Campus Computer Club and the page number on the outline footer.

7. Apply the Elegant animation scheme in the Moderate category to all slides.

8. Animate the clip on Slide 1 using the Blinds Entrance custom animation effect, the clip on Slide 2 using the Diagonal Down Right Motion Paths effect, the clip on Slide 3 using the Checkerboard Entrance effect, and the clip on Slide 5 using the Box Exit effect.

9. Save the presentation on a floppy disk using the file name, Buyer's Guide.

10. Print the presentation outline. Print the presentation slides. Print a handout with all five slides arranged vertically on one page.

11. Quit PowerPoint.

3 Creating a Presentation on the Outline Tab, Inserting Clip Art, and Applying Slide Transitions and Animation Effects

Problem: Chief Malcolm Snipes from the police department at your school has asked you to help him prepare a lecture on the topic of roadside emergencies. He has helped many students when they call his office for assistance. He knows that nearly 3,000 people die in car accidents every year when their cars are parked on the side of a road or on a median, and many of these fatalities started with a breakdown that could have been avoided. He asks you to prepare a PowerPoint presentation to accompany his talk. The slide show will describe how to pull off the road safely, how to obtain help, what supplies to store in your glove compartment, what supplies to keep in your trunk, and what routine maintenance you should perform. You search for appropriate clip art to add to the slides and are unable to find images that are part of the Microsoft Clip Organizer. You connect to the Internet, obtain clip from Microsoft's Web site, and create the presentation using the outline shown in Figure 2-71.

I. Handling Roadside Breakdowns
    A. Stop Problems, Remain Safe
    B. Presented by
    C. Campus Police Department
II. Pull off the Road Safely
    A. Eliminate distractions
        1) Turn off the stereo
    B. Look in mirrors
    C. Reduce speed slowly
    D. Use turn signal
        1) Not flashers
III. Obtain Help
    A. Place 'Call Police' sign in window
    B. Tie scarf or clothing to door handle or antenna
    C. Stay inside the vehicle
        1) Keep seat belt fastened
IV. Glove Compartment Supplies
    A. 'Call Police' sign
    B. Flashlight
    C. Health insurance card
    D. Pen, message pad
    E. Vehicle registration, insurance
V. Trunk Supplies
    A. Fire extinguisher
    B. Jack and lug wrench
    C. Spare tire inflated properly
    D. Jumper cables
VI. Perform Routine Maintenance
    A. Check oil level, tire pressure weekly
    B. Rotate tires every 5,000 miles
    C. Examine tires for cuts, nails, stones

FIGURE 2-71

(continued)

In the Lab

Creating a Presentation on the Outline Tab, Inserting Clip Art, and Applying Slide Transitions and Animation Effects *(continued)*

The clips you find may vary from the clips shown in Figures 2-72a through 2-72f. You then refine the presentation using clip art, animation schemes, and custom animation effects to create the slide show shown in Figures 2-72a through 2-72f.

Instructions: Perform the following tasks.

1. Create a new presentation using the Ripple design template and the outline in Figure 2-71 on the previous page.

2. On the title slide, insert the clip art shown in Figure 2-72a and add the Fly In Entrance custom animation effect. Change the speed to Slow. Size the clip if necessary.

3. On Slide 2, change the slide layout to Title, Text, and 2 Content, and insert the clips shown in Figure 2-72b. Add the Fly In Entrance custom animation effect for the top image and change the Direction to From Top-Right. Add the Fly In Entrance custom animation effect for the bottom image. Size the clips if necessary.

4. On Slide 3, change the slide layout to Title and Text over Content, and insert the clip shown in Figure 2-72c. Add the Grow/Shrink Emphasis custom animation effect. Size the clip if necessary.

5. Change the slide layout on Slide 4 (Figure 2-72d) to Title, 2 Content and Text. Insert the two clip art images shown. Add the Box Entrance custom animation effect to both clips. Size the clips if necessary.

6. On Slide 5 (Figure 2-72e), change the slide layout to Title and 2 Content over Text. Insert the clips shown and add the Fly In Entrance custom animation effect for both. Change the Direction for the fire extinguisher to From Top-Left and for the tire to From Top-Right. Size the clips if necessary.

7. On Slide 6 (Figure 2-72f), change the slide layout to Title, Text, and 2 Content. Insert the clips shown and add the Spin Emphasis custom animation effect to both. Size the clips if necessary.

8. Display your name and the current date on the outline header, and display the page number and the name of your school on the outline footer.

9. Apply the Unfold animation scheme to all slides.

10. Save the presentation on a floppy disk using the file name, Roadside Breakdowns.

11. Run the slide show.

12. Print the presentation outline. Print the presentation slides. Print a handout with all six slides arranged horizontally on one page. E-mail the presentation to Chief Snipes using the address malcolm_snipes@ hotmail.com.

13. Quit PowerPoint.

In the Lab

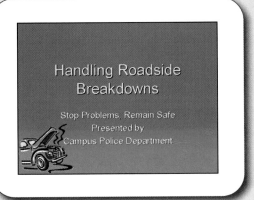

(a) Slide 1

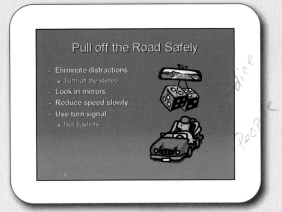

(b) Slide 2

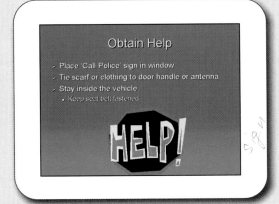

(c) Slide 3

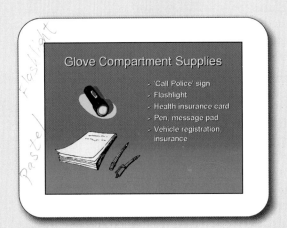

(d) Slide 4

(e) Slide 5

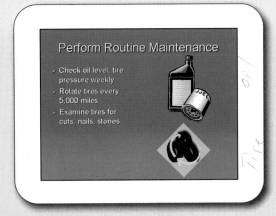

(f) Slide 6

FIGURE 2-72

Cases and Places

The difficulty of these case studies varies:
▶ are the least difficult; ▶▶ are more difficult; and ▶▶▶ are the most difficult.

1 ▶ With the holidays approaching, Janis Lamata, the head librarian at Weber Hills Community Library, wants to present a series of cooking demonstrations. Janis has asked Jean-Luc Richard, the head chef at Chateau la Flambeau Restaurant, to make the presentations. His first program features grilling turkeys and is called, Grilling Is Not Just for Steaks. Jean-Luc provides the outline shown in Figure 2-73 and asks your help in creating a PowerPoint presentation. Using the concepts and techniques introduced in this project, together with Jean-Luc's outline, develop slides for a slide show. Include clip art and animation effects to add interest. Print the outline and slides as handouts so they can be distributed to presentation attendees.

I. Grilling Is Not Just for Steaks
    A. Cooking Turkeys on Your Outdoor Grill
    B. Presented by
    C. Jean-Luc Richard
    D. Head Chef, Chateau la Flambeau Restaurant
II. Before You Start
    A. Pick a turkey less than 24 pounds
        1. Make sure it is thawed completely
    B. Have plenty of fuel
        1. Propane tanks - 5 to 6 hours
        2. Charcoal - 65 to 75 briquettes
    C. Wash hands and utensils thoroughly before touching food
III. Start Cooking
    A. Set grill for indirect grilling and place bird on grill
    B. Cooking times
        1. 12-14 lbs. - 2½ to 3 hours
        2. 15-17 lbs. - 2¾ to 3½ hours
        3. 18-22 lbs. - 3½ to 4¼ hours
    C. No need to turn or baste
IV. Doneness
    A. Cook until meat thermometer reaches 180 degrees
    B. Remove from grill
    C. Let stand 20 minutes
    D. Smoked turkey may appear a little pink
        1. It is cooked thoroughly

FIGURE 2-73

Cases and Places

2 ▶ Dr. Jasmine Lopez wants to make a presentation at the Rest Haven Rehabilitation Center and Clinic where you volunteer on weekends. The presentation is a series of healthy tips for those planning to retire between the ages of 50 and 55 so they can enjoy their retirement for many years. The nursing director, Charles Becker, asks you to create a PowerPoint presentation for Dr. Lopez. The presentation will cover preventive health strategies for those planning early retirement. Dr. Lopez has provided the outline shown in Figure 2-74. Using the concepts and techniques introduced in this project, together with Dr. Lopez's outline, develop slides for a slide show. Include clip art and animation effects to add interest. Print the outline and slides as a one-page handout so they can be distributed to presentation attendees.

I. Staying Healthy as You Age
   A. Presented by
   B. Dr. Jasmine Lopez
   C. Board-certified internist and Director of Adult Health Care
II. Eating to Live Longer
   A. Balance food with physical activity
   B. Eat plenty of whole grains, vegetables, and fruits
   C. Reduce fatty meats
      1. Choose fish and chicken
      2. Concentrate on low-saturated fats
   D. Limit consumption of salt, sugar, and alcoholic beverages
III. Longevity with Vitamins
   A. B vitamins reduce homocysteine protein
      1. Decrease heart disease
   B. As we age, we have difficulty absorbing calcium and vitamins B-12 and D
   C. Vitamin C
      1. Decreases cancer risk by 20%
      2. Reduces the risk of heart attacks by 40%
IV. Do Not Call This a Diet
   A. White blood cells (natural infection fighters) are affected by what we eat
   B. Eat for life
      1. Follow the USDA Food Guide Pyramid
      2. Avoid cooking fats derived from animal products
      3. Avoid trans fats (hydrogenated fats)
        a. They increase triglycerides

FIGURE 2-74

3 ▶▶ Strength training offers many positive benefits. First, it builds power. Athletes who participate in strength training can increase their performance in other sports, such as tennis or golf. Strength training also provides energy. Research shows that strength training increases endurance for runners and swimmers. Another benefit of this training is decreased fatigue. It also improves mood, self-confidence, and self-esteem, which expand beyond sports into personal life. Strength training also helps prevent osteoporosis by strengthening bones and building bone density. It helps burn calories, even while a person is resting, by increasing the body's metabolism for as many as 12 hours after exercising. The training also balances the body by making both sides equally strong. Normally, one side is stronger than the other. A balanced body is less prone to injuries. The director of your campus fitness center wants new members to view a presentation on strength training. Using the techniques introduced in this project, create a slide show about strength training. Include appropriate clip art and animation effects.

Cases and Places

4 ▶▶ As an intern for the Great Lakes Arts Association (GLAA), you have helped the Association's director, Rajish Gupta, with many projects. He asks you to create a PowerPoint presentation for his visits at many community sites. Rajish says the Association's mission is to strengthen the bond between the diverse communities in the Great Lakes area. It also provides opportunities for artistic expression, education, cultural exchanges, and art appreciation. In addition, the Association's commission provides cultural planning, grant writing, information and referral services, and technical assistance. It sponsors exhibits of local, regional, national, and international artists at various locations. Exhibits feature fiber art, photography, paintings, folk art, glass, and sculptures. Educational opportunities include art classes and workshops by prominent artists at local schools, lectures, readings, bus tours narrated by art historians and authorities, and scholarships to send gifted students from low-income families to state colleges and private art schools. Membership levels are student, individual, family, artist, patron, sponsor, benefactor, life member, and organization. Using the techniques introduced in this project, create a presentation about the GLAA. Include appropriate clip art and animation effects.

5 ▶▶ Walking is one of the easiest methods of exercising. Many students have discovered that walking enhances both the body and spirit. Leading researchers believe this form of exercise also prolongs life. Paula Peerman, the director of recreation at your community's park district, wants to organize a walking club and has asked you to help her promote the idea. She wants you to recruit and motivate members by describing various techniques to enhance their walking routines. For example, members can try interval training by increasing their walking speed for 30 seconds and then returning to their normal speed for one minute. They also should walk with a friend to add motivation and help pass the time. If they do not feel like walking on a particular day, they can tell each other they are going to exercise for just a few minutes. Those few minutes might stretch into a half-hour or more. Walkers should swing their arms to increase their heart rates and to burn more calories. Using the techniques introduced in this project, create a presentation about the benefits of walking. Include appropriate clip art and animation effects.

6 ▶▶▶ Bookstores are becoming an integral part of the community. Many have guest speakers, cultural events, and various clubs. Your local bookstore, Bobbie's Books, is sponsoring a book club, where members will meet on four consecutive Monday nights to discuss a famous author. Pick a prominent author, such as Stephen King, Danielle Steel, John Grisham, Michael Crichton, or Margaret Eleanor Atwood. Visit your local bookstore and library, and search the Internet for information about the author. Then, create a presentation to promote Bobbie's Books. Include a short biography of this author, describe his or her best-selling books, discuss critical comments by reviewers, and present relevant Web sites. Include appropriate clip art and animation effects.

7 ▶▶▶ Many homeowners are finding the cost of remodeling prohibitive, so they are taking on do-it-yourself projects. Visit two local lumberyards or building supply stores and collect information about adding a wooden deck to a home. Learn about the different types of wood and stains, the various types of designs, and how to maintain the deck. Then, create a PowerPoint presentation that includes a summary of this information along with a list of the tools and materials needed and the estimated time to complete the project. Add appropriate clip art and animation effects.

Microsoft PowerPoint 2002

Creating a Presentation on the Web Using PowerPoint

CASE PERSPECTIVE

With the Internet transforming the job market, corporations are rethinking the way they advertise their available jobs and market their businesses on Web sites. They list their open positions and describe the positive aspects of their companies on their corporate Web sites. Job seekers, likewise, are changing their traditional methods of searching for jobs and marketing themselves. They now prepare electronic or online resumes and send them via e-mail to businesses. They also search for jobs on employment Web sites, called job boards, such as Monster.com.

The Placement Center director at Highland College, Tina Natella, wants to teach students how to use the Internet to find careers. She decides the most effective way to disseminate this information is to have you prepare a PowerPoint slide show and then make the presentation available on the World Wide Web to all students. The slide show, called Job Search, will contain this information along with clip art and an animation scheme for visual interest. Tina then wants you to publish the presentation on the Web in a file named Jobs on the Internet.

Introduction

The graphic design power of PowerPoint allows you to create vibrant presentations that convey information in a clear, interesting manner. Some of these presentations are created for small, specific audiences, such as a subcommittee planning a department retreat. In this case, the presentation may be shown in an office conference room. Other presentations are designed for large, general audiences, such as workers at a corporation's various offices across the country learning about a new insurance benefits package. These employees can view the presentation on their company's **intranet**, which is an internal network that uses Internet technologies. On a grand scale, you can inform the entire world about the contents of your presentation by posting your slide show to the World Wide Web. To publish to the World Wide Web, you need an **FTP (File Transfer Protocol)** program to copy your presentation and related files to a Web server.

PowerPoint allows you to create a Web page in two ways. First, you can start a new presentation, as you did in Projects 1 and 2 when you produced the Make Friends and Enjoy Spring Break presentations. PowerPoint provides a Web Presentation template in the **AutoContent Wizard** option when you start PowerPoint. The wizard provides design and content ideas to help you develop an effective slide show for an intranet or for the Internet by opening a sample presentation that you can alter by adding your own text and graphics.

Second, by using the **Save as Web Page command**, you can convert an existing presentation to a format compatible with popular Web browsers such as Microsoft Internet Explorer. This command allows you to create a Web page from a single slide or from a multiple-slide presentation.

This Web Feature illustrates opening the Job Search presentation on the Data Disk (Figure 1a) and then saving the presentation as a Web page using the Save as Web Page command. See the inside back cover of this book for instructions for downloading the Data Disk or see your instructor for information on accessing the files required in this book. Then, you will publish your presentation, and PowerPoint will start your default browser and open your HTML file so you can view the presentation (Figures 1b through 1e). Finally, you will edit the presentation, save it again, and view it again in your default browser.

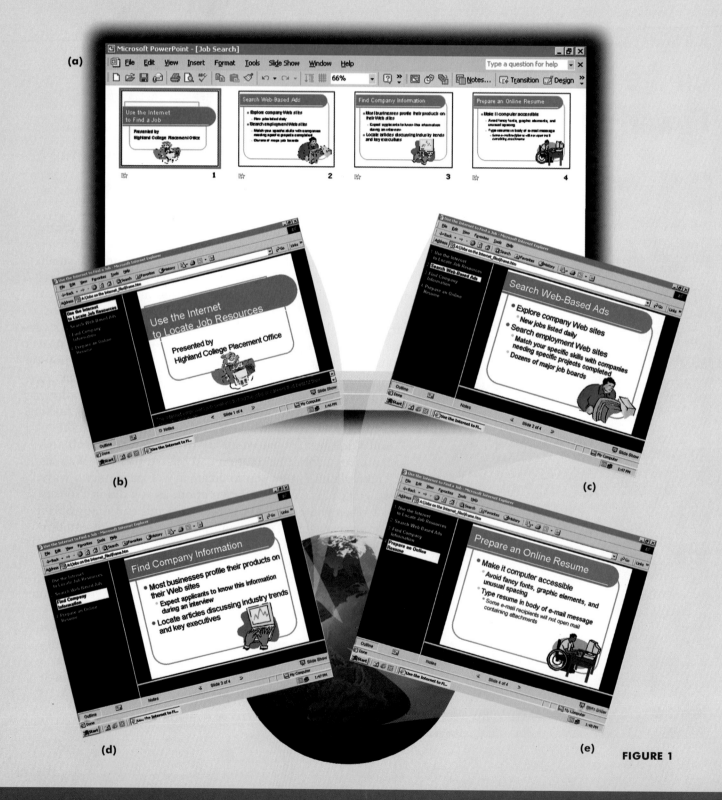

FIGURE 1

You can preview your presentation as a Web page. This action opens the presentation in your default Web browser without saving HTML files. You can use this feature to review and modify your work in progress until you develop a satisfactory presentation.

Because you are converting the Job Search presentation on the Data Disk to a Web page, the first step in this project is to open the Job Search file. Then, you will save the file as a Web page and view the presentation in your default browser. For instructional purposes in this Web Feature, you create and save your Web page on a floppy disk. At times, this saving process may be slow, so you must be patient.

Saving a PowerPoint Presentation as a Web Page

Once a PowerPoint slide show is complete, you want to save it as a Web page so you can publish and then view it in a Web browser. Microsoft Internet Explorer and Netscape Navigator are the two more common browsers installed on computers today. PowerPoint allows you to **publish** the presentation by saving the pages to a Web folder or to an FTP location. When you publish your presentation, it is available for other computer users to view on the Internet or by other means.

You can save and then view the presentation in two ways. First, you can save the entire presentation as a Web page, quit PowerPoint, open your browser, and open the Web page in your browser. Second, you can combine these steps by saving the presentation as a Web page, publishing the presentation, and then viewing the presentation as a Web page. In this case, PowerPoint will start the browser and display your presentation automatically. Perform the following steps to save and publish the Job Search presentation as a Web page.

More *About*

Job Searches on the Internet

Corporations are predicted to spend $4 billion by 2005 on online recruiting and job-placement advertisements, up from $411 million in 1999. Newspaper classified advertising revenues are expected to decrease dramatically. Some human resources personnel claim they can fill vacant positions twice as quickly by posting their ads online rather than placing ads in the newspaper.

Steps **To Save a PowerPoint Presentation as a Web Page**

1 **Start PowerPoint and then open the Job Search file on the Data Disk. Click the notes pane and then type** The Internet empowers job seekers to find the jobs or careers that best fit their interests and goals. **as the note. Click File on the menu bar and then point to Save as Web Page.**

PowerPoint opens and displays the presentation in normal view (Figure 2). The File menu displays. The notes frame contains the speaker notes you typed.

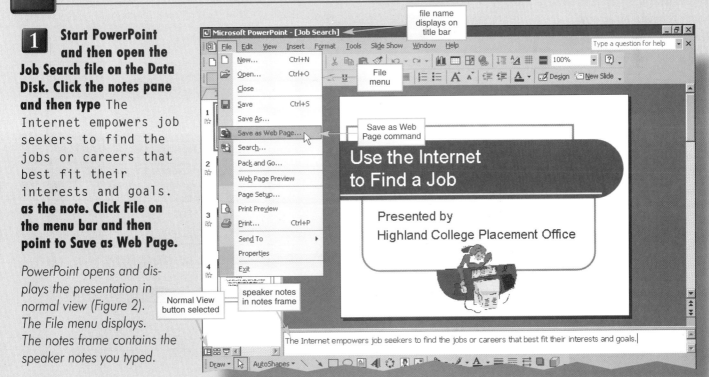

FIGURE 2

2 **Click Save as Web Page. When the Save As dialog box displays, type** Jobs on the Internet **in the File name text box. Point to the Publish button.**

PowerPoint displays the Save As dialog box (Figure 3). Web Page displays in the Save as type box.

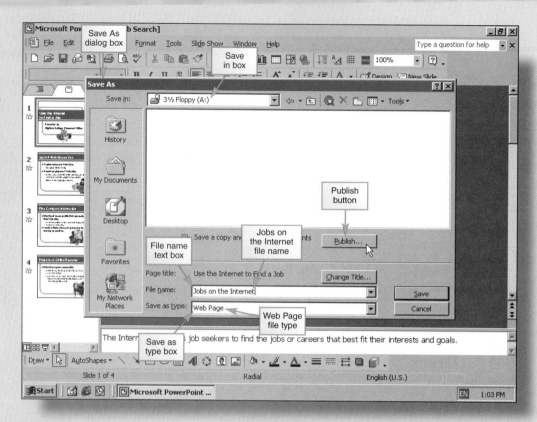

FIGURE 3

3 **Click the Publish button. If the Office Assistant displays, click No, don't provide help now. When the Publish as Web Page dialog box displays, triple-click the File name text box in the Publish a copy as area and then type** A:\Jobs on the Internet **in the text box. If necessary, click Open published Web page in browser to select it. Point to the Publish button.**

*The Publish as Web Page dialog box displays (Figure 4). PowerPoint defaults to publishing the complete presentation, although you can choose to publish one or a range of slides. The **Open published Web page in browser check box** is selected, which means the Jobs on the Internet presentation will open in your default browser when you click the Publish button.*

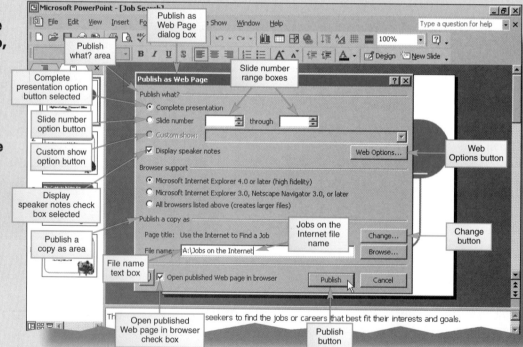

FIGURE 4

4 Click the Publish button.

PowerPoint saves the presentation as Jobs on the Internet.htm on the Data Disk in drive A. After a few seconds, PowerPoint opens your default Web browser in a separate window (Figure 5).

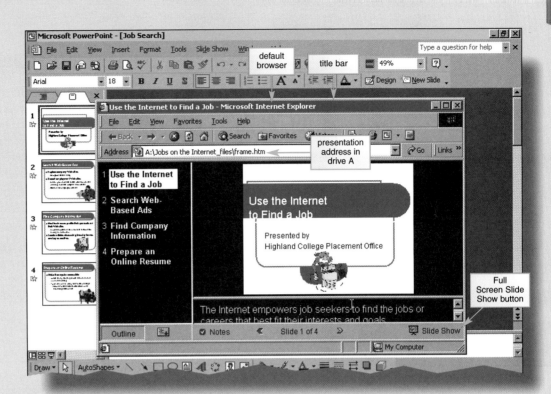

FIGURE 5

Publishing provides customizing options that are not available when you merely save the entire presentation and then start your browser. The **Publish as Web Page dialog box** provides several options to customize your Web page. For example, you can change the page title that displays on the browser's title bar and in the history list. People visiting your Web site can store a link to your Web page, which will display in their favorites list. To change the page title, you click the Change button in the Publish a copy as area (shown in Figure 4) and then type a new title.

The **Publish what? area** of the Publish as Web Page dialog box allows you to publish parts of your presentation. PowerPoint defaults to publishing the complete presentation, but you can select specific slides by clicking the **Slide number option button** and then entering the range of desired slide numbers in the range boxes. In addition, you can publish a custom show you have created previously. A **custom show** is a subset of your presentation that contains slides tailored for a specific audience. For example, you may want to show Slides 1, 2, and 4 to one group and Slides 1, 3, and 4 to another group.

You can choose to publish only the publication slides, and not the accompanying speaker notes. By default, the **Display speaker notes check box** is selected in the Publish what? area. You typed speaker notes for Slide 1 of this presentation, so they will display in the browser window. If you do not want to make your notes available to users, click the Display speaker notes check box to remove the check mark.

The **Web Options button** in the Publish what? area allows you to select options to determine how your presentation will look when viewed in a Web browser. You can choose options such as allowing slide animation to show, selecting the screen size, and having the notes and outline panes display when viewing the presentation in a Web browser.

With the Job Search file opened and the presentation saved as a Web page, the next step is to view the slide show using your default browser.

Other Ways

1. Press ALT+F, press G, type new file name, press SHIFT+TAB two times, press P, change file name in Publish copy as area; press ENTER

2. In Voice Command mode, say "File, Save as Web Page, [type file name], Publish, [type file name], Publish"

More About

Publishing Web Presentations

One advantage of publishing a PowerPoint presentation is the flexibility of using Web discussions to gather comments about the document. Saving the presentation as an .htm or .mht Web-based format provides the most flexibility for reviewers. The .mht format combines multiple pictures and slides into a single file called a Web archive. For more information, visit the PowerPoint 2002 More About Web page (scsite.com/pp2002/more.htm) and then click Publishing.

Viewing a Presentation

Presentations to large groups or distributed over many sites can create problems. Publishing the presentation as a Web page allows individuals to see the slides, but recording a broadcast for later viewing on the Internet is another alternative. For more information, visit the PowerPoint 2002 More About Web page (scsite.com/pp2002/more.htm) and then click Broadcasting.

Viewing a Presentation as a Web Page

PowerPoint makes it easy to create a presentation and then view how it will display on an intranet or the World Wide Web. By viewing your slide show, you can decide which features look good and which need modification. The left side of the window contains the navigation frame, which is the outline of the presentation. The outline displays a table of contents consisting of each slide's title text. You can click the **Expand/Collapse Outline button** below the navigation frame to view the complete slide text. The right side of the window displays the complete slide in the slide frame. The speaker notes display in the notes frame below the slide frame. Perform the following steps to view the Jobs on the Internet presentation as a Web page.

 ## To View a Presentation as a Web Page

1 **Double-click the Microsoft Internet Explorer title bar to maximize the browser window. Point to the Full Screen Slide Show button.**

Slide 1 of the Jobs on the Internet presentation displays in the slide frame in the browser window (Figure 6). The navigation frame contains the table of contents, which consists of the title text of each slide. The notes frame displays the speaker notes.

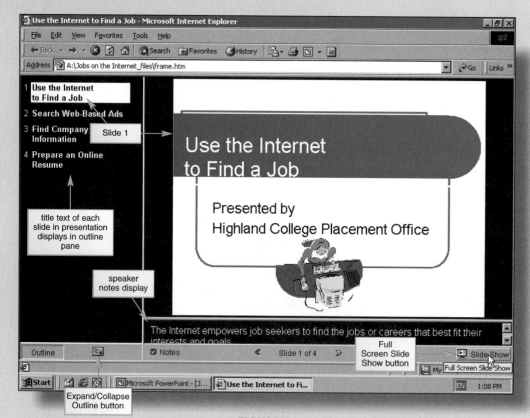

FIGURE 6

2 **Click the Full Screen Slide Show button.**

Slide 1 fills the entire screen (Figure 7). The Slide 1 title text and computer clip art display.

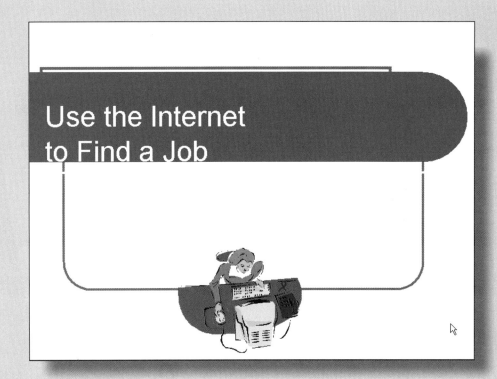

FIGURE 7

3 **Click to display the first line of the subtitle text.**

The first line of the Slide 1 subtitle text displays.

4 **If necessary, continue clicking each slide in the presentation. When the black slide displays, click it. Click the Yes button in the Microsoft PowerPoint dialog box. Point to the Expand/Collapse Outline button below the outline.**

Each of the four slides in the Jobs on the Internet presentation displays. The message on the black slide, End of slide show, click to exit., indicates the conclusion of the slide show.

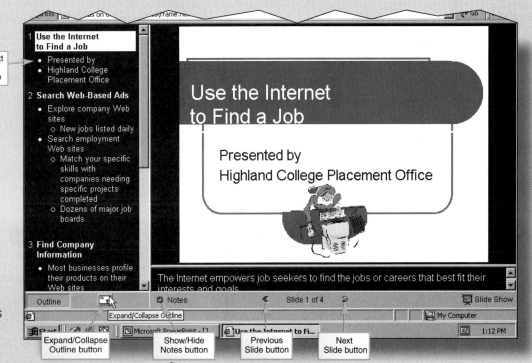

FIGURE 8

5 **Click the Expand/Collapse Outline button.**

The navigation frame displays the text of each slide in an outline (Figure 8). To display only the title of each slide, you would click the Expand/Collapse Outline button again.

More *About*

Connecting to Your Audience

As you choose to show or hide your outline and notes, consider the needs of your audience. Some researchers believe listeners are more attentive on Sundays, Mondays, and Tuesdays because they are more relaxed than at the middle and end of a week. Thus, you may need to provide more information via the outline and notes when your audience is less focused.

You can alter the browser window by choosing to display or hide the navigation and notes frames. To hide the navigation frame, click the **Show/Hide Outline button** below the outline. Later, if you want to redisplay the navigation frame, click the Show/Hide Outline button again. Similarly, the **Show/Hide Notes button** below the slide frame allows you to display or conceal the speaker notes on a particular slide.

To advance through the Web page, click the **Next Slide button** below the slide frame. Likewise, to display a slide appearing earlier in the slide show, click the **Previous Slide button**.

Editing a Web Page through a Browser

You may want to modify your Web page by making small changes to the text or art on some slides. In this presentation, you want to change the title text in Slide 1 to reflect the fact that the presentation covers more than finding a job on the Internet; it describes various resources available for planning a career. The following steps change the second line of the title slide to modify Slide 1.

Steps **To Edit a Web Page through a Browser**

1 Point to the Edit button on the Standard Buttons toolbar.

Slide 1 displays in the browser (Figure 9). The ScreenTip, Edit with Microsoft PowerPoint, indicates you can modify the presentation using PowerPoint directly in the browser window. Your computer may indicate other editing options, such as using Windows Notepad.

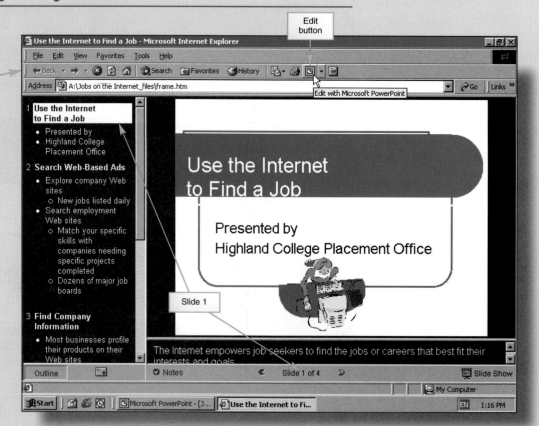

FIGURE 9

2 **Click the Edit button. Select the words, Find a Job, in the second line of the title text placeholder.**

When you click the Edit button, PowerPoint opens a new presentation with the same file name as the Web presentation file name, as indicated by the title bar and the recessed PowerPoint Jobs on the Internet button on the Windows taskbar (Figure 10). A selection rectangle displays around the title text place-holder. The three words are highlighted.

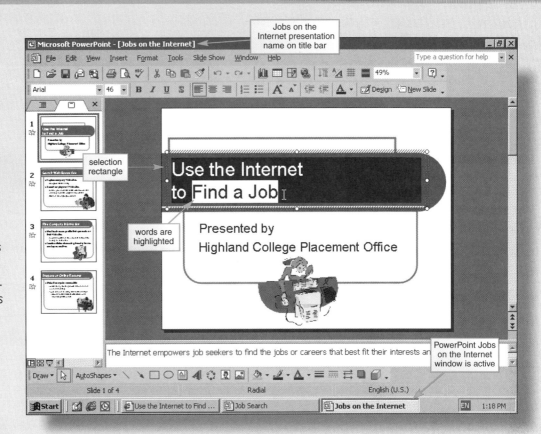

FIGURE 10

3 **Type** Locate Job Resources **and then point to the Save button on the Standard toolbar.**

The second line is modified (Figure 11).

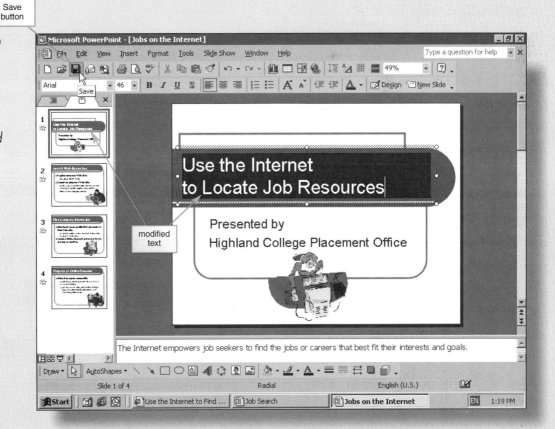

FIGURE 11

4 **Click the Save button. Point to the Use the Internet to Find a Job – Microsoft Internet Explorer button on the taskbar.**

PowerPoint saves the changes to the Jobs on the Internet.htm file on the Data Disk in drive A. The buttons on the taskbar indicate that two PowerPoint presentations and the browser are open (Figure 12).

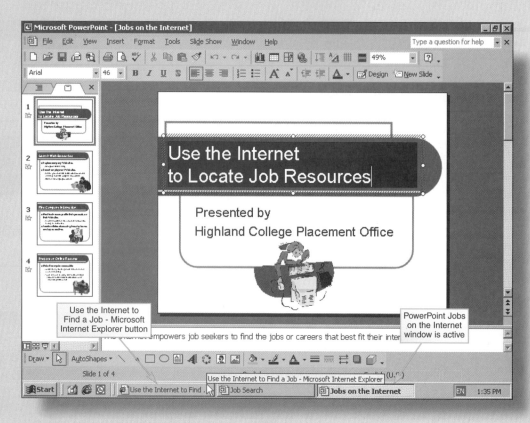

FIGURE 12

5 **Click the Use the Internet to Find a Job – Microsoft Internet Explorer button and then point to the Refresh button on the Standard Buttons toolbar.**

The browser window displays the title text and clip art on Slide 1 (Figure 13). The Refresh button displays the most current version of the Web page.

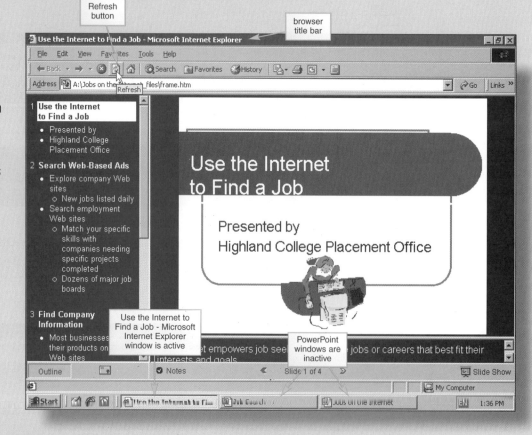

FIGURE 13

6 **Click the Refresh button. Point to the Close button on the browser title bar.**

The complete Slide 1 displays with the editing change (Figure 14).

7 **Click the Close button.**

PowerPoint closes the Jobs on the Internet Web presentation, and the PowerPoint window redisplays in normal view with the Jobs on the Internet presentation active.

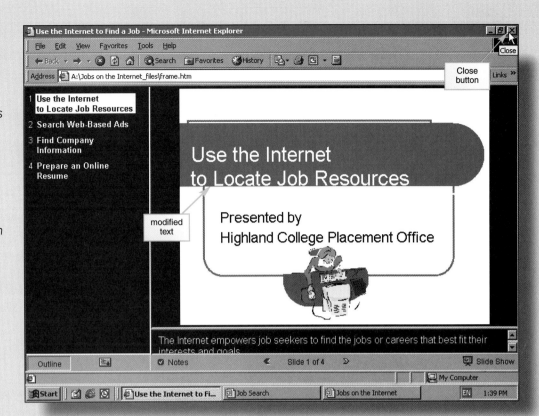

FIGURE 14

The Web page now is complete. The next step is to make your Web presentation available to others on your network, an intranet, or the World Wide Web. Ask your instructor how you can post your presentation.

CASE PERSPECTIVE SUMMARY

Students attending Tina Natella's presentation in the Placement Center should learn information on using the Internet to improve their career searches. The Job Search slide show will help to reinforce the key points presented, including facts about searching Web-based advertisements, finding company information, and preparing an online resume. The students will be able to apply this information when they look for a first job or a new career. Tina can publish your presentation to the World Wide Web so that students who cannot attend the lecture also can gain the useful information presented.

Web Feature Summary

This Web feature introduced you to creating a Web page by saving an existing PowerPoint presentation as an HTML file. You then viewed the presentation as a Web page in your default browser. Next, you modified Slide 1. Finally, you reviewed the Slide 1 change using your default browser. With the Job Search presentation converted to a Web page, you can post the file to an intranet or to the World Wide Web.

What You Should Know

Having completed this Web Feature, you now should be able to perform the following tasks:

▶ Edit a Web Page through a Browser *(PPW 1.08)*
▶ Save a PowerPoint Presentation as a Web Page *(PPW 1.03)*
▶ View a Presentation as a Web Page *(PPW 1.06)*

In the Lab

1 Creating a Web Page from the Make Friends Presentation

Problem: Jennifer Williams, the dean of counseling at Westview College, wants to expand the visibility of the Make Friends presentation you created for the counseling department in Project 1. She believes the World Wide Web would be an excellent vehicle to help students throughout the campus and at other colleges, and she has asked you to help transfer the presentation to the Internet.

Instructions: Start PowerPoint and then perform the following steps with a computer.

1. Open the Make Friends presentation shown in Figures 1-2a through 1-2d on page PP 1.09 that you created in Project 1. (If you did not complete Project 1, see your instructor for a copy of the presentation.)
2. Use the Save as Web Page command on the File menu to convert and publish the presentation. Save the Web page using the file name, Curing Loneliness.
3. View the presentation in a browser.
4. Modify Slide 2 by adding the words, on Campus, to the title.
5. Change the first third-level paragraph to the words, Current events, sports scores, on Slide 4.
6. View the modified Web page in a browser.
7. Ask your instructor for instructions on how to post your Web page so others may have access to it.

2 Creating a Web Page from the Enjoy Spring Break Presentation

Problem: The Enjoy Spring Break presentation you developed in Project 2 for the Office of Student Activities is generating much interest. Students are visiting the office, which has moved to Room 3221, and requesting longer hours for the Caribbean Cruise Reception. Maria Lopez, the student activities director, has asked you to post the presentation to the school's intranet.

Instructions: Start PowerPoint and then perform the following steps with a computer.

1. Open the Enjoy Spring Break presentation shown in Figures 2-1a through 2-1e on page PP 2.05 that you created in Project 2. (If you did not complete Project 2, see your instructor for a copy of the presentation.)
2. Use the Save as Web Page command on the File menu to convert and publish the presentation. Save the Web page using the file name, Caribbean Cruise.
3. View the presentation in a browser.
4. Modify Slide 2 by changing the word, parasailing, to the words, scuba diving, in the third bulleted paragraph.
5. Modify Slide 5 by changing the room number to 3221 and by changing the ending time of the reception to 8:00 p.m.
6. View the modified Web page in a browser.
7. Ask your instructor for instructions on how to post your Web page so others may have access to it.

In the Lab

3 Creating a Personal Presentation

Problem: You have decided to apply for an internship at a not-for-profit organization in Chicago. You are preparing to send your resume and cover letter to the executive director, and you want to develop a unique way to publicize your computer expertise. You decide to create a personalized PowerPoint presentation emphasizing your leadership abilities and scholarly achievements. You refer to this presentation in your cover letter and inform the executive director that she can view this presentation because you have saved the presentation as a Web page and posted the pages on your school's server.

Instructions: Start PowerPoint and then perform the following steps with a computer.

1. Prepare a presentation highlighting your leadership abilities. Create a title slide and at least three additional slides. Use appropriate clip art and an animation scheme.
2. Use the Save as Web Page command to convert and publish the presentation. Save the Web page using the file name, Additional Skills.
3. View the presentation in a browser.
4. Ask your instructor for instructions on how to post your Web page so others may have access to it.

Microsoft PowerPoint 2002

PROJECT

Using Visuals to Enhance a Slide Show

You will have mastered the material in this project when you can:

O B J E C T I V E S

- Create presentations using visuals
- Open a Microsoft Word outline as a presentation
- Modify a clip
- Customize bullets using the slide master
- Insert and format a table
- Create and format an organization chart
- Apply a new design template to a single slide
- Rearrange slides
- Add an animation scheme to selected slides
- Print slides as handouts

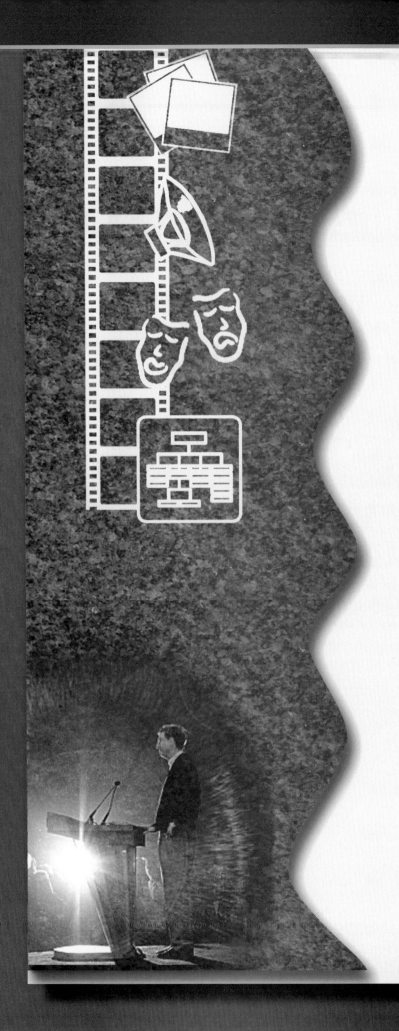

Presenter's Tools

Prepare to Succeed

Audiences remember a personalized, one-of-a-kind, visual presentation. Presenters recall the apprehension of speaking in front of a group. Although speakers sometimes are faced with obstacles of their own making, practicing a few simple strategies can help reduce the stress and anxiety and take the focus away from their nervousness.

Accomplished speakers agree that the key to overcoming nervousness and hesitation and to improve confidence is preparation. To help you prepare, you can create your presentation with PowerPoint as you do in this project for the Wellness Institute at Parkland College. Starting with a template, you will learn the techniques to enhance your slide show by adding visuals that include clip art, a photo, a table, and an organization chart. Appropriate visuals help set the tone, which in turn, helps you create a relaxed atmosphere, putting you at ease with your listeners.

Further prepare by remembering a few indispensable rules. Dress conservatively. Stand tall. Maintain eye contact with your audience. Avoid standing behind a lectern. Use simple language and pause before or after a key point. Conclude your presentation with a challenge, leaving your audience with something to think about. Then, with these rules

LEADERSHIP

SUCCESS

Dress

Stand

Maint

Use Sim

Pause

Chaleng

in mind, spend a few minutes alone before the presentation to collect your thoughts and direct your energy.

Leaders in business, government, science, religion, and virtually all vocations agree that the ability to present one's views clearly, while keeping the audience involved, is fundamental to a successful career. Though you probably spend more time in front of the lectern than behind it, your college years are a good time to get a head start on the competition by learning how to develop power presentations on your personal computer.

Even with this help, however, it is not enough merely to present dry, static details. A presentation needs zest to grab and hold the attention of today's sophisticated audiences.

Among PowerPoint's many features are the capabilities of adding graphical images in a slide show to give the audience a visual association to help assimilate the speaker's words. Going one step further, a variety of pleasing transitions can be achieved to make one image blend into the next, rather than making abrupt frame changes.

Build effects allow a concept to be presented one point at a time, preventing the visual overload that occurs if all the information is presented at once. In psychology, this is called chunking, recognizing that the human brain absorbs information more readily in small bites than in one huge mass.

Finally, be the leader you can be. Step up in front of people confidently and enthusiastically. Focus on your message because you have all the tools you need to make a great presentation.

COURAGE

ENTHUSIASM

Microsoft PowerPoint 2002

Using Visuals to Enhance a Slide Show

CASE PERSPECTIVE

Yesterday's health clubs are today's wellness centers. Designed to help members develop lifelong healthy habits, these former gyms and exercise rooms have been transformed into state-of-the-art facilities tailored to any individual. Programs and services emphasize aerobic conditioning, strength training, proper nutrition, and stress management. Membership rates are designed to fit a variety of budgets.

A new Wellness Institute at Parkland College will open in a few weeks, and the director, Malcolm Perkins, wants to attract potential members. He has asked you to help with the marketing efforts for the upcoming Open House. He knows you have extensive computer experience and wants you to develop a PowerPoint slide show that promotes the Wellness Institute and describes its classes, services, and membership fees. He has asked you to use a variety of visuals, including clip art, a table, and an organization chart. You agree to create the presentation.

Introduction

Bulleted lists and simple graphics are the starting point for most presentations, but they can become boring. Advanced PowerPoint users want exciting presentations — something to impress their audiences. With PowerPoint, it is easy to develop impressive presentations by customizing bullets, embedding organization charts and tables, creating a custom background, and creating new graphics.

One problem you may experience when developing a presentation is finding the proper graphic to convey your message. One way to overcome this obstacle is to modify clip art from the Microsoft Clip Organizer. Another solution is to create a table and an organization chart.

This project introduces several techniques to make your presentations more exciting.

Project Three — Wellness Institute Grand Opening

Project 3 expands on PowerPoint's basic presentation features by importing existing files and embedding objects. This project creates a presentation that is used to promote the new Wellness Institute at Parkland College (Figures 3-1a through 3-1d). The project begins by building the presentation from an outline created in Microsoft Word. Then, several objects are inserted to customize the presentation. These objects include customized bullets, an organization chart, a table, and clip art.

(a) Slide 1

(b) Slide 2

(c) Slide 3

(d) Slide 4

FIGURE 3-1

Starting and Customizing a New Presentation

In Projects 1 and 2, you started a presentation document, chose layouts, applied a design template, and reset your toolbars. You need to repeat the same steps to begin this project. Perform the steps on the next page to start and customize a new presentation and change to the Outline tab. See your instructor if the Competition template is not available on your system.

TO START AND CUSTOMIZE A NEW PRESENTATION AND CHANGE TO THE OUTLINE TAB

1 Click the Start button on the Windows taskbar, point to Programs on the Start menu, and then click Microsoft PowerPoint on the Programs submenu.

2 If the New Presentation task pane displays, click the Show at startup check box to remove the check mark and then click the Close button on the task pane title bar.

3 If the Language bar displays, click its Minimize button.

4 Click the Slide Design button on the Formatting toolbar. When the Slide Design task pane displays, click the down scroll arrow in the Apply a design template list, and then click the Competition template in the Available For Use area.

5 If the Standard and Formatting toolbars display on one row, click the Toolbar Options button on the right side of either toolbar and then click Show Buttons on Two Rows on the Toolbar Options menu.

6 Click the Close button in the Slide Design task pane.

7 Click the Outline tab in the tabs pane.

PowerPoint displays the Title Slide slide layout and the Competition template on Slide 1 in normal view (Figure 3-2).

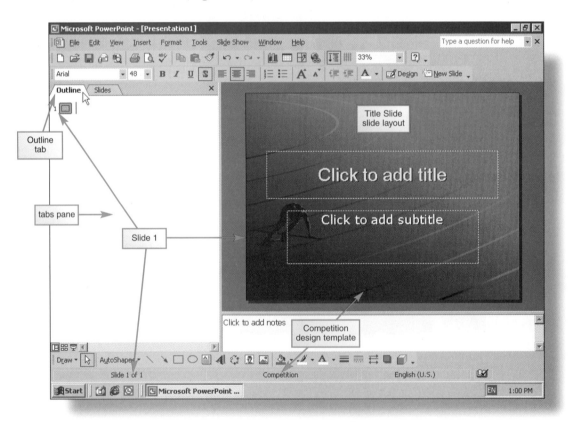

FIGURE 3-2

Importing Text Created in Another Application

In your classes, you may be asked to make an oral presentation. For example, in your English composition class, your instructor may require you to summarize a research paper you wrote. You can use a PowerPoint presentation to help you construct and deliver your presentation.

PowerPoint can use text created in other programs to create a new slide show. This text may have originated in Microsoft Word or another word processing program, or it may have appeared in a Web page. Microsoft Word files use the file extension **.doc** in their file names. Text originating in other word processing programs should be saved in Rich Text Format (.rtf) or plain text format (.txt), and Web page documents should have an HTML extension (.htm).

An outline created in Microsoft Word or another word processing program works well as a shell for a PowerPoint presentation. Instead of typing text in PowerPoint, as you did in Projects 1 and 2, you can import this outline, add visual elements such as clip art, photos, graphical bullets, and animation schemes, and ultimately create an impressive slide show. If you did not create an outline to help you write your word processing document, you can create one by saving your paper with a new file name, removing all text except the topic headings, and then saving the file again.

The advantage of using an outline saved as a Microsoft Word or Rich Text Format document is that PowerPoint uses the heading styles in the document and creates an outline structure. For example, a Heading 1 style becomes a slide title, and a Heading 2 style becomes the first level of body text. If the document does not have any heading styles and has text styled as Normal, PowerPoint creates a slide title from each paragraph.

A file saved as a Text Only file in Microsoft Word is saved without formatting. This **plain text file**, which has the file extension **.txt**, does not contain heading styles, so PowerPoint uses the tabs at the beginning of paragraphs to define the outline structure.

To create a presentation using an existing outline, select **Slides from Outline** on the Insert menu. PowerPoint opens the Insert Outline dialog box, displays All Outlines in the Files of type box, and displays a list of outlines. Next, you select the file that contains the outline. PowerPoint then creates a presentation using your outline. Each major heading in your outline becomes a slide title, and subheadings become a bulleted list.

Opening a Microsoft Word Outline as a Presentation

The next step in this project is to import an outline created in Microsoft Word. PowerPoint can produce slides based on an outline created in Microsoft Word or another word processing program if the outline was saved in a format that PowerPoint can recognize. The outline you import in this project was saved as a file with a .doc extension.

Importing an outline into PowerPoint requires two steps. First, you must tell PowerPoint you are opening an existing document. Then, to open the outline, you need to select the proper file in the Insert Outline dialog box.

The PowerPoint Help System

Need Help? It is no further than the Ask a Question box in the upper-right corner of the window. Click the box that contains the text, Type a question for help (Figure 3-2), type help, and then press the ENTER key. PowerPoint will respond with a list of items you can click to learn about obtaining help on any PowerPoint-related topic. To find out what is new in PowerPoint 2002, type what's new in PowerPoint in the Ask a Question box.

Writing Tools

Use tools such as the thesaurus and readability statistics that are available in word processing programs such as Microsoft Word to help develop effective outlines to import into your slide shows. The goal in constructing powerful PowerPoint presentations is to convey information precisely, and these tools should help you with your organization and creative efforts.

Steps To Open a Microsoft Word Outline as a Presentation

1 Insert your Data Disk into drive A. Click Insert on the menu bar and then point to Slides from Outline.

The Insert menu displays (Figure 3-3). You want to open the outline created in Microsoft Word and saved on your Data Disk.

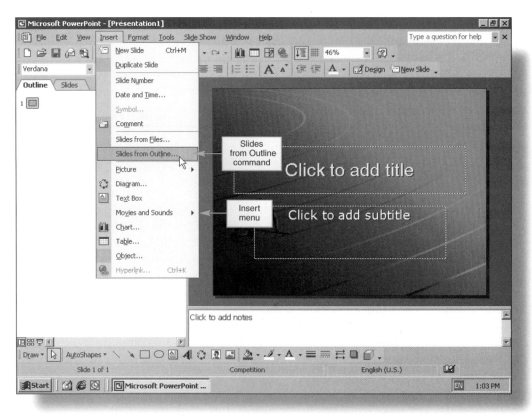

FIGURE 3-3

2 Click Slides from Outline. Click the Look in box arrow and then click 3½ Floppy (A:). Click Wellness Institute Outline in the Look in list. Point to the Insert button.

The Insert Outline dialog box displays (Figure 3-4). A list displays the outline files that PowerPoint can open. Your list may be different depending on the files stored on your floppy disk.

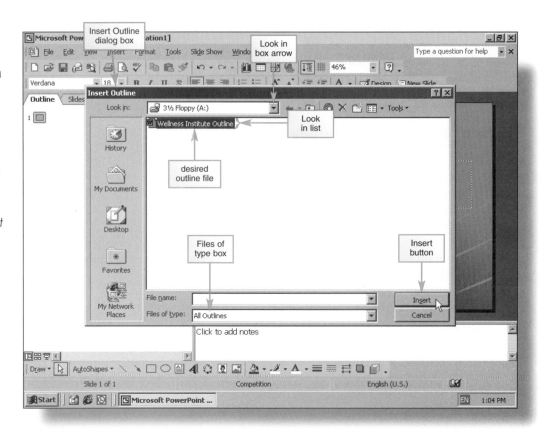

FIGURE 3-4

3 Click the Insert button.

PowerPoint opens the Wellness Institute Outline and creates Slides 2 through 5 (Figure 3-5). See your instructor if you have difficulty displaying the outline. The outline displays in the tabs pane, and Slide 2 displays in the slide pane. The outline text on Slides 2 and 3 displays bulleted, indicating the slide layout is a bulleted list.

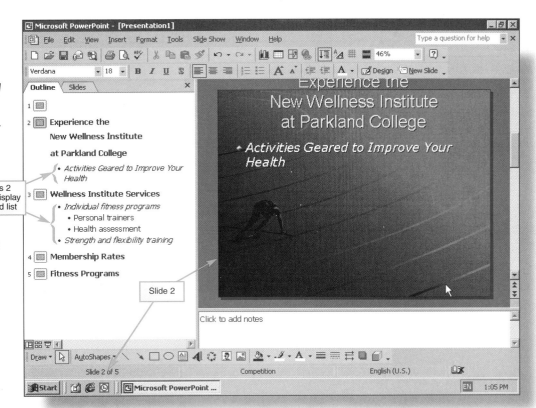

FIGURE 3-5

Imported outlines can contain up to nine outline levels, whereas PowerPoint outlines are limited to six levels (one for the title text and five for body paragraph text). When you import an outline, all text in outline levels six through nine is treated as a fifth-level paragraph.

Deleting a Slide

PowerPoint added Slides 2 through 5 when you imported the Microsoft Word outline. Slide 1 is blank and should be deleted. Perform the the steps on the next page to delete Slide 1.

Other Ways

1. In Microsoft Word, open desired document, on File menu point to Send To, click Microsoft PowerPoint
2. Press ALT+I, press L, press ENTER
3. In Voice Command mode, say "Insert, Slides from Outline, Insert"

Steps **To Delete a Slide**

1 **Click the Slide 1 slide icon on the Outline tab.**

The Slide 1 slide icon is selected, and Slide 1 displays (Figure 3-6).

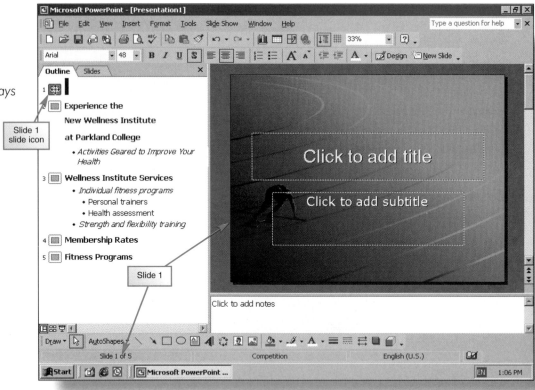

FIGURE 3-6

2 **Click Edit on the menu bar and then point to Delete Slide (Figure 3-7).**

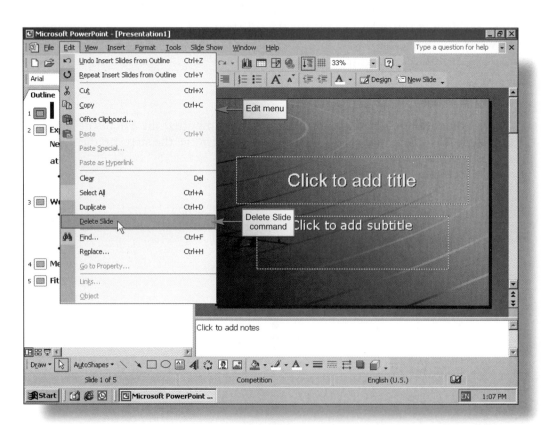

FIGURE 3-7

3 **Click Delete Slide.**

The blank Slide 1 is deleted and is replaced with the original Slide 2 (Figure 3-8).

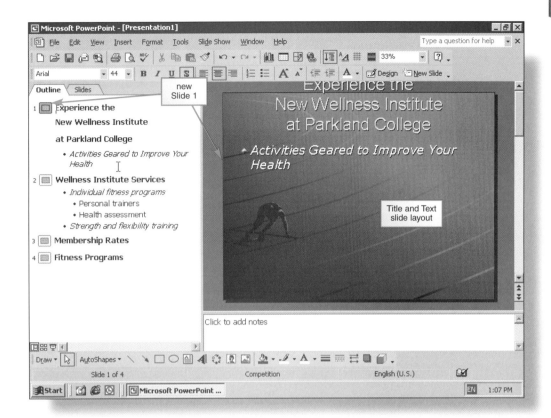

FIGURE 3-8

The current slides in the presentation have the Title and Text slide layout. The next section describes how to apply the Title Slide layout to Slide 1.

Changing the Slide 1 Layout to Title Slide

When you started the new presentation, PowerPoint created Slide 1 and applied the Title Slide slide layout. Now that the original Slide 2 is the new Slide 1, you want to apply the Title Slide slide layout to introduce the presentation. Perform the following steps to change the Slide 1 slide layout.

TO CHANGE THE SLIDE LAYOUT TO TITLE SLIDE

1 Click Format on the menu bar and then click Slide Layout.

2 Click the Title Slide slide layout located in the Text Layouts area of the Slide Layout task pane.

3 Click the Close button in the Slide Layout task pane.

Slide 1 has the desired Title Slide slide layout (Figure 3-9 on the next page).

Other Ways

1. Click Slide 1 slide icon, press DELETE
2. Right-click Slide 1 slide icon, click Delete Slide on shortcut menu
3. Press ALT+E, press D
4. In Voice Command mode, say "Edit, Delete Slide"

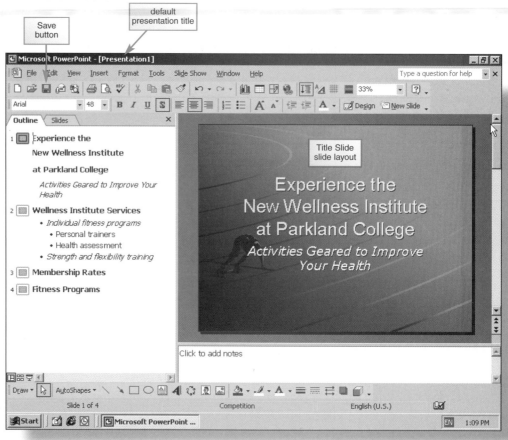

FIGURE 3-9

Saving the Presentation

You now should save the presentation because you applied a design template, created a presentation from an outline file, deleted a slide, and applied a new slide layout. The following steps summarize how to save a presentation.

TO SAVE A PRESENTATION

1 Click the Save button on the Standard toolbar.

2 Type Wellness Institute in the File name text box.

3 Click the Save in box arrow. Click 3½ Floppy (A:) in the Save in list.

4 Click the Save button in the Save As dialog box.

The presentation is saved on the floppy disk in drive A with the file name Wellness Institute. This file name displays on the title bar.

Inserting and Modifying Clips

A **clip art picture** is composed of many objects grouped together to form one object. PowerPoint allows you to modify and enhance the clip by disassembling it into the objects. **Disassembling** a clip art picture, also called **ungrouping**, separates one object into multiple objects. Once ungrouped, you can manipulate the individual objects as needed to form a new object. When you ungroup a clip art picture in PowerPoint, it becomes a **drawing object** and loses its link to the Microsoft Clip Organizer. In addition to clips, other drawing objects are curves, lines, AutoShapes, and WordArt.

Objects usually are saved in one of two **graphic formats**: vector or bitmap. A **vector graphic** is a piece of art that has been created by a drawing program such as CorelDRAW or Adobe Illustrator. The clip art pictures used in this project are vector graphic objects and are created as a collection of lines. Vector graphic files store data either as picture descriptions or as calculations. These files describe a picture mathematically as a set of instructions for creating the objects in the picture. These mathematical descriptions determine the position, length, and direction in which the lines are drawn. These calculations allow the drawing program to re-create the picture on the screen as necessary. Because vector graphic objects are described mathematically, they also can be layered, rotated, and magnified with relative ease. Vector graphics also are known as **object-oriented pictures**. Clip art pictures in the Microsoft Clip Organizer that have the file extension of **.wmf** are examples of vector files. Vector files can be ungrouped and manipulated by their component objects. You will ungroup the workout clips used on Slides 2 and 5 in this project.

PowerPoint allows you to insert vector files because it uses **graphic filters** to convert the various graphic formats into a format PowerPoint can use. These filters are installed with the initial PowerPoint installation or can be added later by running the Setup program.

A **bitmap graphic** is the other major format used to store objects. These art pieces are composed of a series of small dots, called pixels, that form shapes and lines. A **pixel**, short for **picture element**, is one dot in a grid. A picture that is produced on the computer screen or on paper by a printer is composed of thousands of these dots. Just as a bit is the smallest unit of information a computer can process, a pixel is the smallest element that can display or that print hardware and software can manipulate in creating letters, numbers, or graphics.

Bitmap graphics are created by digital cameras or in paint programs such as Microsoft Paint. Bitmap graphics also can be produced from **digitizing** art, pictures, or photographs by passing the artwork through a scanner. A **scanner** is a hardware device that converts lines and shading into combinations of the binary digits 0 and 1 by sensing different intensities of light and dark. The scanner shines a beam of light on the picture being scanned. The beam passes back and forth across the picture, sending a digitized signal to the computer's memory. A **digitized signal** is the conversion of input, such as the lines in a drawing, into a series of discrete units represented by the binary digits 0 and 1. **Scanned pictures** are bitmap pictures and have jagged edges. The jagged edges are caused by the individual pixels that create the picture. Bitmap graphics also are known as **raster images**. Pictures in the Microsoft Clip Organizer that have the file extensions of **.jpg** (Joint Photographic Experts Group), **.bmp** (Windows Bitmap), **.gif** (Graphics Interchange Format), and **.png** (Portable Network Graphics) are examples of bitmap graphic files.

Bitmap files cannot be ungrouped and converted to smaller PowerPoint object groups. They can be manipulated, however, in an imaging program such as Microsoft Photo Editor. This program allows you to rotate or flip the pictures and then insert them in your slides.

Slide 2 contains a modified version of a three people exercising. This clip is from the Microsoft Clip Organizer. You may want to modify a clip art picture for various reasons. Many times you cannot find a clip art picture that precisely illustrates your topic. For example, you want a picture of a man and woman shaking hands, but the only available clip art picture has two men and a woman shaking hands.

More About

Copyrights

Copyright laws protect many pictures and graphics, so you must selectively choose objects to scan, digitize, and import into your presentations. If you scan designs covered under the pictorial and graphic category of these laws, you are violating the owners' intellectual property rights. Choose pictures of landscapes and objects commonly found in nature to avoid copyright violations.

More About

File Size

PowerPoint file sizes are large, and they increase greatly when you add pictures and clips to the slides. When scanning an image, try to make the file size as small as possible. To compress the files, use the .png, .wmf, or .jpeg image file format. Crop unnecessary parts of the image and use a low scanning resolution. For more information on scanning, visit the PowerPoint 2002 More About Web page (scsite.com/pp2002/more.htm) and then click Scanning.

Modifying Pictures

If you plan to save your PowerPoint slide show as a Web page, size imported pictures to a specific dimension less than 50 percent. To crop a picture, first select the picture and then click the Crop button on the Picture toolbar. Place the cropping tool over a sizing handle and drag to frame the portion of the picture you want to include on your slide. You also can specify an exact percentage for the object's height and width. Cropped pictures eliminate the extraneous details and help your viewers focus on the essential elements of the image.

Occasionally you may want to remove or change a portion of a clip art picture or you might want to combine two or more clip art pictures. For example, you can use one clip art picture for the background and another picture as the foreground. Still other times, you may want to combine a clip art picture with another type of object. The types of objects you can combine with a clip art picture depend on the software installed on your computer. The **Object type list** in the Insert Object dialog box identifies the types of objects you can combine with a clip art picture. In this presentation, the picture with three people exercising contains a background that is not required to display on the slide, so you will ungroup the clip art picture and remove the background.

Modifying the clip on Slide 2 requires several steps. First, you display Slide 2 and change the slide layout. Then, you insert the exercising picture into the slide. In the next step, you scale the picture to increase its size. Finally, you ungroup the clip, delete unwanted pieces, and then regroup the component objects. The steps on the following pages explain in detail how to insert, scale, ungroup, modify, and regroup a clip art image.

Changing the Slide 2 Layout to Title, Content and Text

For aesthetic reasons, you want the bulleted list to display on the right side of the slide. To change the slide layout, perform the following steps.

TO CHANGE THE SLIDE LAYOUT TO TITLE, CONTENT AND TEXT

1 Click the Next Slide button to display Slide 2.

2 Click Format on the menu bar and then click Slide Layout.

3 Scroll down and then click the Title, Content and Text slide layout in the Text and Content Layouts area of the Slide Layout task pane.

4 Click the Close button in the Slide Layout task pane.

Slide 2 has the desired Title, Content and Text slide layout (Figure 3-10).

Inserting a Clip into a Content Placeholder

The first step in modifying a clip is to insert the picture on a slide. You insert the exercising clip from the Microsoft Clip Organizer. In later steps, you modify the clip.

The following steps explain how to insert the clip of the three people exercising. See your instructor if this clip is not available on your system.

TO INSERT A CLIP INTO A CONTENT PLACEHOLDER

1 Click the Insert Clip Art button in the content placeholder.

2 Type exercise in the Search text text box and then click the Search button.

3 If necessary, scroll down the list to display the desired clip shown in Figure 3-11, click the clip to select it, and then click the OK button.

The selected clip is inserted into the content placeholder on Slide 2 (Figure 3-11). If the desired clip does not display on your system, see your instructor.

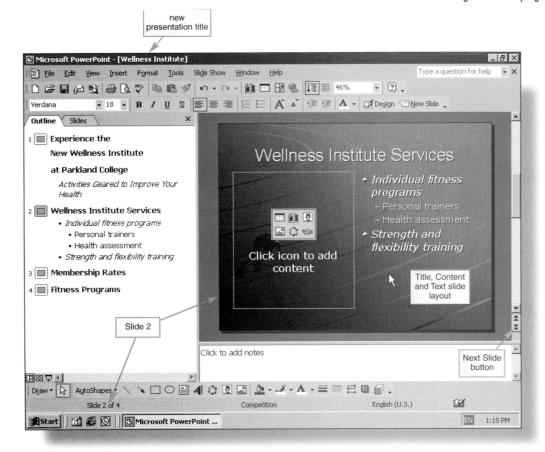

FIGURE 3-10

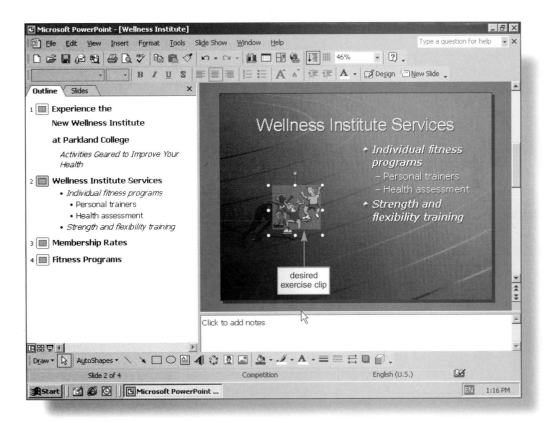

FIGURE 3-11

Sizing and Moving Clips

With the exercising clip inserted on Slide 2, the next step is to increase its size. Perform the following steps to size and move the clip.

TO SIZE AND MOVE A CLIP

1 Right-click the clip and then click Format Picture on the shortcut menu.

2 Click the Size tab in the Format Picture dialog box.

3 Click and hold down the mouse button on the Height box up arrow in the Scale area until 200 % displays and then release the mouse button.

4 Click the OK button.

5 Drag the exercising clip up and to the left so the man's waist is beside the bullet preceding the word, Strength.

The exercising clip art picture doubles in size and displays in the desired location (Figure 3-12).

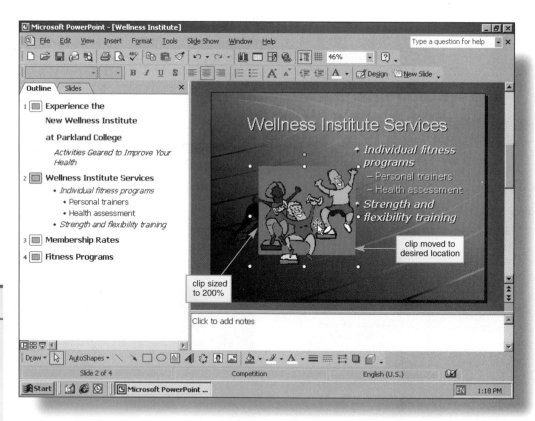

FIGURE 3-12

Saving Images

Be sure to save a backup copy of clip art or other images before you start to ungroup or alter them. If you are dissatisfied with the results of your changes, you then can delete your modifications and begin again with the original image. After making several changes with which you are satisfied, it is a good idea to save the file so you do not have to start from the beginning if you dislike the end product.

Ungrouping a Clip

The next step is to ungroup the exercising clip on Slide 2. When you **ungroup** a clip art picture, PowerPoint breaks it into its component objects. A clip may be composed of a few individual objects or several complex groups of objects. These groups can be ungrouped repeatedly until they decompose into individual objects.

Perform the following steps to ungroup a clip.

1 With the exercising clip selected, right-click the clip. Point to Grouping on the shortcut menu, and then point to Ungroup on the Grouping submenu.

Sizing handles indicate the clip is selected (Figure 3-13).

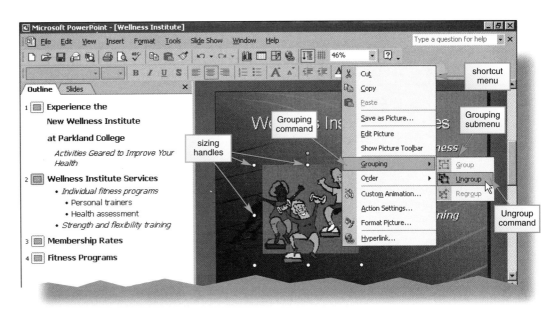

FIGURE 3-13

2 Click Ungroup. Click the Yes button in the Microsoft PowerPoint dialog box.

3 Right-click the clip, point to Grouping on the shortcut menu, and then click Ungroup.

The clip now displays as many objects, and sizing handles display around the ungrouped objects (Figure 3-14). The message in the PowerPoint dialog box explains that this clip is an imported picture. Converting it to a Microsoft Office drawing permanently discards any embedded data or linking information it contains.

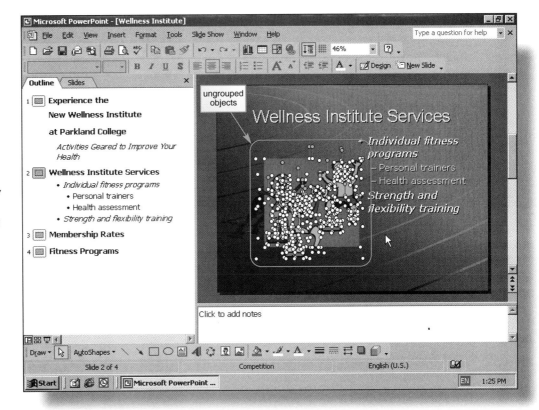

FIGURE 3-14

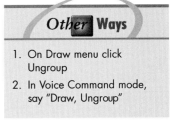

Other Ways

1. On Draw menu click Ungroup
2. In Voice Command mode, say "Draw, Ungroup"

Zooming

Zooming in on the clip art may help you select and deselect objects. To zoom in, click the Zoom box arrow on the Standard toolbar and then click the magnification you desire. When you are finished working with the clip, click the Zoom box arrow and then click Fit to display the entire slide.

Because a clip art picture is a collection of complex groups of objects, you may need to ungroup a complex object into less complex objects before being able to modify a specific object. When you ungroup a clip and click the Yes button in the Microsoft PowerPoint dialog box (Step 2 on the previous page), PowerPoint converts the clip to a PowerPoint object. Recall that a PowerPoint object is an object not associated with a supplementary application.

To replace a PowerPoint object with a clip art picture, click the Insert Clip Art button on the Drawing toolbar or click Insert on the menu bar. Click Object and then click Media Clip. If for some reason you decide not to ungroup the clip art picture, click the No button in the PowerPoint dialog box. Clicking the No button terminates the Ungroup command, and the clip art picture displays on the slide as a clip art picture.

Recall that a clip art picture is an object imported from the Microsoft Clip Organizer. Disassembling imported, embedded, or linked objects eliminates the embedding data or linking information the object contains that ties it back to its original source. Use caution when objects are not completely regrouped. Dragging or scaling affects only the selected object, not the entire collection of objects. To **regroup** the individual objects, select all the objects, click the Draw button on the Drawing toolbar, and then click Group.

Deselecting Clip Art Objects

All of the ungrouped objects in Figure 3-14 on the previous page are selected. Before you can manipulate an individual object, you must **deselect** all selected objects to remove the selection rectangles, and then you must select the object you want to manipulate. For example, on this slide, you will remove the orange background behind the three people. The following step explains how to deselect objects.

TO DESELECT CLIP ART OBJECTS

1 Click outside the clip area.

Slide 2 displays without sizing handles around the objects (Figure 3-15).

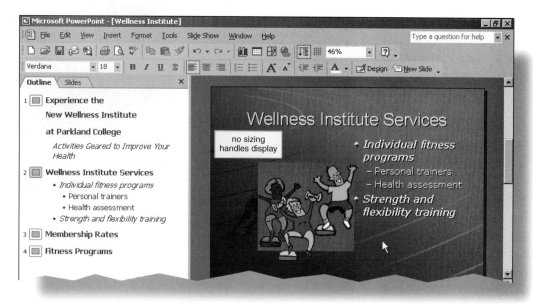

FIGURE 3-15

The exercising clip now is ungrouped into many objects. The next section explains how to delete the unwanted background.

Deleting a PowerPoint Object

Now that the exercising picture is ungrouped, you can delete the background object. Perform the following steps to delete the background.

 To Delete a PowerPoint Object

1 **Click the lower-right corner of the exercising background.**

Sizing handles display around the clip background (Figure 3-16). If you inadvertently select a different area, click below the clip and retry.

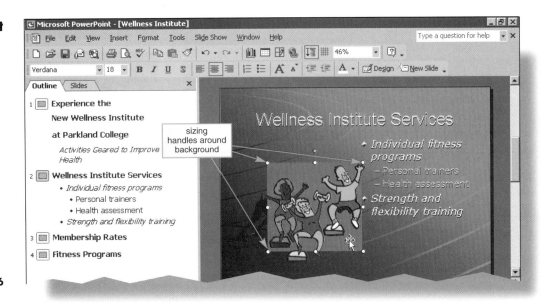

FIGURE 3-16

2 **Press the DELETE key.**

The background object is deleted (Figure 3-17).

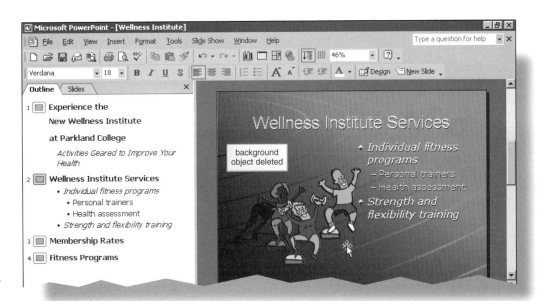

FIGURE 3-17

1. On Edit menu click Clear
2. In Voice Command mode, say "Edit, Clear"

Regrouping Objects

All of the ungrouped objects in the exercise picture must be regrouped so they are not accidentally moved or manipulated. Perform the following steps to regroup these objects.

Steps **To Regroup Objects**

1 **Click the lower-left corner of the slide and then drag diagonally to the upper-right corner of the clip above the man's left hand.**

A dotted-line rectangle displays around the exercising clip as you drag (Figure 3-18). You want to group the objects within this area.

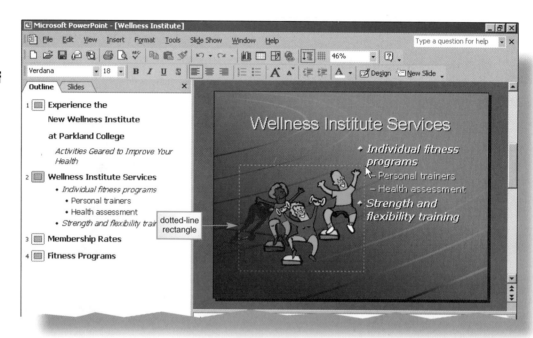

FIGURE 3-18

2 **Release the mouse button. Click the Draw button on the Drawing toolbar and then point to Regroup on the Draw menu.**

Sizing handles display on all the selected components of the exercising clip (Figure 3-19).

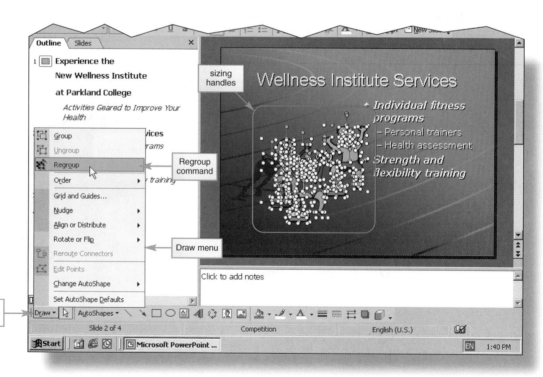

FIGURE 3-19

3 **Click Regroup.**

The eight sizing handles displaying around the entire clip indicate the object is regrouped (Figure 3-20).

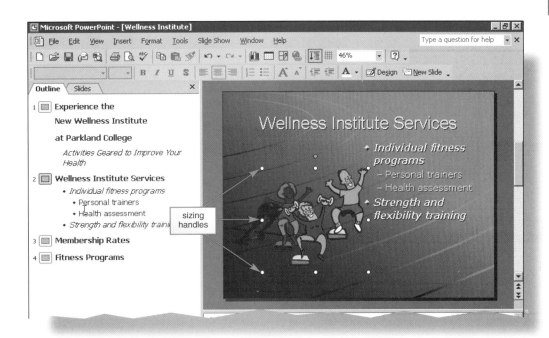

FIGURE 3-20

Other Ways

1. On Draw menu click Regroup
2. In Voice Command mode, say "Draw, Regroup"

All the components of the exercising picture now are grouped into one object. The next change you want to make to Slide 2 is to modify bullets in the list.

Customizing Graphical Bullets Using the Slide Master

PowerPoint allows you to change the appearance of bullets in a slide show. The Slide 2 Title, Content and Text slide layout uses the default bullet styles determined by the Competition design template. You may want to change these characters, however, to add visual interest and variety to your slide show.

The Competition design template uses gold shaded dots for the first-level paragraphs and white en dashes for the second-level paragraphs. An **en dash** is the approximate width of the letter n. Changing the white en dashes to the yin and yang graphical character (☯) would enhance the visual nature of your presentation and emphasize the interplay between aspects of the environment to maintain optimal health. The **yin and yang concepts** originated in China in the seventeenth century and underlie fundamental principles of Chinese medicine and philosophy. Yin represents receptivity and grounding, while yang emphasizes assertion and achievement. Both are equal and necessary for good health and a fulfilling life.

Customizing the graphical bullets requires you to change the default white en dashes to the yin and yang symbol. PowerPoint allows you to change the bullet style for a single list or throughout a presentation. When several slides need to be changed, you should change the slide master. Each **master** stores information about the design template's appearance. Slides have two masters: title master and slide master. The **title master** controls the appearance of the title slide. The **slide master** controls the appearance of the other slides in a presentation.

If you select a design template but want to change one of its components, you can override that component by changing the slide master. The slide master components frequently changed are listed in Table 3-1 on the next page. Any change to the slide master results in changing every slide in the presentation, except the title slide.

More About

Adding Bullets

Bullets are added automatically in the text placeholders, but you also can add them in front of any paragraph you type. Just click the Bullets button on the Formatting toolbar. To remove a bullet, click anywhere in the paragraph and then click the Bullets button.

Table 3-1 Summary of Slide Master Components	
COMPONENT	**DESCRIPTION**
Background items	Any object other than the title object or text object. Typical items include borders and graphics such as a company logo, page number, date, and time.
Color scheme	A coordinated set of eight colors designed to complement each other. Color schemes consist of background color, line and text color, shadow color, title text color, object fill color, and three different accent colors.
Date	Inserts the special symbol used to print the date the presentation was printed.
Font	Defines the appearance and shape of letters, numbers, and special characters.
Size	Specifies the size of the characters on the screen in a measurement system called points.
Slide number	Inserts the special symbol used to print the slide number.
Style	Font styles include regular, bold, italic, and bold italic. Effects include underline, shadow, emboss, superscript, and subscript. Effects can be applied to most fonts.
Text alignment	Position of text in a paragraph is left-aligned, right-aligned, centered, or justified. Justified text is spaced proportionally across the object.
Time	Inserts the special symbol used to print the time the presentation was printed.

For example, if you change the level-2 bullet on the slide master, each slide (except the title slide) changes that bullet. In this project, you will change the bullet style on the slide master to reflect the change throughout the presentation, so the new symbol will display in the bulleted list on Slide 2.

Bullet styles have three components: character, size, and color. A **bullet character** can be a predefined style, a variety of fonts and characters displayed in the Symbol dialog box, or a picture from the Clip Organizer. **Bullet size** is measured as a percentage of the text size and can range from 25 to 400 percent. **Bullet color** is based on the eight colors in the design template's color scheme. Additional standard and custom colors also are available.

To emphasize the wellness message in the slide show, you want to change the bullet style in the second-level paragraphs from an en dash to the yin and yang symbol and from white to brown. You will make these changes on the slide master.

Displaying the Slide Master

To change all second-level bullets throughout the presentation, the bullet should be changed on the slide master. Perform the following steps to display the slide master.

Steps **To Display the Slide Master**

1 **Click View on the menu bar, point to Master, and then point to Slide Master on the Master submenu.**

The View menu and Master submenu display (Figure 3-21). Each PowerPoint component — slides (both title and text), audience handouts, and notes pages — has a master that controls its appearance.

FIGURE 3-21

2 Click Slide Master.

The Competition slide master and Slide Master View tool-bar display (Figure 3-22). The Competition Title Master slide thumbnail and Competition Slide Master slide thumbnail display on the left edge of the screen. The Competition Slide Master slide thumbnail is selected.

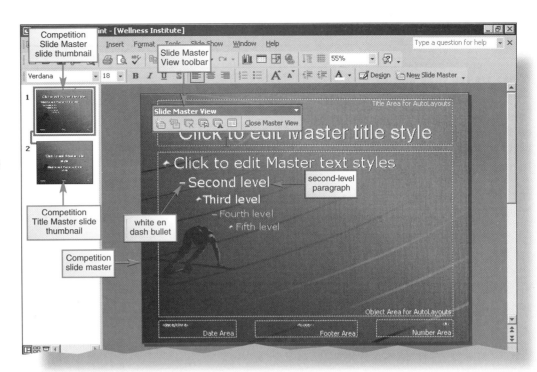

FIGURE 3-22

The **Slide Master View toolbar** contains buttons that are useful when inserting multiple slide masters or title masters in a slide show. Table 3-2 describes the buttons on the Slide Master View toolbar. You will use some of these buttons in Project 4.

Once the slide master is displayed, any changes to the components are reflected throughout the slide show except on the title slide. In Figure 3-22, the text styles and bullets for the five paragraph levels and for the title are shown. The second-level paragraph has an en dash bullet, the Verdana font, a font size of 24, and the shadow effect, and it is left-aligned. These slide master text attributes are modified in a manner similar to changing attributes on an individual slide.

Other Ways

1. Press and hold down SHIFT, click Normal View button
2. In Voice Command mode, say "View, Master, Slide Master"

Changing a Bullet Character on the Slide Master

The first bullet style change replaces the white en dash with the yin and yang symbol. Perform the steps on the next page to change the level-2 bullet character.

Table 3-2	Buttons on the Slide Master View Toolbar	
BUTTON	**BUTTON NAME**	**DESCRIPTION**
	Insert New Slide Master	Adds multiple slide masters to a slide show.
	Insert New Title Master	Adds multiple title masters to a slide show.
	Delete Master	Deletes a slide master from a slide show. When a slide master is deleted, the title master is deleted automatically.
	Preserve Master	Protects a slide master so it is not deleted automatically when all slides following that master are deleted or when another design template is applied to all slides that follow that master.
	Rename Master	Gives slide master a customized name.
	Master Layout	Displays the elements on the master, such as the title and subtitle text, header and footer placeholders, lists, pictures, tables, charts, AutoShapes, and movies.
	Close Master View	Hides the Slide Master View toolbar.

Steps **To Change a Bullet Character on the Slide Master**

1 **On the slide master, click the paragraph, Second level. Click Format on the menu bar and then point to Bullets and Numbering.**

The Format menu displays (Figure 3-23).

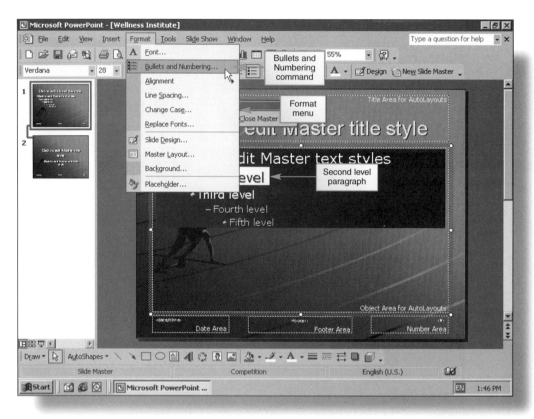

FIGURE 3-23

2 **Click Bullets and Numbering. If necessary, click the Bulleted tab when the Bullets and Numbering dialog box displays. Point to the Customize button.**

The Bullets and Numbering dialog box displays (Figure 3-24). The Bulleted tab displays a variety of bullets and the options of no bullets or custom bullets.

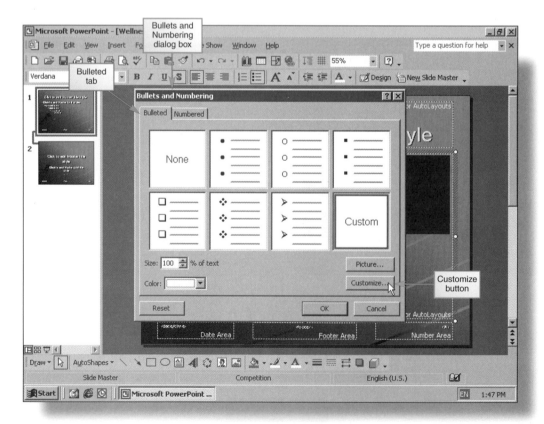

FIGURE 3-24

3 **Click the Customize button. Point to the Font box arrow in the Symbol dialog box.**

The en dash symbol is selected in the Symbol dialog box because it is the default level-2 bullet style for the Competition design template (Figure 3-25). The en dash is part of the General Punctuation subset of symbols for the Times New Roman font.

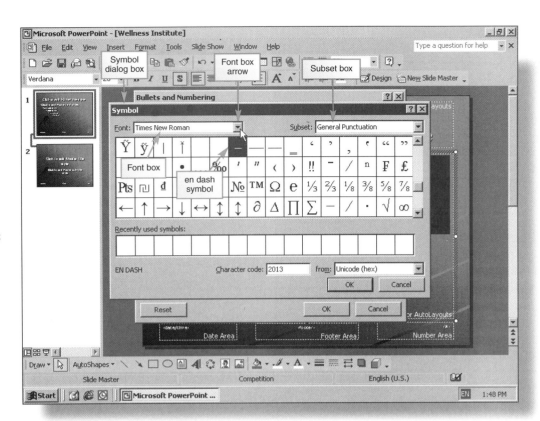

FIGURE 3-25

4 **Click the Font box arrow, scroll through the list until Wingdings displays, and then point to Wingdings.**

PowerPoint displays a list of available fonts (Figure 3-26). Your list of available fonts may differ, depending on the type of printer you are using and the fonts that are installed on your system. The yin and yang symbol is part of the Wingdings font.

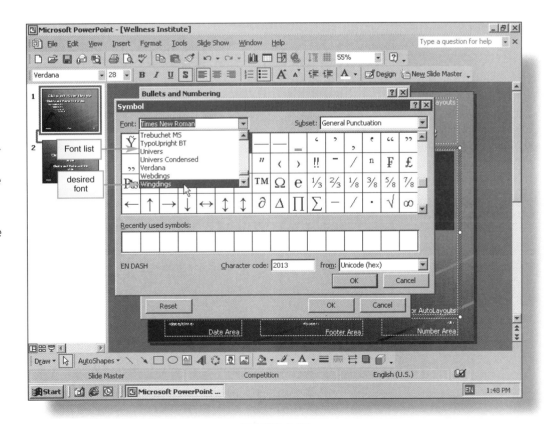

FIGURE 3-26

5 **Click Wingdings and then point to the yin and yang symbol.**

The symbols for the Wingdings font display (Figure 3-27). You may have to scroll through the symbols to locate the yin and yang symbol.

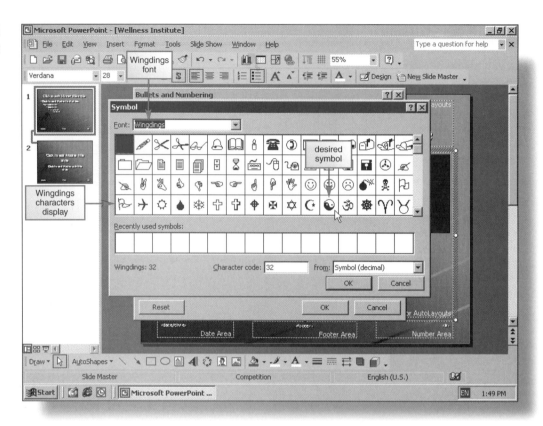

FIGURE 3-27

6 **Click the yin and yang symbol and then point to the OK button in the Symbol dialog box.**

The yin and yang symbol is selected (Figure 3-28). Any Wingdings symbol can be used as a bullet.

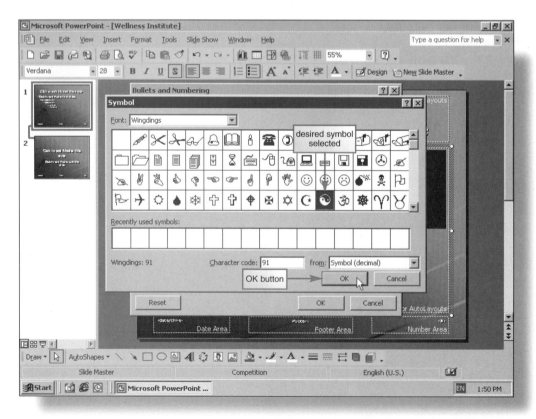

FIGURE 3-28

7 **Click the OK button.**

The Bullets and Numbering dialog box displays (Figure 3-29). PowerPoint applies the yin and yang symbol to the second-level paragraph, which you will see when the dialog box closes.

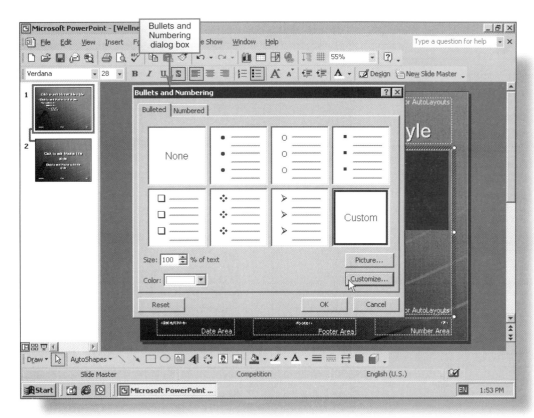

FIGURE 3-29

The yin and yang symbol now will display as the level-2 bullet throughout the slide show. The next step is to change the color of the yin and yang bullet.

Changing a Bullet Color on the Slide Master

The new white bullet blends with the font color. To add contrast to the symbol, a brown bullet works well with the level-1 gold bullet. The color brown is one of the eight default colors of the Competition design template. Perform the steps on the next page to change the level-2 bullet color.

1. Right-click Second level paragraph, click Bullets and Numbering on shortcut menu, click Customize button

2. Press ALT+O, press B, press ALT+U

3. In Voice Command mode, say "Format, Bullets and Numbering, Customize"

More *About*

The Word PowerPoint

The English language is in a constant state of flux. The term, PowerPoint, was used originally as a noun to refer only to the software you are using in these projects. The word now has evolved into a synonym for the word, presentation. As a result, you can tell your friends that you have created a spectacular PowerPoint.

To Change a Bullet Color on the Slide Master

1 **With the Bullets and Numbering dialog box displaying, click the Color box arrow. Point to the color brown in the row of available colors.**

The color white displays in the Color box and is selected in the row of available colors because it is the default bullet color in the Competition design template (Figure 3-30).

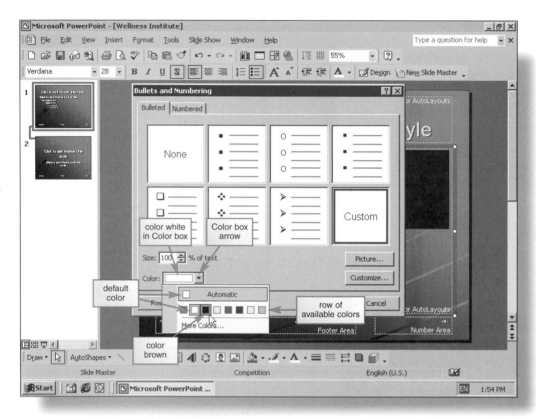

FIGURE 3-30

2 **Click the color brown. Point to the OK button.**

The color brown displays in the Color box (Figure 3-31).

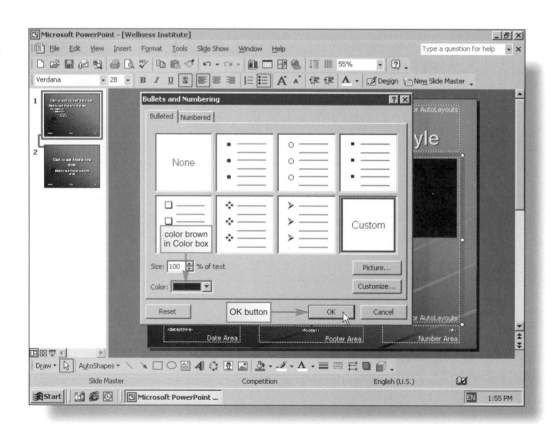

FIGURE 3-31

3 **Click the OK button. Point to the Close Master View button on the Slide Master View toolbar.**

The brown yin and yang custom bullet displays in the level-2 paragraph (Figure 3-32). All changes to the slide master are complete. After closing the slide master view, the presentation returns to normal view.

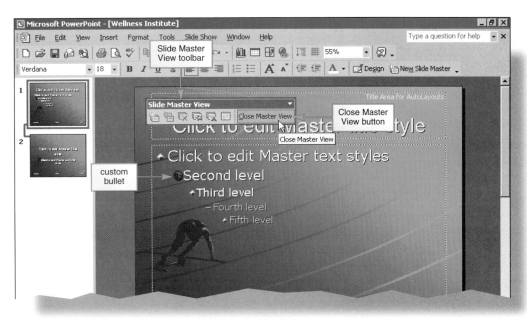

FIGURE 3-32

4 **Click the Close Master View button.**

Slide 2 is complete (Figure 3-33).

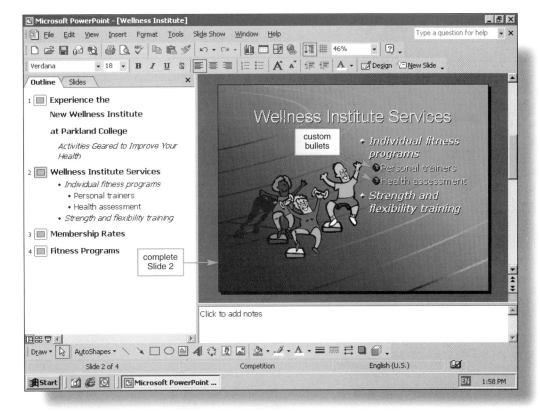

FIGURE 3-33

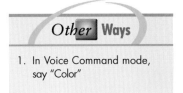

Other Ways

1. In Voice Command mode, say "Color"

PowerPoint displays the new brown bullet symbol in front of each level-2 paragraph on Slide 2. After making this change, save the presentation by clicking the Save button on the Standard toolbar. The next section describes how to add a table to a slide.

More *About*

Plagiarizing Text

Acknowledge the source of information for a table or other content in a presentation. You can type these details on the slide or state them when you give your presentation. The same plagiarism guidelines you use when writing research papers also apply to slide shows. Give credit where credit is due. For more information about acknowledging sources, visit the PowerPoint 2002 More About Web page (scsite.com/pp2002/more.htm) and then click Plagiarism.

Creating a Table on a Slide

Slide 3 is included in this presentation to inform students, employees, and community residents of the costs of joining the Wellness Institute. The enrollment fee and monthly fee for these three groups of potential members are listed. To make this information visually appealing, you can arrange the figures in a table. A **table** is a collection of rows and columns. The intersection of a row and a column is called a **cell**. You fill the cells with data pertaining to the Wellness Institute membership costs. Then you format the table by formatting the column heading font, formatting the border style and color, and making the background dark orange.

Inserting a Basic Table

PowerPoint provides two major methods of creating a table. If the table is basic and has the same number of rows in each column, such as the one for this presentation, use the **Insert Table button** on the Standard toolbar and specify the number of desired rows and columns. If the table is more complex, use the **Tables and Borders toolbar** to draw and format the table.

Steps **To Insert a Basic Table**

1 **Click the Next Slide button to display Slide 3. Point to the Insert Table button on the Standard toolbar.**

Slide 3 displays the slide title and a text placeholder (Figure 3-34).

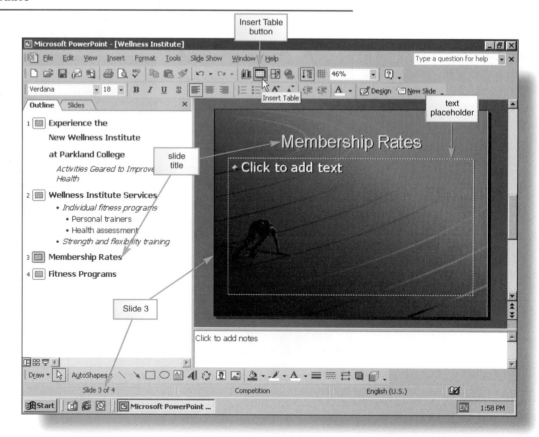

FIGURE 3-34

2 Click the Insert Table button and then point to the upper-left square in the grid.

The first square is dark blue, meaning it is selected. The message at the bottom of the grid states that the table currently has one row and one column (Figure 3-35).

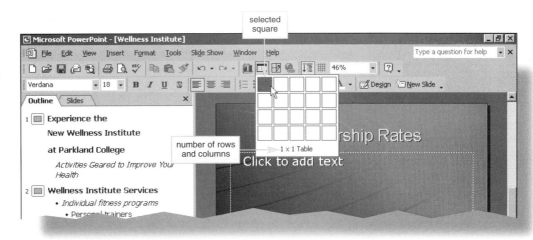

FIGURE 3-35

3 Move the mouse pointer two squares to the right so the first three squares in the grid are selected. Then move the mouse pointer down four squares in the grid.

Four rows and three columns are selected, as indicated by the dark blue squares and the message at the bottom of the grid (Figure 3-36).

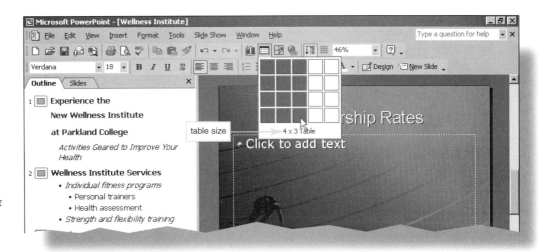

FIGURE 3-36

4 Click the selected square at the bottom-right corner of the grid. If necessary, click the Close button on the Tables and Borders toolbar.

PowerPoint displays a table with four rows and three columns. The insertion point is in the upper-left cell, which is selected (Figure 3-37). Although the Tables and Borders toolbar will be used later in this project, it is not required to display it at this time.

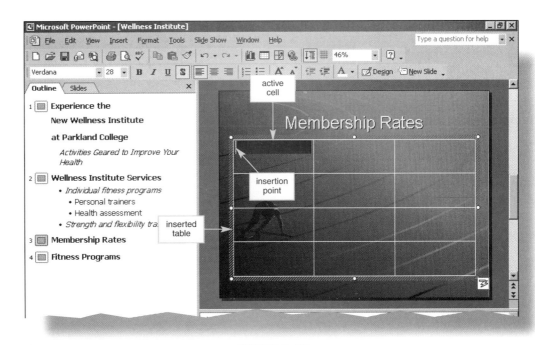

FIGURE 3-37

More*About*

Tables

Tables help show trends and relationships among groups of data. Keep these graphical elements small on slides by using a maximum of four rows and three columns.

Table 3-3	Membership Rates Data	
MEMBERSHIP	**ENROLLMENT FEE**	**MONTHLY FEE**
Student	$70	$5
Employee	$125	$10
Community Resident	$150	$35

Entering Data in a Table

The table on Slide 3 consists of three columns: one for the type of membership, one for enrollment fees, and one for monthly fees. A **heading** identifies each column. The membership types, enrollment fees, and monthly fees are summarized in Table 3-3.

Perform the following steps to enter data in the table.

Steps **To Enter Data in a Table**

1 **Type** Membership **and then press the** RIGHT ARROW **key.**

The first column title, Membership, displays in the top-left cell. The middle cell in the first row is the active cell (Figure 3-38). You also can press the TAB *key to advance to the next cell.*

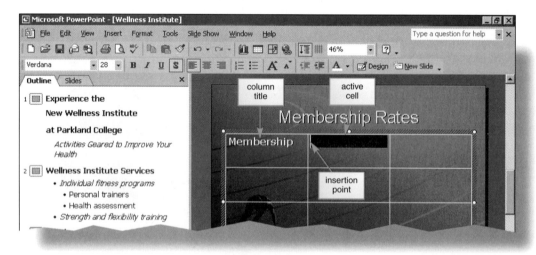

FIGURE 3-38

2 **Repeat Step 1 to enter the remaining column titles and for the other table cells by using Table 3-3 as a guide.**

The three types of memberships and the corresponding enrollment and monthly fees display (Figure 3-39). All entries are left-aligned and display in 28-point Verdana font.

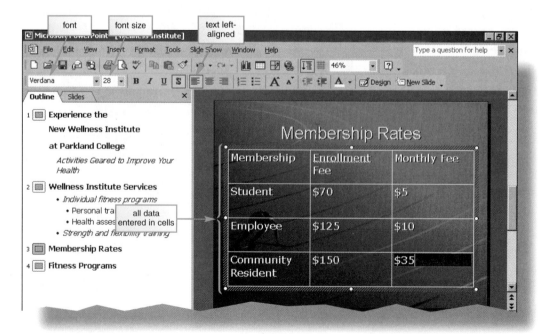

FIGURE 3-39

The next step is to format the table. You **format** the table to emphasize certain entries and to make it easier to read and understand. In this project, you will change the column heading alignment and font style and size, add borders, change the border line color, and make the background dark orange. The process required to format the table is explained in the remainder of this section. Although the format procedures will be carried out in a particular manner, you should be aware that you can make these format changes in any order.

More *About*

Cell Width

If the cells in a table are too narrow or too wide, point to the cell border. When the mouse pointer changes to a double vertical bar, drag the border to the left or right to change the cell width.

Formatting a Table Cell

You format an entry in a cell to emphasize it or to make it stand out from the rest of the table. Perform the following steps to bold and center the column headings and then increase the font size.

Steps ## To Format a Table Cell

1 **Click the top-left cell, Membership. Press and hold the SHIFT key and then click the top-right cell, Monthly Fee. Release the SHIFT key. Click the Font box arrow on the Formatting toolbar. Scroll up and then point to Bookman Old Style.**

The three column headings, Membership, Enrollment Fee, and Monthly Fee, are selected and the Font list displays (Figure 3-40).

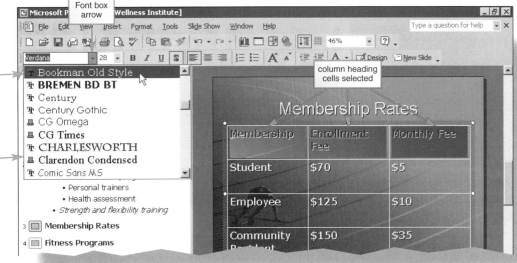

FIGURE 3-40

2 **Click Bookman Old Style. Point to the Bold button on the Formatting toolbar.**

The text in the heading cells displays in 28-point Bookman Old Style font (Figure 3-41).

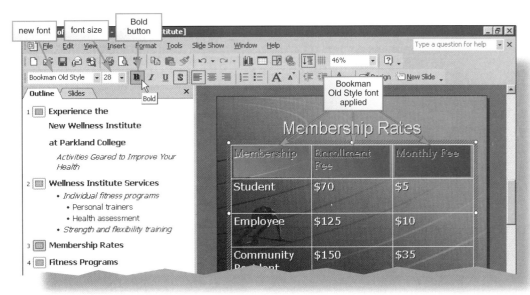

FIGURE 3-41

3 **Click the Bold button and then point to the Center button on the Formatting toolbar.**

The text displays in bold and is left-aligned in the cells (Figure 3-42).

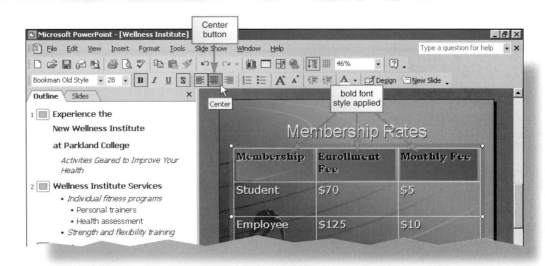

FIGURE 3-42

4 **Click the Center button.**

The text is centered in the cells (Figure 3-43).

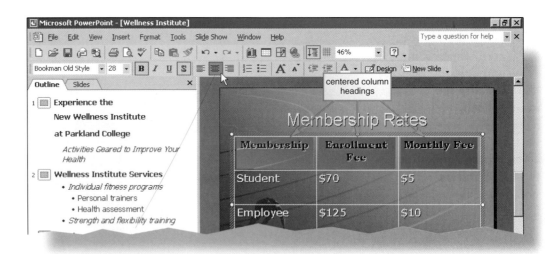

FIGURE 3-43

You can change the font type, size, or style at any time while the table is selected. Some PowerPoint users prefer to change font and cell alignments before they enter any data. Others change the font and alignment while they are building the table or after they have entered all the data.

Displaying the Tables and Borders Toolbar

One method of visually enhancing a table is to use the **Tables and Borders toolbar**. This toolbar contains buttons and menus that allow you to perform frequent table drawing and formatting functions more quickly than when using the menu bar. Figure 3-44 shows the name of each button on the Tables and Borders toolbar.

Perform the following step to display the Tables and Borders toolbar.

TO DISPLAY THE TABLES AND BORDERS TOOLBAR

1 Click View on the menu bar, point to Toolbars, and then click Tables and Borders on the Toolbars submenu.

The Tables and Borders toolbar displays (Figure 3-45).

More *About*

Line Styles

A viewer may pay more attention to a table if it has an attractive border, line style, and color. Thick borders and lines draw more attention than thin borders, and warm colors, such as red and yellow, draw more attention than cool colors, such as green or violet.

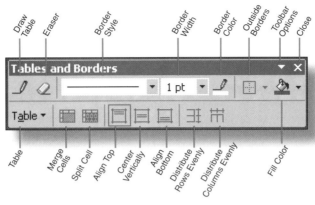

FIGURE 3-44

Formatting a Table

The next step is to format the table by changing the borders and adding a background color. A **border** is the visible line around the edge of an object. The border draws attention to the object by defining its edges. A border has line style and line color attributes. The **line style** determines the line thickness and line appearance of the border. For example, you could choose a thick, solid line for your border. **Line color** determines the color of the line that forms the border. Your table on Slide 3 will have a dashed brown border with a 3-point width.

To draw the attention of the audience to the table, add color to the

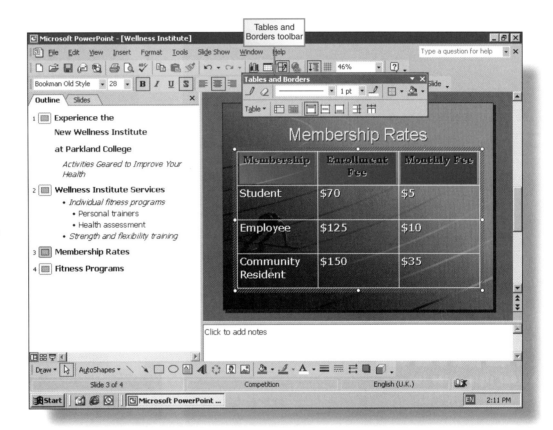

FIGURE 3-45

lines of the border. Recall that the design template establishes the attributes of the title master and the slide master. When you click the Border Color button or the Fill Color button arrow on the Tables and Borders or Drawing toolbar, a list displays line color options. A portion of the list includes the eight colors used to create the design template. One of the colors is identified as the line color, and another is identified as the fill color. Both colors are listed as the **Automatic option** in the color list.

Use the Tables and Borders toolbar to format the table on Slide 3 by adding borders, changing the border style, width, and color, and adding a background color.

Table Colors

Graphic artists know that viewers prefer colorful slides. These colors, however, need to be applied to tables and fonts with care. If you are using more than two colors in a table, put the darkest colors at the bottom. When audience members study slides, they will look at the lighter colors at the top, scan naturally to the bottom, and then return their attention to the speaker.

Steps **To Format a Table**

1 **Click the Table button on the Tables and Borders toolbar and then point to Select Table.**

The formatting changes will be made to the entire table, so you need to select all the cells and borders (Figure 3-46).

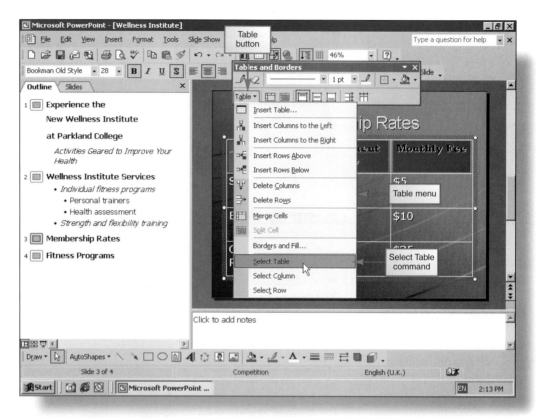

FIGURE 3-46

2 **Click Select Table. Click the Border Style box arrow on the Tables and Borders toolbar and then point to the fourth border style in the list.**

The table is selected and the Border Style list displays (Figure 3-47). PowerPoint provides 10 border styles and a No Border option.

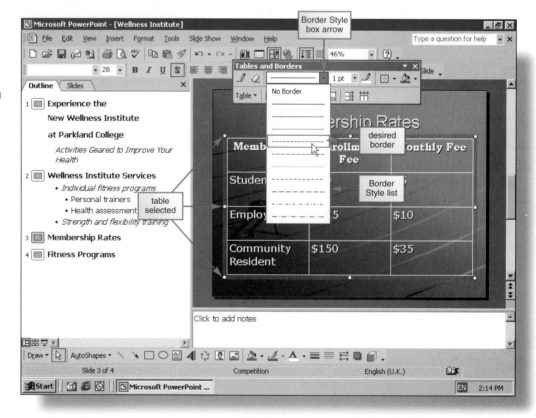

FIGURE 3-47

3 Click the fourth border style. Click the Border Width box arrow on the Tables and Borders toolbar and then point to 3 pt.

The border style is applied (Figure 3-48). The desired border width is 3 pt. PowerPoint provides nine possible widths in the Border Width list.

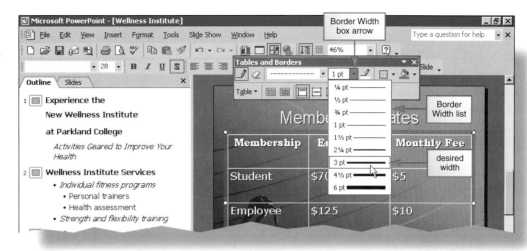

FIGURE 3-48

4 Click 3 pt. Click the Border Color button on the Tables and Borders toolbar and then point to the color brown, the Follow Shadows Scheme Color button (color three in the row), in the list.

The 3 pt. border width is applied (Figure 3-49). The color white is the default border color in the Competition design template color scheme. The default shadows color is brown.

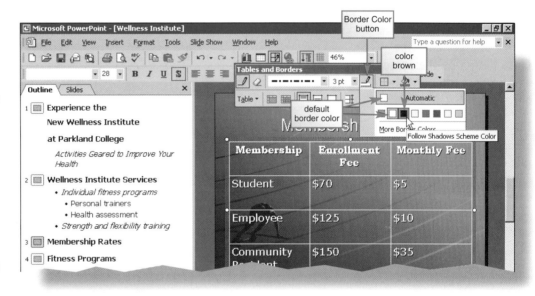

FIGURE 3-49

5 Click the color brown. Click the Outside Borders button arrow on the Tables and Borders toolbar. Point to the All Borders style in row 1, column 2.

The color is applied (Figure 3-50). You can choose 12 possible border styles in the Outside Borders list. The Outside Borders style is the default border style.

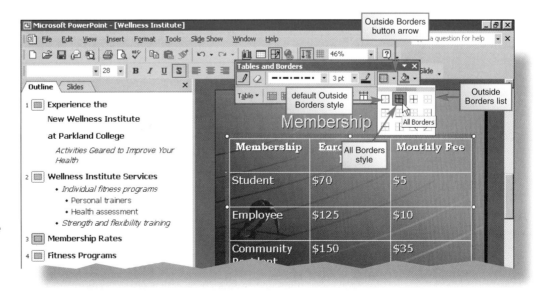

FIGURE 3-50

6 Click the All Borders style. Click the Fill Color button arrow on the Tables and Borders toolbar. Point to the color dark orange, the Follow Accent Scheme Color button (color six in the row), in the list.

The new border style is applied to the table (Figure 3-51). The default fill color is medium orange.

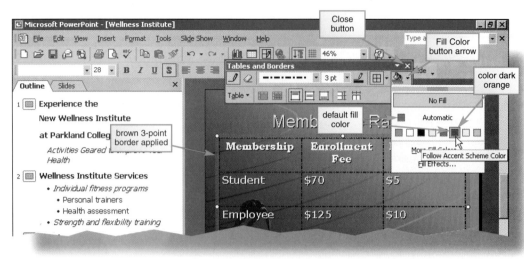

FIGURE 3-51

7 Click the color dark orange. Click the Close button on the Tables and Borders toolbar title bar.

The table background is dark orange (Figure 3-52). The Tables and Borders toolbar is not used in the remainder of this project.

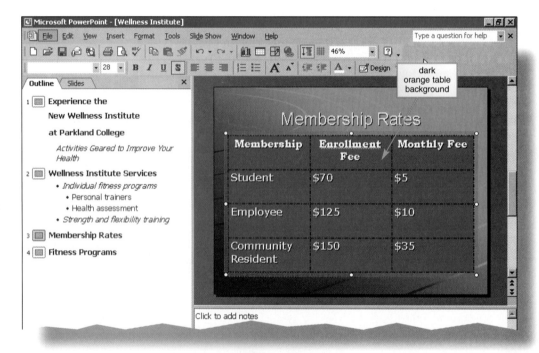

FIGURE 3-52

Other Ways

1. On Format menu click Table, click Borders tab, select style, color, and width preferences, click diagram or use buttons to apply borders, click Fill tab, click Fill color arrow, select background color, click OK button

Slide 3 now is complete. Again, because you have made some significant changes to the presentation, save the slide show by clicking the Save button on the Standard toolbar. The next section describes how to create an organization chart that describes three types of fitness activities available at the Wellness Institute.

Creating an Organization Chart

Slide 4 contains a chart that elaborates on the fitness programs available to Wellness Institute members, as shown in Figure 3-53. This type of chart is called an **organization chart**, which is a hierarchical collection of elements depicting various functions or responsibilities that contribute to an organization or to a collective function.

Typically, you would use an organization chart to show the structure of people or departments within an organization, hence the name, organization chart.

Organization charts are used in a variety of ways to depict relationships. For example, a company uses an organization chart to describe the relationships between the company's departments. In the information sciences, often organization charts show the decomposition of a process or program. When used in this manner, the chart is called a **hierarchy chart**.

Creating an organization chart requires several steps. First, you display the slide that will contain the organization chart and select the Organization Chart diagram from the Diagram Gallery. Then you enter and format the contents of the shapes in the organization chart.

Perform the steps on the following pages to create the organization chart for this project.

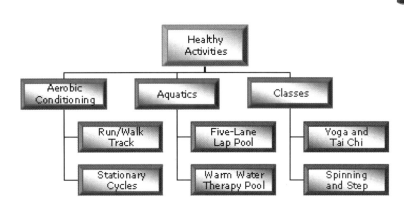

FIGURE 3-53

Displaying the Next Slide and the Organization Chart Diagram

Perform the following steps to display Slide 4 and the Organization Chart Diagram.

Steps **To Display the Next Slide and the Organization Chart Diagram**

1 **Click the Next Slide button to display Slide 4. Point to the Insert Diagram or Organization Chart button on the Drawing toolbar.**

Slide 4 displays the slide title and a text placeholder (Figure 3-54).

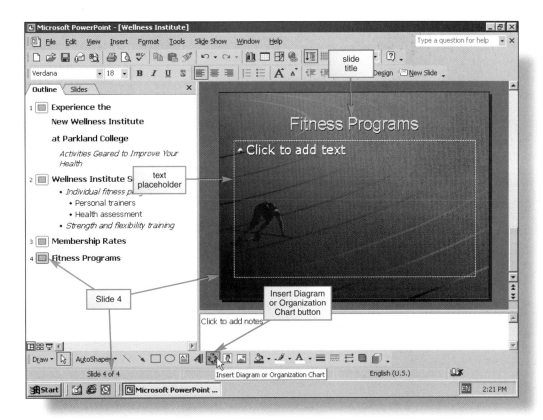

FIGURE 3-54

2 **Click the Insert Diagram or Organization Chart button and then point to the OK button.**

The Diagram Gallery dialog box displays (Figure 3-55). The Organization Chart diagram type is selected. The other diagram types are Cycle Diagram, Radial Diagram, Pyramid Diagram, Venn Diagram, and Target Diagram.

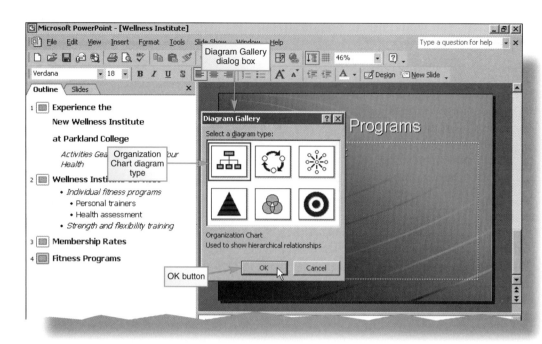

FIGURE 3-55

3 **Click the OK button.**

A sample organization chart and the Organization Chart toolbar display (Figure 3-56). The organization chart is composed of four shapes connected by lines. The top shape, called the superior shape, is selected automatically.

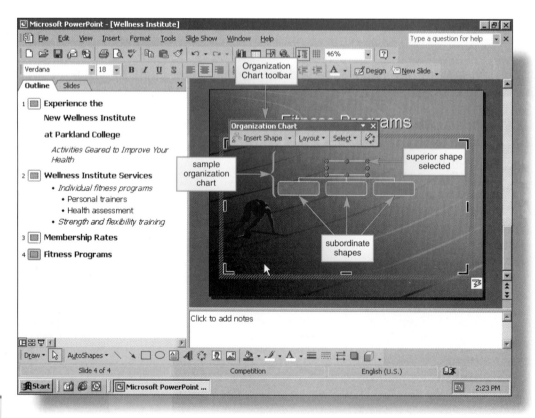

FIGURE 3-56

Other **Ways**

1. On Insert menu point to Picture, click Organization Chart on Picture submenu
2. On Insert menu click Diagram, click OK button
3. In Voice Command mode, say "Insert, Picture, Organization Chart"

PowerPoint displays a sample organization chart to help create the chart. The sample is located in a work area called the **canvas** and is composed of one **superior shape**, located at the top of the chart, and three **subordinate shapes**. Lines to one or more subordinates connect a superior shape, also called a manager. A subordinate shape is located at a lower level than its manager and has only one manager. When a lower-level subordinate shape is added to a higher-level subordinate shape, the higher-level subordinate shape becomes the manager of the lower-level subordinate shape. A whole section of an organization chart is referred to as a **branch**, or an appendage, of the chart.

The Organization Chart toolbar (Figure 3-57) contains buttons to help you create and design your chart. The **Insert Shape button** allows you to add three different shapes to your chart: subordinate, coworker, and assistant. Three subordinate shapes are displayed by default in the sample organization chart. A **coworker shape** is located next to another shape and is connected to the same superior shape. An **assistant shape** is located below another shape and is connected to any other shape with an elbow connector.

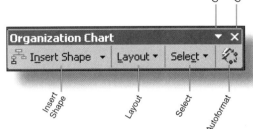

FIGURE 3-57

The **Layout button** changes the location of the lines connecting the subordinate branches. Layout options include Standard, Both Hanging, Left Hanging, and Right Hanging. It also has options to change the size of the entire organization chart by shrinking, expanding, or scaling.

The **Select button** highlights a specific level or branch in the chart. It also allows you to select all assistants or all connecting lines. Once these areas are selected, you easily can change their visual elements, such as text color, fill colors, line style, or line color.

The **Autoformat button** allows you to add a preset design scheme by selecting a style from the Organization Chart Style Gallery. These designs have a variety of colors, background shades, and borders.

The Wellness Institute promotes three types of activities: aerobic conditioning, aquatics, and classes. As a result, your organization chart will consist of three shapes immediately below the manager and two shapes immediately below each subordinate manager. These organization chart layouts for each activity are identical, so you create the structure for the aerobic conditioning and then repeat the steps for the aquatics and classes branches.

Adding Text to the Superior Shape

In this presentation, the organization chart is used to describe the various healthy activities at the Wellness Institute. The topmost shape, called the superior, identifies the purpose of this organization chart: Healthy Activities. Recall that when you inserted the Organization Chart diagram, the superior shape is selected. The step on the next page explains how to create the title for this shape.

More About

The Organization Chart

The organization chart tool in PowerPoint 2002 has greater formatting capability than in earlier versions of PowerPoint. It has been rewritten completely to take advantage of Microsoft Office XP's enhanced drawing capabilities and uses the AutoFormatting feature extensively. Some manual formatting functions no longer exist in the new organization chart tool, so you may have difficulty editing an organization chart that was created in earlier versions of PowerPoint.

Steps **To Add Text to the Superior Shape**

1 **Type** Healthy **in the superior shape and then press the ENTER key. Type** Activities **on the second line.**

Healthy Activities displays in the superior shape (Figure 3-58).

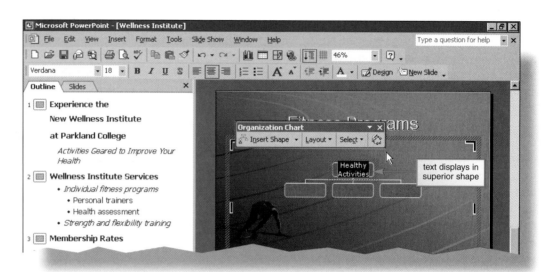

FIGURE 3-58

The text for the superior shape is entered. The next steps are to add text to the three subordinate shapes and then insert and add text to the subordinate and coworker shapes.

Adding Text to the Subordinate Shapes

The process of adding text to a subordinate shape is the same as adding text to the superior shape except that first you must select the subordinate shape. The following steps explain how to add text to subordinate shapes.

Steps **To Add Text to the Subordinate Shapes**

1 **Click the left subordinate shape. Type** Aerobic **and then press the ENTER key. Type** Conditioning **on the second line.**

Aerobic Conditioning displays as the text for the left subordinate shape (Figure 3-59).

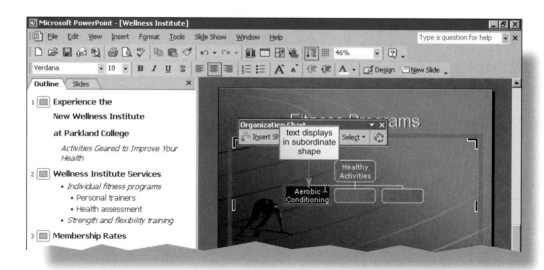

FIGURE 3-59

2 **Click the middle subordinate shape. Type** Aquatics **in the shape.**

Aquatics displays as the text for the middle subordinate shape.

3 **Click the right subordinate shape. Type** Classes **in the shape.**

Classes displays as the text for the right subordinate shape (Figure 3-60).

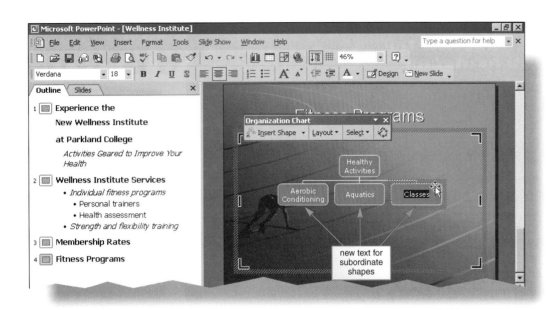

FIGURE 3-60

Inserting Subordinate and Coworker Shapes

You can add three types of shapes to the organization chart: subordinate, coworker, and assistant. Because each of the three Wellness Institute activities has two specific programs, you need to add two subordinate shapes to each of the activities.

To add a single subordinate shape to the chart, click the **Insert Shape button** on the Organization Chart toolbar. The subordinate shape is the default shape. To add a coworker or assistant shape, click the **Insert Shape button arrow** and then click the desired shape.

In this organization chart, the two aerobic conditioning features of the Wellness Institute — Run/Walk Track and Stationary Cycles — are subordinate to the Aerobic Conditioning shape. These two features are coworkers because they both are connected to the same manager. The following steps explain how to use the Insert Shape button to add these two shapes below the Aerobic Conditioning shape.

More About

Typing Text

Avoid using all capital letters as you type text in an organization chart or on slides. Audience members have difficulty reading text typed with all uppercase letters and often have to review the slide a second time to comprehend the message.

Steps **To Insert Subordinate and Coworker Shapes**

1 **Click the Aerobic Conditioning shape. Point to the Insert Shape button on the Organization Chart toolbar.**

The Aerobic Conditioning shape is selected (Figure 3-61).

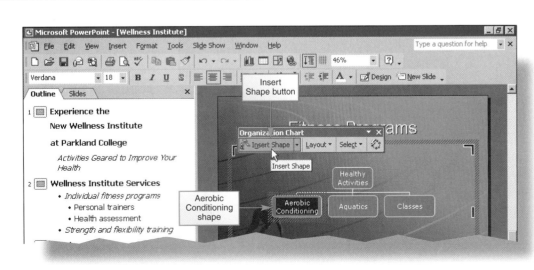

FIGURE 3-61

2 **Click the Insert Shape button. Point to the new subordinate shape.**

A subordinate shape displays below the Aerobic Conditioning shape (Figure 3-62). Aerobic Conditioning now is the manager to the new subordinate shape.

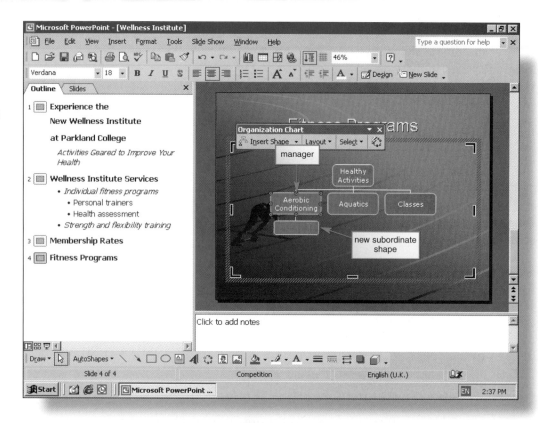

FIGURE 3-62

3 **Click the new subordinate shape. Click the Insert Shape button arrow on the Organization Chart toolbar and then point to Coworker on the Insert Shape menu.**

The new subordinate shape is selected. Three possible shapes display on the Insert Shape menu (Figure 3-63).

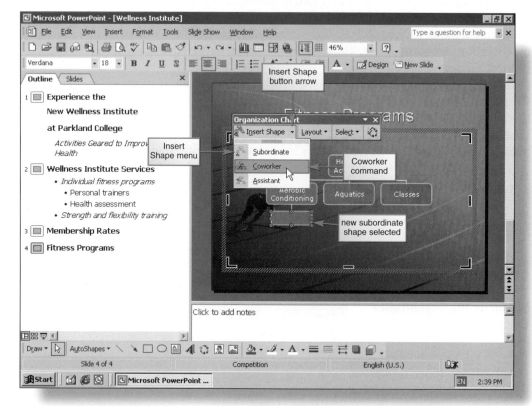

FIGURE 3-63

4 **Click Coworker.**

A new coworker shape is added to the right of the subordinate shape (Figure 3-64).

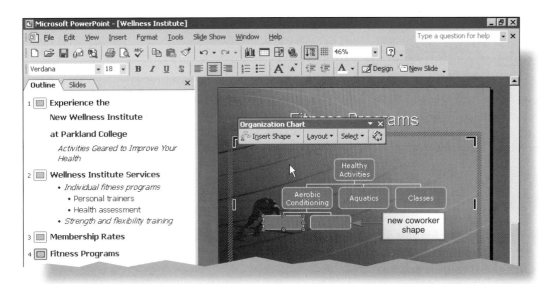

FIGURE 3-64

Other Ways

1. Press ALT+SHIFT+N, press SHIFT+C

2. In Voice Command mode, say "Insert Shape, Coworker"

The basic structure of the left side of the organization chart is complete. You now will add text to the coworker shapes in the chart.

Adding Text to Coworker Shapes

The next step in creating the organization chart is to add text to the two new shapes that are subordinate to the Aerobic Conditioning shape. The following steps summarize adding text to each coworker shape.

TO ADD TEXT TO COWORKER SHAPES

1 If necessary, click the left coworker shape. Type Run/Walk and then press the ENTER key. Type Track in the shape.

2 Click the right coworker shape. Type Stationary and then press the ENTER key. Type Cycles in the shape.

Both coworker shapes contain text related to aerobic conditioning activities (Figure 3-65).

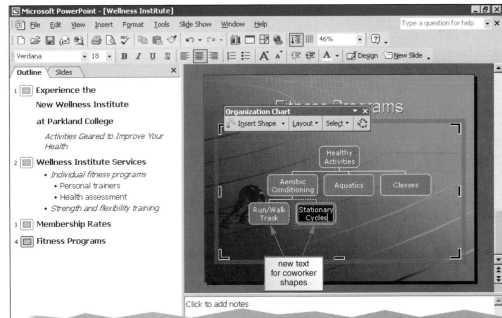

FIGURE 3-65

Changing the Shape Layout

Now that the shapes for the Aerobic Conditioning branch are labeled, you want to change the way the organization chart looks. With the addition of each new shape, the chart expanded horizontally, which is the default layout. Before you add the Aquatics and Classes activities, you will change the layout of the coworker shapes from Standard to Right Hanging. To change the layout, you must select the most superior shape of the branch to which you want to apply the new layout.

Steps **To Change the Shape Layout**

1 **Click the Aerobic Conditioning shape. Click the Layout button on the Organization Chart toolbar and then point to Right Hanging on the Layout menu.**

The default Standard style is selected, which is indicated by the selected icon (Figure 3-66). The Aerobic Conditioning shape is the superior shape of the coworker shapes.

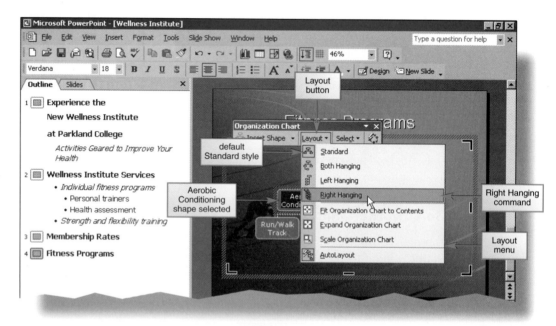

FIGURE 3-66

2 **Click Right Hanging.**

The organization chart displays the two coworker shapes vertically below the Aerobic Conditioning shape (Figure 3-67).

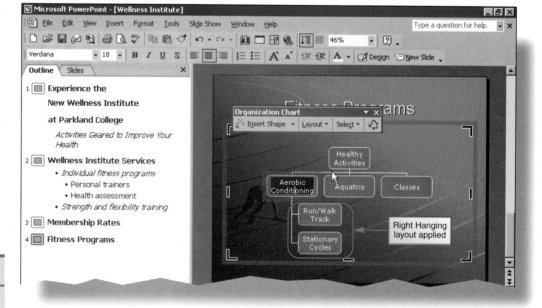

1. Press ALT+L, press R
2. In Voice Command mode, say "Layout, Right Hanging"

FIGURE 3-67

If you select an incorrect style or want to return to the previous style, click the Undo Change Layout command on the Edit menu or press CTRL+Z.

Insert Additional Subordinate and Coworker Shapes

With the aerobic conditioning features of the Wellness Institute added to the organization chart, you need to create the Aquatics and Classes components of the chart. Perform the following steps to add four shapes, enter text, and change the layout.

TO INSERT ADDITIONAL SUBORDINATE AND COWORKER SHAPES

1 Click the Aquatics shape and then click the Insert Shape button on the Organization Chart toolbar.

2 Click the new subordinate shape, type `Five-Lane` and then press the ENTER key. Type `Lap Pool` in the shape.

3 Click the Insert Shape button arrow on the Organization Chart toolbar and then click Coworker.

4 Click the new coworker shape, type `Warm Water` and then press the ENTER key. Type `Therapy Pool` in the shape.

5 Click the Aquatics shape, click the Layout button, and then click Right Hanging.

6 Click the Classes shape and then click the Insert Shape button on the Organization Chart toolbar.

7 Click the new subordinate shape, type `Yoga and` and then press the ENTER key. Type `Tai Chi` in the shape.

8 Click the Insert Shape button arrow on the Organization Chart toolbar and then click Coworker.

9 Click the new coworker shape, type `Spinning` and then press the ENTER key. Type and `Step` in the shape.

10 Click the Classes shape, click the Layout button on the Organization Chart toolbar, and then click Right Hanging.

Four shapes contain text related to aquatics and classes offered at the Wellness Institute (Figure 3-68).

All the desired text now displays on the organization chart. The next section explains how to change the organization chart style.

More About

Animating Chart Elements

Add visual interest to an organization chart by animating its shapes. Click Slide Show on the menu bar and then click Custom Animation. When the Custom Animation task pane opens, click Add Effect, and then click the desired Entrance, Emphasis, or Exit effect. Click the arrow next to the effect you applied and then click Effect Options. When the dialog box displays for that effect, click the Diagram Animation tab and then select how you want to animate the elements of your chart.

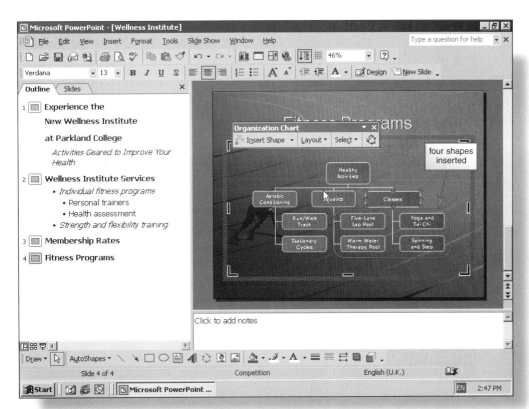

FIGURE 3-68

Changing the Preset Design Scheme

To format the organization chart so it looks like the chart shown in Figure 3-53 on page PP 3.39, select a diagram style in the Organization Chart Style Gallery. The **Organization Chart Style Gallery** contains a variety of styles that use assorted colors, border styles, and shadow effects. The following steps describe how to change the default design scheme.

Steps **To Change the Preset Design Scheme**

1 **Point to the Autoformat button on the Organization Chart toolbar (Figure 3-69).**

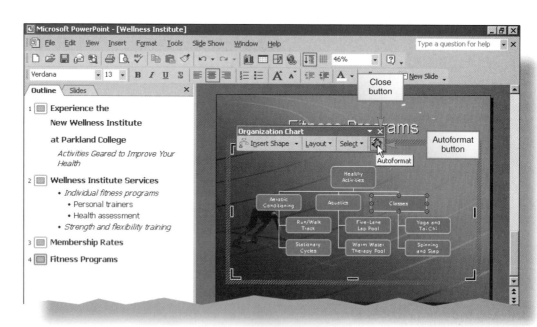

FIGURE 3-69

2 **Click the Autoformat button and then click the Beveled Gradient style in the Diagram Style list. Point to the Apply button in the Organization Chart Style Gallery dialog box.**

Diagram Style names display in the list. When you click a name, PowerPoint previews that style (Figure 3-70).

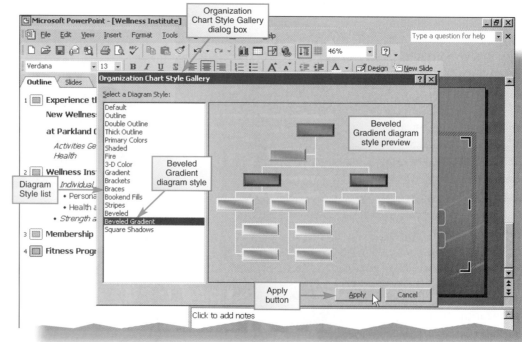

FIGURE 3-70

3 **Click the Apply button. Click the Close button on the Organization Chart toolbar.**

PowerPoint applies the Beveled Gradient style to all the shapes and lines in the chart (Figure 3-71).

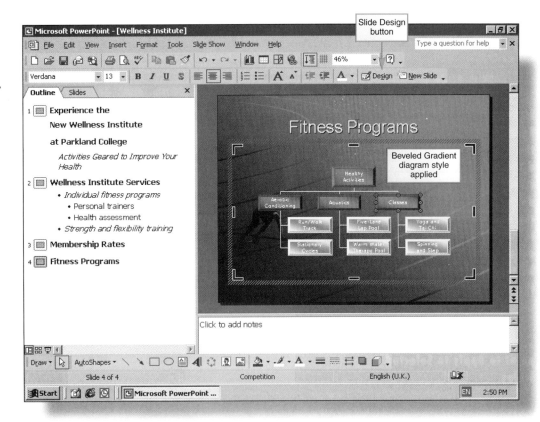

FIGURE 3-71

Applying a New Design Template

You can see that the information in the organization chart will display more prominently if the slide has a different background. One method of changing the look of an individual slide is to change the design template. Perform the steps on the next page to change the design template on Slide 4 from Competition to Edge.

Other Ways

1. Press SHIFT+ALT+C, press RIGHT ARROW, press ENTER, press DOWN ARROW or UP ARROW to scroll through styles, press ENTER

2. In Voice Command mode, say "Autoformat, Beveled Gradient, Apply"

More *About*

Giving Presentations

When you are asked to present your slide show to an audience, help keep stress at a minimum by eating and drinking well. For a burst of energy, eat an apple or a banana instead of snacks with a high fat content, such as potato chips. Drink plenty of water instead of soda and coffee. For more information on giving presentations, visit the PowerPoint 2002 More About Web page (scsite.com/pp2002/more.htm) and then click Giving Presentations.

Steps **To Apply a New Design Template to a Single Slide**

1 **With Slide 4 displaying, click the Slide Design button on the Formatting toolbar. When the Slide Design task pane displays, click the down scroll arrow in the Apply a design template list until the Edge template displays in the Available For Use area. Point to the arrow button on the right side of the Edge template.**

2 **Click the arrow button and then point to Apply to Selected Slides.**

You can apply the Edge template to all slides or the selected slide, or you can see a larger preview of the template (Figure 3-72).

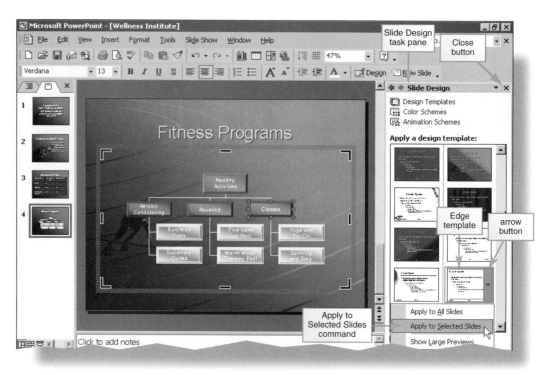

FIGURE 3-72

3 **Click Apply to Selected Slides. Click the Close button in the Slide Design task pane.**

PowerPoint applies the Edge template to Slide 4 (Figure 3-73).

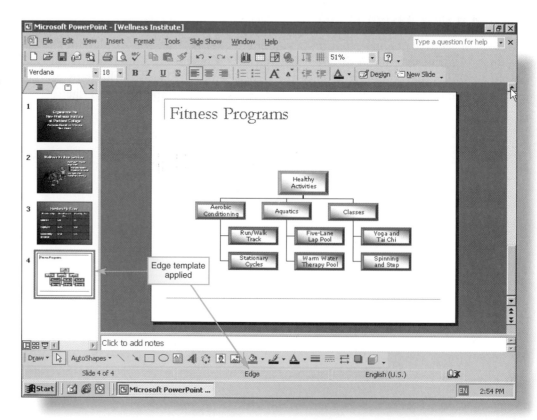

FIGURE 3-73

Slide 4 now is complete. The next section describes how to change the order of individual slides.

Rearranging Slides

The Slide 4 organization chart should display before the Slide 3 table in a slide show. Changing slide order is an easy process. Perform the following steps to rearrange Slides 3 and 4.

More *About*

Quick Reference

For a table that lists how to complete tasks covered in this book using the mouse, menu, shortcut menu, and keyboard, see the Quick Reference Summary at the back of this book or visit the Shelly Cashman Series Office XP Web page (scsite.com/ offxp/qr.htm) and then click Microsoft PowerPoint 2002.

 To Rearrange Slides

1 **Click the Slide 3 slide thumbnail in the tabs pane.**

The Slide 3 slide thumbnail is selected (Figure 3-74).

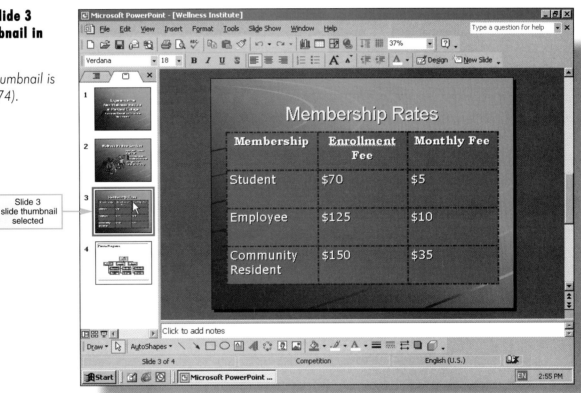

FIGURE 3-74

2 **Drag the Slide 3 slide thumbnail below the Slide 4 slide thumbnail.**

The slide with the organization chart displays above the slide with the chart (Figure 3-75). When you are dragging the slide thumbnail, a line indicates the new location of the selected slide.

new location for organization chart slide

new location for table slide

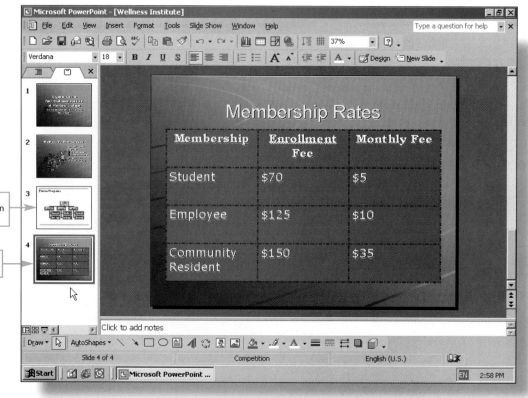

FIGURE 3-75

Other Ways

1. On Outline tab select slide icon, drag icon to new location
2. In slide sorter view select slide thumbnail, drag thumbnail to new location

The order of Slides 3 and 4 is changed. If you want to change the order of multiple consecutive slides, press the SHIFT key before clicking each slide icon or slide thumbnail. Save the presentation.

Adding an Animation Scheme to Selected Slides

The final step in preparing the Wellness Institute presentation is to add an animation scheme to Slides 1, 2, and 4. Perform the following steps to add the Unfold animation scheme to these three slides.

TO ADD AN ANIMATION SCHEME TO SELECTED SLIDES

1 Press and hold down the CTRL key and then click the Slide 2 and Slide 1 slide thumbnails. Release the CTRL key.

2 Click Slide Show on the menu bar and then click Animation Schemes.

3 Scroll down the Apply to selected slides list and then click Unfold in the Moderate category.

4 Click the Close button in the Slide Design task pane.

The Unfold animation scheme is applied to Slides 1, 2, and 4 in the Wellness Institute presentation.

Other Ways

1. In slide sorter view, select slides to add transitions, right-click selected slide, click Animation Schemes on shortcut menu, click desired animation, click Close button
2. Select slides to add transitions, on Slide Show menu click Animation Schemes, click desired animation, click Close button

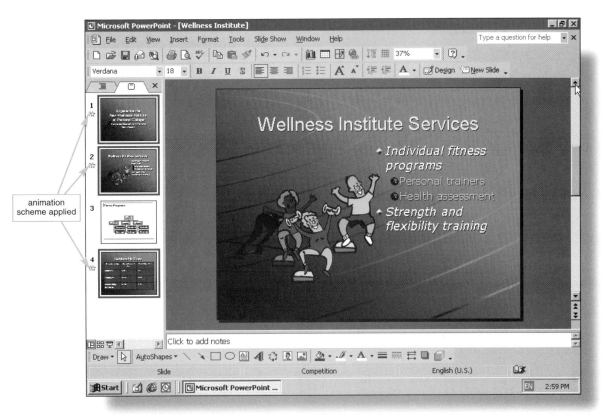

FIGURE 3-76

Printing Slides as Handouts

Perform the following steps to print the presentation slides as handouts, four slides per page.

TO PRINT SLIDES AS HANDOUTS

1 Ready the printer.

2 Click File on the menu bar and then click Print.

3 Click the Print what box arrow and then click Handouts in the list.

4 Click the Slides per page box arrow in the Handouts area and then click 4 in the list.

5 Click the OK button.

The handout prints as shown in Figure 3-77 on the next page.

Microsoft Certification

The Microsoft Office User Specialist (MOUS) Certification program provides an opportunity for you to obtain a valuable industry credential — proof that you have the PowerPoint 2002 skills required by employers. For more information, see Appendix E or visit the Shelly Cashman Series MOUS Web page at scsite.com/offxp/cert.htm.

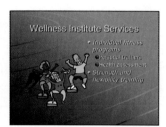

1

FIGURE 3-77

Running the Slide Show, Saving, and Quitting PowerPoint

With the slide show complete, click the Slide Show button and run the presentation to ensure that you are satisfied with the slide content and animation scheme.

If you made any changes to your presentation since your last save, you should save it again before quitting PowerPoint. Perform the following steps to save changes to the presentation and quit PowerPoint.

TO SAVE CHANGES AND QUIT POWERPOINT

1 Click the Close button on the Microsoft PowerPoint window title bar.

2 If prompted, click the Yes button in the Microsoft PowerPoint dialog box.

PowerPoint saves any changes made to the presentation since the last save and then quits PowerPoint.

C A S E   P E R S P E C T I V E   S U M M A R Y

The Wellness Institute slide show should help generate interest among potential members. The people viewing your presentation on your college's intranet and receiving a handout will obtain a good overview of the Wellness Institute's services, the variety of activities offered, and the membership fees. The Institute should expect an overwhelming response to its membership drive.

Project Summary

Project 3 introduced you to several methods of enhancing a presentation with visuals. You began the project by creating the presentation from an outline that was created in Word. Then, when you created Slide 2, you learned how to ungroup and customize clip art. You also learned how to change the bullet character on the slide master. You learned to create and format a table on Slide 3. Slide 4 introduced you to creating an organization chart and applying a design template to a single slide and change the order of slides in the presentation. Finally, you learned how to print your presentation slides as handouts.

What You Should Know

Having completed this project, you now should be able to perform the following tasks:

- Add an Animation Scheme to Selected Slides *(PP 3.52)*
- Add Text to Coworker Shapes *(PP 3.45)*
- Add Text to the Subordinate Shapes *(PP 3.42)*
- Add Text to the Superior Shape *(PP 3.42)*
- Apply a New Design Template to a Single Slide *(PP 3.50)*
- Change a Bullet Character on the Slide Master *(PP 3.24)*
- Change a Bullet Color on the Slide Master *(PP 3.28)*
- Change the Preset Design Scheme *(PP 3.48)*
- Change the Shape Layout *(PP 3.46)*
- Change the Slide Layout to Title, Content and Text *(PP 3.14)*
- Change the Slide Layout to Title Slide *(PP 3.11)*
- Delete a PowerPoint Object *(PP 3.19)*
- Delete a Slide *(PP 3.10)*
- Deselect Clip Art Objects *(PP 3.18)*
- Display the Next Slide and the Organization Chart Diagram *(PP 3.39)*
- Display the Slide Master *(PP 3.22)*
- Display the Tables and Borders Toolbar *(PP 3.34)*
- Enter Data in a Table *(PP 3.32)*
- Format a Table *(PP 3.36)*
- Format a Table Cell *(PP 3.33)*
- Insert a Basic Table *(PP 3.30)*
- Insert a Clip into a Content Placeholder *(PP 3.14)*
- Insert Additional Subordinate and Coworker Shapes *(PP 3.47)*
- Insert Subordinate and Coworker Shapes *(PP 3.43)*
- Open a Microsoft Word Outline as a Presentation *(PP 3.08)*
- Print Slides as Handouts *(PP 3.53)*
- Rearrange Slides *(PP 3.51)*
- Regroup Objects *(PP 3.20)*
- Save a Presentation *(PP 3.12)*
- Save Changes and Quit PowerPoint *(PP 3.54)*
- Size and Move a Clip *(PP 3.16)*
- Start and Customize a New Presentation and Change to the Outline Tab *(PP 3.06)*
- Ungroup a Clip *(PP 3.17)*

Learn It Online

Instructions: To complete the Learn It Online exercises, start your browser, click the Address bar, and then enter scsite.com/offxp/exs.htm. When the Office XP Learn It Online page displays, follow the instructions in the exercises below.

1 Project Reinforcement TF, MC, and SA

Below PowerPoint Project 3, click the Project Reinforcement link. Print the quiz by clicking Print on the File menu. Answer each question. Write your first and last name at the top of each page, and then hand in the printout to your instructor.

2 Flash Cards

Below PowerPoint Project 3, click the Flash Cards link. When Flash Cards displays, read the instructions. Type 20 (or a number specified by your instructor) in the Number of Playing Cards text box, type your name in the Name text box, and then click the Flip Card button. When the flash card displays, read the question and then click the Answer box arrow to select an answer. Flip through Flash Cards. Click Print on the File menu to print the last flash card if your score is 15 (75%) correct or greater and then hand it in to your instructor. If your score is less than 15 (75%) correct, then redo this exercise by clicking the Replay button.

3 Practice Test

Below PowerPoint Project 3, click the Practice Test link. Answer each question, enter your first and last name at the bottom of the page, and then click the Grade Test button. When the graded practice test displays on your screen, click Print on the File menu to print a hard copy. Continue to take practice tests until you score 80% or better. Hand in a printout of the final practice test to your instructor.

4 Who Wants to Be a Computer Genius?

Below PowerPoint Project 3, click the Computer Genius link. Read the instructions, enter your first and last name at the bottom of the page, and then click the Play button. Hand in your score to your instructor.

5 Wheel of Terms

Below PowerPoint Project 3, click the Wheel of Terms link. Read the instructions, and then enter your first and last name and your school name. Click the Play button. Hand in your score to your instructor.

6 Crossword Puzzle Challenge

Below PowerPoint Project 3, click the Crossword Puzzle Challenge link. Read the instructions, and then enter your first and last name. Click the Play button. Work the crossword puzzle. When you are finished, click the Submit button. When the crossword puzzle redisplays, click the Print button. Hand in the printout.

7 Tips and Tricks

Below PowerPoint Project 3, click the Tips and Tricks link. Click a topic that pertains to Project 3. Right-click the information and then click Print on the shortcut menu. Construct a brief example of what the information relates to in PowerPoint to confirm you understand how to use the tip or trick. Hand in the example and printed information.

8 Newsgroups

Below PowerPoint Project 3, click the Newsgroups link. Click a topic that pertains to Project 3. Print three comments. Hand in the comments to your instructor.

9 Expanding Your Horizons

Below PowerPoint Project 3, click the Articles for Microsoft PowerPoint link. Click a topic that pertains to Project 3. Print the information. Construct a brief example of what the information relates to in PowerPoint to confirm you understand the contents of the article. Hand in the example and printed information to your instructor.

10 Search Sleuth

Below PowerPoint Project 3, click the Search Sleuth link. To search for a term that pertains to this project, select a term below the Project 3 title and then use the Google search engine at google.com (or any major search engine) to display and print two Web pages that present information on the term. Hand in the printouts to your instructor.

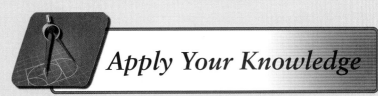

Apply Your Knowledge

1 Creating a Presentation from an Outline, Inserting and Modifying Clips, and Changing Bullets

Instructions: Start PowerPoint. Open the outline, Buying a Car, from the Data Disk. See the inside back cover of this book for instructions for downloading the Data Disk or see your instructor for information about accessing the clips and files required for this book. The outline gives three specific tips for negotiating a selling price. Perform the following tasks.

1. Apply the Fading Grid design template.
2. Delete the blank Slide 1. Change the slide layout for Slide 1 to Title Slide (Figure 3-78a).
3. On Slide 1, insert the car clip. Size the clip to 265%. Ungroup the clip and delete the light green background. Regroup the clip.
4. On Slide 2, insert the checkbook clip shown in Figure 3-78b. Size the clip to 185%. Ungroup the clip and delete the star background. Regroup the clip.
5. Change the first-level paragraph bullets on the slide master to the hand symbol located in the Wingdings font. Change the bullet color to green.
6. Apply the Zoom animation scheme in the Moderate category list to both slides.
7. Save the presentation with the file name, Negotiating Tips.
8. Print the slides as a handout with both slides on one page.
9. Quit PowerPoint.

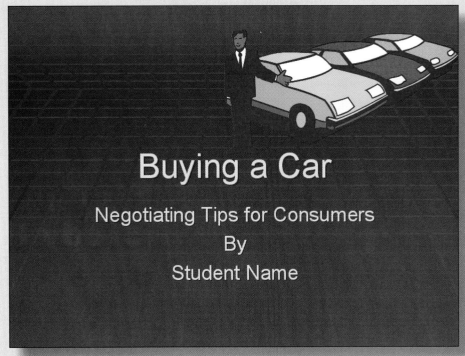

(a) Slide 1

(b) Slide 2

FIGURE 3-78

In the Lab

1 Creating a Custom Slide

Problem: Many colleges ask successful students to become mentors to incoming students. You decide to participate in the mentoring program at your school to help these new students become acclimated to college life during their first semester on campus. The student mentor supervisor asks you to create a presentation for these students on the topic of good study habits. You decide to begin the assignment by creating a title slide with a clip showing students studying. You import a clip, modify it, and then import and modify another clip to create the slide shown in Figure 3-79. See your instructor if the clips are not available on your system.

Instructions: Perform the following tasks.

1. Start PowerPoint and apply the Studio design template to the Title Only slide layout.
2. Type Developing Good Study Habits for the slide title. Change the font size to 48. Bold this text.
3. Insert the clip shown in Figure 3-79. Size the clip to 275%.
4. Ungroup the picture. Then delete the 3 + 2 = 5 formula.
5. Insert the clip with the letter A. Size the clip to 115%.
6. Ungroup this clip and delete the blue background so that only the red dots display on the yellow background.
7. Regroup both clips together as one object.
8. Apply the Ellipse motion animation scheme.
9. Save the presentation with the file name, Mentoring.
10. Print the slide.
11. Quit PowerPoint.

FIGURE 3-79

In the Lab

2 Customizing Bullets and Inserting a Table

Problem: Each year more than 1.25 million people are treated for burn injuries in the United States. More than one-half of these accidents are preventable, especially when they involve children. The fire chief in your community has asked you to help him create a presentation describing some burn prevention tips. He wants you to include a table describing the three types of burns and to give information on preventing children from becoming burn victims. Create the presentation shown in Figures 3-80a, 3-80b, 3-80c, and 3-80d.

Instructions: Perform the following tasks.

1. Start PowerPoint. Open the outline, Burn Outline, from the Data Disk. Apply the Network design template. Delete the blank Slide 1.
2. On Slide 1, apply the Title Slide slide layout. Increase the title font size to 72 point. Italicize the text.
3. On Slide 2, use the slide master to change the first-level bullet to the sad face shown in Figure 3-80b. Change the bullet color to aqua.

(a) Slide 1

(b) Slide 2

(c) Slide 3

(d) Slide 4

FIGURE 3-80

(continued)

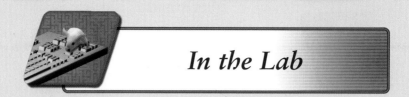

In the Lab

Customizing Bullets and Inserting a Table *(continued)*

4. Change the order of Slides 3 and 4.

5. On Slide 4, create the table shown in Figure 3-80d on the previous page. Format the table by changing the column headings to 32-point Garamond. Center and bold these headings. Change the border style to the second style in the Border Style list, and then change the width to 1½ pt. Change the border color to the color dark blue. Apply the All Borders border style. Finally, change the table fill color to light blue.

6. Apply the Compress animation scheme to Slides 1, 2, and 3.

7. Save the presentation with the file name, Burn Prevention.

8. Print handouts with two slides on one page. Quit PowerPoint.

3 Opening an Existing Outline, Adding Graphical Bullets, Inserting a Table, and Creating an Organization Chart

Problem: The community theater company in the town of Western Oak is seeking subscribers for the upcoming season. You have been asked to help with the recruiting efforts. You decide to develop a presentation that includes information about the newly renovated theater, the performances, and the board of directors. Create the presentation starting with the Theater Outline on your Data Disk. Then insert the clip and table and create the organization chart shown in Figures 3-81a, 3-81b, 3-81c, and 3-81d. See your instructor if the clip is not available on your system.

Instructions: Perform the following tasks.

1. Start PowerPoint. Open the Theater Outline on your Data Disk.

2. Apply the Cascade design template.

3. Delete the blank Slide 1. On Slide 1, apply the Title Slide slide layout. Italicize and center the subtitle text.

4. On Slide 2, use the slide master to change the first-level bullets to the masks shown in Figure 3-81b that are part of the Webdings font. Change the bullet color to gold. Change the second-level bullets to the music symbol that is part of the Webdings font. Change the bullet color to light blue.

5. Insert the masks clip. Size the clip to 125%. Ungroup this clip and delete the purple background and the grapes. Regroup the clip.

6. Change the order of Slides 3 and 4.

7. On Slide 3, insert the table shown in Figure 3-81c. Format the table by changing the column headings to 40-point Comic Sans MS. Center and bold these headings. Change the border style to the last style in the Border Style list, and then change the width to 6 pt. Change the border color to the color gold. Apply the Inside Borders border style. Finally, change the table fill color to medium blue.

8. Create the organization chart shown in Figure 3-81d. Apply the Stripes diagram style.

9. Apply the Rise up animation scheme to Slides 1 and 2.

10. Save the presentation with the file name, Western Oak Theater. Print the presentation and then quit PowerPoint.

In the Lab

(a) Slide 1

(b) Slide 2

FIGURE 3-81

(continued)

In the Lab

Opening an Existing Outline, Adding Graphical Bullets, Inserting a Table, and Creating an Organization Chart *(continued)*

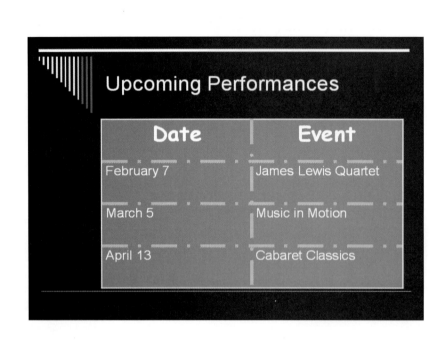

(c) Slide 3

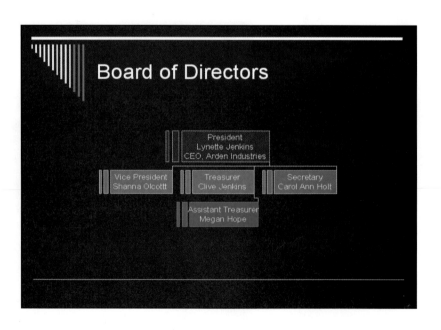

(d) Slide 4

FIGURE 3-81

Cases and Places

The difficulty of these case studies varies:
▶ are the least difficult; ▶▶ are more difficult; and ▶▶▶ are the most difficult.

1 ▶ Human resources employees at Mechan Computers are recruiting students to work at the office near your campus. In an attempt to develop interest in the three-year-old company, the employees want you to create a PowerPoint presentation to show during the campus Job Fair next month. Create a title slide with a clip and a text slide with an organization chart describing the three major benefits of working at Mechan: compensation, environment, and hours. The high compensation includes $12.75 per hour starting pay, 5% commission, 10% employee discount, and a 401K plan. The working environment is casual and friendly, with monthly social events and an annual retreat to Lake Tahoe. Work hours are flexible and include two weeks of vacation during the first year, 10 paid holidays, and 10 personal business days.

2 ▶ According to the U.S. Department of Agriculture, you should eat a maximum of 10 teaspoons of sugar daily. While this amount seems tolerable, you need to examine product labels and nutrition guides to see how much sugar you really do consume. If you are thirsty, you might want to rethink your normal liquid consumption habits. For example, a 20-ounce sweetened ice tea has fifteen teaspoons of sugar, a can of orange soda has thirteen, and a 10-ounce milk shake has nine. Ten reduced-fat Oreo cookies have eleven and one-half teaspoons of sugar, a 2.1-ounce Snickers bar has six, and a 1-ounce chocolate bar has three. One-half cup of fruit canned in heavy syrup has four teaspoons, while the same amount in plain juice has no added sugar. Also, an 8-ounce serving of fruit yogurt has seven added teaspoonfuls of sugar whereas plain yogurt has zero. Create a presentation and a handout with a title slide, a bulleted list, and table that conveys this information. Include a title slide and appropriate clips and animation effects.

3 ▶▶ Handheld computers help many people stay organized when they are on the go. These small devices typically are categorized by the operating system they run: Palm OS or Pocket PC. While prices are plummeting for these computers, features are skyrocketing. Visit an electronics store, read magazines, or perform online research to learn about four of the latest models. What are the prices for these popular handheld computers? What applications do they run? Are the screens color or monochrome? How well do the handwriting recognition features work? How long is the battery life? What accessories are available? Then, use Microsoft Word to create an outline that organizes your research findings. Open this Word document as a PowerPoint presentation and create a slide show with this information. Use a title slide and include appropriate clips and animation effects. Print the presentation and your outline.

Cases and Places

4 ▶▶ The park district director in your town has announced plans to update the classes offered this summer. The changes include classes for all age groups. For children, new classes are Toddler Tumbling, Wrestling Camp, Cheerleading Camp, and Football Fundamentals. For adults, new offerings are Yoga, Advanced Aerobics, Kickboxing, and Modern Jazz. Seniors can experience classes in Flexibility, Indoor Walking, and Self-Defense. New swimming classes are Aqua Babies for children six months to two-years-old, Preschool Swim for children three- to five-years-old, Teen Swim, Aqua Motion, and Senior Water Fitness. Also added to the schedule are Conditioning for Golfers and Tennis Players, Gardening with Perennials and Annuals, Basic Photography, and Acrylic Painting. The marketing director has asked you to help her publicize the class changes and wants you to create a slide show to display at the local mall. Using the techniques introduced in this project, create the presentation by inserting lists, a table, and an organization chart depicting the new offerings. Include appropriate clips and animation effects.

5 ▶▶ The library in your town is promoting its Literacy Fun Walk, an event to raise funds for and awareness of library services and the Literary Foundation. The 2.5-mile walk will occur on August 21 from 11:00 a.m. to 3:00 p.m. through neighborhoods in your community. The registration date is July 31, and registration packets may be obtained at the library or the village hall. The Chamber of Commerce and private businesses will match the $25 registration fee. Walk participants will receive a T-shirt and water bottle. Using the techniques introduced in this project, create a presentation to promote this Literacy Fun Walk. Include a map of your community that you obtain from an online Web site, such as mapquest.com, and draw a walk route on the city streets. Insert clips on the map of significant sites the participants will view, such as the library, the fire station, and the courthouse. Include animation effects and appropriate clips.

6 ▶▶▶ Finding and working with an academic advisor is paramount to a new student's success. The counseling department asks you to create a presentation that includes tips on the benefits of having an academic advisor. The presentation should define academic advising, describe how advisors help students, and list the questions students should ask their advisors. Include a slide with a table that shows registration dates for the coming school year. The first column should show the activity, the second column should give the fall term date, and the third column should show the spring term date. Add appropriate clips, and modify one of the clips by removing any background material.

7 ▶▶▶ Some campus sports teams garner much attention and have an avid fan base. Other teams have smaller turnouts at their events. Select one athletic team at your school that does not attract a lot of publicity and obtain a roster of the players. Using the techniques introduced in this project, create a slide show containing a hierarchy chart of the captain, trainers, coaches, and other key personnel. Then insert a table listing some of the veteran athletes' names, their positions, their year in school, and any records held.

Microsoft PowerPoint 2002

PROJECT
4

Modifying Visual Elements and Presentation Formats

You will have mastered the material in this project when you can:

- Create a presentation using the AutoContent Wizard
- Modify a presentation template by changing the color scheme
- Add information to the Footer Area of the slide master
- Add a bitmap graphic to a background
- Create a WordArt element and add it to a slide
- Scale a WordArt element
- Add sound effects to slides
- Create folders for storing presentations
- Add a chart to a slide
- Insert an Excel chart on a slide
- Insert a Word table on a slide
- Add hyperlinks to slides
- Embed fonts in presentations
- Apply transition effects to a presentation
- Rehearse presentation timings
- Print speaker notes
- Save slide presentations as Rich Text Format outlines
- Run a slide show with hyperlinks

Inspire and Inform Your Audience

Multimedia Presentations Entertain and Educate

I n this era of instant communication, people now can use multimedia technologies to share information, ideas, and news, and to provide entertainment in a way that is efficient, effective, and enjoyable. Using multiple forms of media to communicate can help audiences increase their retention and understanding of information. In fact, learning curves are about 60 percent faster and content retention has been shown to be 25 to 50 percent higher when multimedia technologies are implemented.

Baby boomers and the X Generation both have grown up with technological advances beyond the wildest dreams of former generations. Moviegoers of 50 and 60 years ago viewed reel-to-reel films projected onto the silver screen in movie palaces such as Mann's Chinese Theater in Hollywood. Today's theatergoers sit in stadium seating in mega-theaters that contain custom-designed sound systems and the latest IMAX® theater technology. Three-dimensional images are projected onto giant screens up to eight stories high with such realism that you can almost reach out to touch them. Today's audiences enjoy forms of entertainment that thrill the senses and move the emotions in exciting new ways.

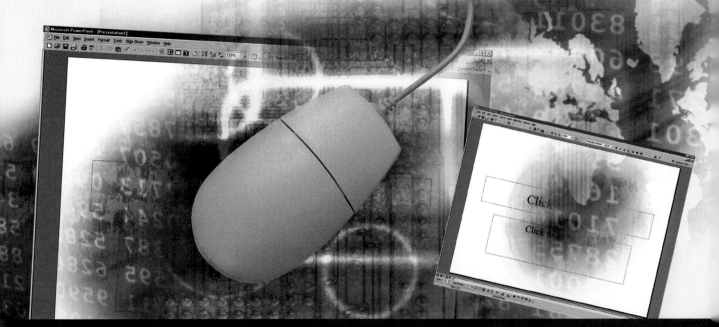

Whether the purpose is to entertain or inform, in a world competing for audiences, higher and more exacting standards have created a high-tech society that demands excitement and stimulation in everything it sees. Presentations are no exception. In exchange for their time and attention, people expect presentations to be entertaining, as well as informative.

PowerPoint provides the multimedia technology required to supply audiences with stimulating presentations. In this project, you will create a PowerPoint presentation about good nutrition and health for the Parkland College Wellness Institute. You will become familiar with the versatility of PowerPoint as you work with various backgrounds, hyperlinks, sound effects, and slide transitions. The presentation also will incorporate a variety of graphics, including charts, tables, and photographs, and you will use PowerPoint to weave these elements together into an inspiring and informative presentation.

PowerPoint provides the freedom to create a picture to any author's specifications, which is a decided advantage over other static presentation tools. After embedding a graphics object, the object can be manipulated in several ways: changing its size, extracting part of the image, rearranging the individual components of the image, or adding objects from other sources to the original.

The capability of importing from other applications, such as Excel or Word, adds another powerful tool to the presenter's collection. Using Word, for instance, interactive documents, graphs, charts, tables, worksheets, and special text effects created with WordArt can add to the excitement of a PowerPoint presentation.

As a creative, diverse, and effective form of multimedia production, PowerPoint presentations provide a means to entertain, inspire, and satisfy audiences.

Microsoft PowerPoint 2002

Modifying Visual Elements and Presentation Formats

PROJECT

Membership at the new Wellness Institute at Parkland College has soared during the past few months. Students are very aware of the need to stay healthy and are happy to have a campus-based center where they can participate in programs geared toward health and fitness. A large part of the membership success is due to the slide show you created in Project 3. Students, faculty, and community members visit the facility on a regular basis to burn calories and tone muscles.

A survey conducted by personal trainers at the Institute indicates members are seeking additional services, including nutritional counseling. The director, Malcolm Perkins, wants to offer a seminar discussing the connection between eating healthy foods and improving general wellness. He has asked you to help with this project by developing a PowerPoint presentation on this subject. You recommend using a variety of graphics, including a photograph, charts, and tables.

Introduction

"The beginning is the most important part of the work," according to the ancient Greek philosopher Plato. The beginning of a PowerPoint slide show also is a critical part of a presentation. The first slide sets the tone, announces the topic, and generates interest. Occasionally you may have trouble when beginning to design a presentation. Selecting a design template, appropriate colors, and a slide layout for a specific audience can be a challenge.

Microsoft designers recognize this undertaking and have developed the AutoContent Wizard to help begin a presentation. This wizard creates up to 12 slides with suggested content about specific topics, such as selling a new product or reporting the status of a project. Based on the user's responses to questions about the presentation type, style, and options, the wizard selects a design template and creates slides with varying layouts and content that can be modified to fit the audience's needs.

Project Four — Get Fit: Eat Better and Feel Great

Project 4 customizes the slide show generated by the AutoContent Wizard. You will add a graphical heading and change the background on Slide 1 to call attention to the fitness slide show topic. You also will add data from other sources, including an Excel chart and a Word table, and insert visual elements to create the slide show shown in Figures 4-1a through 4-1e.

(a) Slide 1

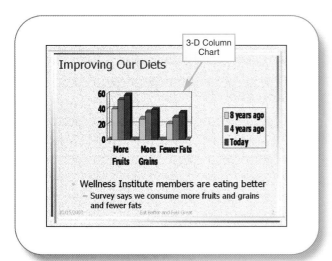

(b) Slide 2

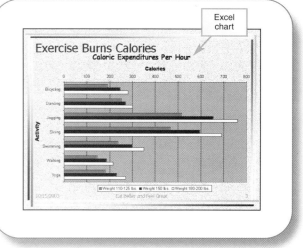

(c) Slide 3

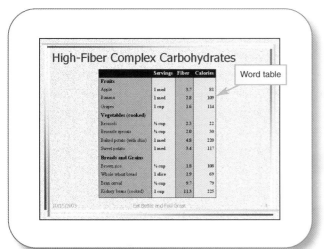

(d) Slide 4

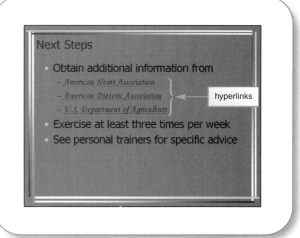

(e) Slide 5

FIGURE 4-1

Starting a New Presentation from the AutoContent Wizard

Beginning the eating well slide show is made easier by using the AutoContent Wizard. This feature helps you get started by supplying organization and ideas for the slides. The 24 presentations are organized in six categories: All, General, Corporate, Projects, Sales / Marketing, and Carnegie Coach. After starting a new presentation, use the AutoContent Wizard to generate slides for the healthy foods presentation.

Starting and Customizing a New Presentation

To begin, start a new presentation. To reset your toolbars and menus so they display exactly as shown in this book, follow the steps in Appendix D. Perform the following steps to create a new presentation.

TO START AND CUSTOMIZE A NEW PRESENTATION

1 Click the Start button on the Windows taskbar, point to Programs on the Start menu, and then click Microsoft PowerPoint on the Programs submenu.

2 If the New Presentation task pane displays, click the Show at startup check box to remove the check mark and then click the Close button on the task pane title bar.

3 If the Language bar displays, click its Minimize button.

4 If the Standard and Formatting toolbars display on one row, click the Toolbar Options button on the right side of either toolbar and then click Show Buttons on Two Rows on the Toolbar Options menu.

A new presentation titled Presentation1 displays in the PowerPoint window (Figure 4-2).

More *About*

The PowerPoint Help System

Need Help? It is no further than the Ask a Question box in the upper-right corner of the window. Click the box that contains the text, Type a question for help (Figure 4-2), type help, and then press the ENTER key. PowerPoint will respond with a list of items you can click to learn about obtaining help on any PowerPoint-related topic. To find out what is new in PowerPoint 2002, type what's new in PowerPoint in the Ask a Question box.

file name

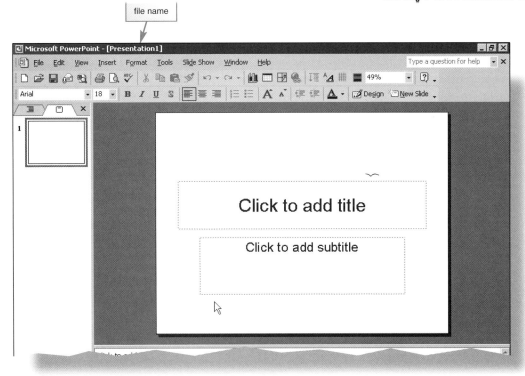

FIGURE 4-2

Using the AutoContent Wizard

With the presentation created, you can use the AutoContent Wizard to generate content. Because the topic of your slide show involves marketing a new healthy eating seminar, the **Selling a Product or Service presentation** that is part of the Sales / Marketing presentation type creates useful ideas to begin developing the presentation. The wizard also will create a footer that displays at the bottom of each slide. Perform the following steps to use the AutoContent Wizard.

More About

PowerPoint Tips

PowerPoint users have discovered many shortcuts and tricks that make using the software a breeze. They often share their discoveries with other PowerPoint users. To learn about their tips, visit the PowerPoint 2002 More About Web page (scsite.com/pp2002/more.htm) and then click Tips.

 To Use the AutoContent Wizard

1 **Click View on the menu bar and then point to Task Pane.**

The View menu displays (Figure 4-3). You want to open the New Presentation task pane and then create a new presentation using the AutoContent Wizard.

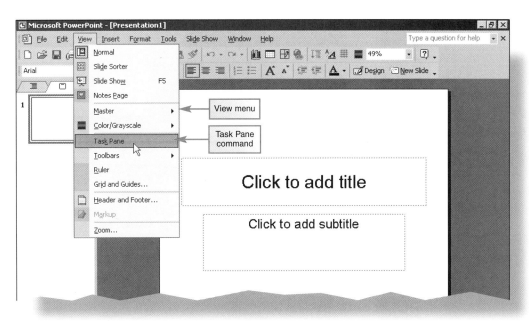

FIGURE 4-3

2 Click Task Pane. Point to From AutoContent Wizard in the New area.

The New Presentation task pane displays (Figure 4-4).

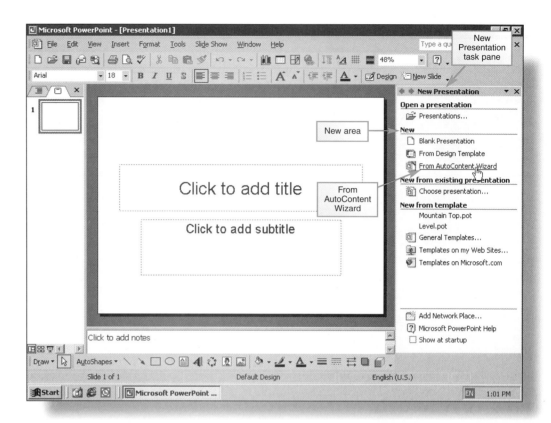

FIGURE 4-4

3 Click From AutoContent Wizard. When the AutoContent Wizard dialog box displays, point to the Next button. If the Office Assistant displays, click No, don't provide help now.

PowerPoint displays the Start panel, describing the function of the AutoContent Wizard (Figure 4-5). You can click the Help button if you desire further explanations from the Office Assistant or the Cancel button to exit the AutoContent Wizard.

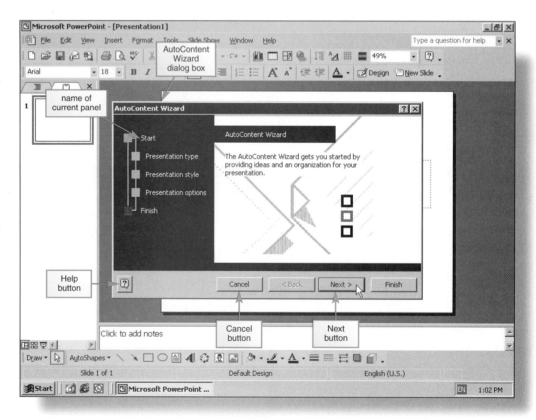

FIGURE 4-5

4 Click the Next button. When the Presentation type panel displays, click the Sales / Marketing button and then point to the Next button.

The 24 presentations are grouped in six categories (Figure 4-6). General is the default category. The names of the presentations within the Sales / Marketing category display in a list. Selling a Product or Service is selected because it is the first name in the list. You can click the Back button to review previous panels.

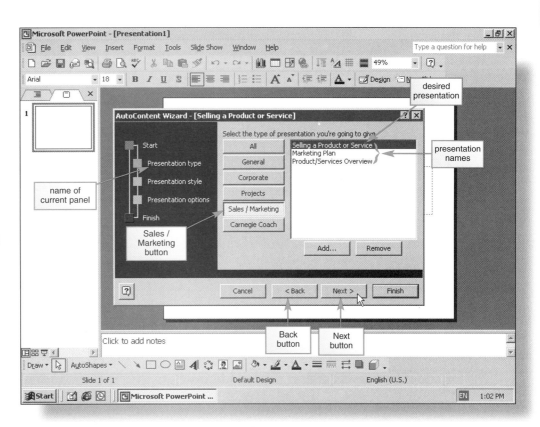

FIGURE 4-6

5 Click the Next button. When the Presentation style panel displays, point to the Next button.

PowerPoint defaults to developing an on-screen presentation. You could select alternate outputs, such as a Web presentation, overhead, or slides.

6 Click the Next button. When the Presentation options panel displays, click the Footer text box and then type Eat Better and Feel Great as the footer text. Point to the Next button.

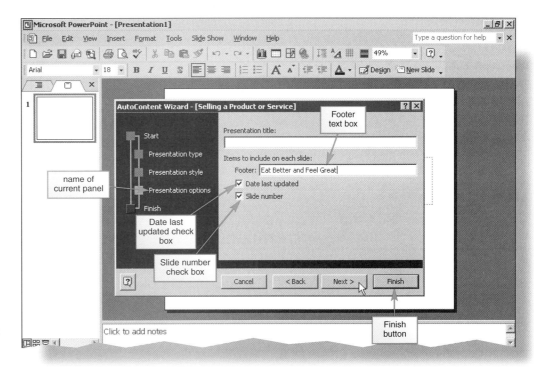

FIGURE 4-7

The AutoContent Wizard creates a footer that will display at the bottom of each slide. The footer will contain the current date, the slide number, and the text you typed (Figure 4-7).

7 **Click the Next button. Point to the Finish button.**

The Finish panel displays a message that the AutoContent Wizard has all the necessary information to develop the slides.

8 **Click the Finish button.**

PowerPoint closes the AutoContent Wizard and displays Slide 1 in the presentation (Figure 4-8). Malcolm Perkins's name displays because his name was entered as the software user when PowerPoint was installed on the system for this project. The footer displays the current date, the Eat Better and Feel Great text, and the slide number. The AutoContent Wizard created a new presentation, so Presentation2 displays as the presentation title in the PowerPoint window.

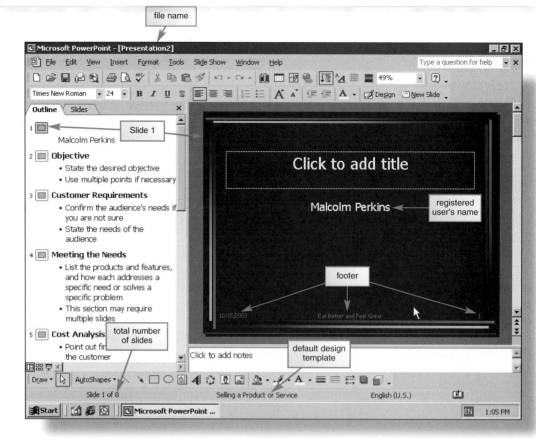

FIGURE 4-8

Other Ways

1. In Voice Command mode, say "View, Task Pane, From AutoContent Wizard, Next, [click Sales / Marketing], Next, Next, [type footer], Next, Finish"

More About

Templates

You can add a customized content template to the AutoContent Wizard. To do this, click New on the File menu and then click From AutoContent Wizard. Click the Next button and then select the category in which you want to display your template. Click Add, locate the template you want to add, and then click OK.

The AutoContent Wizard developed eight slides in the Selling a Product or Service theme. You will modify these slides to fit the eating well topic by changing the presentation color scheme, changing the slide backgrounds, adding a bitmap graphic, creating a WordArt element, inserting an Excel chart and a Word table, and adding a chart, hyperlinks, a sound, and transitions.

Customizing Entire Presentation Elements

With the basic elements of the slide show created, you can modify two default elements that display on all slides in the presentation. First, you must modify the template by changing the color scheme. Then, you will add information to the slide master Footer Area.

Changing the Presentation Template Color Scheme

The first modification to make is to change the color scheme throughout the presentation. The **color scheme** of each slide template consists of eight balanced colors you can apply to all slides, an individual slide, notes pages, or audience handouts. A color scheme consists of colors for a background, text and lines, title text, shadows, fills, accent, accent and hyperlink, and accent and followed hyperlink. Table 4-1 explains the components of a color scheme.

Table 4-1	Color Scheme Components
COMPONENT	**DESCRIPTION**
Background color	The background color is the fundamental color of a PowerPoint slide. For example, if the background color is black, you can place any other color on top of it, but the fundamental color remains black. The black background shows everywhere you do not add color or other objects. The background color on a slide works the same way.
Text and lines color	The text and lines color contrasts with the background color of the slide. Together with the background color, the text and lines color sets the tone for a presentation. For example, a gray background with a black text and lines color sets a dramatic tone. In contrast, a red background with a yellow text and lines color sets a vibrant tone.
Title text color	The title text color contrasts with the background color in a manner similar to the text and lines color. Title text displays in the title text placeholder on a slide.
Shadow color	The shadow color is applied when you color an object. This color usually is a darker shade of the background color.
Fill color	The fill color contrasts with both the background color and the text and lines color. The fill color is used for graphs and charts.
Accent colors	Accent colors are designed as colors for secondary features on a slide. Additionally, accent colors are used as colors on graphs.

More About

Copying Slides

Using the AutoContent Wizard is one way of deriving information for a slide show. Another way is to copy slides from other presentations directly into your new presentation. To do so, display the slide in your presentation that precedes the slide you want to insert, on the Insert menu click Slides from Files, select the presentation containing the slide you want to copy, click Display, select the slide or slides you want to copy to your presentation, and then click Insert. If you want to copy an entire presentation, click Insert All.

Perform the following steps to change the color scheme for the template from a black background and white letters to a white background with dark blue letters.

Steps To Change the Presentation Template Color Scheme

1 **Click the Slide Design button on the Formatting toolbar. Point to Color Schemes in the Slide Design task pane.**

The Slide Design task pane displays (Figure 4-9).

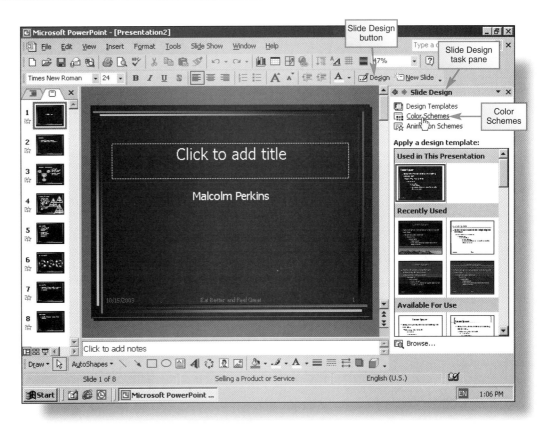

FIGURE 4-9

2 **Click Color Schemes. Point to the top-right color scheme template.**

Four color schemes are available (Figure 4-10). The top-right color scheme is selected and will be applied to all slides in the presentation.

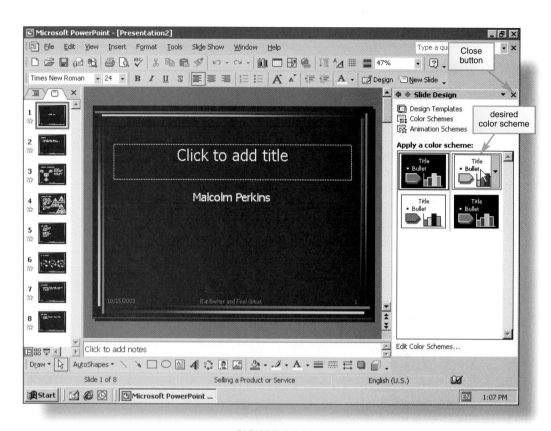

FIGURE 4-10

3 **Click the selected color scheme template and then click the Close button on the Slide Design task pane title bar.**

Slide 1 displays with the new color scheme (Figure 4-11). Slide thumbnails of the slides in the presentation display in the tabs pane.

Other Ways

1. On Format menu click Slide Design, in Slide Design task pane click Color Schemes, click desired color scheme

2. Press ALT+O, press D, press DOWN ARROW key, press ENTER, press arrow keys until desired color selected, press ENTER

3. In Voice Command mode, say "Format, Slide Design, Color Schemes"

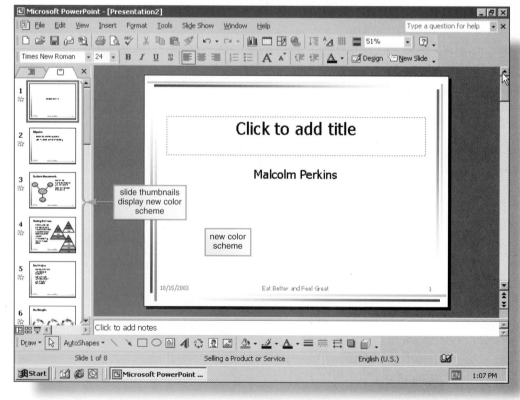

FIGURE 4-11

By default, PowerPoint applies the desired color scheme to all slides in the presentation. If you want to apply it to individual slides or want to see a larger template thumbnail, you would click the arrow button of the selected color scheme and then make your selection. In addition, you can edit the current color scheme by clicking the Edit Color Schemes link at the bottom of the task pane.

Modifying the Footer on the Title Master

With the color scheme changed, you now can revise the text on the title slide footer from Eat Better and Feel Great to Parkland Wellness Institute. One method of making this change is to modify the footer on the title master. In Project 3, you modified the slide master when you customized bullets. In this project, you will display the title master to add information to the Footer Area of that slide. Perform the following steps to modify the title slide footer.

More About

Multiple Masters

Each design template inserts a title master and slide master automatically. When you have more than one design template in your presentation, you have multiple masters. These pairs of slide and title masters display as thumbnails in the Slides tab. When you place your mouse over one of these master thumbnails, a ScreenTip displays the name of the master and indicates which slides have this master applied.

 To Modify the Footer on the Title Master

1 **Click View on the menu bar, point to Master, and then click Slide Master on the Master submenu. Point to the word, <footer>, in the Footer Area on the title master.**

The Selling a Product or Service Title Master and Slide Master View toolbar display (Figure 4-12). The title master and slide master thumbnails display on the left edge of the screen. The title master thumbnail is selected.

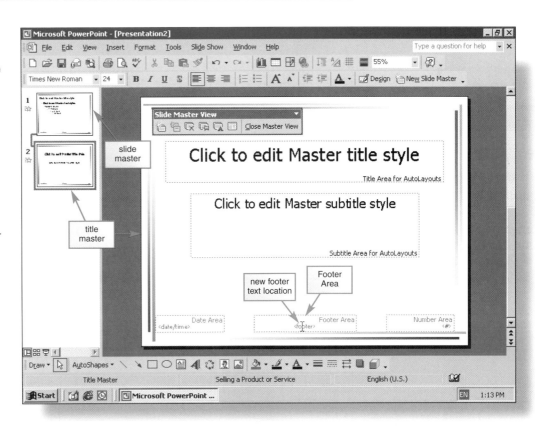

FIGURE 4-12

2 **Click the word, <footer>, in the Footer Area and then type** Parkland Wellness Institute **in the red text box. Point to the Close Master View button on the Slide Master View toolbar.**

The new footer text displays in the title master Footer Area (Figure 4-13).

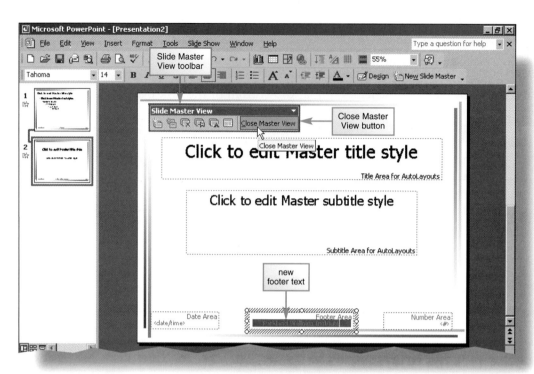

FIGURE 4-13

3 **Click the Close Master View button.**

The new title slide footer text, Parkland Wellness Institute, replaces the Eat Better and Feel Great footer text entered when you were using the AutoContent Wizard (Figure 4-14).

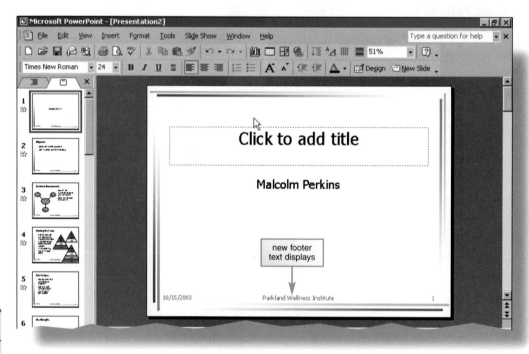

FIGURE 4-14

Other Ways

1. Press and hold down SHIFT key, click Normal View button, click Footer Area, type footer text, click Close Master View button on Slide Master View toolbar

2. Press ALT+V, press M, press S, type footer text, press ALT+C

3. In Voice Command mode, say "View, Master, Slide Master, [type footer text], Close Master View"

You have made a color scheme change on all eight slides in the presentation and a footer change on the title slide in the presentation. The next steps will change the content and graphics on individual slides.

Adding a Picture to Create a Custom Background

The new color scheme creates a white background on all slides. To generate audience interest in a presentation, you can add pictures. The next step is to insert an exercise picture to create a custom background. This picture is a bitmap graphic and is stored on the Data Disk. See the inside back cover of this book for instructions for downloading the Data Disk or see your instructor for information about accessing the files required for this book. Perform the following steps to add this picture to the Slide 1 background.

More About

Backgrounds

Some researchers have determined that audience members prefer viewing photographs instead of line art on a slide, although the line art may be more effective in carrying the desired message. In addition, viewers prefer color graphics as compared to black-and-white objects. The various colors, however, do not affect the amount of information retained. For more information, visit the PowerPoint 2002 More About Web page (scsite.com/ pp2002/more.htm) and then click Backgrounds.

 To Add a Picture to Create a Custom Background

1 **Right-click anywhere on Slide 1 except the title text placeholder. Click Background on the shortcut menu. When the Background dialog box displays, point to the Background fill box arrow.**

The Background dialog box displays (Figure 4-15).

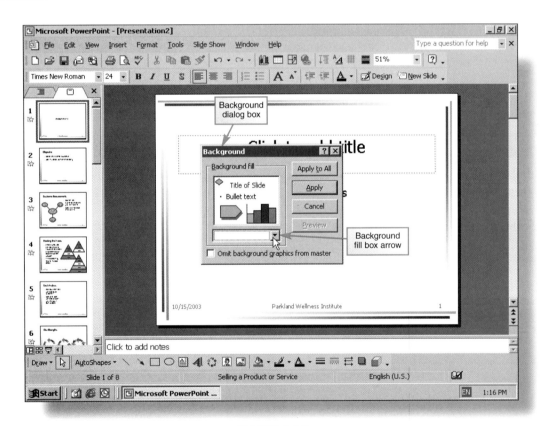

FIGURE 4-15

2 Click the Background fill box arrow. Point to Fill Effects on the menu.

The Background fill menu containing commands and options for filling the slide background displays (Figure 4-16). The current background fill color is Automatic, which is the Selecting a Product or Service design template default. The eight colors in the top row are for the new color scheme; the eight colors below this row are for the original color scheme. Fill Effects is highlighted.

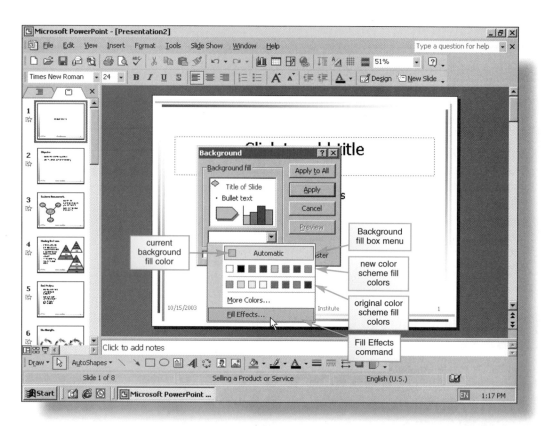

FIGURE 4-16

3 Click Fill Effects. When the Fill Effects dialog box displays, if necessary click the Picture tab and then point to the Select Picture button.

The Fill Effects dialog box displays (Figure 4-17).

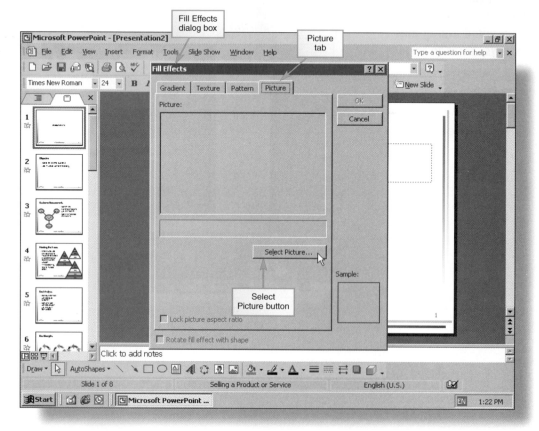

FIGURE 4-17

4 **Click the Select Picture button. When the Select Picture dialog box displays, click the Look in box arrow and then click 3½ Floppy (A:). Click the Workout thumbnail. Point to the Insert button.**

The Select Picture dialog box displays (Figure 4-18). The selected file, Workout, displays in the preview box.

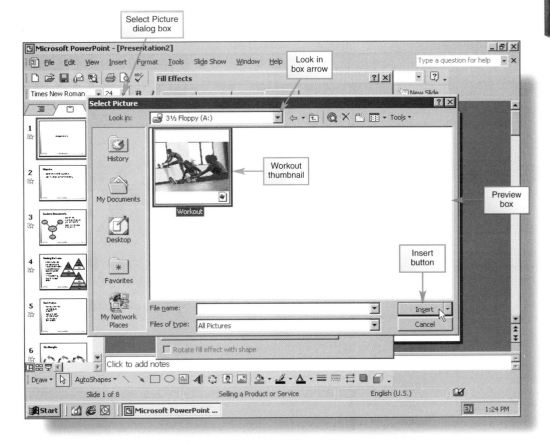

FIGURE 4-18

5 **Click the Insert button. When the picture displays in the Fill Effects dialog box, click the OK button. When the Background dialog box displays, point to the Apply button.**

The Background dialog box displays the Workout picture in the Background fill area (Figure 4-19). You could add the picture to Slide 1 or to all slides in the presentation.

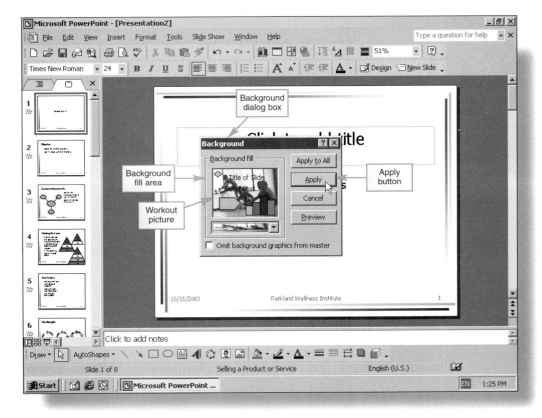

FIGURE 4-19

<table>
<tr><td>

6   **Click the Apply button.**

Slide 1 displays the Workout picture as the slide background (Figure 4-20). The Selling a Product or Service design template text attributes display on the slide.

</td><td>

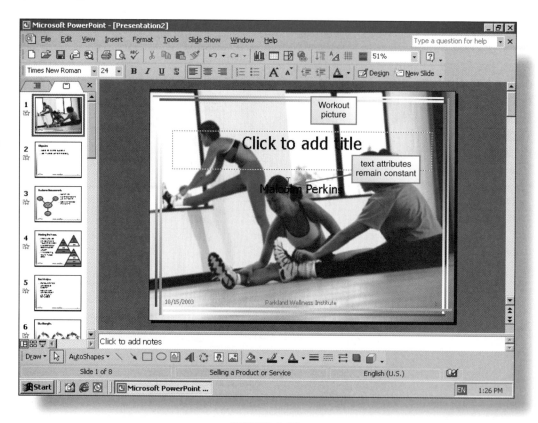

</td></tr>
</table>

FIGURE 4-20

Other Ways

1. On Format menu click Background, click Background fill box arrow, click Fill Effects, click Select Picture button, click Look in box arrow, click 3½ Floppy (A:), click desired picture, click Insert button, click OK button, click Apply button

2. Press ALT+O, press K, press DOWN ARROW key, press F, press LEFT ARROW key, press ALT+L, press ALT+I, press arrow key to select 3½ Floppy (A:), press ENTER, press TAB key three times, press arrow keys to selected desired picture, press ALT+S, press ENTER, press ENTER

3. In Voice Command mode, say "Format, Background"

When you customize the background, the design template text attributes remain the same, but the slide background changes. For example, adding the Workout picture to the slide background changes the appearance of the slide background but maintains the text attributes of the Selling a Product or Service design template.

Creating a WordArt Element and Adding It to a Slide

The Workout picture on Slide 1 is intended to generate interest in the presentation. Another method of attracting viewers is by using a **WordArt element**, which is text that has been altered with special effects. PowerPoint supplies 30 predefined WordArt styles that vary in shape and color.

Creating and adding the Get Fit WordArt element shown in Figure 4-1a on page PP 4.05 requires several steps. First, you delete the title text placeholder because you are going to use the WordArt element as the presentation title. Then, you create the WordArt object. Finally, you position and size the element on the title slide. The next several sections explain how to create the WordArt element and then add it to Slide 1.

Deleting the Title Text Placeholder

The Get Fit WordArt object will display at the top of Slide 1 as a substitution for title text. You need to delete the title text placeholder because you are not going to use it in this presentation.

Perform the following steps to delete the title text placeholder.

To Delete the Title Text Placeholder

1 **Click the title text placeholder and then point to the placeholder's selection rectangle.**

The mouse pointer changes to a four-headed arrow (Figure 4-21).

FIGURE 4-21

2 **Right-click the selection rectangle. Point to Cut on the shortcut menu (Figure 4-22)**

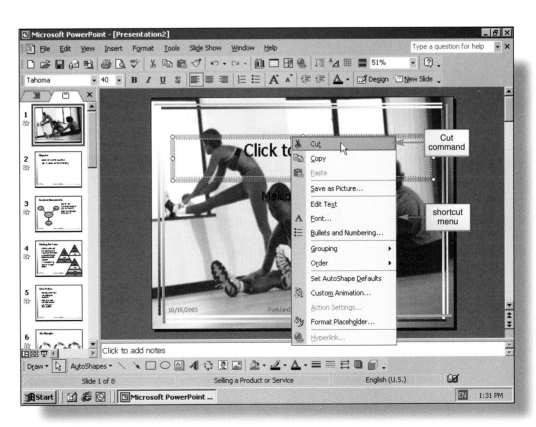

FIGURE 4-22

3 **Click Cut.**

Slide 1 displays without the title text placeholder (Figure 4-23).

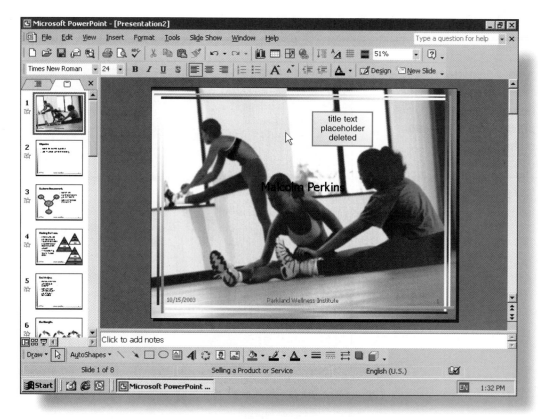

FIGURE 4-23

 Ways

1. Click title text placeholder selection rectangle, click Cut button on Standard toolbar
2. Click title text placeholder selection rectangle, on Edit menu click Cut
3. Click title text placeholder selection rectangle, press CTRL+X
4. In Voice Command mode, say "Edit, Cut"

With the title text placeholder deleted, you can create the WordArt element. The Get Fit title on Slide 1, shown in Figure 4-1a on page 4.05, contains letters that have been altered with special text effects. Using WordArt, first you will select a letter style for this text. Then, you will type the name of the presentation and select a unique height and width for its layout. Many predefined shapes could be used, and buttons on the WordArt toolbar allow you to rotate, slant, curve, and alter the shape of letters. WordArt also can be used in the other Microsoft Office applications. The next several sections explain how to create the text WordArt element.

Selecting a WordArt Style

PowerPoint supplies WordArt styles with a variety of shapes and colors. Perform the following steps to select a style for the Get Fit text.

Steps To Select a WordArt Style

1 **Click the Insert WordArt button on the Drawing toolbar. When the WordArt Gallery dialog box displays, click the WordArt style in row 3, column 2. Point to the OK button.**

The WordArt Gallery dialog box displays (Figure 4-24).

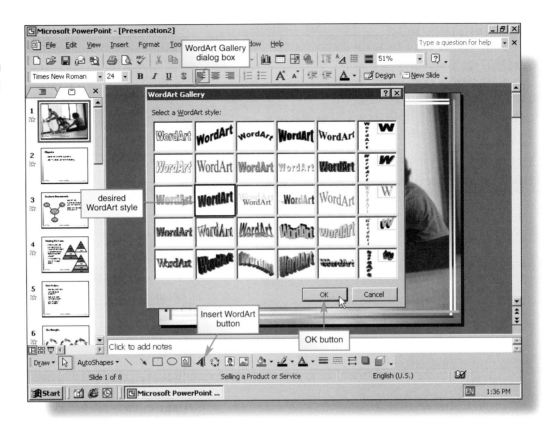

FIGURE 4-24

2 **Click the OK button.**

The Edit WordArt Text dialog box displays (Figure 4-25). The default text, Your Text Here, in the Text text box is selected.

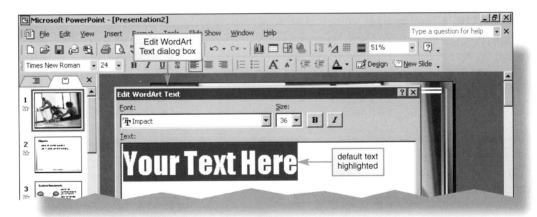

FIGURE 4-25

Entering the WordArt Text

To create a text element, you must enter text in the Edit WordArt Text dialog box. By default, the words, Your Text Here, in the Text text box are selected. When you type the text for your title object, it replaces the selected text. When you want to start a new line, press the ENTER key. Perform the steps on the next page to enter the text for the Get Fit heading.

Other Ways

1. On Insert menu point to Picture, click WordArt, click desired style, click OK
2. Press ALT+I, press P, press W, press arrow keys to select desired style, press ENTER
3. In Voice Command mode, say "Insert, Picture, WordArt, [click desired style], OK"

Steps **To Enter the WordArt Text**

1 **If necessary, select the text in the Edit WordArt Text dialog box. Type** Get Fit **in the Text text box. Point to the OK button.**

The text displays in the Text text box in the Edit WordArt Text dialog box (Figure 4-26). The default font is Impact, and the font size is 36.

FIGURE 4-26

2 **Click the OK button. If necessary, display the WordArt toolbar by right-clicking a toolbar and then clicking WordArt.**

The Get Fit text displays (Figure 4-27). The WordArt toolbar displays in the same location and with the same shape as it displayed the last time it was used. You can move the WordArt toolbar by dragging its title bar.

1. Type text, press ENTER
2. In Dictation mode, say "Get Fit"

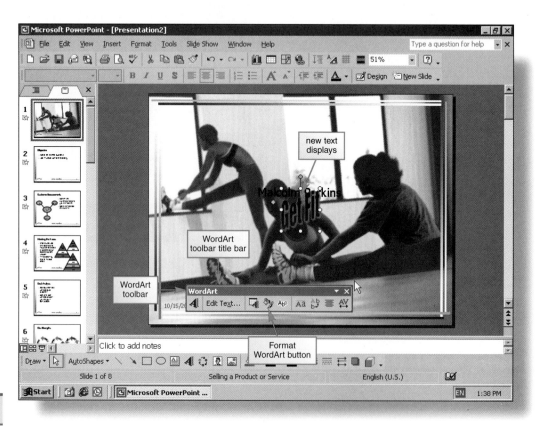

FIGURE 4-27

The WordArt toolbar contains buttons that allow you to change an object's appearance. For example, you can rotate the letters, change the character spacing and alignment, scale the size, and add different fill and line colors. Table 4-2 explains the purpose of each button on the WordArt toolbar.

Table 4-2	WordArt Toolbar Button Functions	
BUTTON	**BUTTON NAME**	**DESCRIPTION**
	Insert WordArt	Creates a WordArt element
Edit Te<u>x</u>t...	Edit Text	Changes the text characters, font, and font size
	WordArt Gallery	Chooses a different WordArt style for the selected WordArt object
	Format WordArt	Formats the color, lines, size, pattern, position, and other properties of the selected object
Abc	WordArt Shape	Modifies the text into one of 30 shapes
Aa	WordArt Same Letter Heights	Makes all letters the same height, regardless of case
Ab bJ	WordArt Vertical Text	Stacks the text in the selected WordArt object vertically — one letter on top of the other — for reading from top to bottom
	WordArt Alignment	Left-aligns, centers, right-aligns, word-justifies, letter-justifies, or stretch-justifies text
AV	WordArt Character Spacing	Displays options (Very Tight, Tight, Normal, Loose, Very Loose, Custom, Kern Character Pairs) for adjusting spacing between text

The next section explains how to change the WordArt height and width.

Changing the WordArt Height and Width

WordArt objects actually are drawing objects, not text. Consequently, WordArt objects can be modified in various ways, including changing their height, width, line style, fill color, and shadows. Unlike text, however, they neither can display in outline view nor be spell checked. In this project, you will increase the height and width of the WordArt object. The Size tab in the Format WordArt dialog box contains two areas used to change an object's size. The first, the **Size and rotate area**, allows you to enlarge or reduce an object, and the rotate area allows you to turn an object around its axis. The second, the **Scale area**, allows you to change an object's size while maintaining its height-to-width ratio, or **aspect ratio**. If you want to retain the object's original settings, you click the Reset button in the **Original size area**. Perform the steps on the next page to change the height and width of the WordArt object.

More About

Compressing Pictures

Pictures, graphics, and other visual images increase the presentation file size tremendously. PowerPoint 2002 includes a feature that compresses these elements. To reduce the size, click the Compress Pictures button on the Picture toolbar and then click All pictures in document. In the Change resolution area, click either Web/Screen or Print. Click Compress pictures and Delete cropped areas of pictures if you are certain you will not need to restore these images to their original sizes and resolutions. Click the OK button.

To Change the WordArt Height and Width

1 **Click the Format WordArt button on the WordArt toolbar. Click the Size tab in the Format WordArt dialog box. Point to the Height text box in the Size and rotate area.**

The Size sheet displays in the Format WordArt dialog box (Figure 4-28). The Get Fit text currently is 1.41 inches high and 1.26 inches wide.

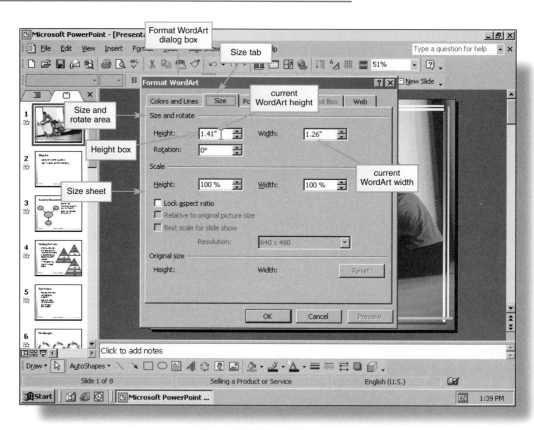

FIGURE 4-28

2 **Triple-click the Height text box in the Size and rotate area. Type 2.85 in the Height text box. Triple-click the Width text box in the Size and rotate area. Type 4.1 in the Width text box. Point to the OK button.**

The Height and Width text boxes display the new entries (Figure 4-29).

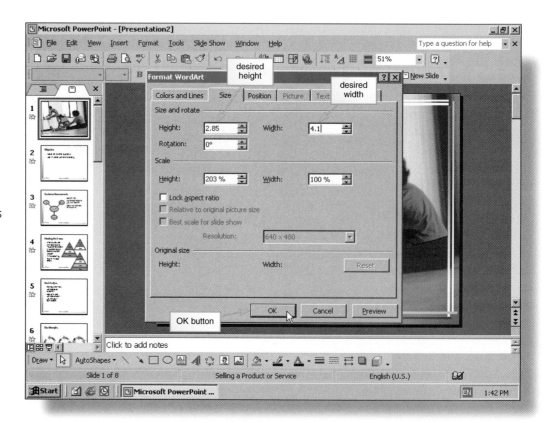

FIGURE 4-29

3   **Click the OK button.**

The WordArt text object displays.

4   **Drag the text object until the bottom of the letter G displays above the M in Malcolm Perkins's name. If necessary, you can make small adjustments in the position of the object by pressing the arrow keys on the keyboard that correspond to the direction in which to move.**

The WordArt text object is positioned correctly (Figure 4-30).

FIGURE 4-30

Entering the Presentation Subtitle and Adding a Sound Effect

The final modifications to the title slide are entering and positioning the subtitle text and then adding music to play when the subtitle displays during a slide show.

Entering and Positioning the Presentation Subtitle

Perform the steps on the next page to enter information about the healthy eating seminar in the subtitle text placeholder.

Other Ways

1. Right-click WordArt object, click Format WordArt on shortcut menu, click Size tab, triple-click Height text box in Size and rotate area, type new value, triple-click Width text box in Size and rotate area, type new value, click OK button

2. Press ALT+O, press O, press ALT+E, enter percent, press ALT+D, type new value, press ENTER

3. In Voice Command mode, say "Format, WordArt, Size, Height, [type new value], Width, [type appropriate percent], OK"

Steps **To Enter and Position the Presentation Subtitle**

1 **If the WordArt toolbar displays, click the Close button on the WordArt toolbar. Triple-click the text, Malcolm Perkins, in the subtitle text placeholder to select the name. Type** Eat Better and Feel Great **but do not press the ENTER key. Point to the middle sizing handle on the bottom edge of the subtitle text placeholder.**

The default text inserted by the AutoContent Wizard is replaced with the desired text. The mouse pointer changes to a double-headed arrow (Figure 4-31).

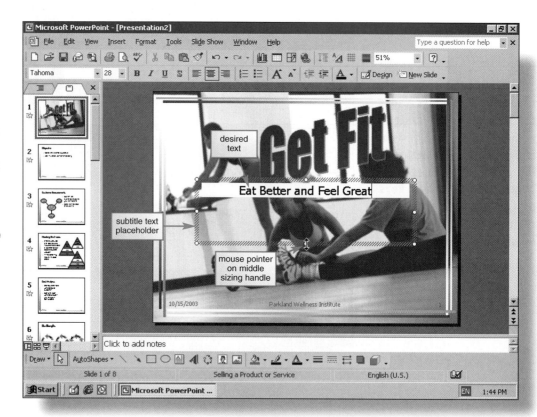

FIGURE 4-31

2 **Drag the sizing handle up until it is below the new subtitle text. Point to the placeholder's selection rectangle.**

The subtitle text placeholder size fits the new text. The mouse pointer changes to a four-headed arrow (Figure 4-32). If the AutoFit Options smart tag displays, click it and then click, Stop Fitting Text to This Placeholder.

FIGURE 4-32

3 Drag the subtitle text down until it displays above the Parkland Wellness Institute footer text. If necessary, you can make small adjustments in the position of the object by pressing the arrow keys on the keyboard that correspond to the direction in which you want to move.

The subtitle text is positioned correctly (Figure 4-33).

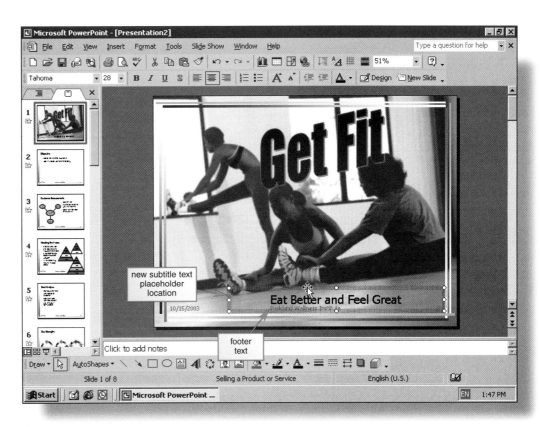

FIGURE 4-33

Adding a Sound Effect

Using a **sound effect** calls attention to areas of interest or importance to which a presenter may want to call attention, such as the subtitle text in this presentation. PowerPoint allows you to add sounds and music to a presentation. These sounds can be from the Microsoft Clip Organizer, files you have stored on your computer, a CD, and the Internet. To hear the sound effects, you need speakers and a sound card on your system. An upbeat sports theme works well with this fitness presentation. During the slide show, the sound clip, Sports Open, should play when the Slide 1 subtitle text displays. This clip is available from the Microsoft Clip Organizer and the Microsoft Design Gallery Live site, and it is on your Data Disk. It is a **Musical Instrument Digital Interface** (**MIDI**) file, which uses a standard format to encode and communicate music and sound between computers, music synthesizers, and instruments. Perform the steps on the next page to add the music to Slide 1.

More About

Playing a CD

If you have a CD track that adds interest and variety to the presentation, insert the CD into the CD-ROM drive, click the slide that you want to display when the track starts, click Insert on the menu bar, point to Movies and Sounds, and then click Play CD Audio Track. Click Loop until stopped to keep the track playing throughout the presentation. Then enter the specific track and the starting and ending times.

Steps **To Add a Sound Effect**

1 **Click Insert on the menu bar and then point to Movies and Sounds. Point to Sound from File on the Movies and Sounds submenu.**

The Insert menu and Movies and Sounds submenu display (Figure 4-34).

FIGURE 4-34

2 **Click Sound from File. When the Insert Sound dialog box displays, click the Look in box arrow and then click 3½ Floppy (A:). Click Sports Open. Point to the OK button.**

The Insert Sound dialog box displays the Sports Open file (Figure 4-35). The music note icon preceding the file name indicates the file is a MIDI Sequence file. Your list of file names may vary.

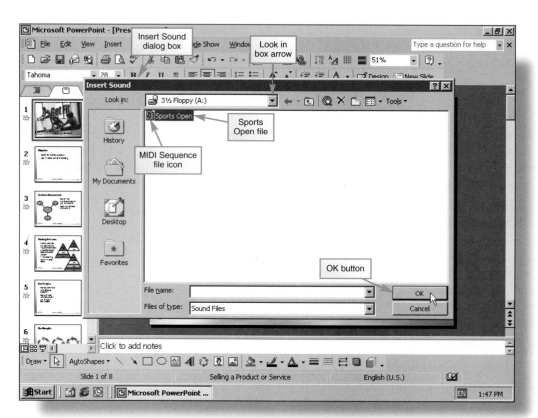

FIGURE 4-35

3 Click the OK button. When the Microsoft PowerPoint dialog box displays, click the Yes button.

The speaker icon indicates the sound is added to Slide 1. Clicking the Yes button instructs PowerPoint to play the Sports Open sound file automatically when the subtitle text displays during a slide show. Clicking the No button tells PowerPoint to play the sound when you click Slide 1 after the subtitle text displays.

4 Drag the speaker icon off the slide to the lower-right corner of the screen.

You cannot hide the speaker icon, but you can drag it off the slide because it is set to play automatically during the slide show (Figure 4-36). If you had not selected the automatic option, you would have to click the speaker icon to play the sound effect.

FIGURE 4-36

Creating a Folder and Saving a Presentation

You now should create a folder and save the presentation because you changed the subtitle text to reflect the purpose of the new presentation, deleted the title text and replaced it with a WordArt object, and inserted a picture to create a custom background. A **folder** is a specific location on a disk. Saving the presentation in a folder helps organize your files. Perform the steps on the next page to create a folder and save the presentation.

Other Ways

1. Press ALT+I, press V, press N, press ALT+I, press UP ARROW key to select 3½ Floppy (A:), press ENTER, press TAB three times, press arrow keys to select desired file, press ENTER, press ENTER

2. In Voice Command mode, say "Insert, Movies and Sounds, Sound from File, [click desired file], OK, Yes"

Steps **To Create a Folder and Save a Presentation**

1 **Click the Save button on the Standard toolbar. When the Save As dialog box displays, type** Eating Well **in the File name text box.**

2 **Click the Save in box arrow. Click 3½ Floppy (A:) in the Save in list. Point to the Create New Folder button on the Save As dialog box toolbar.**

The buttons on the Save As dialog box toolbar allow you to select folders or change the display (Figure 4-37).

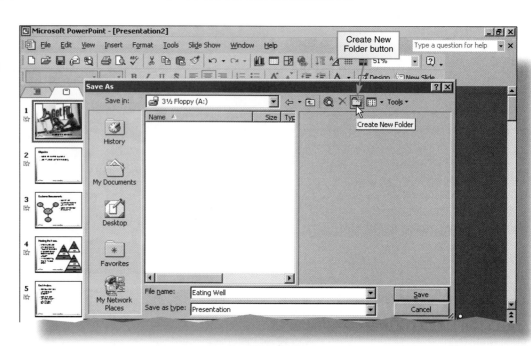

FIGURE 4-37

3 **Click the Create New Folder button. When the New Folder dialog box displays, type** Wellness Institute **in the Name text box. Point to the OK button.**

Wellness Institute is the name of the folder being created (Figure 4-38).

4 **Click the OK button.**

The Wellness Institute folder displays in the Save in box.

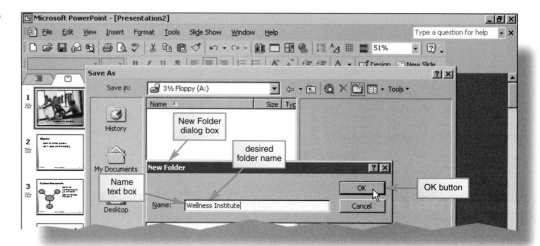

FIGURE 4-38

5 **Click the Save button.**

The presentation is saved in the Wellness Institute folder on the floppy disk in drive A with the file name Eating Well. This file name displays on the title bar (Figure 4-39).

FIGURE 4-39

Deleting Slides

This section adds a chart on Slide 5; deletes the graphics on Slide 6; inserts a Word table and an Excel chart on Slide 7; and modifies Slide 8. Slides 2, 3, and 4 are not needed in this presentation. One quick method of deleting multiple slides is to use the **SHIFT+click technique** to select more than one slide. To perform the SHIFT+click technique, press and hold down the SHIFT key as you click the starting and ending range of desired slides. After you click the slides, release the SHIFT key. Perform the following steps to delete these slides.

More About

Deleting Slides

PowerPoint does not display a warning message when you press the DELETE key to delete a slide. If you delete a slide inadvertently, click the Undo button to insert the slide.

TO DELETE SLIDES

1 Click the Slide 2 slide thumbnail on the Slides tab.

2 Press and hold down the SHIFT key and then click Slide 4. Release the SHIFT key.

3 Press the DELETE key.

Slides 2, 3, and 4 are deleted (Figure 4-40). The presentation now is composed of five slides.

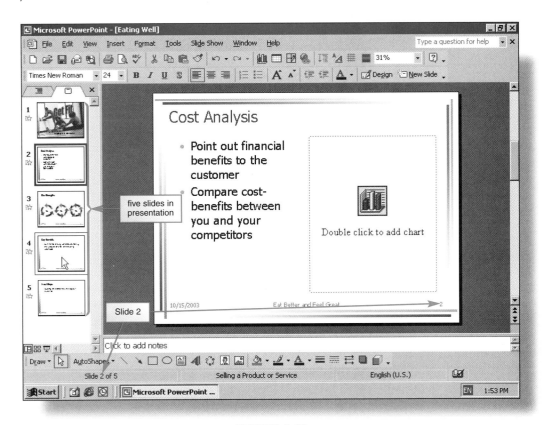

FIGURE 4-40

More About

Copyrights

Some PowerPoint users download files illegally from the Internet and then insert these graphics and text documents into their slides. Congress passed the Online Copyright Infringement Liability Limitation Act of 1998 to address the widespread practice of online copyright infringement. This law makes it difficult for Internet service providers to be found liable for the actions of their subscribers. To learn about the legal cases and legislative process that led to this law, visit the PowerPoint 2002 More About Web page (scsite.com/pp2002/more.htm) and then click Copyrights.

Adding a Chart to a Slide

The chart on Slide 2 shows survey results that indicate how the eating habits of members of the Wellness Institute have changed during the past eight years. The findings denote that members have been eating more vegetables and fruits, and they have been cutting fats from their diets. The chart on Slide 2, shown in Figure 4-41, shows how the diets have improved. You will build this chart directly within the PowerPoint presentation using the supplementary application called **Microsoft Graph**, which is installed automatically with PowerPoint.

When you start to create this diet improvement chart, Microsoft Graph opens and displays a chart and associated data. The default Microsoft Graph chart style is a **3-D Column chart**. This style compares values across categories and across series. The 3-D Column chart is appropriate when comparing two or more items in specified intervals, such as in this Slide 2 chart depicting how the Wellness Institute members have varied their consumption of vegetables, fruits, and fats during the previous four- and eight-year periods.

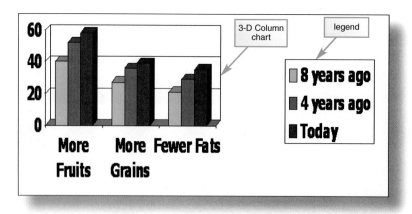

FIGURE 4-41

More About

Sample Data

The Microsoft Graph sample datasheet displays five rows and six columns. To display additional rows and columns, click the scroll boxes and scroll arrows. Drag the window corner in the lower-right corner of the datasheet to increase the datasheet size.

The figures for the chart are entered in a corresponding **datasheet**, which is a rectangular grid containing columns (vertical) and rows (horizontal). Column letters display above the grid to identify particular **columns**, and row numbers display on the left side of the grid to identify particular **rows**. **Cells** are the intersections of rows and columns, and they are the locations for the chart data and text labels. For example, cell A1 is the intersection of column A and row 1. Numeric and text data are entered in the **active cell**, which is the one cell surrounded by a heavy border. You will replace the sample data in the datasheet by typing entries in the cells, but you also can import data from a text file or Lotus 1-2-3 file, import a Microsoft Excel worksheet or chart, or paste data obtained in another program.

Editing the Title and Bulleted List Text

Before you create the 3-D Column chart, you first must edit the text generated by the AutoContent Wizard. The following steps describe these tasks.

TO EDIT THE TITLE AND BULLETED LIST TEXT

1 With Slide 2 displaying, triple-click the title text, Cost Analysis. Type Improving Our Diets in the title text placeholder.

2 Triple-click the first first-level paragraph in the text placeholder.

3 Type Wellness Institute members are eating better as the new text.

4 Triple-click the second first-level paragraph in the text placeholder.

5 Type Survey shows we consume more fruits and grains and fewer fats as the new text.

6 Click the Increase Indent button on the Formatting toolbar.

Slide 2 displays with the edited text (Figure 4-42).

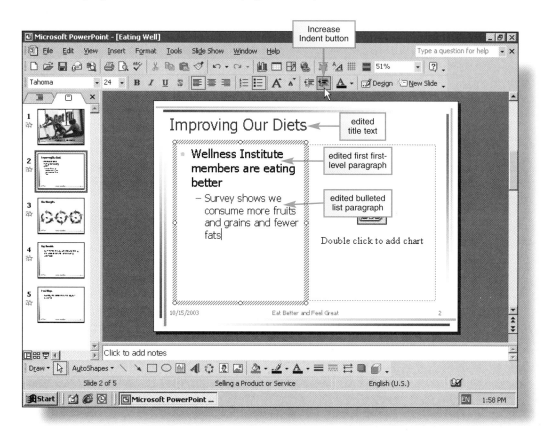

FIGURE 4-42

Changing the Slide Layout and Positioning the Text Placeholder

The next steps require changing the layout so the chart displays above the text placeholder and then positioning the text placeholder above the footer. The steps on the next page describe this procedure.

More *About*

AutoNumber Bullets

Graphical bullets allow you to customize your presentation. Numbered bullets also give your slides a customized look. PowerPoint's AutoNumber feature adds numbers to the beginning of each slide paragraph. To use this feature, first remove any bullets by pressing the BACKSPACE key. Then type the number 1 or the Roman numeral one and either a period or a closing parenthesis. Type the paragraph text and then press the ENTER key. PowerPoint will add the next consecutive number or Roman numeral. You can modify the slide master to change the default numbering settings.

TO CHANGE THE SLIDE LAYOUT AND POSITION THE TEXT PLACEHOLDER

1 Click Format on the menu bar and then click Slide Layout.

2 Click the Title and Content over Text slide layout in the Text and Content Layouts area of the Slide Layout task pane.

3 Click the Close button in the Slide Layout task pane.

4 Drag the middle sizing handle on the bottom edge of the text placeholder up until it is below the second first-level paragraph.

5 Drag the text placeholder down until it displays above the Eat Better and Feel Great footer text. If the AutoFit Options smart tag displays, click it and then click, Stop Fitting Text to This Placeholder.

Slide 2 has the desired Title and Content over Text slide layout. The text placeholder displays in the desired position (Figure 4-43).

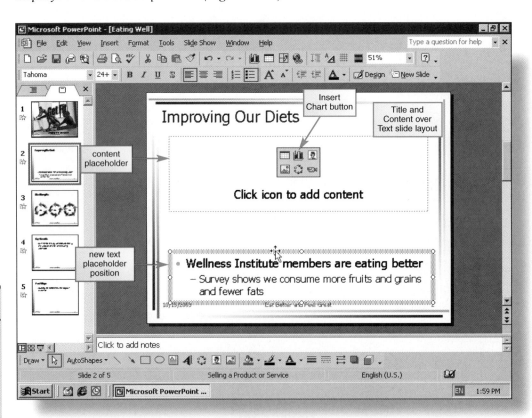

FIGURE 4-43

Adding Data

In this presentation you add your own data to the datasheet. At times, however, you may want to import data from a text file, a Lotus 1-2-3 file, a Microsoft Excel worksheet or chart, or another program. This data can be a maximum of 4,000 rows by 4,000 columns, and a maximum of 255 data series can be displayed on the chart. To add this data, select the cell where the imported data will begin, click the Import File button on the Standard toolbar, click the data location in the Look in box, and then double-click the file you want to import. If you import a text file, the Text Import Wizard will help you arrange the data on the datasheet.

Adequate space has been allocated for the chart. Creating the chart shown in Figure 4-41 on page PP 4.32 requires replacing the sample data. The following section describes how to perform this action.

Inserting a Chart and Replacing the Sample Data

Microsoft Graph provides sample data to create the default chart. You need to change these figures to the numbers representing the members' consumption of fruits, grains, and fats eight years ago, four years ago, and today. Table 4-3 summarizes the survey data. Each column represents the percentage of Wellness Institute members who modified their diets eight years ago, four years ago, and today by eating more fruits and grains and fewer fats. The numbers are entered into rows 1 through 3, and the titles are entered above the data rows in columns A, B, and C. The legend titles are entered in the first column. The chart **legend** identifies each bar in the chart. In this case, the aqua bar identifies the 1st quarter results, the pink bar identifies the 2nd quarter, and the purple bar identifies the 3rd quarter. The sample data displays in four columns; the Wellness Institute survey requires only three categories: fruits, grains, and fats. You therefore need to delete one column of sample data. The following steps describe how to replace the sample data.

More About

Formatting Text

You can format the font used for the legend and axes. To format the legend, right-click the legend, click Format Legend on the shortcut menu, click the Font tab, and then select font attributes, such as font style, size, color, and effects. To format the axes, right-click an axis, click Format Axis on the shortcut menu, click the Font tab, and then make the selections.

Table 4-3	Diet Improvement Survey Data		
	MORE FRUITS	*MORE GRAINS*	*FEWER FATS*
8 years ago	40	27	21
4 years ago	52	36	29
Today	58	39	35

Steps **To Insert a Chart and Replace the Sample Data**

1 **Click the Insert Chart button in the content placeholder. Right-click the letter D at the top of column D in the datasheet and then point to Clear Contents on the shortcut menu.**

Microsoft Graph displays the sample datasheet and chart (Figure 4-44). The cells in column D are selected.

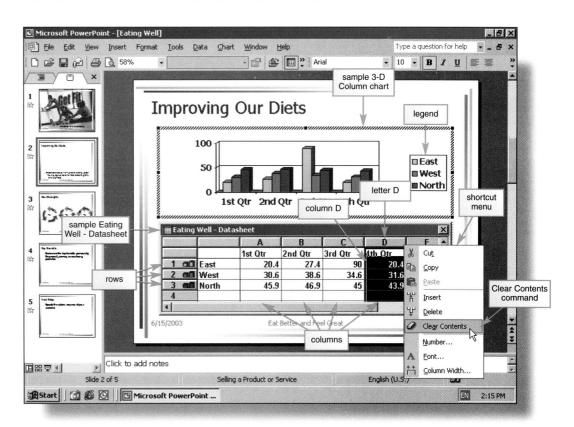

FIGURE 4-44

2 **Click Clear Contents. Click cell A1, which is the intersection of column A and row 1.**

Cell A1 is selected (Figure 4-45). The mouse pointer changes to a block plus sign.

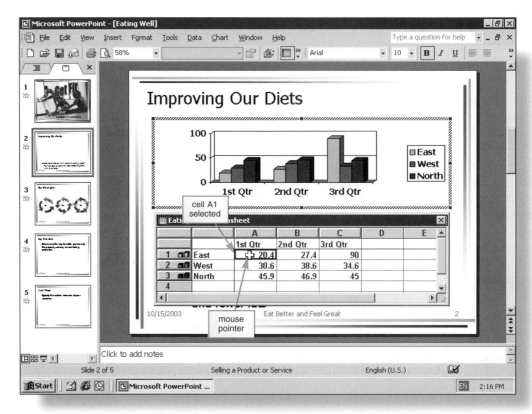

FIGURE 4-45

3 **Type 40 in cell A1 and then press the RIGHT ARROW key. Enter the remaining figures and data labels by using Table 4-3 on the previous page as a guide. Point to the Close button on the datasheet.**

As you type these figures and data labels in the datasheet, they modify the chart (Figure 4-46).

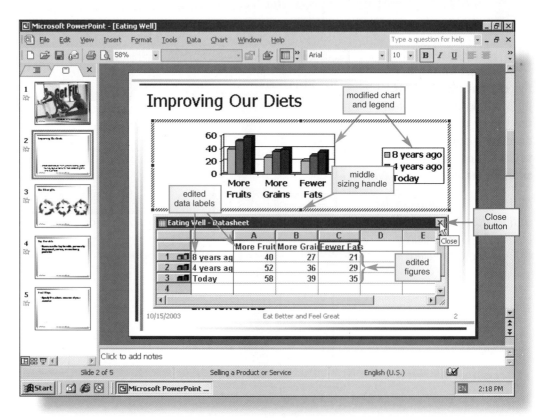

FIGURE 4-46

4 **Click the Close button. Click the slide anywhere except the chart window.**

The datasheet closes and the revised chart and legend display.

5 **Drag the middle sizing handle on the bottom edge of the chart window down until it is above the first bulleted paragraph in the text placeholder.**

The chart and legend display in the desired location on Slide 2 (Figure 4-47).

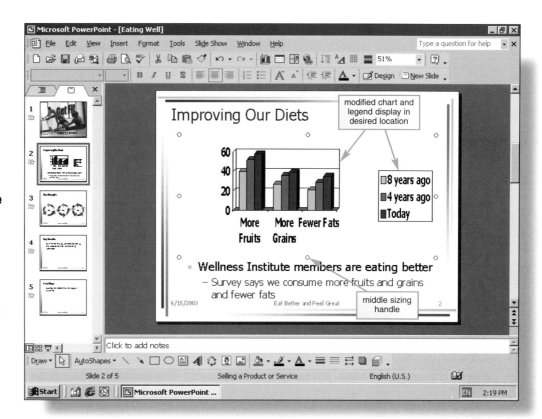

FIGURE 4-47

The diet data has been entered in the Microsoft Graph datasheet. The three categories surveyed — more fruits, more grains, and fewer fats — display. Slide 2 is complete. You should save the presentation by clicking the Save button on the Standard toolbar.

The next slide in the presentation also will have a chart. Unlike the chart you just created using Microsoft Graph, this chart was created in Microsoft Excel. You will insert this chart into Slide 3. This graphic describes the calories burned when specific aerobic activities are performed for one hour.

Inserting an Excel Chart

Aerobic activity helps burn calories and strengthen the cardiovascular system. These important benefits should be of interest to Wellness Institute members, so you want to emphasize the aerobic qualities of various exercises. A chart created in Microsoft Excel can depict how common sports activities burn calories depending on an individual's weight. A **Clustered Bar chart** compares values across categories. Similarly, the caloric expenditure chart shown in Figure 4-48 on the next page illustrates the number of calories burned per hour for each sport depending on the individual's weight.

Other **Ways**

1. On Insert menu click Chart, click column D, on Edit menu point to Clear, click All, enter data, on View menu click Datasheet

2. Press ALT+I, press H, click column D, press ALT+E, press A, press A, enter data, press ALT+V, press D

3. In Voice Command mode, say "Insert, Chart, [click column D], Edit, Clear, All, [enter data], View, Datasheet"

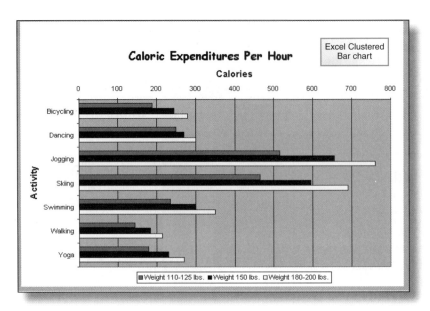

FIGURE 4-48

Modifying a Chart

If you work on a chart, return to PowerPoint, and then click Undo before you make any changes to the presentation, you will undo all the changes you made to your chart. In fact, you may delete the chart itself. To undo individual changes made to a chart, double-click the chart to activate it. Then manually undo the changes.

PowerPoint allows you to insert, or **embed**, many types of objects into a presentation. You inserted clips into slides in Projects 2 and 3, and you will embed a Microsoft Word table into Slide 4. Other objects you can embed include video clips, Microsoft PhotoDraw pictures, and Adobe Acrobat documents.

Displaying the Next Slide, Editing the Title Text, and Deleting AutoShape Objects

Before you insert the Excel chart from the Data Disk, you need to display the next slide, change the title text, and delete the AutoShape objects. The AutoContent Wizard generated a slide with three circular AutoShapes. An **AutoShape** is a ready-made object, such as a line, star, banner, arrow, connector, or callout. These shapes can be sized, rotated, flipped, colored, and combined to add unique qualities to a presentation. Most of the shapes contain an **adjustment handle** that allows changes to the object, such as changing the size of an arrow. The AutoShapes are available on the Drawing toolbar and in the Clip Organizer. Text boxes with the word, Text, display in the three AutoShapes on Slide 3. A **text box** is a moveable, resizable area that can contain text or graphics. Perform the following steps to display the slide, enter a title, and delete the three AutoShape objects.

TO DISPLAY THE NEXT SLIDE, EDIT THE TITLE TEXT, AND DELETE THE AUTOSHAPE OBJECTS

1 Click the Next Slide button to display Slide 3.

2 Triple-click the title text, Our Strengths. Type Exercise Burns Calories in the title text placeholder.

3 Click one of the arrows in the left AutoShape and then press the DELETE key.

4 Repeat Step 3 for the middle and right AutoShapes.

Slide 3 displays with the new title text and deleted AutoShapes (Figure 4-49).

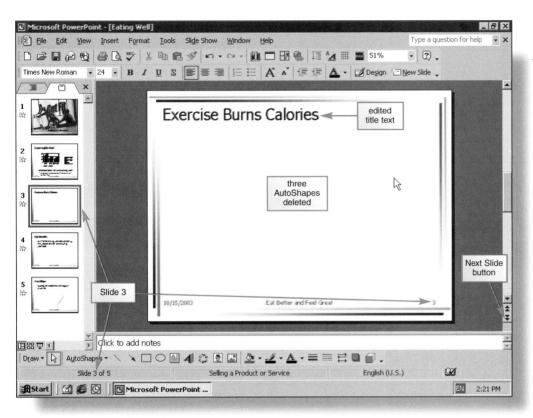

FIGURE 4-49

Slide 3 now displays the slide title and a blank area for the Excel chart. The next section explains how to insert this Excel chart.

Inserting an Excel Chart

The Clustered Bar chart on the Data Disk compares how many calories people with varying weights burn per hour when they are engaging in athletic activities.
Perform the steps on the next page to insert an Excel chart.

Editing Excel Charts

To edit an Excel chart you import into your slide, double-click the chart, use the Microsoft Excel tools and menus to modify the chart, and then click outside the chart to return to PowerPoint.

To Insert an Excel Chart

1 **Click Insert on the menu bar and then point to Object.**

The Insert menu displays (Figure 4-50). You want to insert the chart created in Microsoft Excel and saved on your Data Disk.

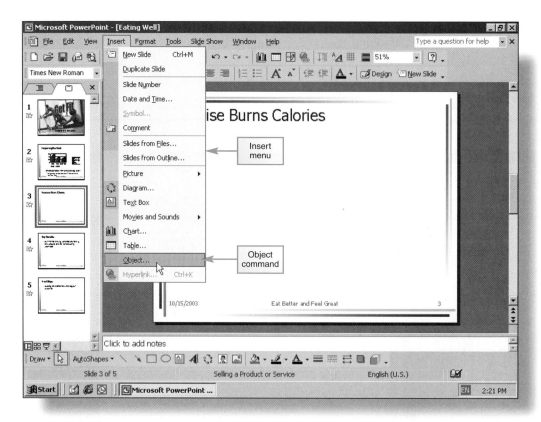

FIGURE 4-50

2 **Click Object. When the Insert Object dialog box displays, click Create from file. Point to the Browse button.**

The Insert Object dialog box displays (Figure 4-51). The Create from file option allows you to select an object created in another application or in PowerPoint.

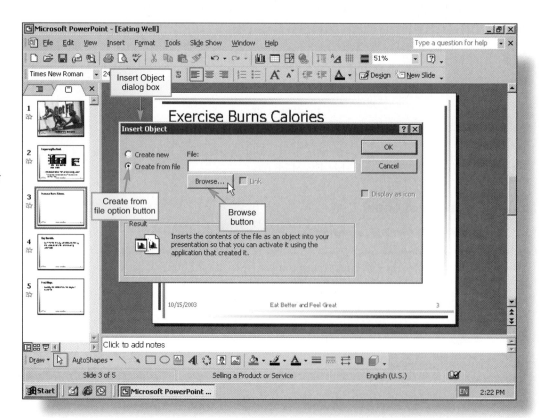

FIGURE 4-51

3 **Click the Browse button. When the Browse dialog box displays, click the Look in box arrow and then click 3½ Floppy (A:). Click Calories in the Look in list. Point to the OK button.**

The Browse dialog box displays the files on the Data Disk (Figure 4-52). Your list of file names may vary. Calories is the Excel file you will insert into Slide 3.

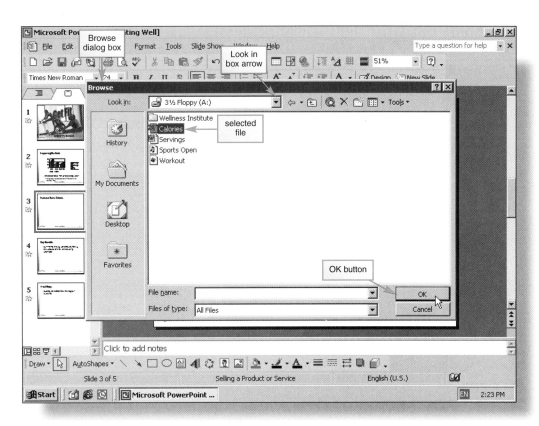

FIGURE 4-52

4 **Click the OK button. When the Insert Object dialog box redisplays, point to the OK button.**

*The Insert Object dialog box now displays A:\Calories.xls in the File text box. The **.xls extension** indicates the file is a Microsoft Excel file.*

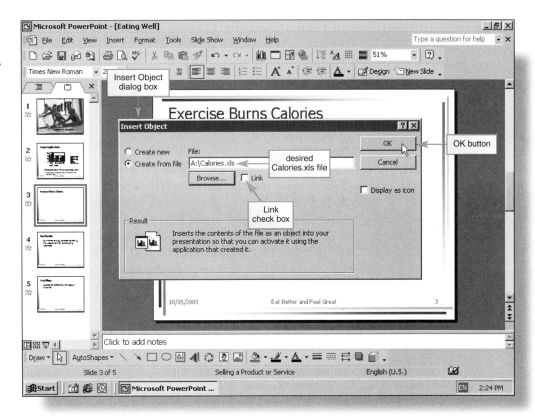

FIGURE 4-53

5 **Click the OK button.**

Slide 3 displays the Calories chart (Figure 4-54).

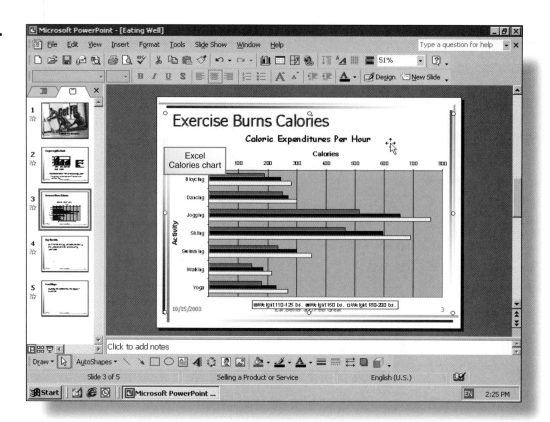

FIGURE 4-54

Other Ways

1. Press ALT+I, press O, press ALT+F, type file name, click OK button
2. In Voice Command mode, say "Insert, Object, Create from file, [type file name], OK"

File Formats

Having problems distinguishing .ppt from .pps? Microsoft PowerPoint Help includes a table listing file types, extensions, and uses. Type `file formats for saving presentations` in the Ask a Question box and then press the ENTER key. When the list of topics displays, click File formats for saving presentations. To print the table, click the Print button in the Microsoft PowerPoint Help window.

When you click the Create from file option button in the Insert Object dialog box, the dialog box changes. The File box replaces the Object type box. Another change to the dialog box is the addition of the Link check box. If the **Link check box** is selected, the object is inserted as a linked, instead of an embedded, object. Like an embedded object, a **linked object** also is created in another application; however, the linked object maintains a connection to its source. If the original object is changed, the linked object on the slide also changes. The linked object is stored in the **source file**, the file in which the object was created.

For example, the Excel chart you embedded into the slide is stored on the Data Disk. If you were to link rather than embed the Calories file, then every time the Calories file changed in Excel, the changes would display on the chart on Slide 3. Your PowerPoint presentation would store a representation of the original Calories file and information about its location. If you later moved or deleted the source file, the link would be broken, and the object would not be available. Consequently, if you make a presentation on a computer other than the one on which the presentation was created and the presentation contains a linked object, be certain to include a copy of the source files. The source files must be stored in the exact location as originally specified when you linked them to your presentation.

When you select a source file from the Browse dialog box, PowerPoint associates the file with a specific application, which is based on the file extension. For example, if you select a source file with the file extension **.doc**, PowerPoint recognizes the file as a Microsoft Word file. Additionally, if you select a source file with the file extension **.xls**, PowerPoint recognizes the file as a Microsoft Excel file.

Scaling and Moving an Excel Chart

Sufficient space exists on Slide 3 to reduce the chart so the legend does not overlap the footer. Perform the following steps to scale the chart object.

TO SCALE AND MOVE AN EXCEL CHART

1 Right-click the Calories chart and then click Format Object on the shortcut menu.

2 If necessary, click the Size tab in the Format Object dialog box.

3 Click and hold down the mouse button on the Height box down arrow in the Scale area until 95 % displays and then release the mouse button.

4 Click the OK button.

5 Drag the Calories chart to the right so it is centered on the slide. If necessary, you can make small adjustments by pressing the arrow keys on the keyboard that correspond to the direction in which to move.

The Excel chart is reduced and moved to the desired position (Figure 4-55).

Other Ways

1. On Format menu click Object, click Size tab, click Scale Height box up arrow to display desired height, click OK button

2. Press ALT+O, press O, press RIGHT ARROW key, press ALT+H, press UP ARROW key to display desired height, press ENTER

3. In Voice Command mode, say "Format, Object, Height, [type height], OK"

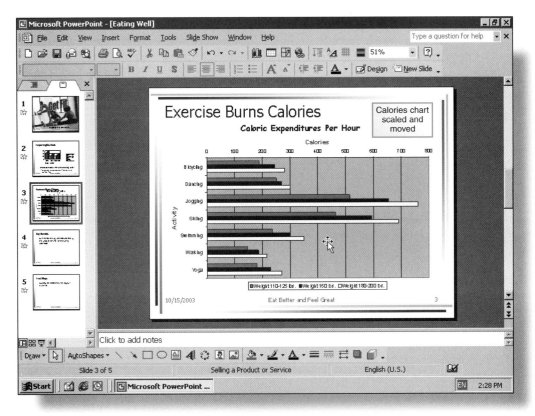

FIGURE 4-55

Slide 3 now is complete. Again, because you have changed the presentation significantly, save the slide show by clicking the Save button on the Standard toolbar. The next slide also will have a graphic that shows the amount of fiber and calories contained in fruits, cooked vegetables, and breads.

More About

Objects in Notes

Pictures and objects can be included in your notes. To add these objects, click Notes Page on the View menu and add the desired objects. These visuals will print when you specify Notes Pages in the Print dialog box. They will not, however, display in the notes pane.

Editing a Word Table

To edit a Word table you import into your slide, double-click the table and then use the Word tools and menus to format the table. For example, to change the width of the table, click the Table Properties command on the Table menu, click the Table tab, click Preferred width in the Size area, and then enter the new measurement in the Preferred width text box.

Adding a Table from Word

The Eating Well presentation now shows how Wellness Institute members' diets have been improving and how many calories are burned per hour during various activities. Figure 4-56 shows a Microsoft Word table that lists the number of calories and amount of fiber in a serving of some fruits, vegetables, and bread and grains. The Servings file was created using Microsoft Word and enhanced with Word's Table AutoFormat feature. PowerPoint allows you to embed this table into a presentation. The same steps used to insert the Excel Calories chart into a slide are used to insert a Microsoft Word table. In the following sections, you will display the next slide, edit the title text, and insert the Word table from the Data Disk.

	Servings	Fiber	Calories
Fruits			
Apple	1 med	3.7	81
Banana	1 med	2.8	109
Grapes	1 cup	1.6	114
Vegetables (cooked)			
Broccoli	½ cup	2.3	22
Brussels sprouts	½ cup	2.0	30
Baked potato (with skin)	1 med	4.8	220
Sweet potato	1 med	3.4	117
Breads and Grains			
Brown rice	½ cup	1.8	108
Whole wheat bread	1 slice	1.9	69
Bran cereal	½ cup	9.7	79
Kidney beans (cooked)	1 cup	11.3	225

Word Servings table

FIGURE 4-56

Displaying the Next Slide, Editing the Title Text, and Changing the Slide Layout

Before you insert the Word table, you need to display the next slide, edit the slide title text, and change the slide layout.

TO DISPLAY THE NEXT SLIDE, EDIT THE TITLE TEXT, AND CHANGE THE SLIDE LAYOUT

1 Click the Next Slide button to display Slide 4.

2 Triple-click the title text, Key Benefits. Type High-Fiber Complex Carbohydrates in the title text placeholder.

3 Triple-click the bullet text paragraph in the text placeholder. Press the DELETE key.

4 Click Format on the menu bar and then click Slide Layout.

5 Click the Title Only slide layout in the Text Layouts area in the Slide Layout task pane.

6 Click the Close button in the Slide Layout task pane.

Slide 4 has a new title and the desired Title Only slide layout (Figure 4-57).

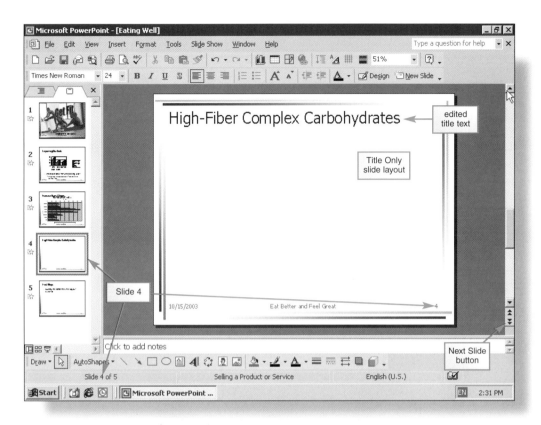

FIGURE 4-57

Inserting a Word Table

Slide 4 now displays the slide title and a blank area for the Servings table. The following steps explain how to insert this Word table, which has the file name Servings.doc.

TO INSERT A WORD TABLE

1 Click Insert on the menu bar and then click Object.

2 When the Insert Object dialog box displays, click Create from file. Click the Browse button.

3 When the Browse dialog box displays, click the Look in box arrow and then click 3½ Floppy (A:). Click Servings in the Look in list. Click the OK button.

4 When the Insert Object dialog box displays, click the OK button.

Slide 4 displays the Servings table (Figure 4-58 on the next page).

1. Press ALT+I, press O, press ALT+F, type file name, press ENTER
2. In Voice Command mode, say, "Insert, Object, Create from file, [type file name], OK"

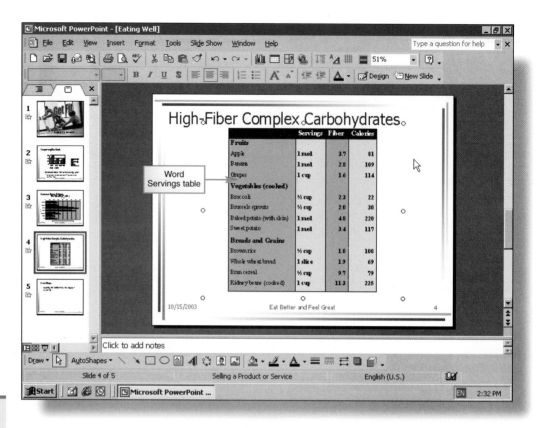

FIGURE 4-58

More *About*

Saving a Slide as a Graphic

Each slide can be saved in .gif format and then inserted as a picture into another program or on a Web page. To save a slide as a graphic, display the slide, click Save As on the File menu, and then click Windows Metafile or GIF Graphics Interchange Format in the Save as type box.

If you want to edit the Servings table, double-click the table. This action starts Microsoft Word and opens the Servings table as a Word document. Then, make the desired changes or use the Word tools and menus to modify the table, save the table, and then click outside the table to quit Word and return to PowerPoint. These editing changes will appear in the Servings table embedded into Slide 4. The source file in Word remains unchanged, however.

Scaling and Moving a Word Table

Sufficient space exists on Slide 4 to enlarge the table. Perform the following steps to scale the Servings Word table.

Other Ways

1. On Format menu click Object, click Size tab, click Scale Height box up arrow to display desired height, click OK button
2. Press ALT+O, press O, press RIGHT ARROW key, press ALT+H, press UP ARROW key to display desired height, press ENTER
3. In Voice Command mode, say "Format, Object, Height, [type height], OK

TO SCALE AND MOVE A WORD TABLE

1 Right-click the Servings table and then click Format Object on the shortcut menu.

2 If necessary, click the Size tab in the Format Object dialog box.

3 Click and hold down the mouse button on the Height box up arrow in the Scale area until 105 % displays and then release the mouse button.

4 Click the OK button.

5 Drag the Servings table up and to the left so it is centered on the slide. If necessary, you can make small adjustments by pressing the arrow keys on the keyboard that correspond to the direction in which to move.

The Servings table chart is enlarged and moved to the desired position (Figure 4-59).

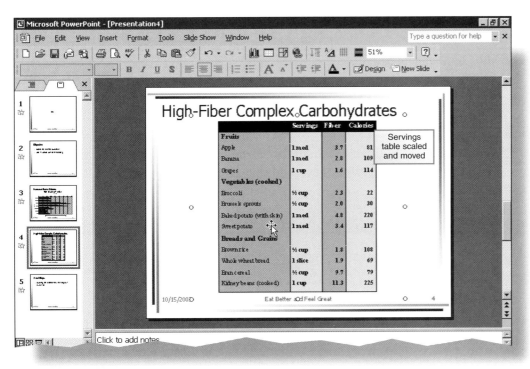

FIGURE 4-59

Slide 4 is complete, so you should save the slide show by clicking the Save button on the Standard toolbar. The Eating Well presentation informs Wellness Institute members viewing the slide show about the need to eat well and choose healthy foods. The final slide in the presentation will give information on locating additional information on these nutritional topics.

Adding Hyperlinks and Embedding Fonts

Slide 5 in the Eating Well slide show presents resources for additional information. Wellness Institute members can refer to these sources to learn more about the topics presented in the slide show or to obtain specific information that would benefit them personally.

Part of this slide will contain hyperlinks. A **hyperlink**, also called a **link**, is a connection from one slide to a Web page, another slide, a custom show consisting of specific slides in a presentation, or a file. Hyperlinks can be text or an object, such as a picture, graph, shape, or WordArt. On Slide 5, the text hyperlinks will be **absolute links** because they will specify the exact location of a page on the World Wide Web. This location is encoded as a **Uniform Resource Locator** (**URL**), also called a **Web address**.

To call attention to these hyperlinks, you will change the font from the default Tahoma to Monotype Corsiva. While Monotype Corsiva is a font included with PowerPoint 2002, it may not be available on all computers. Users sometimes delete fonts on their computers if they are not using that style and want to save space on the hard drive or network server. Consequently, you will need to embed that font in your presentation. Like the Excel chart you inserted into Slide 3 and Word table you inserted into Slide 4, an **embedded font** is inserted into a presentation and becomes part of the file to guarantee it displays. The following sections explain how to create the hyperlinks and embed the Monotype Corsiva font.

More **About**

Quick Reference

For a table that lists how to complete tasks covered in this book using the mouse, menu, shortcut menu, and keyboard, see the Quick Reference Summary at the back of this book, or visit the Shelly Cashman Series Office XP Web page (scsite.com/offxp/qr.htm) and then click Microsoft PowerPoint 2002.

Displaying the Next Slide and Editing the Text

Before you create the hyperlinks to the World Wide Web, you need to display the next slide and edit the slide text.

TO DISPLAY THE NEXT SLIDE AND EDIT THE TEXT

1 Click the Next Slide button to display Slide 5.

2 Triple-click the bullet text paragraph in the text placeholder. Type Obtain additional information from and then press the ENTER key.

3 Press the TAB key. Type American Heart Association and then press the ENTER key.

4 Type American Dietetic Association and then press the ENTER key.

5 Type U.S. Department of Agriculture and then press the ENTER key.

6 Press SHIFT+TAB, and then type Exercise at least three times per week and then press the ENTER key.

7 Type See personal trainers for specific advice but do not press the ENTER key.

The edited bulleted list displays on Slide 5 (Figure 4-60).

1. In Dictation mode, say "Obtain additional information from, New Line, Tab, American Heart Association, New Line, American Dietetic Association, New Line, U.S. Department of Agriculture, New Line, [type Backspace], Exercise at least three times per week, New Line, See personal trainers for specific advice"

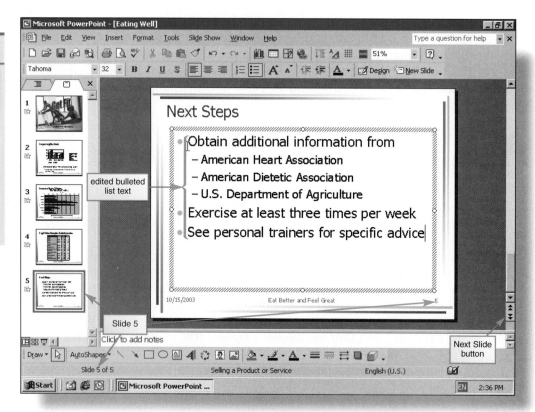

FIGURE 4-60

All editing changes are complete. The next step is to create hyperlinks for the three second-level paragraphs.

Adding a Hyperlink to a Slide

Each second-level paragraph will be a hyperlink to an organization's Web page. If you are connected to the Internet when you run your presentation, you can click a hyperlink, and your default Web browser will access the URL you specified. The following steps will describe how to create the first hyperlink.

Steps **To Add a Hyperlink to a Slide**

1 **Triple-click the first second-level paragraph, American Heart Association. Point to the Insert Hyperlink button on the Standard toolbar.**

The first second-level paragraph is selected (Figure 4-61).

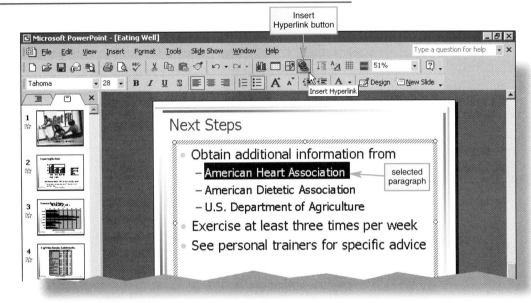

FIGURE 4-61

2 **Click the Insert Hyperlink button. When the Insert Hyperlink dialog box displays, if necessary click the Existing File or Web Page button on the Link to bar. Type** www.americanheart.org **in the Address text box. Point to the OK button.**

The URL for the American Heart Association hyperlink text is http://www.americanheart.org (Figure 4-62). PowerPoint automatically appends the http:// to the URL.

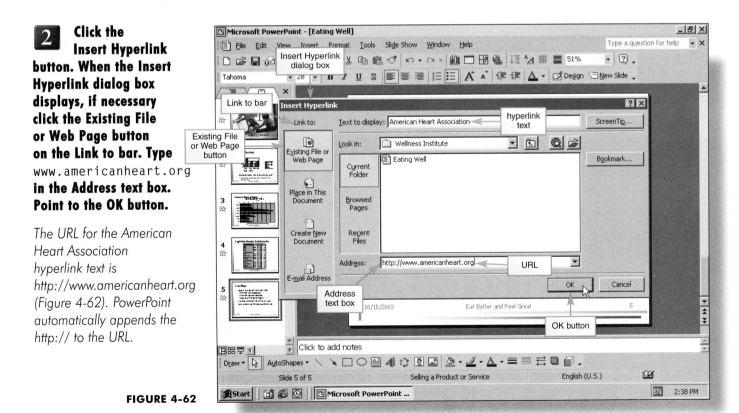

FIGURE 4-62

3 **Click the OK button.**
Click Slide 5 anywhere
except the text placeholder.

The American Heart
Association hyperlink text is
underlined and has the font
color purple (Figure 4-63).

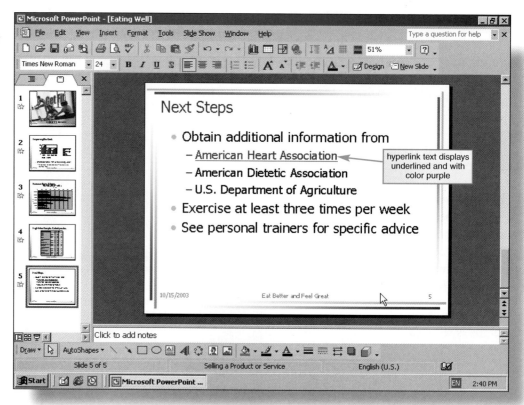

FIGURE 4-63

Other **Ways**

1. On Insert menu click
   Hyperlink, type address,
   click OK button

2. Press ALT+I, press I, press
   ENTER

3. Press CTRL+K, type address,
   press ENTER

4. In Voice Command mode,
   say "Insert Hyperlink, [type
   address], OK"

Adding Remaining Hyperlinks to a Slide

The hyperlink for the first second-level paragraph is complete. The next task is to create hyperlinks for the two other second-level paragraphs on Slide 5.

TO ADD REMAINING HYPERLINKS TO A SLIDE

1 Triple-click the second second-level paragraph, American Dietetic Association.

2 Click the Insert Hyperlink button and then type `www.eatright.org` in the Address text box. Click the OK button.

3 Triple-click the third second-level paragraph, U.S. Department of Agriculture.

4 Click the Insert Hyperlink button and then type `www.usda.gov` in the Address text box. Click the OK button. Click Slide 5 anywhere except the text placeholder.

The hyperlinks for the two second-level paragraphs are added (Figure 4-64).

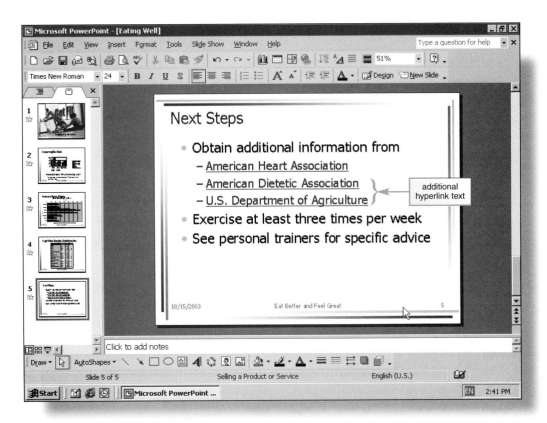

FIGURE 4-64

If you are connected to the Internet when you run the presentation, you will click each of the three second-level paragraphs. Your browser will display the corresponding Web page for each paragraph.

Changing the Font

The three hyperlinks are indicated by the purple, underlined text. To call additional attention to these links, you will change the font from Tahoma to Monotype Corsiva. To perform this task, you could select each paragraph individually and then change the font. It is quicker to select all three paragraphs and then change the font. Perform the steps on the next page to change the font of the three hyperlink text paragraphs.

Microsoft Certification

The Microsoft Office User Specialist (MOUS) Certification program provides an opportunity for you to obtain a valuable industry credential — proof that you have the PowerPoint 2002 skills required by employers. For more information, see Appendix E or visit the Shelly Cashman Series MOUS Web page at scsite.com/offxp/cert.htm.

Steps **To Change the Font**

1 **Click between the first second-level bullet and the letter A in American Heart Association. Drag downward and to the right until the three second-level paragraphs are highlighted.**

PowerPoint selects the three hyperlink text paragraphs (Figure 4-65).

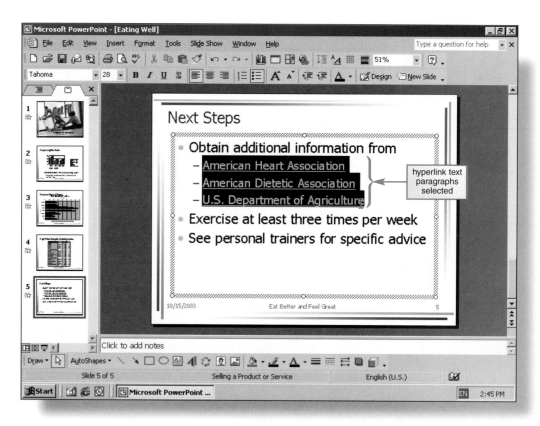

FIGURE 4-65

2 **Click the Font box arrow on the Formatting toolbar, scroll through the font list until Monotype Corsiva displays, and then point to Monotype Corsiva.**

PowerPoint displays a list of available fonts (Figure 4-66). Your list of available fonts may differ depending on the type of printer you are using. The current font is Tahoma.

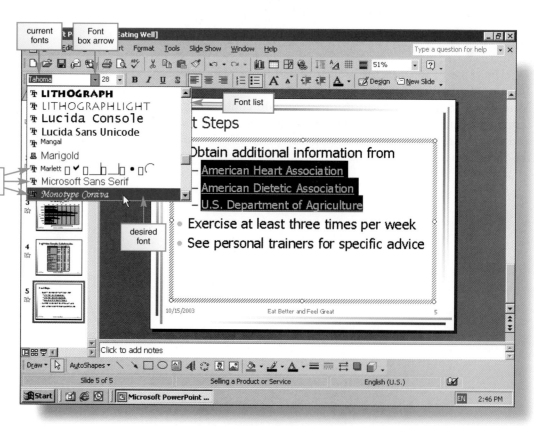

FIGURE 4-66

3 **Click Monotype Corsiva. Click to the right of any of the hyperlink text paragraphs.**

PowerPoint changes the font of the selected text to Monotype Corsiva (Figure 4-67).

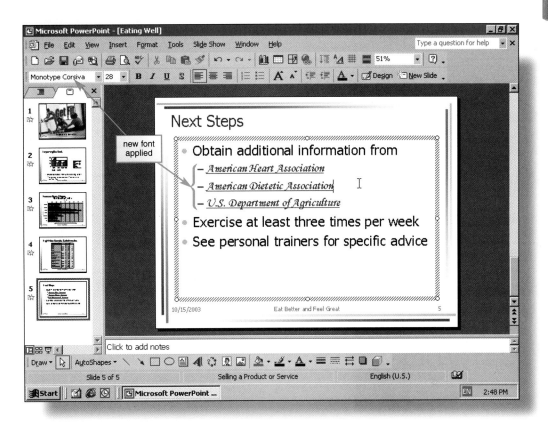

FIGURE 4-67

The hyperlink text is differentiated from the other text on Slide 5 by the underlined purple Monotype Corsiva font.

Embedding Fonts in a Presentation

To ensure the Monotype Corsiva font displays on any computer that runs the slide show, you must embed the fonts in the slide show. The embedded letters become part of the file. The Microsoft Windows license allows you to embed any TrueType fonts that come with that software. A **TrueType font** displays with the symbol **T** in the Font list and is a high-grade set of specifically designed characters. Printed output of TrueType fonts matches the screen display. Other TrueType fonts on a system can be embedded if they do not have any license restrictions and can be edited and installed.

Other Ways

1. Select text, on Format menu click Font, select desired font in Font list, click OK button
2. Right-click selected text, click Font on shortcut menu, select desired font in Font list, click OK button
3. With insertion point at beginning of first second-level paragraph, press CTRL+SHIFT+DOWN ARROW, press CTRL+SHIFT+F, press DOWN ARROW key until desired font displays, press ENTER
4. In Voice Command mode, say "Select Paragraph, Font, [desired font name]"

The file size increases substantially when a font is embedded. To keep the size as small as possible, embed only the characters used in the presentation. If, however, other users may edit your slides, the full set of font characters needs to be embedded. Perform the following steps to embed only the characters used in this slide show.

 To Embed Fonts in a Presentation

1 **Click File on the menu bar and then click Save As. When the Save As dialog box displays, click the Tools button on the toolbar and then point to Save Options.**

The *Tools menu* gives options for saving files, including adding passwords, sharing documents, and compressing the size of pictures (Figure 4-68).

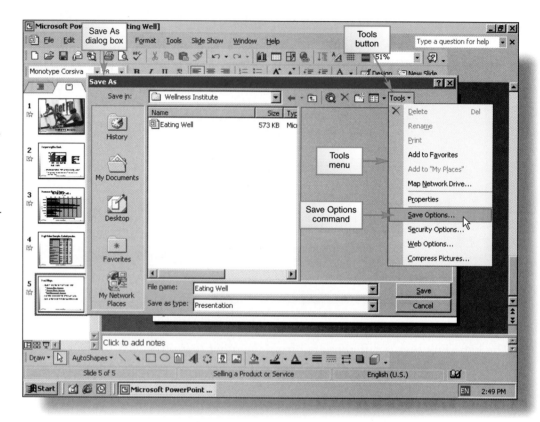

FIGURE 4-68

2 **Click Save Options. When the Save Options dialog box displays, click the Embed TrueType fonts check box and then click Embed characters in use only (best for reducing file size). Point to the OK button.**

Only the Monotype Corsiva letters used in the three hyperlink text paragraphs and the Tahoma letters used in the presentation will be embedded (Figure 4-69). To embed all the characters in the Monotype Corsiva and Tahoma font sets, select Embed all characters (best for editing by others).

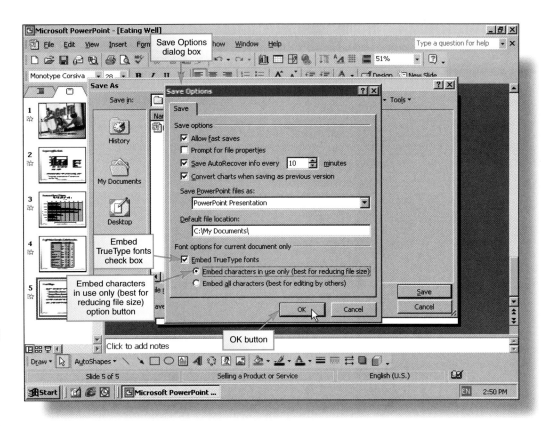

FIGURE 4-69

3 **Click the OK button. When the Save As dialog box displays, click the Save button. Click the Yes button when the Microsoft PowerPoint dialog box displays informing you that you already have a file named Eating Well saved in the Wellness Institute folder. If your system displays a Microsoft PowerPoint dialog box with the message that your Data Disk is full, insert another disk in drive A and repeat these three steps.**

The file with the embedded fonts replaces the Eating Well file on your floppy disk in drive A. The presentation does not change in appearance after this operation and displays as shown in Figure 4-67 on page PP 4.53.

The text for all five slides in the Eating Well presentation has been entered. You now will modify the presentation format by adding transition and sound effects and rehearsing the presentation timing.

Other Ways

1. Press ALT+F, press A, press ALT+L, press S, press E, press U, press ENTER, press ALT+S, click Yes button

2. In Voice Command mode, say "File, Save As, Tools, Save Options, Embed TrueType fonts, Embed characters in use only, OK, Save"

Rehearsing Presentations

More than three million people worldwide have benefited from participating in Toastmasters International, a non-profit organization established in California in 1924. Members meet frequently and practice various types of public speaking, including giving prepared and impromptu speeches, conducting meetings, and giving constructive feedback. To learn more about this organization and to find a local chapter near you, visit the PowerPoint 2002 More About Web page (scsite.com/pp2002/more.htm) and then click Rehearsing.

Modifying the Presentation Format

PowerPoint allows you to control the way you advance from one slide to another by adding a **slide transition**. The AutoContent Wizard added animations to the slides, but it did not apply a slide transition. Some animation schemes include transitions, but if the one you select does not or if you want to change the transition, PowerPoint allows you to apply this effect using the Slide Transition task pane. A slide transition can be applied to a single slide, a group of slides, or an entire presentation.

The second modification you will make is to rehearse the slide timing. When you **rehearse timings**, you start the slide show in **rehearsal mode** and then specify the number of seconds you want each slide to display on the screen when you run the slide show.

The final modification you will make to this slide is to change the slide background. Earlier in this project, you added a picture to Slide 1 to add interest in the presentation. Now you will add a speckled background to Slides 2, 3, and 4 and add a solid blue background to Slide 5.

Adding a Slide Transition to a Slide Show

PowerPoint has more than 50 different slide transitions, and you can vary the speed of each in a presentation. The name of the slide transition characterizes the visual effect that displays. For example, the slide transition effect, **Split Vertical In**, displays the next slide by covering the previous slide with two vertical boxes moving from the left and right edges of the screen until the two boxes reach the center of the screen. The effect is similar to closing draw drapes over a window.

PowerPoint requires you to select at least one slide before applying slide transition effects. In this presentation, you apply slide transition effects to all slides except the title slide. Because Slide 5 already is selected, you must select Slides 2, 3, and 4. The quickest method of selecting these slides is by using the SHIFT+click technique you used to delete slides in this project.

The slide show includes the **Shape Circle slide transition effect** between slides. That is, all slides begin stacked on top of one another, like a deck of cards. As you click the mouse button to view the next slide, the new slide enters the screen by starting at the center of the slide and opening up in a circle to the edges.

Perform the following steps to apply the Shape Circle slide transition effect to the Eating Well presentation.

Steps | **To Add a Slide Transition to a Slide Show**

1 **With Slide 5 selected on the Slides tab, press and hold down the SHIFT key and then click Slide 2. Release the SHIFT key.**

Slides 2 through 5 are selected, as indicated by the heavy border around each slide.

2 **Point to Slide 2 and right-click. Point to Slide Transition on the shortcut menu (Figure 4-70).**

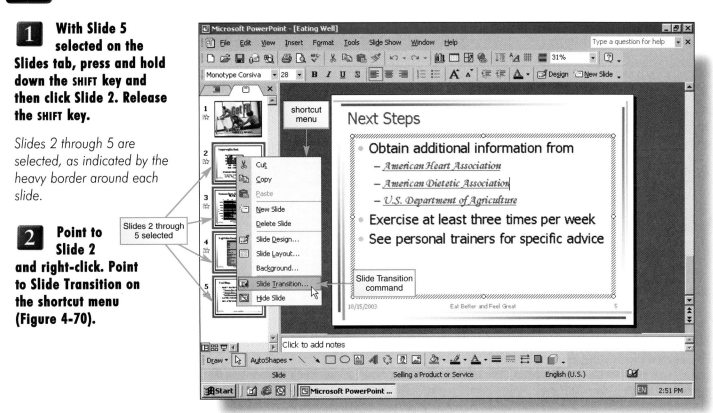

FIGURE 4-70

3 **Click Slide Transition. When the Slide Transition task pane displays, click the down scroll arrow in the Apply to selected slides list until Shape Circle displays. Click Shape Circle.**

The Slide Transition task pane displays (Figure 4-71). The Apply to selected slides list displays available slide transition effects. The effect is previewed in the slide pane because the AutoPreview check box is checked. To see the preview again, click the Play button. To preview the effect on all slides in the presentation, click the Slide Show button.

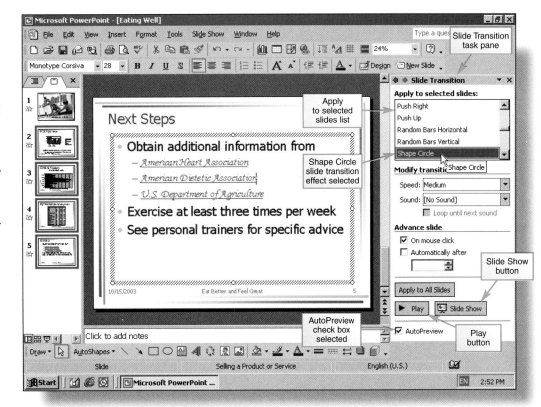

FIGURE 4-71

 **4** Click the Modify Transition Speed box arrow and then click Slow. Point to the Close button in the Slide Transition task pane.

The effect is previewed again in the slide pane. Slow displays in the Modify transition Speed box (Figure 4-72). You can select a transition speed of Slow, Medium, or Fast.

5 Click the Close button.

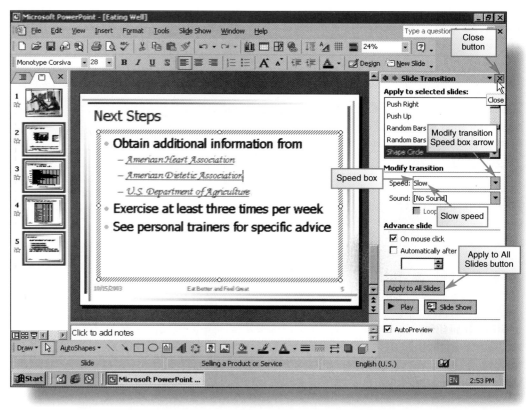

FIGURE 4-72

Other Ways

1. Select slides, on Slide Show menu click Slide Transition, select desired transition, select desired transition speed, click Close button

2. Select slides, press ALT+D, press T, press arrow keys to select desired transition, press ENTER, press arrows keys to select desired transition speed, click Close button

3. In Voice Command mode, say "Slide Show, Slide Transition"

To apply slide transition effects to every slide in the presentation, right-click a slide, click Slide Transition on the shortcut menu, choose the desired slide transition effect, and then click the **Apply to All Slides button** in the Slide Transition task pane. To remove slide transition effects, select the slides to which slide transition effects are applied, click the up scroll arrow in the Apply to selected slides list until No Transition displays, and then click No Transition.

The Shape Circle slide transition effect has been applied to the presentation. You should save the slide show again. The next step in creating this slide show is to set timings for the slide show.

Rehearsing Timings

In previous slide shows, you clicked to advance from one slide to the next. Because all slide components have been added to the five slides in the presentation, you now can set the time each slide displays on the screen. You can set these times in two ways. One method is to specify each slide's display time manually in the Slide Transition task pane. The second method is to use PowerPoint's **rehearsal feature**, which allows you to advance through the slides at your own pace, and the amount of time you view each slide is recorded. You will use the second technique in this project.

When you begin rehearsing a presentation, the Rehearsal toolbar displays. The **Rehearsal toolbar** contains buttons that allow you to start, pause, and repeat viewing the slides in the slide show and to view the times for each slide and the elapsed time. Table 4-4 describes the buttons on the Rehearsal toolbar.

Table 4-4 Rehearsal Toolbar Buttons

BUTTON	BUTTON NAME	DESCRIPTION
➡	Next	Displays the next slide or next animated element on the slide.
⏸	Pause	Stops the timer. Click the Next or Pause button to resume timing.
0:00:00	Slide Time	Indicates the length of time a slide has displayed. You can enter a slide time directly in the Slide Time box.
↺	Repeat	Clears the Slide Time box and resets the timer to 0:00.
0:00:00	Elapsed Time	Time indicates slide show total time.

Table 4-5 Slide Rehearsal Timings

SLIDE NUMBER	DISPLAY TIME	ELAPSED TIME
1		
Title Text	0:10	0:10
Subtitle Text	0:20	0:30
2	0:30	1:00
3	0:30	1:30
4	0:30	2:00
5	2:00	4:00

Table 4-5 indicates the desired timings for the five slides in the Eating Well presentation. The subtitle text on Slide 1 displays when you click the mouse button, and then the sound effect plays for 10 seconds. Slide 5 has the three hyperlinks, so you need to allow time to view the three Web sites.

Perform the following steps to add slide timings to the slide show.

Steps **To Rehearse Timings**

1 **Click Slide Show on the menu bar and then point to Rehearse Timings.**

The Slide Show menu displays (Figure 4-73).

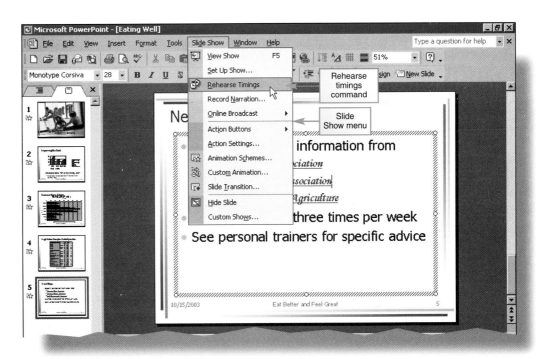

FIGURE 4-73

2 **Click Rehearse Timings. Point to the Next button on the Rehearsal toolbar. When the Elapsed Time box displays 0:10, click the Next button.**

The subtitle text displays and the Sports Open sound effect plays (Figure 4-74).

FIGURE 4-74

3 **When the Elapsed Time box displays 0:30, click the Next button.**

Slide 2 displays.

4 **When the Elapsed Time box displays 1:00, click the Next button to display Slide 3. When the Elapsed Time box displays 1:30, click the Next button to display Slide 4. When the Elapsed time box displays 2:00, click the Next button to display Slide 5. When the Elapsed Time box displays 4:00, click the Next button to display the black slide. Point to the Yes button in the Microsoft PowerPoint dialog box.**

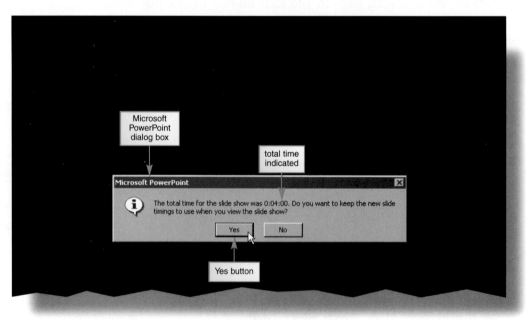

FIGURE 4-75

The Microsoft PowerPoint dialog box displays the total time and asks if you want to keep the new slide timings with a total elapsed time of 0:04:00 (Figure 4-75).

5 **Click the Yes button.**

Each slide's timing displays in the lower-left corner in slide sorter view (Figure 4-76).

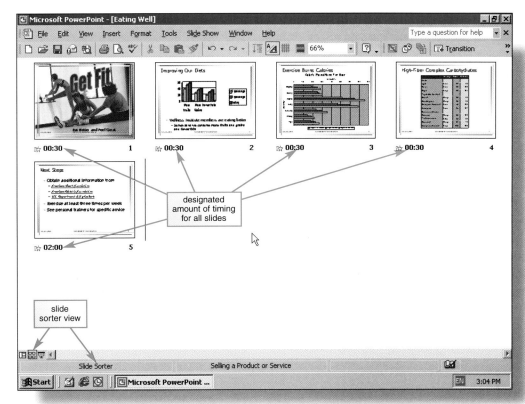

FIGURE 4-76

Other **Ways**

1. Press ALT+D, press R
2. In Voice Command mode, say "Slide Show, Rehearse Timings"

The Eating Well slide timing is complete. The presentation will run four minutes.

Formatting Slide Backgrounds

The five slides in slide sorter view look plain. A colored background would add contrast and increase visual appeal. The next step is to add a texture to the background on Slides 2, 3, and 4 and change the background color on Slide 5 to medium blue. The steps on the next page change the background for these four slides.

To Format Slide Backgrounds

1 **In slide sorter view, click Slide 2, hold down the SHIFT key, and then click Slide 4.**

Slides 2, 3, and 4 are selected.

2 **Click Format on the menu bar and then click Background. When the Background dialog box displays, click the Background fill box arrow. Click Fill Effects, and then point to the Texture tab in the Fill Effects dialog box.**

In addition to a picture as used on Slide 1, possible backgrounds are gradients, textures, and patterns (Figure 4-77).

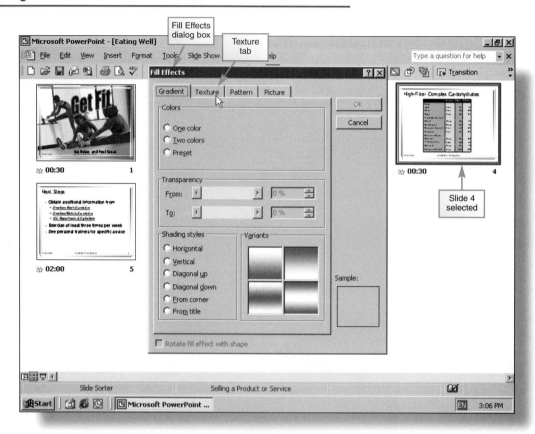

FIGURE 4-77

3 **Click the Texture tab. Click the Newsprint texture in column 1, row 1. Point to the OK button.**

The Newsprint sample displays in the Sample box (Figure 4-78). Twenty-four textures are available, including wood, water, cork, and granite.

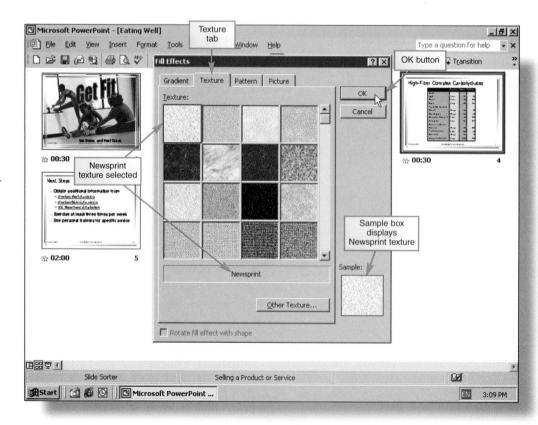

FIGURE 4-78

4 **Click the OK button. Click the Apply button.**

The Newsprint texture is applied to Slides 2, 3, and 4 (Figure 4-79).

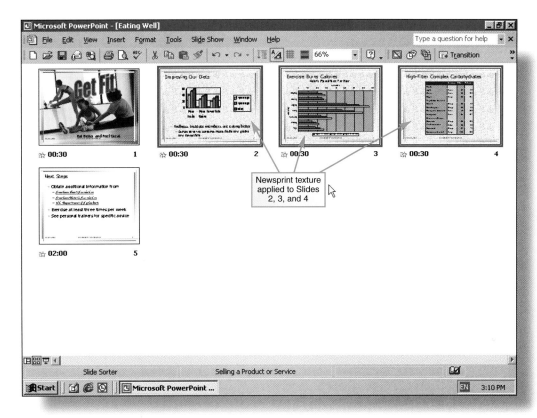

FIGURE 4-79

5 **Click Slide 5. Click Format on the menu bar and then click Background. When the Background dialog box displays, click the Background fill box arrow. Click the color medium blue (color 3 in the top row). Point to the Apply button.**

The color medium blue displays in the Background fill area (Figure 4-80). When you click the Apply button, the medium blue color is displayed on only the one selected slide.

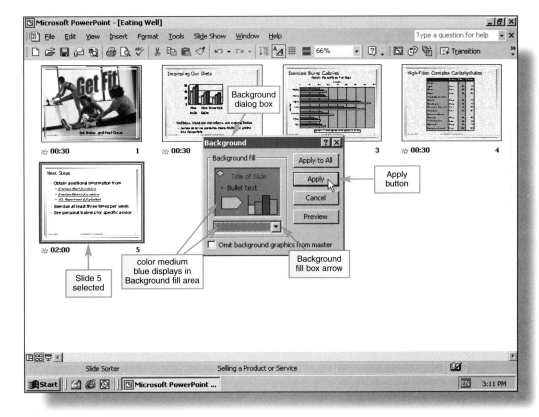

FIGURE 4-80

<table>
<tr><td>6</td><td>**Click the Apply button.**</td></tr>
</table>

Slide 5 displays with the medium blue background (Figure 4-81).

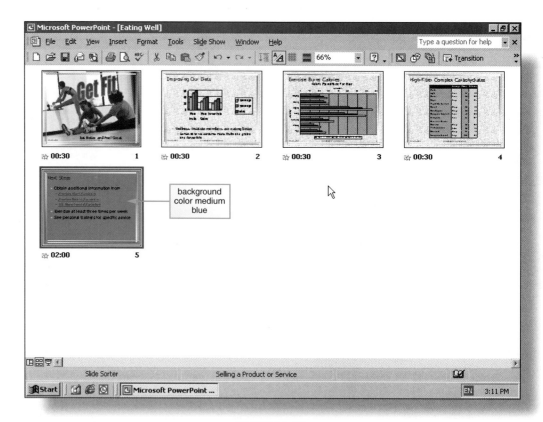

FIGURE 4-81

Other **Ways**

1. Press ALT+O, press K
2. In Voice Command mode, say "Format, Background, Background fill, Fill Effects, [select texture], OK, Apply, Format, Background, Background fill, [select color], Apply"

Each slide in the presentation now has a custom background. You should save the presentation again by clicking the Save button on the Formatting toolbar.

Adding Notes and Printing Speaker Notes

Slides and handouts usually are printed to distribute to audience members. These printouts also are helpful to speakers so they can write notes that will guide them through a presentation. As you create slides, you may find material you want to state verbally and do not want to include on the slide. You can type and format notes in the **notes pane** as you work in normal view and then print this information as **notes pages**. Notes pages print with a small image of the slide at the top and the comments below the slide. Charts, tables, and pictures added to the notes pane also print on these pages. You can make changes to the **notes master** if you want to alter the default settings, such as the font or the position of page elements, such as the slide area and notes area.

Adding Notes

In this project, comments are added to Slides 2, 4, and 5. After adding comments, you can print a set of speaker notes. Perform the following steps to add text to the notes pane on these slides and then print the notes.

More About

Printing Speaker Notes

As you add visual elements to your presentations, think about how you are going to discuss these objects in an oral presentation. When you get an idea, type it in the notes pane. You can add headers and footers to the speaker notes master that contain page numbers and the current date and time.

Steps **To Add Notes**

1 **In slide sorter view, double-click Slide 2. In normal view, click the notes pane and then type** People today are making healthy dietary choices. Nutrient information is found on nearly every food package.

The **notes** *provide supplementary information for a speaker at a presentation (Figure 4-82).*

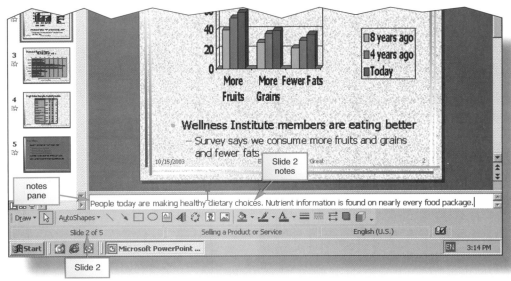

FIGURE 4-82

2 **Click the Next Slide button two times to display Slide 4. Click the notes pane and then type** Carbohydrates, proteins, fats, vitamins, and minerals are important nutrients in a well-balanced diet.

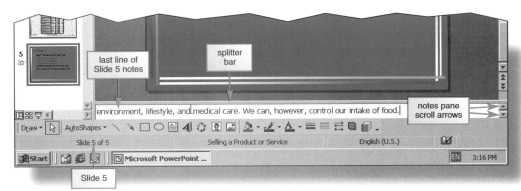

FIGURE 4-83

3 **Click the Next Slide button to display Slide 5. Click the notes pane and then type** People do not become healthy or unhealthy based solely on food. General health is influenced by heredity, environment, lifestyle, and medical care. We can, however, control our intake of food.

Only the last line of these notes displays (Figure 4–83). Dragging the splitter bar up enlarges the notes pane. Clicking the notes pane scroll arrows allows you to view the entire text.

Printing Speaker Notes

These notes give additional information that supplements the text on the slides. To print the speaker notes, perform the steps on the next page.

Other **Ways**

1. In Dictation mode, say "People today are making healthy dietary choices. Nutrient information is found on nearly every food package, [select Slide 4 notes pane], Carbohydrates, proteins, fats, vitamins, and minerals are important nutrients in a well-balanced diet, [select Slide 5 notes pane], People do not become healthy or unhealthy based solely on food. General health is influenced by heredity, environment, lifestyle, and medical care. We can, however, control our intake of food"

To Print Speaker Notes

1 **Click File on the menu bar and then click Print. When the Print dialog box displays, click the Print what box arrow and then point to Notes Pages.**

The Print dialog box displays (Figure 4-84). Notes Pages displays highlighted in the Print what list.

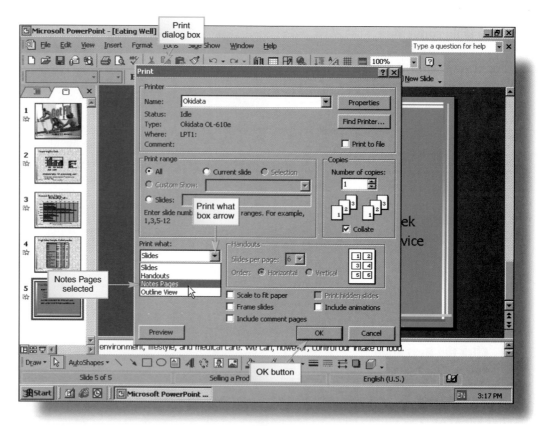

FIGURE 4-84

2 **Click Notes Pages in the list and then click the OK button.**

The five PowerPoint notes pages display (Figure 4-85a through 4-85e). The notes display on Slides 2, 4, and 5.

(a) Page 1

FIGURE 4-85

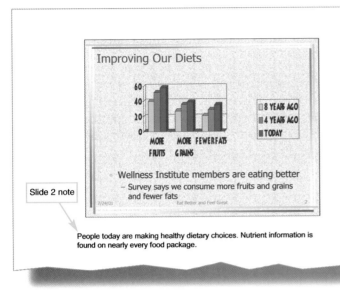

Slide 2 note

People today are making healthy dietary choices. Nutrient information is found on nearly every food package.

(b) Page 2

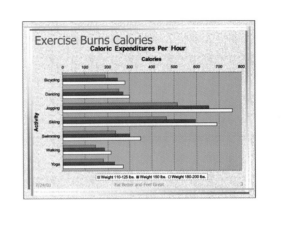

(c) Page 3

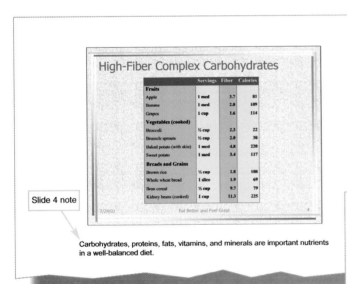

Slide 4 note

Carbohydrates, proteins, fats, vitamins, and minerals are important nutrients in a well-balanced diet.

(d) Page 4

Other Ways

1. On File menu click Print Preview, click Notes Pages in Print What list, click Print button on Print Preview toolbar
2. Press CTRL+P, press ALT+W, press DOWN ARROW key until Notes Pages is selected, press ENTER, press ENTER
3. In Voice Command mode, say "File, Print, Print What, Notes Pages, OK"

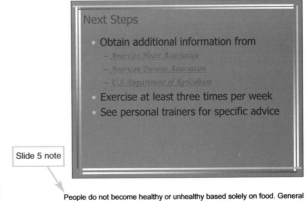

Slide 5 note

People do not become healthy or unhealthy based solely on food. General health is influenced by heredity, environment, lifestyle, and medical care. We can, however, control our intake of food.

(e) Page 5

FIGURE 4-85

Saving the Presentation in Rich Text Format

The presentation is complete. You now should spell check and then save it again by clicking the Spelling and Save buttons, respectively, on the Standard toolbar. So you can import the text into a Word document or another word processing package, you will save the presentation in **Rich Text Format** (**.rtf**). When you save the file as an .rtf outline, you lose any graphics, such as the Word table and Excel worksheet. Perform the steps on the next page to save the presentation as an .rtf outline.

Steps **To Save the Presentation in Rich Text Format**

---

1 **Click File on the menu bar and then click Save As.**

2 **When the Save As dialog box displays, click the Save as type box arrow, scroll down, and then point to Outline/RTF.**

You can save the presentation in a variety of formats (Figure 4-86).

3 **Click Outline/RTF. Click the Save button.**

PowerPoint saves the text of the presentation with the file name Eating Well.rtf. If no more space remains on your Data Disk, insert another floppy disk.

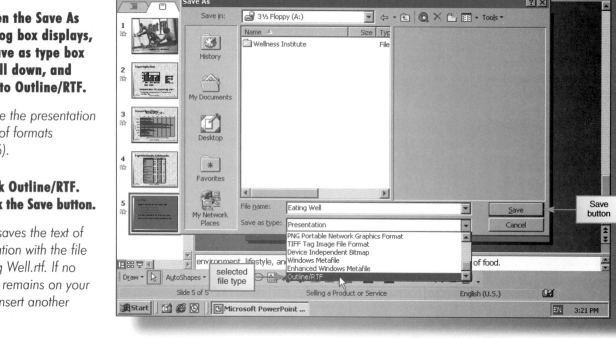

FIGURE 4-86

Other Ways

1. Press ALT+F, press A, press ALT+T, press DOWN ARROW key, press ENTER, press ENTER
2. In Voice Command mode, say "File, Save As, Save as type, Outline RTF, Save"

Running a Slide Show with Hyperlinks

Running a slide show that contains hyperlinks is the same as running any other slide show. When a presentation contains hyperlinks and you are connected to the Internet, you can click the hyperlink text to command your default browser to locate the hyperlink file. Perform the following steps to run the Eating Well presentation.

TO RUN A SLIDE SHOW WITH HYPERLINKS

1 Click Slide 1 on the Slides tab. Click the Slide Show button in the lower-left corner of the PowerPoint window.

2 Click Slide 1. The subtitle text will display and the sound effect will play automatically. Slides 2, 3, 4, and 5 will display according to the slide timings.

3 When Slide 5 displays, click the first hyperlink to start your browser and view the American Heart Association Web page. If necessary, maximize the Web page window when the page displays. Click the Close button on the Web page title bar to stop the browser.

4 Repeat Step 3 for the second and third hyperlinks.

5 Click the black slide. Click the Close button on the PowerPoint title bar.

Slide 1 displays in normal view, PowerPoint quits, and then control returns to the desktop.

CASE PERSPECTIVE SUMMARY

The Eating Well presentation should satisfy the members' interest in learning the basics of nutrition. Malcolm Perkins now can schedule the seminar discussing the connection between eating healthy foods and improving general wellness. He can emphasize the need to exercise regularly, consume more fruits and grains, decrease the intake of fats, and monitor the carbohydrates in common foods. Your presentation, which includes a photograph, a table, and two charts, helps reinforce the message that members must continue to monitor their eating habits and engage in regular physical exercise if they want to burn calories quickly and live long, healthy lives.

Project Summary

Project 4 started by using the AutoContent Wizard to generate some text and graphics using the Selling a Product or Service design template. You then customized presentation elements by changing the color scheme and modifying the footer. After adding a picture to the title slide background, you created a WordArt title and added a sound effect to that slide. Next, you used Microsoft Graph to create a chart and then inserted an Excel chart and added a Word table. You then created a slide containing hyperlinks to Web sites containing additional nutritional information. After adding and modifying the slide elements, you embedded the fonts, added slide transitions, rehearsed timings, and formatted the slide backgrounds. To assist the individual who is presenting the slide show, you added notes to the slides and printed speaker notes. Finally, you saved the presentation in Rich Text Format and then ran the slide show to display the hyperlinks.

What You Should Know

Having completed this project, you now should be able to perform the following tasks:

▶ Add a Hyperlink to a Slide *(PP 4.49)*

▶ Add a Picture to Create a Custom Background *(PP 4.15)*

▶ Add a Slide Transition to a Slide Show *(PP 4.57)*

▶ Add a Sound Effect *(PP 4.28)*

▶ Add Notes *(PP 4.65)*

▶ Add Remaining Hyperlinks to a Slide *(PP 4.50)*

▶ Change the Font *(PP 4.52)*

▶ Change the Presentation Template Color Scheme *(PP 4.11)*

▶ Change the Slide Layout and Position the Text Placeholder *(PP 4.34)*

▶ Change the WordArt Height and Width *(PP 4.24)*

▶ Create a Folder and Save a Presentation *(PP 4.30)*

▶ Delete Slides *(PP 4.31)*

▶ Delete the Title Text Placeholder *(PP 4.19)*

▶ Display the Next Slide and Edit the Text *(PP 4.48)*

▶ Display the Next Slide, Edit the Title Text, and Change the Slide Layout *(PP 4.44)*

▶ Display the Next Slide, Edit the Title Text, and Delete the AutoShape Objects *(PP 4.39)*

▶ Edit the Title and Bulleted List Text *(PP 4.32)*

▶ Embed Fonts in a Presentation *(PP 4.54)*

▶ Enter and Position the Presentation Subtitle *(PP 4.26)*

▶ Enter the WordArt Text *(PP 4.22)*

▶ Format Slide Backgrounds *(PP 4.62)*

▶ Insert a Chart and Replace the Sample Data *(PP 4.35)*

▶ Insert a Word Table *(PP 4.45)*

▶ Insert an Excel Chart *(PP 4.40)*

▶ Modify the Footer on the Title Master *(PP 4.13)*

▶ Print Speaker Notes *(PP 4.66)*

▶ Rehearse Timings *(PP 4.59)*

▶ Run a Slide Show with Hyperlinks *(PP 4.69)*

▶ Save the Presentation in Rich Text Format *(PP 4.68)*

▶ Scale and Move a Word Table *(PP 4.46)*

▶ Scale and Move an Excel Chart *(PP 4.43)*

▶ Select a WordArt Style *(PP 4.21)*

▶ Start a New Presentation *(PP 4.06)*

▶ Use the AutoContent Wizard *(PP 4.07)*

Learn It Online

Instructions: To complete the Learn It Online exercises, start your browser, click the Address bar, and then enter scsite.com/offxp/exs.htm. When the Office XP Learn It Online page displays, follow the instructions in the exercises below.

1 Project Reinforcement TF, MC, and SA

Below PowerPoint Project 4, click the Project Reinforcement link. Print the quiz by clicking Print on the File menu. Answer each question. Write your first and last name at the top of each page, and then hand in the printout to your instructor.

2 Flash Cards

Below PowerPoint Project 4, click the Flash Cards link. When Flash Cards displays, read the instructions. Type 20 (or a number specified by your instructor) in the Number of Playing Cards text box, type your name in the Name text box, and then click the Flip Card button. When the flash card displays, read the question and then click the Answer box arrow to select an answer. Flip through Flash Cards. Click Print on the File menu to print the last flash card if your score is 15 (75%) correct or greater and then hand it in to your instructor. If your score is less than 15 (75%) correct, then redo this exercise by clicking the Replay button.

3 Practice Test

Below PowerPoint Project 4, click the Practice Test link. Answer each question, enter your first and last name at the bottom of the page, and then click the Grade Test button. When the graded practice test displays on your screen, click Print on the File menu to print a hard copy. Continue to take practice tests until you score 80% or better. Hand in a printout of the final practice test to your instructor.

4 Who Wants to Be a Computer Genius?

Below PowerPoint Project 4, click the Computer Genius link. Read the instructions, enter your first and last name at the bottom of the page, and then click the Play button. Hand in your score to your instructor.

5 Wheel of Terms

Below PowerPoint Project 4, click the Wheel of Terms link. Read the instructions, and then enter your first and last name and your school name. Click the Play button. Hand in your score to your instructor.

6 Crossword Puzzle Challenge

Below PowerPoint Project 4, click the Crossword Puzzle Challenge link. Read the instructions, and then enter your first and last name. Click the Play button. Work the crossword puzzle. When you are finished, click the Submit button. When the crossword puzzle redisplays, click the Print button. Hand in the printout.

7 Tips and Tricks

Below PowerPoint Project 4, click the Tips and Tricks link. Click a topic that pertains to Project 4. Right-click the information and then click Print on the shortcut menu. Construct a brief example of what the information relates to in PowerPoint to confirm you understand how to use the tip or trick. Hand in the example and printed information.

8 Newsgroups

Below PowerPoint Project 4, click the Newsgroups link. Click a topic that pertains to Project 4. Print three comments. Hand in the comments to your instructor.

9 Expanding Your Horizons

Below PowerPoint Project 4, click the Articles for Microsoft PowerPoint link. Click a topic that pertains to Project 4. Print the information. Construct a brief example of what the information relates to in PowerPoint to confirm you understand the contents of the article. Hand in the example and printed information to your instructor.

10 Search Sleuth

Below PowerPoint Project 4, click the Search Sleuth link. To search for a term that pertains to this project, select a term below the Project 4 title and then use the Google search engine at google.com (or any major search engine) to display and print two Web pages that present information on the term. Hand in the printouts to your instructor.

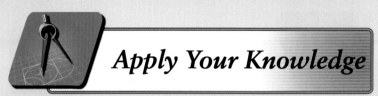
Apply Your Knowledge

1 Creating a WordArt Object, Changing a Background, and Applying Sound and Transition Effects

Instructions: Start PowerPoint. Open the presentation Food Drive from the Data Disk. See the inside back cover of this book for instructions for downloading the Data Disk or see your instructor for information on accessing the clips and files required for this book. Perform the following tasks to modify the slides as shown in Figures 4-87a and 4-87b.

1. Click File on the menu bar and then click Save As. Create a new folder with the name, Food Drive. Save the presentation with the file name, Food Drive Update, in the new folder.
2. Apply the Studio design template.
3. On Slide 1, change the first paragraph of the subtitle text, Summer Solstice Food Drive, to Holiday Food Drive. Change the font to Impact. Increase the font size to 48.
4. On Slide 1, delete the second paragraph of the subtitle text, June 20. Create a WordArt element using the WordArt style in row 1, column 1 of the WordArt Gallery. Enter November 24 as the WordArt text. Change the WordArt object height in the Size and rotate area to 1.25 and the width to 4.52. Position the WordArt object as shown in Figure 4-87a.
5. Format both slide backgrounds by applying the Blue tissue paper texture.
6. Apply the Newsflash slide transition to both slides with the Slow transition speed.
7. Add the sound file, Clock Ticking, to Slide 2. Instruct PowerPoint to play the sound file automatically. Drag the speaker icon off the slide to the lower-right corner of the screen.
8. Add your name and today's date to the slide footer.
9. Save the Food Drive Update file again and embed the characters used on the slides.
10. Run the Food Drive Update presentation.
11. Print the slides as a handout with both slides on one page. Quit PowerPoint.

Apply Your Knowledge

ςηπ
**Zeta Eta Pi
Fraternity's**

Holiday Food Drive
November 24

November 3, 2003   Student Name

(a) Slide 1

Help the Less Fortunate

- Need non-perishable food items
  - Soups
    - Cans or mixes
  - Canned vegetables and fruit
- Miscellaneous dry goods
- Time is ticking away

November 3, 2003   Student Name

(b) Slide 2

FIGURE 4-87

In the Lab

1 Creating Slides with WordArt and a Chart

Problem: Your local park district holds an annual summer golf outing to raise money for civic organizations. This year the park board commissioners want to use the proceeds to purchase computers. They read a report showing that many desktop and notebook computers currently are obsolete or will become obsolete in the next few years. The statistics for that report are summarized in Table 4-6.

Table 4-6	Obsolete Computers Data			
	1997	*1999*	*2003*	*2007*
Desktop	17.5	21.1	63.3	61.3
Notebook	16.8	20.9	64.1	65.7

You have volunteered to help publicize the outing by creating a PowerPoint presentation to run on the computer at the park district office. The park board commissioners want to approve the title slide before you work on the entire project, and you agree to create that slide and a slide showing the number of obsolete computers. The title slide contains a WordArt object and a picture as the background. You create the slides shown in Figures 4-88a and 4-88b.

Instructions: Start PowerPoint and perform the following tasks with a computer.

1. Open a new presentation and apply the Echo design template to the Title Slide slide layout. Add the Golf picture from the Data Disk to the Slide 1 background. Change the color scheme to the scheme in row 2, column 1.
2. Type `Match Your Skills` as the first paragraph in the title text placeholder, `Help Raise Money` as the second paragraph in the title text placeholder, and `Have Fun` as the third paragraph in the title text placeholder.
3. Change the font of these three paragraphs to Tahoma and decrease the font size to 32.
4. Drag the middle sizing handle on the right edge of the title text placeholder to the left until it is at the right edge of the new title text. Drag the title text placeholder to the upper-right corner of the slide as shown in Figure 4-88a.
5. Delete the subtitle text placeholder.

FIGURE 4-88a

In the Lab

6. Create the WordArt object by clicking the Insert WordArt button on the Drawing toolbar. In the WordArt Gallery dialog box, select the WordArt style in row 4, column 5. Type Go for Birdies and Bogeys in the Edit WordArt Text dialog box. Scale the WordArt height and width to 125%. Drag the WordArt down to the position shown in Figure 4-88a.

7. Insert a new slide and apply the Title and Content slide layout. Change the slide design on Slide 2 to Fading Grid. Change the color scheme for Slide 2 only to the scheme in row 5, column 1.

8. Type Obsolete Computers in the title text placeholder. Press the ENTER key. Type (in millions) as the second paragraph in the title text placeholder. Change the font for both paragraphs to Book Antiqua. Use a similar font if Book Antiqua is not installed on your system. Decrease the font size of the second paragraph, (in millions), to 20.

9. Add a chart to Slide 2 using the data in Table 4-6. To delete the data in row 3 of the datasheet, right-click the number 3 on the left edge of row 3, and then click Clear Contents on the shortcut menu. Scale the chart to 110% and position the chart as shown Figure 4-88b.

10. Add the Uncover Right slide transition to both slides. Modify the transition speed to slow.

11. In the Slide 1 notes pane, type This golf outing is the most successful fund-raising event for the park district. In the past five years, we have raised more than $25,000. In the Slide 2 notes pane, type The data for the year 2007 is an estimate based on the current trends in computer hardware development.

12. Save the presentation with the file name, Golf Outing, and embed the characters used on the slides.

13. Run the Golf Outing presentation.

14. Print speaker notes. Quit PowerPoint.

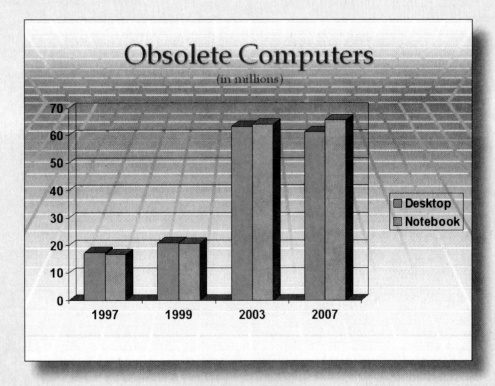

FIGURE 4-88b

In the Lab

2 Inserting a Picture and a Word Table and Adding a Sound Effect

Problem: As a biology major, you have an internship with Friends of Nipper Creek. This community group sponsors several events throughout the year, including the Nipper Creek Ecology day. You have been asked to create a presentation that will run on a computer at the Nipper Creek Nature Center on that day. The slide show will focus on the day's activities and provide advice for the volunteers. It will include WordArt on the title slide and a table listing natural alternatives to pesticides.

Instructions: Start PowerPoint and perform the following tasks with a computer.

1. Open a new presentation and apply the Grass Layers design template. Add the Creek picture from the Data Disk to the Slide 1 background.

2. On Slide 1, enter the title and subtitle text shown in Figure 4-89a. Italicize the subtitle text, change the font to Garamond, and increase the font size to 40.

3. Add a new slide and enter the title and subtitle text shown in Figure 4-89b. Change the first-level paragraph bullet to a bird, which is part of the Webdings font.

4. Add a new slide and change the color scheme to the scheme in row 2, column 1. Change the slide layout to Title Only. Enter the title text shown in Figure 4-89c. Insert the Word table, Insecticides, from the Data Disk. Scale the table to 130% and center the table under the title text placeholder.

5. Add a new slide and delete the title text placeholder. Apply the Capsules design template to this slide. Change the first-level paragraph bullet to the bird used in Step 3. Change the bullet color to dark green. Enter the bulleted list shown in Figure 4-89d. Add the sound file, Laughter, from the Data Disk. Instruct PowerPoint to play the sound file automatically. Drag the speaker icon off the slide to the lower-right corner of the screen.

6. Create the WordArt element shown in Figure 4-89d. Use the WordArt style in row 5, column 4. Change the WordArt height to 2 and the width to 5. Position the object as shown in Figure 4-89d.

7. Apply the Dissolve in animation scheme to all slides, the Comb Horizontal slide transition to Slides 1, 2, and 4, and the Shape Diamond slide transition to Slide 3.

8. Add your name, today's date, and the page number to the slide footer.

9. Create a new folder with the name, Nipper Creek. Save the presentation with the file name, Ecology Day, in the new folder and embed the characters used on the slides. Save the presentation as a Rich Text Format outline.

10. Run the Ecology Day presentation.

11. Print the slides as a handout with two slides on one page. Quit PowerPoint.

In the Lab

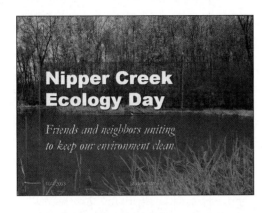

(a) Slide 1

(b) Slide 2

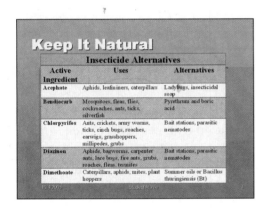

(c) Slide 3

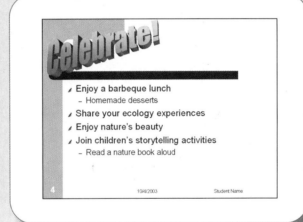

(d) Slide 4

FIGURE 4-89

In the Lab

3 Using the AutoContent Wizard, Changing the Color Scheme and Background, and Inserting an Excel Chart

Problem: You work for the international advertising agency, Donner and Blitzen. Your supervisor, Nick Krouse, has asked you to research which types of businesses are doing the most advertising on the Internet. He wants you to make an oral report on your findings and to make a recommendation of where your agency should concentrate its efforts to secure new accounts. You decide to create a PowerPoint slide show to accompany your presentation and use the AutoContent Wizard to help you develop the key ideas for the slides. You create the presentation shown in Figures 4-90a through 4-90d.

Instructions: Start PowerPoint and perform the following tasks with a computer.

1. Create a new presentation, and use the AutoContent Wizard to generate content for the on-screen presentation. Use the Recommending a Strategy presentation type in the General category. Type Targeting Advertisers as the presentation title and Donner and Blitzen Advertising as the footer text. Include the date and slide number in the footer.

2. Enter your name as the subtitle text.

3. Insert WordArt with the text, Make the Sale, using the WordArt style in row 4, column 4. Scale the WordArt height and width to 130% and position the art as shown in Figure 4-90a.

4. Delete Slides 2, 5, and 6.

5. On Slide 2, replace the title text, Goal and Objective, with the text shown in Figure 4-90b. Italicize the title text and change the font to Sylfaen.

6. On Slide 3, replace the title text, Today's Situation, with the title text, Who Are Today's Advertisers? and then italicize this text and change the font to Sylfaen. Delete the bulleted text, change the slide layout to Title and Content, and then change the color scheme only for Slide 3 to the scheme in row 1, column 2. Insert the Excel chart, Advertising.xls, from the Data Disk. Size the chart height to 4.7 and the width to 9.3. Position the chart as shown in Figure 4-90c. Insert the sound file, Market, from your Data Disk and instruct PowerPoint to play the sound automatically. Drag the speaker icon off the slide to the lower-right corner of the screen.

7. On Slide 4, Recommendation, enter the text shown in Figure 4-90d. Italicize the title text and change the font to Sylfaen. Change the font of the three second-level text paragraphs to Sylfaen.

8. On Slide 4, create a hyperlink for the Financial bullet text with the URL, www.barrons.com. Create a hyperlink for the Automotive bullet text with the URL, www.gm.com. Create a hyperlink for the Computer bullet text with the URL, www.microsoft.com.

9. On Slide 4, change the design template to Radial. Format the slide background with the color aqua (color 5 in the top row).

10. Apply the Wedge slide transition effect to Slides 2, 3, and 4. Modify the transition speed to Slow.

11. Rehearse timings for the slide show. Have Slide 1 display for 30 seconds, Slide 2 for 20 seconds, Slide 3 for 40 seconds, and Slide 4 for 2 minutes.

In the Lab

(a) Slide 1

(b) Slide 2

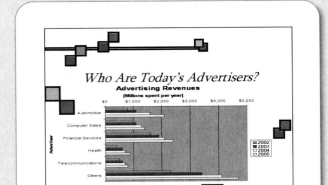

(c) Slide 3

(d) Slide 4

FIGURE 4-90

12. In the Slide 1 notes pane, type American companies outspend all their counterparts worldwide on advertising. These costs include developing the advertising campaigns and then placing the ads in various mass media outlets. In the Slide 2 notes pane, type Celebrities often promote products and services. Michael Jordan earned more than $30 million annually by endorsing products for General Motors, Nike, McDonalds, and other companies. In the Slide 4 notes pane, type The automotive industry is the largest advertiser. General Motors has spent more than $2.2 billion annually. Dell and Gateway are the largest catalog marketers.

13. Run the Donner presentation.

14. Save the presentation with the file name, Donner, and embed the fonts. Save the presentation as a Rich Text Format outline. Print speaker notes. Quit PowerPoint.

Cases and Places

The difficulty of these case studies varies:
▶ are the least difficult; ▶▶ are more difficult; and ▶▶▶ are the most difficult.

1 ▶ In-line skating has grown in popularity and is one of the fastest-growing recreational sports in the world. In 1989, three million skaters spent $20 million on their skates and protective gear. In 1994, sales soared when nearly 14 million skaters spent $250 million. Today, the more than 27 million in-line skaters are purchasing more than $300 million in equipment yearly. Females account for 52 percent of skaters, and youths ranging in age from 7 to 17 are 58 percent of the total skaters. In-line skaters can participate more safely if they follow these steps: Wear full protective gear, including a helmet, wrist guards, and knee and elbow pads; practice basic skills, including braking, turning, and balancing, in a parking lot or other flat surface; always skate under control; and avoid hills until mastering speed control. The public relations director of your local park district has asked you to prepare a slide show emphasizing these safety tips and illustrating the in-line skating popularity surge. You decide to develop a slide show to run at the sporting goods store. Prepare a short presentation aimed at encouraging skaters to practice safe skating. Include a chart showing the increase in skaters and equipment sales. The title slide should include WordArt for visual appeal. The final slide should have hyperlinks to the Rollerblade and Aggressive Skaters Association (ASA) Web sites.

2 ▶ People are living longer lives today. Americans born one hundred years ago could expect to live approximately 47 years; now they can expect to live more than 76 years. Table 4-7 lists the years of expected life for individuals born in four years: 1920, 1960, 1980, and 2000.

The decrease in the death rate is due to better nutrition, health care, and sanitation. Death rates are lower for college graduates than for people not completing high school and for people living in cities than in rural areas. Seventeen children are born in the world every four seconds, and seven people die. These rates account for a net increase of three people every two seconds, or 9,000 more people in the world every hour. One of the requirements in your health class is to write a research paper and then give an oral report on your findings. You decide to study population growth and want to prepare a PowerPoint presentation explaining the major concepts. Using the techniques introduced in this project, create a short slide show. Use the statistics in Table 4-7 to add a chart to one slide. Include WordArt on the title slide, sound effects, and transition effects.

Table 4-7 Life Expectancies in the United States				
	1920	1960	1980	2000
Average	54.1	70.1	73.2	75.8
Male	54.3	68.7	70.6	71.4
Female	55.4	72.3	78.5	79.2

Cases and Places

3 ▶ Volunteers believe they make a contribution to society while they gain much more in return. They do everything from repairing computers to preparing meals. Community organizations and not-for-profit businesses frequently seek volunteers for various projects. You decide to visit and telephone several local civic groups to determine volunteer opportunities. The first number you call is 555-3425, which is the local television station. The program director, Shelly Moore, tells you she is seeking week-day volunteers to help with membership drives during the last two weeks of this month. Shifts are from 8:00 a.m. to 1:00 p.m., 1:00 p.m. to 5:00 p.m., and 5:00 p.m. to 9:00 p.m. The next place you call is the After School Learning Center (555-6458). The coordinator, Chris Jackson, informs you that volun-teer tutors are needed to help with after-school activities from 4:00 p.m. to 7:00 p.m. Responsibilities include helping elementary school children with their math and English skills. You then visit the Vocational Services Center, located at 483 Main Street. You talk with Marla Collins, the organization's director, and discover that volunteers train nearly 50 people each month to use software applications, including Microsoft Office and Windows. Other volunteers repair and upgrade donated computer equip-ment. Classes are offered weekdays from 6:00 p.m. to 8:00 p.m. and on Saturdays from 9:00 a.m. to 11:00 a.m. You decide to help publicize these volunteer opportunities by developing a slide show that will run at the local library. You start by designing a title slide that captures the spirit of volunteering. Use a picture as the background on Slide 1 and add a WordArt element. Create a Word table that organizes the information you gathered in the categories of organization name, telephone number or location, contact person, hours, and description. Enhance the presentation by adding sound clips and slide transition effects.

4 ▶▶ Credit cards can offer opportunities for consumers to purchase items when they are short on cash. But when the credit card debt exceeds household income, credit cards can become a burden. Credit card debt has risen to one of the highest levels on record: in 1980, the average amount of debt per household was 61.3 percent, in 1990 it rose to 79.8 percent, and in 2000 it was 85.7 percent. The average credit card bill has grown nearly 270 percent in the past 10 years. Managers at the local lending institution, We Save U National Bank, want to alert students about the dangers of near-record levels of debt as com-pared with disposable income. They report that one student accumulated more than $270,000 of debt on his credit cards after charging his tuition, books, rent, and other educational expenses. The managers want to encourage students to charge wisely and to take advantage of financial services offered at its main office. You have agreed to develop a persuasive PowerPoint slide show explaining how credit card debt can lead to financial problems, including bankruptcy. Include a chart with the household credit card debt percentages. Add slides featuring the bank's services and savings plans, such as certificates of deposit and Individual Retirement Accounts. Enhance the presentation by adding slide transition effects and an animation scheme. Visit local branches of banks and credit unions or search the Internet to find information for the presentation.

Cases and Places

5 ▶▶ Repair technicians at your neighborhood appliance store receive many telephone calls from customers placing service calls because they think their dishwashers are not working properly. Common complaints are that the dishes are not completely clean and that the glasses are cloudy. When the technicians arrive at the customers' kitchens, they discover that many of the dishwashers are not broken and that the problems often are due to other factors. For example, dirty dishes may be due to using old powdered detergent, improper loading, and excessive dirt and length of time between wash cycles. Cloudy dishes can be due to hard water or soft water. Water hardness is measured in grains per million, and the correct amount of detergent depends on the water hardness. If the water has 0 to 3 grains per million, it is considered soft. Use 3 teaspoons of powder detergent. If it has 4 to 9 grains, it is considered medium. Use 4 to 9 teaspoons of detergent. If it has 10 to 12 grains, it is considered hard. Use 10 to 12 teaspoons of detergent. Visit an appliance store near campus or search the Internet to find the answers to common questions regarding dishwasher operation. Using this information and the techniques introduced in the project, prepare a presentation that provides information about optimizing a dishwasher's performance. Include a Word table describing water hardness and the proper amount of detergent. Enhance the presentation by modifying the slide background, adding clips, applying animation schemes and transition effects, and rehearsing timings. Include hyperlinks to three Web sites. Add speaker notes to the slides and print these notes.

6 ▶▶▶ Leisure time is at a premium today. More than 44 percent of men and 61 percent of women believe their amount of free time has decreased during the past 10 years. One of the consequences of this loss of free time is less time for hobbies and crafts. To fill this void, many people attend arts and crafts shows to buy handmade and personalized items. These events are held throughout the year and can feature fine art, photography, country crafts, and painted clothing and accessories. Develop an informative slide show about upcoming craft shows in your area during the next two months. Scan bulletin boards at local supermarkets and read local newspapers to find information for the presentation. Include a chart listing the location, dates, times, sponsors, and craft types.

7 ▶▶▶ Home insulation helps to retain interior heat in the winter and cold in the summer. It also reduces energy consumption and the amount of pollution and greenhouse gases emitted into the atmosphere. Tiny pockets of trapped air keep heat from being transferred through the material. It can be installed in attics, side walls, basement walls, crawl spaces, garage doors, and around heating and cooling ducts. One of the measures of the product's insulating power is the R-value, which refers to the capability of slowing the transfer of heat. The higher the R-value, the better the material's resistance to the flow of heat through it. The U.S. Department of Energy recommends an R-value of 38 for attic insulation in most areas of the country. Visit a local home improvement store or search the Internet to find information on various types of insulation, such as blanket, blown-in, foamed-in, rigid, and reflective. Determine the R-value recommendations for new and existing homes in your town. Then, develop a PowerPoint presentation on your findings. Include tables comparing the products' R-values and the recommended values for various locations in a house. Enhance the presentation by modifying the slide background, applying an animation scheme and transition effects, and rehearsing timings. Include hyperlinks to three Web sites.

Microsoft PowerPoint 2002

Delivering Presentations to and Collaborating with Workgroups

CASE PERSPECTIVE

Students walking and traveling alone can be vulnerable to crime. They must be alert when they are walking to parking lots and garages and driving on city streets. Mark Klein, the campus police chief, presents several seminars each semester on safety procedures and techniques.

The chief has asked you to help him develop a PowerPoint presentation to accompany his talk discussing driving alone in a vehicle. He would like you to develop the presentation and then deliver it to him and two members of his staff for review. You set up a review cycle so the chief and two members of his staff can comment on your presentation. When you have incorporated their comments in your final document, you will schedule and deliver an online broadcast to these three reviewers.

In addition, Chief Klein wants to put his PowerPoint presentation on a floppy disk to take to his speaking engagements on campus. You agree to help by using the Pack and Go Wizard, which compresses the files and optionally includes the Viewer.

Introduction

The phrase, the whole is greater than the sum of its parts, certainly can apply to a PowerPoint slide show. Often presentations are enhanced when individuals collaborate to fine-tune text, visuals, and design elements on the slides. PowerPoint offers an effective method of sending presentations for review and for sharing comments. A **review cycle** occurs when a slide show author e-mails a file to multiple reviewers so they can make comments and changes to their copies of the slides and then return the file to the author. If the author uses Microsoft Outlook to send the presentation for review, this e-mail program automatically **tracks changes** to the file by displaying who made the changes and comments.

Another method of collaborating with colleagues is by broadcasting the presentation over the Web. **Presentation broadcasting** delivers the slide show to remote audiences who are on the same intranet or are using the Internet. An **intranet** is an internal network that applies Internet technologies and is used to distribute company information to employees.

PowerPoint file sizes often are much larger than those produced by other Microsoft Office programs, such as Word and Excel. Presentations with embedded pictures and video easily can grow beyond the 1.44 MB capacity of floppy disks. The large file size may present difficulties if you need to transport your presentation to show on another computer. One solution to this file size limitation is using the **Pack and Go Wizard**. This program compresses and saves all the components of a presentation so it can be delivered on a computer other than the one on which it was created. Linked documents and multimedia files are included in this packaged file. The Wizard can embed any TrueType font that is included in Windows; however, it cannot embed other TrueType fonts that have built-in copyright restrictions.

Part 1: Workgroup Collaboration Using a Review Cycle

The slide show consists of four slides that provide guidelines for drivers when they are traveling alone. Topics address parking safely, avoiding carjackings, and remaining alert (Figures 1a through 1h). The presentation uses a picture, clips, and WordArt to add visual interest.

ORIGINAL

(a) Slide 1

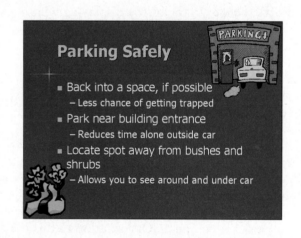

(b) Slide 2

REVISED

(e) New Slide 1

(f) New Slide 2

FIGURE 1

ORIGINAL

REVISED

(c) Slide 3

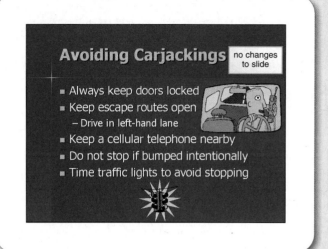

(g) New Slide 3

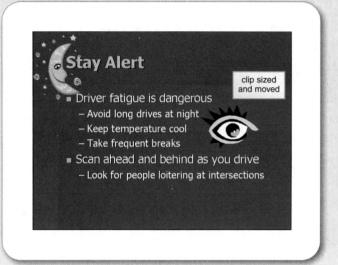

(d) Slide 4

(h) New Slide 4

FIGURE 1

To avoid reading notes and changes made on printouts of a presentation, you can send the PowerPoint file to reviewers using Microsoft Outlook or any other 32-bit e-mail program that is compatible with the Messaging Application Programming Interface (MAPI), a network or Microsoft Exchange server, or a disk. Reviewers can edit the file using any version of PowerPoint.

The review cycle consists of inserting a comment on a slide, sending the presentation to reviewers, receiving the edited file, and evaluating the reviewers' suggestions by accepting and rejecting each comment using the Revisions Pane task pane and Reviewing toolbar.

More About

Reviewing Presentations

Linked files and graphics must be included in the attachment or embedded in the presentation if you want your reviewers to examine the entire slide show.

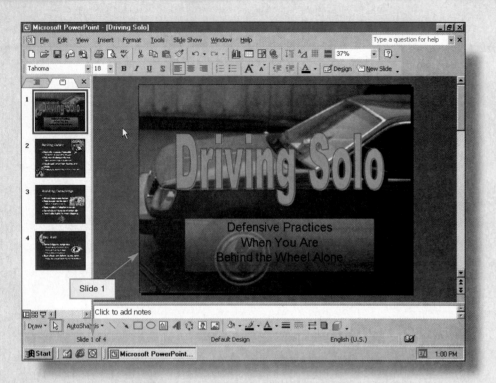

FIGURE 2

Starting PowerPoint and Opening a File

Perform the steps on the next page to start PowerPoint and open the presentation, Driving Solo, from the Data Disk. See the inside back cover for instructions for downloading the Data Disk or see your instructor for information about accessing the files required for this book.

TO START POWERPOINT AND OPEN A PRESENTATION

1 Insert your Data Disk into drive A.

2 Click the Start button on the Windows taskbar and then click Open Office Document.

3 When the Open Office Document dialog box displays, click the Look in box arrow and then click 3½ Floppy (A:) in the Look in list. Double-click the file name, Driving Solo.

4 If the Language bar displays, click its Minimize button.

Slide 1 of the Driving Solo presentation displays in normal view (Figure 2).

Displaying the Reviewing Toolbar and Inserting a Comment

To prepare a presentation for review, you might want to insert a comment containing information for the reviewers. A **comment** is a description that does not normally display as part of the slide show. It can be used to clarify information that may be difficult to understand, to pose questions, or to communicate suggestions. The first step in the review cycle for this project is to display the

Table 1	Buttons on the Reviewing Toolbar	
BUTTON	**BUTTON NAME**	**DESCRIPTION**
	Markup	Displays comments on slides. It is activated when the first comment is entered.
Reviewers...	Reviewers	Displays the user name for all presentation reviewers.
	Previous Item	Selects the previous comment.
	Next Item	Selects the next comment.
	Apply	Incorporates the change into the presentation. Also applies all changes to the current slide or presentation.
	Unapply	Reverses the change made to the document. Also reverses all changes made to the current slide or presentation.
	Insert Comment	Adds a comment to a slide.
	Edit Comment	Changes the comment text.
	Delete Comment	Deletes a comment from a slide.
End Review...	End Review	Stops the reviewing process. All unapplied changes are lost.
	Revisions Pane	Displays or hides the Revisions Pane task pane.
	Toolbar Options	Allow you to select the particular buttons you want to display on the toolbar.

Reviewing toolbar and then insert a comment on Slide 1 asking the reviewers to openly express their opinions.

One method of inserting a comment is by clicking the Insert Comment button on the Reviewing toolbar. This toolbar is shown in Figure 4, and the buttons are described in Table 1.

Perform the following steps to display this toolbar and insert a comment on Slide 1.

Steps ## To Display the Reviewing Toolbar and Insert a Comment

1 **Click View on the menu bar and then point to Toolbars. Point to Reviewing on the Toolbars submenu.**

The View menu and Toolbars submenu display (Figure 3).

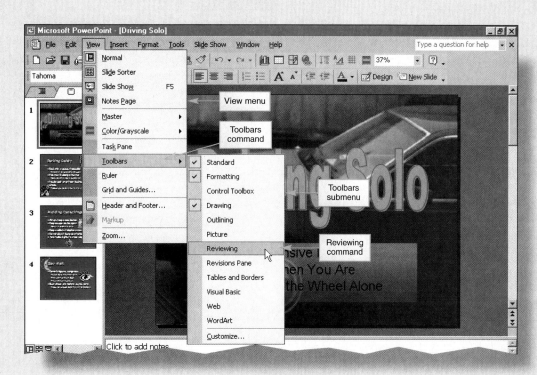

FIGURE 3

2 **Click Reviewing. Point to the Insert Comment button on the Reviewing toolbar.**

The Reviewing toolbar displays (Figure 4).

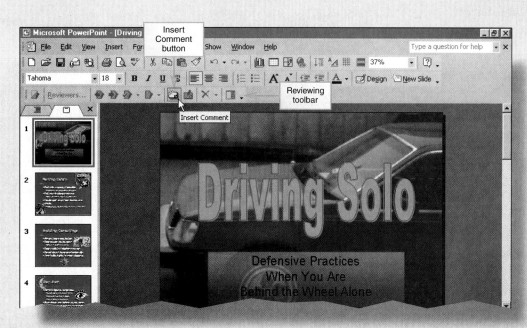

FIGURE 4

3 **Click the Insert Comment button. When the comment box displays, type** Please review this presentation and make suggestions about the art and text. Thanks.

*PowerPoint opens a **comment box** at the top of the slide (Figure 5). The presentation author's name is Sherrie Coleman, and her initials are SC. The author's initials, date, and comments display in the comment box. Your author's initials may differ from this figure. PowerPoint adds a small rectangle, called a **comment marker**, to the upper-left corner of the slide. The number, 1, following the author's initials indicates the comment is the first comment made by this reviewer.*

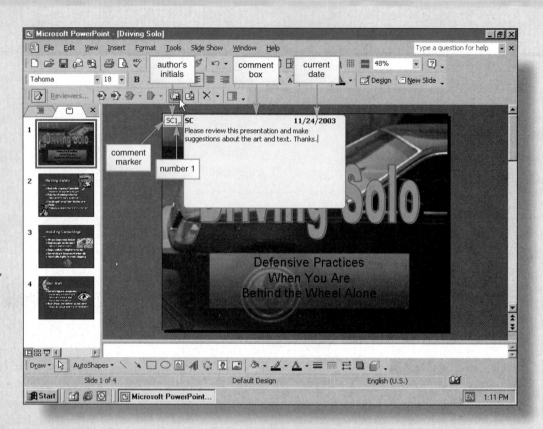

FIGURE 5

4 **Click anywhere outside the comment box and then click the Save button on the Standard toolbar to save the presentation.**

*Clicking outside the comment box hides the text and **locks in** the comment. The author's initials and the comment number display (Figure 6).*

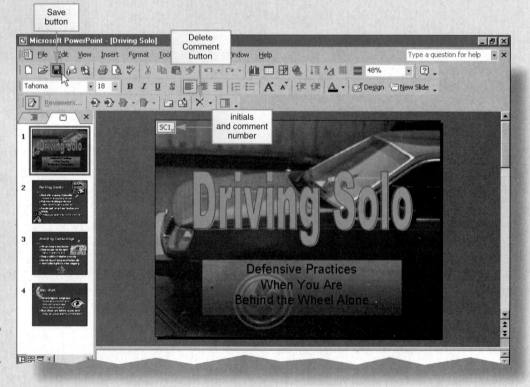

FIGURE 6

Other **Ways**

1. On Insert menu click Comment
2. Press ALT+I, press M
3. In Voice Command mode, say "Insert, Comment"

When PowerPoint closes the comment box, the comment disappears from the screen. If you want to redisplay the comment, point to the comment marker. You can drag the comment to move its position on the slide. To change the reviewer's name and initials, click Tools on the menu bar, click Options, click the General tab, and then edit the Name and Initials fields. If you want to delete a comment, click the Delete Comment button on the Reviewing toolbar or click the comment marker and then press the DELETE key.

Collaborating with Workgroups

If you plan to have others edit your slide show or suggest changes, PowerPoint provides four ways to collaborate with others. **Collaborating** means working together in cooperation on a document with other PowerPoint users.

First, you can **distribute** your slide show to others, physically on a disk or through e-mail using the Send To command on the File menu. With the Send To command, you may choose to embed the document as part of the e-mail message or attach the file as an e-mail attachment, which allows recipients of the e-mail message to open the file if the application is installed on their systems.

Second, you can **route** your slide show to a list of people who pass it along from one to another on the routing list using e-mail. The Send To command on the File menu includes a Routing Recipient command. You specify e-mail addresses, the subject, and the message in the **routing slip**, which is similar to an e-mail message. PowerPoint creates the e-mail message with routing instructions and reminds people who open the document to pass it along to the next person in the routing list when they are finished.

Third, you can **collaborate** interactively with other people through discussion threads or online meetings. The integration of **NetMeeting** with Microsoft Office XP allows you to share and exchange files with people at different locations. When you start an online meeting from within PowerPoint, NetMeeting automatically starts in the background and allows you to share the contents of your file(s).

Fourth, you can collaborate by sharing the slide show. **Sharing** means more than simply giving another user a copy of your file. Sharing implies that multiple people can work independently on the same slide show simultaneously.

With any of the collaboration choices, you should keep track of the changes that others make to your slide show.

Distributing the Slide Show for Review

The next step is to send the slide show to Chief Klein and two of his assistants, Jessica Cantero and Mary Halen. If you are completing this project on a personal computer, you will be prompted to choose the e-mail addresses of the recipients. You can use the recipients specified in the steps in this project, or you can substitute the e-mail addresses shown with e-mail addresses from your address book or class. Your return e-mail contact information must be valid to round trip the file back to yourself. The term **round trip** refers to sending a document to recipients and then receiving it back at some point in time.

Perform the steps on the next page to distribute the presentation for review.

More About

Routing Presentations

Options for deadlines, deliveries, and status checks are available when you prepare a presentation for routing. The Add Routing Slip dialog box allows you to select whether the presentation should be sent to all the recipients simultaneously or sequentially in the order you specify. Reviewers can make changes and insert comments using any version of PowerPoint. You also can choose to have the presentation returned to you automatically after the last recipient closes it.

More About

Using NetMeeting

Microsoft has integrated its Office and NetMeeting programs so a number of people can view a presentation and share the contents of a file. This integration enables you to collaborate with and receive feedback from other people simultaneously as you complete your presentation. You can schedule the meeting in advance by using Microsoft Outlook or start an impromptu online meeting from within an active PowerPoint presentation. If your colleagues are available and they decide to accept your invitation, the online meeting begins. They can use such tools as a whiteboard, video, and audio to present their opinions and comments. For more information, visit the PowerPoint 2002 More About Web page (scsite.com/pp2002/more.htm) and then click NetMeeting.

To Send the Presentation for Review

1 Click File on the menu bar, point to Send To, and then point to Mail Recipient (for Review).

The File menu and Send To submenu display (Figure 7).

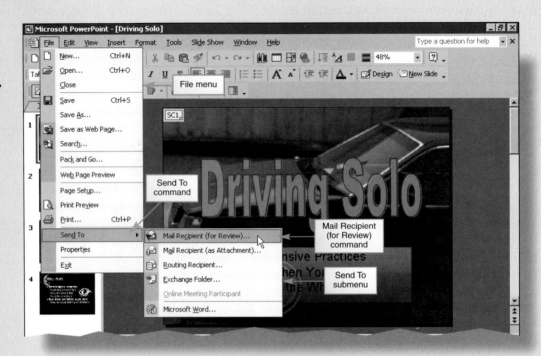

FIGURE 7

2 Click Mail Recipient (for Review). If the Choose Profile dialog box displays, choose your user profile and then click the OK button. When the e-mail Message window displays, **type** Chief_Klein@ hotmail.com; Jessica_ Cantero@hotmail.com; Mary_Halen@hotmail .com **in the To text box. Point to the Send button.**

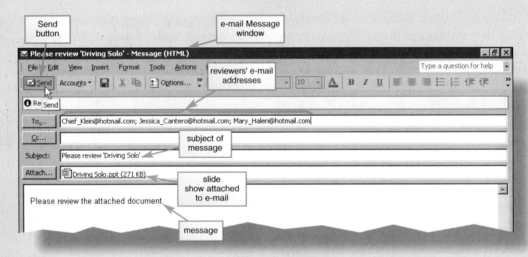

FIGURE 8

PowerPoint displays the e-mail Message window (Figure 8). If you are working on a networked system, see your instructor or network administrator for the correct e-mail account to use.

3 Click the Send button on the Standard Buttons toolbar.

The e-mail with the attached presentation is sent to the three reviewers.

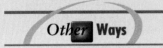

1. Press ALT+F, press D, press C, enter addresses, press ALT+S

Each of the reviewers opens the presentation and makes comments and suggestions about the presentation. The Chief Klein comments include changes to the Slide 1 background and a suggestion about the clip on Slide 3. The Jessica Cantero comment suggests a change to the text on Slide 2 to make the presentation conform to the 7 × 7 rule. The Mary Halen comments recommend adding a slide transition to each slide, reducing the size of the clip on Slide 4, and then repositioning it on the slide. All the reviewers make the proposed changes to the presentation. The next section describes how you will merge these files and review the suggestions.

Merge Slide Shows and Print Comments

PowerPoint keeps a **change history** with each shared slide show. The slide show owner reviews each presentation comment and then makes a decision about whether to accept the suggested change. After the reviewers commented on the Driving Solo presentation, they changed the file name to include their last names and then e-mailed the revised file back to you. If you and your reviewers use Microsoft Outlook as your e-mail program, PowerPoint automatically combines the reviewed presentations with your original slide show. If you used another e-mail program, a server, or a hard disk, you must merge the reviewers' files with your original.

Three slide shows — Driving Solo-Klein, Driving Solo-Cantero, and Driving Solo-Halen — are stored on the Data Disk. As the owner of the original presentation, you review their comments and modifications and make decisions about whether to accept these suggestions. In this Web Feature, you will see a printout of each slide and the comments each reviewer has made about the presentation before you begin to accept and reject each suggestion.

PowerPoint can print these slides and comments on individual pages. The following steps use this slide show to illustrate printing these suggestions.

More About

Printing Transparencies

Print slides, comments, notes, and outlines on overhead transparencies made especially for laser or inkjet printers. Before printing, change the page setup by clicking File on the menu bar and then clicking Page Setup. When the Page Setup dialog box displays, click the Slides sized for box arrow and then click Overhead.

Steps **To Merge Slide Shows and Print Comments**

1 **With the Driving Solo presentation active, click Tools on the menu bar and then point to Compare and Merge Presentations.**

The Tools menu displays (Figure 9).

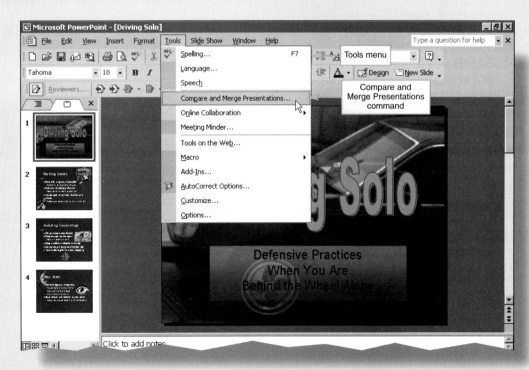

FIGURE 9

2 **Click Compare and Merge Presentations.** When the Choose Files to Merge with Current Presentation dialog box displays, if necessary click the Look in box arrow and then click 3½ Floppy (A:). Click **Driving Solo-Klein.** Press the CTRL key, click **Driving Solo-Cantero** and **Driving Solo-Halen.** Release the CTRL key. Point to the Merge button.

The Choose Files to Merge with Current Presentation dialog box displays (Figure 10). The files displayed on your computer may vary. The three selected files contain comments and revisions from the three reviewers. The steps instructed you to select the files to merge in the order they were sent to the reviewers, but you can merge files in any order.

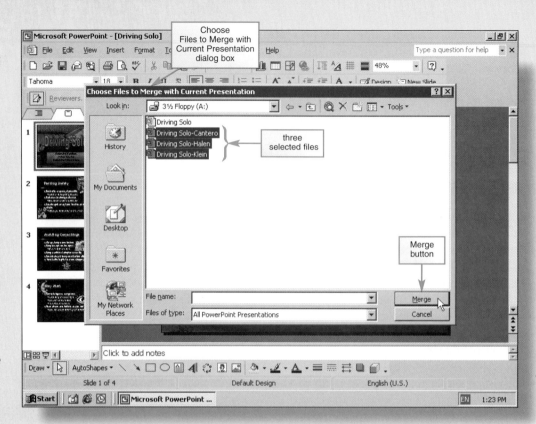

FIGURE 10

3 **Click the Merge button. If a Microsoft PowerPoint dialog box displays asking if you want to browse your presentation, click the Continue button. If a Microsoft PowerPoint dialog box displays asking if you want to merge these changes with your original presentation, click the Yes button. Click File on the menu bar and then point to Print.**

The Revisions Pane task pane and File menu display (Figure 11). Each reviewer's comments in the Slide changes area are marked in a distinct color, which helps identify the author of each suggestion. The order of the comments in the list depends upon the order in which the files were merged with the original presentation. Your comments may display in a different sequence.

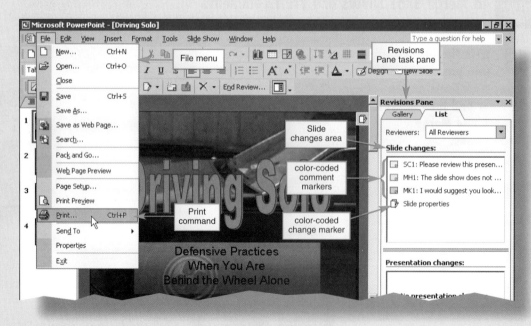

FIGURE 11

4 **Click Print. When the Print dialog box displays, click Include comment pages to select the check box. Point to the Preview button.**

The Print dialog box displays (Figure 12).

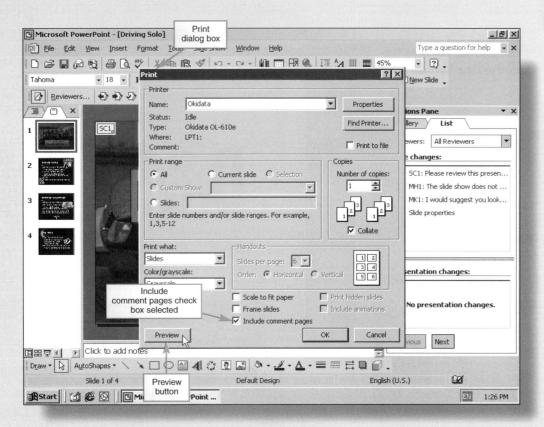

FIGURE 12

5 **Click the Preview button. Point to the Print button.**

Slide 1 displays in the Print Preview window (Figure 13). To preview all eight pages, click the Next Page button.

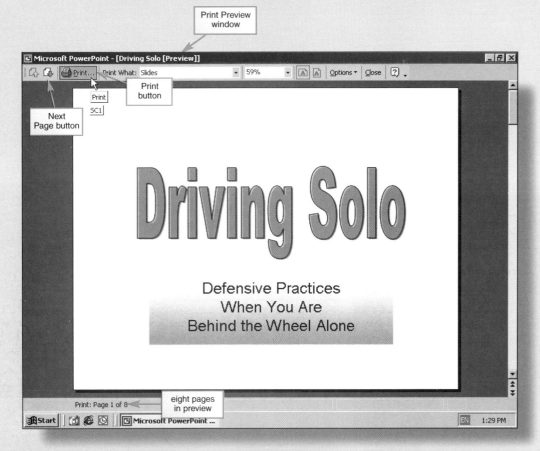

FIGURE 13

Click the Print button. Point to the Close Preview button.

The Close Preview button closes the Print Preview window (Figure 14). The four slides and three comment pages print, as shown in Figure 15 on this page and next two pages.

 Click the Close Preview button.

PowerPoint returns to normal view.

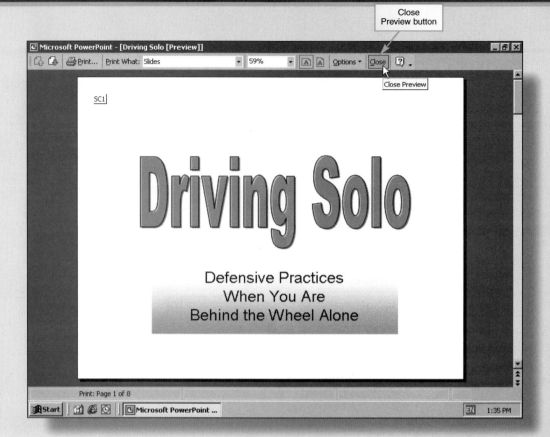

FIGURE 14

SC1

Driving Solo

Defensive Practices
When You Are
Behind the Wheel Alone

(a) Page 1

Slide 1	
SC1	Please review this presentation and make suggestions about the art and text. Thanks. SC, 11/24/03
MH1	The slide show does not have an animation scheme or transition effects. I applied the Split Vertical Out transition to all the slides to give you an idea of what I thought looked good. Mary Halen, 11/24/03
MK1	I would suggest you look for a picture of a more modern car. I have inserted a photo of me in my car. I think it adds to the students' interest. Chief Mark Klein, 11/24/03

(b) Page 2

FIGURE 15

JC1

Parking Safely

- Back into a space, if possible
  - Less chance of getting trapped
- Park near building entrance
  - Reduces time alone outside car
- Locate spot away from bushes and shrubs
  - Allows you to see around and under car

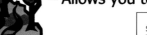

(c) Page 3

Slide 2	
JC1	This slide does not follow the 7 x 7 rule. I changed the final first-level paragraph by deleting the last two words, and shrubs, to follow the rule. Jessica Cantero, 11/24/03

(d) Page 4

MK2

Avoiding Carjackings

- Always keep doors locked
- Keep escape routes open
  - Drive in left-hand lane
- Keep a cellular telephone nearby
- Do not stop if bumped intentionally
- Time traffic lights to avoid stopping

(e) Page 5

Slide 3	
MK2	Could you find a clip with a cellular phone being used in the hands-free mode? It is very dangerous to drive while talking on the telephone. Chief Mark Klein, 11/24/03

(f) Page 6

FIGURE 15

MH2

Stay Alert

- Driver fatigue is dangerous
  - Avoid long drives at night
  - Keep temperature cool
  - Take frequent breaks
- Scan ahead and behind as you drive
  - Look for people loitering at intersections

Slide 4

MH2   I think the eye clip on this slide is too big. I reduced the size to 45% for you.
               Mary Halen, 11/24/03

(g) Page 7

(h) Page 8

FIGURE 15

1. In Voice Command mode, say "Tools, Compare and Merge Presentations, [select file names], Merge, Continue, File, Print, Include comment pages, Preview, Print, Close"

Personal Information

The three reviewers' names and initials display in the Revisions Pane. You may, however, not want your personal information displayed in a comment or macro or saved in a presentation. This information includes your name, initials, and company. To remove this information, click Tools on the menu bar and then click Options. When the Options dialog box displays, click the Security tab. In the Privacy Options area, click Remove personal information from this file on save.

The eight printouts show each of the four slides and the comments each reviewer made about the slides. These pages are helpful to reference as you evaluate the reviewers' suggestions and changes.

Reviewing, Accepting, and Rejecting Comments

The Revisions Pane task pane and Reviewing toolbar help you review each comment and then decide whether to accept the change or delete the suggestion. Color-coded comment and change markers display in the Revisions Pane task pane. Perform the following steps to view each reviewer's comments for each slide in the presentation.

Steps **To Review and Accept Comments on Slide 1**

1 **With Slide 1 displaying, click the SC1 comment marker on the List tab in the Revisions Pane task pane.**

The SC comment box displays (Figure 16). The presentation author's name is Sherrie Coleman, and her initials are SC. The initials in your comment box may vary. The blue comment marker indicates the first comment inserted before sending the presentation to the reviewers. Clicking the comment marker displays the comment.

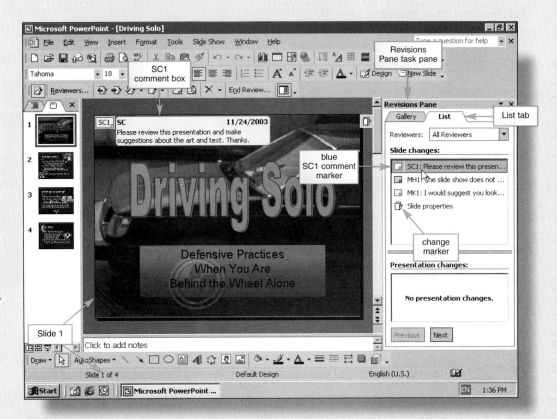

FIGURE 16

2 **Point to the Delete Comment button on the Reviewing toolbar (Figure 17).**

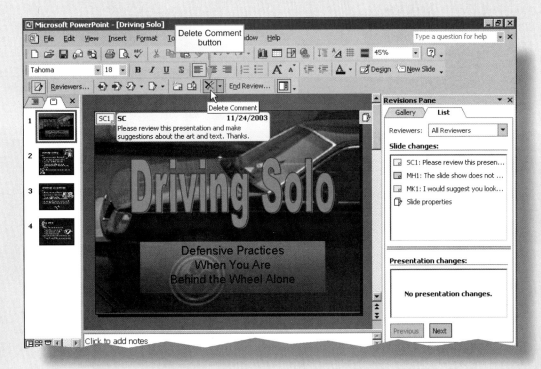

FIGURE 17

3 **Click the Delete Comment button. Click the Next Item button on the Reviewing toolbar to display the MH1 comment. Point to the Gallery tab in the Revisions Pane task pane.**

Sherrie Coleman's comment is deleted from Slide 1 (Figure 18). Mary Halen's first comment regarding animation schemes and transition effects displays. The Slide properties change marker is blank, which indicates you have not applied any changes to the slide.

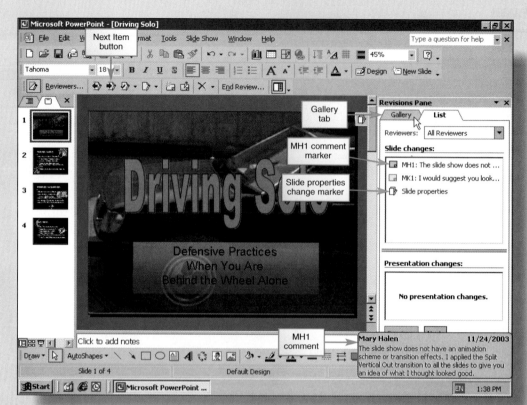

FIGURE 18

4 **Click the Gallery tab and then point to the Mary Halen check box above the Mary Halen slide preview.**

The Gallery tab displays (Figure 19). Slide 1 does not have a slide transition effect. Clicking the check box above Mary Halen's slide preview applies the slide transition effect she added to the presentation.

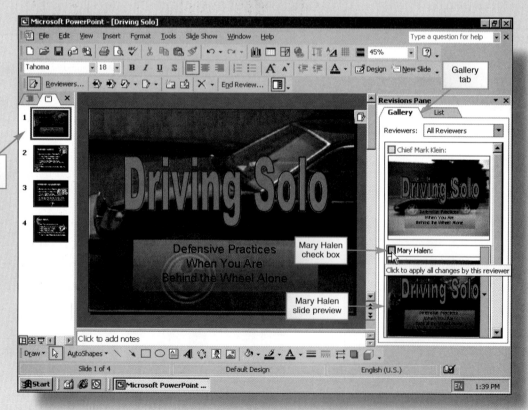

FIGURE 19

5 **Click Mary Halen and then point to the List tab.**

The Split Vertical Out slide transition effect is applied to Slide 1 (Figure 20). You can accept the slide transition change by clicking the check box, clicking the slide preview, or clicking the Apply button on the Reviewing toolbar.

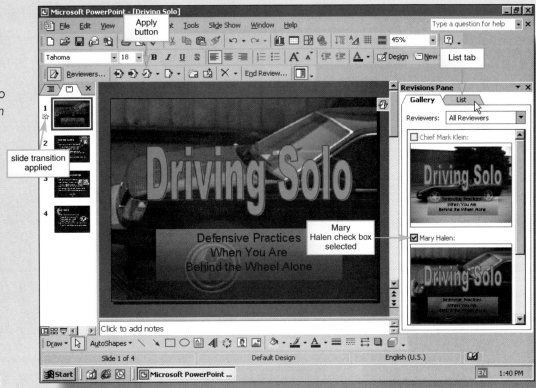

FIGURE 20

6 **Click the List tab and then click the Delete Marker button. Click the green MK1 comment marker and then point to the Gallery tab.**

Mary Halen's change marker is deleted and Chief Mark Klein's first comment displays (Figure 21). Because the Chief Klein changes modified Slide 1, you need to view the change before accepting or rejecting the modification.

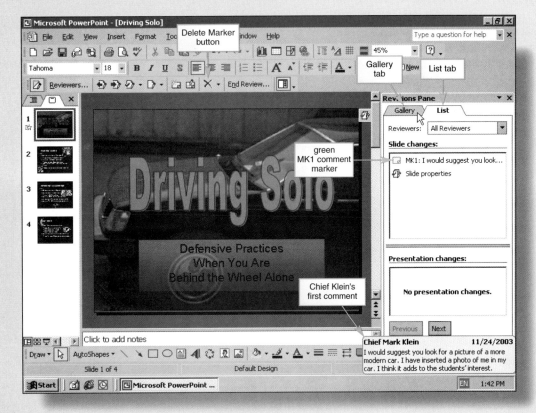

FIGURE 21

7 **Click the Gallery tab, click the Chief Mark Klein check box, and then point to the List tab.**

Slide 1 displays with the new background (Figure 22).

FIGURE 22

8 **Click the List tab and then click the Delete Comment button. Click the Slide Properties change marker and then point to the Delete Marker button on the Reviewing toolbar.**

Mark Klein's first comment is deleted (Figure 23). The checks indicate the changes you have applied. If you decide to unapply one or both of the Slide 1 changes, click the check boxes. A check mark displays in the Slide properties change marker, which indicates you have applied a change to the slide.

FIGURE 23

9 **Click the Delete Marker button. Point to the Next button on the List tab in the Revisions Pane task pane.**

The new background and slide transition effect changes remain (Figure 24). The message in the Slide changes area of the Revisions Pane task pane indicates that no more changes from the reviewers are available for Slide 1 and that the next comments are on Slide 2.

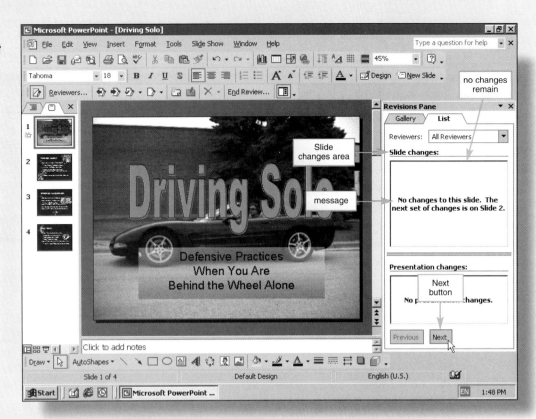

FIGURE 24

All the desired changes from the reviewers have been made to Slide 1. You now can review additional suggestions on the remaining slides in the slide show.

Reviewing, Accepting, and Rejecting Comments on Slides 2, 3, and 4

The three reviewers have made suggestions regarding the text and clip art on the next three slides. The steps on the next page review and accept comments on Slide 2.

Digitizing

Chief Klein added a digitized picture of himself to the Slide 1 background. Digitizing produces some dazzling objects that add interest to presentations. Many artists have traded their paintbrushes and easels for the mouse and monitor. To view some of their creations, visit the PowerPoint 2002 More About Web page (scsite.com/pp2002/more. htm) and then click Digitizing.

Steps To Review and Accept Comments on Slide 2

1 **Click the Next button. Click the orange JC1 comment marker on the List tab in the Revisions Pane task pane. Read the comment and then point to the Delete Comment button on the Reviewing toolbar.**

The Jessica Cantero first comment displays on Slide 2 (Figure 25).

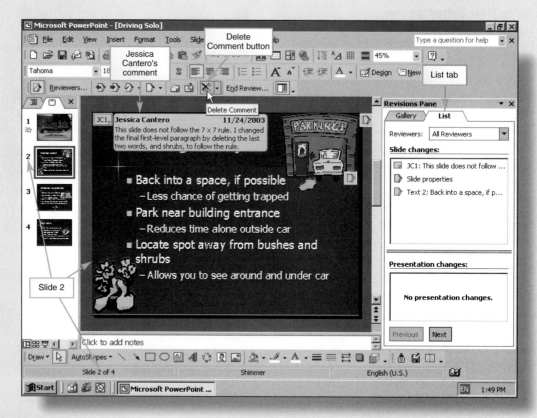

FIGURE 25

2 **Click the Delete Comment button. Click the purple Slide properties change marker in the Revisions Pane task pane and then point to the Slide transition (Mary Halen) check box.**

The Jessica Cantero comment is deleted from Slide 2 (Figure 26). The Mary Halen comment suggested and then applied a slide transition to Slide 2 in the presentation. Clicking the check box accepts the change.

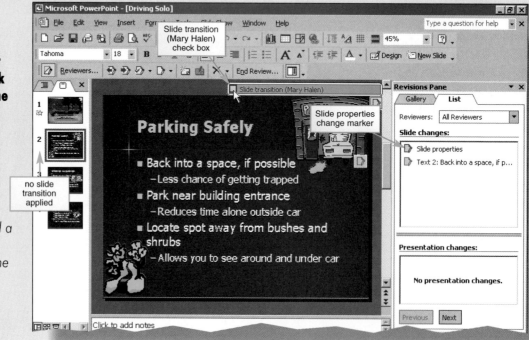

FIGURE 26

3 **Click the Slide transition (Mary Halen) check box and then point to the Delete Marker button on the Reviewing toolbar.**

The check marks and animation icon indicate the Split Vertical Out slide transition effect is applied to Slide 2 (Figure 27).

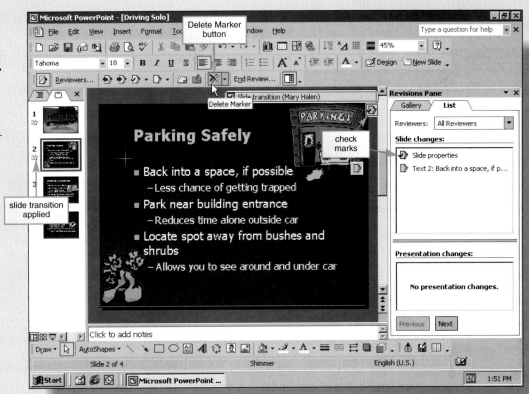

FIGURE 27

4 **Click the Delete Marker button. Click the orange Text 2 change marker and then point to the Deleted "and shrubs" (Jessica Cantero) check box.**

The Mary Halen change marker is deleted (Figure 28). When you point to the check box, the borders around the words, and shrubs, indicate the words that are to be deleted by applying the Jessica Cantero change.

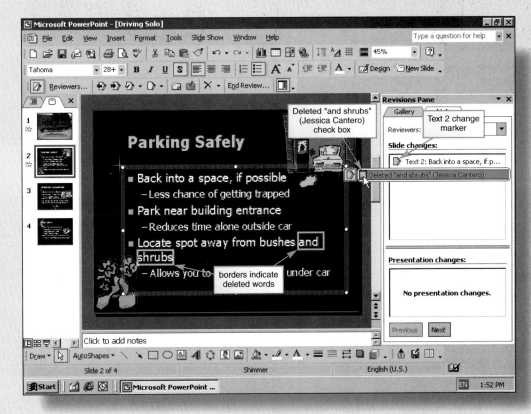

FIGURE 28

5 **Click the Deleted "and shrubs" (Jessica Cantero) check box and then point to the Delete Marker button on the Reviewing toolbar.**

The Jessica Cantero change is accepted (Figure 29).

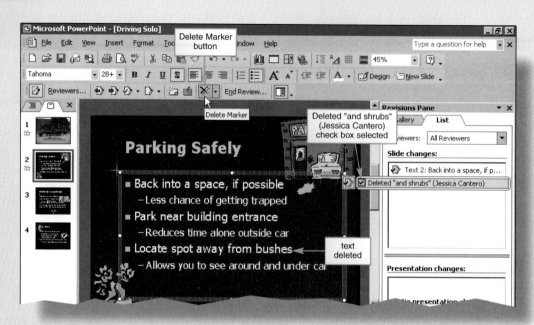

FIGURE 29

6 **Click the Delete Marker button.**

The Jessica Cantero change marker is deleted (Figure 30). The message in the Slide changes area in the Revisions Pane task pane indicates that no more changes from the reviewers are available for Slide 2 and that the next comments are on Slide 3.

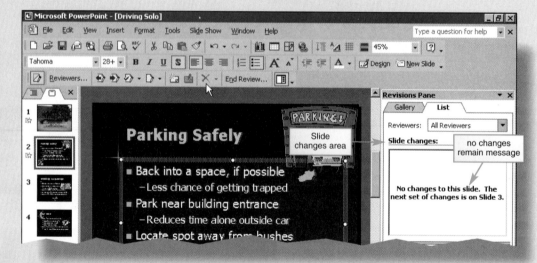

FIGURE 30

All the desired changes from the reviewers have been made to Slide 2. You now can review additional suggestions for the two remaining slides. Perform the following steps to review the comments on Slides 3 and 4 of the presentation using the instructions in Table 2.

TO REVIEW AND ACCEPT COMMENTS ON SLIDES 3 AND 4

1 Click the Next button on the List tab in the Revisions Pane task pane.

2 Be certain to delete each comment marker or change marker after you have performed the action in Table 2.

3 Review the additional comments in the slide show and perform the actions indicated in Table 2.

4 When you have reviewed all the comments, click the Close button in the Revisions Pane task pane.

5 Save the Driving Solo presentation.

6 Run the Driving Solo presentation to see the modifications.

The process of reviewing and accepting the changes to the slide show is complete. The Driving Solo presentation has been updated with suggestions from the three reviewers (Figure 31).

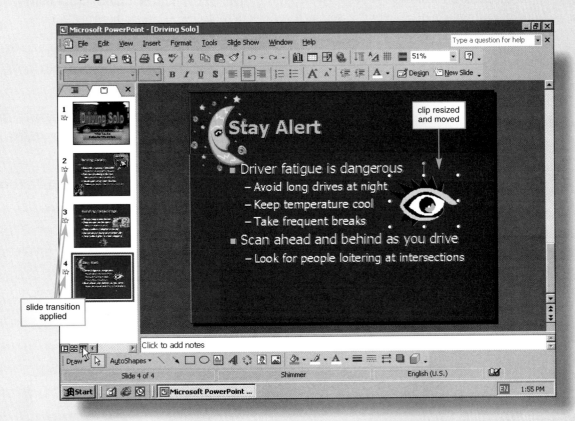

FIGURE 31

Table 2	Changes for Slides 3 and 4		
SLIDE NUMBER	**COMMENT MARKER**	**CHANGE MARKER**	**ACTION**
3	MK2		Read and then delete the comment.
		Slide properties	Apply the Mary Halen slide transition and then delete the change marker.
4	MH2		Read and then delete the comment.
		Slide properties	Apply the Mary Halen slide transition and then delete the change marker.
		Picture frame 77	Apply the changes to the Picture frame 77 and then delete the change marker.i

These changes complete the Driving Solo slide show. The next step is to schedule and deliver this presentation as a broadcast to remote audiences.

More About

Voice Commands

If you use PowerPoint's new Voice Command mode, you may have discovered that this feature may not work with the Microsoft Clip Organizer. Clip Organizer uses Voice Command mode only if it is started when the Insert Clip Art task pane displays. It will not work if you try to run Clip Organizer from the Start menu or from an icon on the desktop or if you click the Clip Organizer link at the bottom of the Clip Organizer task pane to start the stand-alone version.

More *About*

Updating Broadcasts

If you need to change the content in a presentation that is scheduled for broadcast, you must open the presentation, make the changes, resave it, and then reschedule the broadcast. To reschedule, click Slide Show on the menu bar, point to Online Broadcast, and then click Reschedule a Live Broadcast. Save and close the message when Outlook or another e-mail program opens.

Part 2: Scheduling and Delivering Online Broadcasts

PowerPoint's **broadcasting feature** allows remote viewers to see live performances of presentations. While saving slide shows as Web pages creates static versions of presentations, **delivering** broadcasts actually allows presenters to give presentations and include their voices and video.

Windows Media Services or a third-party Windows Media Services provider must be used if a presentation is broadcast to more than 10 computers, and the files must be placed on a shared network server for viewers to access via their Internet connections. The file location must be specified in the form of \\servername\sharename\. If the presentation includes video, Microsoft recommends using Windows Media Services. Prepare to deliver the broadcast about 30 minutes prior to the broadcast time so you can upload the file to the Windows Media Server and send e-mail reminder messages to your audience.

When setting up a broadcast, you must decide when to schedule it, whether you will record and save the broadcast for airing at a later date, and what attributes you want to include, such as video and audio. Broadcasts are set up automatically to include audio and video streams.

The following steps describe how to set up and schedule an online broadcast. You must be connected to a network or to the Internet to perform these steps.

Steps **To Set Up and Schedule an Online Broadcast**

---

1 **Click Slide Show on the menu bar, point to Online Broadcast, and then point to Schedule a Live Broadcast.**

The Slide Show menu and Online Broadcast submenu display (Figure 32).

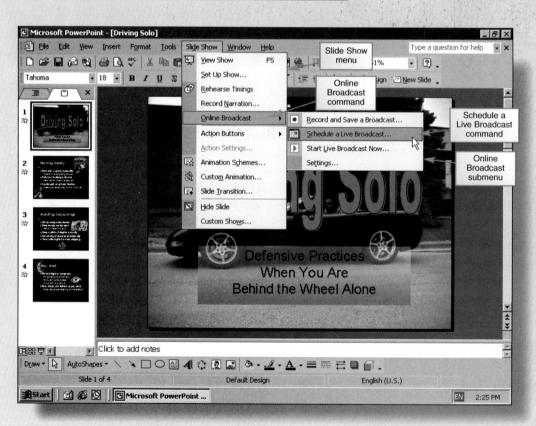

FIGURE 32

2 Click **Schedule a Live Broadcast** on the Online Broadcast submenu. When the Schedule Presentation Broadcast dialog box displays, click the Description text box and then type The purpose of this presentation is to present advice for people who are traveling alone in their vehicles. Double-click the current name in the Speaker text box, and then type Chief Klein as the speaker name. If necessary, type a semicolon and your name in the Keywords text box. Delete any text in the Copyright and Email text boxes. Point to the Settings button.

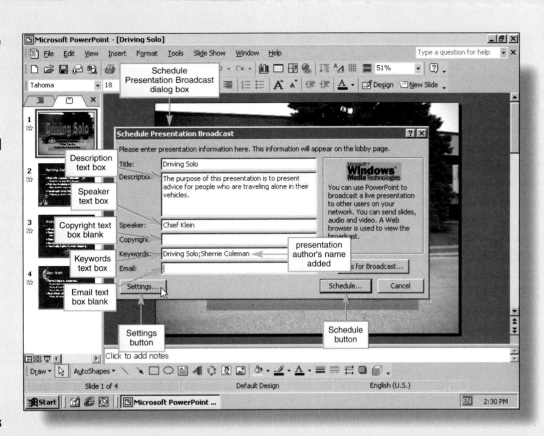

FIGURE 33

The Schedule Presentation Broadcast dialog box displays as shown (Figure 33). The information in the text boxes will be displayed in the e-mail message sent to audience members.

3 Click the Settings button. When the Broadcast Settings dialog box displays, if necessary click None in the Audio/Video area on the Presenter tab. If necessary, click Display speaker notes with the presentation in the Presentation options area to remove the check mark. Ask your instructor where the broadcast files will be stored on your computer network, and then, in the Save broadcast files in text box, type the location where these broadcast files will be stored. Point to the OK button.

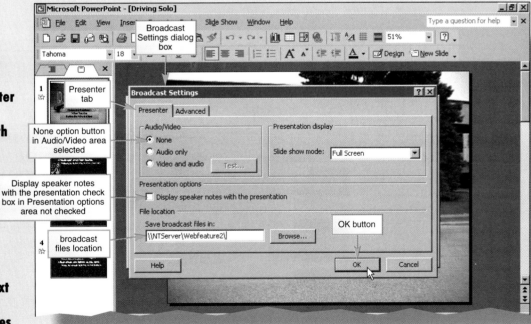

FIGURE 34

The Broadcast Settings dialog box displays as shown (Figure 34). This presentation does not have audio or video components or speaker notes.

4 **Click the OK button. Click the Schedule button. When the Driving Solo – Meeting window displays, click the Maximize button. On the Appointment tab, type** Jessica_Cantero@hotmail.com; Mary_Halen@hotmail.com **in the To text box. Click the Start time date box arrow, click the right arrow at the top of the calendar until the desired month displays, and then click the desired date. Click the Start time time box arrow and then click the desired time in the list.**

The Driving Solo – Meeting window displays as shown (Figure 35). Semicolons or commas can separate recipients' names. Sending the e-mail notifies the two reviewers that the broadcast has been scheduled for a particular date and time and can be viewed at the Event Address (URL) listed in the message. Meetings are scheduled automatically for 30 minutes on the same date.

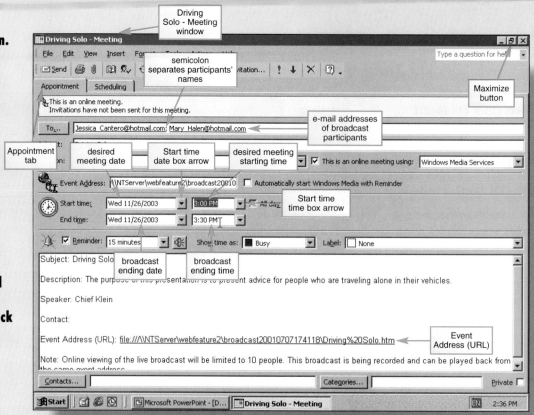

FIGURE 35

5 **Click the Send button on the Standard toolbar. When the Microsoft PowerPoint dialog box displays indicating the broadcast has been scheduled successfully and the broadcast settings have been saved, point to the OK button.**

The message indicates the broadcast settings have been saved in your Driving Solo file (Figure 36).

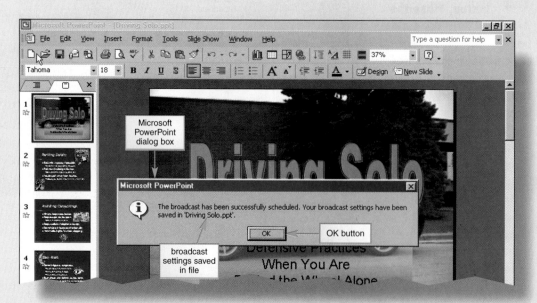

FIGURE 36

6 **Click the OK button.**

Mary Halen and Jessica Cantero will receive an e-mail message indicating that the Driving Solo broadcast has been scheduled.

The presentation has been set up and scheduled. When you are ready to begin the broadcast, click Slide Show on the menu bar, point to Online Broadcast, and then click Start Live Broadcast Now on the Online Broadcast submenu. When the Live Presentation Broadcast dialog box displays, click the Driving Solo broadcast and then click the Broadcast button. Mary Halen and Jessica Cantero can view the slides by launching their Internet browsers and typing the link listed in their e-mail message invitations.

Broadcasting is one method of sharing a presentation with viewers. The next part of this project prepares the Driving Solo presentation so that you can present the slide show with audience members at remote locations.

Part 3: Saving the Presentation Using the Pack and Go Wizard

The **Pack and Go Wizard** will compress the presentation. If desired, you can package it with the PowerPoint Viewer so you can show it on another computer. As you proceed through the Wizard, PowerPoint will prompt you to select the presentation file, a destination drive, linking and embedding options, and whether to add the Viewer.

The Driving Solo file size is 307 KB; and the Pack and Go Wizard will create a compressed file with the file name pres0.ppz with a file size of 243 KB. In addition, the Wizard creates another file, PNGSETUP.EXE, which is needed to unpack, or extract, the presentation file and copy it onto a remote computer. Perform the following steps to use the Pack and Go Wizard.

More About

Packing Animations

Not all animations will show when a PowerPoint presentation has been compressed using the Pack and Go Wizard and then viewed using the PowerPoint Viewer. These animations include any exit, emphasis, or motion path effects. Only entrance effects are supported. The Viewer also cannot run macros or Microsoft ActiveX controls. Compatible transition animations are: blinds, box, checkerboard, cover, cut, dissolve, fade, random bars, split, strips, uncover, and wipe. Other compatible animation effects are: fly in, flash once, typewriter, and appear.

Steps To Save the Presentation Using the Pack and Go Wizard

1 **With the Driving Solo presentation active, click File on the menu bar and then point to Pack and Go.**

The File menu displays (Figure 37). Depending on your computer system installation, you may be prompted to install the Pack and Go Wizard. If this message displays, see your instructor.

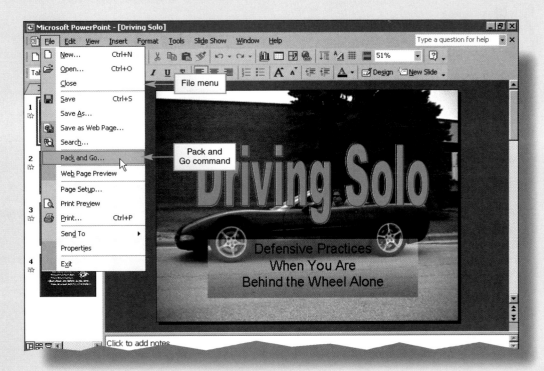

FIGURE 37

2 **Click Pack and Go.
When the Pack and
Go Wizard dialog box
displays, point to the Next
button. If the Office
Assistant displays, click No,
don't provide help now.**

*PowerPoint displays the Start
panel, describing the function
of the Pack and Go Wizard
(Figure 38). You can click the
Help button if you desire further explanations from the
Office Assistant or the Cancel
button to exit the Pack and
Go Wizard.*

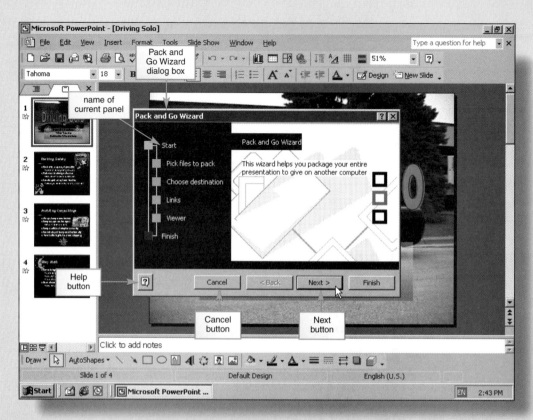

FIGURE 38

3 **Click the Next
button. When the
Pick files to pack panel
displays, point to the Next
button.**

*The Active presentation check
box is selected (Figure 39).
You can choose to package
the Driving Solo file or other
PowerPoint files. You can click
the Back button to review
previous panels.*

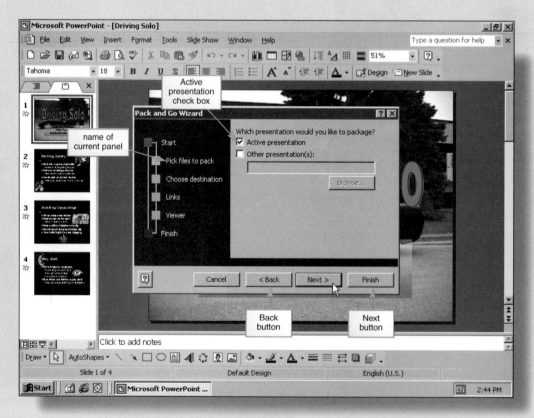

FIGURE 39

4 **Click the Next button. When the Choose destination panel displays, point to the Next button.**

PowerPoint defaults to saving the packed file on the floppy disk in drive A (Figure 40). You could select an alternate destination, such as your hard drive, a Zip drive, or another computer on your network.

FIGURE 40

5 **Click the Next button. When the Links panel displays, click Include linked files to remove the check mark. Point to the Next button.**

The Driving Solo presentation does not contain any linked files, so you do not need to select this option (Figure 41). If the presentation had linked files, such as embedded PowerPoint charts and Word tables, you would need to include these files in the package. The presentation uses the TrueType Tahoma font, but this standard font is available on most computers. Embedding fonts ensures the text displays correctly if the font is not installed on the destination computer.

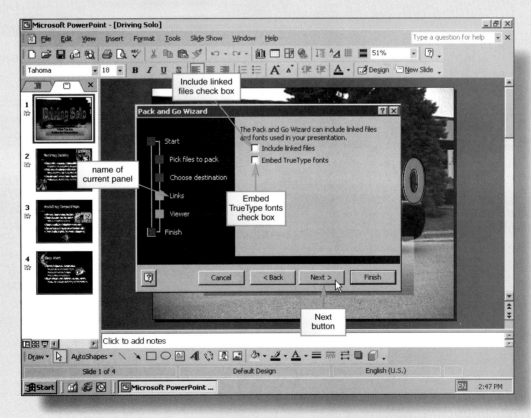

FIGURE 41

6 **Click the Next button. When the Viewer panel displays, point to the Next button.**

You are going to pack only the Driving Solo presentation (Figure 42). You would include the Viewer to run the presentation on a remote computer if PowerPoint was not installed on that machine. If the Viewer is not available, you would need to click the Download the Viewer button to connect to the Microsoft site, obtain this program, and install it on your system.

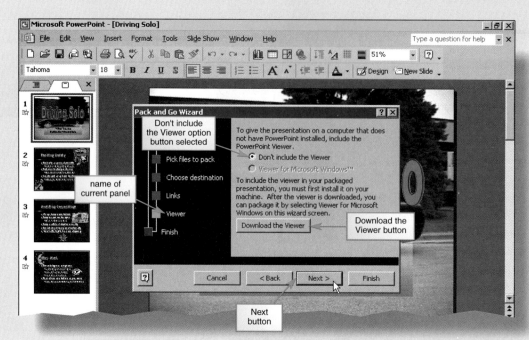

FIGURE 42

7 **Click the Next button. Point to the Finish button.**

The Finish panel displays a message that PowerPoint will compress the Driving Solo presentation to drive A (Figure 43).

8 **Click the Finish button. When the Microsoft PowerPoint dialog box displays, point to the OK button.**

PowerPoint packs the presentation files and displays status messages of which files are being added to the package.

9 **Click the OK button in the Microsoft PowerPoint dialog box.**

PowerPoint closes the Pack and Go Wizard and displays the Driving Solo presentation in normal view.

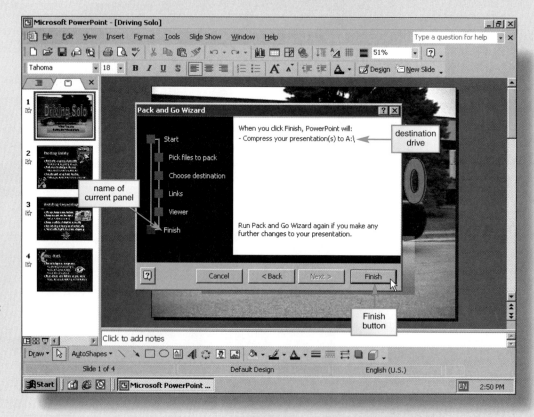

FIGURE 43

The Pack and Go Wizard saves the presentation on your floppy disk. You now are ready to transport the presentation to a remote site.

Unpacking a Presentation

When you arrive at a remote location, you will need to open the packed presentation. Perform the following steps to unpack the presentation.

TO UNPACK A PRESENTATION

1 Insert your first floppy disk of packed files in drive A. Right-click the Start button on the taskbar and then click Open on the shortcut menu.

2 Click the Up button on the Standard Buttons toolbar until the My Computer window displays. Double-click 3½ Floppy (A:).

3 When the 3½ Floppy (A:) window opens, double-click PNGSETUP.

4 When the Pack and Go Setup dialog box displays, create or select a destination folder, and then click the OK button. Ask your instructor if you are uncertain of the destination folder name.

5 When the Pack and Go Setup dialog box displays the message that the presentation has been installed successfully in the directory, click the Yes button to run the slide show now.

PowerPoint unpacks the Driving Solo presentation and runs the slide show.

This project is complete. You now should close the Driving Solo presentation.

Closing the Presentation

Perform the following step to close the presentation but leave PowerPoint running.

TO CLOSE THE PRESENTATION

1 Click File on the menu bar and then click Close on the File menu.

PowerPoint closes the Driving Solo presentation.

More About

Disabling New Features

To use only animations that are compatible with the PowerPoint Viewer, click Tools on the menu bar and then click Options. When the Options dialog box displays, click the Edit tab. In the Disable new features area, click New animation effects and then click the OK button. The Custom Animation dialog box will display instead of the Custom Animation task pane.

Other Ways

1. Press ALT+F, press C
2. In Voice Command mode, say "File, Close"

CASE PERSPECTIVE SUMMARY

The Driving Solo presentation has been enhanced with comments and changes obtained from three reviewers. In addition, Chief Klein can share the slide show with remote viewers by broadcasting this presentation via the Internet. Now he can show the presentation to students at various locations across the campus. By using the Pack and Go Wizard, he can transport the presentation file to these locations.

Web Feature Summary

This Web Feature demonstrated three methods of sharing a presentation with others. In Part 1, you set up a review cycle and sent the presentation for review. In Part 2, you learned to set up and schedule an online broadcast. In Part 3, you learned to use the Pack and Go Wizard to condense files.

What You Should Know

Having completed this Web Feature, you now should be able to perform the following tasks:

▶ Close the Presentation *(PPW 2.31)*
▶ Display the Reviewing Toolbar and Insert a Comment *(PPW 2.05)*
▶ Merge Slide Shows and Print Comments *(PPW 2.09)*
▶ Review and Accept Comments on Slide 1 *(PPW 2.15)*
▶ Review and Accept Comments on Slide 2 *(PPW 2.20)*
▶ Review and Accept Comments on Slides 3 and 4 *(PPW 2.22)*
▶ Save the Presentation Using the Pack and Go Wizard *(PPW 2.27)*
▶ Send the Presentation for Review *(PPW 2.08)*
▶ Set Up and Schedule an Online Broadcast *(PPW 2.24)*
▶ Start PowerPoint and Open a Presentation *(PPW 2.04)*
▶ Unpack a Presentation *(PPW 2.31)*

In the Lab

1 Reviewing and Accepting Comments, Scheduling a Broadcast, and Using the Pack and Go Wizard

Problem: Lori Jackson, the director of community education at your school, wants to promote the new dance class that will be offered next semester. To spread the message, she wants to show the Dance Lessons presentation shown in Figures 44a through 44d. Lori wants two dance instructors on her staff, Janita and Phillip, to review the presentation, so she asks you to send the slide show to them and would like to review their comments. She creates the final presentation shown in Figures 44e through 44h. In addition, she wants you to broadcast the revised presentation to your instructor. She knows that the cafeteria and student union are equipped with computers that have PowerPoint 2002 installed, so she would like for you to use the Pack and Go Wizard to transfer the presentation to floppy disks so she can run the slide show on those computers.

Instructions: Start PowerPoint and then perform the following steps with a computer.

1. Open the presentation, Dance Lessons, from the Data Disk. The slides are shown in Figures 44a through 44d on this page and the next two pages.
2. Merge the two instructors' revised files, Dance Lessons-Janita and Dance Lessons-Phillip, on the Data Disk. Print the slides and the comments.
3. On Slide 1, accept all the changes.
4. On Slide 2, reject Janita's changes and accept Phillip's changes.
5. On Slide 3, accept Phillip's design template change and reject all other changes.
6. On Slide 4, accept all the changes.
7. Schedule the broadcast for on October 6 at 9:00 a.m. Invite your instructor to the broadcast.
8. Save the presentation with the file name, New Dance Lessons.
9. Save the presentation using the Pack and Go Wizard. Do not embed TrueType fonts, and do not include the Viewer.
10. Quit PowerPoint. Hand in the floppy disk containing the presentation to your instructor.

ORIGINAL

(a) Slide 1

REVISED

(e) New Slide 1

FIGURE 44

(continued)

In the Lab

Reviewing and Accepting Comments, Scheduling a Broadcast, and Using the Pack and Go Wizard *(continued)*

ORIGINAL

Have Fun and Get Fit

➤ *Have two left feet?*
  ➤ *We will have you on your toes in no time*
➤ *Want to lose weight?*
  ➤ *Dancing burns hundreds of calories*
➤ *Want to meet people?*
  ➤ *You will have dance partners every night*

(b) Slide 2

REVISED

Have Fun and Get Fit

● Have two left feet ?
  ▪ You will be dancing the first night
● Want to lose weight?
  ▪ Dancing burns hundreds of calories
● Want to meet people?
  ▪ You will have dance partners every night

(f) New Slide 2

Learn Several Dances

➤ *Fox trot*
  ➤ *The classic ballroom dance*
➤ *Stepping*
  ➤ *Organized rhythmic dance steps*
➤ *Latin line dancing*
  ➤ *Tango, salsa-mambo, and merengue*

(c) Slide 3

● ● ● Learn Several Dances

  ○ Fox trot
    ● The classic ballroom dance
  ○ Stepping
    ● Organized rhythmic dance steps
  ○ Latin line dancing
    ● Tango, salsa-mambo, and merengue

(g) New Slide 3

FIGURE 44

In the Lab

ORIGINAL

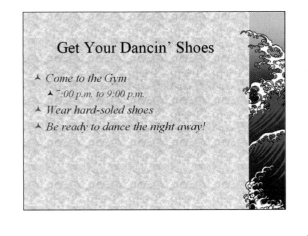

REVISED

(d) Slide 4

(h) New Slide 4

FIGURE 44

2 Reviewing a Presentation and Saving Changes Using the Pack and Go Wizard

Problem: Malcolm Perkins has shown the Get Fit: Eat Better and Feel Great slide show you created for him in Project 4 successfully to several groups of Wellness Institute members. He has made a few changes to the presentation and has e-mailed you his revised file, Eating Well-Malcolm. He informs you that he would like to present the slide show at the local health food store and at the library. Both of these locations have computers, so he would like to transport the slide show on floppy disks and install it on the computers at these sites instead of taking his notebook computer to these events. You agree to make his suggested changes to the presentation and to help him by using the Pack and Go Wizard to transfer the slide show to floppy disks. Create the final presentation shown in Figures 45a through 45e on the next page.

Instructions: Start PowerPoint and then perform the following steps with a computer.

1. Open the Eating Well presentation shown in Figures 4-1a through 4-1e on page PP 4.05. (If you did not complete Project 4, see your instructor for a copy of the presentation.)
2. Merge the Eating Well-Malcolm file on your Data Disk. Print the slides and his comments. Accept all of Malcolm's changes except the one on Slide 5.
3. Save the presentation with the file name, Eating Well Revised.
4. Save the file using the Pack and Go Wizard. Include the linked files and embed TrueType fonts.
5. Hand in the floppy disks containing the presentation to your instructor. Quit PowerPoint.

(continued)

In the Lab

Reviewing a Presentation and Saving Changes Using the Pack and Go Wizard *(continued)*

(a) Slide 1

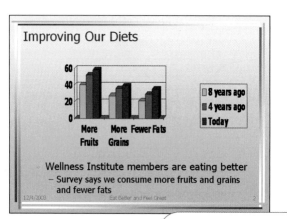

(b) Slide 2

(c) Slide 3

FIGURE 45

In the Lab

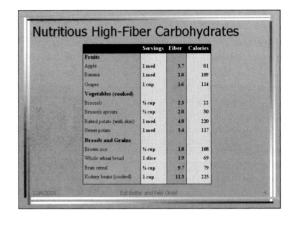

Nutritious High-Fiber Carbohydrates

	Servings	Fiber	Calories
Fruits			
Apple	1 med	3.7	81
Banana	1 med	2.8	109
Grapes	1 cup	1.6	114
Vegetables (cooked)			
Broccoli	½ cup	2.3	22
Brussels sprouts	½ cup	2.0	30
Baked potato (with skin)	1 med	4.8	220
Sweet potato	1 med	3.4	117
Breads and Grains			
Brown rice	½ cup	1.8	108
Whole wheat bread	1 slice	1.9	69
Bran cereal	½ cup	9.7	79
Kidney beans (cooked)	1 cup	11.3	225

1/24/2003   Eat Better and Feel Great   4

(d) Slide 4

Next Steps

- Obtain additional information from
  - *American Heart Association*
  - *American Dietetic Association*
  - *U.S. Department of Agriculture*
- Exercise at least three times per week
- See personal trainers for specific advice

(e) Slide 5

FIGURE 45

3 Broadcasting a Presentation and Reviewing Comments

Problem: After viewing the Enjoy Spring Break presentation in Project 2, you decide to create a similar presentation highlighting your favorite vacation destinations. You create the slide show and decide to solicit comments regarding the presentation from your professors, friends, classmates, or family members. You ask your network administrator or instructor to upload this file to a shared folder on your school's Web server.

Instructions: Start PowerPoint and perform the following tasks with a computer.

1. Invite two people and your instructor to view the online broadcast. Schedule the broadcast for 10:00 a.m. next Monday or a day and time that is convenient for the three invitees.
2. Insert a comment on Slide 1 of the presentation. Send the presentation to two professors, friends, classmates, or family members. Ask the reviewers to make comments and changes to the presentation and have them send their files back to you.
3. Merge their files with your original presentation. Print the slides and their comments.
4. Review their comments and accept or reject their suggestions. Print the revised slides. Hand in the printed original slides, comments, and revised slides to your instructor. Quit PowerPoint.

Microsoft PowerPoint 2002

Working with Macros and Visual Basic for Applications (VBA)

You will have mastered the material in this project when you can:

O B J E C T I V E S

- Create a toolbar
- Customize a toolbar by adding buttons
- Use the macro recorder to create a macro
- Customize a menu by adding a command
- Open a presentation and print it by executing a macro
- Create a form to customize a presentation
- Create a user interface
- Add controls, such as command buttons and combo boxes, to a form
- Assign properties to controls
- Write VBA code to create a unique presentation

The Perfect Portfolio

Customized and Creative

After all your hard work as a student, you are ready to leap into a profession in your chosen field of study. Many college graduates search for career choice information at campus placement centers and job fairs and in employment classified advertisements in local papers and career Web sites.

As you read job descriptions and begin interviewing for positions, you will discover that computer skills are an important priority with employers. CareerLab®, an online occupation advisement Web site, indicates that a high number of middle- and upper-level management job seekers do not own a computer, cannot create a word-processed document or copy a disk, and never have used the Internet. These individuals are at a disadvantage in the job market.

People with up-to-date computer skills are in high demand, and top executives are expected to take their notebook computers on the road. Many employers look for candidates with more than a basic knowledge

of computers; they desire individuals proficient in the latest version of software, especially Microsoft Word, Microsoft Excel, and Microsoft PowerPoint. An added bonus for employers is a candidate who has become certified as a Microsoft Office User Specialist (MOUS). When writing your cover letter and resume, emphasize your competency in these and any other programs in which you are proficient.

After you receive a call to schedule an interview, you must prepare for presenting yourself in the most persuasive manner. Career books and Web sites abound with advice on what questions to expect, what questions to ask, and what clothes to wear. In the typical 30-minute interview, you will be judged on your communications skills, leadership ability, maturity, and intelligence.

No doubt you also will be asked questions about your computer expertise. While you can list these skills on your resume and discuss them with the interviewer, nothing is more persuasive than actually demonstrating your proficiency. One of the most influential methods of showing this technological knowledge is with an electronic portfolio.

The portfolio concept is not new; artists, architects, and journalists routinely bring binders, scrapbooks, and folders to interviews to showcase their drawings, plans, and writings. Today, technology-savvy students have transformed these tangible notebooks to electronic notebooks using PowerPoint to display their projects, describe their experiences, and demonstrate their skills.

In this project, you will develop an electronic career portfolio slide show for Bernie Simpson, an elementary education major who is seeking a position teaching middle school science. The presentation highlights Bernie's teaching and leisure activities using video clips and digital photographs. With a form developed in Visual Basic for Applications, a programming language that extends PowerPoint's capabilities, the slide show can be tailored for each prospective school district.

Eye-catching, professional-looking electronic portfolios provide employment candidates with cutting-edge skills recruiters seek. The techniques you will learn in this project, coupled with organized interview plans and a well-thought-out portfolio, will benefit you as you embark on your chosen career path.

Microsoft PowerPoint 2002

Working with Macros and Visual Basic for Applications (VBA)

C A S E   P E R S P E C T I V E

Creative job seekers are developing innovative methods of presenting their educational background and work experiences. One of these techniques is running an electronic career portfolio slide show on a notebook computer during an interview. Your classmate, Bernie Simpson, has asked you to help him develop such a slide show. Bernie is an elementary education major and is seeking a position teaching science at a middle school. He wants to tailor his slide show for each prospective school district for several interviews next month. He has two video clips and three digital photos highlighting his teaching and leisure activities.

After examining the information Bernie wants to emphasize, you determine that the best method for customizing each presentation is to use a form you develop using Visual Basic for Applications. Bernie's responses on the form will create a unique slide show for each interview. You also will create a toolbar and add buttons and then add a command to the File menu to simplify the related tasks he must perform: saving the presentation as a Web page, using the Pack and Go Wizard, printing a handout, and displaying the form.

Introduction

Before a computer can take an action and produce a desired result, it must have a step-by-step description of the task to be accomplished. This series of precise instructions is called a **procedure**, which also is called a **program** or **code**. The process of writing a procedure is called **computer programming**. Every PowerPoint command on a menu and button on a toolbar has a corresponding procedure that executes when the command or button is clicked. When the computer **executes** a procedure, it carries out the step-by-step instructions. In a Windows environment, the instructions associated with a task are executed when an **event** takes place, such as clicking a button, an option button, or a check box.

Because a command or button in PowerPoint does not exist for every possible task, Microsoft has included a powerful programming language called **Visual Basic for Applications** (**VBA**). This programming language allows you to customize and extend the capabilities of PowerPoint.

In this project, you will learn how to create macros using a code generator called a **macro recorder**. A **macro** is a procedure composed of VBA code that automates multi-step tasks. By simply executing a macro, the user can perform tasks that otherwise would require many keystrokes. You also will learn how to add buttons to toolbars. You will add a command to a menu and associate it with a print macro. Finally, you will learn the basics of VBA as you create an interface, set properties, and write the code.

The slide show you create in this project is intended to help the user, Bernie Simpson, in his job search. The goal is that he will open the Teaching Portfolio file on his notebook computer at each job interview, open the form, and then make selections on the form to indicate which slide template, video clip, and picture to insert. VBA will create the presentation corresponding to these selections. Two possible slide shows are shown in Figures 5-1a through 5-1h.

Presentation 1

(a) Slide 1

(b) Slide 2

(c) Slide 3

(d) Slide 4

Presentation 2

(e) Slide 1

(f) Slide 2

(g) Slide 3

(h) Slide 4

FIGURE 5-1

Project Five — Creating an Electronic Resume

The following requirements are necessary to create the Teaching Portfolio:

Needs: The portfolio requires an easy-to-use interface. This interface will be implemented in three phases:

Phase 1 — Create a toolbar and add two buttons (Save as Web Page and Pack and Go) that normally do not display on any toolbar (Figure 5-2).

Phase 2 — Use the macro recorder to create a macro that prints handouts that display four slides per page vertically using the Pure Black and White option. Assign the macro to a command on the File menu (Figure 5-3) so the user can execute the macro by clicking the command.

Phase 3 — Add a button to the toolbar created in Phase 1 that displays a form allowing the user to design a custom presentation (Figure 5-4). This form lets the user select one of two slide design templates, video clips, and pictures.

FIGURE 5-2

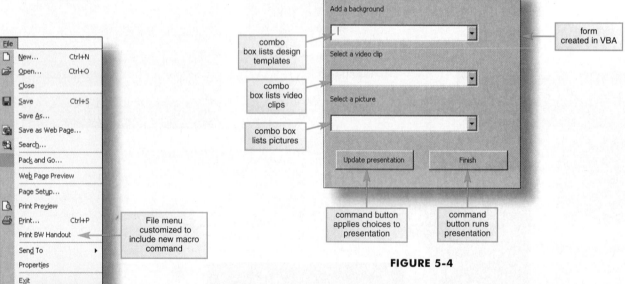

FIGURE 5-3

FIGURE 5-4

Source of Data: You develop a preliminary presentation the user will complete by making appropriate selections on a form. This slide show, shown in Figures 5-5a through 5-5d, has the file name, Teaching, and is located on the Data Disk.

Opening a Presentation and Saving It with a New File Name

To begin, start PowerPoint and open the Teaching file on the Data Disk. Then reset the toolbars and menus so they display exactly as shown in this book (see Appendix D). Perform the following steps.

TO OPEN A PRESENTATION AND SAVE IT WITH A NEW FILE NAME

1 Click the Start button on the Windows taskbar, point to Programs on the Start menu, and then click Microsoft PowerPoint on the Programs submenu.

(a) Slide 1

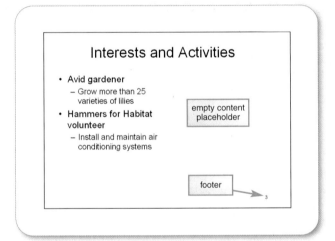

(c) Slide 3

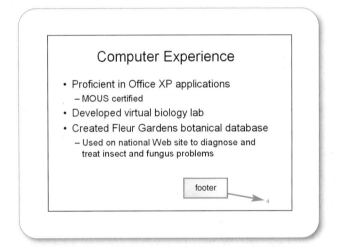

(b) Slide 2

(d) Slide 4

FIGURE 5-5

2 If the New Presentation task pane displays, click the Show at startup check box to remove the check mark and then click the Close button on the task pane title bar.

3 If the Language bar displays, click its Minimize button.

4 If the Standard and Formatting toolbars display on one row, click the Toolbar Options button on the right side of either toolbar and then click Show Buttons on Two Rows on the Toolbar Options menu.

5 Open the presentation, Teaching, from the Data Disk. See the inside back cover of this book for instructions for downloading the Data Disk or see your instructor for information about accessing the files required for this book.

6 Save the presentation with the file name, Teaching Portfolio.

The presentation is saved with the file name, Teaching Portfolio (Figure 5-6 on the next page).

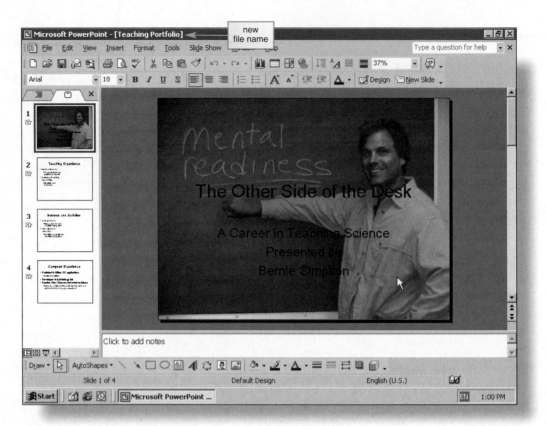

FIGURE 5-6

The PowerPoint Help System

Need Help? It is no further than the Ask a Question box in the upper-right corner of the window. Click the box that contains the text, Type a question for help (Figure 5-6), type help, and then press the ENTER key. PowerPoint will respond with a list of items you can click to learn about obtaining help on any PowerPoint-related topic. To find out what is new in PowerPoint 2002, type what's new in PowerPoint in the Ask a Question box.

The Teaching Portfolio presentation is composed of four slides (Figures 5-5a through 5-5d on the previous page). The first is a title slide with a picture of Bernie as the background. The subtitle text gives the purpose of the slide show and Bernie's identifying information. You will select one of two slide design templates, Clouds or Orbit, to format the text and position the placeholders.

Slide 2 describes Bernie's teaching experience, and it uses the Title, Text, and Content slide layout. The content placeholder is empty, but it will contain one of two possible video clips, golf or motorcycle, based on the selection made in the Visual Basic form. A digital video camera was used to shoot this video, and then later it was edited and the clips were compressed to use in this presentation.

Slide 3 highlights Bernie's interests and activities. One of his pastimes is gardening, growing many types of lilies, and another is volunteering at the local Hammers for Habitat organization, which builds and repairs low-income housing for community residents. The slide also uses the Title, Text, and Content slide layout; one of two photos of Bernie gardening or testing an air conditioning unit will be inserted into the content placeholder.

Slide 4 emphasizes Bernie's computer expertise and his Microsoft Office User Specialist (MOUS) certification in Office XP. His accomplishments include creating a virtual lab for biology classes and developing the botanical database for Fleur Gardens, which are emphasized in the presentation.

Slides 2, 3, and 4 have a footer that contains the slide number, as seen in Figure 5-7. In addition, they use the Float animation scheme. Slide 1 automatically advances in 10 seconds or when you click the mouse, and Slides 2, 3, and 4 advance 15 seconds after they display or when you click the mouse.

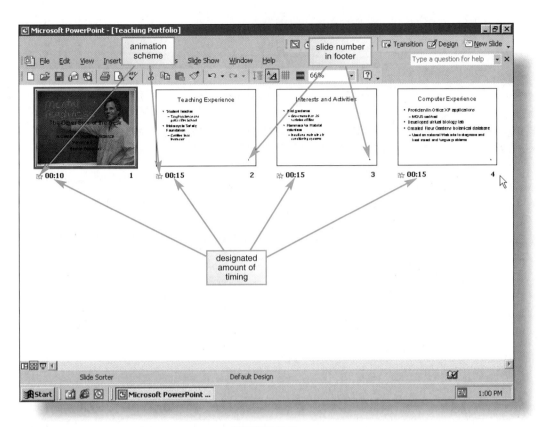

FIGURE 5-7

Phase 1 — Creating a Toolbar and Adding Two Buttons

The first phase of this project creates a toolbar that displays in the lower-right corner of the screen beside the Drawing toolbar. PowerPoint provides more than a dozen toolbars for a variety of purposes. A **custom toolbar**, however, allows you to display the buttons specific to your needs.

Creating and Customizing a Toolbar

One of the buttons you will add to the custom toolbar is the Save as Web Page button. Although users can save a file as a Web page by clicking the Save as Web Page command on the File menu, they also can click a button to make the presentation available for potential employers to view on the Internet. The second button you will add to the custom toolbar in this phase of the project will launch the Pack and Go Wizard. Users can click this button to compress and store the presentation files. They then can transport the presentation on floppy disks to show on a computer at the interviewing site, rather than view it on their notebook computers.

You can customize toolbars and menus by adding, deleting, and changing the function of buttons and commands. Once you add a button to a toolbar or a command to a menu, you can assign a macro to the button or command. You customize a toolbar or menu by invoking the **Customize command** on the Tools menu. The key to understanding how to customize a toolbar or menu is to recognize that when the Customize dialog box is open, PowerPoint's toolbars and menus are in edit mode. **Edit mode** allows you to modify the toolbars and menus.

More **About**

Job Hunting

Are you looking for a job or do you need information about a career? Turn to the Internet for a wealth of information about the fastest-growing careers, employment databases, salaries, freelance work, and resume writing. For more information, visit the PowerPoint 2002 More About Web page (scsite.com/pp2002/more.htm) and then click Jobs.

Perform the following steps to create a custom toolbar.

Steps **To Create a Custom Toolbar**

1 **Click Tools on the menu bar and then point to Customize.**

The Tools menu displays (Figure 5-8).

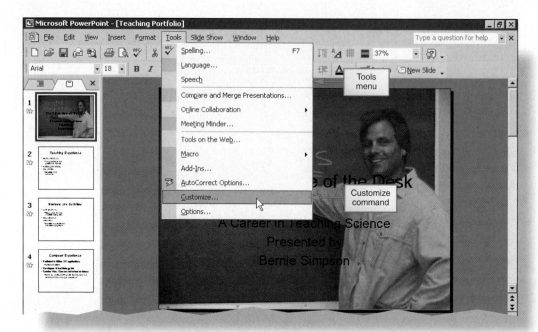

FIGURE 5-8

2 **Click Customize. When the Customize dialog box displays, if necessary, click the Toolbars tab, and then point to the New button.**

The Toolbars sheet in the Customize dialog box displays (Figure 5-9).

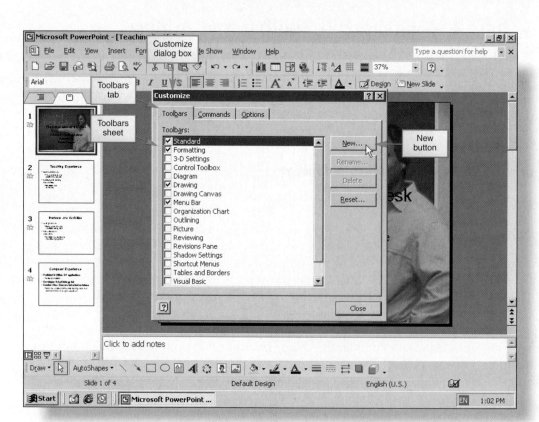

FIGURE 5-9

3 **Click the New button. When the New Toolbar dialog box displays, type** Resume **in the Toolbar name text box and then point to the OK button.**

Resume will be the name of the new toolbar (Figure 5-10).

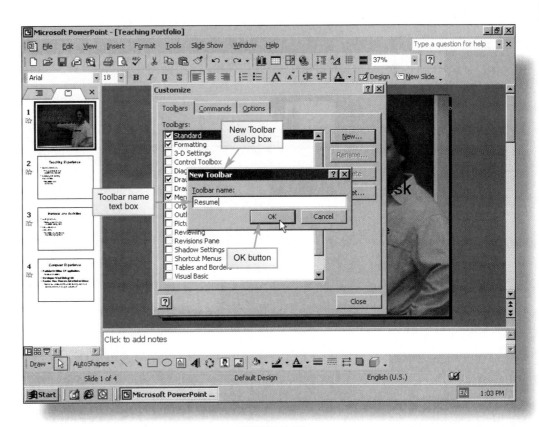

FIGURE 5-10

4 **Click the OK button and then point to the Close button in the Customize dialog box.**

The Resume toolbar displays (Figure 5-11).

FIGURE 5-11

5 **Click the Close button, and then click the toolbar and drag it to the bottom-right corner of the screen beside the Drawing toolbar.**

The Resume toolbar displays in the desired location (Figure 5-12). The toolbar title does not display.

FIGURE 5-12

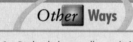

Other Ways

1. Right-click a toolbar, click Customize on shortcut menu, click Toolbars tab, click New button
2. Click More buttons on a toolbar, click Add or Remove buttons, click Customize, click Toolbars tab, click New button

The Resume toolbar is positioned beside the Drawing toolbar. The next step is to add two buttons to it. One button will save the presentation as a Web page, and the second will start the Pack and Go Wizard. Perform the following steps to add these buttons to the Resume toolbar.

Steps **To Add Two Buttons to the Resume Toolbar**

1 **Click the Toolbar Options button on the new toolbar, point to Add or Remove Buttons, and then point to Customize on the Add or Remove Buttons submenu.**

The Add or Remove Buttons submenu displays (Figure 5-13).

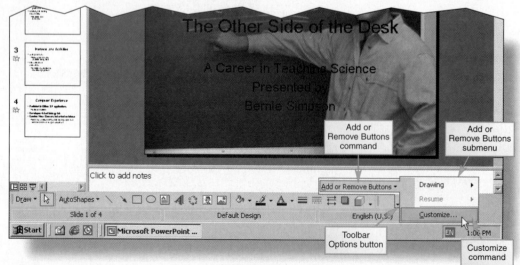

FIGURE 5-13

2 **Click Customize. When the Customize dialog box displays, click the Commands tab. Scroll down in the Commands list and then click Save as Web Page.**

You can select buttons from several categories, and each category has a variety of commands (Figure 5-14). File is the default category. Some commands have images associated with them.

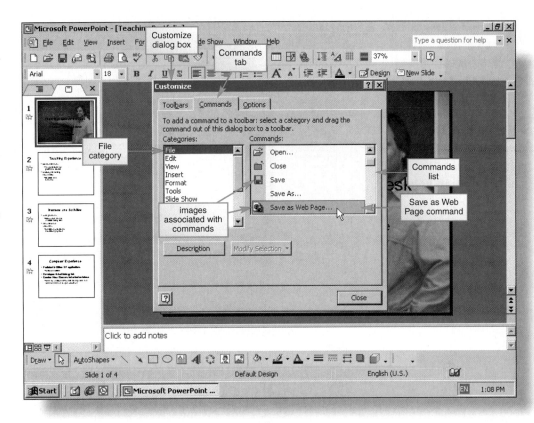

FIGURE 5-14

3 **Drag the Save as Web Page command from the Commands list to the new Resume toolbar.**

The Save as Web Page button displays with an image on the Resume toolbar (Figure 5-15). The heavy border surrounding the button indicates PowerPoint is in edit mode.

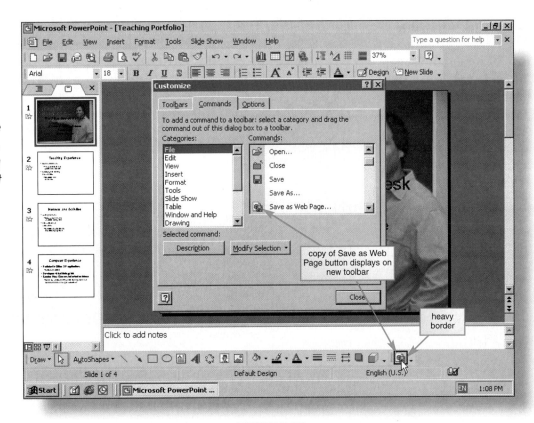

FIGURE 5-15

4 Scroll down in the Commands list and then click Pack and Go. Drag the Pack and Go command from the Commands list to the right of the Save as Web Page button on the Resume toolbar. Point to the Modify Selection button.

The Pack and Go button displays on the Resume toolbar with its name displaying on the face of the button (Figure 5-16). A heavy border surrounds the button, indicating that PowerPoint is in edit mode.

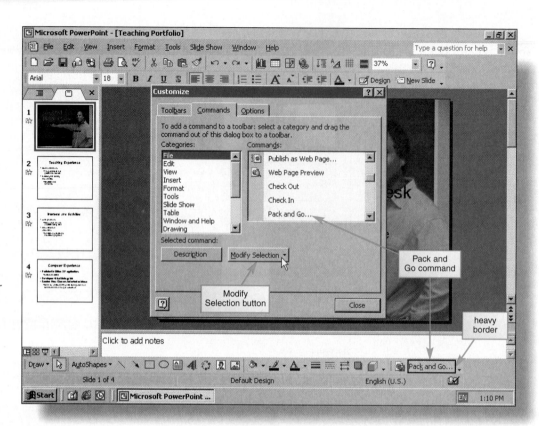

FIGURE 5-16

5 Click the Modify Selection button and then point to Change Button Image. When the Change Button Image palette displays, point to the button with a blue arrow pointing toward a floppy disk (row 1, column 6).

PowerPoint displays a palette of button images from which to choose (Figure 5-17).

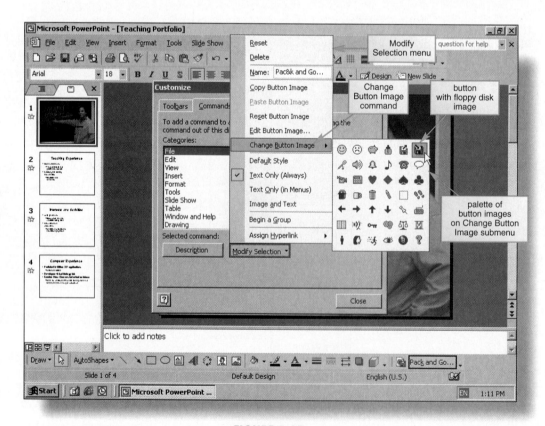

FIGURE 5-17

6 **Click the button with the floppy disk image. Point to the Modify Selection button.**

The Pack and Go button displays on the toolbar with the floppy disk image and the text, Pack and Go (Figure 5-18).

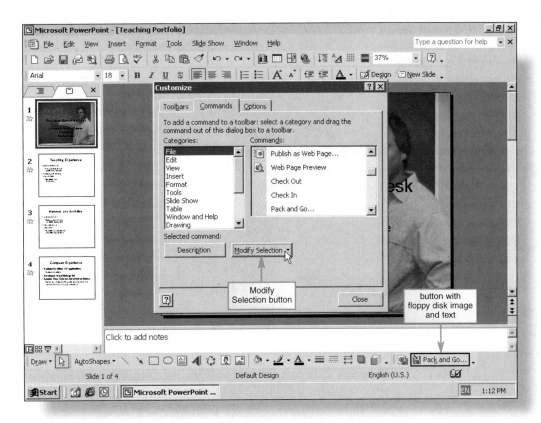

FIGURE 5-18

7 **Click the Modify Selection button and then point to Default Style.**

The default style includes only the image, not text (Figure 5-19). The ampersand in the Name box, Pac&k and Go, underlines the letter k on the button, indicating a keyboard shortcut.

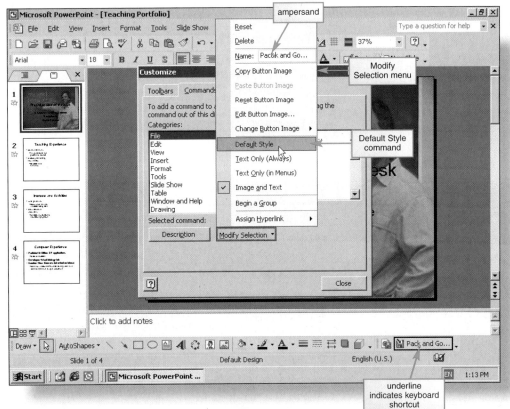

FIGURE 5-19

8 Click Default Style. Point to the Close button in the Customize dialog box.

The Pack and Go button image displays with the floppy disk only (Figure 5-20).

9 Click the Close button.

PowerPoint quits edit mode.

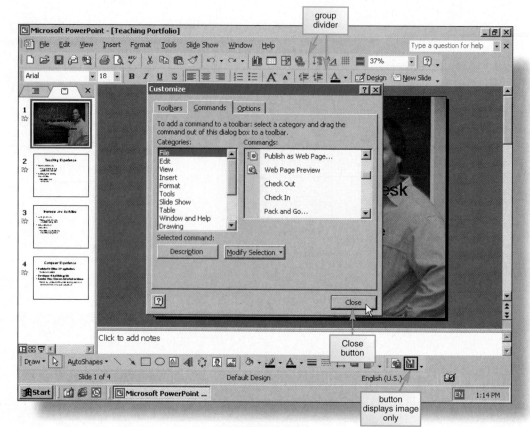

FIGURE 5-20

The previous steps illustrate how a toolbar is created easily and how buttons are added. PowerPoint includes a complete repertoire of commands for editing buttons on a toolbar, as shown on the Modify Selection menu in Figure 5-19 on the previous page. Table 5-1 briefly describes each of the commands on this menu.

Table 5-1 Summary of Commands on the Modify Selection Menu	
COMMAND	**DESCRIPTION**
Reset	Changes the image on the selected button to the original image and disassociates the macro with the button
Delete	Deletes the selected button
Name box	Changes the ScreenTip for a button and changes the command name for a command on a menu
Copy Button Image	Copies the button image to the Office Clipboard
Paste Button Image	Pastes the button image on the Office Clipboard onto selected button
Reset Button Image	Changes the button image back to the original image
Edit Button Image	Edits the button image
Change Button Image	Chooses a new button image
Default Style; Text Only (Always); Text Only (in Menus); Image and Text	Chooses one of the four styles to indicate how the button should display
Begin a Group	Groups buttons by drawing a vertical line (divider) on the toolbar (see the group dividing lines in Figure 5-20)
Assign Hyperlink	Assigns a hyperlink to a Web page or document

You can add as many buttons as you want to a toolbar. You also can change any button's function. For example, when in edit mode with the Customize dialog box displaying, you can right-click the Save button on the Standard toolbar and assign it a macro or hyperlink. The next time you click the Save button, the macro will execute, so PowerPoint will launch the application associated with the hyperlink rather than save the presentation.

Reset the toolbars to their installation default by clicking the Toolbars tab in the Customize dialog box, selecting the toolbar in the Toolbars list, and clicking the Reset button. Because it is so easy to change the buttons on a toolbar, each project in this book begins by resetting the toolbars.

More *About*

Modifying Buttons

If the Change Button Image palette does not contain an image to your liking, you can modify one of the icons or draw a new one. Click the Edit Button Image command and then design a unique image using the Button Editor dialog box.

Saving the Presentation

The changes to Phase 1 of the presentation are complete. Perform the following step to save the presentation before recording a macro in Phase 2 of this project.

TO SAVE A PRESENTATION

 Click the Save button on the Standard toolbar.

PowerPoint saves the presentation by saving the changes made to the presentation since the last save.

Phase 2 — Recording a Macro and Assigning It to a Menu Command

The second phase of the project creates a macro to print a handout displaying four slides per page vertically using the Pure Black and White option. The default PowerPoint print setting is Slides, with one slide printing on each sheet of paper. When the Print what setting is changed to handouts, the default setting is six slides per page in a horizontal order, meaning Slides 1 and 2 display at the top of the page, Slides 3 and 4 display in the middle of the page, and Slides 5 and 6 display at the bottom of the page. The user can distribute a one-page handout, shown in Figure 5-21, of the four slides in this presentation printed using the Pure Black and White option and displayed vertically, meaning Slides 1 and 3 display on the top, and Slides 2 and 4 display below.

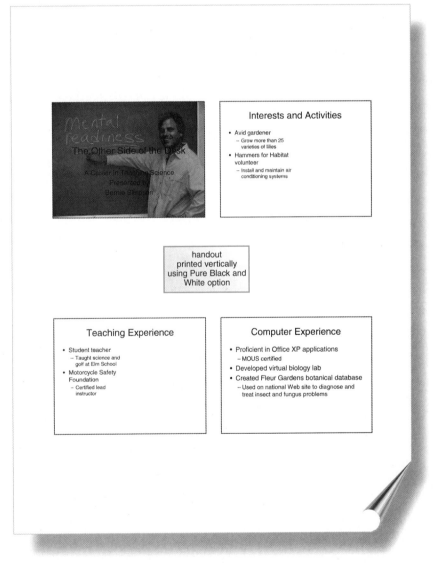

FIGURE 5-21

Deleting Toolbars

You may decide to delete a toolbar once you have created it. To delete a custom toolbar, click Tools on the menu bar, click Customize, and then click the Toolbars tab. Select the custom toolbar in the Toolbars list that you want to delete, and then click the Delete button. You cannot delete a built-in toolbar. If you select a built-in toolbar in the Toolbars list, the Reset button displays. When you click the Reset button, PowerPoint restores that toolbar to its default buttons, menus, and submenus.

Undoing Macros

Occasionally, you may want to undo the changes created by a macro you have executed. Clicking the Undo button on the Standard toolbar once often does not reverse all the changes. You probably will need to click the Undo button arrow and then select several commands in the list.

The planned macro will change the output from slides to handouts and will change the slide order on the handout from horizontal to vertical. The handout will print using the Pure Black and White option instead of Grayscale or another default setting on your computer, so all shades of gray will change to either black or white. The macro then will reset the Print dialog box to its original settings.

With the macro, users can print a one-page handout by executing a single command, rather than performing the several steps otherwise required. They can click the Print button on the Standard toolbar and change the settings in the Print dialog box to print these handouts, or they can execute the macro to print the handout. Once the macro is created, it will be assigned to a command on the File menu.

Recording a Macro

PowerPoint has a **macro recorder** that creates a macro automatically based on a series of actions performed while it is recording. Like a tape recorder, the macro recorder records everything you do to a presentation over a period of time. The macro recorder can be turned on, during which time it records your activities, and then turned off to stop the recording. Once the macro is recorded, it can be **played back** or **executed** as often as desired.

It is easy to create a macro. All you have to do is turn on the macro recorder and perform these steps:

1. Name the macro.
2. Change the output settings from slides to handouts, the slides per page from six to four, the slide order on the handout from horizontal to vertical, and the print option from Grayscale (or the default print setting on your computer) to Pure Black and White.
3. Print the handout.
4. Restore the output settings from four slides per page to six, from vertical to horizontal slide order, from handouts to slides, and from Pure Black and White to Grayscale (or the default print setting on your computer).
5. Stop the macro recorder.

What is impressive about the macro recorder is that you actually step through the task as you create the macro. You will see exactly what the macro will do before you use it.

When you create the macro, you first must name it. The name is used to reference the macro when you want to execute it. The name PrintHandout is used for the macro in this project. **Macro names** can be up to 255 characters long; they can contain numbers, letters, and underscores; and they cannot contain spaces and other punctuation. Perform the following steps to record the macro.

To Record a Macro to Print Handouts in Vertical Slide Order
Steps ## in Pure Black and White

1 **Click Tools on the menu bar, point to Macro, and then point to Record New Macro on the Macro submenu.**

The Tools menu and Macro submenu display (Figure 5-22).

FIGURE 5-22

2 **Click Record New Macro. When the Record Macro dialog box displays, type** PrintHandout **in the Macro name text box. Type** Macro prints Pure Black and White handouts in vertical slide order **in the Description text box. Make sure the Store macro in text box displays Teaching Portfolio. Point to the OK button.**

The Record Macro dialog box displays as shown in Figure 5-23.

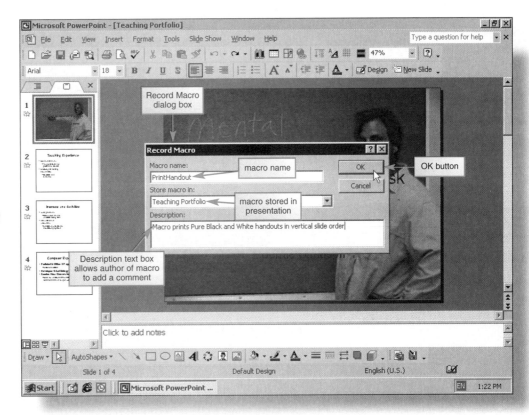

FIGURE 5-23

3 **Click the OK button. Click File on the menu bar and then point to Print.**

The Stop Recording toolbar and the File menu display (Figure 5-24). Any task you perform after the Stop Recording toolbar displays will be part of the macro. When you are finished recording the macro, you will click the Stop Recording button on the Stop Recording toolbar to end the recording.

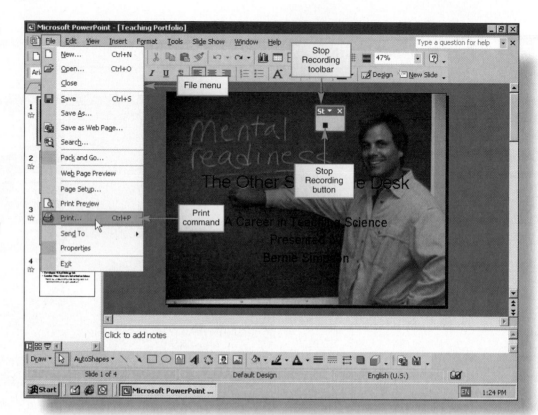

FIGURE 5-24

4 **Click Print. When the Print dialog box displays, click the Print what box arrow and click Handouts, click the Slides per page box arrow in the Handouts area and click 4, click Vertical order in the Handouts area, click the Color/grayscale box arrow, click Pure Black and White, and then point to the OK button.**

The Print dialog box displays as shown in Figure 5-25.

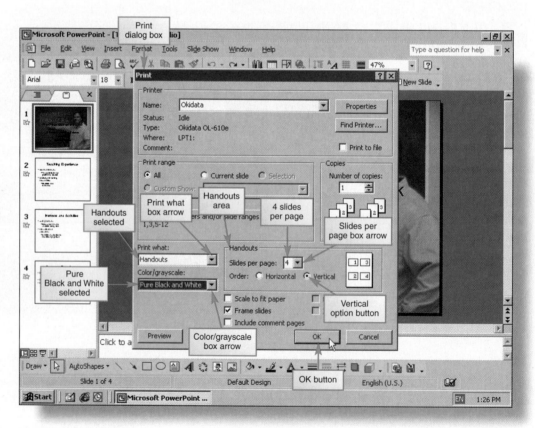

FIGURE 5-25

5 Click the OK button. Click File on the menu bar and then click Print. When the Print dialog box displays, click the Color/grayscale box arrow and then click Grayscale, click the Slides per page box arrow in the Handouts area and click 6, click Horizontal order in the Handouts area, click the Print what box arrow and click Slides, and then point to the OK button.

The Print dialog box displays as shown in Figure 5-26. Your computer is restored to its default print settings. The printout resembles the handout shown in Figure 5-21 on page PP 5.17.

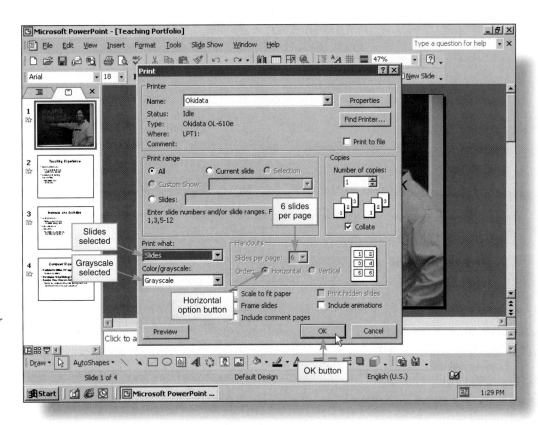

FIGURE 5-26

6 Click the OK button. Point to the Stop Recording button.

The Print dialog box closes (Figure 5-27). The four slides in the presentation print in grayscale or your computer's default print option.

7 Click the Stop Recording button.

PowerPoint stops recording the printing activities and hides the Stop Recording toolbar.

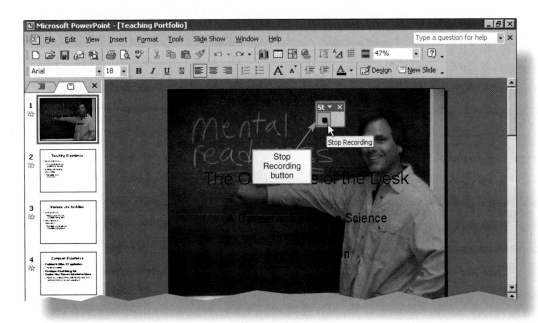

FIGURE 5-27

If you recorded the wrong actions, delete the macro and record it again. You delete a macro by clicking Tools on the menu bar, pointing to Macro on the Tools menu, and then clicking Macros on the Macro submenu. When the Macro dialog box displays, click the name of the macro (PrintHandout), and then click the Delete button. Then record the macro again.

Other Ways

1. Click Record Macro button on Visual Basic toolbar

2. Press ALT+T, press M, press R

3. In Voice Command mode, say "Tools, Macro, Record New Macro"

Customizing a Menu

As you use PowerPoint to create presentations and print handouts, you may find yourself repeating many steps. It is convenient to simplify these repetitive processes by adding a button to a toolbar or a command to a menu that you can click to perform the tasks automatically. PowerPoint allows you to add commands to a button or to a menu. The following steps show how to add a command to the File menu to execute the PrintHandout macro.

Steps

To Add a Command to a Menu, Assign the Command to a Macro, and Invoke the Command

1 **Click Tools on the menu bar and then click Customize. When the Customize dialog box displays, if necessary, click the Commands tab. Scroll down in the Categories list and then click Macros. Click File on the menu bar to display the File menu.**

The Customize dialog box and File menu display (Figure 5-28). A heavy border surrounds the File menu name, indicating PowerPoint is in edit mode.

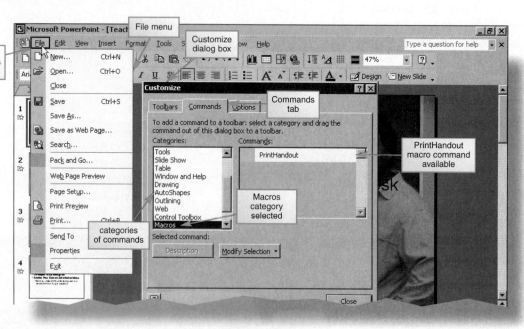

FIGURE 5-28

2 **Drag the PrintHandout entry from the Commands list in the Customize dialog box immediately below the Print command on the File menu.**

PowerPoint adds PrintHandout to the File menu (Figure 5-29). The heavy border surrounding PrintHandout on the File menu indicates edit mode.

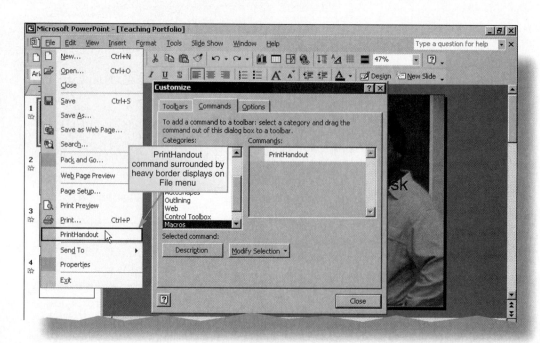

FIGURE 5-29

3 Right-click PrintHandout on the File menu and then click the Name box on the shortcut menu. Type `Print BW Handout` **as the new name of this command. Point to the Close button at the bottom of the Customize dialog box.**

The shortcut menu displays with the new command name in the Name box (Figure 5-30).

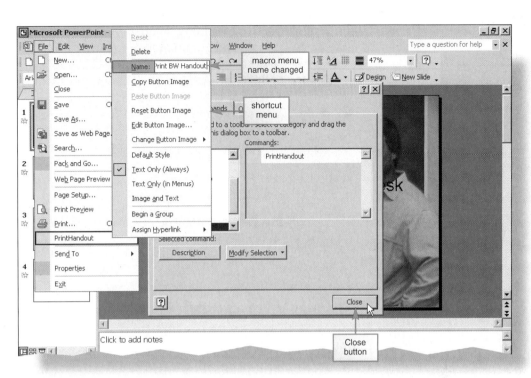

FIGURE 5-30

4 Click the Close button. Click File on the menu bar and then point to Print BW Handout.

PowerPoint quits edit mode. The File menu displays with the new command, Print BW Handout, on the menu (Figure 5-31).

5 Click Print BW Handout on the File menu.

After several seconds, the handout and slides print as shown in Figures 5-5 and 5-21 on pages PP 5.07 and PP 5.17.

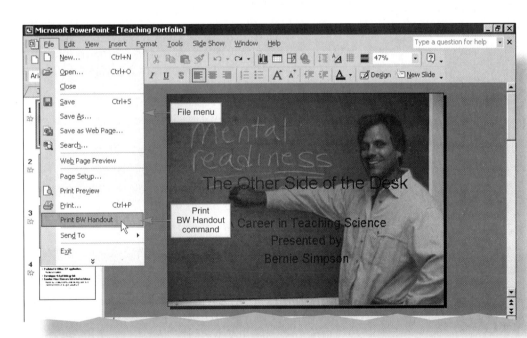

FIGURE 5-31

You have the same customization capabilities with menus as you do with toolbars. All of the commands described in Table 5-1 on page PP 5.16 apply to menus as well. Any command specific to buttons pertains to editing the button on the left side of a command on a menu.

Other Ways

1. Right-click toolbar, click Customize on shortcut menu, click Commands tab
2. On View menu click Toolbars, click Customize, click Commands tab
3. In Voice Command mode, say "View, Toolbars, Customize, Commands"

An alternative to adding a command to a menu is to add a new menu name to the menu bar and add commands to its menu. You can add a new menu name to the menu bar by selecting New Menu in the Categories list of the Customize dialog box and dragging New Menu from the Commands list to the menu bar.

With the toolbar and macro added to the presentation, save the file and then close the presentation. Perform the following steps.

TO SAVE AND CLOSE THE PRESENTATION

1 Click the Save button on the Standard toolbar.

2 Click the presentation's Close button on the menu bar to close the presentation and leave PowerPoint open.

PowerPoint saves the Teaching Portfolio presentation on drive A and then closes the presentation.

Opening a Presentation Containing a Macro and Executing the Macro

A **computer virus** is a potentially damaging computer program designed to affect a computer negatively by infecting it and altering the way it works without the user's knowledge or permission. Currently, more than 13,000 known computer viruses exist, and an estimated six new viruses are discovered each day. The increased use of networks, the Internet, and e-mail has accelerated the spread of computer viruses.

To combat this evil, most computer users run antivirus programs that search for viruses and destroy them before they ever have a chance to infect the computer. Macros are a known carrier of viruses because people can add code easily to them. For this reason, each time you open a presentation with a macro associated with it, PowerPoint may display a Microsoft PowerPoint dialog box warning that a macro is attached and that macros can contain viruses. Table 5-2 summarizes the buttons users can use to continue the process of opening a presentation with macros.

Macro Security

If you change the macro security setting for a PowerPoint file, that setting takes effect only for PowerPoint presentations. It does not apply to Microsoft Word and Excel files. You can specify different security levels for the three Office applications.

Table 5-2	Buttons in the Microsoft PowerPoint Dialog Box When Opening a Presentation with Macros
BUTTONS	**DESCRIPTION**
Disable Macros	Macros are unavailable to the user
Enable Macros	Macros are available to the user to execute
More Info	Opens the Microsoft PowerPoint Help window and displays information on viruses and macros

If you are confident of the source (author) of the presentation and macros, click the Enable Macros button. If you are uncertain about the reliability of the source, then click the Disable Macros button. For more information on this topic, click the More Info button.

The following steps open the Teaching Portfolio presentation to illustrate the Microsoft PowerPoint dialog box that displays when a presentation contains a macro. The steps then show how to execute the recorded macro, PrintHandout.

To Open a Presentation with a Macro and Execute the Macro

1 **With PowerPoint active, click File on the menu bar and then click Open. When the Open dialog box displays, click the Look in box arrow, and if necessary, click 3½ Floppy (A:). Double-click the file name Teaching Portfolio.**

The Microsoft PowerPoint dialog box displays (Figure 5-32).

2 **Click the Enable Macros button. When Slide 1 of the Teaching Portfolio displays, click File on the menu bar and then click Print BW Handout.**

PowerPoint opens the Teaching Portfolio presentation, executes the macro, and then prints the handout and the four slides shown in Figures 5-5 and 5-21 on pages PP 5.07 and PP 5.17.

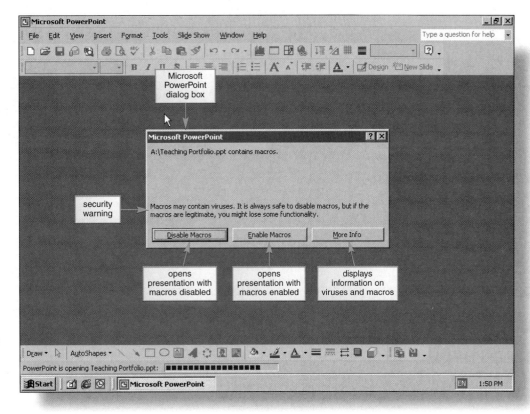

FIGURE 5-32

If you are running antivirus software, you may want to turn off the security warning shown in Figure 5-32. You can turn off the security warning by clicking Tools on the menu bar, pointing to Macro, and then clicking Security on the Macro submenu. When the Security dialog box displays, click the Low button. Then, the next time you open a presentation with an attached macro, PowerPoint will open the presentation immediately, rather than display the dialog box shown in Figure 5-32.

Viewing a Macro's VBA Code

As described earlier, a macro is composed of VBA code, which is created automatically by the macro recorder. You can view the VBA code through the Visual Basic Editor. The **Visual Basic Editor** is used by all Office applications to enter, modify, and view VBA code.

Other **Ways**

1. Click Run Macro button on Visual Basic toolbar
2. On Tools menu point to Macro, click Macros, double-click macro name
3. Press ALT+F8, double-click macro name
4. In Voice Command mode, say "Tools, Macro, Macros"

Steps To View a Macro's VBA Code

1 Click Tools on the menu bar, point to Macro, and then point to Macros on the Macro submenu.

The Tools menu and Macro submenu display (Figure 5-33).

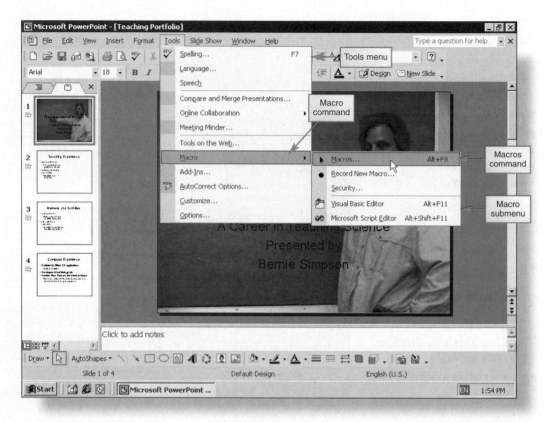

FIGURE 5-33

2 Click Macros. When the Macro dialog box displays, if necessary click PrintHandout in the list, and then point to the Edit button.

The Macro dialog box displays (Figure 5-34).

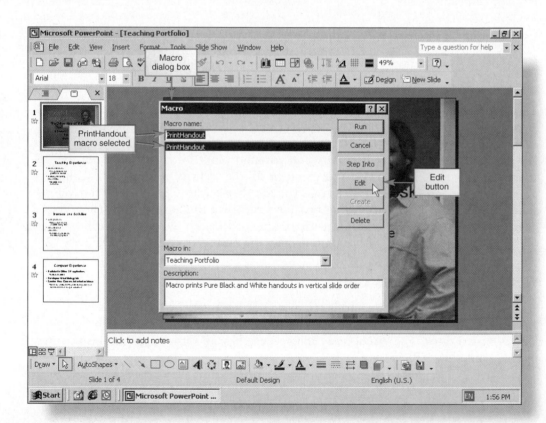

FIGURE 5-34

3 **Click the Edit button.**

The Visual Basic Editor starts and displays the VBA code in the PrintHandout macro (Figure 5-35).

4 **Scroll through the VBA code. When you are finished, click the Close button on the right side of the Microsoft Visual Basic – Teaching Portfolio title bar.**

The Visual Basic Editor closes, and Slide 1 in the Teaching Portfolio presentation displays.

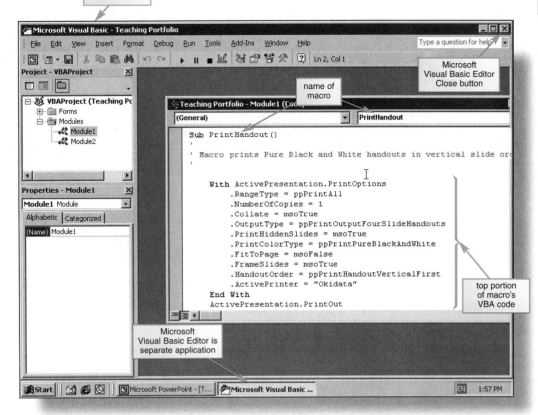

FIGURE 5-35

This set of instructions, beginning with line 1 in Figure 5-35 and continuing sequentially to the last line, executes when you invoke the macro. By scrolling through the VBA code, you can see that the macro recorder generates many instructions. In this case 32 lines of code are generated to print the handout vertically using the Pure Black and White option.

Phase 3 — Creating a Form to Customize the Presentation

With a toolbar and buttons added and the macro recorded to print handouts, you are ready to develop a form that allows users to design custom presentations for each interview. This form, called a **user interface**, allows users to input data and then display results. The user interface and the step-by-step procedure for its implementation are called an **application**. Thus, Microsoft created the name Visual Basic for Applications (VBA) for its programming language used to customize PowerPoint and other Office XP programs.

Programmers build applications using the three-step process shown in Figures 5-36a through 5-36c (on the next page): (1) create the user interface; (2) set the properties; and (3) write the VBA code.

Other Ways

1. Click Visual Basic Editor button on Visual Basic toolbar
2. Press ALT+T, press M, press V

More About

Narration

Add audio and video narration to your slides with add-ins that several companies, including Microsoft and RealNetworks, have developed. These powerful and inexpensive tools can make your presentations powerful and dynamic. Simply start these programs, run your slide show, and speak into a microphone or look into a camera. You then can broadcast the integrated presentation over the Web. For more information, visit the PowerPoint 2002 More About Web page (scsite.com/pp2002/more.htm) and then click Narration.

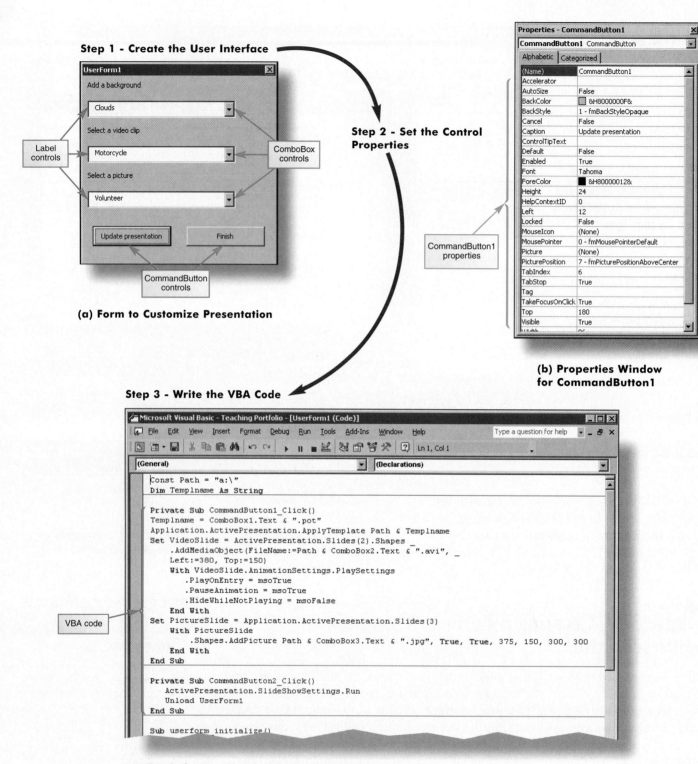

FIGURE 5-36

Step 1 – Create the User Interface

The form shown Figure 5-36a displays the application's user interface. The **interface** allows the user to specify a template, video clip, and digital picture and place them in the presentation. The form contains three label controls, three combo box controls, and two command button controls. The **labels** identify the contents of the combo boxes. Each **combo box** allows a choice of two items. The **command buttons** update the presentation, close the interface form, and run the presentation.

The first element on the form is a label indicating the use of the combo box directly below the label. The label instructs the user to select one of two slide design templates listed in the combo box. This label-and-combo-box set is repeated twice. The second set allows the user to select one of two video clips, and the final set tells the user to choose one of two photos. The two command buttons at the bottom of the form execute the VBA procedure. The **Update presentation button** applies the design template and inserts the video clip and picture into the slides, and the **Finish button** hides the user form, unloads it from memory, and runs the presentation.

Creating the interface consists of sizing the form, adding each of the controls to the form, and adjusting their sizes and positions. When beginning to create a user interface, position the controls as close as possible to their final locations on the form; after setting the properties, you can finalize their positions. As you create the form, try to locate the controls as shown in Figure 5-36a.

The Standard toolbar (Figure 5-37) displays when you use VBA. Alternately, you can right-click a toolbar and then click Standard on the shortcut menu to display it.

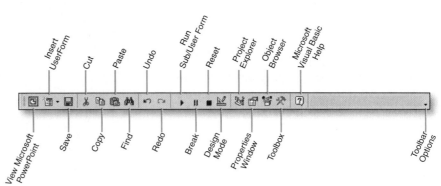

FIGURE 5-37 - VBA Standard Toolbar

Opening the Visual Basic IDE and a New Form

Before you begin creating the interface, you must start the **Visual Basic integrated development environment (IDE)**, which contains nine different windows and four toolbars. The windows can be **docked**, or anchored, to other windows that are dockable, and the four toolbars can be docked or can float in their own windows. Perform the following steps to open the Visual Basic IDE and open a new form.

More About

Docking

To customize the Visual Basic environment, you can move, dock, and resize a toolbar, a window, or the toolbox. To move an element, click the title bar and then drag the object to the desired location. This element will dock, or attach itself, to the edge of another window. To see more content in a docked element, drag one of its borders.

Steps | To Open the Visual Basic IDE and a New Form

1 With the **Teaching Portfolio presentation still open, click Tools on the menu bar, point to Macro, and then point to Visual Basic Editor.**

The Tools menu and Macro submenu display (Figure 5-38).

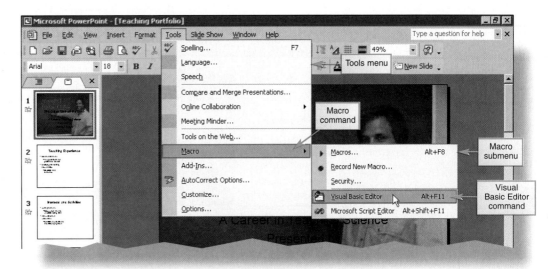

FIGURE 5-38

2 **Click Visual Basic Editor. Click Insert on the menu bar and then point to UserForm.**

The Visual Basic Editor opens and displays a Project window and a Properties window. The Insert menu displays (Figure 5-39).

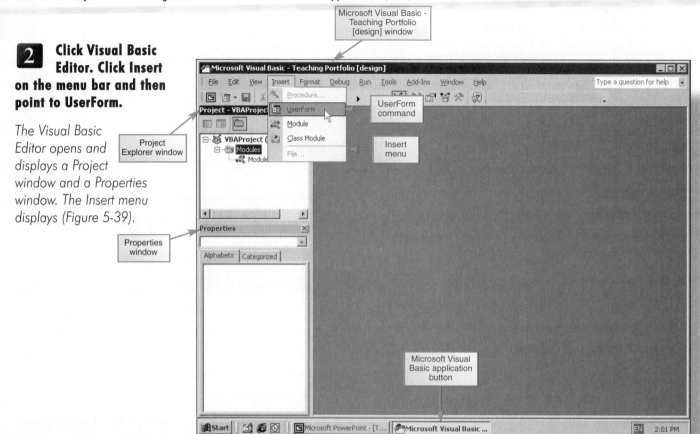

FIGURE 5-39

3 **Click UserForm. If the Toolbox does not display, click the Toolbox button on the Standard toolbar.**

A new form, UserForm1, opens and the Toolbox displays (Figure 5-40). Your form may display in a different location, and your Toolbox may have a different shape.

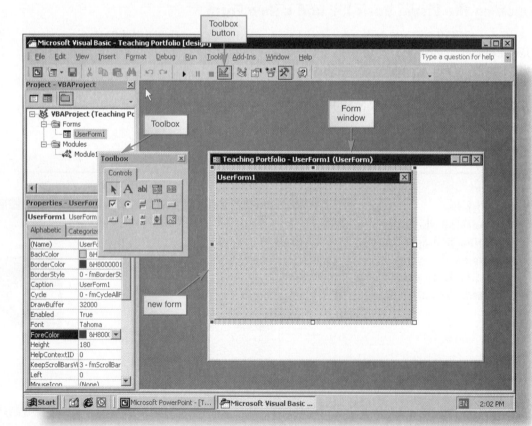

FIGURE 5-40

Changing the Form Size and the Toolbox Location

In design mode, you can resize a form by changing the values of its **Height property** and **Width property** in the Properties window, and you can change a form's location on the screen by changing the values of its **Top property** and **Left property**. You also can resize a form by dragging its borders and change its location by dragging and dropping. Perform the following steps to set the size of the form by dragging its borders and set the location by dragging and dropping.

More *About*

File Names

If you modify a macro, you need to resave it to preserve the changes. To see the file name that will be used, point to the Save button on the Standard toolbar. The ScreenTip will display the current file name.

 To Change the Form Size and the Toolbox Location

1 **Point to the form window's bottom border. Without releasing the mouse button, drag the window border down.**

Dragging the bottom border increases the height of the form window (Figure 5-41). The mouse pointer displays as a two-headed arrow.

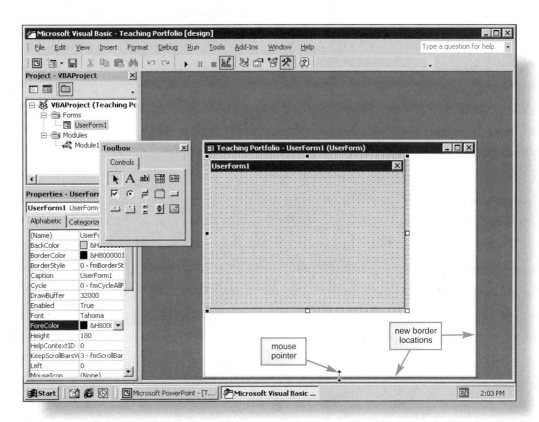

FIGURE 5-41

2 **Release the mouse button. Point to the form's bottom-center sizing handle. Without releasing the mouse button, drag the form border down.**

Dragging the border of the form increases the height of the form. The mouse pointer displays as a two-headed arrow (Figure 5-42).

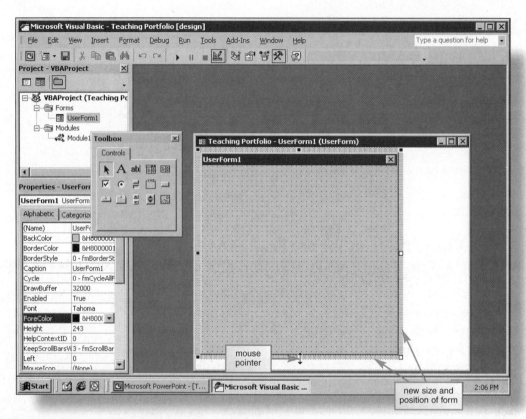

FIGURE 5-42

3 **Release the mouse button. Click the Toolbox title bar and drag it to the lower-right side of the form window.**

The form's size displays as shown in Figure 5-43. The Toolbox displays to the right of the form window.

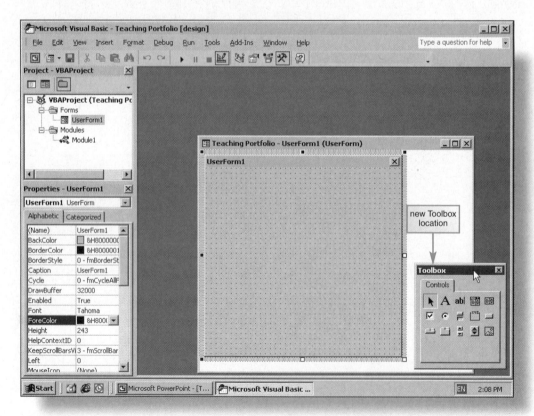

FIGURE 5-43

Adding Controls

Graphical images, or objects, in Windows applications include buttons, check boxes, tabs, and text boxes. Visual Basic calls these objects **controls**. The user form in this project contains three types of controls (see Figure 5-36a on page PP 5.28). Table 5-3 describes these controls and their functions.

You add controls to a form using tools in the **Toolbox**. To use a tool, you click its respective button in the Toolbox. Table 5-4 identifies the Toolbox buttons.

Table 5-3	VBA Controls Used in UserForm1
CONTROL	DESCRIPTION
Label	Displays text such as the words, Company Name, on a form. At run time, the user cannot change the text on a label.
ComboBox	Presents a list of choices. When an item is selected from the list by clicking it, the item displays in a highlighted color.
CommandButton	Represents a button that initiates an action when clicked.

Table 5-4	Summary of Buttons in the Toolbox	
BUTTON	NAME	FUNCTION
	Select Objects pointer	Draws a rectangle over the controls you want to select
	Label	Adds a label control
	TextBox	Adds a text box control
	ComboBox	Adds a custom edit box, drop-down list box, or combo box on a menu bar, toolbar, menu, submenu, or shortcut menu
	ListBox	Adds a list box control
	CheckBox	Adds a check box control
	OptionButton	Adds an option button control
	ToggleButton	Adds a toggle button control
	Frame	Creates an option group or groups controls with closely related contents
	CommandButton	Adds a command button control
	TabStrip	Contains a collection of one or more tabs
	MultiPage	Contains a collection of one or more pages
	ScrollBar	Adds a scroll bar control
	SpinButton	Adds a spin button control
	Image	Adds an image control

ADDING LABEL AND COMBO BOX CONTROLS The next steps are to add the three label and combo box controls shown in Figure 5-36a on page PP 5.28. Perform the steps on the next page to add these controls to the form.

Steps **To Add Label and Combo Box Controls to a Form**

1 **Click the Label button in the Toolbox. Position the mouse pointer in the upper-left corner of the form.**

The Label button in the Toolbox is selected, and the mouse pointer changes to a cross hair and a copy of the Label button when it is over the form (Figure 5-44). The upper-left corner of the Label control will be positioned in this location.

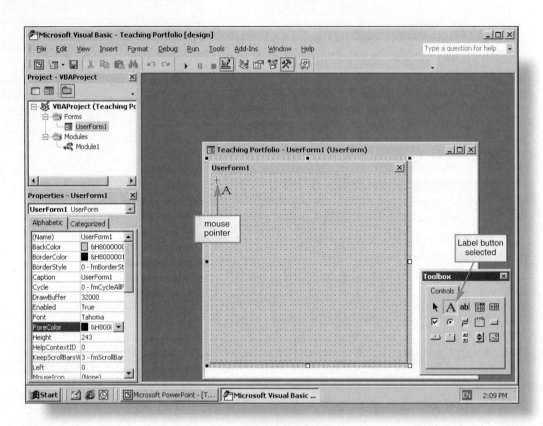

FIGURE 5-44

2 **Click the mouse button. Point to the ComboBox button in the Toolbox.**

The label displays on the form with the default caption, Label1 (Figure 5-45). The label is surrounded by a selection rectangle and sizing handles.

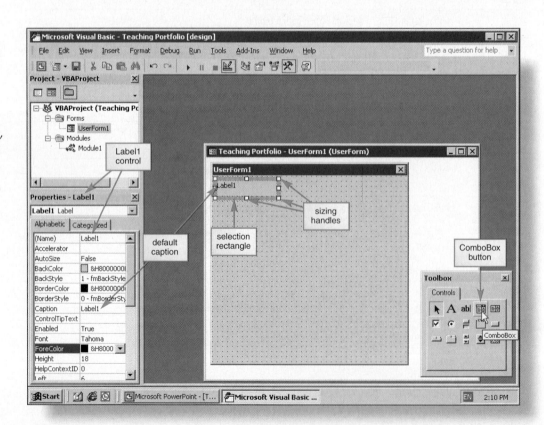

FIGURE 5-45

3 **Click the ComboBox button in the Toolbox. Position the mouse pointer below the Label1 control.**

The ComboBox button in the Toolbox is recessed, and the mouse pointer changes to a cross hair and a copy of the ComboBox button when it is over the form (Figure 5-46). The upper-left corner of the ComboBox control will be positioned in this location.

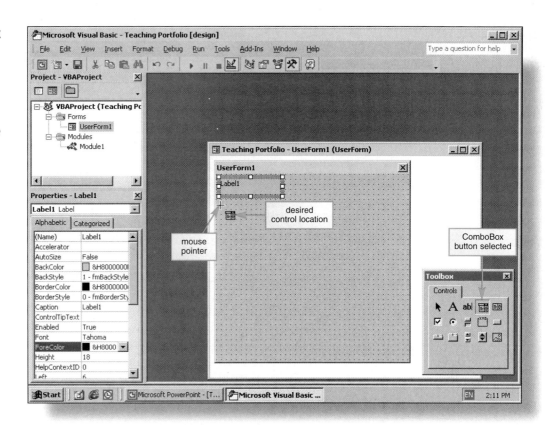

FIGURE 5-46

4 **Click the mouse button.**

The ComboBox control is added to the form (Figure 5-47).

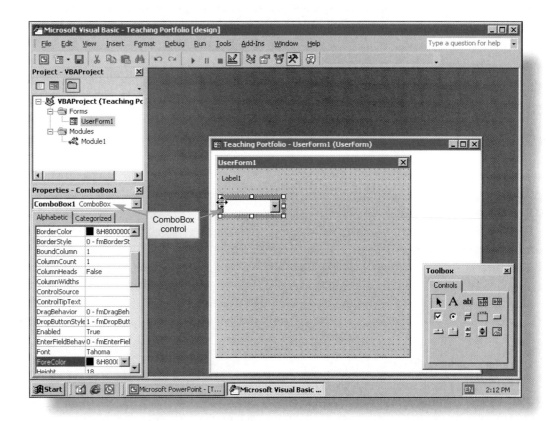

FIGURE 5-47

5 **Repeat Steps 1 through 4 to add the second and third Label controls and second and third ComboBox controls to the form as shown in Figure 5-48.**

The three Label and ComboBox controls display on the form (Figure 5-48).

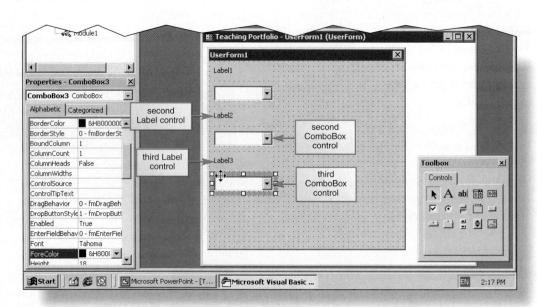

FIGURE 5-48

With the labels and combo boxes added to the form, the next step is to add the two CommandButton controls below the third ComboBox control.

ADDING COMMAND BUTTON CONTROLS   When users finish making selections on the form, they can click the Update presentation button to assemble the presentation by applying the design template and inserting the video clip and picture into the slides. After clicking the Update presentation button, they can click the Finish button to hide the user form, unload it from memory, and run the presentation. Perform the following steps to add these two command button controls to the form.

Steps **To Add Command Button Controls to a Form**

1 **Click the CommandButton button in the Toolbox. Position the mouse pointer in the lower-left corner of the form.**

The CommandButton button in the Toolbox is recessed, and the mouse pointer changes to a cross hair and a copy of the CommandButton button when it is over the form (Figure 5-49). The upper-left corner of the first command button control will be positioned in this location.

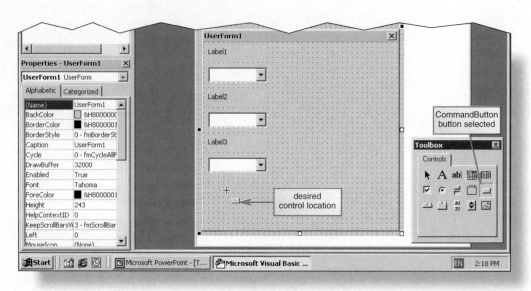

FIGURE 5-49

2 **Click the mouse button.**

The CommandButton1 control is added to the form (Figure 5-50).

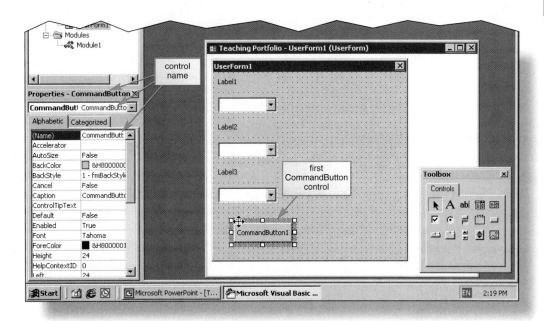

FIGURE 5-50

3 **Repeat Steps 1 and 2 to add a second CommandButton control, CommandButton2, as shown in Figure 5-51.**

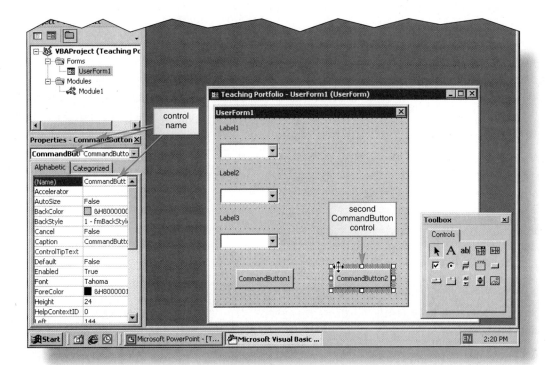

FIGURE 5-51

Step 2 – Set Control Properties

Controls have several different **properties** (Figure 5-52 on the next page), such as caption (the words on the face of the button), background color, foreground color, height, width, and font. Once you add a control to a form, you can change any property to improve its appearance and modify how it works.

SETTING THE CONTROL CAPTION PROPERTIES The controls on the form are not very informative because they do not state their functions. You must provide meaningful descriptions of the choices the user can make when using the form. These descriptions are called **captions**. You type the captions in the Properties window. This window has two tabs, Alphabetic and Categorized. The **Alphabetic list** displays the properties in alphabetical order. The **Categorized list** displays the properties in categories, such as appearance, behavior, font, and miscellaneous. The following steps change the controls' caption properties.

Steps **To Set the Controls' Caption Properties**

1 **Click the Label1 control. With the Label1 control selected, click Caption on the Alphabetic tab in the Properties window.**

The Properties window for the Label1 control displays (Figure 5-52). The default Caption property is Label1. Sizing handles indicate Label1 is selected.

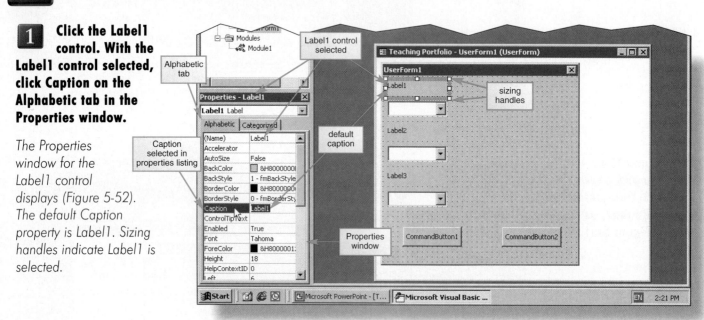

FIGURE 5-52

2 **Double-click the current caption, Label1, to select it, type** Add a background **as the caption, and then press the ENTER key.**

Add a background is the new caption for Label1 (Figure 5-53). The new caption displays on the form.

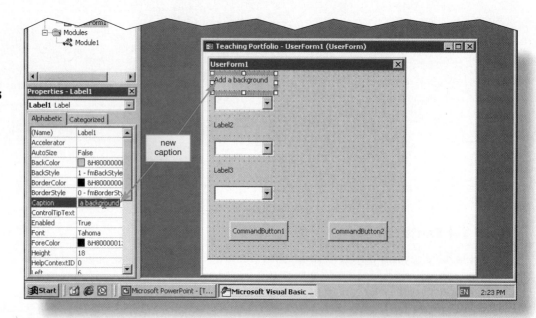

FIGURE 5-53

3 **Change the captions for the remainder of the controls on the form using Table 5-5.**

The captions for the form display (Figure 5-54).

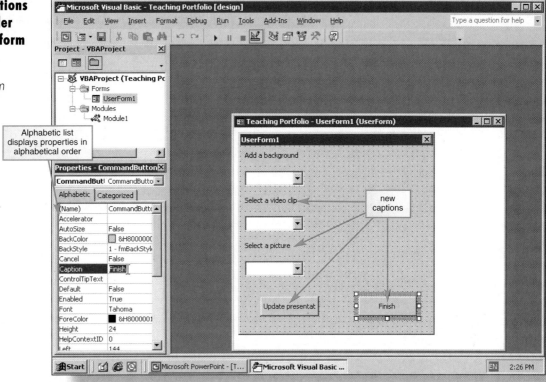

FIGURE 5-54

FINE-TUNING THE USER INTERFACE After setting the properties for all the controls, you can fine-tune the size and location of the controls on the form. You can reposition a control in three ways:

1. Drag the control to its new location.
2. Select the control and use the arrow keys to reposition it.
3. Select the control and set the control's Top and Left properties in the Properties window.

To use the third technique, you need to know the distance the control is from the top of the form and the left edge of the form in points. One point is equal to 1/72 of an inch. Thus, if the Top property of a control is 216, then the control is 3 inches (216 / 72) from the top of the form.

Controls also may require resizing. You need to increase the size of the CommandButton1 control so the entire caption displays. You can resize a control in two ways:

1. Drag the sizing handles.
2. Select the control and set the control's Height and Width properties in the Properties window.

As with the Top and Left properties, the Height and Width properties are measured in points. Table 5-6 on the next page lists the exact points for the Top, Left, Height, and Width properties of each of the controls on the form.

Table 5-5	Control Captions
CONTROL CAPTION	*NEW CAPTION*
Label2	Select a video clip
Label3	Select a picture
CommandButton1	Update presentation
CommandButton2	Finish

More About

Electronic Portfolios

Electronic portfolios help emphasize a job seeker's accomplishments and strengths. The presentations are shown during interviews, mailed to potential employers along with a paper resume, and posted on personal home pages. Employers are impressed with the creativity and efforts these interviewees display in these presentations. For more information, visit the PowerPoint 2002 More About Web page (scsite.com/pp2002/more.htm) and then click Portfolios.

Table 5-6	Exact Locations of Controls on the Form			
CONTROL	*TOP*	*LEFT*	*HEIGHT*	*WIDTH*
Label1	6	6	18	96
Label2	60	6	18	96
Label3	114	6	18	96
ComboBox1	30	6	20	180
ComboBox2	84	6	20	180
ComboBox3	138	6	20	180
CommandButton1	180	12	24	96
CommandButton2	180	126	24	96

The following steps resize and reposition the controls on the form using the values in Table 5-6.

Steps **To Resize and Reposition Controls on a Form**

1 **Click the Label1 control, Add a background. Change its Top, Left, Height, and Width properties in the Properties window to those listed in Table 5-6.**

The Label1 control Properties window displays (Figure 5-55).

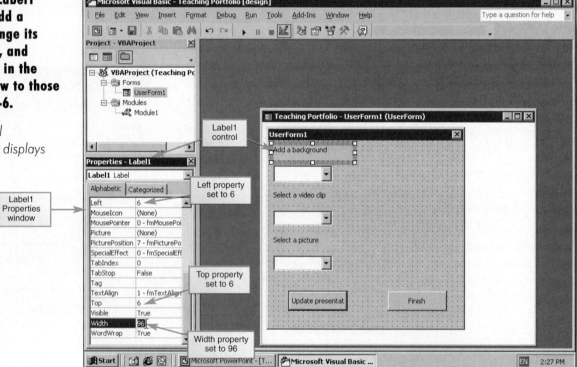

FIGURE 5-55

2 **One at a time, select the controls and change their Top, Left, Height and Width properties to those listed in Table 5-6.**

The form displays with the resized and repositioned controls (Figure 5-56).

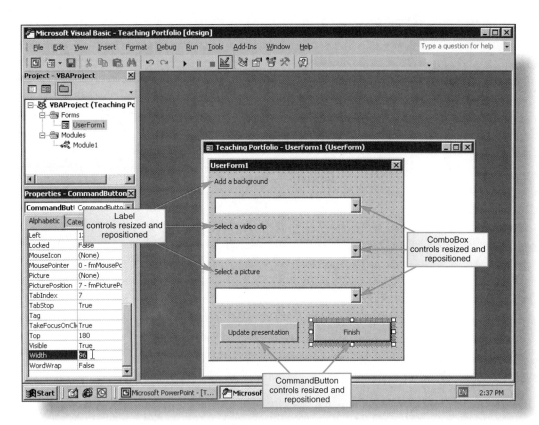

FIGURE 5-56

Step 3 – Write the VBA Code

You have created the interface and set the properties of the controls for this project. The next step is to write and then enter the procedure that will execute when you click the Create Presentation button on the Resume toolbar. You will create this button near the end of this project. Clicking this button is the event that triggers execution of the procedure that assembles the custom presentation. As mentioned earlier, Visual Basic for Applications (VBA) is a powerful programming language that can automate many activities described thus far in this book. The code for this project will include events and modules. The events in this program are the buttons on the form. To begin the process, you need to write a module that will serve as a macro that will display the form.

PLANNING A PROCEDURE When you trigger the event that executes a procedure, PowerPoint steps through the Visual Basic statements one at a time beginning at the top of the procedure. When you plan a procedure, therefore, remember that the order in which you place the statements in the procedure is important because the order determines the sequence of execution.

Once you know what you want the procedure to do, write the VBA code on paper in a similar format as that shown in Table 5-7 on the next page. Then, before entering the procedure into the computer, test it by putting yourself in the position of PowerPoint and stepping through the instructions one at a time. As you do so, think about how the instructions affect the slide show. Testing a procedure before entering it is called **desk checking**, and it is an important part of the development process.

VBA Topics

The Microsoft Visual Basic for Applications Home Page gives information geared toward independent software vendors and corporate developers. The site includes VBA news and related topics that help programmers customize their applications. To view this page, visit the PowerPoint 2002 More About Web page (scsite.com/pp2002/more.htm) and then click VBA Topics.

Customizing the VBA Appearance

To customize the appearance of VBA code, click Tools on the VBA menu bar, click Options, and then click the Editor Format tab. You can specify the foreground and background colors used for different types of text, such as Comments Text and Syntax Error Text. You also can change the font and font size.

Adding comments before a procedure will help you remember its purpose at a later date. In Table 5-7, the first seven lines are comments. **Comments** begin with the word Rem or an apostrophe ('). These comments contain overall documentation about the procedure and may be placed anywhere in the procedure. Most developers place comments before the Sub statement. Comments have no effect on the execution of a procedure; they simply provide information about the procedure, such as name, creation date, and function.

Table 5-7	Create Presentation Procedure
LINE	**VBA CODE**
1	' Create Presentation Procedure Author: Lakesha Helms
2	' Date Created: 12/1/2003
3	' Run from: Click Update presentation button
4	' Function: When executed, this procedure accepts data that causes
5	' PowerPoint to build a custom presentation that adds
6	' a template, video clip, and digital picture.
7	'
8	Sub createpresentationteaching()
9	UserForm1.userform_initialize
10	UserForm1.Show
11	End Sub

A procedure begins with a **Sub statement** and ends with an **End Sub statement** (lines 8 and 11 in Table 5-7). The Sub statement begins with the name of the procedure. The parentheses following the procedure name allow the passing of data values, or arguments, from one procedure to another. Passing arguments is beyond the scope of this project, but the parentheses still are required. The End Sub statement signifies the end of the procedure and returns PowerPoint to normal view.

The first executable statement in Table 5-7 is line 9, which calls the userform_ initialize procedure on the form, indicated by the object name, UserForm1. You use the UserForm1 object name, so VBA can find the userform_initalize procedure. Line 10, issues the command to display the form in the PowerPoint normal view window. Again, you must use the form name so VBA knows which form to display. Line 11 is the end of the procedure. Every procedure must conclude with an End Sub statement.

To enter a procedure, use the Visual Basic Editor. To activate the Visual Basic Editor, you can click the **View Code button** in the VBA Project window or click the **Module command** on the Insert menu.

The Visual Basic Editor is a full-screen editor, which allows you to enter a procedure by typing the lines of VBA code as if you were using word processing software. At the end of a line, press the ENTER key to move to the next line. If you make a mistake in a statement, you can use the arrow keys and the DELETE or BACKSPACE key to correct it. You also can move the insertion point to previous lines to make corrections.

USING THE VISUAL BASIC EDITOR TO ENTER A PROCEDURE The following steps activate the Visual Basic Editor and create the procedure for the Create Presentation module.

VBA Help

Microsoft offers a variety of VBA help on its Web site. Topics include understanding VBA syntax, setting References, using Object Variables, and writing efficient code. To view this site, visit the PowerPoint 2002 More About Web page (scsite.com/pp2002/more.htm) and then click VBA Help.

Steps | **To Enter the Create Presentation Procedure**

1 **Click the Insert UserForm button arrow on the Standard toolbar and then point to Module.**

The Insert UserForm list displays (Figure 5-57).

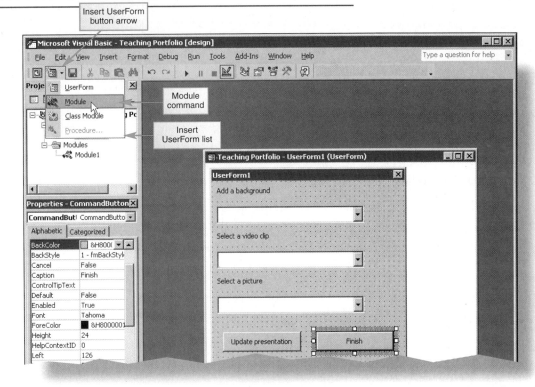

FIGURE 5-57

2 **Click Module in the Insert UserForm list. When the Visual Basic Editor opens, click the maximize button in the Teaching Portfolio – Module2 (Code) window. Type the seven comment statements (lines 1 through 7) in Table 5-7. Be certain to enter an apostrophe at the beginning of each comment line.**

PowerPoint starts the Visual Basic Editor, adds Module2, and displays the Microsoft Visual Basic window (Figure 5-58). The comment lines display in green. Module1 contains the code for the Print BW Handout macro you recorded in Phase 2 of this project.

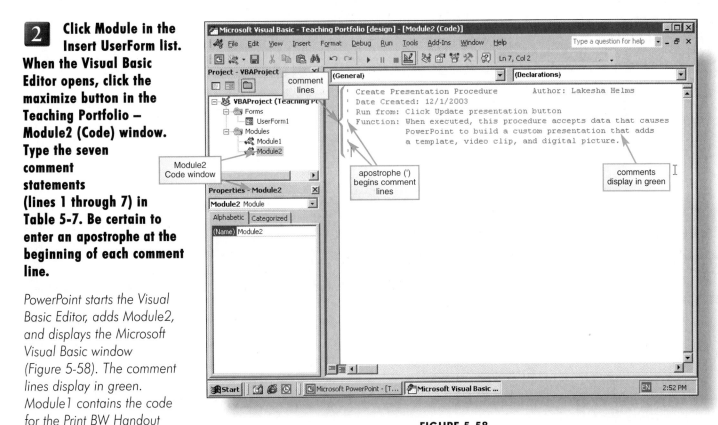

FIGURE 5-58

3 Press the ENTER key to position the insertion point on the next line. Enter lines 8 through 10 in Table 5-7. Do not enter the End Sub statement (line 11). For clarity, indent all lines between the Sub statement and End Sub statement by three spaces. Point to the Close Window button on the right side of the menu bar.

The Create Presentation procedure is complete (Figure 5-59). You do not need to enter the End Sub statement in line 11 of Table 5-7 because the Visual Basic Editor displays that line automatically when you type the Sub statement in line 8.

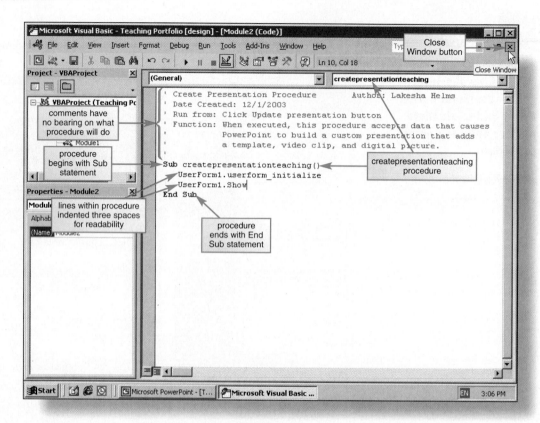

FIGURE 5-59

4 Click the Close Window button.

The Module2 Code window closes, and the form displays in the UserForm1 window (Figure 5-60). The UserForm1 window is maximized.

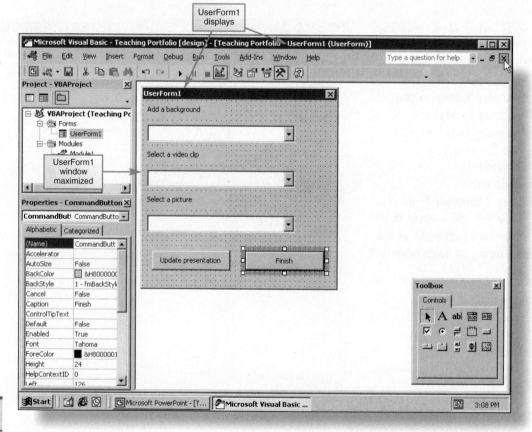

FIGURE 5-60

Other Ways

1. On Insert menu click Module
2. Press ALT+I, press M

More About Visual Basic for Applications

Visual Basic for Applications uses many more statements than those presented here. Even this simple procedure, however, should help you understand the basic makeup of a Visual Basic statement. Lines 9 and 10 in the procedure shown in Figure 5-59 include a period. The entry on the left side of the period tells PowerPoint which object you want to affect.

An **object** is a real-world thing. Your textbook, your car, your pets, and even your friends are objects. Visual Basic uses objects in its association with applications. This technique is described as **object-oriented (OO)**. When it refers to programming it is called **Object-Oriented Programming (OOP)**. The development of OOP provides a way to represent the world in conceptual terms that people understand. People relate to their everyday objects and easily can understand that these objects can have properties and behaviors.

An object is described by its properties. **Properties** are attributes that help differentiate one object from another. For example, your car has a color, a certain body style, and a certain type of interior. These properties are used to describe the car. The Visual Basic programming language has specific rules, or **syntax**. In Visual Basic syntax, you separate an object and its property with a period. For example, car.color, specifies a car object and the property color. You would write the statement, car.color = "red", to set the value of the color property to red.

An object also has certain behaviors, or methods. A **method** is a function or action you want the object to perform or an action that will be performed on an object. You can write your own functions, or you can use the built-in methods supplied with Visual Basic. Methods associated with car, pet, and friend objects might be drive, feed, and talk, respectively. The drive method would be written, car.drive, just as in the statement, UserForm1.Show, where UserForm1 is the object and Show is the method.

The following example shows that you can change an object's property value during execution of a procedure. Similar statements often are used to clear the properties of controls or to set them to initial values. This process is called **initialization**. The object in this case is a text box control.

$$\underbrace{\text{textbox1}}_{\text{control name}} . \underbrace{\text{text}}_{\text{property}} = \text{" "}$$

WRITING THE FORM'S INITIALIZATION PROCEDURE The next step is to write the procedure to initialize some of the control properties. Recall in Step 2 – Set Control Properties of this project that you added the controls to the form and then set some of the properties. With respect to VBA, PowerPoint has two modes: design mode and run mode. In **design mode**, you can resize controls, assign properties to controls, and enter VBA code. In **run mode**, all controls are active. That is, if you click a control, it triggers the event, and PowerPoint executes the procedure associated with the control.

Properties such as the label and command button caption properties were set in Step 2 of this project at design time. Data items can be added to a combo box at run-time using the AddItem method. The **AddItem method** is used to add items to a combo box. Table 5-8 shows the general form of the AddItem method.

More About

VBA Web Sites

The Internet contains a variety of Visual Basic information. Many Web sites offer information on coding, magazines, games, and tips. To view these sites, visit the PowerPoint 2002 More About Web page (scsite.com/pp2002/more.htm) and then click VBA Web Sites.

More About

Variables

When variables are initialized, a numeric variable is initialized to zero, a variable-length string is initialized to a zero-length string (" "), which also is called a null string, and a fixed-length string is filled with zeros.

Table 5-8	AddItem Method Format		
General Form:	`ComboBox1.AddItem "item name"`		
Comment:	The AddItem method places the item name string into the text list of the combo box.		
Example:	`ComboBox1.AddItem "Clouds"`		
	`ComboBox1.AddItem "Golf"`		
	`ComboBox3.AddItem "Volunteer"`		

Table 5-9	General Form of the Clear Method
General Form:	ComboBox1.Clear
Comment:	All the items in the combo box are deleted.
Example:	ComboBox2.Clear

A good practice is to issue the **Clear method** before adding items to the combo box. Table 5-9 shows the general form of the Clear method to clear all the items in a combo box.

The initialize procedure code in Table 5-10 sets some controls' property values during run mode. The **Initialize Form procedure** ensures the combo boxes are clear and adds the text items to the combo boxes. To add items to a combo box, use the AddItem method. Before adding items to a combo box, the Initialize Form procedure clears the entries in the combo boxes.

The statements in lines 3, 4, and 5 use the Clear method to make sure the combo boxes are empty. Lines 6 through 11 use the AddItem method to add the items to the combo boxes. To complete the section of code for the InitializeForm() procedure, an End Sub statement closes the procedure at line 12.

Table 5-10   Initialize Form Procedure

LINE	VBA CODE
1	Sub userform_initialize()
2	' Initialize the drop down list choices
3	ComboBox1.Clear
4	ComboBox2.Clear
5	ComboBox3.Clear
6	ComboBox1.AddItem "Clouds"
7	ComboBox1.AddItem "Orbit"
8	ComboBox2.AddItem "Motorcycle"
9	ComboBox2.AddItem "Golf"
10	ComboBox3.AddItem "Garden"
11	ComboBox3.AddItem "Volunteer"
12	End Sub

Steps **To Enter the InitializeForm() Procedure**

1 **Point to the View Code button at the top of the Project Explorer window.**

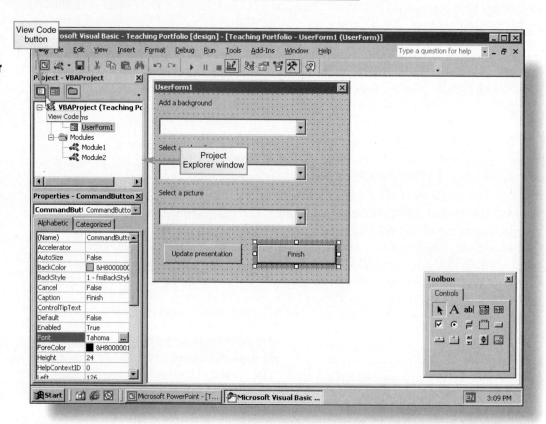

FIGURE 5-61

2 **Click the View Code button. Enter the VBA code shown in Table 5-10.**

The initialize procedure displays in the Code window (Figure 5-62). The word, UserForm, displays in the Object box, and the word, initialize, displays in the Procedure box.

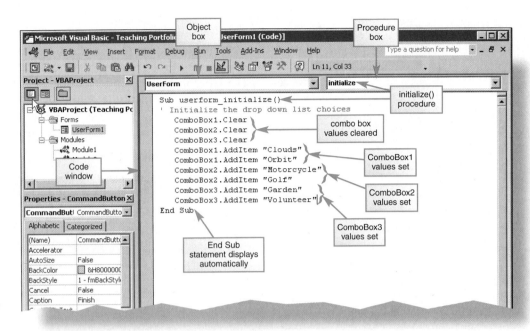

FIGURE 5-62

WRITING THE COMMANDBUTTON1 PROCEDURE Whenever you need to work with an object's properties or methods in more than one line of code, you can use the With statement to eliminate some coding. The **With statement** accepts an object as a parameter and is followed by several lines of code that pertain to this object. You therefore do not need to retype the object name in these lines. Table 5-11 describes the general form of the With statement.

The next step is to write the code for the CommandButton1 procedure as shown in Table 5-12. The CommandButton1 procedure is activated when the user clicks the Update Presentation button on the form. The code for this procedure is associated with the Click event.

Table 5-11	With Statement Format

General Form:	`With object`
	`    Visual Basic code`
	`End With`

Comment:	Object is any valid Visual Basic or user-defined object

Example:	`With textbox1`
	`    .text = ""`
	`End With`

Table 5-12	CommandButton1 Procedure
LINE	**VBA CODE**
1	`Templname = ComboBox1.Text & ".pot"`
2	`Application.ActivePresentation.ApplyTemplate Path & Templname`

3	`Set VideoSlide = ActivePresentation.Slides(2).Shapes _`
	`    AddMediaObject(FileName:=Path & ComboBox2.Text & ".avi", _`
	`    Left:=380, Top:=150)`

4	`With VideoSlide.AnimationSettings.PlaySettings`
5	`    PlayOnEntry = msoTrue`
6	`    PauseAnimation = msoTrue`
7	`    HideWhileNotPlaying = msoFalse`
8	`End With`
9	`Set PictureSlide = Application.ActivePresentation.Slides(3)`
10	`With PictureSlide`
11	`    .Shapes.AddPicture Path & ComboBox3.Text & ".jpg", True, True, 375, 150, 300, 300`
12	`End With`

Presenter View

Dual-monitor capability is available in PowerPoint 2002 if your desktop personal computer has two video cards. One card can display the presentation to your audience, and the other card can display PowerPoint's Presenter view, which helps you navigate through the slides. Presenter view allows you to show slides out of sequence, read speaker notes with an enlarged font size, preview the text that is going to display on the next slide, and black out the screen.

Line 1 defines the name of the template. Line 2 assigns the template to the presentation object. The Set statement in line 3 does several things. It sets an object name, VideoSlide, that represents Slide 2. The statement then assigns the video file selected in ComboBox2 to Slide 2 using the **AddMediaObject() method**. Table 5-13 shows the general form of the AddMediaObject() method. The method places the video at a specific location on the slide using the Left and Top coordinates. The underscore at the end of the line indicates that the statement continues on the next line.

Table 5-13	AddMediaObject() Method Format
General Form:	`Shape_Object.AddMediaObject(FileName, Left, Top, Width, Height)`
Comment:	Shape_Object is the name of the shape on the slide. The file name is required and is the name of the media file. If a path is not specified, the current working folder is path. Left and Top are the positions (in points) of the upper-left corner of the media location relative to the upper-left corner of the document. You also may supply optional Width and Height positions.
Example:	`ActivePresentation.Slides(2).Shapes.AddMediaObject(FileName:=` `"golf.avi", Left:=380, Top:=150)`

Controls

If you press the F1 key when you are running your presentation, PowerPoint displays a list of controls that help you navigate through the slide show. For example, the list describes which keys to press or actions to take to return to the first slide, change the mouse pointer to a pen, and stop and restart an automatic slide show.

Lines 4 through 8 use the same object, VideoSlide, and assign the animation and play settings. The **PauseAnimation property** set to True indicates the animation will pause when the user clicks the shape. When the user clicks the shape again, the animation will continue to play. The **HideWhileNotPlaying property** is set to False, so the video displays and stays on the slide even when not running.

Line 9 sets Slide 3 to a new object called PictureSlide. Lines 10 through 12 add the picture selected from the Picture combo box to the specific coordinates using the **AddPicture method**. Table 5-14 shows the general form of the AddPicture method.

Table 5-14	AddPicture Method Format
General Form:	`Shape_Object.AddPicture(FileName, LinkToFile, SaveWithDocument,` `Left, Top, Width, Height)`
Comment:	The file name is required and represents the file from which the OLE object is created. LinkToFile value is True, to link the picture to the file or False to make the picture an independent copy of the file. SaveWithDocument value True saves the linked picture with the presentation or False to store only the linked information in the document. If LinkToFile is False, this value must be True. Left and Top are the points location for the picture, and Width and Height are the width and height of the picture.
Example:	`.Shapes.AddPicture "mypicture.jpg", True, True, 375, 150, 300, 300`

Steps **To Enter the CommandButton1 Procedure**

1 Click the Object box arrow at the top of the Code window, and then point to CommandButton1 in the Object list (Figure 5-63).

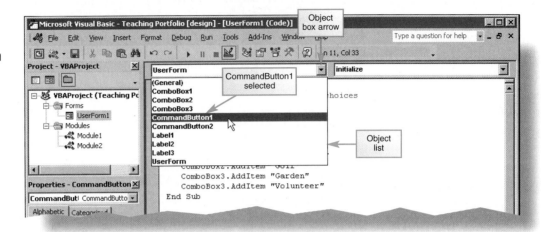

FIGURE 5-63

2 Click CommandButton1. Make sure Click is in the Procedure box.

The Visual Basic Editor displays the Sub and End Sub statements for the CommandButton1 procedure and positions the insertion point between the two statements (Figure 5-64).

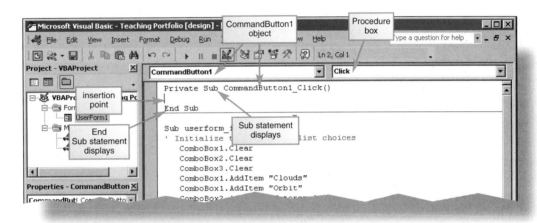

FIGURE 5-64

3 Enter the VBA code shown in lines 1 through 12 in Table 5-12. Do not press the ENTER key after typing the End With statement in line 12.

CommandButton1_Click() displays as the procedure (Figure 5-65).

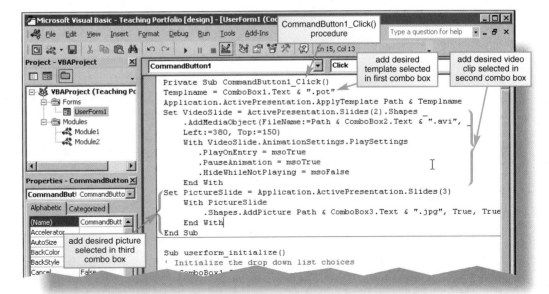

FIGURE 5-65

Table 5-15   CommandButton2 Procedure

LINE	VBA CODE
1	ActivePresentation.SlideShowSettings.Run
2	Unload UserForm1

WRITING THE COMMANDBUTTON2 PROCEDURE The next step is to write the CommandButton2 procedure. This procedure executes when the user clicks the Finish button. The procedure hides and unloads the form and starts the presentation.

Line 1 starts the current active presentation. Line 2 unloads the form (UserForm1).

Steps **To Enter the CommandButton2 Procedure**

1 **Click the Object box arrow in the Code window, and then click CommandButton2 in the Object box. Make sure Click is in the Procedure box.**

The Visual Basic Editor displays the Sub and End Sub statements for the CommandButton2 procedure and positions the insertion point between the two statements (Figure 5-66).

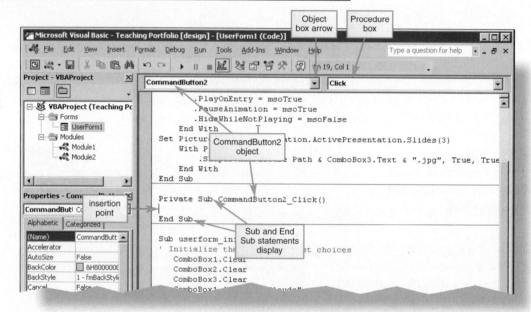

FIGURE 5-66

2 **Enter the VBA code shown in Table 5-15.**

CommandButton2_Click() displays as the procedure (Figure 5-67).

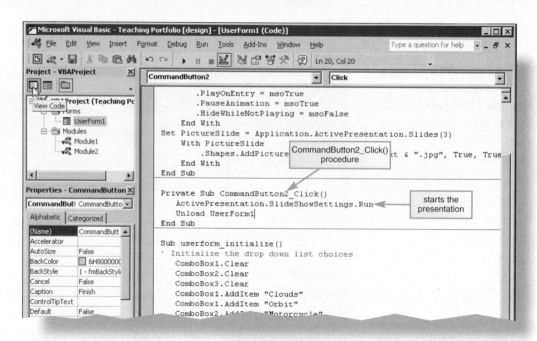

FIGURE 5-67

WRITING THE GENERAL DECLARATIONS   At the beginning of a Visual Basic program, it may be necessary to declare some variables or constant values. In this application, a **Path constant** is declared, which tells PowerPoint where to find files on a disk. PowerPoint needs to locate the templates, video, and digital images. The basic form of a **Constant statement** is shown in Table 5-16.

Table 5-16	Constant Statement Format
General Form:	`Public | Private] Const constname [As type] = expression`
Comment:	Public or Private indicates whether the value is available to all Visual Basic modules or just the current module. The constname must be a valid Visual Basic identifier and type must be a valid Visual Basic data type. The expression can be any valid Visual Basic expression.
Examples:	`Const Path = "a:\"` `Const Tax = 0.065`

Similar to the Const statement is the Dim statement. The general form of the Dim statement is shown in Table 5-17.

This project uses the Path constant because the video clip and digital images used are too large to fit on a floppy disk. By assigning the Path value once, the Path constant can be used in several modules as needed. If the location of the files changes, the programmer need only change the value of the Path constant. This procedure reduces the possibility of errors. To initialize a Path constant, perform the following steps.

Table 5-17	Dim Statement Format
General Form:	`Public | Private] DIM VariableName [As type] = expression`
Comment:	Public or Private indicates whether the value is available to all Visual Basic modules or just the current module. The VariableName must be a valid Visual Basic identifier and type must be a valid Visual Basic data type. The expression can be any valid Visual Basic expression.
Examples:	`Dim Area As Single` `Dim Templname As String`

Steps **To Initialize a Path Constant**

1   **Click the Object box arrow and then click (General).**

(General) displays in the Object box, and (Declarations) displays in the Procedure box (Figure 5-68).

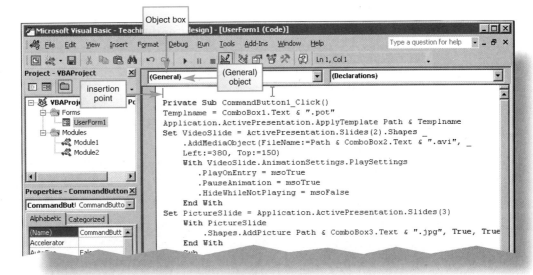

FIGURE 5-68

 **Type** `Const Path = "a:\"` **and then press the ENTER key. Type** `Dim Templname As String` **and then press the ENTER key.**

The constant and variable are declared for all procedures. A line displays and separates the General Declarations from the CommandButton1 procedure (Figure 5-69). You need to specify the location of your files.

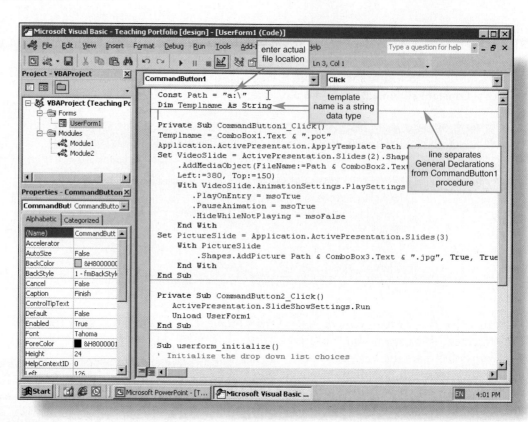

FIGURE 5-69

Other Ways

1. Click File on menu bar, click Close and Return to Microsoft PowerPoint
2. Press ALT+Q
3. Press ALT+F, press C

The VBA code is complete. The next step is to close the Visual Basic Editor and save the presentation. Before closing the Visual Basic Editor, you should verify your code by comparing it to Figures 5-58 through 5-69.

TO SAVE THE VISUAL BASIC CODE, CLOSE THE VISUAL BASIC EDITOR, AND SAVE THE PRESENTATION

1 Click the Save button on the Standard toolbar.

2 Click the Close button on the right side of the Visual Basic Editor title bar.

3 When the PowerPoint window displays, click the Save button on the Standard toolbar to save the presentation using the file name, Teaching Portfolio.

Adding a Button to Run the Form

The third button you will add to the custom Resume toolbar is the Create Presentation button. Users click this button and then make selections on the form to create a custom presentation. Perform the following steps to add this button.

TO ADD THE CREATE PRESENTATION BUTTON

1 Click Tools on the menu bar and then click Customize.

2 When the Customize dialog box opens, if necessary, click the Commands tab. Scroll down in the Categories box and then click Macros. Click createpresentationteaching in the Commands box.

3 Drag the createpresentationteaching entry from the Commands list in the Customize dialog box to the right of the Pack and Go button on the Resume toolbar.

4 Click the Modify Selection button and then point to Change Button Image on the submenu. When the Change Button Image palette displays, click the button with a key (row 6, column 3).

5 Click the Modify Selection button and then click Name on the shortcut menu. Type Create Presentation as the new name of this button.

6 Click Default Style on the submenu.

7 Click the Close button in the Customize dialog box.

The Create Presentation button displays with a key image (Figure 5-70).

button added to Resume toolbar

FIGURE 5-70

Saving the Presentation

The changes to the presentation are complete. Perform the following step to save the finished presentation before testing the controls.

TO SAVE A PRESENTATION

1 Click the Save button on the Standard toolbar.

PowerPoint saves the presentation by saving the changes made to the presentation since the last save.

Testing the Controls

The final step is to test the controls on the form. Use the following data: Orbit design template; Motorcycle video clip; and Volunteer picture. Perform the steps on the next page to test the controls.

More About

Quick Reference

For a table that lists how to complete tasks covered in this book using the mouse, menu, shortcut menu, and keyboard, see the Quick Reference Summary at the back of this book, or visit the Shelly Cashman Series Office XP Web page (scsite.com/offxp/qr.htm) and then click Microsoft PowerPoint 2002.

Steps **To Test the Control on the Form**

1 **Click the Create Presentation button on the Resume toolbar. When the form displays, click the Add a background box arrow and then click Orbit. Click the Select a video clip box arrow and then click Motorcycle. Click the Select a picture box arrow and then click Volunteer. Point to the Update presentation button.**

The form displays as shown (Figure 5-71).

2 **Click the Update Presentation button and then click the Finish button.**

The Teaching Portfolio slide show runs automatically.

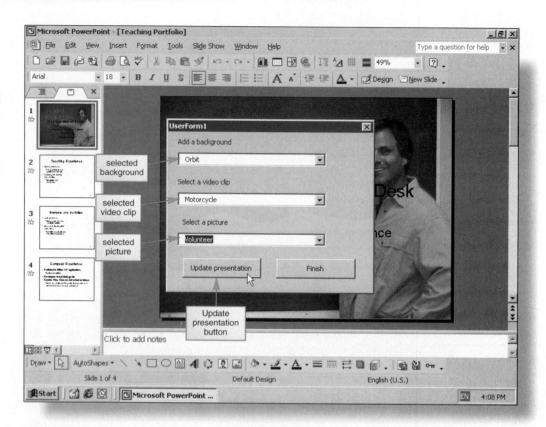

FIGURE 5-71

3 **Click the black slide to end the slide show. Print the four slides and a handout.**

Microsoft Certification

The Microsoft Office User Specialist (MOUS) Certification program provides an opportunity for you to obtain a valuable industry credential — proof that you have the PowerPoint 2002 skills required by employers. For more information, see Appendix E or visit the Shelly Cashman Series MOUS Web page at scsite.com/offxp/cert.htm.

The Orbit design template is applied to the presentation, the motorcycle video displays on Slide 2, and the air conditioning digital picture displays on Slide 3. If the slides do not display as shown, then click Tools on the menu bar, point to Macro, and then click Visual Basic Editor. Click the View Code button on the VBA Project toolbar, and then check the controls' properties and VBA code. Save the presentation again and repeat Steps 1 and 2 above.

Quitting PowerPoint

The project is complete. To quit PowerPoint, perform the following steps.

TO QUIT POWERPOINT

1 Click the Close button on the title bar.

2 If the Microsoft PowerPoint dialog box displays, click the Yes button to save changes made since the last save.

PowerPoint closes.

CASE PERSPECTIVE SUMMARY

The Teaching Portfolio slide show should assist Bernie with his job search. The form you developed using Visual Basic for Applications allows him to create a unique presentation for each interview. He can select a template, video clip, and digital picture. In addition, the buttons on the Resume toolbar you created and the new command on the File menu easily allow him to save the presentation as a Web page, to use the Pack and Go Wizard to transport this file, and to print a handout for the interviewer. Bernie's extraordinary and professional custom presentation should impress interviewers and help him land the best job possible.

Project Summary

Project 5 presented the principles of customizing a presentation. In Phase 1, you learned how to create a toolbar and add two buttons, Save as Web Page and the Pack and Go Wizard. In Phase 2, you learned how to use the macro recorder to create a macro that prints handouts displaying four slides per page and assign this macro to a command on the File menu. In Phase 3, you learned how to create a form composed of label controls, combo box controls, and command button controls. In this phase, you also learned how to write VBA code.

What You Should Know

Having completed this project, you now should be able to perform the following tasks:

▶ Add a Command to a Menu, Assign the Command to a Macro, and Invoke the Command *(PP 5.22)*

▶ Add Two Buttons to the Resume Toolbar *(PP 5.12)*

▶ Add Command Button Controls to a Form *(PP 5.36)*

▶ Add Label and Combo Box Controls to a Form *(PP 5.34)*

▶ Add the Create Presentation Button *(PP 5.52)*

▶ Change the Form Size and the Toolbox Location *(PP 5.31)*

▶ Create a Custom Toolbar *(PP 5.10)*

▶ Enter the CommandButton1 Procedure *(PP 5.49)*

▶ Enter the CommandButton2 Procedure *(PP 5.50)*

▶ Enter the Create Presentation Procedure *(PP 5.43)*

▶ Enter the InitializeForm() Procedure *(PP 5.46)*

▶ Initialize a Path Constant *(PP 5.51)*

▶ Open a Presentation and Save It with a New File Name *(PP 5.06)*

▶ Open a Presentation with a Macro and Execute the Macro *(PP 5.25)*

▶ Open the Visual Basic IDE and a New Form *(PP 5.29)*

▶ Quit PowerPoint *(PP 5.54)*

▶ Record a Macro to Print Handouts in Vertical Slide Order in Pure Black and White *(PP 5.19)*

▶ Resize and Reposition Controls on a Form *(PP 5.40)*

▶ Save a Presentation *(PP 5.17, PP 5.53)*

▶ Save and Close the Presentation *(PP 5.24)*

▶ Save the Visual Basic Code, Close the Visual Basic Editor, and Save the Presentation *(PP 5.52)*

▶ Set the Controls' Caption Properties *(PP 5.38)*

▶ Test the Control on the Form *(PP 5.54)*

▶ View a Macro's VBA Code *(PP 5.26)*

Learn It Online

Instructions: To complete the Learn It Online exercises, start your browser, click the Address bar, and then enter scsite.com/offxp/exs.htm. When the Office XP Learn It Online page displays, follow the instructions in the exercises below.

1 Project Reinforcement TF, MC, and SA

Below PowerPoint Project 5, click the Project Reinforcement link. Print the quiz by clicking Print on the File menu. Answer each question. Write your first and last name at the top of each page, and then hand in the printout to your instructor.

2 Flash Cards

Below PowerPoint Project 5, click the Flash Cards link. When Flash Cards displays, read the instructions. Type 20 (or a number specified by your instructor) in the Number of Playing Cards text box, type your name in the Name text box, and then click the Flip Card button. When the flash card displays, read the question and then click the Answer box arrow to select an answer. Flip through Flash Cards. Click Print on the File menu to print the last flash card if your score is 15 (75%) correct or greater and then hand it in to your instructor. If your score is less than 15 (75%) correct, then redo this exercise by clicking the Replay button.

3 Practice Test

Below PowerPoint Project 5, click the Practice Test link. Answer each question, enter your first and last name at the bottom of the page, and then click the Grade Test button. When the graded practice test displays on your screen, click Print on the File menu to print a hard copy. Continue to take practice tests until you score 80% or better. Hand in a printout of the final practice test to your instructor.

4 Who Wants to Be a Computer Genius?

Below PowerPoint Project 5, click the Computer Genius link. Read the instructions, enter your first and last name at the bottom of the page, and then click the Play button. Hand in your score to your instructor.

5 Wheel of Terms

Below PowerPoint Project 5, click the Wheel of Terms link. Read the instructions, and then enter your first and last name and your school name. Click the Play button. Hand in your score to your instructor.

6 Crossword Puzzle Challenge

Below PowerPoint Project 5, click the Crossword Puzzle Challenge link. Read the instructions, and then enter your first and last name. Click the Play button. Work the crossword puzzle. When you are finished, click the Submit button. When the crossword puzzle redisplays, click the Print button. Hand in the printout.

7 Tips and Tricks

Below PowerPoint Project 5, click the Tips and Tricks link. Click a topic that pertains to Project 5. Right-click the information and then click Print on the shortcut menu. Construct a brief example of what the information relates to in PowerPoint to confirm you understand how to use the tip or trick. Hand in the example and printed information.

8 Newsgroups

Below PowerPoint Project 5, click the Newsgroups link. Click a topic that pertains to Project 5. Print three comments. Hand in the comments to your instructor.

9 Expanding Your Horizons

Below PowerPoint Project 5, click the Articles for Microsoft PowerPoint link. Click a topic that pertains to Project 5. Print the information. Construct a brief example of what the information relates to in PowerPoint to confirm you understand the contents of the article. Hand in the example and printed information to your instructor.

10 Search Sleuth

Below PowerPoint Project 5, click the Search Sleuth link. To search for a term that pertains to this project, select a term below the Project 5 title and then use the Google search engine at google.com (or any major search engine) to display and print two Web pages that present information on the term. Hand in the printouts to your instructor.

Apply Your Knowledge

1 Creating a Macro and Customizing a Menu and Toolbar

Instructions: Start PowerPoint. Open the presentation, Beach, from the Data Disk. See the inside back cover of this book for instructions for downloading the Data Disk or see your instructor for information on accessing the files required for this book. Perform the following tasks.

1. Use the Record New Macro command to create a macro that exports the presentation outline to Microsoft Word. Call the macro ExportWord. Change the name of the author in the Description box to your name. Make sure the Store macro in box displays Beach Vacation. Click the OK button. When the Stop Recording toolbar displays, do the following:
   (a) Click File on the menu bar and then click Save As. (b) When the Save As dialog box displays, type Beach Outline in the File name box. (c) Click the Save as type box arrow and then click Outline/RTF in the Save as type list. (d) Be certain the Save in box location is 3½ Floppy (A:). (e) Click the Save button. (f) Click the Stop Recording button on the Stop Recording toolbar.

2. Add a button to the Standard toolbar (Figure 5-72a) and a command to the File menu (Figure 5-72b on the next page). Use the image of a pencil (row 4, column 4) and the Default Style for the button. Change the macro name on the File menu to Export to Word.

3. View the ExportWord's VBA code. When the Visual Basic Editor displays the macro (Figure 5-72c on the next page), click File on the menu bar, click Print, and then click the OK button. Close the Visual Basic Editor.

4. Run the macro as follows: (a) Click the button you added to the Standard toolbar. (b) Click File on the menu bar and then click the Export to Word command.

5. Save the presentation with the file name, Beach Vacation.

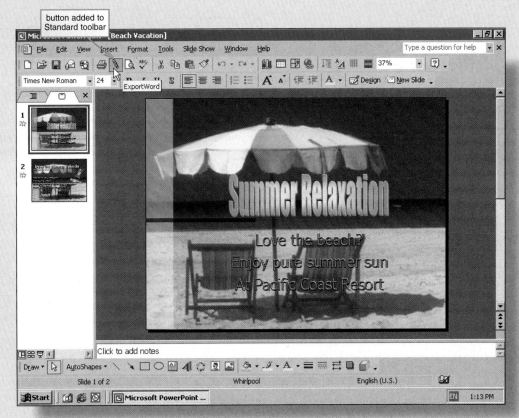

FIGURE 5-72a

(continued)

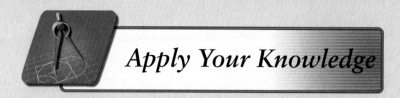

Apply Your Knowledge

Creating a Macro and Customizing a Menu and Toolbar *(continued)*

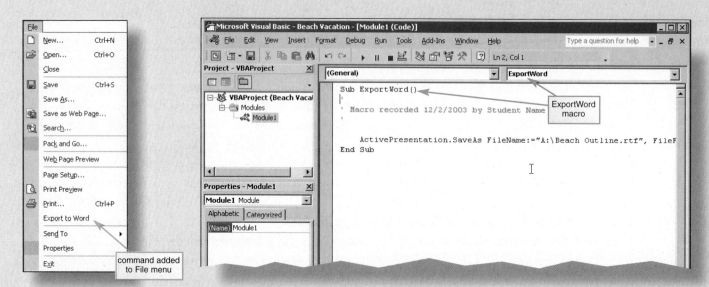

FIGURE 5-72b   **FIGURE 5-72c**

6. Reset the toolbars to their installation settings (see Appendix D). Quit PowerPoint. Hand in the printout to your instructor.

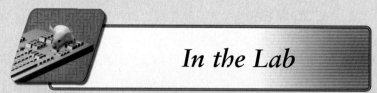

In the Lab

1 Create a New Toolbar, Record New Macros, and Place New Macros on a Toolbar

Problem: You are employed as an administrative assistant at the local bank. Part of your job responsibilities includes greeting customers and arranging appointments with loan officers. Many of the customers are in the process of applying for used car loans, and they have many questions regarding buying these vehicles efficiently and obtaining the best price. Your manager has asked you to prepare a PowerPoint presentation for these customers to view as they are waiting for their appointments with the loan officers. You agree to create this presentation and decide to write a macro that changes the slide backgrounds. You also add a button to save the presentation using the Pack and Go Wizard. A third macro prints Notes Pages for handouts to distribute to these customers. Slide 1 and the new buttons display in Figure 5-73.

Instructions: Start PowerPoint and perform the following tasks with a computer.

1. Open the file, Road Tips, from your Data Disk. Save the presentation with the file name, Road Tips Revised.

In the Lab

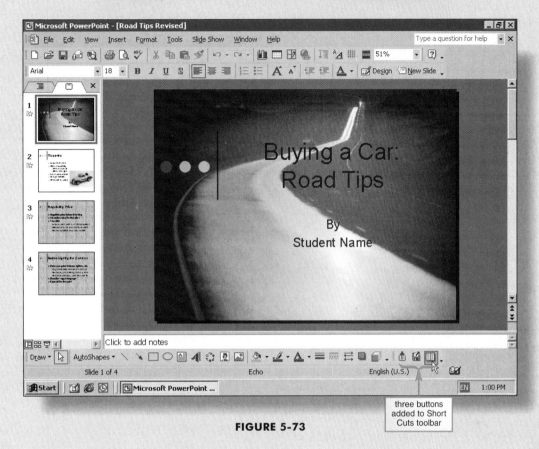

FIGURE 5-73

three buttons added to Short Cuts toolbar

2. Create a new toolbar and name it Short Cuts. Place the new toolbar next to the Drawing toolbar.

3. Use the Record New Macro command to create a macro that changes the backgrounds on Slides 3 and 4. Name the macro, Background, change the name of the author in the Description box to your name, and then store the macro in the Road Tips Revised file.

4. With the Stop Recording toolbar on the screen, do the following: (a) Select Slides 3 and 4 on the Slides tab. (b) Click Format on the menu bar and then click Background. (c) Click the Background fill area arrow in the Background dialog box, click Fill Effects, click the Texture tab, click Papyrus, click the OK button, and then click the Apply button in the Background dialog box. (d) Click the Stop Recording button on the Stop Recording toolbar.

5. Use the Record New Macro command to create a macro that saves the presentation using the Pack and Go Wizard. Call the macro, PackandGo, change the name of the author in Description box to your name, and store the macro in the Road Tips Revised file.

6. With the Stop Recording toolbar displaying, perform the following steps: (a) Click File on the menu bar and then click Pack and Go. (b) Follow the instructions for the Pack and Go Wizard using the active presentation and save it on your Data Disk. Do not include linked files, embedded True Type fonts, or the Viewer. (c) Click the Stop Recording button on the Stop Recording toolbar.

7. Use the Record New Macro command to create a macro that prints Notes Pages. Call the macro, PrintNotes, change the name of the author in Description box to your name, and then store the macro in the Road Tips Revised file.

(continued)

In the Lab

Create a New Toolbar, Record New Macros, and Place New Macros on a Toolbar *(continued)*

8. With the Stop Recording toolbar displaying, perform the following steps: (a) Click File on the menu bar and then click Print. (b) In the Print what box, click Handouts. (c) In the Slides per page box, click 4; make sure Order is Horizontal; and then click the OK button. (d) After the handouts print, click File on the menu bar and then click Print. (e) In the Slides per page box, click 6. (f) In the Print what box, click Slides. (g) Click the OK button. (h) After the four slides print, click the Stop Recording button on the Stop Recording toolbar.

9. Add the three macros to the new Short Cuts toolbar. Modify the selection for the Background macro, and change the image to the ink bottle icon (row 1, column 4). On the Modify Selection menu, select the Default Style. Change the image icon for the PackandGo macro to the floppy disk with the arrow pointing out (row 1, column 5). Select the Default Style on the Modify Selection menu. Modify the selection for the PrintNotes macro and change the image to the book pages (row 6, column 1).

10. Add the PrintNotes macro to the File menu above the Print menu command. Change the Name to Print Notes.

11. Save the presentation again. Print the macro code for all three macros. Reset the menus and toolbars to their installation settings (see Appendix D). Quit PowerPoint. Hand in the macro code and Notes Pages to your instructor.

2 Creating a New Toolbar and Writing a Visual Basic Program to Add Preset Gradient Backgrounds

Problem: You are a summer intern at New Century Credit Union working in the Information Technology (IT) department. The IT director wants you to work with Shalanda Green, who is developing a presentation on investing. Shalanda will be giving the presentation several times to various groups and wants the presentation to have a different look each time. You tell Shalanda you can write a Visual Basic program to display a form (Figure 5-74a) and let her change the background to preset gradient colors. The two of you agree to change the background on Slides 2 and 4. To streamline the process, you will create a toolbar and place a Start button for the Visual Basic program on the new toolbar (Figure 5-74b).

Instructions: Start PowerPoint and perform the following tasks.

1. Open the Investing presentation on the Data Disk. Save the presentation with the file name, New Century.
2. Create a new toolbar with the name, Invest. Place this toolbar to the right of the Formatting toolbar.
3. Open the Visual Basic Editor and insert a new module.
4. Click the View Code button. In the General Declarations window, enter the code from Table 5-18, which will run the Visual Basic program. The End Sub statement will display automatically after entering line 1.
5. Close the Visual Basic Editor. Add this module, createpresentationInvesting(), to the new toolbar as a button.

Table 5-18	General Declarations
LINE	**VBA CODE**
1	Sub createpresentationInvesting()
2	UserForm1.UserForm_Initialize
3	UserForm1.Show

In the Lab

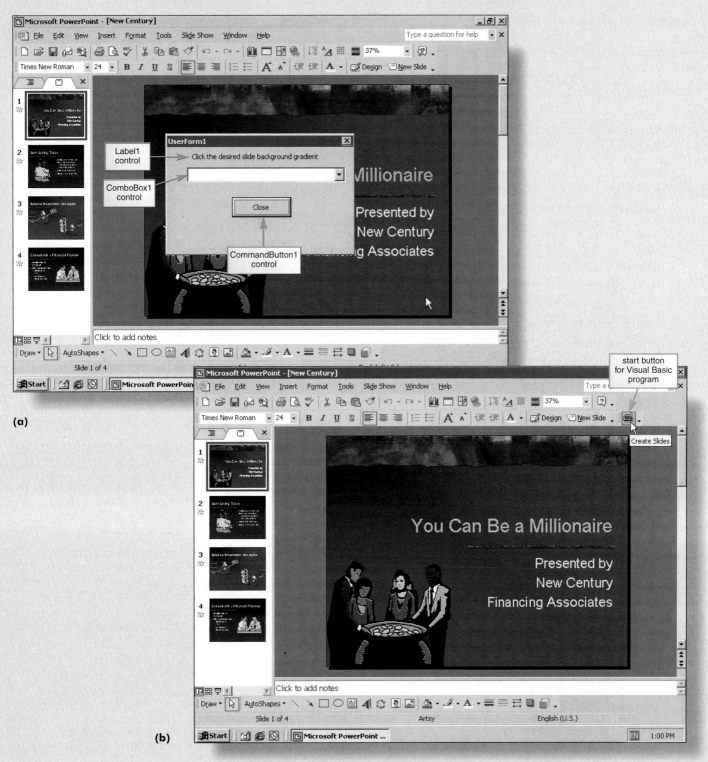

(a)

(b)

FIGURE 5-74

(continued)

In the Lab

Creating a New Toolbar and Writing a Visual Basic Program to Add Preset Gradient Backgrounds *(continued)*

6. Modify the new toolbar button by clicking the Modify Selection button. Change the button image to the keyboard (row 5, column 6) and select the Default style. Click the Modify Selection button and then click Name on the shortcut menu. Change the name of this button to Create Slides.

7. Save the presentation again.

8. Open the Visual Basic Editor. A new User Form (UserForm1) already exists. Add a label, a combo box, and a command button.

9. Click anywhere in UserForm1. In the Properties window, change the Height to 147 and Width to 230. Place a label, combo box, and command button on the form as shown in Figure 5-74a on the previous page. Use the data in Table 5-19 to set the properties for these controls.

10. Click the View Code button. After the End Sub in the Code window for the ComboBox1 control, enter the code from Table 5-20 to add the preset gradient names to the combo box (ComboBox1). The End Sub will display automatically.

11. Click the Object box arrow and then select CommandButton1. Make sure Click is in the Procedure box. Enter the code in Table 5-21 between the Sub and End Sub statements.

Table 5-19	Control Properties	
CONTROL	*PROPERTY*	*VALUE*
Label1	Caption	Click the desired slide background gradient
	Height	18
	Width	222
	Top	6
	Left	30
ComboBox1	Height	18
	Width	192
	Top	24
	Left	24
CommandButton1	Caption	Close
	Height	24
	Width	72
	Top	60
	Left	78

Table 5-20	Initialize Form Procedure
LINE	*VBA CODE*
1	Sub UserForm_Initialize()
2	ComboBox1.AddItem "Brass"
3	ComboBox1.AddItem "Calm Water"
4	ComboBox1.AddItem "Day Break"
5	ComboBox1.AddItem "Desert"
6	ComboBox1.AddItem "Early Sunset"
7	ComboBox1.AddItem "Fire"
8	ComboBox1.AddItem "Horizon"
9	ComboBox1.AddItem "Late Sunset"
10	ComboBox1.AddItem "Night Fall"
11	ComboBox1.AddItem "Ocean"
12	ComboBox1.AddItem "Parchment"
13	ComboBox1.AddItem "Wheat"

Table 5-21	CommandButton1 Procedure
LINE	*VBA CODE*
1	ActivePresentation.SlideShowSettings.Run
2	UserForm1.Hide
3	Unload UserForm1
4	End

12. Save the Visual Basic code. Close the Visual Basic Editor. Run the presentation.

13. Print the presentation. Print the form and the Visual Basic code by clicking File on the menu bar and then clicking Print, clicking Current Project in the Range area, making sure the Form Image and Code boxes are checked in the Print What area, and then clicking the OK button. Quit PowerPoint. Hand in the printouts to your instructor.

In the Lab

3 Writing a Visual Basic Program to Place Picture Images as the Background

Problem: You are working part time for the Community Park District. The director, Fernando Leva, wants a kiosk to display a PowerPoint presentation listing the monthly activities the park district offers. The kiosk will display in the foyer of the town hall, and the presentation will be started every morning. Fernando wants to show a different background picture every day. For the month of July, the district has these programs scheduled: a trip to see a major league soccer game; a golf outing; a fishing trip; a visit to the zoo; a trip to a remote beach; and a nature photography course. You tell Fernando that you can create a Visual Basic program with a form that allows him to select a background picture. Fernando wants to see a prototype before you complete the entire project.

Instructions: Start PowerPoint and then perform the following tasks.

1. Open the Park presentation on the Data Disk. Save the presentation with the file name, Park District.
2. Open the Visual Basic Editor.
3. Create the form shown in Figure 5-75a on page PP 5.65. Position the controls as shown in the figure, and then change the properties for each control as indicated in Table 5-22.
4. Write the Visual Basic code for the OptionButton1 control. Double-click the OptionButton1 control and enter the code from Table 5-23 between the Private Sub and End Sub statements.

Table 5-23   OptionButton1 Procedure

LINE	VBA CODE
1	`With ActiveWindow.Selection.SlideRange`
2	`.FollowMasterBackground = msoFalse`
3	`.DisplayMasterShapes = msoTrue`
4	`With .Background`
5	`.Fill.Visible = msoTrue`
6	`.Fill.Transparency = 0#`
7	`.Fill.UserPicture "a:\soccer.jpg"`
8	`End With`
9	`End With`

Table 5-22   Control Properties

CONTROL	PROPERTY	VALUE
Label1	Caption	Select Background Pictures
	Height	18
	Width	114
	Top	24
	Left	66
OptionButton1	Caption	Soccer
	Height	18
	Width	108
	Top	60
	Left	6
OptionButton2	Caption	Golfing
	Height	18
	Width	108
	Top	90
	Left	6
OptionButton3	Caption	Fishing
	Height	18
	Width	108
	Top	126
	Left	6
OptionButton4	Caption	Zoo
	Height	18
	Width	108
	Top	60
	Left	126
OptionButton5	Caption	Beach
	Height	18
	Width	108
	Top	90
	Left	126
OptionButton6	Caption	Photography
	Height	18
	Width	108
	Top	90
	Left	126
CommandButton1	Caption	Run Show
	Height	24
	Width	72
	Top	156
	Left	78

(continued)

In the Lab

Writing a Visual Basic Program to Place Picture Images as the Background *(continued)*

5. Repeat the process for option buttons 2 through 5. Change the file name for the picture in line 7 for each option button as indicated in Table 5-24.

Table 5-24	Option Button File Names
CONTROL	**VALUE**
OptionButton2	A:\golf.jpg
OptionButton3	A:\fishing.jpg
OptionButton4	A:\zoo.jpg
OptionButton5	A:\beach.jpg
OptionButton6	A:\camera.jpg

6. Create a new toolbar with the name, Park District. Place the toolbar to the right of the Drawing toolbar.
7. With the Visual Basic Editor still open, insert a new module.
8. Click the View Code button. In the General Declarations window, enter the code from Table 5-25, which will run the Visual Basic program. The End Sub statement will display automatically after entering line 1.

Table 5-25	General Declarations
LINE	**VBA CODE**
1	`Sub ParkDistrictStart()`
2	`UserForm1.userform_initialize`
3	`UserForm1.Show`
4	`End Sub`

9. Add this module, ParkDistrictStart(), to the new toolbar as a button.
10. Click the Modify Selection button to modify the new toolbar button. Change the button image to the runner (row 7, column 3) and use the Default Style (Figure 5-75b). Change the button name to Run Show.
11. Save the Visual Basic code.
12. Print the form and the Visual Basic code by clicking File on the menu bar and then clicking Print. Click the Current Project in the Range area. Make sure the Form Image and Code boxes are checked in the Print What area. Click the OK button. Close the Visual Basic Editor and reset the toolbars to their installation settings (see Appendix D). Quit PowerPoint. Hand in the printouts to your instructor.

In the Lab

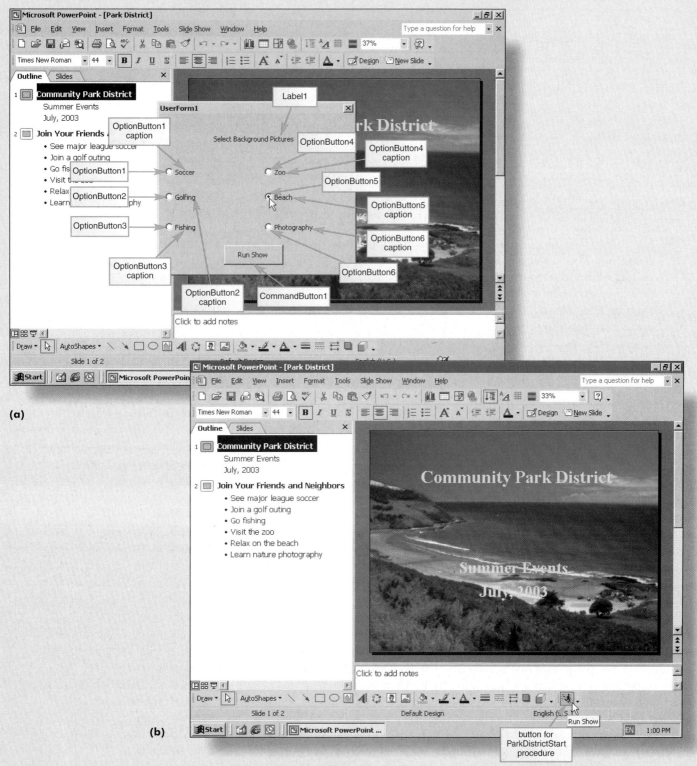

(a)

(b)

FIGURE 5-75

Cases and Places

The difficulty of these case studies varies:
▶ are the least difficult; ▶▶ are more difficult; and ▶▶▶ are the most difficult.

1 ▶ Open the Wellness Institute presentation you created in Project 3. See your instructor if you did not complete this project. Record a macro that changes the background to a preset gradient. Name the macro BWGradient. On the Gradient tab in the Fill Effects dialog box, click the Two colors option. Assign Color 1 the color, light blue and Color 2 the color, white. In the Shading styles area, click the From title style and click the first Variants style (row 1, column 1). Apply the background to all slides. Assign the macro to a new button on the Standard toolbar. View the macro and then print the code. Hand in the printouts to your instructor.

2 ▶ Open The Blues about the Flu presentation from the Data Disk. Create a new toolbar with the name, Flu Tools. Record a macro to save the presentation as a Web page and then preview the Web pages. Assign the macro to a button on the Flu Tools toolbar to execute this module. Record a second macro to add a footer with today's date, your school's name, and the page number on all slides except the title slide. Assign the macro to a command on the View menu. View the macros and then print the code. Hand in the printouts to your instructor.

3 ▶▶ Open The Blues about the Flu presentation from the Data Disk and delete the clips on Slides 4 and 5. Create a form that allows the user to select one of five templates from a combo box. Slides 3 and 4 have clip art, and the user can select one of five clips for Slide 3 and one of five clips for Slide 4. These five images may be used as choices for both slides. Write the Visual Basic module that executes this form. Name the module, AddTemplates_ClipArt, and then add a button on the Formatting toolbar to execute this module. Print the form, the Visual Basic code, and the presentation. Hand in the printouts to your instructor.

4 ▶▶ Using Microsoft Internet Explorer, go to the Microsoft Office Developer's Web site: msdn.microsoft.com/library/. In the Table of Contents frame, click Office Solutions Development, and then click Microsoft PowerPoint. Click the links and find a technical article, such as Create a Presentation from a Word Document. Read and summarize the article. Hand in the article and the summary to your instructor.

5 ▶▶ Your local park district is expanding the classes offered for residents during the summer months. Two of the new classes are Golf Fundamentals for Children and Motorcycle Safety Basics. Create a slide show for the park district using the video clips, motorcycle.avi and golf.avi, used in this project. Add four pictures or clip art files showing various outdoors activities, such as swimming, baseball, boating, and camping. Create a new toolbar with the name, Classes. Record a macro that prints handouts and notes. Place this macro on the new toolbar, and change the text of the button to an appropriate image. Next, create a form that allows the user to modify the slides to select various video clips, pictures, clip art, and design templates. Execute the print macro, and then display the form. Print slides, the Visual Basic code, and the form. Submit the printouts to your instructor.

Cases and Places

6 ▶▶▶ PowerPoint cannot record a macro for every keystroke. For example, PowerPoint will not record the keystrokes to make a Summary Slide automatically. Open the completed Enjoy Spring Break presentation you created in Project 2. See your instructor if you did not complete this project. Write a Visual Basic module that creates a new blank slide at the end of the slide sequence and reads the title text of Slides 2 through the end of the slides. By incorporating the Count method and using Visual Basic For/Next statements, you can create this slide.

(a) Start a new subroutine for this module called SummarySlide().

(b) In the General Declarations window, enter the code from Table 5-26 to declare the variables used in the module.

(c) Type Sub Summary_Slide() and then press the ENTER key. The End Sub statement should display automatically.

(d) Enter the Visual Basic code in Table 5-27 to determine the total number of slides in the presentation. Do not press the ENTER key after typing the End With statement in line 12.

Table 5-26	General Declarations
LINE	VBA CODE
1	Dim mySlide As Integer
2	Dim SumText As String
3	Dim SummarySlideLines(5) As String

Table 5-27	Determine Slide Count Procedure
LINE	VBA CODE
4	' Determine the total number of slides
5	With ActivePresentation.Slides
6	SlideCount = .Count + 1
7	End With

(e) Enter the Visual Basic code in Table 5-28 to collect the titles from every slide.

Table 5-28	Collect Titles Procedure
LINE	VBA CODE
8	' Collect the titles from every slide
9	For mySlide = 2 To SlideCount - 1
10	Set myPresentation = ActivePresentation.Slides(mySlide)
11	SummarySlideLines(mySlide) = myPresentation.Shapes.Title.TextFrame.TextRange.Text
12	Next mySlide

(f) Add the Visual Basic code from Table 5-29 to add a slide at the end of the presentation and then insert the slide title.

Table 5-29	Add Summary Slide Procedure
LINE	VBA CODE
13	' Add the summary slide
14	Set SumSlide = ActivePresentation.Slides.Add(SlideCount, ppLayoutText).Shapes
15	' Insert the title for the summary slide
16	SumSlide.Title.TextFrame.TextRange.Text = "In Conclusion"

(continued)

Cases and Places

(g) Using the For/Next loop in Table 5-30, collect the slide titles into one long string of text. Press the ENTER key at the end of each title so the titles will display on separate lines in the slide.

Table 5-30 Collect Slide Titles Procedure	
LINE	**VBA CODE**
17	`For mySlide = 2 To SlideCount - 1`
18	`  SumText = SumText & SummarySlideLines(mySlide) & Chr(13)`
19	`Next mySlide`

(h) Insert the SumText module in Table 5-31 that places text into the text placeholder.

Table 5-31 Insert Summary Text Procedure	
LINE	**VBA CODE**
20	`' Insert the titles in the slide text placeholder`
21	`SumSlide.Placeholders(2).TextFrame.TextRange.Text = SumText`
22	`End Sub`

(i) Create a button on the Formatting toolbar to execute the Summary_Slide() module.

(j) Save the Visual Basic code, and then save the presentation with the file name, Spring Break Update.

(k) Execute the Visual Basic program. Print the Visual Basic code and the slides using the Pure Black and White option. Quit PowerPoint.

7 ▶▶▶ Open the Teaching Portfolio presentation you created in this project. You would like to share the layout of your form with various colleagues to obtain their feedback on the forms layout. With the Visual Basic Editor open, search the Help files for the code to write a module that prints the form. Save the module as PrintThisForm. Using the Customize command on the Tools menu, locate your module in the Macro commands. Drag the PrintThisForm entry to the right of the Create Presentation button on the Resume toolbar. Modify this new button using the open pages image (row 6, column 1) on the Change Button Image palette. Name the button Print Form and then set the new button to the default style. Execute and then print the macro. Hand in the printouts to your instructor.

Microsoft PowerPoint 2002

PROJECT

Creating a Self-Running Presentation Containing Interactive Documents

You will have mastered the material in this project when you can:

O B J E C T I V E S

- Insert a slide from another presentation
- Add action buttons and action settings to slides
- Use guides to position an object
- Format action buttons by adding fill color, shadows, and lines
- Add captions to action buttons
- Format action button caption text
- Insert, size, and format a Radial diagram
- Add text to Radial diagram shapes
- Insert and format an AutoShape
- Add and format AutoShape text
- Apply a motion path animation effect to an AutoShape
- Create a self-running presentation
- Set slide show timings manually
- Start the self-running presentation and view interactive documents

Innovative Images Create Meaningful Messages

Films of the silent era launched the motion picture industry in the early twentieth century. Movies consisted of one-reel films only a few minutes long. At first a novelty, and then increasingly an art form, silent films reached greater intricacy and length in the early 1910s. Even without sound, these films portrayed numerous types of emotions and messages. Humans have relied on imagery to communicate since the beginning of time. Images play a vital role in relaying messages and promoting communication.

Individuals long have used pictures, or graphics, as guides for building structures involving complex spatial relationships. Imagine trying to build the pharaohs' pyramids without a plan drawn out on papyrus or a Boeing jet without engineering drawings.

Yet, in recent years, graphics, onscreen presentations, self-running presentations, online meetings, presentations on the Web, overhead transparencies, and 35mm slide shows have played an even greater role in the art of communication. People understand more easily when visual elements are combined. From sales presentations, to impressive slide shows in courtroom dramas, to disseminating information in kiosks, people turn to images to persuade others, to influence buying choices, or to adopt

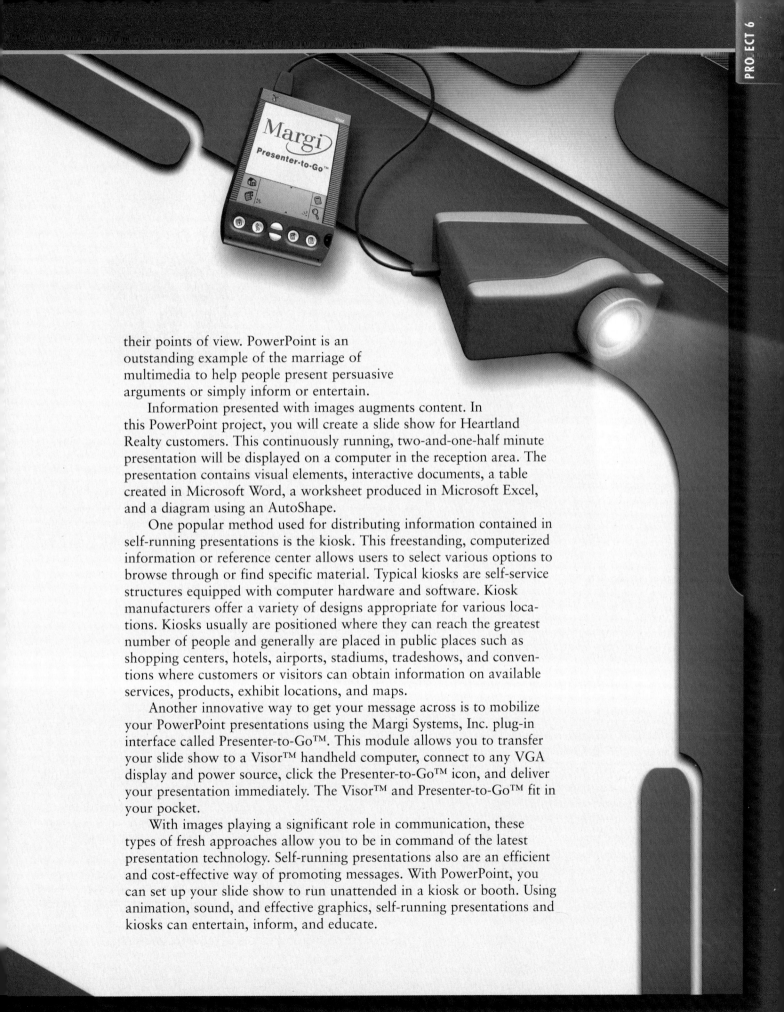

their points of view. PowerPoint is an outstanding example of the marriage of multimedia to help people present persuasive arguments or simply inform or entertain.

Information presented with images augments content. In this PowerPoint project, you will create a slide show for Heartland Realty customers. This continuously running, two-and-one-half minute presentation will be displayed on a computer in the reception area. The presentation contains visual elements, interactive documents, a table created in Microsoft Word, a worksheet produced in Microsoft Excel, and a diagram using an AutoShape.

One popular method used for distributing information contained in self-running presentations is the kiosk. This freestanding, computerized information or reference center allows users to select various options to browse through or find specific material. Typical kiosks are self-service structures equipped with computer hardware and software. Kiosk manufacturers offer a variety of designs appropriate for various locations. Kiosks usually are positioned where they can reach the greatest number of people and generally are placed in public places such as shopping centers, hotels, airports, stadiums, tradeshows, and conventions where customers or visitors can obtain information on available services, products, exhibit locations, and maps.

Another innovative way to get your message across is to mobilize your PowerPoint presentations using the Margi Systems, Inc. plug-in interface called Presenter-to-Go™. This module allows you to transfer your slide show to a Visor™ handheld computer, connect to any VGA display and power source, click the Presenter-to-Go™ icon, and deliver your presentation immediately. The Visor™ and Presenter-to-Go™ fit in your pocket.

With images playing a significant role in communication, these types of fresh approaches allow you to be in command of the latest presentation technology. Self-running presentations also are an efficient and cost-effective way of promoting messages. With PowerPoint, you can set up your slide show to run unattended in a kiosk or booth. Using animation, sound, and effective graphics, self-running presentations and kiosks can entertain, inform, and educate.

Microsoft PowerPoint 2002

Creating a Self-Running Presentation Containing Interactive Documents

CASE PERSPECTIVE

Owning a home is the ultimate dream for many people, but buying the right home can be complicated. Potential buyers must be financially qualified, and they need to understand mortgage options and how much money they can afford to buy a house. Buyers often use worksheets to determine their eligibility in order to investigate various lending options.

At Heartland Realty, you assist real estate agents in scheduling workshops on financing options and loan documentation. They want to conduct a workshop for first-time home buyers, but no slide show exists on that topic. You decide to use your PowerPoint skills to create this presentation. The slide show will consist of one slide from an existing presentation and three new slides to cover prequalification review, the maximum affordable home price, and the benefits of home ownership. You will create an interactive slide show that includes a program to determine the debt-to-income ratio, a worksheet created in Microsoft Excel that allows buyers to determine the maximum selling price, a table created in Microsoft Word that shows the interest rate factor, and a diagram using an AutoShape that shows the benefits of home ownership.

Introduction

People thirst for information. From catching the breaking news on cable television to downloading their latest e-mail messages, individuals keep up with the day's events.

One method used for disseminating information is a **kiosk**. This freestanding, self-service structure is equipped with computer hardware and software and is used to provide information or reference materials to the public. Some have a touch screen or keyboard that serves as an input device and allows users to select various options to browse through or find specific information. Kiosks frequently are found in public places, such as shopping centers, hotels, museums, libraries, and airport terminals.

Every presentation is created for a specific audience. Sometimes, when running a slide show, you want to open another application to show more detailed information about a particular topic. For example, when presenting mortgage information, you may want to show an estimated affordable home price based on the buyer's income and debts and the percentage and term of the loan. PowerPoint allows you to show these figures without leaving the presentation by using interactive documents. An **interactive document** is a file created in another application, such as Microsoft Word or Excel, and then opened during the running of a slide show.

In this project, you will create a slide show for Heartland Realty customers. This show will run continuously on a computer in the reception area, so potential first-time home buyers can view five slides during the brief two-and-one-half-minute presentation that gives them information on purchasing a property. The five presentation slides are shown in Figures 6-1a, 6-1b, 6-1d, 6-1f, and 6-1h. The users also can advance the slides manually to interact with the presentation. The interactive documents are shown in Figures 6-1c, 6-1e, and 6-1g.

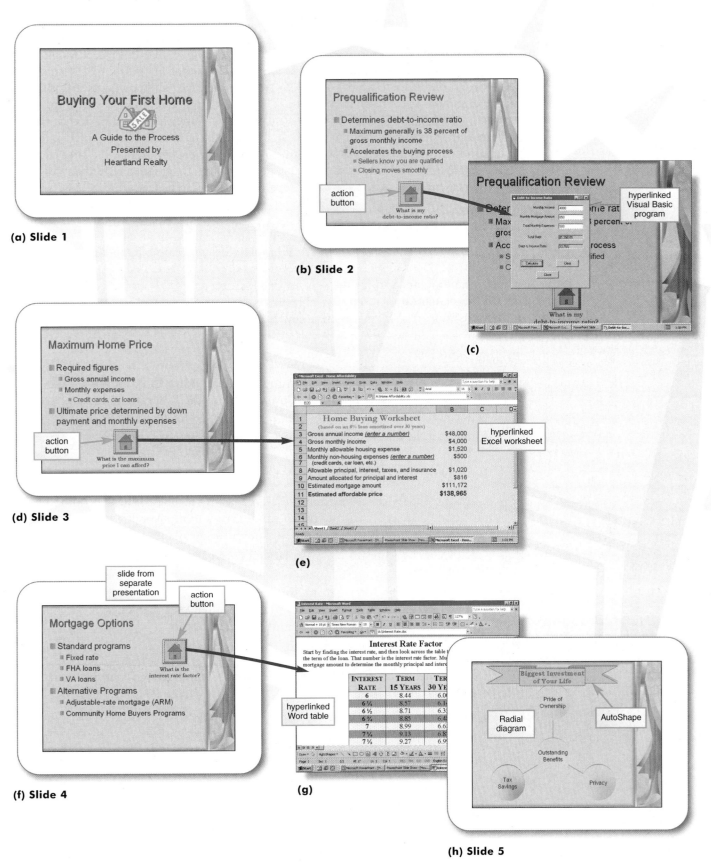

(a) Slide 1

(b) Slide 2

(c)

(d) Slide 3

(e)

(f) Slide 4

(g)

(h) Slide 5

FIGURE 6-1

Project Six — Buying Your First Home

The self-running two-and-one-half-minute presentation created in Project 6 contains several visual elements, including three action buttons that hyperlink to a Visual Basic program, an Excel chart, and a Word table. The last slide contains a Radial diagram and an AutoShape that emphasize the advantages of home ownership. Automatic slide timings are set so these slides display after a desired period of time. The presentation then is designated to be a self-running presentation so that it restarts when it is finished. As with other PowerPoint presentations, the first steps are to create a new presentation, select a design template, create a title slide, and save the presentation. The following steps illustrate these procedures.

Starting and Customizing a New Presentation

To begin, create a new presentation, apply a design template, and change the color scheme. The following steps review accomplishing these tasks. You also need to reset the toolbars and menus so they display exactly as shown in this book. For a detailed explanation of resetting the toolbars and menus, see Appendix D. Perform these steps to start and customize a new presentation.

TO START AND CUSTOMIZE A NEW PRESENTATION

1. Click the Start button on the Windows taskbar, point to Programs on the Start menu, and then click Microsoft PowerPoint on the Programs submenu.

2. If the New Presentation task pane displays, click the Show at startup check box to remove the check mark and then click the Close button on the task pane title bar.

3. If the Language bar displays, click its Minimize button.

4. Click the Slide Design button on the Formatting toolbar. When the Slide Design task pane displays, click the down scroll arrow in the Apply a design template list, and then click the Kimono template in the Available For Use area.

5. Click Color Schemes in the Slide Design task pane, and then click the bottom-left color scheme template (row 4, column 1).

6. If the Standard and Formatting toolbars display on one row, click the Toolbar Options button on the right side of either toolbar and then click Show Buttons on Two Rows on the Toolbar Options menu.

7. Click the Close button in the Slide Design task pane.

Slide 1 has the desired Title Slide slide layout and Kimono design template with a revised color scheme (Figure 6-2).

More About

Kiosks

Kiosks allow customers to place orders, make payments, and access the Internet. Many kiosks have multimedia devices for playing sound and video. Military bases have installed kiosks that allow personnel to conduct personal business and communicate with friends and family by sending video clips and photographs. Governments worldwide have installed kiosks that provide Internet access to public services and information. For more information, visit the PowerPoint 2002 More About Web page (scsite.com/pp2002/more.htm) and then click Kiosk.

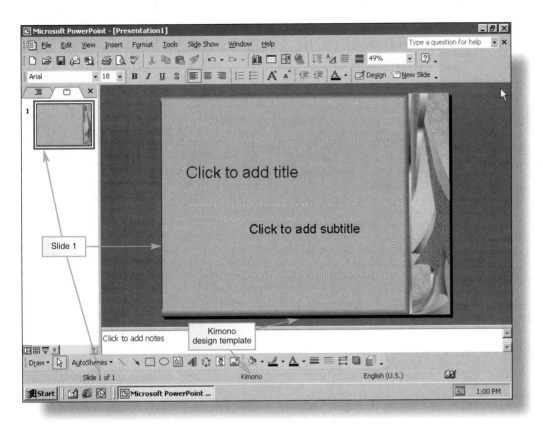

FIGURE 6-2

Creating the Title Slide

The purpose of this presentation is to guide potential homeowners through the buying process. The slide show will give helpful pointers to enhance their meetings with real estate agents. The opening slide should introduce this concept. Perform the following steps to create a title slide.

TO CREATE A TITLE SLIDE

1 Click the title text placeholder to select it.

2 Type Buying Your First Home in the title text placeholder.

3 Press CTRL+ENTER to move the insertion point to the subtitle text placeholder.

4 Type A Guide to the Process and then press SHIFT+ENTER to create a line break.

5 Type Presented by and then press SHIFT+ENTER.

6 Type Heartland Realty but do not press the ENTER key.

The title text and subtitle text display on Slide 1 as shown in Figure 6-3 on the next page.

More *About*

The PowerPoint Help System

Need Help? It is no further than the Ask a Question box in the upper-right corner of the window. Click the box that contains the text, Type a question for help (Figure 6-2), type help, and then press the ENTER key. PowerPoint will respond with a list of items you can click to learn about obtaining help on any PowerPoint-related topic. To find out what is new in PowerPoint 2002, type what's new in PowerPoint in the Ask a Question box.

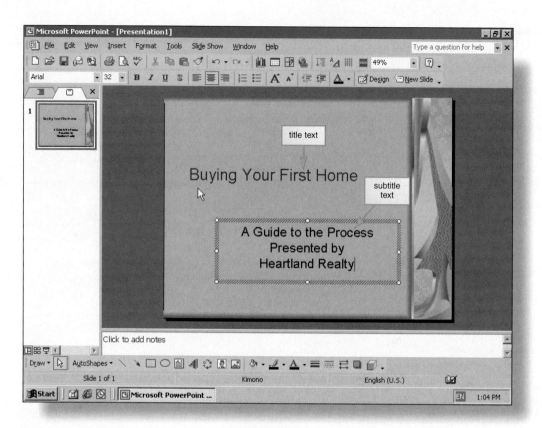

FIGURE 6-3

Home Buying

First-time house buyers can find a wealth of information on the Internet. Web sites offer information about mortgages, inspections, closings, and checklists. For more information, visit the PowerPoint 2002 More About Web page (scsite.com/pp2002/more.htm) and then click Home Buying.

Creating Slide 2

The **prequalification review process** gives potential home buyers an accurate idea of the maximum home price they can afford. As a standard real estate industry guideline, lenders desire monthly debt to not exceed 38 percent of monthly income. When buyers meet this financial requirement, they can shop for a home with confidence, and sellers can appreciate they are dealing with serious buyers. This debt-to-income ratio is described on the second slide in the presentation. It contains a button that runs a Visual Basic program that allows users to determine if their debt-to-income ratio exceeds 38 percent. Perform the following steps to create Slide 2.

TO CREATE SLIDE 2

1 Click the New Slide button on the Formatting toolbar.

2 Type Prequalification Review in the title text placeholder.

3 Press CTRL+ENTER to move the insertion point to the body text placeholder.

4 Type Determines debt-to-income ratio and then press the ENTER key.

5 Press the TAB key. Type Maximum generally is 38 percent of gross monthly income and then press the ENTER key.

6 Type Accelerates the buying process and then press the ENTER key.

7 Press the TAB key. Type Sellers know you are qualified and then press the ENTER key.

8   Type Closing moves smoothly but do not press the ENTER key. Point to the New Slide button on the Formatting toolbar.

The Slide 2 title text and body text display (Figure 6-4).

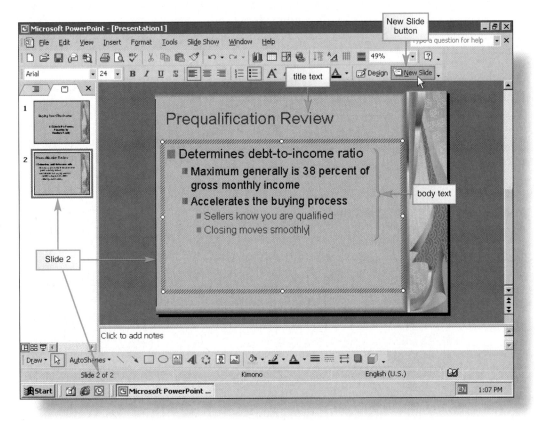

FIGURE 6-4

Creating Slide 3

The maximum home price is computed based on the buyer's monthly annual income; housing expenses, such as utilities and repairs; non-housing expenses, such as tuition loans, credit card payments, and car loans; housing obligations, including taxes and insurance; and mortgage payment. The third slide in the presentation describes the maximum home price. It contains a button that displays an Excel worksheet allowing buyers to compute their estimated affordable home price. Perform the following steps to create Slide 3.

TO CREATE SLIDE 3

1   Click the New Slide button on the Formatting toolbar.

2   Type Maximum Home Price in the title text placeholder.

3   Press CTRL+ENTER to move the insertion point to the body text placeholder.

4   Type Required figures and then press the ENTER key.

5   Press the TAB key. Type Gross annual income and then press the ENTER key.

More About

Inserting Slide Numbers

Slide numbers help organize the slides. To insert a slide number on every side except the title slide, click Insert on the menu bar and then click Slide Number. When the Header and Footer dialog box displays, click Date and time in the Include on slide area, click Slide number, click Footer, click Don't show on title slide, and then click the Apply to All button.

6   Type Monthly expenses and then press the ENTER key.

7   Press the TAB key. Type Credit cards, car loans and then press the ENTER key.

8   Press SHIFT+TAB two times. Type Ultimate price determined by down payment and monthly expenses but do not press the ENTER key.

The Slide 3 title text and body text display (Figure 6-5).

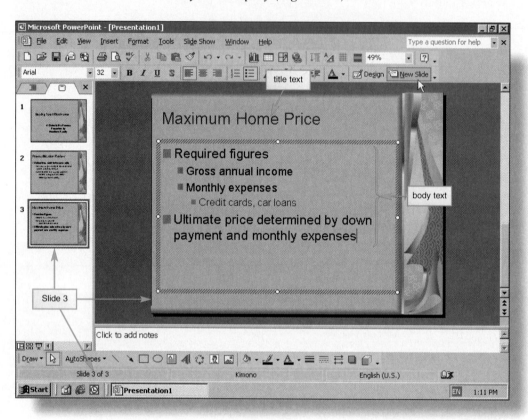

FIGURE 6-5

More About

Audiences

A relaxed and refreshed audience often is willing to listen to new concepts. Researchers suggest that audiences are most prone to feel these emotions on Sundays, Mondays, and Tuesdays. Viewers generally have less time to consider the major points of a presentation at the end of the week.

Adding a Presentation within a Presentation

Occasionally, you may need a slide from another presentation in the presentation you are creating. PowerPoint makes it easy to insert one or more slides from other presentations.

Inserting a Slide from Another Presentation

The PowerPoint presentation with the file name, Mortgage Basics, describes various mortgage types. It contains four slides, and the third slide, shown in Figure 6-6c, lists standard and alternative mortgage types. The Mortgage Basics file is on your Data Disk. See the inside back cover of this book for instructions for downloading the Data Disk or see your instructor for information on accessing the files required for this book. The steps on page PP 6.12 demonstrate how to insert Slide 3 from that file into your presentation.

(a) Slide 1

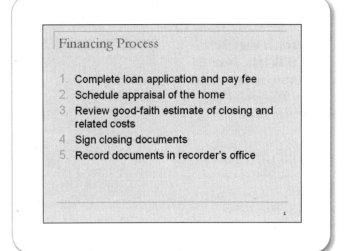

(b) Slide 2

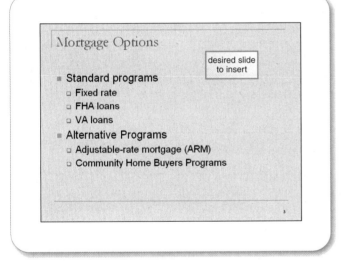

(c) Slide 3

(d) Slide 4

FIGURE 6-6

To Insert a Slide from Another Presentation

 Insert your Data Disk into drive A. Click Insert on the menu bar and then point to Slides from Files.

The Insert menu displays (Figure 6-7). The Slides from Files command allows you to insert a slide from another PowerPoint file.

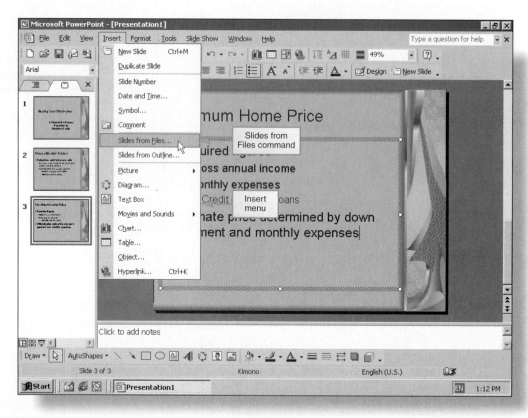

FIGURE 6-7

2 **Click Slides from Files. When the Slide Finder dialog box displays, if necessary, click the Find Presentation tab and then point to the Browse button.**

The Slide Finder dialog box displays (Figure 6-8). If you use several presentations on a regular basis, you can add them to your List of Favorites so you can find them easily.

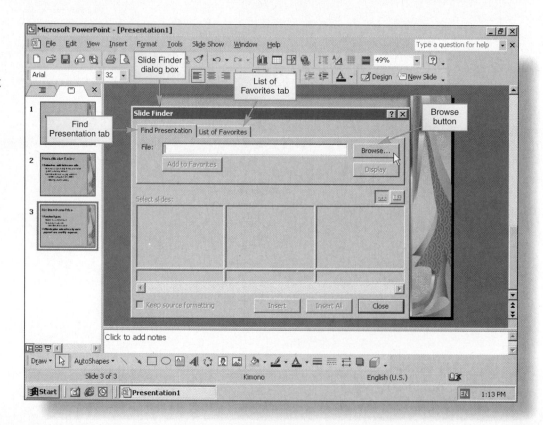

FIGURE 6-8

3 Click the Browse button. Click the Look in box arrow and then click 3½ Floppy (A:). Click Mortgage Basics in the list. Point to the Open button.

The Browse dialog box displays (Figure 6-9). A list displays the files that PowerPoint can open. Your list of file names may vary. Mortgage Basics is the file that contains the slide you will insert.

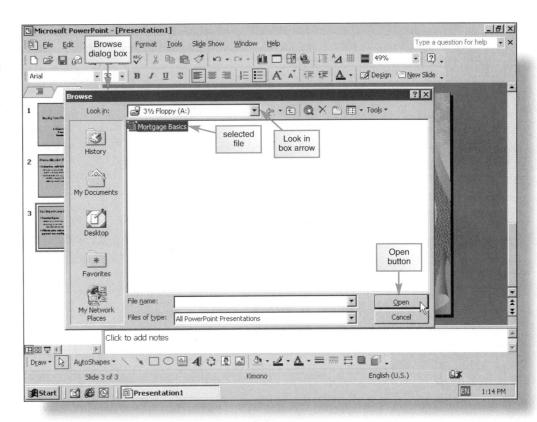

FIGURE 6-9

4 Click the Open button. Click the Slide 3 image, Mortgage Options, in the Select slides area. Point to the Insert button.

The Slide Finder dialog box displays (Figure 6-10). The selected file, A:\Mortgage Basics.ppt, displays in the File text box. Slide 3 of this presentation is the slide to insert in your presentation.

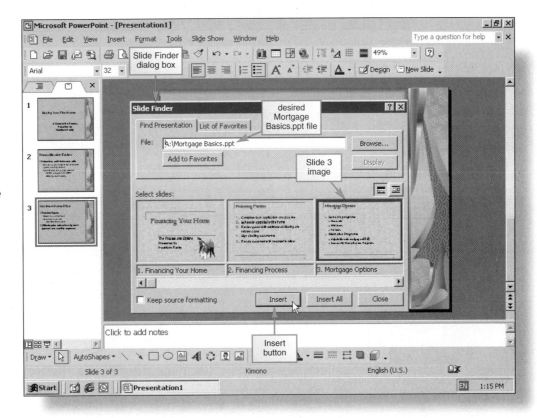

FIGURE 6-10

5 **Click the Insert button. Point to the Close button.**

PowerPoint inserts the Mortgage Basics Slide 3 in your presentation (Figure 6-11). The Slide Finder dialog box remains open to allow you to insert additional slides.

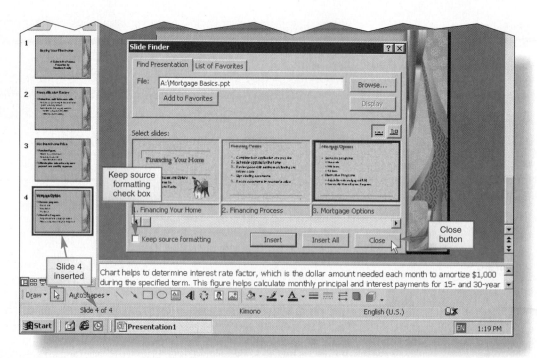

FIGURE 6-11

6 **Click the Close button.**

Your presentation consists of four slides (Figure 6-12).

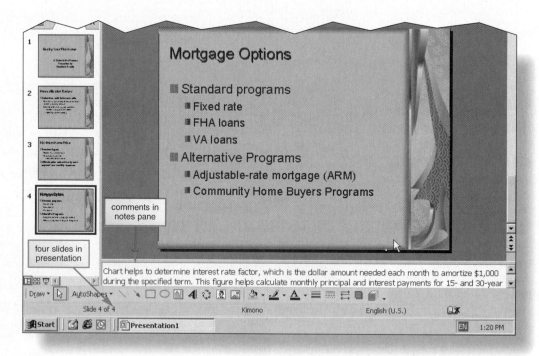

FIGURE 6-12

1. Press ALT+I, press F, press ALT+B, select desired file, press ALT+O, select desired slide, press I, press ESC

2. In Voice Command mode, say "Insert, Slides from Files, Browse, [type file name], Open, [select slide], Insert, Close"

The Kimono design template and revised color scheme are applied to the new Slide 4. To retain the Edge design template that is applied to the Mortgage Basics slides, you would click Keep source formatting in the Slide Finder dialog box. If desired, you could have selected additional slides from the Mortgage Basics presentation or from other slide shows. If you might use the Mortgage Basics file later, you can add that file to your Favorites folder so it is accessible readily.

Adding Notes to Slides

In this project, Slides 2 and 4 have comments. Slide 4 retains the comments that were inserted for the Mortgage Basics presentation. Perform the following step to add text to the notes pane on Slide 2.

TO ADD NOTES

1 Click the Slide 2 slide thumbnail in the tabs pane, click the notes pane, and then type A prequalification review is a simple, quick process that tells only how much of a loan a potential buyer can afford.

The information in this note supplements the text in the slide (Figure 6-13).

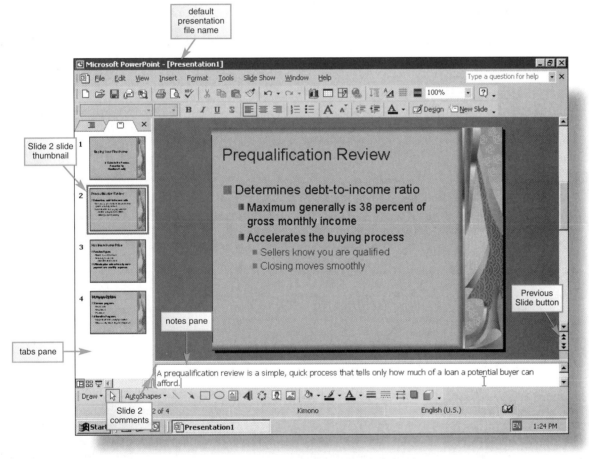

FIGURE 6-13

Saving the Presentation

You now should save your presentation because you have done a substantial amount of work. The following steps save the presentation.

TO SAVE A PRESENTATION

1 Click the Save button on the Standard toolbar.

2 Type House Buying in the File name text box.

3 Click the Save in box arrow. Click 3½ Floppy (A:) in the Save in list.

4 Click the Save button in the Save As dialog box.

The presentation is saved on the floppy disk in drive A with the file name, House Buying. This file name displays on the title bar.

The presentation contains four slides with text. The next section inserts a clip and adds timings to Slide 1.

Inserting, Sizing, and Moving a Clip on a Slide

With all the desired text added to the slides in the presentation, the next step is to add the animated house clip to Slide 1. Perform the following steps to add and size this clip and then move it to the center of the slide.

TO INSERT, SIZE, AND MOVE A CLIP ON A SLIDE

1 Click the Previous Slide button to display Slide 1. Click the Insert Clip Art button on the Drawing toolbar. When the Insert Clip Art task pane displays, type for sale in the Search text text box and then click the Search button. Click the animated pink and gray house or another appropriate clip. Click the Close button on the Insert Clip Art task pane title bar.

2 Right-click the clip and then click Format Picture on the shortcut menu. If necessary, click the Size tab when the Format Picture dialog box displays. Double-click the Height text box in the Scale area and then type 250 in the box. Click the OK button.

3 If necessary, use the arrow keys to move the clip to the center of the slide between the title text and the subtitle text.

The selected clip is inserted into Slide 1, sized, and moved to the desired location (Figure 6-14).

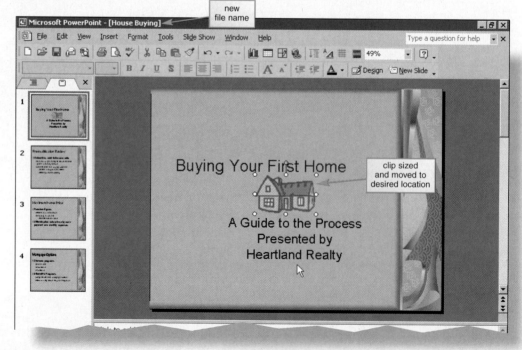

FIGURE 6-14

Creating an Interactive Document

The next step in customizing the House Buying presentation is to edit slides so they connect to three files with additional information. You edit Slides 2, 3, and 4 to contain three hyperlinks: one to a Visual Basic program, debtratio; another to a Microsoft Excel worksheet, Home Affordability; and a third to a Microsoft Word document, Interest Rate. These files are stored on the Data Disk. Figure 6-1(b) on page PP 6.05 contains an action button to reference the debtratio program. This program determines the buyer's debt-to-income ratio.

An **action button** is a built-in 3-D button that can perform specific tasks such as display the next slide, provide help, give information, and play a sound. In addition, the action button can activate a **hyperlink**, which is a shortcut that allows users to jump to another program, in this case Visual Basic, Microsoft Excel, and Microsoft Word, and load a specific file. A hyperlink also allows users to move to specific slides in a PowerPoint presentation or to an Internet address. In this slide, you will associate the hyperlink with an action button, but you also can use text or any object, including shapes, tables, or pictures. You specify which action you want PowerPoint to perform by using the **Action Settings** command on the Slide Show menu.

When you run the House Buying presentation and click the action button on Slide 2, PowerPoint runs the Visual Basic program. Once you have finished running the Visual Basic program, you will return to Slide 2 by clicking the Close button on the Debt-to-Income Ratio form.

Creating the slide requires several steps. First, add an action button and create a hyperlink to the Visual Basic program. Then, scale the button, add color, and add a caption. The next several sections explain how to add an action button and an action setting to the slide.

Adding an Action Button and Action Settings

You will display additional information about qualifying for a mortgage by running the Visual Basic program without quitting PowerPoint. To obtain details on the buyer's debt-to-income ratio, you will click the action button. When you click the button, a coin sound will play. The next section describes how to create the action button and place it on Slide 2.

More About

Activating Hyperlinks

In this presentation, you activate a hyperlink by clicking an action button. You also have the option of activating the hyperlink by placing the mouse pointer over the button. To specify this option, click the Mouse Over tab in the Action Settings dialog box and then select the desired controls.

More About

Visual Basic

Millions of developers worldwide use the Visual Basic language and programming system to create computer software components and applications. This set of tools and technologies is an extremely powerful, versatile, and complex system for Windows desktop applications, reusable software components for building other applications, and applications targeted for the Internet and intranets. For more information, visit the PowerPoint 2002 More About Web page (scsite.com/pp2002/more.htm) and then click Visual Basic.

To Add an Action Button and Action Settings

1 Click the Next Slide button to display Slide 2. Click Slide Show on the menu bar, point to Action Buttons, and then point to Action Button: Home on the Action Buttons submenu.

The Action Buttons submenu displays 12 built-in 3-D buttons (Figure 6-15).

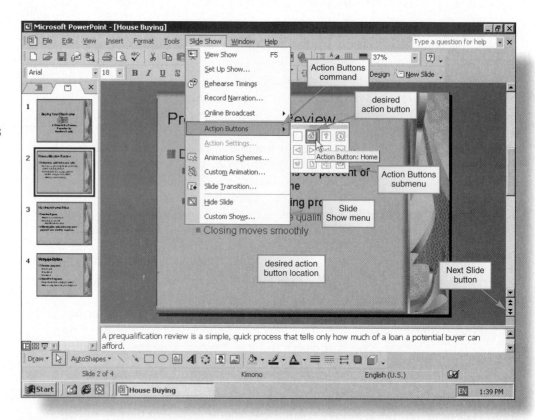

FIGURE 6-15

2 Click Action Button: Home. Click the bottom center of Slide 2 below the last text paragraph. When the Actions Settings dialog box displays, if necessary, click the Mouse Click tab. Point to the Hyperlink to box arrow.

The Action Settings dialog box displays (Figure 6-16) with the action button placed on Slide 2. Hyperlink to is the default Action on click.

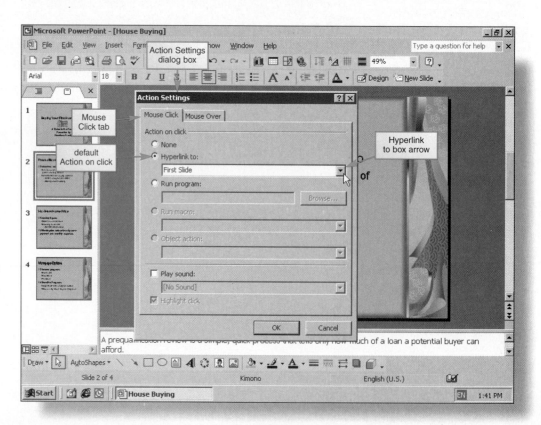

FIGURE 6-16

3 Click the Hyperlink to box arrow, click the down scroll arrow to scroll through the list of locations, and then point to Other File.

The list box displays the possible locations in the slide show or elsewhere where a hyperlink can be established (Figure 6-17). Other File is selected.

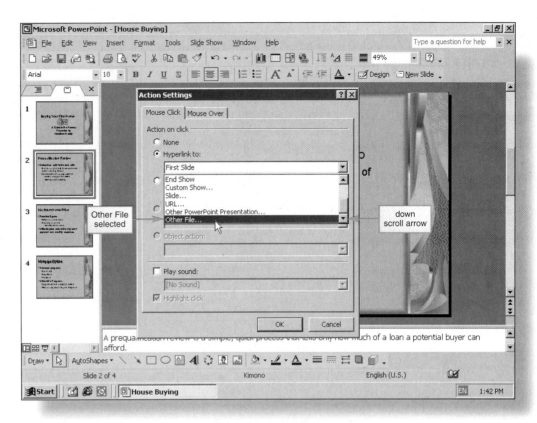

FIGURE 6-17

4 Click Other File. When the Hyperlink to Other File dialog box displays, if necessary, click the Look in box arrow and then click 3½ Floppy (A:). Click debtratio. Point to the OK button.

The debtratio file name is the Visual Basic file you will link to the action button (Figure 6-18). Your list of file names may vary.

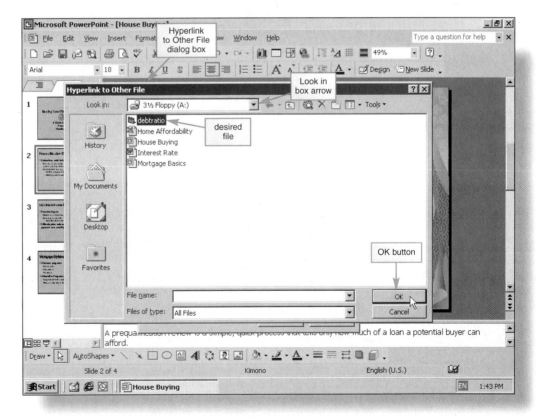

FIGURE 6-18

5 Click the OK button. Click Play sound, click the Play sound box arrow, click the down scroll arrow, and then point to Coin.

The Hyperlink to box displays the Visual Basic program file name, debtratio (Figure 6-19). A check mark displays in the Play sound check box. The Play sound list displays sounds that can play when you click the action button.

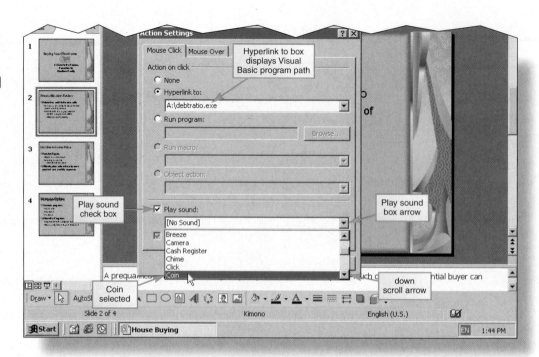

FIGURE 6-19

6 Click Coin. Click the OK button.

The action button is selected on Slide 2 as indicated by the sizing handles (Figure 6-20).

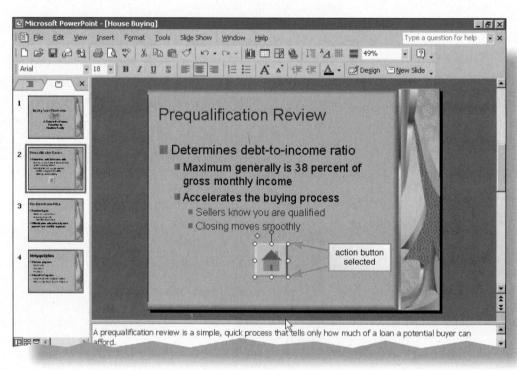

FIGURE 6-20

Other **Ways**

1. Click AutoShapes button on Drawing toolbar, on AutoShapes menu point to Action Buttons, on Action Buttons submenu click desired action button

2. Press ALT+D, press I

3. In Voice Command mode, say "Slide Show, Action Buttons"

With the action button created and linked to the Visual Basic program, debtratio, you need to repeat the procedure for the Excel worksheet action button on Slide 3 and the Word table action button on Slide 4. Perform the following steps to create action buttons on Slides 3 and 4 and to hyperlink the Excel and Word documents to the PowerPoint presentation.

TO CREATE ADDITIONAL ACTION BUTTONS AND HYPERLINKS

1 Click the Slide 3 slide thumbnail in the tabs pane. Click Slide Show on the menu bar, point to Action Buttons, and then click Action Button: Home on the Action Buttons submenu.

2 Click the bottom center on Slide 3 below the last text paragraph.

3 Click the Hyperlink to box arrow in the Action Settings dialog box, click the down scroll arrow to scroll through the list of locations, and then click Other File.

4 Double-click Home Affordability in the list.

5 Click Play sound. Click the Play sound box arrow, click the down scroll arrow, and then click Typewriter.

6 Click the OK button.

7 Click the Slide 4 slide thumbnail in the tabs pane. Click Slide Show on the menu bar, point to Action Buttons, and then click Action Button: Home on the Action Buttons submenu.

8 Click the area to the right of the first first-level paragraph on Slide 4.

9 Click the Hyperlink to box arrow, click the down scroll arrow, and then click Other File.

10 Double-click Interest Rate in the list.

11 Click Play sound. Click the Play sound box arrow, and then scroll down and click Cash Register.

12 Click the OK button.

Slides 3 and 4 display with the action buttons for the Excel worksheet and Word document hyperlinks (Figure 6-21).

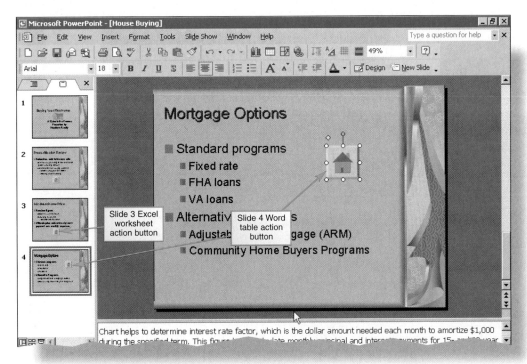

FIGURE 6-21

When you select a file in the Look in list, PowerPoint associates the file with a specific application, which is based on the file extension. For example, when you select the Home Affordability file with the file extension **.xls**, PowerPoint recognizes the file as a Microsoft Excel file. Additionally, when you select the Interest Rate file with the file extension **.doc**, PowerPoint recognizes the file as a Microsoft Word file.

Scaling Action Buttons

The size of the action buttons can be increased. Perform the following steps to scale the three action buttons.

TO SCALE ACTION BUTTONS

1 With Slide 4 active, right-click the action button and then click Format AutoShape on the shortcut menu.

2 If necessary, click the Size tab. Click Lock aspect ratio in the Scale area and then double-click the Height text box. Type 110 in the Height box.

3 Click the OK button.

4 Repeat these steps for the action buttons on Slides 2 and 3.

The action buttons are resized to 110 percent of their original size (Figure 6-22).

Other Ways

1. On Format menu click AutoShape, click Size tab, click Lock aspect ratio
2. Press ALT+O, press O, RIGHT ARROW
3. In Voice Command mode, say "Format, AutoShape, Size, Lock aspect ratio"

Sounds

The sounds that play when you click an action button fit a variety of applications. You can, however, add custom sounds, such as a human voice, music, or sound effects, to a slide show. Many Web sites on the Internet provide these sound files, which have the file extension .wav, and allow you to download them free. For an example of one of these Web sites, visit the PowerPoint 2002 More About Web page (scsite.com/pp2002/more.htm) and then click Sounds.

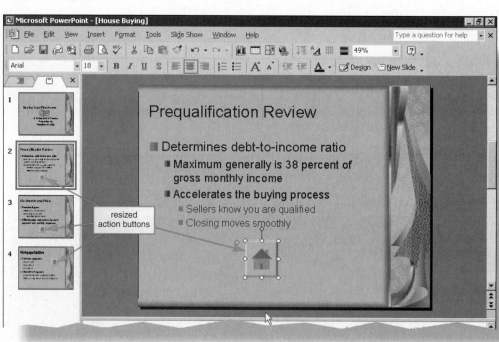

FIGURE 6-22

Displaying Guides and Positioning Action Buttons

PowerPoint guides are used to align objects. The **guides** are two straight dotted lines, one horizontal and one vertical. When an object is close to a guide, its corner or its center (whichever is closer) **snaps**, or attaches itself, to the guide. You can move the guides to meet your alignment requirements. In this project, you use the vertical and horizontal guides to help position the action buttons and captions on Slides 2, 3, and 4. The center of a slide is 0.00 on both the vertical and the horizontal guides. You position a guide by dragging it to a new location. When you point to a guide and then press and hold the mouse button, PowerPoint displays a ScreenTip containing the exact position of the guide on the slide in inches. An arrow displays below the guide position to indicate the vertical guide either left or right of center. An arrow displays to the right of the guide position to indicate the horizontal guide either above or below center. Perform the following steps to display the guides and position the action button on Slide 2.

Steps **To Display Guides and Position the Slide 2 Action Button**

1 **With Slide 2 selected, right-click anywhere in the gray area of the slide except the title text or body text placeholders or the action button. Point to Grid and Guides on the shortcut menu (Figure 6-23).**

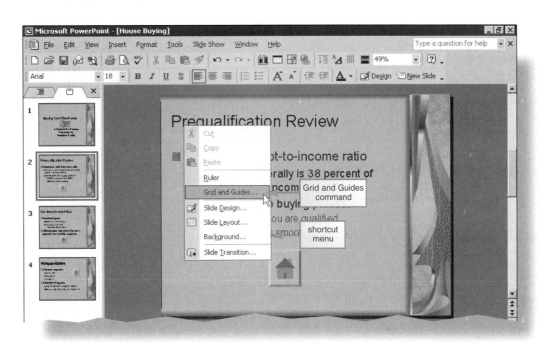

FIGURE 6-23

2 **Click Grid and Guides. When the Grid and Guides dialog box displays, click Display drawing guides on screen in the Guide settings area and then point to the OK button.**

The Snap objects to grid check box indicates the action buttons and other objects will snap to the drawing guides that display on the screen (Figure 6-24).

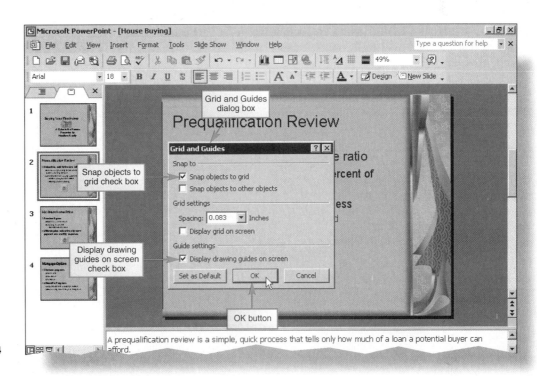

FIGURE 6-24

3 **Click the OK button.**

The horizontal and vertical guides display (Figure 6-25).

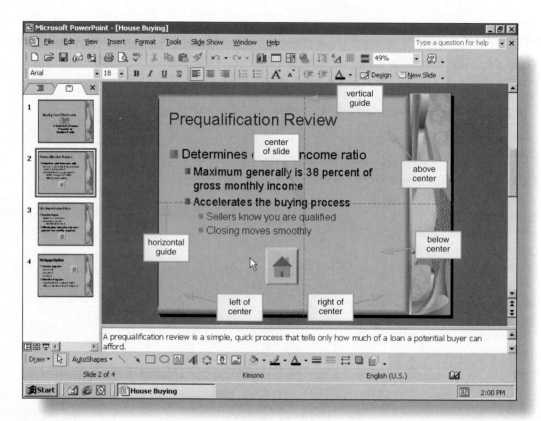

FIGURE 6-25

4 **Point to the horizontal guide anywhere in the gray area of the slide except the title text or body text placeholders. Click and then drag the guide to 1.50 inches below center. Do not release the mouse button.**

While holding down the mouse button, a ScreenTip displays indicating the position of the horizontal guide (Figure 6-26). This guide will be used to position the top edge of the action button.

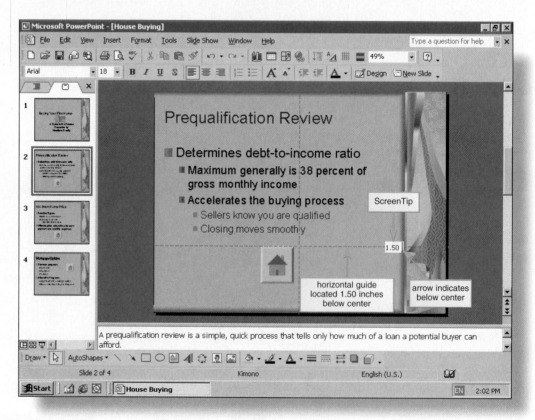

FIGURE 6-26

5 **Release the mouse button. Drag the action button until the top edge snaps to the horizontal guide and the right edge snaps to the vertical guide.**

The top of the action button aligns with the horizontal guide, and the right edge of the button aligns with the vertical guide (Figure 6-27).

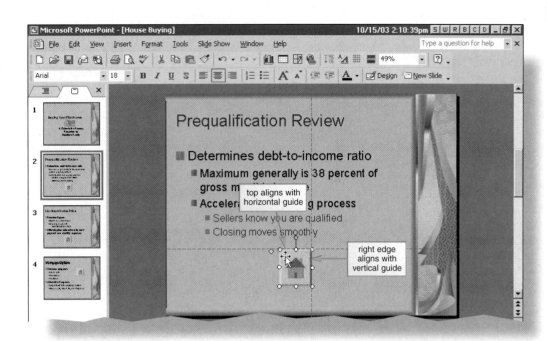

FIGURE 6-27

The Slide 2 action button displays in the desired location. Perform the following steps to align the action buttons on Slides 3 and 4.

TO POSITION THE SLIDE 3 AND SLIDE 4 ACTION BUTTONS

1 Click the Next Slide button to display Slide 3. Drag the action button until the top edge snaps to the horizontal guide and the right edge snaps to the vertical guide.

2 Click the Next Slide button to display Slide 4. Drag the horizontal guide to 0.75 inches above center. Drag the vertical guide to 1.25 inches right of center.

3 Drag the action button until the bottom edge snaps to the horizontal guide and the left edge snaps to the vertical guide.

The action buttons for Slides 3 and 4 display in the desired locations (Figure 6-28).

Other **Ways**

1. On View menu click Grid and Guides, click Display drawing guides on screen

2. Press ALT+V, press I, press I

3. In Voice Command mode, say "View, Grid and Guides, Display drawing guides on screen"

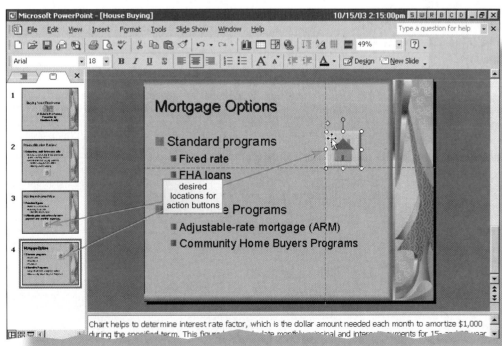

FIGURE 6-28

Hiding Guides

When you no longer want to control the exact placement of objects on the slide, you can **hide guides**. Perform the following steps to hide guides.

TO HIDE GUIDES

1 Right-click Slide 4 anywhere except the title or body text placeholders or the action buttons. Click Grid and Guides on the shortcut menu.

2 When the Grid and Guides dialog box displays, click Display drawing guides on screen in the Guide settings area.

3 Click the OK button.

Other Ways

1. On View menu click Grid and Guides, click Display drawing guides on screen
2. Press ALT+V, press I, press I
3. In Voice Command mode, say "View, Grid and Guides, Display drawing guides on screen"

The guides are hidden.

The action buttons are positioned in the desired locations. Changing the fill color, shadow, and lines can enhance them.

Adding a Fill Color to the Action Buttons

To better identify the action buttons from the slide background, you can add fill color. **Fill color** is the interior color of a selected object. Perform the following steps to add fill color to the action button on Slide 4.

Steps To Add a Fill Color to the Slide 4 Action Button

1 **With Slide 4 active, click the action button and then click the Fill Color button arrow on the Drawing toolbar. Point to the color green (row 1, column 6).**

The Fill Color list displays (Figure 6-29). Automatic is selected, indicating that beige is the current default fill color based on the Kimono design template color scheme. Green is the default Follow Accent Scheme Color.

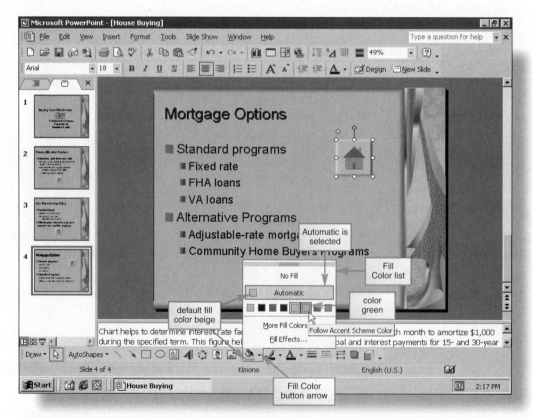

FIGURE 6-29

2 **Click the color green.**

The action button displays filled with the color green (Figure 6-30).

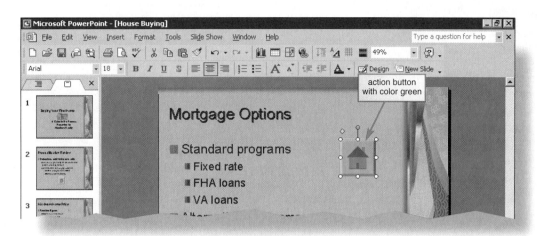

FIGURE 6-30

The Slide 2 action button is filled with the color green. The fill color now is set to this color. Perform the following steps to change the fill color of the action buttons on Slides 2 and 3 to this color.

TO ADD A FILL COLOR TO THE SLIDE 2 AND SLIDE 3 ACTION BUTTONS

1 Click the Previous Slide button to display Slide 3. Click the action button and then click the Fill Color button on the Drawing toolbar.

2 Repeat Step 1 for the Slide 2 action button.

The action buttons on Slides 2 and 3 display filled with the color green (Figure 6-31).

Other Ways

1. On Format menu click AutoShape, click Colors and Lines tab
2. Right-click action button, click Format AutoShape on shortcut menu, click Colors and Lines tab
3. Press ALT+O, press O
4. In Voice Command mode, say "Format, AutoShape, Colors and Lines"

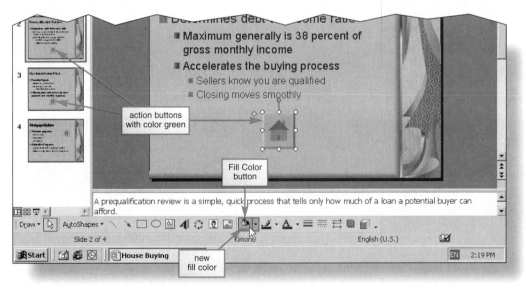

FIGURE 6-31

Adding a Shadow to the Action Buttons

To add depth to an object, you **shadow** it by clicking the Shadow button on the Drawing toolbar. Perform the steps on the next page to add a shadow to the three action buttons.

To Add a Shadow to the Action Buttons

1 **With the Slide 2 action button selected, click the Shadow Style button on the Drawing toolbar. Point to Shadow Style 14 (row 4, column 2) in the Shadow Style list.**

Twenty shadow styles display along with a No Shadow option (Figure 6-32).

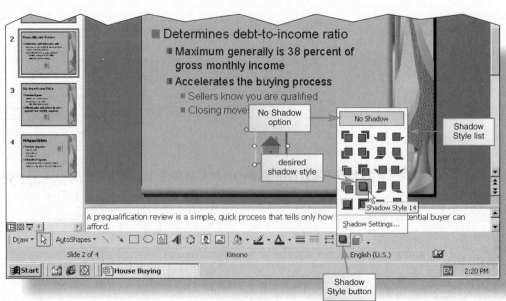

FIGURE 6-32

2 **Click Shadow Style 14.**

PowerPoint adds the shadow effect to the action button (Figure 6-33).

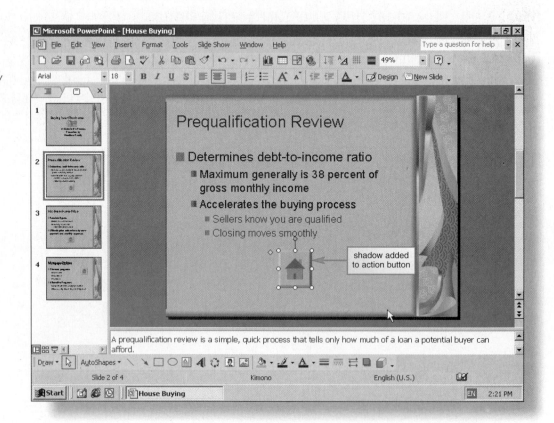

FIGURE 6-33

Slide 2 is defined with a green fill color and shadow. The buttons on Slides 3 and 4 also will be modified with shadows. Perform the following steps to add shadow effects to the remaining action buttons on Slides 3 and 4.

TO ADD A SHADOW TO THE SLIDE 3 AND SLIDE 4 ACTION BUTTONS

1 Click the Next Slide button to display Slide 3. Click the action button, click the Shadow Style button on the Drawing toolbar, and then click Shadow Style 14 (row 4, column 2).

2 Repeat Step 1 for the Slide 4 action button.

The action buttons on Slides 3 and 4 display with shadows (Figure 6-34).

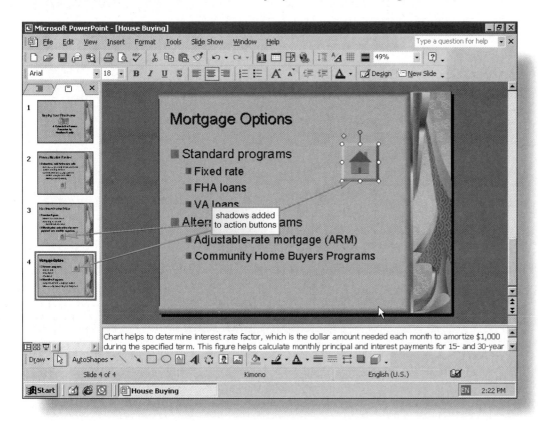

FIGURE 6-34

The green color and shadows help to identify the buttons. Lines further identify their shapes. The next section describes how to add lines to the action buttons.

Adding Lines to the Action Buttons

Lines define the edges of a shape. To add lines, click the Line Style button on the Drawing toolbar. Thirteen line styles are available, and you can modify them by clicking More Lines and then changing colors, size, and positions. Perform the steps on the next page to add lines to the three action buttons.

More *About*

Action Buttons

The 12 action buttons in the Action Buttons submenu are a subset of PowerPoint's AutoShapes, which are convenient visuals designed to add visual interest to slides. To add an action button with one of these other AutoShapes, click the AutoShapes button on the Drawing toolbar, select one of the categories of shapes, such as lines, connectors, basic shapes, flowchart elements, stars and banners, and callouts, click an AutoShape, and then click the slide in the location where you want the AutoShape to display.

To Add Lines to the Slide 4 Action Button

1 **With the Slide 4 action button selected, click the Line Style button on the Drawing toolbar and then point to the ¾ pt line style in the Line Style list.**

PowerPoint provides 13 line styles (Figure 6-35).

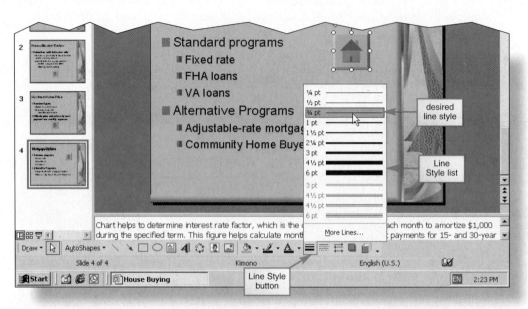

FIGURE 6-35

2 **Click the ¾ pt style.**

PowerPoint adds lines to the Slide 4 action button (Figure 6-36).

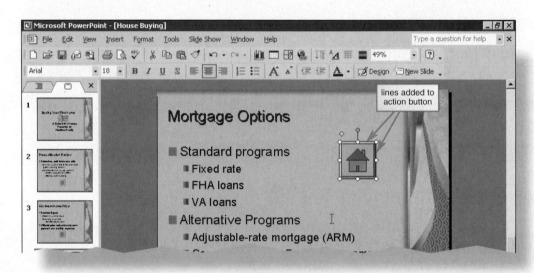

FIGURE 6-36

1. On Format menu click AutoShape, click Colors and Lines tab
2. Right-click action button, click Format AutoShape on shortcut menu, click Colors and Lines tab
3. Press ALT+O, press O
4. In Voice Command mode, say "Format, AutoShape, Colors and Lines"

The Slide 4 action button is enhanced with lines. The buttons on Slides 2 and 3 also will be modified. Perform the following steps to add lines to the action buttons on Slides 2 and 3.

TO ADD LINES TO THE SLIDE 2 AND SLIDE 3 ACTION BUTTONS

1 Click the Previous Slide button to display Slide 3. Click the action button, click the Line Style button on the Drawing toolbar, and then click the ¾ pt style.

2 Repeat Step 1 for the Slide 2 action button.

The action buttons on Slides 2 and 3 display with lines (Figure 6-37).

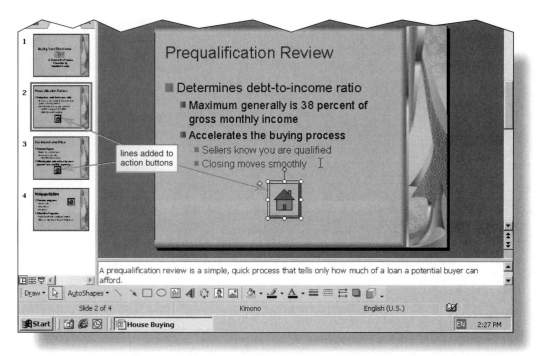

FIGURE 6-37

The three action buttons are distinguished from the background with a new fill color, shadows, and lines. Captions will identify their functions to users, as discussed in the following section.

Adding Captions to the Action Buttons

Captions for the three action buttons are the final components that need to be added to Slides 2, 3, and 4. Perform the following steps to add a caption to the action button on Slide 2.

More About

Hiding Slides

As a presenter, you can decide whether to show a particular slide. To hide a slide, click the Slide Sorter View button at the lower left of the PowerPoint window, right-click the desired slide, and then click Hide Slide on the shortcut menu. The null sign, a square with a slash, displays over the slide number to indicate the slide is hidden. When you no longer want to hide a slide, change views to slide sorter view, right-click the slide, and then click Hide Slide on the shortcut menu. This action removes the square with a slash surrounding the slide number. When you run the presentation, the hidden slide does not display unless you press the H key when the slide preceding the hidden slide is displaying. You skip the hidden slide by clicking the mouse and advancing to the next slide.

Steps **To Add a Caption to the Slide 2 Action Button**

1 **With Slide 2 displaying, click the Text Box button on the Drawing toolbar and then point to the area below and to the left of the action button.**

The Text Box button is selected (Figure 6-38). The mouse pointer is positioned where the left edge of the text box will be located.

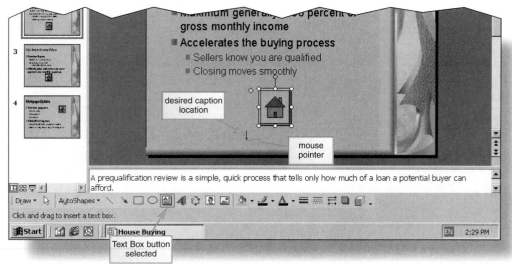

FIGURE 6-38

2 **Click the slide at this location. Type** What is my **and then press SHIFT+ENTER. Type** debt-to-income ratio? **as the second caption line.**

The caption for the Slide 2 action button displays (Figure 6-39).

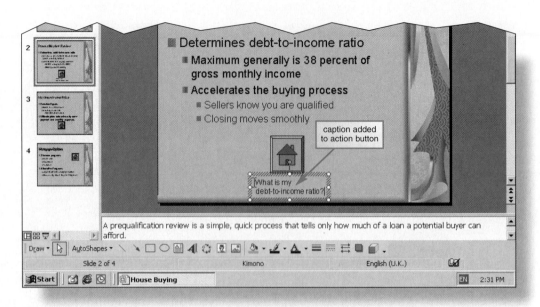

FIGURE 6-39

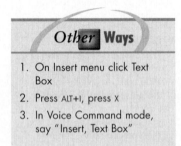

Other Ways

1. On Insert menu click Text Box
2. Press ALT+I, press X
3. In Voice Command mode, say "Insert, Text Box"

A caption helps identify the Slide 2 action button. The buttons on Slides 3 and 4 also need captions. Perform the following steps to add captions to the action buttons on Slides 3 and 4.

TO ADD CAPTIONS TO THE SLIDE 3 AND SLIDE 4 ACTION BUTTONS

1 Click the Next Slide button to display Slide 3. Click the Text Box button on the Drawing toolbar and then click below and to the left of the action button. Type What is the maximum and then press SHIFT+ENTER. Type price I can afford? as the second caption line.

2 Click the Next Slide button to display Slide 4. Click the Text Box button on the Drawing toolbar and then click below and to the left of the action button. Type What is the and then press SHIFT+ENTER. Type interest rate factor? as the second caption line.

The captions for the Slide 3 and Slide 4 action buttons display (Figure 6-40).

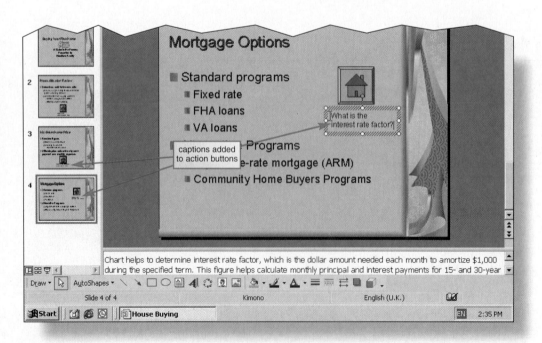

FIGURE 6-40

The three captions are added to the slides. To enhance the display, you can format the text by changing the font, font size, and font color.

Formatting the Action Button Caption Text

Changing the characteristics of the caption text adds visual appeal to the action buttons. The following steps format the captions by changing the font to Bookman Old Style, increasing the font size to 20, and changing the font color to gold.

More About

Black Slides

A black slide may help an audience focus on the speaker. To create this slide, click the New Slide button on the Standard toolbar, select the Blank slide layout, click Format on the menu bar, click Background, click the Background fill box arrow, and then click the color black.

Steps **To Format the Slide 4 Action Button Caption Text**

1 **If necessary, click the Slide 4 action button caption text and then click the Center button on the Formatting toolbar. Click Edit on the menu bar and then point to Select All.**

The caption text is centered in the text box and the Edit menu displays (Figure 6-41). The Select All command will select all letters in the caption by highlighting them.

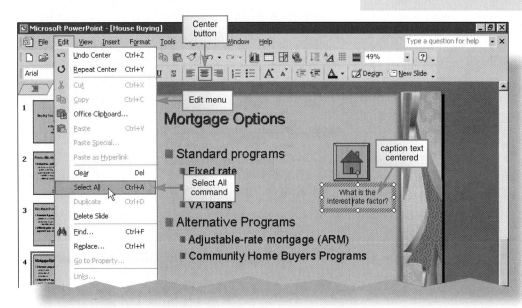

FIGURE 6-41

2 **Click Select All. Right-click the caption text and then click Font on the shortcut menu. When the Font dialog box displays, click the down scroll arrow in the Font list and then click Bookman Old Style in the Font list. Click 20 in the Size list. Point to the Color box arrow.**

Bookman Old Style displays in the Font box, and 20 displays in the Size box (Figure 6-42).

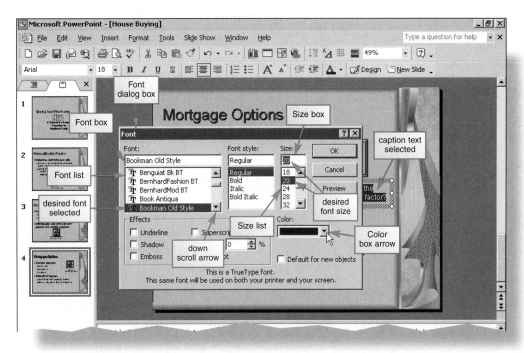

FIGURE 6-42

3 Click the Color box arrow and then click the color gold (row 1, column 7). Point to the OK button.

The color gold is the Follow Accent and Hyperlink Scheme Color in the Kimono design template color scheme (Figure 6-43). The color gold displays in the Color box.

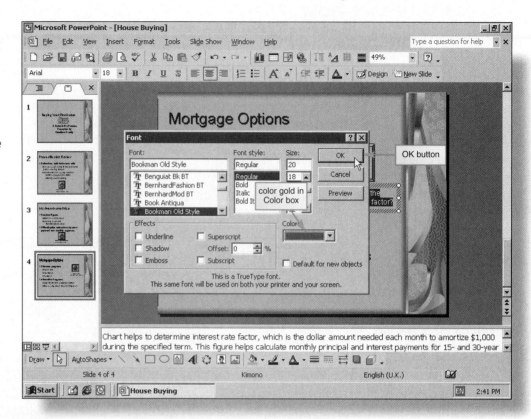

FIGURE 6-43

4 Click the OK button and then click anywhere on the slide other than the title and body text placeholders.

PowerPoint displays the Slide 4 caption with the Bookman Old Style font, a font size of 20, and the color gold (Figure 6-44).

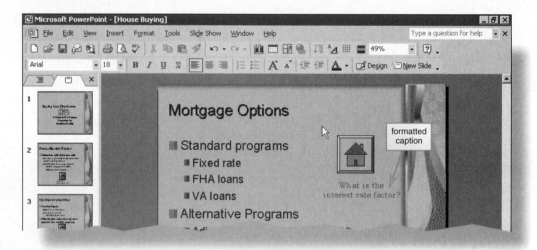

FIGURE 6-44

The Slide 4 action button caption text is formatted, and you need to repeat the procedure to format the caption text for the action buttons on Slides 2 and 3. Perform the following steps to format these captions.

TO FORMAT THE SLIDE 2 AND SLIDE 3 ACTION BUTTON CAPTION TEXT

1 Click the Previous Slide button to display Slide 3. Click the action button caption and then click the Center button on the Formatting toolbar. Press CTRL+A.

2 Right-click the text and then click Font on the shortcut menu. When the Font dialog box displays, click the down scroll arrow in the Font list and then click Bookman Old Style.

3 Click 20 in the Size list.

4 Click the Color box arrow and then click the color gold (row 1, column 7).

5 Click the OK button and then click anywhere on a blank area of the slide.

6 Repeat these steps for Slide 2 in the presentation.

Slides 2, 3, and 4 are complete (Figure 6-45).

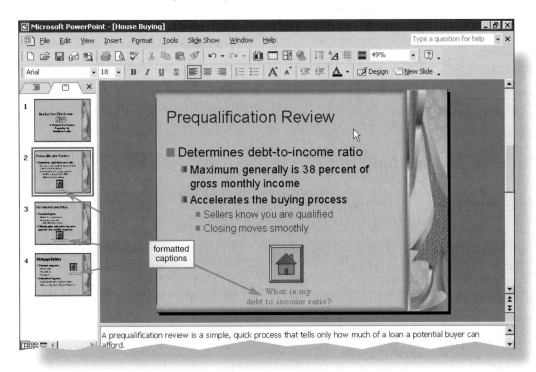

FIGURE 6-45

The captions are added and formatted, and you may need to make slight modifications to center their placements below the action buttons. If so, click a caption, click the border, and use the arrow keys to position the text box as shown in Figure 6-45.

You now should save your presentation because you have done a substantial amount of work.

Inserting, Formatting, and Animating a Diagram

Diagrams help users understand concepts by showing the relationship among parts of a process or visualizing how something works. One of the new features in PowerPoint 2002 is the capability of inserting predesigned diagrams by clicking the Insert Diagram or Organization Chart button on the Drawing toolbar or by selecting the slide layout with a content placeholder and then clicking the Insert Diagram or Organization Chart button in the content placeholder. The five diagram types are described in Table 6-1 on the next page.

Fonts

Designers have developed hundreds of unique fonts that you can download and then use in your presentations. Many of these fonts are available free. For examples of these fonts, visit the PowerPoint 2002 More About Web page (scsite.com/pp2002/more.htm) and then click Fonts.

Table 6-1	Diagram Types and Functions	
TYPE	NAME	FUNCTION
	Cycle	Shows process with continuous action
	Pyramid	Shows relationship between elements based on a foundation
	Radial	Shows elements relating to a core element
	Target	Shows steps leading to a goal
	Venn	Shows overlap between and among different elements

More *About*

Summary Slides

A summary slide contains bulleted titles from selected slides and can be used to recap the main points of the presentation or as an agenda of topics. To add a summary slide in slide sorter view, select the slides you want to include in the summary and then click the Summary Slide button on the Slide Sorter toolbar. You then can rearrange the summary slide by moving it to the end of the presentation.

Diagrams have a **drawing space** around them that extends to the non-printing border and drawing handles. More drawing space can be added if additional objects are needed, or this space can be reduced to fit tightly around the diagram.

Inserting a Radial Diagram

PowerPoint inserts a **Radial diagram** composed of a central core element and three related elements. You easily can add elements by using the Diagram toolbar buttons. Perform the following steps to insert the Radial diagram.

Steps **To Insert a Radial Diagram**

1 **Click the Slide 4 slide thumbnail in the tabs pane and then click the New Slide button on the Formatting toolbar to insert a new slide. Click Format on the menu bar and then click Slide Layout. When the Slide Layout task pane displays, point to the Content slide layout in the Content Layouts area.**

The Slide Layout task pane displays (Figure 6-46). The new Slide 5 displays with Title and Text layout.

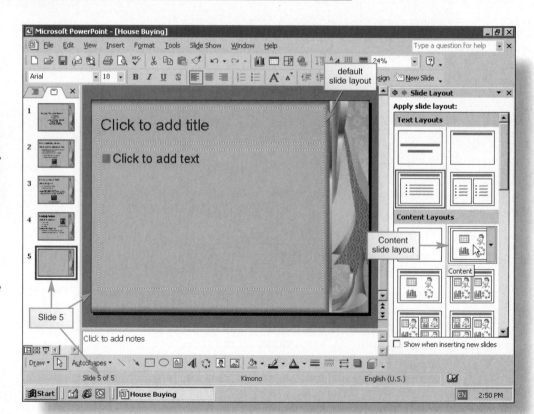

FIGURE 6-46

2 Click the Content slide layout. Point to the Insert Diagram or Organization Chart button in the content placeholder.

The Insert Diagram or Organization Chart button is selected (Figure 6-47). A ScreenTip describes its function.

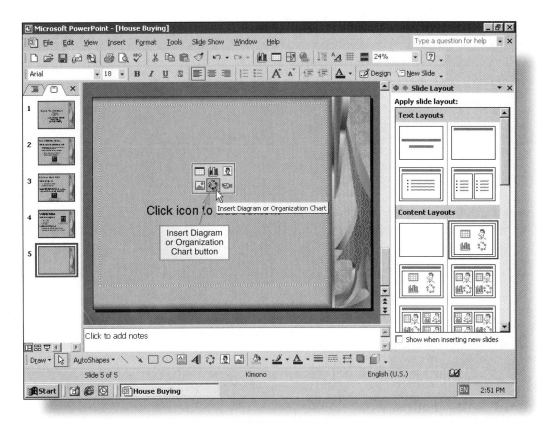

FIGURE 6-47

3 Click the Insert Diagram or Organization Chart button. When the Diagram Gallery dialog box displays, click the Radial Diagram diagram type. Point to the OK button.

Radial Diagram is selected (Figure 6-48).

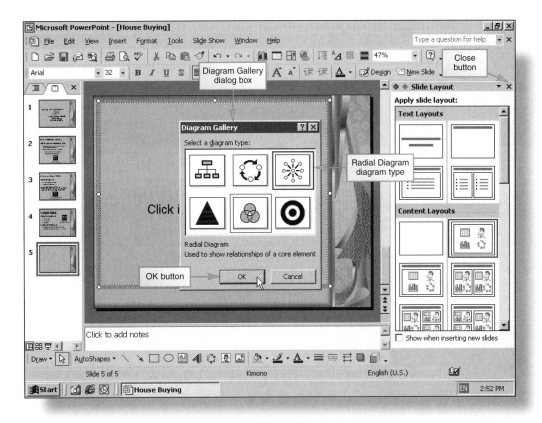

FIGURE 6-48

4 **Click the OK button. Click the Close button in the Slide Layout task pane.**

The Radial diagram and Diagram toolbar display (Figure 6-49).

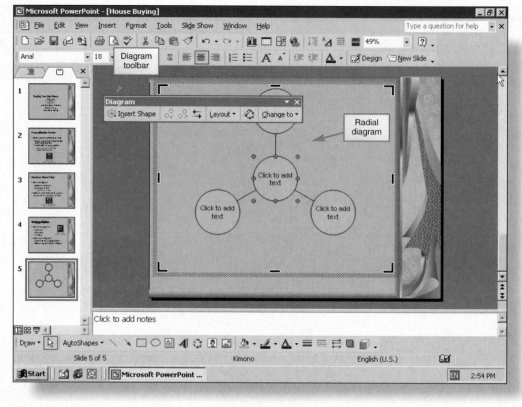

FIGURE 6-49

Other Ways

1. Click Insert Diagram or Organization Chart button on Drawing toolbar
2. On Insert menu click Diagram
3. Press ALT+I, press G
4. In Voice Command mode, say "Insert, Diagram"

The Diagram toolbar displays automatically when you select any diagram other than an organization chart. It contains buttons that allow you to create and design a diagram. Table 6-2 describes the functions of each button on the Diagram toolbar.

Table 6-2 Diagram Toolbar Buttons and Functions

BUTTON	NAME	FUNCTION
Insert Shape	Insert Shape	Adds a new shape next to the selected shape in the diagram, such as a new level to a Pyramid diagram
	Move Shape Backward	Rotates the shape within the diagram
	Move Shape Forward	Rotates the shape within the diagram
	Reverse Diagram	Reverses the order of shapes in the diagram
Layout ▾	Layout	Adjusts the size of the drawing area containing the diagram
	AutoFormat	Customizes the overall style of a diagram with a preset design scheme in the Diagram Style Gallery dialog box
Change to ▾	Change to	Converts the diagram to another type of diagram or chart, such as from a Radial diagram to a Venn diagram

Changing the Radial Diagram Size

Each object inserted into a slide is placed on a drawing layer. Each **drawing layer** is stacked on top of each other and can be rearranged, in a manner similar to shuffling a deck of cards, so that it displays in front of or behind other objects. The Radial diagram drawing layer should display as the top layer of Slide 5, but it is too large. The diagram can be sized and scaled in the same manner as clip art and other objects are sized. Perform the following steps to scale the diagram.

Steps **To Change the Radial Diagram Size**

1 **Right-click the gray slide background in the drawing area and then point to Format Diagram on the shortcut menu.**

The shortcut menu displays and a border displays around the drawing area (Figure 6-50).

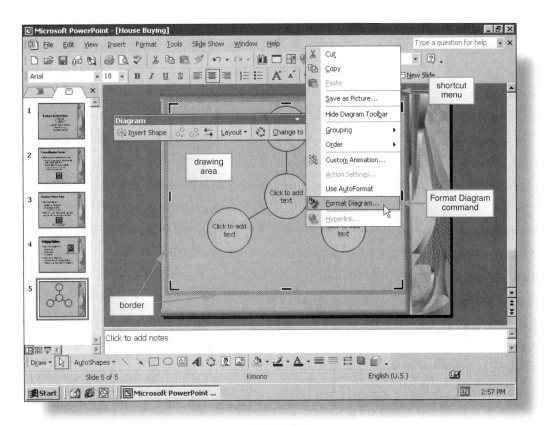

FIGURE 6-50

2 **Click Format Diagram. When the Format Diagram dialog box displays, if necessary, click the Size tab and then click and hold down the Height box up arrow in the Scale area until 120 % displays. Point to the OK button.**

Both the Height and Width boxes in the Scale area display 120 % (Figure 6-51).

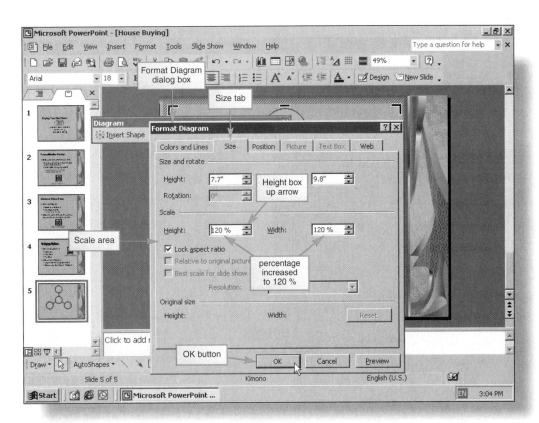

FIGURE 6-51

3 **Click the OK button. Click the Layout button on the Diagram toolbar and then point to Fit Diagram to Contents.**

The *Fit Diagram to Contents command* reduces the unnecessary space around the diagram (Figure 6-52).

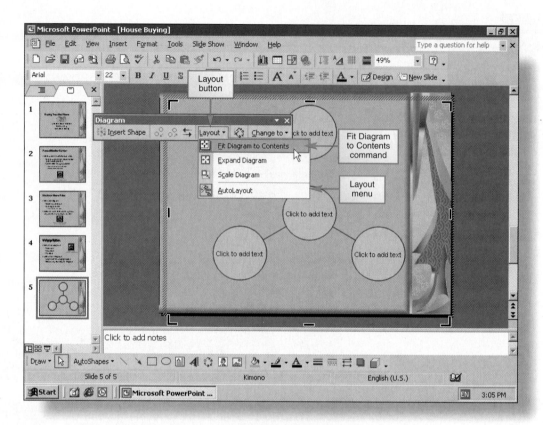

FIGURE 6-52

4 **Click Fit Diagram to Contents. Click the border of the diagram and then drag the border down and to the center of the gray area.**

The *Radial diagram* is the desired size and is positioned in the correct location (Figure 6-53).

1. On Format menu click Diagram, click Size tab
2. Press ALT+O, press D, press D
3. In Voice Command mode, say "Format, Diagram, Size"

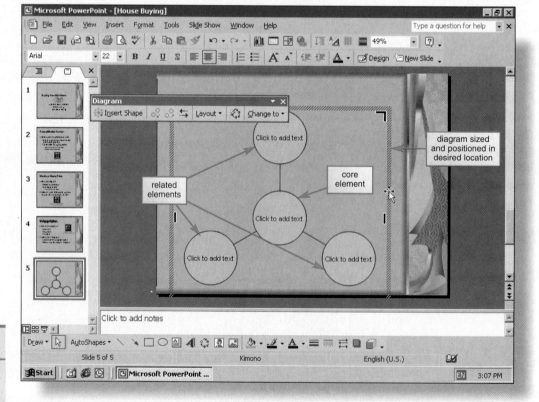

FIGURE 6-53

The Radial diagram displays in the center of Slide 5. It consists of a central core element and three related elements. If necessary, you can use the Diagram toolbar to add and connect additional elements to the core element and to move them forward or backward in the diagram. You also can delete elements by selecting them and then pressing the DELETE key.

Adding Text to the Diagram Shapes

Text helps users identify the relationships among these objects. Because buying a home has many advantages, placing the words, Outstanding Benefits, in the Radial diagram core element is appropriate and carries the most weight. Three major benefits of home ownership are pride, tax savings, and privacy. These three concepts will be placed in the three shapes connected to the core element. Perform the following steps to add text to the four shapes in the Radial diagram.

More About

Adding Text

In the Target and Cycle diagrams, you can add text only to the text boxes provided. In the other diagrams, you can add text by inserting a text box.

 To Add Text to the Radial Diagram Shapes

1 **Click the center shape. Type** Outstanding **and then press the ENTER key. Type** Benefits **and then point to the top shape.**

The desired text is added to the core element (Figure 6-54).

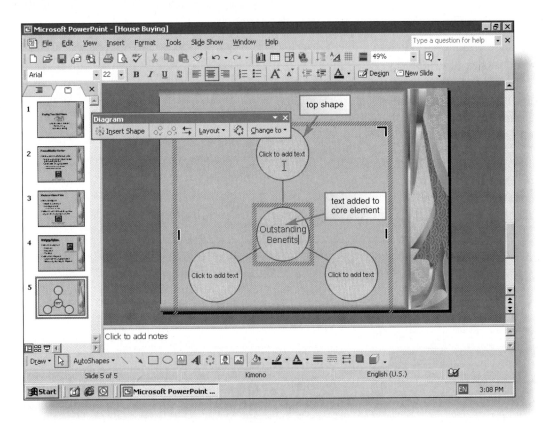

FIGURE 6-54

2 **Click the top shape. Type** Pride of **and then press the ENTER key. Type** Ownership **and then point to the left shape.**

The text for the first benefit of home ownership is described in the top shape.

3 **Click the left shape. Type** Tax **and then press the ENTER key. Type** Savings **and then point to the right shape.**

The text for the second benefit of home ownership is described in the left shape.

4 **Click the right shape. Type** Privacy **and then point to the AutoFormat button on the Diagram toolbar.**

The text for the third benefit of home ownership is described in the right shape (Figure 6-55).

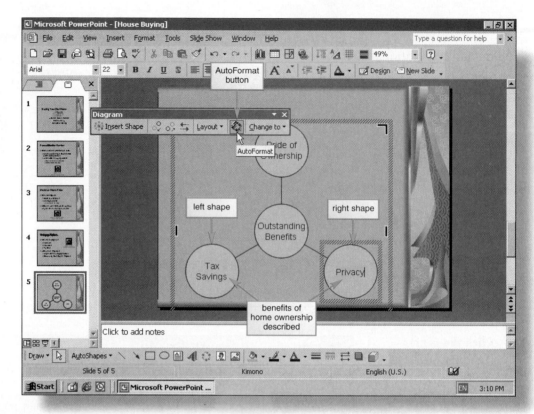

FIGURE 6-55

Adding Sound

You can add sound to a diagram to direct focus to different pieces of a diagram during a presentation. You can, for example, have PowerPoint play the sound of applause as an element displays.

All elements of the Radial diagram have been added. Formatting the diagram would create visual interest. The next section describes the preset design schemes that can enliven a presentation.

Formatting the Radial Diagram

PowerPoint provides nine preset styles in addition to the default style in the **Diagram Style Gallery**. These styles use assorted colors, shadows, and lines to add interest and variety. You also can custom format the diagram by adding color, changing the line style and weight, changing the fill color, inserting a background, and adding texture. The following steps show how to format the diagram by applying the 3-D Color diagram style.

To Format the Radial Diagram

1 **Click the AutoFormat button on the Diagram toolbar. When the Diagram Style Gallery dialog box displays, click the 3-D Color diagram style. Point to the Apply button.**

Diagram Style names display in the list. When you click a name, PowerPoint previews that style (Figure 6-56).

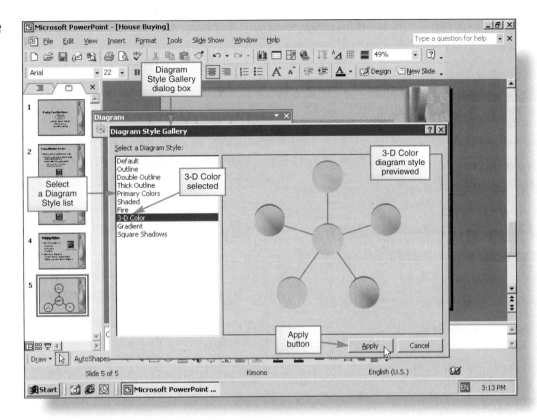

FIGURE 6-56

2 **Click the Apply button. Click a gray area of the slide not in the diagram placeholder.**

PowerPoint applies the 3-D Color diagram style to the Radial diagram (Figure 6-57).

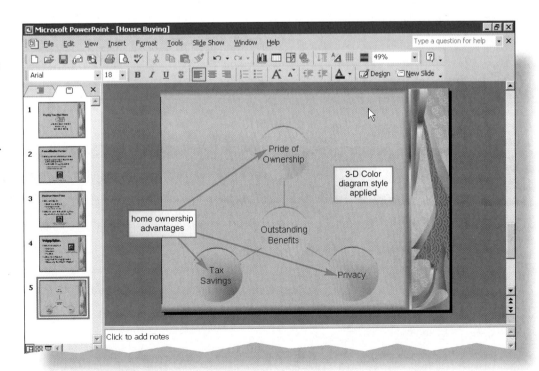

FIGURE 6-57

Transforming AutoShapes

After you insert and format one AutoShape, you may decide to substitute a different AutoShape. Rather than delete the AutoShape, convert it to the shape you desire by selecting the object, clicking the Draw button on the Drawing toolbar, clicking Change AutoShape, and then selecting the new AutoShape on the Change AutoShape submenu.

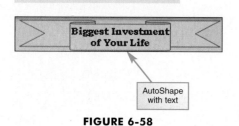

FIGURE 6-58

The elements of the Radial diagram are complete. If you want to move one of the shapes, select that shape and then click the Move Shape Forward or Move Shape Backward button on the Diagram toolbar.

Inserting and Formatting an AutoShape

As shown in the Radial diagram on Slide 5, three advantages of owning a home are pride of ownership, tax savings, and privacy. To emphasize the value of the investment and these benefits, you want to add an AutoShape that calls attention to this remarkable investment. An **AutoShape** is a ready-made object, such as a line, star, banner, arrow, connector, or callout. These shapes can be sized, rotated, flipped, colored, and combined to add unique qualities to a presentation.

You click the AutoShapes button on the Drawing toolbar to select a category, such as Block Arrows or Flowchart. Then, you choose the desired AutoShape and click the area of the slide where you want to insert the AutoShape. You then can add text by clicking the AutoShape and typing the desired information.

Figure 6-58 shows the AutoShape you are to create to accompany the Radial diagram. Creating this object requires several steps. First, you must choose the desired AutoShape and insert it into the slide. You then add text and resize the AutoShape to accommodate this text. The next several sections explain how to create this AutoShape.

Inserting an AutoShape

PowerPoint has a variety of AutoShapes organized in the categories of Lines, Connectors, Basic Shapes, Block Arrows, Flowchart, Stars and Banners, Callouts, and Action Buttons. In addition, the More AutoShapes category displays AutoShapes in the Clip Gallery. The first step in creating the AutoShape object is to select the desired shape. Perform the following steps to insert an AutoShape into Slide 5.

Steps **To Insert an AutoShape**

 Click the AutoShapes button on the Drawing toolbar, point to Stars and Banners, and then point to Down Ribbon (row 3, column 2) on the Stars and Banners submenu.

The Stars and Banners submenu displays (Figure 6-59). The desired AutoShape, Down Ribbon, is selected.

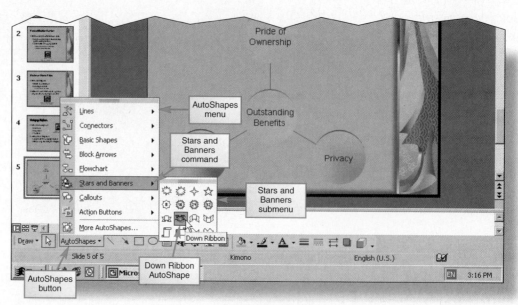

FIGURE 6-59

2 **Click Down Ribbon. Point to the gray area at the top of the slide above the Pride of Ownership object.**

The mouse pointer changes shape to a cross hair (Figure 6-60). The AutoShape will display in this area of the slide.

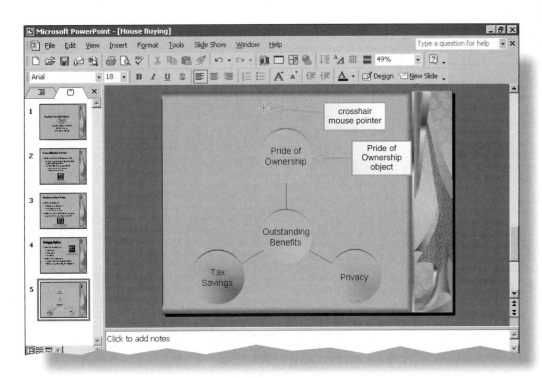

FIGURE 6-60

3 **Click the area at the top of the slide.**

The Down Ribbon AutoShape displays in the desired location (Figure 6-61).

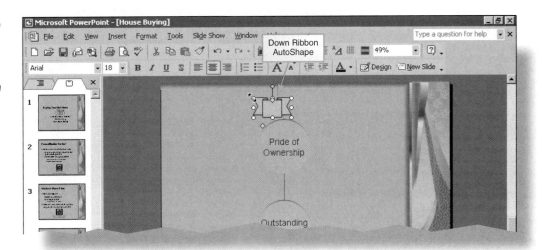

FIGURE 6-61

Other Ways

1. Press ALT+U

2. In Voice Command mode, say "AutoShapes, Stars and Banners, Down Ribbon"

If desired, you now could add special effects and text to the AutoShape. One special effect, for example, is a shadow you can create by clicking Shadow Settings in the Shadow Style list. To allow you to accomplish this, PowerPoint displays the Shadow Settings toolbar containing buttons to turn the shadow on or off, to nudge the shadow up, down, left, or right, and to change the shadow color. Another addition is text. The next section describes adding text to the AutoShape.

Adding Text to an AutoShape

The AutoShape displays on Slide 5 in the correct location. The next step is to add text stating that buying a house is a tremendous investment. The steps on the next page describe how to add this information.

Steps **To Add Text to an AutoShape**

1 **With the AutoShape selected, type** Biggest Investment **and then press** SHIFT+ENTER. **On the next line, type** of Your Life **as the text.**

The AutoShape text displays on two lines (Figure 6-62). Pressing SHIFT+ENTER *creates a line break, which moves the insertion point to the beginning of the next line and does not create a new paragraph.*

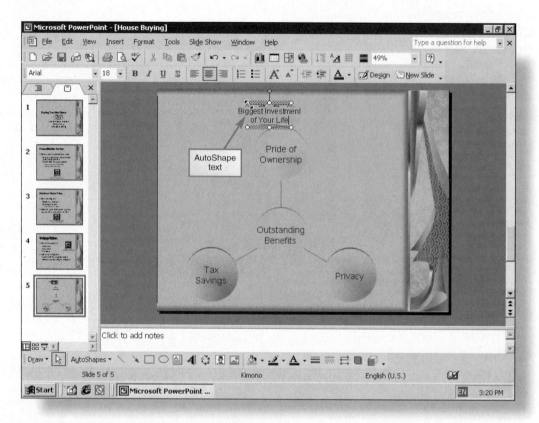

FIGURE 6-62

2 **Right-click the AutoShape, click Format AutoShape on the shortcut menu, and then click the Text Box tab in the Format AutoShape dialog box. Click Resize AutoShape to fit text and then point to the OK button.**

The Text Box sheet in the Format AutoShape dialog box displays (Figure 6-63). The default text placement is in the middle of the object, as indicated by the entry in the Text anchor point box. You can click the Preview button to see the resized AutoShape.

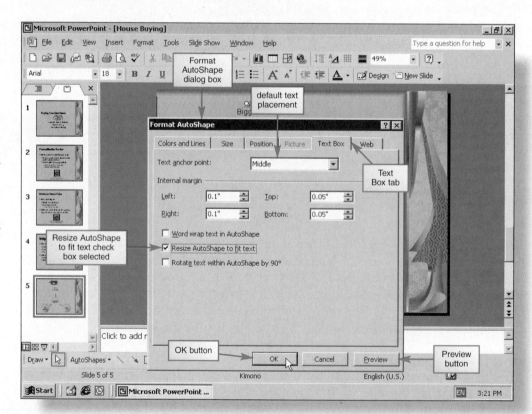

FIGURE 6-63

3 Click the OK button. Click the AutoShape border and drag the object so it is centered above the Pride of Ownership shape.

PowerPoint changes the size of the AutoShape automatically based on the amount of text entered and the amount of space allocated for the AutoShape's margins. The AutoShape displays in the desired location (Figure 6-64). Press the arrow keys to adjust the location.

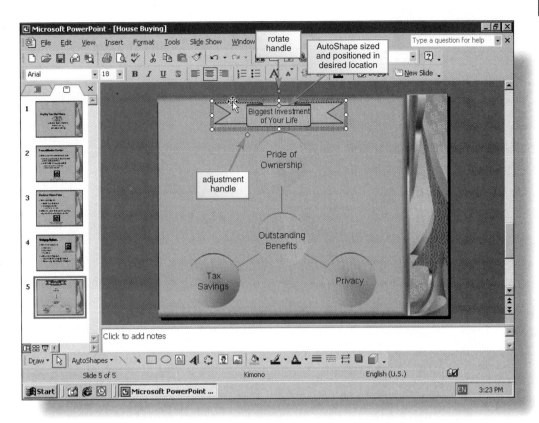

FIGURE 6-64

You can rotate the AutoShape by dragging the green **rotate handle** on the object in the desired direction. The shape also contains two yellow, diamond-shaped **adjustment handles** that allow appearance changes to the most prominent features of the object. For example, you can change the width of the front part of the ribbon by dragging the bottom adjustment handle to the right or to the left to reduce or expand this area.

Applying an AutoShape Entrance Animation Effect

The next steps in creating Slide 5 are to animate the AutoShape object. Perform the following steps to apply an entrance effect.

TO APPLY AN AUTOSHAPE ENTRANCE ANIMATION EFFECT

1 With the AutoShape selected, click Slide Show on the menu bar, click Custom Animation, and then click the Add Effect button in the Custom Animation task pane.

2 Point to Entrance and then click Dissolve In on the More Effects menu.

3 Click the Start box arrow and then click After Previous in the Add Entrance Effect dialog box.

4 Click the Speed box arrow and then click Slow.

The AutoShape will display slowly in the presentation using the Dissolve In animation effect during the slide show (Figure 6-65 on the next page).

Other Ways

1. Type desired text, on Format menu click AutoShape, click Text Box tab, click Resize AutoShape to fit text, click OK button
2. Type desired text, press ALT+O, press O, press CTRL+TAB to select Text Box tab, press TAB to select Resize AutoShape to fit text check box, press SPACEBAR, press ENTER
3. Click AutoShape object, drag a sizing handle until object is desired shape and size

Other Ways

1. Right-click AutoShape, Click Custom Animation on shortcut menu, click Add Effect button
2. Press ALT+D, press M
3. In Voice Command mode, say "Slide Show, Custom Animation, Add Effect, Entrance"

AutoShape Defaults

AutoShapes automatically have a medium shade of green and a thin black border. To change these defaults, double-click a shape to open the Format AutoShape dialog box, make line and color modifications, and then click the Default for new objects check box in the lower-left corner of the Colors and Lines tab. Click the OK button to return to the slide. This formatting will apply to every new AutoShape you insert into a slide. To return to the default settings, click Format on the menu bar, click Apply Design Template, and then reapply the existing presentation template. These settings will override the new default settings.

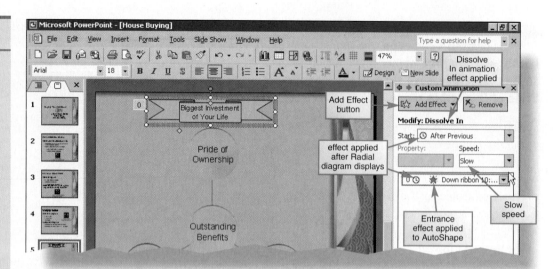

FIGURE 6-65

When you run the slide show, the four shapes in the Radial diagram will display, and then the AutoShape will dissolve into the slide. The next section describes how the AutoShape will move in a triangular pattern around the top object.

Applying a Motion Path Animation Effect to an AutoShape

The next step is applying a motion path to the AutoShape. A **motion path** is a pre-drawn path the shape will follow. In this presentation, the shape will display and then move on the slide in a triangular shape. Perform the following steps to apply a motion path animation effect.

 To Apply a Motion Path Animation Effect to an AutoShape

1 **With the AutoShape selected, click the Add Effect button in the Custom Animation task pane. Point to Motion Paths and then point to More Motion Paths on the Motion Paths submenu.**

The effects in your list may differ (Figure 6-66).

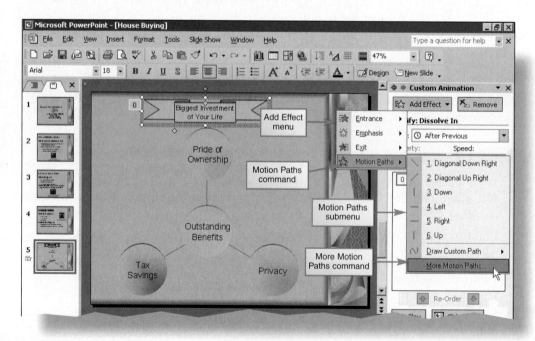

FIGURE 6-66

2 **Click More Motion Paths. When the Add Motion Path dialog box displays, click Equal Triangle in the Basic category and then point to the OK button.**

The Equal Triangle effect is previewed on Slide 5 behind the dialog box because the Preview Effect check box is selected (Figure 6-67).

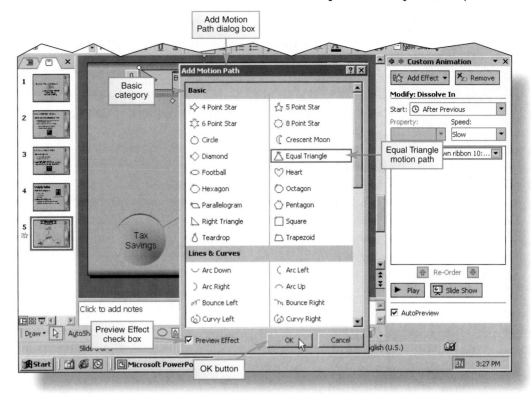

FIGURE 6-67

3 **Click the OK button. Click the Start box arrow in the Custom Animation task pane and then click After Previous. Click the Speed box arrow and then click Very Slow.**

The Equal Triangle motion path is applied (Figure 6-68).

4 **Click the Close button in the Custom Animation task pane.**

The AutoShape will move very slowly in a triangular path after the Radial diagram displays.

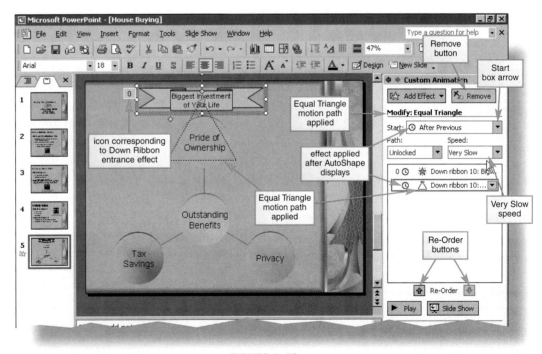

FIGURE 6-68

Effects display in the Custom Animation list in the order they were applied to the slide. This animation sequence can be changed easily by clicking the item you want to move in the list and either dragging it to another position or clicking the Re-Order buttons. The changes are reflected in the renumbered list and in the corresponding icons attached to the placeholders. To remove an effect, click the animation item in the Custom Animation list and then click the Remove button.

Graphics

The art field has expanded with the emergence of computer-generated graphics. Web sites profile artists and their works. They also provide resources for computer artists, designers, and technicians. To view these graphics, visit the PowerPoint 2002 More About Web page (scsite.com/pp2002/more.htm) and then click Graphics.

1. Right-click AutoShape, click Custom Animation on shortcut menu, click Add Effect button
2. Press ALT+D, press M
3. In Voice Command mode, say "Slide Show, Custom Animation, Add Effect, Motion Paths"

AutoShape Text

AutoShape text displays in 24-point Times New Roman font. To change the default formatting of text, select the text or AutoShape, click Format on the menu bar, click Font, and then choose a font style, size, color, and effect. Then, click the Default for new objects check box in the lower-right corner of the Font dialog box. Click the OK button to return to the slide.

A motion path also can be changed. Positioning the mouse pointer over the path and then dragging the path to the desired area on the slide, for example, changes its location. To reverse the movement, right-click the path and then click Reverse Path Direction on the shortcut menu. To apply a different motion path, click the Change button in the Custom Animation task pane, point to Motion Paths, and then click the desired animation.

Formatting AutoShape Text

The Kimono design template determines the AutoShape's text attributes. You can, however, change these characteristics. For example, you can modify the font color, change the font, increase the font size, and add bold and italic styles and underline and shadow effects. Perform the following steps to change the AutoShape's font, font size, and font style.

TO FORMAT AUTOSHAPE TEXT

1 Triple-click the AutoShape text. Click the Font box arrow and then click Bookman Old Style.

2 Click the Font Size box arrow and then click 24.

3 Click the Bold button on the Formatting toolbar.

4 Click the slide in an area other than the AutoShape or placeholders.

The bold AutoShape text has the Bookman Old Style font and a font size of 24 (Figure 6-69).

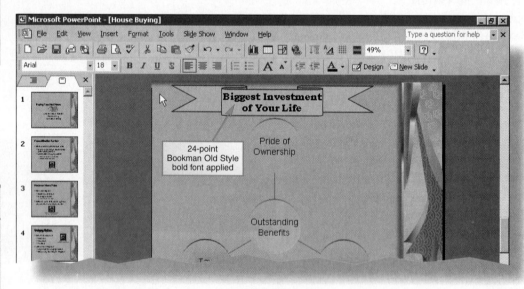

FIGURE 6-69

Text added to an AutoShape becomes part of the shape, which means that it increases font size if the AutoShape is enlarged or that it rotates or flips if the shape is rotated or flipped. If you do not want to attach text to the object, add text instead by using the Text Box button on the Drawing toolbar and then placing the text on top of the object.

All slide elements have been added to the presentation. The next section describes how to set the controls so the slide show runs automatically without user intervention.

Creating a Self-Running Presentation

The House Buying presentation is designed to run unattended. When the last slide in the presentation displays, the slide show **loops**, or restarts, at Slide 1.

PowerPoint has the option of running continuously until a user presses the ESC key. The following steps explain how to set the slide show to run in this manner.

Steps   **To Create a Self-Running Presentation**

1   **Click Slide Show on the menu bar and then point to Set Up Show.**

The Set Up Show options let you decide how much control, if any, you will give to your audience (Figure 6-70).

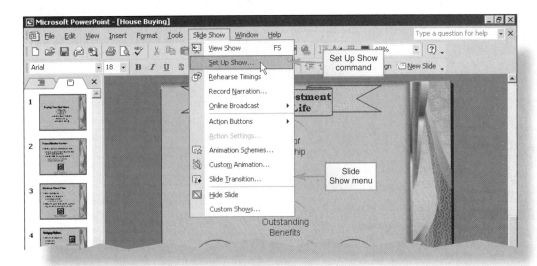

FIGURE 6-70

2   **Click Set Up Show. When the Set Up Show dialog box displays, point to Browsed at a kiosk (full screen) in the Show type area.**

The Set Up Show dialog box displays (Figure 6-71). The default show type is Presented by a speaker (full screen). The Set Up Show dialog box is used to specify the show type, which slides to display, how to advance slides, how multiple monitors are used, and performance enhancements.

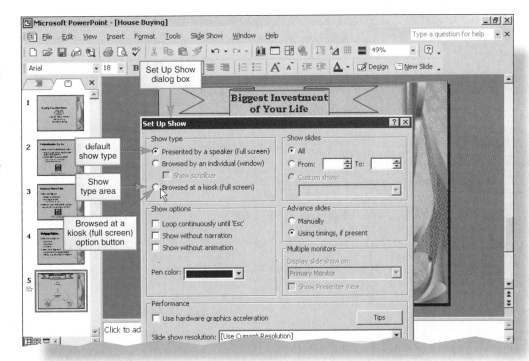

FIGURE 6-71

Click Browsed at a kiosk (full screen). Point to the OK button.

A check mark displays in the Loop continuously until 'Esc' check box, and the text box and label are dimmed (Figure 6-72). The slides will advance automatically based on the timings you specify.

4 **Click the OK button.**

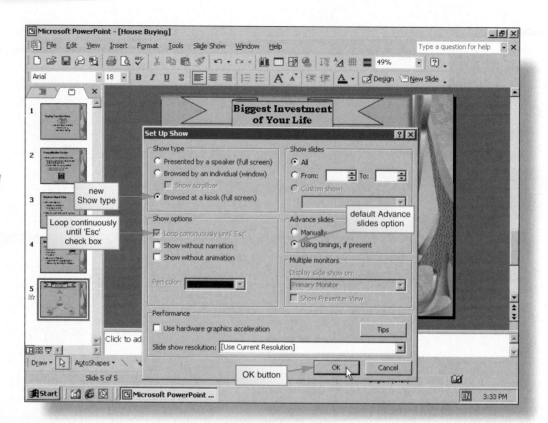

FIGURE 6-72

1. Press ALT+D, press S, press ALT+K, press ENTER

2. In Voice Command mode, say "Slide Show, Set Up Show, Browsed at a kiosk, OK"

This slide show will run by itself without user intervention. The user can, however, advance through the slides manually and click the action buttons.

Adding an Animation Scheme

The next step in preparing the House Buying presentation is to add an animation scheme. Perform the following steps to add the Ellipse motion animation scheme.

TO ADD AN ANIMATION SCHEME

1 Click Slide Show on the menu bar and then click Animation Schemes.

2 Scroll down and then click the Ellipse motion animation scheme in the Exciting category.

3 Click the Apply to All Slides button.

4 Click the Close button on the Slide Design task pane title bar.

The Ellipse motion animation scheme is applied to all slides in the presentation (Figure 6-73).

Quick Reference

For a table that lists how to complete tasks covered in this book using the mouse, menu, shortcut menu, and keyboard, see the Quick Reference Summary at the back of this book or visit the Shelly Cashman Series Office XP Web page (scsite.com/offxp/qr.htm) and then click Microsoft PowerPoint 2002.

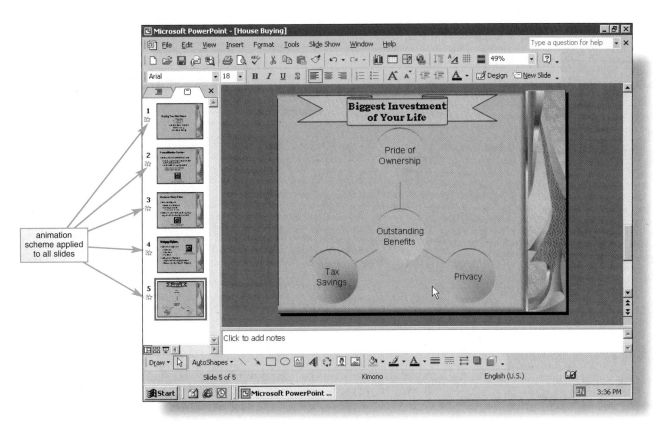

FIGURE 6-73

Setting Slide Show Timings Manually

The slide show is designed to loop continuously at a kiosk for two-and-one-half minutes unless the user moves through the slides manually. Consequently, you must determine the length of time each slide will display on the screen. You can set these times in two ways. One method is to use PowerPoint's **rehearsal** feature, which allows you to advance through the slides at your own pace, and the amount of time you view each slide is recorded. The other method is to set each slide's display time manually. You will use this second technique in the steps on the next page.

Effective Presentations

Major corporations hire graphic designers and speech coaches who work together and develop guidelines that help executives develop effective presentations. These individuals focus on aesthetically pleasing presentations and a fluent delivery. For more information, visit the PowerPoint 2002 More About Web page (scsite.com/pp2002/more.htm) and then click Guidelines.

Steps **To Set Slide Show Timing Manually for Slide 1**

1 **Click the Slide Sorter View button. Right-click Slide 1 and then point to Slide Transition.**

Slide 1 is selected (Figure 6-74).

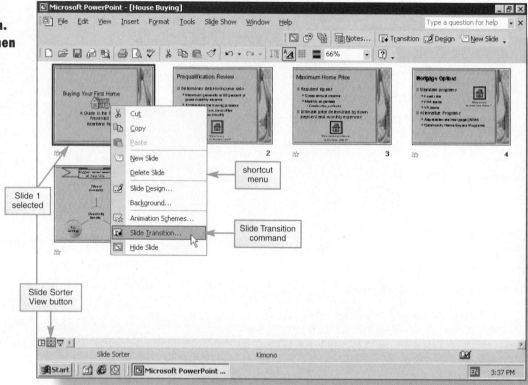

FIGURE 6-74

2 **Click Slide Transition. Point to Automatically after in the Advance slide area.**

The Slide Transition task pane displays (Figure 6-75). The On mouse click check box is selected. A speaker generally uses this default setting to advance through the slides in a presentation. The Strips Right-Down transition effect is part of the Ellipse motion animation scheme.

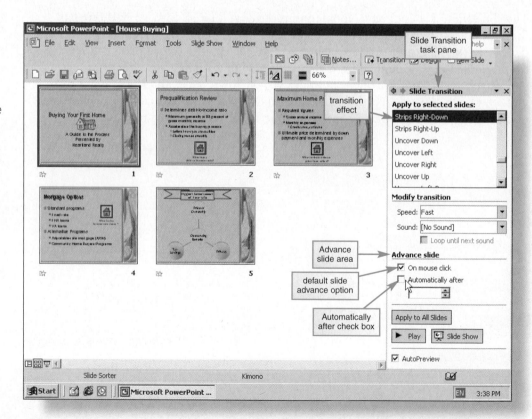

FIGURE 6-75

3 Click Automatically after and then point to the Automatically after box up arrow.

This slide show advances the slide automatically after it has displayed for a designated period or allows users to display the slides manually (Figure 6-76). You specify the length of time you want the slide to display in the Automatically after text box.

4 Click and hold down the mouse button on the Automatically after box up arrow until 00:15 displays and then point to the Play button.

The Automatically after text box displays 00:15 seconds (Figure 6-77). Another method of entering the time is to type the specific number of minutes and seconds in the text box.

5 Click the Play button.

The Strips Right-Down slide transition displays in the Slide 1 slide thumbnail. Below Slide 1, 00:15 displays indicating the designated slide timing.

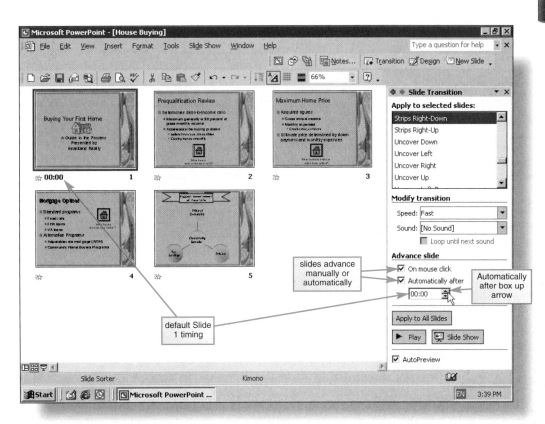

FIGURE 6-76

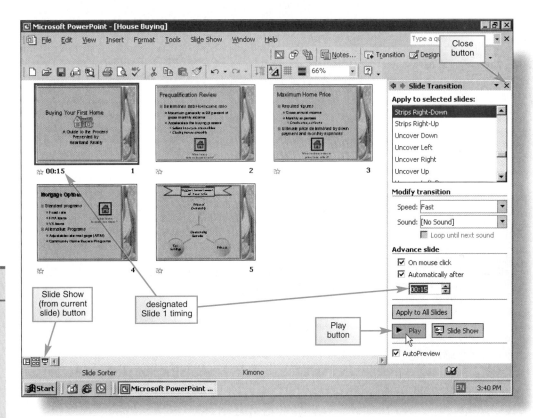

FIGURE 6-77

Other Ways

1. On Slide Show menu click Slide Transition, click Automatically after, click Automatically after box up arrow, click Apply button
2. Press ALT+D, press T, type desired time, press ENTER
3. In Voice Command mode, say "Slide Show, Slide Transition, Automatically after, [type time], Close"

The timing for Slide 1 is complete. You need to repeat this procedure for Slides 2 through 5 in the House Buying presentation. Perform the following steps to set these timings.

TO SET SLIDE SHOW TIMINGS MANUALLY FOR THE REMAINING SLIDES

1 Click the Slide 2 slide thumbnail, press and hold down the SHIFT key, and then click Slide 4. Click Automatically after in the Advance Slide area in the Slide Transition task pane. Click and hold down the Automatically after box up arrow until 00:30 displays.

2 Click the Slide 5 slide thumbnail. Click Automatically after in the Advance Slide area in the Slide Transition task pane. Click and hold down the Automatically after box up arrow until 00:45 displays.

3 Click the Play button.

4 Click the Close button in the Slide Transition task pane title bar.

Each slide's timing displays in the lower-left corner (Figure 6-78).

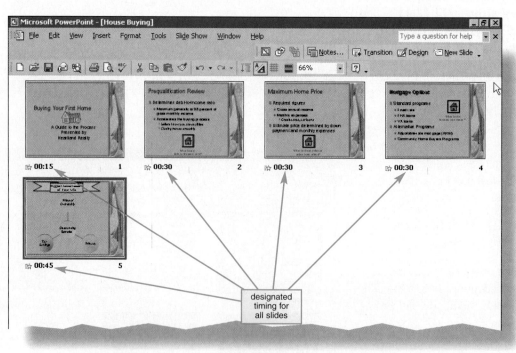

FIGURE 6-78

The House Buying slide timing is complete. The presentation will run for two-and-one-half minutes.

Saving the Presentation

The presentation is complete. You now should save it again.

Starting the Self-Running Presentation

Starting a self-running slide show basically is the same as starting any other slide show. Perform the following steps to run the presentation.

More About

Microsoft Certification

The Microsoft Office User Specialist (MOUS) Certification program provides an opportunity for you to obtain a valuable industry credential — proof that you have the PowerPoint 2002 skills required by employers. For more information, see Appendix E or visit the Shelly Cashman Series MOUS Web page at scsite.com/offxp/cert.htm.

TO START THE SELF-RUNNING PRESENTATION

1 Click Slide 1 and click the Slide Show (from current slide) button.

2 When Slide 2 displays, click the action button. If a security warning displays, click the OK button. Type 4000 in the Monthly Income text box. Click the Monthly Mortgage Amount text box and then type 850 in the box. Click the Total Monthly Expenses text box and then type 500 in the box. Click the Calculate button.

3 Click the OK button, click the Clear button and then enter 2500 in the Monthly Income text box, 650 in the Monthly Mortgage Amount text box, and 500 in the Total Monthly Expenses text box. Click the Calculate button. Click the OK button. Click the Close button.

4 When Slide 3 displays, click the action button. If necessary, maximize the Microsoft Excel window when the worksheet displays. Click the Gross annual income figure (cell B3) and then type 48000 in that cell. Press the ENTER key. Click the Monthly non-housing expenses figure (cell B6) and then type 500 in that cell. Press the ENTER key.

5 After you review the figures, including the Estimated affordable price, click the Gross annual income figure (cell B3) and then type 30000 in that cell. Press the ENTER key. Click the Monthly non-housing expenses figure (cell B6) and then type 500 in that cell. Press the ENTER key.

6 After you review the figures, click the Close button on the Microsoft Excel title bar to return to the presentation.

7 When Slide 4 displays, click the action button. If necessary, maximize the Microsoft Word window when the table displays. Review the table and then click the Close button on the Microsoft Word title bar to return to the presentation.

8 When Slide 5 displays, review the information on the diagram.

9 When Slide 1 displays, press the ESC key to stop the presentation.

The presentation will run for two-and-one-half minutes, and then it will loop back to the beginning and start automatically.

Printing Slides as Handouts

Perform the following steps to print the presentation slides as handouts, three slides per page.

TO PRINT SLIDES AS HANDOUTS

1 Ready the printer.

2 Click File on the menu bar and then click Print.

3 Click the Print what box arrow and then click Handouts in the list.

4 Click the Slides per page box arrow in the Handouts area and then click 3 in the list.

5 Click the OK button.

The handouts print as shown in Figure 6-79 on the next page.

FIGURE 6-79

The House Buying presentation now is complete. If you made any changes to your presentation since your last save, you now should save it again before quitting PowerPoint.

CASE PERSPECTIVE SUMMARY

The House Buying slide show should help first-time buyers understand the process of purchasing real estate. When they arrive for their appointments at Heartland Realty, they can view your presentation at a kiosk and learn the basics of prequalification, determine the approximate home price they can afford, preview mortgage options, and understand the advantages of owning a home. The real estate agents should find your presentation beneficial for introducing their customers to the house-buying process.

Project Summary

Project 6 presented the principles of creating a self-running presentation that can run at a kiosk. You began the project by starting a new presentation and then inserting a slide from another presentation. Next, you embedded a Visual Basic program, an Excel worksheet, and a Word table. You then inserted, formatted, and animated a Radial diagram. Next, you inserted and formatted an AutoShape and added text and a motion path animation effect. You then added an animation scheme and set automatic slide timings to display each slide for a designated period of time. Finally, you printed your presentation slides as handouts with three slides displaying on each page.

What You Should Know

Having completed this project, you now should be able to perform the following tasks:

- Add a Caption to the Slide 2 Action Button (PP 6.31)
- Add a Fill Color to the Slide 2 and Slide 3 Action Buttons (PP 6.27)
- Add a Fill Color to the Slide 4 Action Button (PP 6.26)
- Add a Shadow to the Action Buttons (PP 6.28)
- Add a Shadow to the Slide 3 and Slide 4 Action Buttons (PP 6.29)
- Add an Action Button and Action Settings (PP 6.18)
- Add an Animation Scheme (PP 6.52)
- Add Captions to the Slide 3 and Slide 4 Action Buttons (PP 6.32)
- Add Lines to the Slide 2 and Slide 3 Action Buttons (PP 6.30)
- Add Lines to the Slide 4 Action Button (PP 6.30)
- Add Notes (PP 6.15)
- Add Text to an AutoShape (PP 6.46)
- Add Text to the Radial Diagram Shapes (PP 6.41)
- Apply a Motion Path Animation Effect to an AutoShape (PP 6.48)
- Apply an AutoShape Entrance Animation Effect (PP 6.47)
- Change the Radial Diagram Size (PP 6.39)
- Create a Self-Running Presentation (PP 6.51)
- Create a Title Slide (PP 6.07)
- Create Additional Action Buttons and Hyperlinks (PP 6.21)
- Create Slide 2 (PP 6.08)
- Create Slide 3 (PP 6.09)
- Display Guides and Position the Slide 2 Action Button (PP 6.23)
- Format AutoShape Text (PP 6.50)
- Format the Radial Diagram (PP 6.43)
- Format the Slide 2 and Slide 3 Action Button Caption Text (PP 6.34)
- Format the Slide 4 Action Button Caption Text (PP 6.33)
- Hide Guides (PP 6.26)
- Insert a Radial Diagram (PP 6.36)
- Insert a Slide from Another Presentation (PP 6.12)
- Insert an AutoShape (PP 6.44)
- Insert, Size, and Move a Clip on a Slide (PP 6.16)
- Position the Slide 3 and Slide 4 Action Buttons (PP 6.25)
- Print Slides as Handouts (PP 6.57)
- Save a Presentation (PP 6.15)
- Scale Action Buttons (PP 6.22)
- Set Slide Show Timing Manually for Slide 1 (PP 6.54)
- Set Slide Show Timings Manually for the Remaining Slides (PP 6.56)
- Start and Customize a New Presentation (PP 6.06)
- Start the Self-Running Presentation (PP 6.57)

Learn It Online

Instructions: To complete the Learn It Online exercises, start your browser, click the Address bar, and then enter scsite.com/offxp/exs.htm. When the Office XP Learn It Online page displays, follow the instructions in the exercises below.

1 Project Reinforcement TF, MC, and SA

Below PowerPoint Project 6, click the Project Reinforcement link. Print the quiz by clicking Print on the File menu. Answer each question. Write your first and last name at the top of each page, and then hand in the printout to your instructor.

2 Flash Cards

Below PowerPoint Project 6, click the Flash Cards link. When Flash Cards displays, read the instructions. Type 20 (or a number specified by your instructor) in the Number of Playing Cards text box, type your name in the Name text box, and then click the Flip Card button. When the flash card displays, read the question and then click the Answer box arrow to select an answer. Flip through Flash Cards. Click Print on the File menu to print the last flash card if your score is 15 (75%) correct or greater and then hand it in to your instructor. If your score is less than 15 (75%) correct, then redo this exercise by clicking the Replay button.

3 Practice Test

Below PowerPoint Project 6, click the Practice Test link. Answer each question, enter your first and last name at the bottom of the page, and then click the Grade Test button. When the graded practice test displays on your screen, click Print on the File menu to print a hard copy. Continue to take practice tests until you score 80% or better. Hand in a printout of the final practice test to your instructor.

4 Who Wants to Be a Computer Genius?

Below PowerPoint Project 6, click the Computer Genius link. Read the instructions, enter your first and last name at the bottom of the page, and then click the Play button. Hand in your score to your instructor.

5 Wheel of Terms

Below PowerPoint Project 6, click the Wheel of Terms link. Read the instructions, and then enter your first and last name and your school name. Click the Play button. Hand in your score to your instructor.

6 Crossword Puzzle Challenge

Below PowerPoint Project 6, click the Crossword Puzzle Challenge link. Read the instructions, and then enter your first and last name. Click the Play button. Work the crossword puzzle. When you are finished, click the Submit button. When the crossword puzzle redisplays, click the Print button. Hand in the printout.

7 Tips and Tricks

Below PowerPoint Project 6, click the Tips and Tricks link. Click a topic that pertains to Project 6. Right-click the information and then click Print on the shortcut menu. Construct a brief example of what the information relates to in PowerPoint to confirm you understand how to use the tip or trick. Hand in the example and printed information.

8 Newsgroups

Below PowerPoint Project 6, click the Newsgroups link. Click a topic that pertains to Project 6. Print three comments. Hand in the comments to your instructor.

9 Expanding Your Horizons

Below PowerPoint Project 6, click the Articles for Microsoft PowerPoint link. Click a topic that pertains to Project 6. Print the information. Construct a brief example of what the information relates to in PowerPoint to confirm you understand the contents of the article. Hand in the example and printed information to your instructor.

10 Search Sleuth

Below PowerPoint Project 6, click the Search Sleuth link. To search for a term that pertains to this project, select a term below the Project 6 title and then use the Google search engine at google.com (or any major search engine) to display and print two Web pages that present information on the term. Hand in the printouts to your instructor.

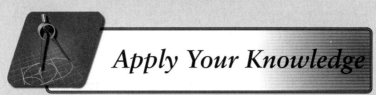

1 Designing a Title Slide Using AutoShapes

Instructions: Members of the astronomy club, the Moonstrucks, have asked you to help them promote their organization. Perform the following tasks to create the title slide shown in Figure 6-80 on the next page.

1. Start PowerPoint. Create a new presentation using the Title Slide slide layout and the Fireworks design template. Apply the color scheme in row 2, column 1.
2. Type the text for the title slide as shown in Figure 6-80. Add a shadow to the title text by selecting the text and clicking the Shadow button on the Formatting toolbar. Bold and italicize the subtitle text.
3. Display the drawing guides. Click the AutoShapes button on the Drawing toolbar, point to Basic Shapes, and then click Moon (row 6, column 4) on the Basic Shapes submenu. Click the slide to display the moon object.
4. Right-click the moon object and then click Format AutoShape on the shortcut menu. If necessary, click the Size tab. Click Lock aspect ratio, scale the moon to 200 %, and then click the OK button.
5. Click the Fill Color button arrow on the Drawing toolbar and then click the color white in the row of available colors.
6. Drag the horizontal guide to 1.50 inches above center and the vertical guide to 3.25 inches left of center. Drag the moon to the upper-left corner of the slide so the top and bottom edges snap to the guides.
7. Click the AutoShapes button on the Drawing toolbar, point to Stars and Banners, and then click 4-Point Star (row 1, column 3). Click the slide to display the star object.
8. Click the Fill Color button arrow on the Drawing toolbar, and then click the color yellow in the row of available colors.
9. Click the Fill Colors button arrow again and then click Fill Effects. If necessary, click the Gradient tab, and then click the lower-left variant sample in the Variants area. Click the OK button in the Fill Effects dialog box.
10. Right-click the 4-Point Star AutoShape, and then click Format AutoShape on the shortcut menu. If necessary, click the Size tab. Click Lock aspect ratio, scale the star to 175 %, and then click the OK button.
11. Drag the horizontal guide to 2.00 inches below center and the vertical guide to 3.25 inches right of center. Drag the star to the lower-right corner of the slide so the top and left edges snap to the guides.
12. Click the AutoShapes button on the Drawing toolbar, point to Basic Shapes, and then click Lightning Bolt (row 6, column 2). Click the slide to display the lightning bolt object.
13. Right-click the lightning bolt object, and then click Format AutoShape on the shortcut menu. If necessary, click the Size tab. Scale the lightning bolt to 200 % without clicking Lock aspect ratio, and then click the OK button.
14. Drag the vertical guide to 3.75 inches left of center and the horizontal guide to 0.42 inch below center. Drag the lightning bolt so the left and top points align with the guides.
15. Click the Insert WordArt button on the Drawing toolbar. Choose the WordArt style in row 3, column 1, and then click the OK button. Enter the club information shown in the bottom of the slide, and substitute your name for the words, Student Name. Click the OK button in the Edit WordArt Text dialog box. Click the WordArt Shape button on the WordArt toolbar, and then apply the Inflate shape (row 4, column 1). Scale the text to 110 %.

(continued)

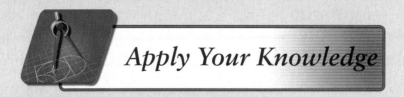

Apply Your Knowledge

Designing a Title Slide Using AutoShapes *(continued)*

FIGURE 6-80

16. Drag the vertical guide to 2.00 inches left of center and the horizontal guide to 2.00 inches below center. Align the top and left edges of the WordArt object with these guides. You might need to make minor adjustments with the scaling to accommodate your name.

17. Apply the Flash bulb animation scheme. Save the presentation with the file name, Moonstrucks. Print the slide using the Pure Black and White option. Quit PowerPoint.

In the Lab

1 Formatting Backgrounds, Linking Slides, and Inserting a Diagram

Problem: The Tri-Circle Ranch has expanded its activities for vacationers. In the past year, the owners have added a variety of hikes through the Rocky Mountains, fishing lessons and trips, and white-water rafting. You have visited the ranch during your summer vacations, and you agree to help the owners market their new programs. You develop a self-running PowerPoint presentation to display at trade shows throughout the country. To make the slide show useful and interesting, you add clip art, hyperlinks to slides within the presentation, and a slide with a Venn diagram. You create the presentation shown in Figures 6-81a through 6-81f on the next page.

Instructions: Start PowerPoint and perform the following tasks. If the picture and clip art images are not available on your computer, see your instructor for copies of these files or substitute similar objects and a picture.

1. Open a new presentation and apply the Title Slide slide layout and the Default Design design template.
2. Create the title slide shown in Figure 6-81a by inserting the picture as a background and moving the placeholder locations. Use the Garamond font. Bold the text, and use a font size of 54 for the title text and 36 for the subtitle text. The title text font color is dark blue, and the subtitle color is white.
3. Insert a new slide and then apply the Blank slide layout. Insert the Venn diagram and then apply the Thick Outline AutoFormat. Scale the Venn diagram to 170 %, click the Layout button on the Diagram toolbar, and then click Fit Diagram to Contents. Center the Venn diagram on the slide.
4. Add a caption shown in Figure 6-81b to each of the areas marked, Click to add text. Apply the Blue tissue paper texture to the Slide 2 background.
5. Add the AutoShape shown in Figure 6-81b by clicking the AutoShapes button on the Drawing toolbar, pointing to Stars and Banners, and then clicking 8-Point Star (row 2, column 1). Insert the AutoShape in the center of the Venn diagram. Type Tri-Circle Ranch and then change the font to Garamond and the font size to 32. Bold this text. Right-click the AutoShape, click Format AutoShape on the shortcut menu, and then click the Text Box tab when the Format AutoShape dialog box displays. Click Resize AutoShape to fit text, and then click the OK button.
6. Add the Circle entrance animation effect and the Circle motion path to the AutoShape.
7. Insert a new slide and apply the Title Only slide layout. Type the title text shown on Slide 3 (Figure 6-81c).
8. Insert a new slide and apply the Title and Text slide layout. Type the text shown on Slide 4 (Figure 6-81d). Repeat this step to create Slides 5 and 6.
9. Insert the clips shown. Scale the clip on Slide 4 to 270 %, Slide 5 to 170 %, and Slide 6 to 285 %.
10. Create the slide backgrounds for Slides 3 through 6 by pressing and holding down the SHIFT key and then clicking the Slide 3 slide thumbnail on the Slides tab. Right-click the Slide 3 slide thumbnail, and then click Background on the shortcut menu. When the Background dialog box displays, click the Background fill arrow, and then click Fill Effects. If necessary, click the Gradient tab in the Fill Effects dialog box. Click From title in the Shading styles area. Click the Color 1 box arrow, and then click the color dark blue in the row of available colors. Click the OK button, and then click the Apply button.
11. Change the font color for all text on Slides 3, 4, 5, and 6 to light blue. Apply the Big title animation scheme to all slides.

(continued)

In the Lab

Formatting Backgrounds, Linking Slides, and Inserting a Diagram *(continued)*

(a) Slide 1

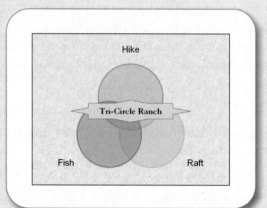

(b) Slide 2

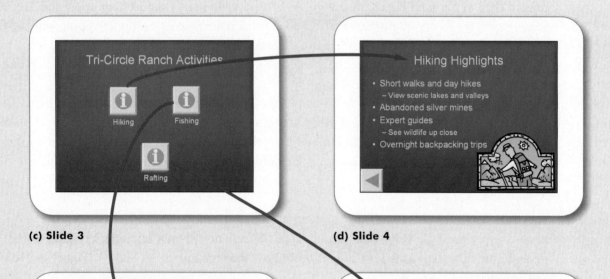

(c) Slide 3

(d) Slide 4

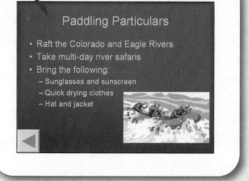

(e) Slide 5

(f) Slide 6

FIGURE 6-81

In the Lab

12. Add the three action buttons and captions shown in Figure 6-81c to Slide 3. Hyperlink the Hiking action button to the Next Slide. Hyperlink the Fishing action button to Slide 4 by clicking the Hyperlink to arrow, clicking Slide, clicking 4. Hiking Highlights, and then clicking the OK button. Hyperlink the Rafting action button to Slide 5. Scale the action buttons to 120 % and apply Shadow Style 5. Change the font to light blue and change the font size to 28 point.

13. Add an action button to the lower-left corner of Slides 4, 5, and 6, and hyperlink each action button to the Previous Slide.

14. Save the presentation with the file name, Rocky Mountains. Run the slide show. When Slide 3 displays, click the Hiking action button to jump to Slide 4. When Slide 4 displays, click the action button to return to Slide 2. Click the Fishing action button to jump to Slide 5. When Slide 5 displays, click the action button to return to Slide 2. Click the Rafting button to jump to Slide 6. When Slide 6 displays, click the slide anywhere except the action button. When Slide 1 displays, press the ESC key.

15. Print the six presentation slides as a handout with two slides per page. Quit PowerPoint.

2 Linking Slides, Inserting an AutoShape, and Setting Timings

Problem: Wireless technology has taken the world by storm. From cellular telephones to notebook computers with high-speed Internet access, these devices have simplified and expanded communication capabilities. Asia and Europe have emerged as global leaders in wireless device use, and during the next few years more than 1.2 billion of these products will be used in most areas of the world. Technology experts gather several times a year to learn about the latest wireless trends and to view new products. One of these conferences is scheduled for San Francisco, and you have offered to create a PowerPoint presentation to help publicize the event. You decide a self-running interactive slide show would be the best vehicle to share information. Develop the presentation shown in Figures 6-82a through 6-82f.

Instructions: Start PowerPoint and perform the following tasks.

1. Open a new presentation and apply the Satellite Dish design template. Add the Golden Gate Bridge picture to the Slide 1 background.

2. On Slide 1, enter the title and subtitle text shown in Figure 6-82a. Bold the text and change the font color of the title text to white and the subtitle text to green (color 8 in the row of available colors). Add the animated cellular telephone clip and scale it to 300 %.

3. Insert a new slide and apply the Title and Text slide layout. Enter the title and bulleted list shown in Figure 6-82b. Add an action button and hyperlink it to the Wireless Use worksheet (Figure 6-82c) on your Data Disk. See the inside back cover of this book for instructions for downloading the Data Disk or see your instructor for information on accessing this file. Play the Voltage sound when the mouse is clicked.

4. Change the button fill color to green, scale it to 90 %, and apply Shadow Style 5. Display the drawing guides and then drag the horizontal guide to 0.58 inch left of center and the vertical guide to 1.75 inches below center. Position the upper-left corner of the button at the intersection of these guides. Add the caption shown in Figure 6-82b and change the font size to 20 point.

(continued)

In the Lab

Linking Slides, Inserting an AutoShape, and Setting Timings (*continued*)

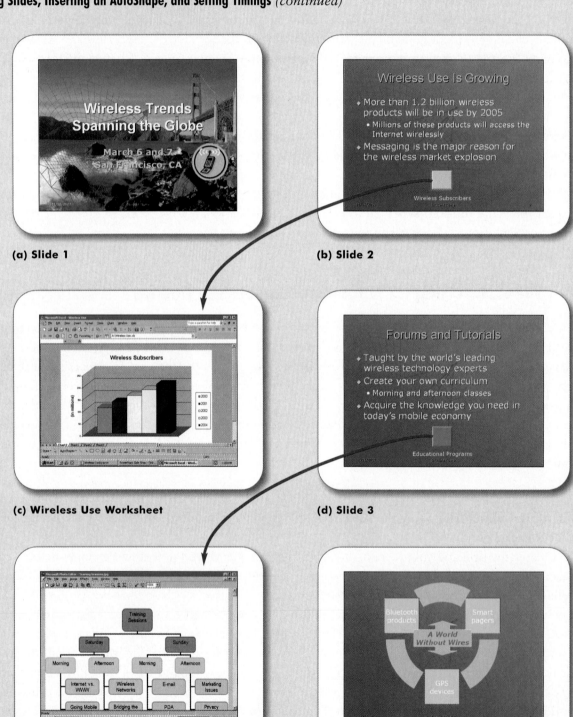

(a) Slide 1

(b) Slide 2

(c) Wireless Use Worksheet

(d) Slide 3

(e) Training Sessions Picture

(f) Slide 4

FIGURE 6-82

In the Lab

5. Insert a new slide and then enter the title and bulleted list shown in Figure 6-82d. Add an action button and hyperlink it to the Training Sessions picture (Figure 6-82e) on your Data Disk. Play the Wind sound when the mouse is clicked.

6. Change the button fill color to aqua, scale it to 90 %, and apply Shadow Style 6. Position the upper-left corner of the button at the intersection of the guides used for Slide 2. Add the caption shown in Figure 6-82d and change the font size to 20 point. Hide the guides.

7. Insert a new slide and apply the Blank slide layout. Insert the Cycle diagram, scale it to 130 %, and position it in the center of the slide. Add the text shown in Figure 6-82f to each of the areas marked, Click to add text. Apply the Square Shadows diagram style.

8. Click the AutoShapes button on the Drawing toolbar, point to Block Arrows, and then click Up-Down Arrow Callout (row 7, column 2). Click the center of the Cycle diagram, and then add the text shown in Figure 6-82f. Increase the font to 24 point and italicize the text. Change the font color to dark green (color 3 in the list) and then resize the AutoShape to fit the text. Add the Spinner entrance effect and 8 Point Star motion path to the AutoShape.

9. Set the slide timings to 30 seconds for Slide 1 and 15 seconds for the other three slides.

10. Set the show type as Browsed at a kiosk.

11. Add your name, today's date, and the slide number to the slide footer.

12. Apply the Float animation scheme to all slides. Save the presentation with the file name, Wireless Conference.

13. Run the slide show. When Slide 2 displays, click the action button to view the Excel chart. Click the Close button on the Wireless Use title bar to return to the presentation. When Slide 3 displays, click the action button to view the class schedule. If necessary, click the maximize button on the Training Sessions title bar. After you have viewed the training sessions, click the Close button on the Training Sessions title bar. When Slide 4 displays, review the information and wait for Slide 1 to display. When Slide 1 displays, press the ESC key.

14. Print handouts with two slides per page. Quit PowerPoint.

3 Inserting a Slide and Adding AutoShapes and Diagrams

Problem: Triathlon Training Techniques (T³) holds camps in Orlando, Florida, during the summer and winter months for athletes preparing to participate in triathlons. The training sessions feature quality instruction from world-class athletes and include demonstrations and lectures. Many camp participants compete in the Calumet Triathlon, which is held annually in November. T³ trainers have asked you to prepare a short slide show promoting their training camp. They have given you a file composed of four slides promoting the Calumet Triathlon, and they want you to insert one slide from that presentation in your new T³ presentation.

Instructions Part 1: Start PowerPoint and open the Calumet Triathlon presentation from the Data Disk. Slides 2 and 4 have information that can be presented visually using diagrams. Perform the tasks on the next page to modify these slides as shown in Figures 6-83a through 6-83d on the next page.

(continued)

In the Lab

Inserting a Slide and Adding AutoShapes and Diagrams *(continued)*

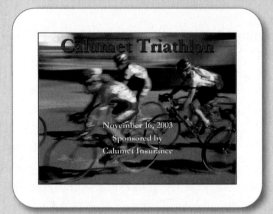

(a) Slide 1

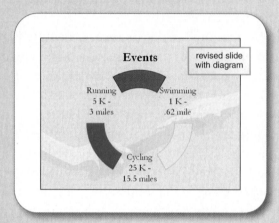

(b) Slide 2

(c) Slide 3

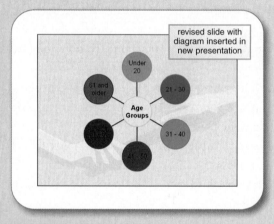

(d) Slide 4

FIGURE 6-83

1. Save the presentation with the new file name, Revised Calumet Triathlon. Click the Next Slide button to display Slide 2. Apply the Title Only slide layout and then delete the text placeholder. Insert a Cycle diagram and then add the text shown in Figure 6-83b to each of the areas marked, Click to add text. Change the font size to 32 point. Apply the Primary Colors diagram style. Scale the diagram to 125 %. Fit the diagram to contents.

2. Click the Slide 4 slide thumbnail on the Slides tab. Apply the Blank slide layout and then delete the title text and two text placeholders. Insert a Radial diagram. Click the Insert Shape button on the Diagram toolbar three times. Add the text shown in Figure 6-83d to each of the areas marked, Click to add text. Change the font to Arial. Bold the center core element. Apply the Primary Colors diagram style. Scale the diagram to 130 %. Fit the diagram to contents. Save the presentation again.

Instructions Part 2:   Perform the following tasks to create the presentation shown in Figures 6-84a through 6-84d.

In the Lab

1. Click the New button on the Formatting toolbar to create a new presentation. Save the presentation with the file name, Triathlon Camps. Apply the Pixel design template. Type the Slide 1 title and subtitle text shown in Figure 6-84a.

2. Create the T^3 AutoShape by clicking the AutoShape button on the Drawing toolbar, pointing to Flowchart, and then clicking the Flowchart: Manual Operation shape. Insert the shape in the white area above the title text placeholder. Size the AutoShape to a height of 1.75 inches and a width of 1.83 inches. Type T3 and then increase the font size to 72. Change the font to Bookman Old Style. Select the number 3. Superscript the number 3 by clicking Format on the menu bar and then clicking Font. When the Font dialog box displays, click Superscript in the Effects area and then click the OK button. Apply the Blinds entrance effect and have the effect Start After Previous. Apply the Spin emphasis effect and have the effect Start After Previous. Apply the Curvy Left motion path. Display the guides. Drag the horizontal guide to 3.25 inches above center and the vertical guide to 0.25 inch right of center. Drag the AutoShape so the top-left corner snaps to the guides.

(a) Slide 1

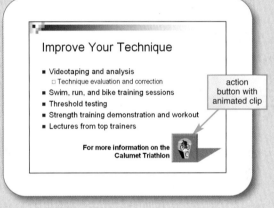

(b) Slide 2

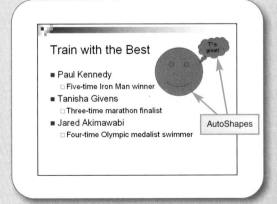

(c) Slide 3

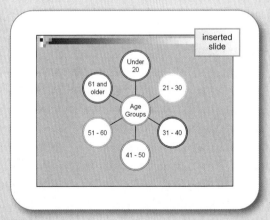

(d) Slide 4

FIGURE 6-84

(continued)

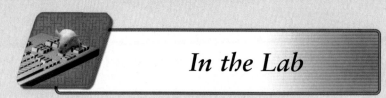

In the Lab

Inserting a Slide and Adding AutoShapes and Diagrams *(continued)*

3. Insert a new slide and then enter the title and body text shown in Figure 6-84b on the previous page. Add the Custom action button (row 1, column 1), and then hyperlink it to the Revised Calumet Triathlon presentation. When the Hyperlink to Slide dialog box displays, click 1. Calumet Triathlon and then click the OK button. Play the Drum Roll sound when the mouse is clicked. Size the button to 120 %. Apply Shadow Style 4 (row 1, column 4). Insert the animated bike clip, size it to 125 %, and then drag it to the middle of the action button. Group the action button and the clip.

4. Add the action button caption shown in Figure 6-84b. Click the Align Right button on the Formatting toolbar, select the caption text, and then bold the text and change the font size to 24 point.

5. Insert a new slide and then enter the title and body text shown in Figure 6-84c on the previous page. Insert the Smiley Face AutoShape (row 5, column 1) in the Basic Shapes category and size it to 250 %. If the AutoShape size is not correct, be certain the Lock aspect ratio check box in the Scale area is checked. Drag the horizontal guide to 2.58 inches above center and the vertical guide to 0.92 inch right of center. Drag the AutoShape so the top and left edges snap to the guides. Insert the Cloud Callout AutoShape (row 1, column 4) in the Callouts category and size it to 175 %. If the AutoShape size is not correct, be certain the Lock aspect ratio check box in the Scale area is checked. Drag the horizontal guide to 3.08 inches above center and the vertical guide to 3.08 inches right of center. Drag the AutoShape so the top and left edges snap to the guides. Add the text shown in Figure 6-84c to the Cloud Callout AutoShape. Hide the guides.

6. Insert Slide 4 from the Revised Calumet Triathlon presentation. Click the Radial diagram and then change the AutoFormat to Double Outline. Right-click the slide in an area other than the Radial diagram and then click Background on the shortcut menu. When the Background dialog box displays, click the Background fill box arrow, click the color light blue (color 8 in the row of available colors), and then click the Apply button.

7. Apply the Spin animation scheme to all slides in the new presentation. Save the presentation again. Display the Revised Calumet Triathlon presentation and then delete Slide 4. Right-click the runners clip on Slide 3, click Hyperlink on the shortcut menu, click Triathlon Camps in the Look in list, click the Address text box, and then type #Train with the Best at the end of the address so that the entire hyperlink address is Triathlon Camps.ppt#Train with the Best. Click the OK button. Save the Revised Calumet Triathlon presentation again.

8. Display and then run the Triathlon Camps presentation. When Slide 2 displays, click a blue area of the action button to run the Revised Calumet Triathlon presentation. After you have reviewed Slide 3 in the Calumet Triathlon presentation, click the clip to return to Slide 3 of the Triathlon Camps presentation. When the complete Slide 3 displays, right-click the slide, point to Pointer Options on the shortcut menu and then click Pen on the Pointer Options submenu. Click and make a check mark in front of each of the solid blue bullets, and then circle each athlete's name.

9. Print handouts for both presentations with two slides per page. Quit PowerPoint.

Cases and Places

The difficulty of these case studies varies:
▶ are the least difficult; ▶▶ are more difficult; and ▶▶▶ are the most difficult.

1 ▶ This past summer you joined the Midwest SUV Club. This organization sponsors many road rallies throughout the summer. At the early spring meeting, the members discuss and plan the first summer rally for June. You volunteer to help publicize the club's activities. You create two presentations, one with the file name, Off-Road Rally, and the second with the file name, Rally Information. The Off-Road Rally presentation contains two slides; Slide 2 contains four action buttons linking to one of four slides in the Rally Information slide show. The captions for these four action buttons are: Who sponsors the rally? What distance is covered? Where does the rally start? How is the scoring conducted? The first action button should link to Rally Information Slide 2, which has the title text, Midwest SUV Club. The body text states that Tanaka Kobiashi and Kenny Park founded the organization, which is composed of conscientious owners of off-road vehicles. Another item on this slide states that the members are safety minded, with excitement in mind. They hold yearly road rallies and vehicle exhibitions. The last item emphasizes that rallies bring friends together and help form new friendships. The second action button links to Slide 3, which has the title text, The Rally. The bulleted text states that a road rally is held each Saturday in June or on Sunday if the weather is inclement. Each rally's distance is approximately 300 miles. The winner is determined at the end of the month and is the individual with the most points. The third action button links to Slide 4, which has the title, Rally Departure Information. It states that the departure point is the Avery High School parking lot. Registration begins at 7:00 a.m., and technical information is provided from 7:30 a.m. to 8:00 a.m. The first car departs at 8:01 a.m. Awards are given at the end of the rally. The fourth action button links to Slide 5, which has the title, Scoring Points. This slide explains that each team consists of two members: a driver and a navigator. These two people may switch places if they are fatigued. Points are based on distance, time, and accomplishment. Accomplishment is defined as the number of directions that are followed. Road speed is not a factor. Slides 2, 3, 4, and 5 in the Rally Information slide show have an action button that hyperlinks back to Slide 2 of the Off-Road Rally slide show. Using the techniques introduced in this project, create these two slide shows. Enhance the presentations with sound and art clips and animation schemes.

2 ▶ Many employees telecommute, meaning they work some hours in an office and other hours at home. A recent survey found that 21 percent of telecommuters work at home at least 40 hours weekly, 10 percent between 30 to 39 hours, 24 percent between 20 to 29 hours, 31 percent between 10 to 19 hours, and 14 percent fewer than 10 hours. Sixty-one percent of employees say they would take a pay cut to work at home. Teleworkers cite many reasons for using this flexible employment option, including reduced gasoline or public transportation costs, less stress, the ability to work during unconventional hours, fewer distractions from office workers, and fewer clothing purchases and cleaning bills. The work practice has its negative aspects, however. They include lack of supervision, reduced contact with managers and co-workers, technical problems, and fewer opportunities for career advancement and raises. The highest proportions of telecommuters are in the New England, Mountain, and Pacific states. Using the techniques introduced in this project, create a slide show describing the telecommuting practice. Use a Target diagram to present the advantages of telecommuting and a Pyramid diagram to present the disadvantages. Create a Word table containing the hours employees spend telecommuting and an Excel table showing the growing trend in the number of telecommuters. Insert action buttons into one slide to hyperlink to these tables. Add an animation scheme and appropriate clips.

Cases and Places

3 ▶▶ Many home owners find satisfaction when they tackle remodeling and building projects themselves. The local home improvement store, Yancy's Home Center, sponsors several Do It Yourself (DIY) clinics throughout the year. As a part-time employee, you agree to help publicize these workshops by creating a short slide show that will run continuously at a kiosk near the service desk. The next clinic is designed to help customers select materials to build decks. Possible materials are cypress, cedar, and synthetics. Cypress is inexpensive and has a soft, even texture. It installs easily and accepts stains and preservatives easily. One negative aspect is that it requires periodic maintenance. Cedar, particularly Western Red Cedar, resists decay naturally and is a very stable, beautiful softwood. It stays flat, resists checking, is lightweight, and is easy to install. Both clear and knotty boards are available. Synthetics are durable because they are created from recycled wood and polymers. They are maintenance free and do not require staining. They will not split or rot and are resilient to weather. Synthetics are excellent to use around pools and hot tubs. Create a presentation using this information, and include an animation scheme and appropriate clips. Use the 32-Point Star AutoShape in your title slide and a footer with the current date, your name, and the slide number on all slides except the title slide. Include an action button to hyperlink to the Excel worksheet, Deck Estimator, which is on your Data Disk. Yancy's has several other PowerPoint presentations on a variety of topics that you can view. Locate the presentation, Yancy, which is on your Data Disk. Insert Slides 2 and 3 from this presentation into your slide show.

4 ▶▶ Recycling is a common practice in many households. Paper, plastics, and glass often are separated and disposed in special bins or bags. Electronic equipment, too, can be recycled. Your county has developed a special program for broken or obsolete computers and peripherals, office equipment and products, small home appliances, and entertainment equipment. These items include personal computers, printers, telephones, toasters, televisions, videocassette recorders, and video games. County officials will be collecting these items during the next two Saturdays at your local high school and a nearby shopping center. They will not accept air conditioners, humidifiers, and hazardous wastes. Develop a short slide show that can be viewed at kiosks throughout the county. Emphasize that recycling is important because electronic products' short useful lives produce waste, these items may contain hazardous materials, and many components can be salvaged. Include a slide with clips of acceptable products, and insert a green arrow AutoShape on this slide to call attention to these items. Include another slide with unacceptable products, and insert a red "No Symbol" AutoShape to emphasize that these products are not included in this recycling project.

5 ▶▶▶ Your economics instructor has assigned a project comparing three cellular telephone services. This task requires you to research monthly fees, the cost of minutes during peak and off-peak hours, current incentives, and the service area range. Then, you must develop a persuasive PowerPoint presentation showing the service with the most favorable plan for your needs. Create this slide show and include the following components: an action button to an Excel worksheet showing fees for various packages; an action button to a Word document promoting the features of a cellular telephone included in these packages; an action button to an Excel chart comparing the talk time and range; and a Cycle diagram showing the three best features of the service you selected. Set the slide timings to 10 seconds for Slide 1 and 15 seconds for the other slides in the presentation. Set the show type as Browsed at a kiosk. Include an animation scheme and appropriate clips.

Microsoft PowerPoint 2002

Importing Templates and Clips from the Microsoft Web Site

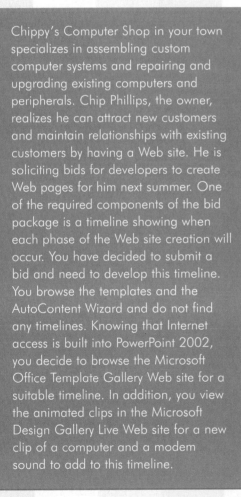

CASE PERSPECTIVE

Chippy's Computer Shop in your town specializes in assembling custom computer systems and repairing and upgrading existing computers and peripherals. Chip Phillips, the owner, realizes he can attract new customers and maintain relationships with existing customers by having a Web site. He is soliciting bids for developers to create Web pages for him next summer. One of the required components of the bid package is a timeline showing when each phase of the Web site creation will occur. You have decided to submit a bid and need to develop this timeline. You browse the templates and the AutoContent Wizard and do not find any timelines. Knowing that Internet access is built into PowerPoint 2002, you decide to browse the Microsoft Office Template Gallery Web site for a suitable timeline. In addition, you view the animated clips in the Microsoft Design Gallery Live Web site for a new clip of a computer and a modem sound to add to this timeline.

Introduction

Although the design templates included in PowerPoint 2002 are varied and versatile, they sometimes do not fit your needs. The Microsoft Clip Organizer likewise has a wide variety of picture images, but at times these images are not exactly to your liking. Microsoft has created the Template Gallery and the Design Gallery Live, which are sources of additional templates, pictures, sounds, and movie clips on the World Wide Web. To access the Template Gallery, you click the Templates on Microsoft.com hyperlink in the New Presentation task pane. To access the Design Gallery Live, you click the Clips Online hyperlink in the Insert Clip Art task pane. If you have an open connection to the Internet, PowerPoint connects you directly to the Template Gallery or the Design Gallery Live home pages (Figures 1a and 1b on the next page).

In this Web Feature, you download the three-month timeline and then modify the slide by adding an animated clip of a computer and a sound file from the Web, as shown in Figure 1c on the next page.

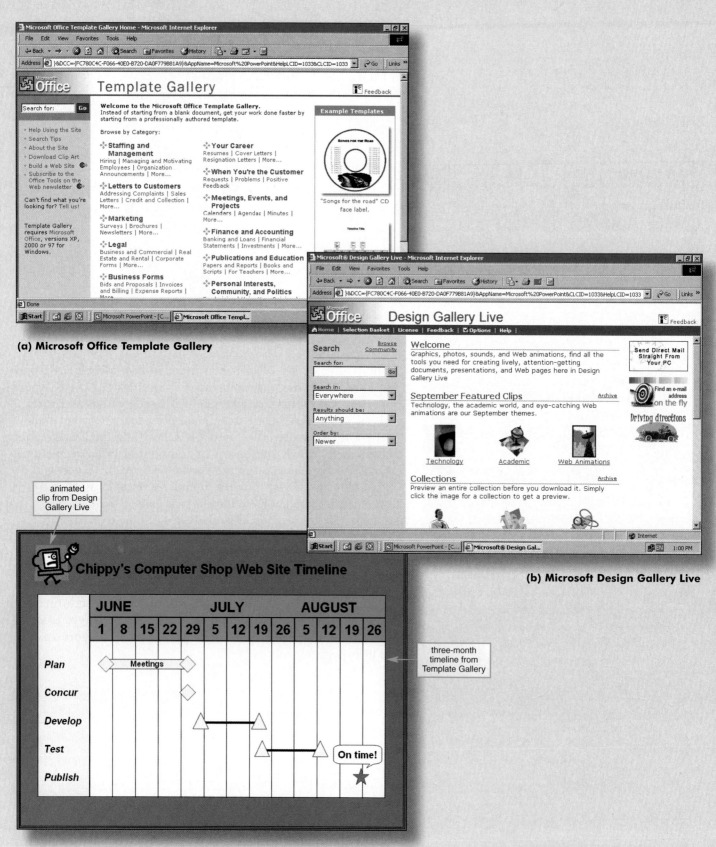

animated clip from Design Gallery Live

three-month timeline from Template Gallery

(a) Microsoft Office Template Gallery

(b) Microsoft Design Gallery Live

(c) Slide 1

FIGURE 1

Importing a Design Template from the Microsoft Office Template Gallery on the World Wide Web

Downloading a template from the Microsoft Office Template Gallery is an easy process. To begin, perform the following steps to start and customize a new PowerPoint presentation.

TO START AND CUSTOMIZE A NEW PRESENTATION

1 Click the Start button on the Windows taskbar, point to Programs on the Start menu, and then click Microsoft PowerPoint on the Programs submenu.

2 If the Language bar displays, click its Minimize button.

3 If the Standard and Formatting toolbars display on one row, click the Toolbar Options button on the right side of either toolbar and then click Show Buttons on Two Rows on the Toolbar Options menu.

A new presentation titled Presentation1 displays in the PowerPoint window.

Content experts have developed hundreds of templates for PowerPoint, Word, Excel, and Access. The templates are arranged in a variety of categories, including Staffing and Management, Marketing, Legal, Your Career, and Publications and Education. These categories are subdivided into organized groupings. For example, the Stationery, Labels, and Cards category is subdivided into the Business Cards, Labels, Fax and Transmission Covers, Cards and Binders, Letterhead and Envelopes, and For the holidays categories. Three timelines are included in the Calendars subcategory within the Meetings, Events, and Projects category.

To use the Microsoft Office Template Gallery and Design Gallery Live Web sites, you must have access to the World Wide Web through an **Internet service provider (ISP)** and then use **Web browser** software to find the Microsoft site. This project uses **Microsoft Internet Explorer** for the Web browser. If you do not have Internet access, your instructor will provide the template used in this part of the project. To simplify connecting to the Template Gallery, the New Presentation task pane contains a Templates on Microsoft.com hyperlink to connect directly to the Template Gallery Web site.

Connecting to the Microsoft Office Template Gallery Web Site

You want to use a template with a three-month timeline. Once you connect to the Web, the Microsoft Office Template Gallery Live home page displays. A **home page** is a specially designed page that serves as a starting point for a Web site. Microsoft updates this home page frequently to reflect additions and features.

Perform the steps on the next page to open the New Presentation task pane, if necessary, connect to the World Wide Web, and then display the Microsoft Office Template Gallery home page.

More About

Templates

Microsoft states that users frequently visit the Office Update Web site to request templates. The initial templates in the Template Gallery were created based on this customer feedback, and Microsoft promises to continue to add new templates to the Web site. If you need a specific template, request one using the Suggestion/Feedback area of the Template Gallery.

More About

Creating Templates

Microsoft partnered with industry leaders to create the hundreds of templates on the Template Gallery Web site. For example, Avery Dennison helped create templates that work with Avery brand labels and other printing supplies, ranging from business cards to CD-ROM labels. Lawoffice.com designed the legal forms and documents and the connection to local attorneys who can provide legal advice in using these forms.

To Connect to the Microsoft Office Template Gallery Web Site

1   **If the New Presentation task pane does not display, click File on the menu bar and then point to New.**

The File menu displays (Figure 2). You want to open the New Presentation task pane and then connect to the Microsoft Web site.

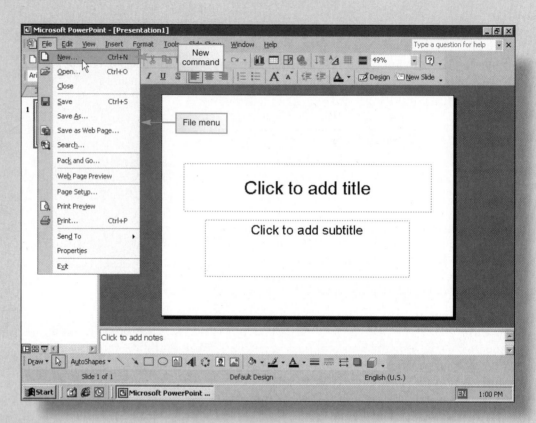

FIGURE 2

2   **Click New. When the New Presentation task pane displays, point to Templates on Microsoft.com in the New from template area.**

The New Presentation task pane displays (Figure 3). If the Templates on Microsoft.com hyperlink does not display, point to the down arrow at the bottom of the task pane.

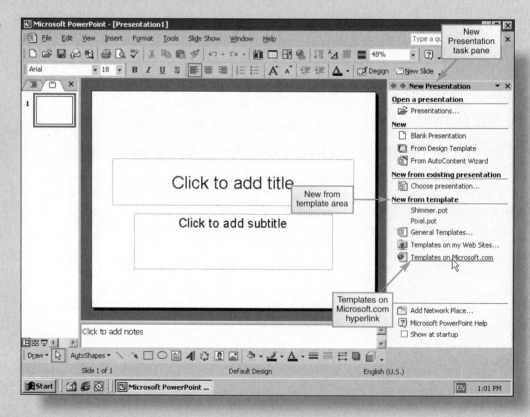

FIGURE 3

3 **Click Templates on Microsoft.com. Connect to the World Wide Web as required by your browser software and ISP. Point to the Calendars hyperlink in the Meetings, Events, and Projects category.**

If you are using a modem, a dialog box displays that connects you to the Web via your ISP. If you are connected directly to the Web through a computer network, the dialog box does not display. Microsoft Internet Explorer displays the Microsoft Office Template Gallery home page, which contains information about Microsoft Office Template Gallery features (Figure 4). The Calendars link is underlined and has the font color red.

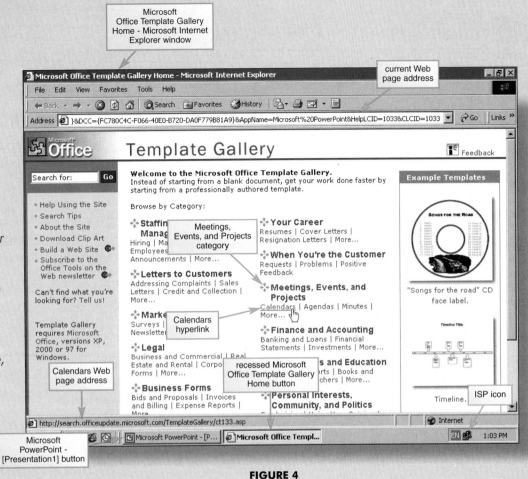

FIGURE 4

The Template Gallery contains hundreds of templates. To find a specific template, you can browse the categories or perform a search by typing a description of the content you want to find. When you locate a desired template, preview the template and then click the Edit in Office button to jump to a Microsoft Office program. You then can customize and edit the template. When you open this new document, the Template Gallery displays a list of hyperlinks in your Web browser. This list may have links to related templates, Help topics about using the Template Gallery, features in the template, and sign-up information to learn about new templates.

Locating and Downloading a Template

Templates are located by browsing the categories or by using keywords to search for a particular type of file. In this Web feature, you will locate a timeline template by browsing the Calendars subcategory in Meetings, Events, and Projects category.

When you find a template to add to your presentation, you can **download**, or copy, it instantly by previewing the template and then clicking the Edit in Microsoft PowerPoint button. Perform the steps on the next page to locate and download the three-month timeline template in the Template Gallery.

Templates

Although many varieties of design templates are available in PowerPoint 2002 and the Microsoft Office Template Gallery, many more are available on Web sites. Designers create these templates and allow you to download and then apply them to your presentations. To view some of these templates, visit the PowerPoint 2002 More About Web page (scsite.com/pp2002/more.htm) and then click Templates.

Steps **To Locate and Download a Template Gallery Template**

1 **Click the Calendars subcategory. When the Calendars page displays, click the down arrow to scroll and then point to Timeline for three months (PowerPoint).**

The Timeline for three months template is required for this project (Figure 5). Other PowerPoint templates in the Calendar subcategory are timelines for six and twelve months.

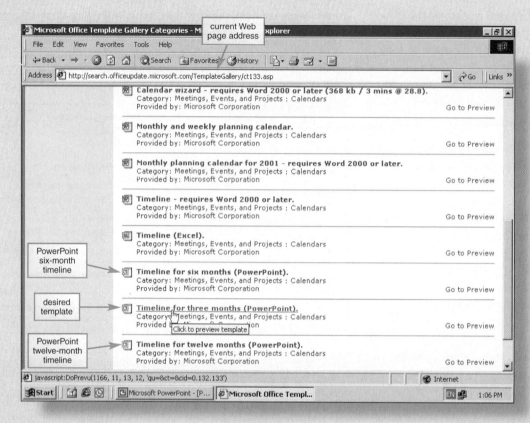

FIGURE 5

2 **Click Timeline for three months (PowerPoint). If the Security Warning dialog box displays asking you to install and run "Microsoft Office Tools on the Web Control," click the Yes button. If the End-User License Agreement for Templates displays, read the agreement and then click the Accept button. Point to the Edit in Microsoft PowerPoint hyperlink.**

Once connected to the Web, the Microsoft Office Template Gallery Live home page displays the Microsoft End-User License Agreement. When you click the Accept button, the Microsoft End-User License Agreement area no longer displays. The Timeline for three months template is previewed in the Web page (Figure 6).

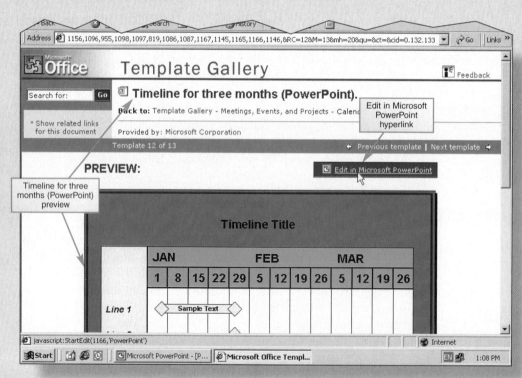

FIGURE 6

<table>
<tr><td>

3 **Click the Edit in Microsoft PowerPoint hyperlink. Click the Close button in the New Presentation task pane.**

PowerPoint opens a new presentation, downloads the Timeline for three months (PowerPoint) template, and displays it in Slide 1 (Figure 7).

</td><td>

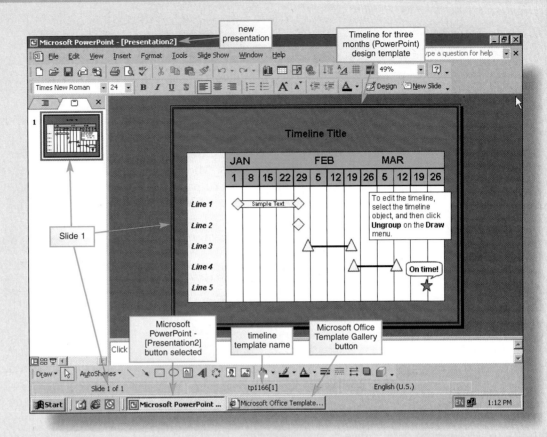

</td></tr>
</table>

FIGURE 7

Saving the Presentation

You now should save the presentation because you applied a design template. The following steps summarize how to save a presentation.

TO SAVE A PRESENTATION

1 Click the Save button on the Standard toolbar.

2 Type `Chippy Timeline` in the File name text box.

3 Click the Save in box arrow. Click 3½ Floppy (A:) in the Save in list.

4 Click the Save button in the Save As dialog box.

The presentation is saved on the floppy disk in drive A with the file name Chippy Timeline. This file name displays on the title bar.

The Chippy Timeline displays in Slide 1. The next section describes downloading clips from the Microsoft Design Gallery Live Web site.

More About

The End-User License Agreement

When you view the Microsoft Office Template Gallery for the first time, you may be asked to read the Microsoft End-User License Agreement (EULA). When you click the Accept button, you agree to abide by the copyright restrictions Microsoft imposes to protect the use of its software. Read the EULA to see what rights and restrictions you have to use the templates found at this site. For more information, visit the PowerPoint 2002 More About Web page (scsite.com/pp2002/more.htm) and then click EULA.

More About

Downloaded Clips

The clips you download while working on your PowerPoint presentation can be used in other Microsoft Office applications. For example, the computer you import in this project can be part of a flyer created in Microsoft Word, and the modem sound can play while users view a Microsoft Excel chart. The clips also can be used and reused in Microsoft Publisher, Microsoft FrontPage, Microsoft PhotoDraw, and Microsoft Works.

Importing Clips from the Microsoft Design Gallery Live on the World Wide Web

The Microsoft Clip Organizer is a useful source for drawings, photographs, sounds, video, and other media files. Many companies provide clip art images on the Web; some sites offer clips free of charge, and others charge a fee.

For additional clips, Microsoft maintains a Web site called the Design Gallery Live that contains clips of pictures, photographs, sounds, and videos. To use the Microsoft Design Gallery Live Web site, as with the Template Gallery Web site, you must have access to an ISP and then use a Web browser. If you do not have Internet access, your instructor will provide the two clips used in this part of the project.

Connecting to the Microsoft Design Gallery Live Web Site

To simplify connecting to the Design Gallery Live Web site, the Insert Clip Art task pane contains a Clips Online hyperlink. You want to insert a motion clip of a computer and a sound file into Slide 1. Once you connect to the Web, the Microsoft Design Gallery Live home page displays. Microsoft updates this home page frequently to reflect seasons, holidays, new collections, artists, special offers, and events.

Perform the following steps to open the Insert Clip Art task pane, connect to the World Wide Web, and then display the Microsoft Design Gallery Live home page.

Steps **To Connect to the Microsoft Design Gallery Live Web Site**

1 **Click the Insert Clip Art button on the Drawing toolbar. Point to Clips Online in the Insert Clip Art task pane.**

The Insert Clip Art task pane displays (Figure 8).

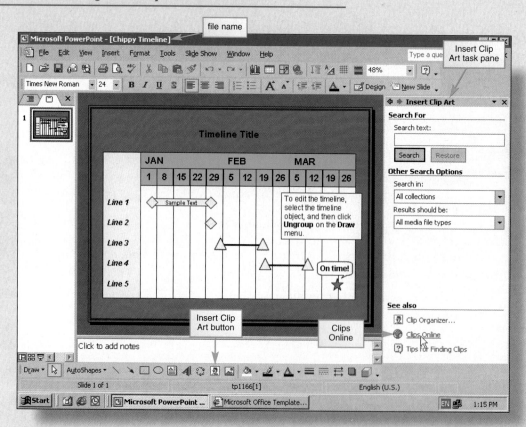

FIGURE 8

2 **Click Clips Online. If necessary, click the OK button in the Connect to Web for More Clip Art, Photos, Sounds dialog box and connect to the Internet. When the Microsoft Design Gallery Live home page displays, if necessary maximize the screen, read the Addendum to the Microsoft End-User License Agreement, and then click the Accept button.**

If you are using a modem and are not already connected to the Web, a dialog box displays that connects you to the Web via your ISP. If you are connected directly to the Web through a computer network, the dialog box does not display. Once connected to the Web, the Microsoft

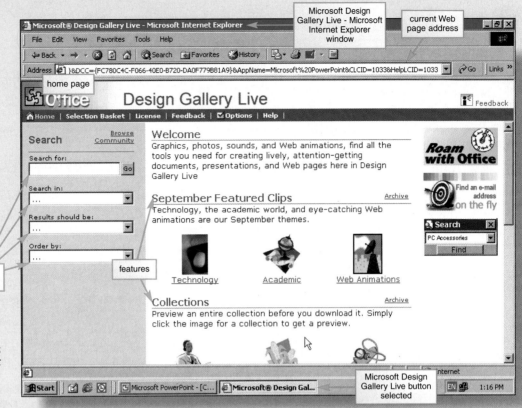

FIGURE 9

Design Gallery Live home page displays the Addendum to the Microsoft End-User License Agreement. When you click the Accept button, the Microsoft End-User License Agreement area no longer displays. The home page displays information about the Microsoft Design Gallery Live features and boxes to locate specific types of clips (Figure 9).

Searching for and Downloading Microsoft Design Gallery Live Clips

The Microsoft Design Gallery Live is similar to the Microsoft Office Template Gallery and the Microsoft Clip Organizer in that you can use keywords to search for clips. You want to locate a motion clip animating a computer and a sound clip containing the sound of a modem. You first will search the Microsoft Design Gallery Live for motion files with the keyword, computers. Then, you will search for sound files with the keyword, technology.

When you find a clip to add to your presentation, you can download it instantly to the Microsoft Clip Organizer on your computer by clicking the Immediate Download icon below the desired clip. You also can select several clips individually and then download them simultaneously. In this project, you want to download motion and sound clips, so you will choose a motion file and then select the check box below the clip to add the file to the selection basket. The **selection basket** holds your selections temporarily until you are ready to add them to your presentation. You then will add the sound clip to the selection basket. The downloaded clips will be added to the Microsoft Clip Organizer in the Downloaded Clips category. To remove a clip from the selection basket, clear the clip's check box.

Perform the steps on the next page to search for clips in the Microsoft Design Gallery Live Web site.

More About

Accepting the EULA

When you accept the terms of the Microsoft End-User License Agreement, your computer sends a message to the Microsoft Design Gallery Live Web site stating that you agree to the licensing restrictions. Microsoft, in turn, sends a message, called a cookie, to your computer so that you will not be asked to accept the EULA each time you visit this Web site. If you are using Internet Explorer 4.0 or later and are asked to accept the agreement each time you go to this site, your computer probably has been instructed not to accept cookies.

1 **Click the Results should be box arrow in the Microsoft Design Gallery Live window. Point to Motion in the list.**

Microsoft groups the clips in five categories: Anything, Clip Art, Photos, Sounds, and Motion (Figure 10).

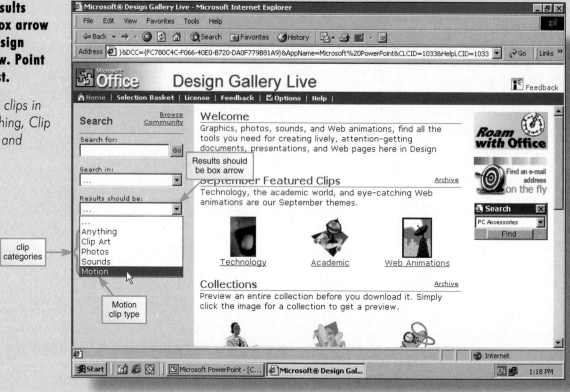

FIGURE 10

2 **Click Motion. Click the Search for text box and type** `computer` **in the box. Point to the Go button (Figure 11).**

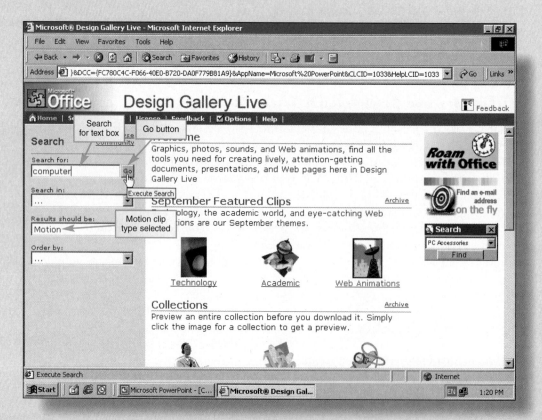

FIGURE 11

3 **Click the Go button. When the search results display, click the check box below the purple animated walking computer and plug. Click the Results should be box arrow. Point to Sounds in the list.**

Design Gallery Live executes the search and displays the results (Figure 12). When you click the check box associated with the thumbnail-sized clip, the motion clip is added to the selection basket, as indicated by the Download 1 Clip hyperlink. The search status displays at the upper-right corner of the page and indicates the number of pages of clips matching the search criteria. The number below each file name is the clip's file size.

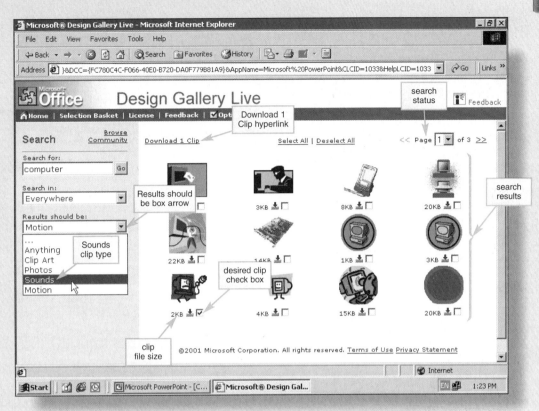

FIGURE 12

4 **Click Sounds. Click the Search for text box, select the current text, and then type** technology **in the box. Click the Go button.**

Design Gallery Live executes the search. After a few moments, several speaker icons with the keyword, technology, display (Figure 13). The speaker icons identify the sound clips. The hyperlink below each clip is its file name. The numbers below each file name are the clip's estimated download time and file size.

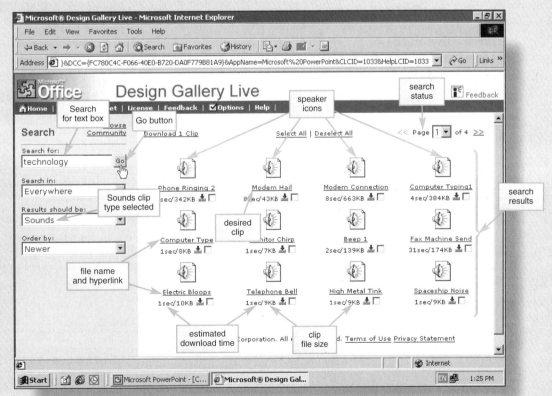

FIGURE 13

5 Click the check box below the clip with the file name, Modem Hail. Point to the Download 2 Clips hyperlink.

When you click the check box, the sound clip is added to the selection basket, as indicated by the underlined Download 2 Clips hyperlink that displays with the font color red (Figure 14).

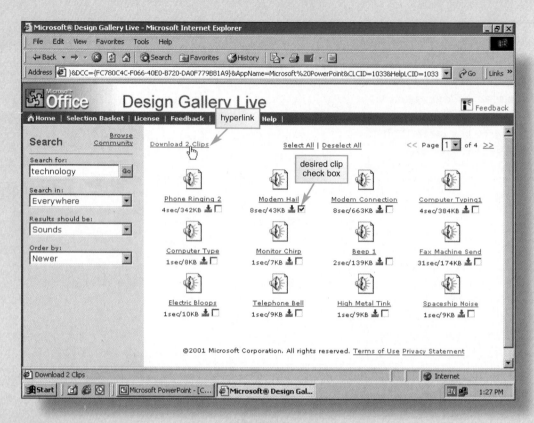

FIGURE 14

6 Click the Download 2 Clips hyperlink. Point to the Download Now! button in the Selection Basket sheet.

Clicking the button will download the two clips stored temporarily in the selection basket (Figure 15).

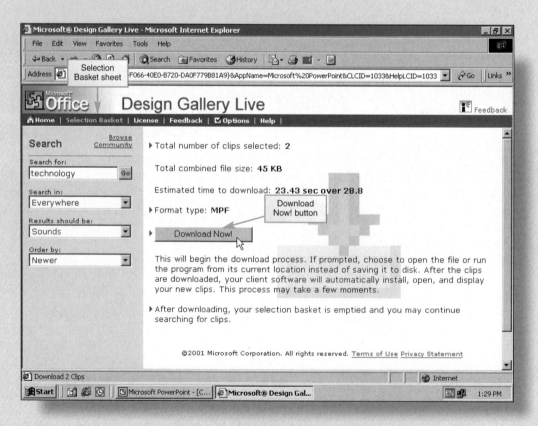

FIGURE 15

7 **Click the Download Now! button. Point to the Microsoft PowerPoint - [Chippy Timeline] button on the taskbar.**

PowerPoint downloads the two clips into the Science & Technology category of the Microsoft Clip Organizer (Figure 16).

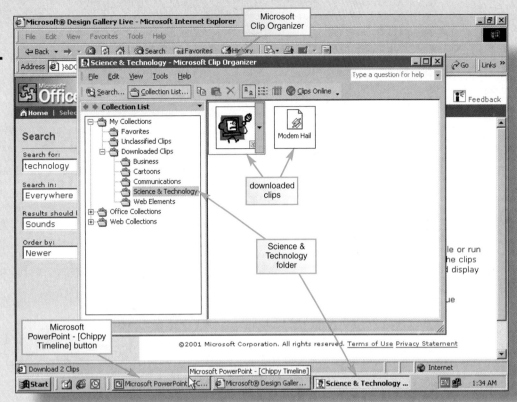

FIGURE 16

8 **Click the Microsoft PowerPoint - [Chippy Timeline] button. Click the Search text text box in the Insert Clip Art task pane, type** computer **and then point to the Search button (Figure 17).**

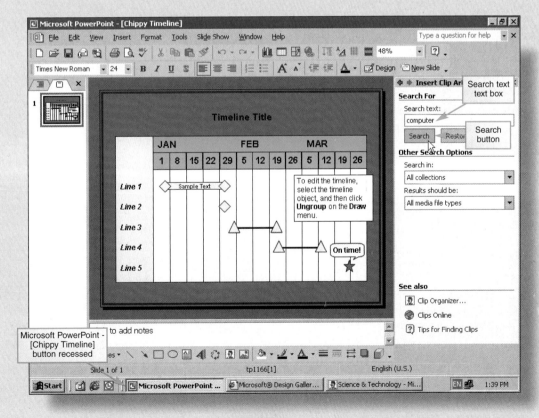

FIGURE 17

9 **Click the Search button. Click the computer clip and then point to the Modem Hail thumbnail.**

When you click the computer clip, PowerPoint inserts the clip into Slide 1 (Figure 18).

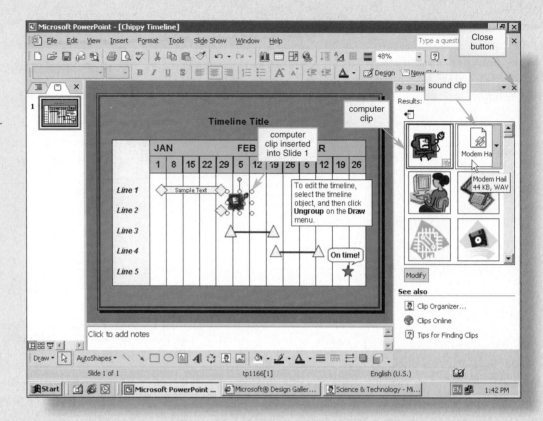

FIGURE 18

10 **Click the Modem Hail clip. When the Microsoft PowerPoint dialog box displays, click the Yes button to play the sound automatically. Click the Close button on the Insert Clip Art task pane title bar.**

The speaker icon displays on top of the animated computer in Slide 1 (Figure 19). You want the music to play automatically when Slide 1 displays. Microsoft Design Gallery Live and the Microsoft Clip Organizer Science & Technology folder still are open, and you are connected to the ISP.

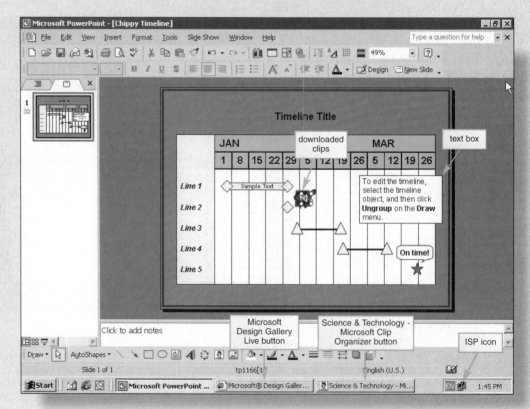

FIGURE 19

Quitting a Web Session

Once you have downloaded the template and clips, quit the Web session. Because Windows displays buttons on the taskbar for each open application, you quickly can quit an application by right-clicking an application button and then clicking the Close button on the shortcut menu. Perform the following steps to quit your current Web session.

TO QUIT A WEB SESSION

1 Right-click the Microsoft Design Gallery Live - Microsoft Internet Explorer button on the taskbar. If you are not using Microsoft Internet Explorer, right-click the button for your browser.

2 Click Close on the shortcut menu.

3 When the dialog box displays, click the Yes button to disconnect. If your ISP displays a different dialog box, terminate your connection to your ISP.

4 Right-click the Science & Technology - Microsoft Clip Organizer button on the taskbar.

5 Click Close on the shortcut menu.

The browser software and Microsoft Clip Organizer close, and the ISP connection is terminated.

Slide 1 displays with the two downloaded objects in the center of the timeline template. The speaker icon represents the Modem Hail sound file.

Editing Text and Moving the Clips

You want to edit the default timeline text and then move the speaker icon to the lower-right corner of the slide and the computer to the upper-left corner. Perform the following steps to edit the text and move the clips to these respective locations.

TO EDIT TEXT AND MOVE THE CLIPS

1 Triple-click the text, Timeline Title, at the top of Slide 1 and then type `Chippy's Computer Shop Web Site Timeline` to replace the current text.

2 Click each of the text items in Slide 1 and replace the text with the words and numbers shown in Figure 20 on the next page.

3 Drag the speaker icon to the lower-right corner of Slide 1.

4 Scale the computer clip to 160 % and then drag it to the upper-left corner of Slide 1.

5 Click the text box with instructions of how to edit the timeline, click the text box border, and then press the DELETE key.

The revised text and downloaded clips display in the appropriate locations in the Slide 1 timeline (Figure 20).

More About

Quick Reference

For a table that lists how to complete tasks covered in this book using the mouse, menu, shortcut menu, and keyboard, see the Quick Reference Summary at the back of this book, or visit the Shelly Cashman Series Office XP Web page (scsite.com/offxp/qr.htm) and then click Microsoft PowerPoint 2002.

More About

Common Questions

Many Web sites feature frequently asked questions (FAQs) about PowerPoint and provide a wealth of information and tips. They give answers to common PowerPoint questions, provide templates and add-ins, and contain tutorials. Some sites allow users to submit questions and to comment about the Web pages' content. To view some of these FAQs, visit the PowerPoint 2002 More About Web page (scsite.com/pp2002/more.htm) and then click FAQ.

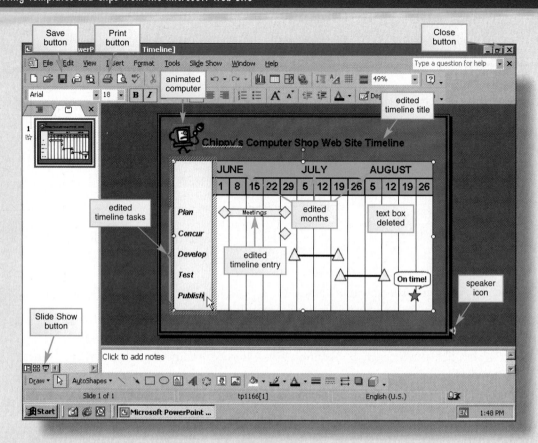

FIGURE 20

Running and Printing the Presentation

The changes to the presentation are complete. Save the presentation again before running the slide show.

Microsoft Certification

The Microsoft Office User Specialist (MOUS) Certification program provides an opportunity for you to obtain a valuable industry credential — proof that you have the PowerPoint 2002 skills required by employers. For more information, see Appendix E or visit the Shelly Cashman Series MOUS Web page at scsite.com/offxp/cert.htm.

Running a Slide Show

To verify the timeline looks as expected, run the presentation. Perform the following step to run the Chippy Timeline slide show.

TO RUN A SLIDE SHOW

1 Click the Slide Show button in the lower-left corner of the PowerPoint window. When Slide 1 displays, click the slide anywhere except on the Pop-up menu buttons.

The presentation displays the animated computer, plays the sound file, and then returns to normal view when finished.

The presentation is complete. If the timeline elements do not display in the desired locations, you can move them on the slide. The next step is to print the presentation slide.

Printing a Presentation Slide

Perform the following step to print the timeline.

TO PRINT A PRESENTATION SLIDE

1 Click the Print button on the Standard toolbar.

Slide 1 prints.

Quitting PowerPoint

To quit PowerPoint, perform the following steps.

TO QUIT POWERPOINT

1 Click the Close button on the Microsoft PowerPoint title bar.

2 If the Microsoft PowerPoint dialog box displays, click the Yes button to save changes made since the last save.

PowerPoint closes.

CASE PERSPECTIVE SUMMARY

The timeline now has edited text, the modem sound, and an animated computer in Slide 1. The design template from the Template Gallery allowed you to create this timeline easily. The clips from the Microsoft Design Gallery Live Web site enhance the slide show and should catch Chip Phillips's attention.

Web Feature Summary

This Web Feature introduced importing design templates and sound and animation clips from the Microsoft Office Template Gallery and the Microsoft Design Gallery Live sites on the World Wide Web. You began by opening a new presentation and then accessing the Template Gallery home page by clicking the Templates on Microsoft.com hyperlink in the New Presentation task pane. You then downloaded the Timeline for three months (PowerPoint) design template. The next step was to access the Microsoft Design Gallery Live home page on the World Wide Web by clicking the Clips Online hyperlink in the Insert Clip Art task pane. Once connected to the Microsoft Design Gallery Live home page, you searched for an animated computer and a technology sound. Then you imported these clips to the Clip Organizer by downloading the files from the Web page. You moved the clips to appropriate locations in Slide 1, edited the timeline text, and then quit the Web session by closing the browser software and disconnecting from the ISP. Finally, you saved the presentation, ran the presentation in slide show view to check for continuity, printed the presentation slide, and quit PowerPoint.

What You Should Know

Having completed this Web Feature, you now should be able to perform the following tasks:

▶ Connect to the Microsoft Design Gallery Live Web Site *(PPW 3.08)*

▶ Connect to the Microsoft Office Template Gallery Web Site *(PPW 3.04)*

▶ Edit Text and Move the Clips *(PPW 3.15)*

▶ Locate and Download a Template Gallery Template *(PPW 3.06)*

▶ Print a Presentation Slide *(PPW 3.17)*

▶ Quit PowerPoint *(PPW 3.17)*

▶ Quit a Web Session *(PPW 3.15)*

▶ Run a Slide Show *(PPW 3.16)*

▶ Save a Presentation *(PPW 3.07)*

▶ Search for and Download Microsoft Design Gallery Live Clips *(PPW 3.10)*

▶ Start and Customize a New Presentation *(PPW 3.03)*

In the Lab

1 Importing a Template and Sound and Motion Clips

Problem: Real estate agents devote much time explaining the home-buying process to first-time buyers. The agents at Heartland Realty have asked you to enhance the presentation you created in Project 6. They believe a Personal Budget worksheet would help home buyers accurately assess their financial situations. In addition, they believe the sound of a coin dropping and an animated clip from the Microsoft Design Gallery Live Web site would make the presentation even more impressive. You decide to use the Microsoft Web Site to find appropriate clips and to modify Slides 3 and 5 of the House Buying presentation.

Instructions: Start PowerPoint and then perform the following steps.

1. Open the House Buying presentation shown in Figures 6-1a through 6-1h on page PP 6.05 that you created in Project 6. (If you did not complete Project 6, see your instructor for a copy of the presentation.)
2. Save the House Buying presentation with the new file name, Enhanced House Buying.
3. Display Slide 3, click View on the menu bar, click Task Pane, and then click Templates on Microsoft.com in the New Presentation task pane. If necessary, connect to the Internet. When the Template Gallery displays, download the Personal Budget worksheet from the Budgeting subcategory in the Finance and Accounting category. Save the worksheet with the file name, Personal Budget.
4. Click the Microsoft PowerPoint - [Enhanced House Buying] button on the taskbar. Add an action button to the upper-right corner of Slide 3 and hyperlink it to the Personal Budget file. Add the caption, What is my Personal Budget? Format the caption font to Bookman Old Style, the font size to 20 point, the font color to black, and no effects. Apply Shadow Style 14 to the action button with a ¾ pt line.
5. Display Slide 5. Click the Insert Clip Art button on the Drawing toolbar, and then click the Clips Online hyperlink in the Insert Clip Art task pane.
6. Search for motion clips with the keyword, money. Select a clip with a rotating coin. Then search for sound clips with the same keyword, money. Select the Coin Drops 1 clip. Download the two clips.
7. Click the Microsoft PowerPoint - [Enhanced House Buying] button on the taskbar. Insert the clips into Slide 5, and have the sound play automatically. Size the rotating coin clip to 300 %. Move the speaker icon to the lower-right corner of Slide 5, and then move the coin clip above the Tax Savings shape.
8. Disconnect from the Web and save the file again.
9. Run the slide show and then print Slides 3 and 5. Quit PowerPoint.

In the Lab

2 Importing a Template and Multiple Sound and Motion Clips

Problem: Administrators running the Triathlon Training Techniques (T³) training camps are pleased with the Triathlon Camps presentation you developed in the In the Lab 3 exercise in Project 6. They want you to add more clips and an action button that hyperlinks to a weight-training log. You decide to search the Microsoft Design Gallery Live Web site for the clips and the Microsoft Office Template Gallery for a training log.

Instructions: Start PowerPoint and then perform the following steps.

1. Open the Triathlon Camps presentation shown in Figures 6-83a through 6-83d and 6-84a through 6-84d on pages PP 6.68 and PP 6.69 that you created in Project 6. (If you did not complete this exercise, see your instructor for a copy of the presentation.) Save the Triathlon Camps presentation with the new file name, Revised Triathlon Camps.

2. Click the Insert Clip Art button on the Drawing toolbar and then click Clips Online in the Insert Clip Art task pane. Search for a photo clip with the keyword, swimming, and select a clip with people swimming at a beach. Search for a motion clip with the keyword, marathons, and select a clip with a male runner. Search for a sound clip with the file name, splashes. Download these three clips.

3. Click the Microsoft PowerPoint - [Revised Triathlon Camps] button on the taskbar. Click View on the menu bar, click Task Pane, and then click Templates on Microsoft.com in the New Presentation task pane. If necessary, connect to the Internet. When the Template Gallery displays, download the Weight training log located in the Hobbies, Sports, and Collections subcategory of the Personal Interests, Community, and Politics category. Click the Edit in Microsoft Word button hyperlink, and then save the document with the file name, Weight Training Log.

4. Click the Microsoft PowerPoint - [Revised Triathlon Camps] button on the taskbar. Display Slide 2 and insert the swimming photo. Size the swimming photo to 60 %. Move the swimming clip to the upper-right corner of the slide. Insert the Splash sound clip into Slide 2 and have the sound play automatically. Move the speaker icon to the lower-left corner of Slide 2.

5. Click the Next Slide button to display Slide 3. Add an action button to the lower-left corner and hyperlink it to the Weight Training Log file. Add the caption, Weight Training Log, to the right of the action button. Format the caption font to Arial, the font size to 24 point, and the font color to black. Bold and left-align the text. Apply Shadow Style 3 to the action button.

6. Insert the marathon clip. Size the runner to 15 % and then drag the clip to the middle of the action button. If the clip image disappears, right-click the action button and then click Bring Forward on the shortcut menu. Group the action button and the clip.

7. Disconnect from the Web and save the file again.

8. Run the slide show and then print Slides 2 and 3. Quit PowerPoint.

In the Lab

3 Modifying a Personal Presentation

Problem: You have been asked to speak to the Campus Computer Club about the usefulness of Microsoft PowerPoint. You decide to prepare a slide show to enhance your speech and want the first slide to list your name and qualifications. The Microsoft Office Template Gallery has an appropriate template, so you download it, add clips from the Design Gallery Live, and then edit the text.

Instructions: Start PowerPoint and perform the following tasks.

1. Start a new presentation. Connect to the Microsoft Office Template Gallery Web site and then locate and download the Introducing and thanking a speaker template. This template is found in the Preparations subcategory of the Meetings, Events, and Projects category.
2. Search the Microsoft Design Gallery Live Web site for appropriate motion, picture, and sound clips. Add these clips to the slide.
3. Edit the Slide 1 text to reflect your qualifications.
4. Delete the text in the notes pane and then add information about yourself.
5. Save the presentation with the file name, Introducing Yourself.
6. Run the slide show and then print the slide. Quit PowerPoint.

APPENDIX A
Microsoft PowerPoint Help System

Using the PowerPoint Help System

This appendix shows you how to use the PowerPoint Help system. At anytime while you are using PowerPoint, you can interact with its Help system and display information on any PowerPoint topic. It is a complete reference manual at your fingertips.

As shown in Figure A-1, you can access PowerPoint's Help system in four primary ways:

1. Ask a Question box on the menu bar
2. Function key F1 on the keyboard
3. Microsoft PowerPoint Help command on the Help menu
4. Microsoft PowerPoint Help button on the Standard toolbar

If you use the Ask a Question box on the menu bar, PowerPoint responds by opening the Microsoft PowerPoint Help window, which gives you direct access to its Help system. If you use one of the other three ways to access PowerPoint's Help system, PowerPoint responds in one of two ways:

1. If the Office Assistant is turned on, then the Office Assistant displays with a balloon (lower-right side in Figure A-1).
2. If the Office Assistant is turned off, then the Microsoft PowerPoint Help window opens (lower-left side in Figure A-1).

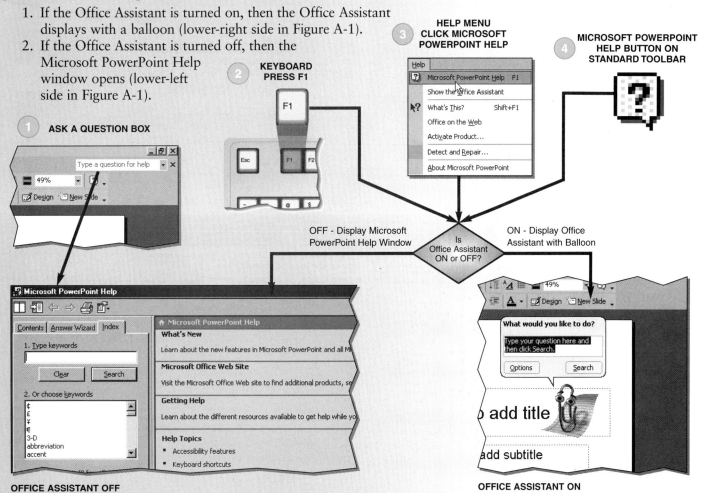

FIGURE A-1

The best way to familiarize yourself with the PowerPoint Help system is to use it. The next several pages show examples of how to use the Help system. Following the examples is a set of exercises titled Use Help that will sharpen your PowerPoint Help system skills.

Ask a Question Box

The **Ask a Question box** on the right side of the menu bar lets you type questions in your own words, or you can type terms, such as animation scheme, Outline tab, or bulleted list. PowerPoint responds by displaying a list of topics related to the term(s) you entered. The following steps show how to use the Ask a Question box to obtain information on bullet styles.

Steps **To Obtain Help Using the Ask a Question Box**

1 **Click the Ask a Question box on the right side of the menu bar, type** bullet styles, **and then press the ENTER key. Point to the Change the bullet style in a list link in the Ask a Question list.**

The Ask a Question list displays (Figure A-2). Your list may display with different entries. Clicking the See more link displays additional links.

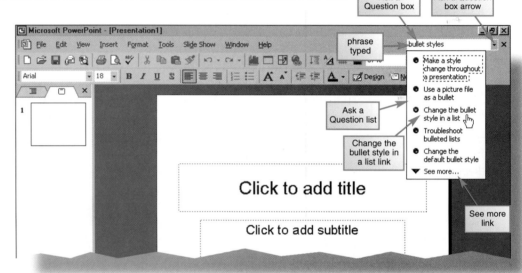

FIGURE A-2

2 **Click Change the bullet style in a list. When the Microsoft PowerPoint Help window displays, double-click its title bar to maximize it. Click the Contents tab on the Contents sheet. Point to the Change the bullet style for a single list link.**

PowerPoint opens a Microsoft PowerPoint Help window that provides information about changing bullet styles (Figure A-3).

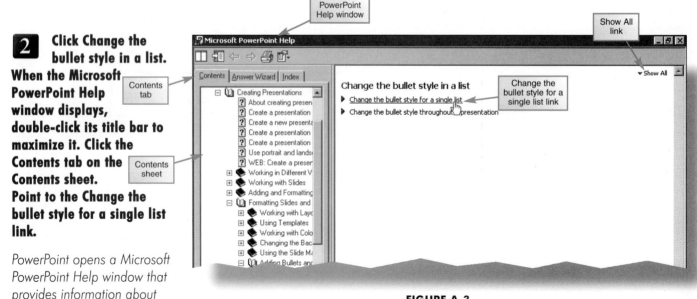

FIGURE A-3

3 **Click Change the bullet style for a single list. Read the information on this topic. Point to the Close button on the Microsoft PowerPoint Help window title bar.**

The Microsoft PowerPoint Help window provides information about changing the bullet style in a list (Figure A-4). You can click the links in item three to obtain additional information on changing the bullet character, size, or color.

4 **Click the Close button.**

The Microsoft PowerPoint Help window closes and the presentation is active.

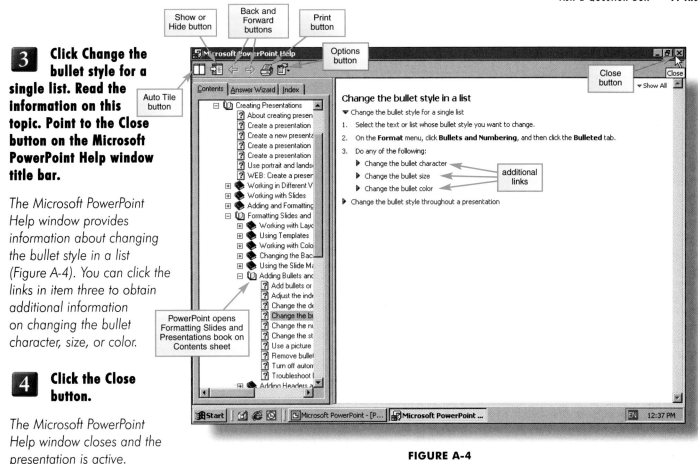

FIGURE A-4

If the Contents sheet is active on the left side of the Microsoft PowerPoint Help window, then PowerPoint opens the book pertaining to the topic for which you are requesting help. In this case, PowerPoint opens the Formatting Slides and Presentations book and the Adding Bullets and Numbering book, which includes a list of topics related to bullets. If the information on the right side is not satisfactory, you can click one of the topics in the Contents sheet to display alternative information related to bullet styles.

As you enter questions and terms in the Ask a Question box, PowerPoint adds them to its list. Thus, if you click the Ask a Question box arrow, a list of previously asked questions and terms will display.

Use the six buttons in the upper-left corner of the Microsoft PowerPoint Help window (Figure A-4) to navigate through the Help system, change the display, and print the contents of the window. Table A-1 lists the function of each of these buttons.

Table A-1	Microsoft PowerPoint Help Toolbar Buttons	
BUTTON	**NAME**	**FUNCTION**
	Auto Tile	Tiles the Microsoft PowerPoint Help window and Microsoft PowerPoint window when the Microsoft PowerPoint Help window is maximized
or	Show or Hide	Displays or hides the Contents, Answer Wizard, and Index tabs
	Back	Displays the previous Help topic
	Forward	Displays the next Help topic
	Print	Prints the current Help topic
	Options	Displays a list of commands

The Office Assistant

The **Office Assistant** is an icon (lower-right side of Figure A-1 on page PP A.01) that displays in the PowerPoint window when it is turned on and not hidden. It has dual functions. First, it will respond in the same way the Ask a Question box does with a list of topics relating to the entry you make in the text box at the bottom of the balloon. The entry can be in the form of a word, phrase, or question written as if you were talking to a human. For example, if you want to learn more about saving a presentation, you can type any of the following terms or phrases in the balloon text box: save, save a presentation, how do I save a presentation, or anything similar. The Office Assistant responds by displaying a list of topics from which you can choose. Once you choose a topic, it displays the corresponding information.

Second, the Office Assistant monitors your work and accumulates tips during a session on how you might increase your productivity and efficiency. You can view the tips at anytime. The accumulated tips display when you activate the Office Assistant balloon. Also, if at anytime you see a lightbulb above the Office Assistant, click it to display the most recent tip.

You may or may not want the Office Assistant to display on the screen at all times. You can hide it and then show it at a later time. You may prefer not to use the Office Assistant at all. Thus, not only do you need to know how to show and hide the Office Assistant, you also need to know how to turn the Office Assistant on and off.

Showing and Hiding the Office Assistant

When PowerPoint initially is installed, the Office Assistant may be off. You turn on the Office Assistant by clicking the **Show the Office Assistant command** on the Help menu. If the Office Assistant is on the screen and you want to hide it, you click the **Hide the Office Assistant command** on the Help menu. You also can right-click the Office Assistant to display its shortcut menu and then click the **Hide command** to hide it. You can move it to any location on the screen. You can click it to display the Office Assistant balloon, which allows you to request Help.

Turning the Office Assistant On and Off

The fact that the Office Assistant is hidden does not mean it is turned off. To turn the Office Assistant off, it must be displaying in the PowerPoint window. You right-click it to display its shortcut menu (right side of Figure A-5). Next, click Options on the shortcut menu. When you click the **Options command**, the **Office Assistant dialog box** displays (left side of Figure A-5).

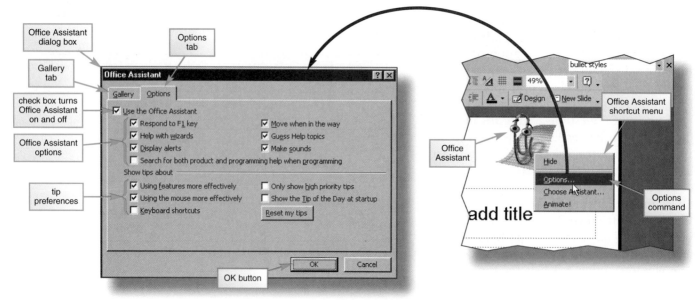

FIGURE A-5

In the **Options sheet** in the Office Assistant dialog box, the **Use the Office Assistant check box** at the top of the sheet determines whether the Office Assistant is on or off. To turn the Office Assistant off, remove the check mark from the Use the Office Assistant check box and then click the OK button. As shown in Figure A-1 on page PP A.01, if the Office Assistant is off when you invoke Help, then PowerPoint opens the Microsoft PowerPoint Help window instead of displaying the Office Assistant. To turn the Office Assistant on later, click the **Show the Office Assistant command** on the Help menu.

Through the Options command on the Office Assistant shortcut menu, you can change the look and feel of the Office Assistant. For example, you can hide the Office Assistant, turn the Office Assistant off, change the way it works, choose a different Office Assistant icon, or view an animation of the current one. These options also are available by clicking the **Options button** that displays in the Office Assistant balloon (Figure A-6).

The **Gallery sheet** (Figure A-5) in the Office Assistant dialog box allows you to change the appearance of the Office Assistant. The default is the paper clip (Clippit). You can change it to a bouncing red happy face (The Dot), a robot (F1), the Microsoft Office logo (Office Logo), a magician (Merlin), the earth (Mother Nature), a cat (Links), or a dog (Rocky).

Using the Office Assistant

As indicated earlier, the Office Assistant allows you to enter a word, phrase, or question and then responds by displaying a list of topics from which you can choose to display Help. The following steps show how to use the Office Assistant to obtain Help on changing a slide design.

Steps **To Use the Office Assistant**

1 **If the Office Assistant is not turned on, click Help on the menu bar and then click Show the Office Assistant. Click the Office Assistant. When the Office Assistant balloon displays, type** how do i change a slide layout **in the text box immediately above the Options button. Point to the Search button.**

The Office Assistant balloon displays as shown in Figure A-6.

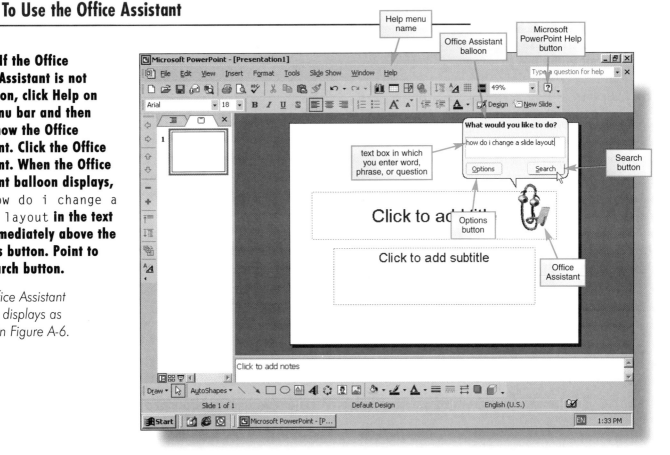

FIGURE A-6

2 **Click the Search button. When the Office Assistant balloon redisplays, point to the topic, Apply a slide layout (Figure A-7).**

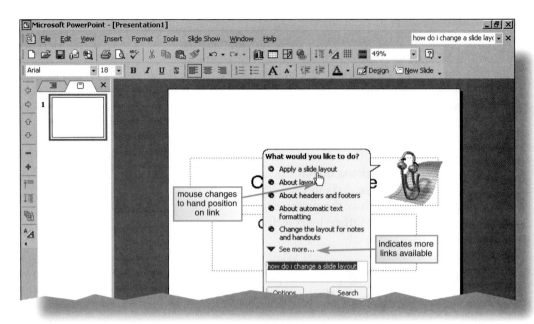

FIGURE A-7

3 **Click the topic, Apply a slide layout. If necessary, move or hide the Office Assistant so you can view all of the text in the Microsoft PowerPoint Help window.**

The Microsoft PowerPoint Help window displays the information on applying a slide layout (Figure A-8).

4 **Click the Close button on the Microsoft PowerPoint Help window title bar to close Help.**

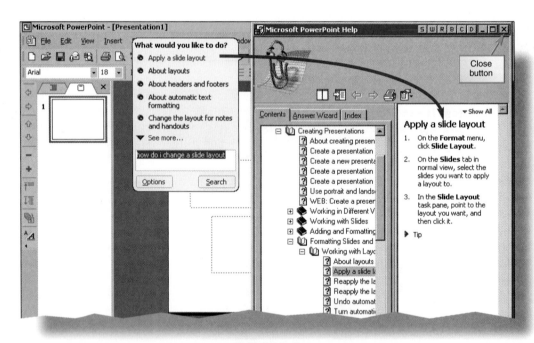

FIGURE A-8

The Microsoft PowerPoint Help Window

If the Office Assistant is turned off and you click the Microsoft PowerPoint Help button on the Standard toolbar, the Microsoft PowerPoint Help window opens (Figure A-9). The left side of this window contains three tabs: Contents, Answer Wizard, and Index. Each tab displays a sheet with powerful look-up capabilities.

Use the Contents sheet as you would a table of contents at the front of a book to look up Help. The Answer Wizard sheet answers your queries the same as the Office Assistant. You use the Index sheet in the same fashion as an index in a book to look up Help. Click the tabs to move from sheet to sheet.

Besides clicking the Microsoft PowerPoint Help button on the Standard toolbar, you also can click the Microsoft PowerPoint Help command on the Help menu, or press the F1 key to display the Microsoft PowerPoint Help window to gain access to the three sheets. To close the Microsoft PowerPoint Help window, click the Close button in the upper-right corner on the title bar.

Using the Contents Sheet

The **Contents sheet** is useful for displaying Help when you know the general category of the topic in question, but not the specifics. The following steps show how to use the Contents sheet to obtain information on printing in black and white.

TO OBTAIN HELP USING THE CONTENTS SHEET

1 With the Office Assistant turned off, click the Microsoft PowerPoint Help button on the Standard toolbar (shown in Figure A-6 on page PP A.05).

2 When the Microsoft PowerPoint Help window displays, double-click the title bar to maximize the window. If necessary, click the Show button to display the tabs.

3 Click the Contents tab. Click the Printing Presentations book on the left side of the window.

4 Click the subtopic, About printing in black and white, below the Printing Presentations book (Figure A-9).

5 Close the Microsoft PowerPoint Help window.

PowerPoint displays Help on the subtopic, About printing in black and white (Figure A-9).

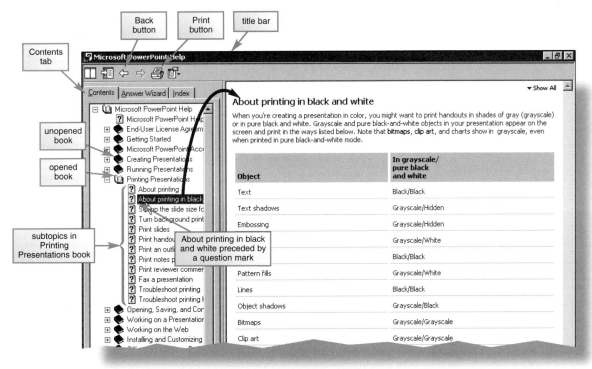

FIGURE A-9

Once the information on the subtopic displays, you can scroll through and read it or you can click the Print button to obtain a printed copy. If you decide to click another subtopic on the left or a link on the right, you can get back to the Help page shown in Figure A-9 by clicking the Back button.

Each topic in the Contents list is preceded by a book icon or question mark icon. A **book icon** indicates subtopics are available. A **question mark icon** means information on the topic will display if you double-click the title. The book icon opens when you double-click the book (or its title) or click the plus sign (+) to the left of the book icon.

Using the Answer Wizard Sheet

The **Answer Wizard sheet** works like the Office Assistant in that you enter a word, phrase, or question and it responds by listing topics from which you can choose to display Help. The following steps show how to use the Answer Wizard sheet to obtain Help on using clip art contained in the Microsoft Clip Organizer.

TO OBTAIN HELP USING THE ANSWER WIZARD SHEET

1 With the Office Assistant turned off, click the Microsoft PowerPoint Help button on the Standard toolbar (shown in Figure A-6 on page PP A.05).

2 When the Microsoft PowerPoint Help window displays, double-click the title bar to maximize the window. If necessary, click the Show button to display the tabs.

3 Click the Answer Wizard tab. Type use clip art in the What would you like to do? text box on the left side of the window and then click the Search button.

4 When a list of topics displays in the Select topic to display list, click Rotate an object (Figure A-10). Click the Rotate to any angle link on the right side of the Microsoft PowerPoint Help window.

5 Close the Microsoft PowerPoint Help window.

PowerPoint displays Help on the topic, Rotate an object (Figure A-10).

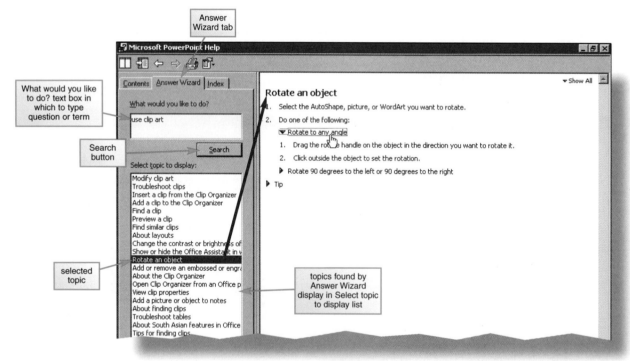

FIGURE A-10

If the topic, Rotate an object, does not include the information you are seeking, you can click another topic in the list. Continue to click topics until you find the desired information.

Using the Index Sheet

The third sheet in the Microsoft PowerPoint Help window is the Index sheet. Use the **Index sheet** to display Help when you know the keyword or the first few letters of the keyword you want to look up. The following steps show how to use the Index sheet to obtain Help on adding sounds to animated text or objects.

What's This? Command and Question Mark Button • **PP A.09**

APPENDIX A

TO OBTAIN HELP USING THE INDEX SHEET

1 With the Office Assistant turned off, click the Microsoft PowerPoint Help button on the Standard toolbar (shown in Figure A-6 on page PP A.05).

2 When the Microsoft PowerPoint Help window displays, double-click the title bar to maximize the window. If necessary, click the Show button to display the tabs.

3 Click the Index tab. Type animation in the Type keywords text box on the left side of the window. Click the Search button.

4 When a list of topics displays in the Choose a topic list, click Add a sound to an animation (Figure A-11).

5 Close the PowerPoint Help window.

PowerPoint displays Help on selecting sounds in the Custom Animation task pane (Figure A-11).

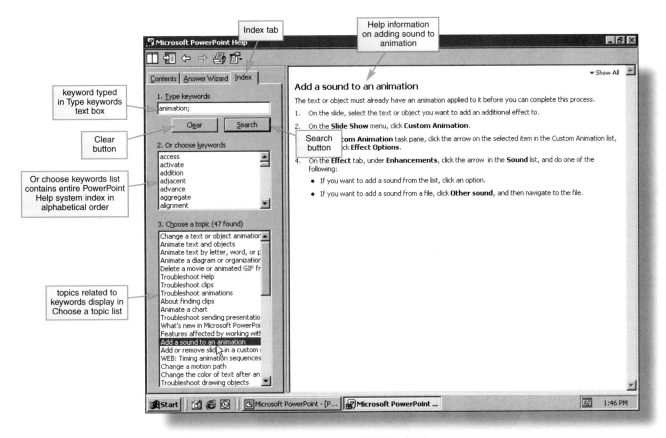

FIGURE A-11

An alternative to typing a keyword in the Type keywords text box is to scroll through the Or choose keywords list (the middle list on the left side of the window). When you locate the keyword you are searching for, double-click it to display Help on the topic. Also in the Or choose keywords list, the PowerPoint Help system displays other topics that relate to the new keyword. As you begin typing a new keyword in the Type keywords text box, PowerPoint jumps to that point in the middle list box. To begin a new search, click the Clear button.

What's This? Command and Question Mark Button

Use the What's This? command on the Help menu or the Question Mark button in a dialog box when you are not sure what an object on the screen is or what it does.

What's This? Command

You use the **What's This? command** on the Help menu to display a detailed ScreenTip. When you click this command, the mouse pointer changes to an arrow with a question mark. You then click any object on the screen, such as a button, to display the ScreenTip. For example, after you click the What's This? command on the Help menu and then click the Show Formatting button on the Formatting toolbar, a description of the Show Formatting button displays (Figure A-12). You can print the ScreenTip by right-clicking it and then clicking Print Topic on the shortcut menu.

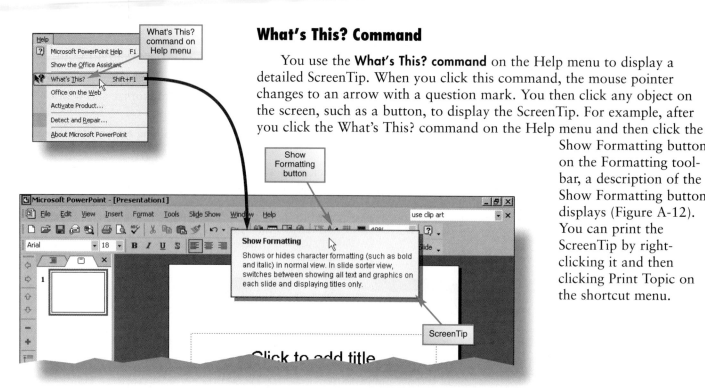

FIGURE A-12

Question Mark Button

Similarly to the What's This? command, the **Question Mark button** displays a ScreenTip. You use the Question Mark button with dialog boxes. It is located in the upper-right corner on the title bar of dialog boxes, next to the Close button. For example, in Figure A-13, the Save As dialog box displays on the screen. If you click the Question Mark button in the upper-right corner of the dialog box and then click the Save as type box, an explanation displays. You can print the ScreenTip by right-clicking it and then clicking Print Topic on the shortcut menu.

If a dialog box does not include a Question Mark button, press SHIFT+F1. This combination of keys displays an explanation or changes the mouse pointer to an arrow with a question mark. You then can click any object in the dialog box to display the ScreenTip.

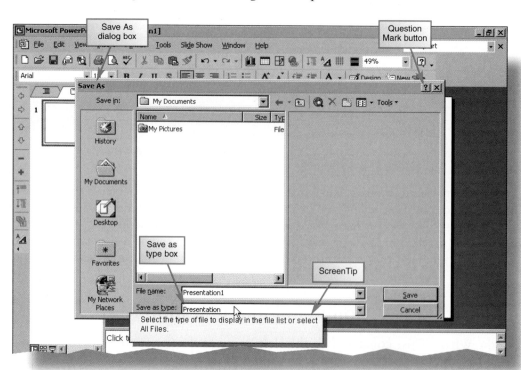

FIGURE A-13

Office on the Web Command

The **Office on the Web command** on the Help menu displays a Microsoft Web page containing up-to-date information on a variety of Office-related topics. To use this command, you must be connected to the Internet. When you invoke the Office on the Web command, the Assistance Center Home page displays. Read through the links that in general pertain to topics that relate to all Office XP topics. Scroll down and click the PowerPoint link in the Help By Product area to display the Assistance Center PowerPoint Help Articles Web page (Figure A-14). This Web page contains numerous helpful links related to PowerPoint.

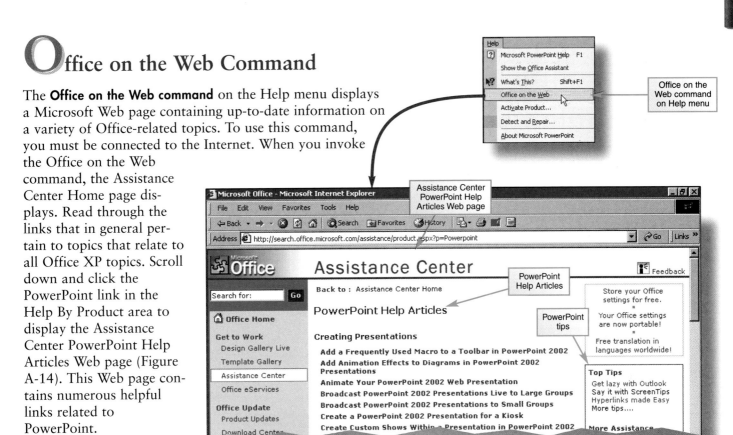

FIGURE A-14

Other Help Commands

Three additional commands available on the Help menu are Activate Product, Detect and Repair, and About Microsoft PowerPoint.

Activate Product Command

The **Activate Product command** on the Help menu lets you activate PowerPoint if it has not already been activated.

Detect and Repair Command

Use the **Detect and Repair command** on the Help menu if PowerPoint is not running properly or if it is generating errors. When you invoke this command, the Detect and Repair dialog box displays. Click the Start button in the dialog box to initiate the detect and repair process.

About Microsoft PowerPoint Command

The **About Microsoft PowerPoint command** on the Help menu displays the About Microsoft PowerPoint dialog box. The dialog box lists the owner of the software and the product identification. You need to know the product identification if you call Microsoft for assistance. The three buttons below the OK button are the System Info button, the Tech Support button, and the Disabled Items button. The **System Info button** displays system information, including hardware resources, components, software environment, and applications. The **Tech Support button** displays a Microsoft PowerPoint window with product support services information. The **Disabled Items button** allows you to enable items that prevented PowerPoint from functioning correctly.

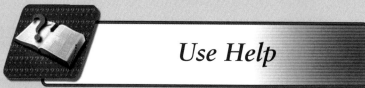

Use Help

1 Using the Ask a Question Box

Instructions: Perform the following tasks using the PowerPoint Help system.

1. Click the Ask a Question box on the menu bar, type how do i change the color scheme, and then press the ENTER key.
2. Click Modify a color scheme in the Ask a Question list. Double-click the Microsoft PowerPoint Help window title bar. Read and print the information. One at a time, click each of the three links in item two on the right side of the window to learn about modifying color schemes for slides, notes, and handouts. Print the information. Hand in the printouts to your instructor. Click the Close button in the Microsoft PowerPoint Help window.
3. Click the Ask a Question box and then press the ENTER key. Click Change text color in the Ask a Question list. If this list does not display, click the See more link and then click Change text color. When the Microsoft PowerPoint Help window displays, maximize the window.
4. Click the Show button on the Help toolbar to display the tabs. Click the Contents tab. Read and print the information. Click each of the two items on the right side of the Microsoft PowerPoint Help window; Change text color in a placeholder, AutoShape, or text box; and Change text color in WordArt. Print the information for each. Close the Microsoft PowerPoint Help window.

2 Expanding on the PowerPoint Help System Basics

Instructions: Use the PowerPoint Help system to understand the topics better and answer the questions listed below. Answer the questions on your own paper, or hand in the printed Help information to your instructor.

1. Right-click the Office Assistant. If it is not turned on, click Show the Office Assistant on the Help menu. When the shortcut menu displays, click Options. Click Use the Office Assistant to remove the check mark, and then click the OK button.
2. Click the Microsoft PowerPoint Help button on the Standard toolbar. Maximize the Microsoft PowerPoint Help window. If the tabs are hidden on the left side, click the Show button on the Help toolbar. Click the Index tab. Type slide show in the Type keywords text box. Click the Search button. Click Add transitions between slides. Print the information. Click the Hide button and then the Show button on the Help toolbar. Click the two links below Do one of the following. Read and print the information for each link. Close the Microsoft PowerPoint Help window. Hand in the printouts to your instructor.
3. Press the F1 key. Maximize the Microsoft PowerPoint Help window. Click the Answer Wizard tab. Type speech recognition in the What would you like to do? text box, and then click the Search button. Click Things you can do and say with speech recognition. Read the information that displays. Print the information. Click the two links in item one, Using Voice Command mode and Using Dictation mode. Read and print the information for both.
4. Click the Contents tab. Click the plus sign (+) to the left of the Creating Presentations book, and then click the plus sign to the left of the Adding Clip Art book. One at a time, click the first three topics below the Adding Clip Art book. Read and print each one. Close the Microsoft PowerPoint Help window. Hand in the printouts to your instructor.

APPENDIX B
Speech and Handwriting Recognition

Introduction

This appendix discusses how you can create and modify worksheets using Office XP's new input technologies. Office XP provides a variety of **text services**, which enable you to speak commands and enter text in an application. The most common text service is the keyboard. Two new text services included with Office XP are speech recognition and handwriting recognition.

When Windows was installed on your computer, you specified a default language. For example, most users in the United States select English (United States) as the default language. Through text services, you can add more than 90 additional languages and varying dialects such as Basque, English (Zimbabwe), French (France), French (Canada), German (Germany), German (Austria), and Swahili. With multiple languages available, you can switch from one language to another while working in PowerPoint. If you change the language or dialect, then text services may change the functions of the keys on the keyboard, adjust speech recognition, and alter handwriting recognition.

The Language Bar

You know that text services are installed properly when the Language Indicator button displays by the clock in the tray status area on the Windows taskbar (Figure B-1a) or the Language bar displays on the screen (Figure B-1b or B-1c). If the Language Indicator button displays in the tray status area, click it, and then click the **Show the Language bar command** (Figure B-1a). The Language bar displays on the screen in the same location it displayed last time.

You can drag the Language bar to any location in the window by pointing to its move handle, which is the vertical line on its left side (Figure B-1b). When the mouse pointer changes to a four-headed arrow, drag the Language bar to the desired location.

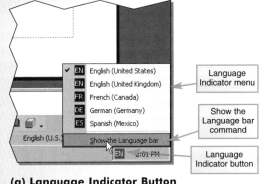

(a) Language Indicator Button in Tray Status Area on Windows Taskbar and Its Menu

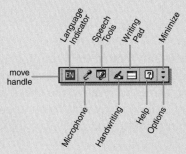

(b) Language Bar with Text Labels Disabled

(c) Language Bar with Text Labels Enabled

FIGURE B-1

If you are sure that one of the services was installed and neither the Language Indicator button nor the Language bar displays, then do the following:

1. Click Start on the Windows taskbar, point to Settings, click Control Panel, and then double-click the Text Services icon in the Control Panel window.
2. When the Text Services dialog box displays, click the Language Bar button, click the Show the Language bar on the desktop check box to select it, and then click the OK button in the Language Bar Settings dialog box.
3. Click the OK button in the Text Services dialog box.
4. Close the Control Panel window.

You can perform tasks related to text services by using the **Language bar**. The Language bar may display with just the icon on each button (Figure B-1b) or it may display with text labels to the right of the icon on each button (Figure B-1c). Changing the appearance of the Language bar will be discussed shortly.

Buttons on the Language Bar

The Language bar shown in Figure B-2a contains eight buttons. The number of buttons on your Language bar may be different. These buttons are used to select the language, customize the Language bar, control the microphone, control handwriting, and obtain help.

When you click the **Language Indicator button** on the far left side of the Language bar, the Language Indicator menu displays a list of the active languages (Figure B-2b) from which you can choose. The **Microphone button**, the second button from the left, enables and disables the microphone. When the microphone is enabled, text services adds two buttons and a balloon to the Language toolbar (Figure B-2c). These additional buttons and the balloon will be discussed shortly.

The third button from the left on the Language bar is the Speech Tools button. The **Speech Tools button** displays a menu of commands (Figure B-2d) that allow you to hide or show the balloon on the Language bar; train the Speech Recognition service so that it can better interpret your voice; add and delete words from its dictionary, such as names and other words not understood easily; and change the user profile so more than one person can use the microphone on the same computer.

The fourth button from the left on the Language bar is the Handwriting button. The **Handwriting button** displays the **Handwriting menu** (Figure B-2e), which lets you choose the Writing Pad (Figure B-2f), Write Anywhere (Figure B-2g), or the on-screen keyboard (Figure B-2h). The **On-Screen Symbol Keyboard command** on the Handwriting menu displays an on-screen keyboard that allows you to enter special symbols that are not available on a standard keyboard. You can choose only one form of handwriting at a time.

The fifth button indicates which one of the handwriting forms is active. For example, in Figure B-2a the Writing Pad is active. The handwriting recognition capabilities of text services will be discussed shortly.

The sixth button from the left on the Language bar is the Help button. The **Help button** displays the Help menu. If you click the Language Bar Help command on the Help menu, the Language Bar Help window displays (Figure B-2i). On the far right of the Language bar are two buttons stacked above and below each other. The top button is the Minimize button and the bottom button is the Options button. The **Minimize button** minimizes (hides) the Language bar so that the Language Indicator button displays in the tray status area on the Windows taskbar. The next section discusses the Options button.

Customizing the Language Bar

The down arrow icon immediately below the Minimize button in Figure B-2a is called the Options button. The **Options button** displays a menu of text services options (Figure B-2j). You can use this menu to hide the Speech Tools, Handwriting, and Help buttons on the Language bar by clicking their names to remove the check mark to the left of each button. The Settings command on the Options menu displays a dialog box that lets you customize the Language bar. This command will be discussed shortly. The Restore Defaults command redisplays hidden buttons on the Language bar.

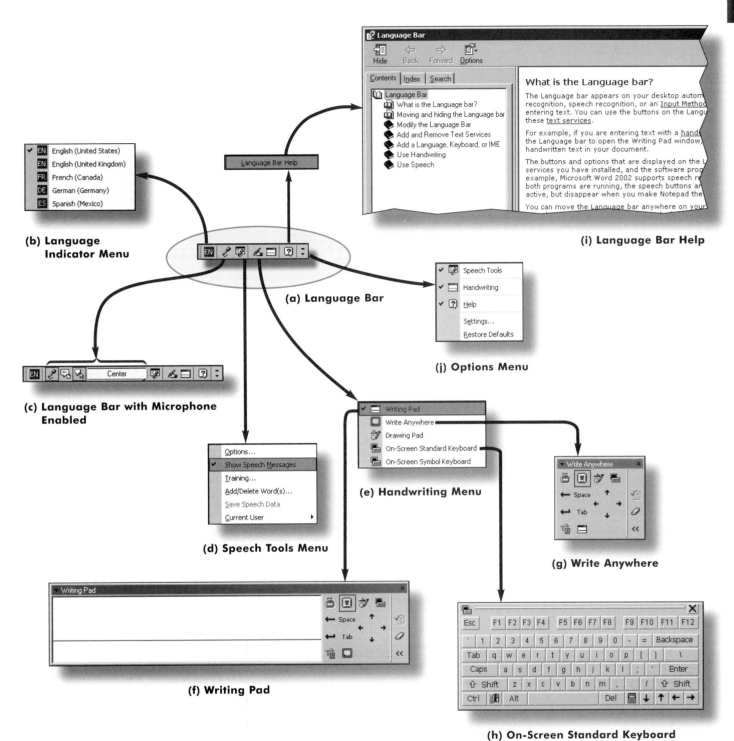

(b) Language Indicator Menu

(i) Language Bar Help

(a) Language Bar

(j) Options Menu

(c) Language Bar with Microphone Enabled

(d) Speech Tools Menu

(e) Handwriting Menu

(g) Write Anywhere

(f) Writing Pad

(h) On-Screen Standard Keyboard

FIGURE B-2

If you right-click the Language bar, a shortcut menu displays (Figure B-3a on the next page). This shortcut menu lets you further customize the Language bar. The **Minimize command** on the shortcut menu minimizes the Language bar the same as the Minimize button on the Language bar. The **Transparency command** toggles the Language bar between being solid and transparent. You can see through a transparent Language bar (Figure B-3b). The **Text Labels command** toggles text labels on the Language bar on (Figure B-3c) and off (Figure B-3a). The **Additional icons in taskbar command** toggles between only showing the Language Indicator button in the tray status area and showing icons that represent the text services that are active (Figure B-3d).

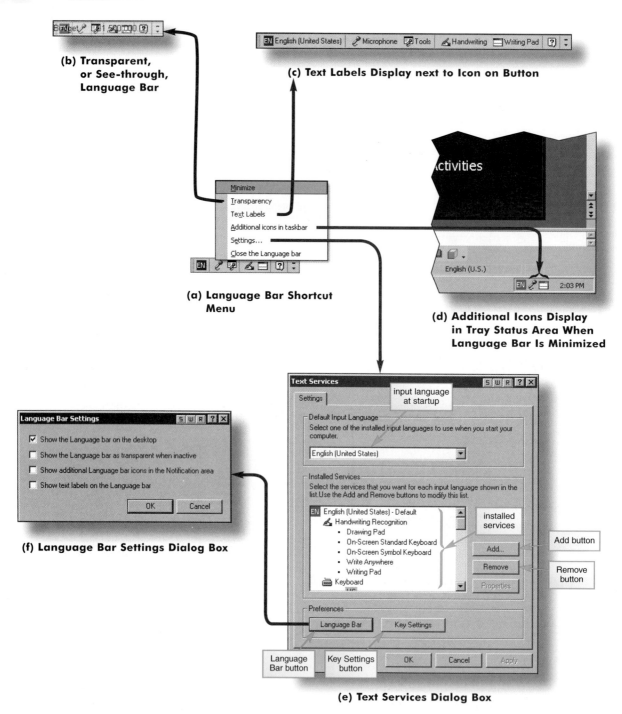

(b) Transparent, or See-through, Language Bar

(c) Text Labels Display next to Icon on Button

(a) Language Bar Shortcut Menu

(d) Additional Icons Display in Tray Status Area When Language Bar Is Minimized

(f) Language Bar Settings Dialog Box

(e) Text Services Dialog Box

FIGURE B-3

The **Settings command** displays the Text Services dialog box (Figure B-3e). The **Text Services dialog box** allows you to select the language at startup; add and remove text services; modify keys on the keyboard; and modify the Language bar. If you want to remove any one of the entries in the Installed Services list, select the entry, and then click the Remove button. If you want to add a service, click the Add button. The Key Settings button allows you to modify the keyboard. If you click the **Language Bar button** in the Text Services dialog box, the **Language Bar Settings dialog box** displays (Figure B-3f). This dialog box contains Language bar options, some of which are the same as the commands on the Language bar shortcut menu described earlier.

The **Close the Language bar command** on the shortcut menu shown in Figure B-3a closes the Language bar and hides the Language Indicator button in the tray status area on the Windows taskbar. If you close the Language bar and want to redisplay it, follow the instructions at the top of page PP B.02.

Speech Recognition

The **Speech Recognition service** available with Office XP enables your computer to recognize human speech through a microphone. The microphone has two modes: dictation and voice command (Figure B-4). You switch between the two modes by clicking the Dictation button and the Voice Command button on the Language bar. These buttons display only when you turn on Speech Recognition by clicking the **Microphone button** on the Language bar (Figure B-5 on the next page). If you are using the Microphone button for the very first time in PowerPoint, it will require that you check your microphone settings and step through voice training before activating the Speech Recognition service.

The **Dictation button** places the microphone in Dictation mode. In **Dictation mode**, whatever you speak is entered as text in the active cell. The **Voice Command button** places the microphone in Voice Command mode. In **Voice Command mode**, whatever you speak is interpreted as a command. If you want to turn off the microphone, click the Microphone button on the Language bar or in Voice Command mode say, "Mic off" (pronounced mike off). It is important to remember that minimizing the Language bar does not turn off the microphone.

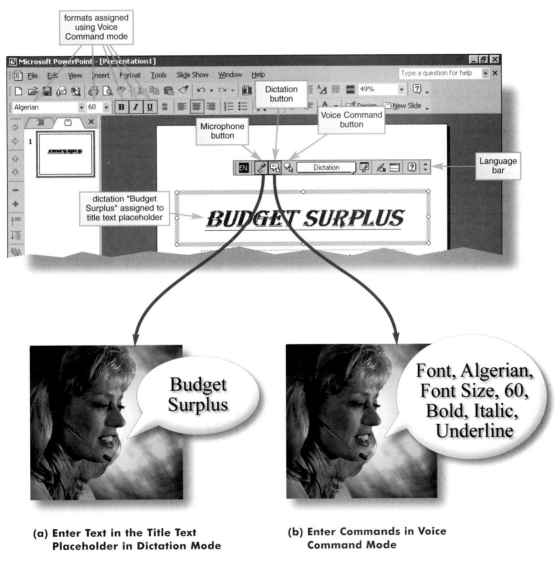

(a) Enter Text in the Title Text
Placeholder in Dictation Mode

(b) Enter Commands in Voice
Command Mode

FIGURE B-4

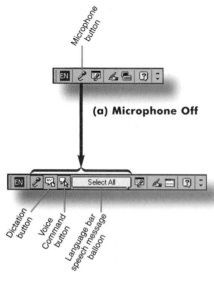

(a) Microphone Off

(b) Microphone On

FIGURE B-5

The **Language bar speech message balloon** shown in Figure B-5b displays messages that may offer help or hints. In Voice Command mode, the name of the last recognized command you said displays. If you use the mouse or keyboard instead of the microphone, a message will appear in the Language bar speech message balloon indicating the word you could say. In Dictation mode, the message, Dictating, usually displays. The Speech Recognition service, however, will display messages to inform you that you are talking too soft, too loud, too fast, or to ask you to repeat what you said by displaying, What was that?

Getting Started with Speech Recognition

For the microphone to function properly, you should follow these steps:

1. Make sure your computer meets the minimum requirements.
2. Install Speech Recognition.
3. Set up and position your microphone, preferably a close-talk headset with gain adjustment support.
4. Train Speech Recognition.

The following sections describe these steps in more detail.

SPEECH RECOGNITION SYSTEM REQUIREMENTS For Speech Recognition to work on your computer, it needs the following:

1. Microsoft Windows 98 or later or Microsoft Windows NT 4.0 or later
2. At least 128 MB RAM
3. 400 MHz or faster processor
4. Microphone and sound card

INSTALLING SPEECH RECOGNITION If Speech Recognition is not installed on your computer, start Microsoft Word and then click Speech on the Tools menu.

SETUP AND POSITION YOUR MICROPHONE Set up your microphone as follows:

1. Connect your microphone to the sound card in the back of the computer.
2. Position the microphone approximately one inch out from and to the side of your mouth. Position it so you are not breathing into it.
3. On the Language bar, click the Speech Tools button, and then click Options (Figure B-6a).
4. When the Speech Properties dialog box displays (Figure B-6b), if necessary, click the Speech Recognition tab.
5. Click the Configure Microphone button. Follow the Microphone Wizard directions as shown in Figures B-6c, B-6d, and B-6e. The Next button will remain dimmed in Figure B-6d until the volume meter consistently stays in the green area.
6. If someone else installed Speech Recognition, click the New button in the Speech Properties dialog box and enter your name. Click the Train Profile button and step through the Voice Training Wizard. The Voice Training Wizard will require that you enter your gender and age group. It then will step you through voice training.

You can adjust the microphone further by clicking the **Settings button** (Figure B-6b) in the Speech Properties dialog box. The Settings button displays the **Recognition Profile Settings dialog box** that allows you to adjust the pronunciation sensitivity and accuracy versus recognition response time.

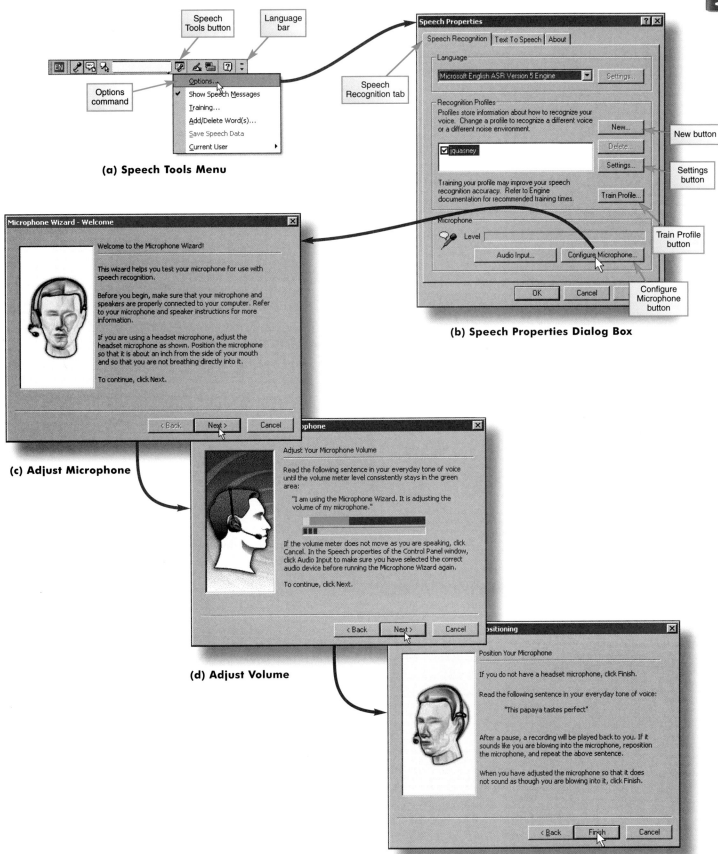

FIGURE B-6

TRAIN THE SPEECH RECOGNITION SERVICE The Speech Recognition service will understand most commands and some dictation without any training at all. It will recognize much more of what you speak, however, if you take the time to train it. After one training session, it will recognize 85 to 90 percent of your words. As you do more training, accuracy will rise to 95 percent. If you feel that too many mistakes are being made, then continue to train the service. The more training you do, the more accurately it will work for you. Follow these steps to train the Speech Recognition service:

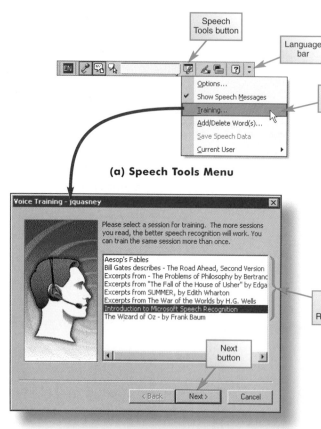

(a) Speech Tools Menu

(b) Voice Training Dialog Box

FIGURE B-7

1. Click the Speech Tools button on the Language bar and then click Training (Figure B-7a).
2. When the **Voice Training dialog box** displays (Figure B-7b), click one of the sessions and then click the Next button.
3. Complete the training session, which should take less than 15 minutes.

If you are serious about using a microphone to speak to your computer, you need to take the time to go through at least three of the eight training sessions listed in Figure B-7b.

Using Speech Recognition

Speech recognition lets you enter text into a worksheet similarly to speaking into a tape recorder. Instead of typing, you can dictate text that you want to assign to cells, and you can issue voice commands. In **Voice Command mode**, you can speak menu names, commands on menus, toolbar button names, and dialog box option buttons, check boxes, list boxes, and button names. Speech Recognition, however, is not a completely hands-free form of input. Speech recognition works best if you use a combination of your voice, the keyboard, and the mouse. You soon will discover that Dictation mode is far less accurate than Voice Command mode. Table B-1 lists some tips that will improve the Speech Recognition service's accuracy considerably.

Table B-1	Tips to Improve Speech Recognition
NUMBER	**TIP**
1	The microphone hears everything. Though the Speech Recognition service filters out background noise, it is recommended that you work in a quiet environment.
2	Try not to move the microphone around once it is adjusted.
3	Speak in a steady tone and speak clearly.
4	In Dictation mode, do not pause between words. A phrase is easier to interpret than a word. Sounding out syllables in a word will make it more difficult for the Speech Recognition service to interpret what you are saying.
5	If you speak too loudly or too softly, it makes it difficult for the Speech Recognition service to interpret what you said. Check the Language bar speech message balloon for an indication that you may be speaking too loudly or too softly.
6	If you experience problems after training, adjust the recognition options that control accuracy and rejection by clicking the Settings button shown in Figure B-6b on the previous page.
7	When you are finished using the microphone, turn it off by clicking the Microphone button on the Language bar or in Voice Command mode say, "Mic off." Leaving the microphone on is the same as leaning on the keyboard.
8	If the Speech Recognition service is having difficulty with unusual words, then add the words to its dictionary by using the Add/Delete Word(s) command on the Speech Tools menu (Figure B-8a). The last names of individuals and the names of companies are good examples of the types of words you should add to the dictionary.
9	Training will improve accuracy; practice will improve confidence.

The last command on the Speech Tools menu is the Current User command (Figure B-8a). The **Current User command** is useful for multiple users who share a computer. It allows them to configure their own individual profiles, and then switch between users as they use the computer.

For additional information on the Speech Recognition service, click the Help button on the Standard toolbar, click the Answer Wizard tab, and search for the phrase, Speech Recognition.

Handwriting Recognition

Using the Office XP handwriting recognition capabilities, you can enter text and numbers into PowerPoint by writing instead of typing. You can write using a special handwriting device that connects to your computer or you can write on the screen using your mouse. Four basic methods of handwriting are available by clicking the **Handwriting button** on the Language bar: Writing Pad; Write Anywhere; On-Screen Standard Keyboard; and On-Screen Symbol Keyboard. Although the on-screen keyboards do not involve handwriting recognition, they are part of the Handwriting menu and, therefore, will be discussed in this section. While the Drawing Pad command displays on the Handwriting menu, it functions only in Microsoft Word and Outlook.

If your Language bar does not include the Handwriting button (Figures B-1b or B-1c on page PP B.01), then for installation instructions click the Help button on the Standard toolbar, click the Answer Wizard tab, and search for the phrase Install Handwriting Recognition.

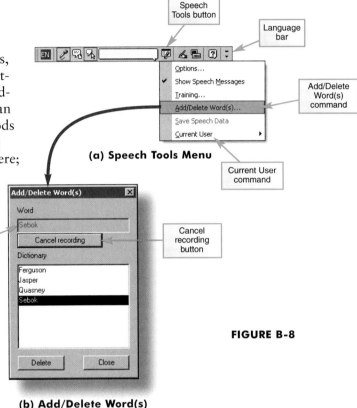

(a) Speech Tools Menu

(b) Add/Delete Word(s) Dialog Box

FIGURE B-8

Writing Pad

To display the Writing Pad, click the Handwriting button on the Language bar and then click Writing Pad (Figure B-9 on the next page). The **Writing Pad** resembles a note pad with one or more lines on which you can use freehand to print or write in cursive. With the **Text button** enabled, you can form letters on the line by moving the mouse while holding down the mouse button. To the right of the note pad is a rectangular toolbar. Use the buttons on this toolbar to adjust the Writing Pad, select cells, and activate other handwriting applications.

Consider the example in Figure B-9. With the subtitle text placeholder selected, the word, State, is written in cursive on the **Pen line** in the Writing Pad. As soon as the word is complete, the Handwriting Recognition service automatically assigns the word to the subtitle text placeholder.

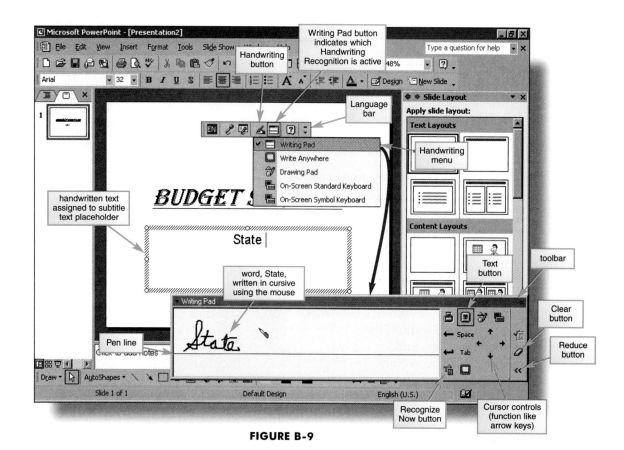

FIGURE B-9

You can customize the Writing Pad by clicking the **Options button** on the left side of the title bar and then clicking the Options command (Figure B-10a). Invoking the **Options command** causes the Handwriting Options dialog box to display. The **Handwriting Options dialog box** contains two sheets: Common and Writing Pad. The **Common sheet** lets you change the pen color and pen width, adjust recognition, and customize the toolbar area of the Writing Pad. The **Writing Pad sheet** allows you to change the background color and the number of lines that display in the Writing Pad. Both sheets contain a **Restore Default button** to restore the settings to what they were when the software was installed initially.

When you first start using the Writing Pad, you may want to remove the check mark from the **Automatic recognition check box** on the Common sheet in the Handwriting Options dialog box (Figure B-10b). With the check mark removed, the Handwriting Recognition service will not interpret what you write in the Writing Pad until you click the **Recognize Now button** on the toolbar (Figure B-9). This allows you to pause and adjust your writing.

The best way to learn how to use the Writing Pad is to practice with it. Also, for more information, click the Help button on the Standard toolbar, click the Answer Wizard tab, and search for the phrase, Handwriting Recognition.

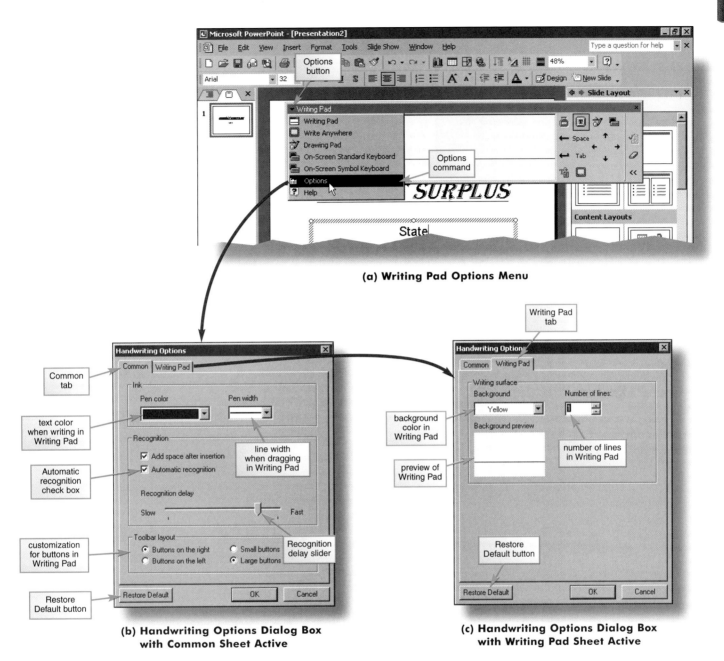

(a) Writing Pad Options Menu

(b) Handwriting Options Dialog Box
with Common Sheet Active

(c) Handwriting Options Dialog Box
with Writing Pad Sheet Active

FIGURE B-10

Write Anywhere

Rather than use a Writing Pad, you can write anywhere on the screen by invoking the **Write Anywhere command** on the Handwriting menu (Figure B-11 on the next page) that displays when you click the Handwriting button on the Language bar. In this case, the entire window is your writing pad.

In Figure B-11, the word, By, is written in cursive using the mouse button. Shortly after you finish writing the word, the Handwriting Recognition service interprets it, assigns it to the subtitle text placeholder, and erases what you wrote.

It is recommended that when you first start using the Writing Anywhere service that you remove the check mark from the Automatic recognition check box in the Common sheet in the Handwriting Options dialog box (Figure B-10b). With the check mark removed, the Handwriting Recognition service will not interpret what you write on the screen until you click the Recognize Now button on the toolbar (Figure B-11).

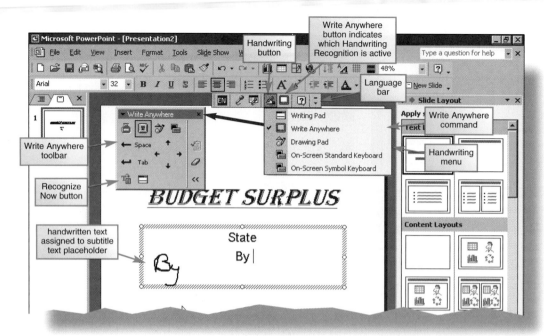

FIGURE B-11

On-Screen Standard Keyboard

The **On-Screen Standard Keyboard command** on the Handwriting menu (Figure B-12) displays an on-screen keyboard. An **on-screen keyboard** lets you enter data into a cell by using your mouse to click the keys. The on-screen keyboard is similar to the type found on handheld computers.

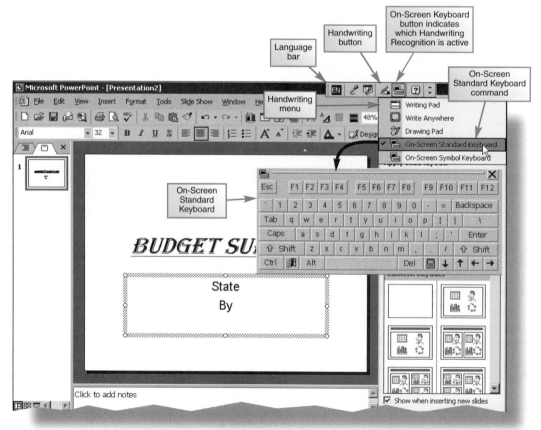

FIGURE B-12

On-Screen Symbol Keyboard

The **On-Screen Symbol Keyboard** command on the Handwriting menu displays a special on-screen keyboard that allows you to enter symbols that are not on your keyboard. To display this keyboard, click the Handwriting button on the Language bar and then click On-Screen Symbol Keyboard (Figure B-13). Clicking the Shift key displays capital letters.

Some symbols are letters in various languages, such as the Latin Þ (thorn), Greek β (beta) and the Latin letter o with slash (Ø). A few of these symbols also are used in mathematical and scientific applications. For example, Ø represents the null set in mathematics when a set has no elements. It also is used to indicate a zero reading when current or voltage is measured on a scale.

The **diacritic symbols** on the keyboard are marks, points, or signs printed above or below a letter to indicate its exact pronunciation or accent. For example, the acute accent on the letter e (é) is used in French words such as attaché and cliché. The cedilla (ç) and circumflex accent (^) are used in the French translation for the phrase, the more that changes, the more it is the same thing: plus ça change, plus c'est la même chose, shown in Figure B-13.

The **ligature symbols** on the keyboard are characters consisting of two or more letters joined together. The Latin small ligature œ, for example, is used in the French word cœur, meaning heart.

Three currency abbreviations also are located on the On-Screen Symbol Keyboard. They include the Euro (€), the British pound (£), and the Japanese yen (¥).

Table B-2 lists some of the symbols on the On-Screen Symbol Keyboard and their uses.

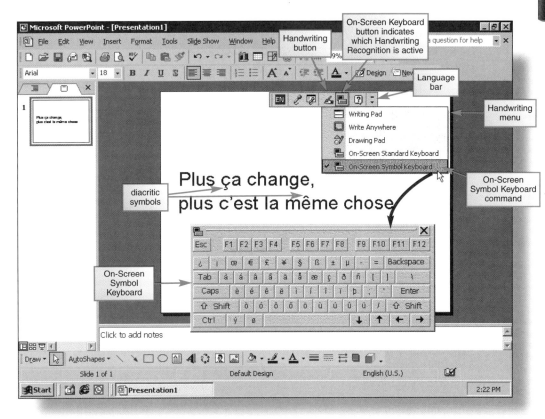

FIGURE B-13

Table B-2	On-Screen Symbol Keyboard Keys	
KEY	**NAME**	**EXAMPLE**
Currency		
€	Euro sign	€875
£	Pound sign	£250
¥	Yen sign	¥500
Mathematics and Science		
β	Beta	$\beta = \omega \,^* c / \lambda$
Ø	Empty (null) set	$A \cap B = Ø$
/	Fraction slash	4/2
μ	Micro sign (mu)	μ-inches
δ	Partial differential (delta)	δy/δx
±	Plus-minus sign	12 ± 2 inches
Diacritic		
´	Acute accent	Attaché, cliché
ç	Cedilla	Façade
^	Circumflex accent	Même
à	Grave accent	À la mode
˜	Tilde	Niño
ü	Umlaut	Naïve
Ligature		
æ	Latin small ligature æ	Encyclopædia Britannica
œ	Latin small ligature œ	Cœur
Miscellaneous		
¿	Inverted question mark	¿Qué pasa?
§	Section	15 U.S. Code §1601

APPENDIX C
Publishing Office Web Pages to a Web Server

With the Office applications, you use the Save as Web Page command on the File menu to save the Web page to a Web server using one of two techniques: Web folders or File Transfer Protocol. A **Web folder** is an Office shortcut to a Web server. **File Transfer Protocol** (**FTP**) is an Internet standard that allows computers to exchange files with other computers on the Internet.

You should contact your network system administrator or technical support staff at your ISP to determine if their Web server supports Web folders, FTP, or both, and to obtain necessary permissions to access the Web server. If you decide to publish Web pages using a Web folder, you must have the Office Server Extensions (OSE) installed on your computer.

Using Web Folders to Publish Office Web Pages

When publishing to a Web folder, someone first must create the Web folder before you can save to it. If you are granted permission to create a Web folder, you must obtain the URL of the Web server, a user name, and possibly a password that allows you to access the Web server. You also must decide on a name for the Web folder. Table C-1 explains how to create a Web folder.

Office adds the name of the Web folder to the list of current Web folders. You can save to this folder, open files in the folder, rename the folder, or perform any operations you would to a folder on your hard disk. You can use your Office program or Windows Explorer to access this folder. Table C-2 explains how to save to a Web folder.

Using FTP to Publish Office Web Pages

When publishing a Web page using FTP, you first must add the FTP location to your computer before you can save to it. An **FTP location**, also called an **FTP site**, is a collection of files that reside on an FTP server. In this case, the FTP server is the Web server.

To add an FTP location, you must obtain the name of the FTP site, which usually is the address (URL) of the FTP server, and a user name and a password that allows you to access the FTP server. You save and open the Web pages on the FTP server using the name of the FTP site. Table C-3 explains how to add an FTP site.

Office adds the name of the FTP site to the FTP locations list in the Save As and Open dialog boxes. You can open and save files using this list. Table C-4 explains how to save to an FTP location.

Table C-1   Creating a Web Folder

1. Click File on the menu bar and then click Save As (or Open).
2. When the Save As dialog box (or Open dialog box) displays, click My Network Places (or Web Folders) on the Places Bar. Double-click Add Network Place (or Add Web Folder).
3. When the Add Network Place Wizard dialog box displays, click the Create a new Network Place option button and then click the Next button. Type the URL of the Web server in the Folder location text box, enter the folder name you want to call the Web folder in the Folder name text box, and then click the Next button. Click Empty Web and then click the Finish button.
4. When the Enter Network Password dialog box displays, type the user name and, if necessary, the password in the respective text boxes and then click the OK button.
5. Close the Save As or the Open dialog box.

Table C-2   Saving to a Web Folder

1. Click File on the menu bar and then click Save As.
2. When the Save As dialog box displays, type the Web page file name in the File name text box. Do not press the ENTER key.
3. Click My Network Places on the Places Bar.
4. Double-click the Web folder name in the Save in list.
5. If the Enter Network Password dialog box displays, type the user name and password in the respective text boxes and then click the OK button.
6. Click the Save button in the Save As dialog box.

Table C-3   Adding an FTP Location

1. Click File on the menu bar and then click Save As (or Open).
2. In the Save As dialog box, click the Save in box arrow and then click Add/Modify FTP Locations in the Save in list; or in the Open dialog box, click the Look in box arrow and then click Add/Modify FTP Locations in the Look in list.
3. When the Add/Modify FTP Locations dialog box displays, type the name of the FTP site in the Name of FTP site text box. If the site allows anonymous logon, click Anonymous in the Log on as area; if you have a user name for the site, click User in the Log on as area and then enter the user name. Enter the password in the Password text box. Click the OK button.
4. Close the Save As or the Open dialog box.

Table C-4   Saving to an FTP Location

1. Click File on the menu bar and then click Save As.
2. When the Save As dialog box displays, type the Web page file name in the File name text box. Do not press the ENTER key.
3. Click the Save in box arrow and then click FTP Locations.
4. Double-click the name of the FTP site to which you wish to save.
5. When the FTP Log On dialog box displays, enter your user name and password and then click the OK button.
6. Click the Save button in the Save As dialog box.

APPENDIX D
Resetting the PowerPoint Toolbars and Menus

PowerPoint customization capabilities allow you to create custom toolbars by adding and deleting buttons and to personalize menus based on their usage. Each time you start PowerPoint, the toolbars and menus display using the same settings as the last time you used it. This appendix shows you how to reset the Standard and Formatting toolbars and menus to their installation settings.

Steps **To Reset the Standard and Formatting Toolbars**

1 **Click the Toolbar Options button on the Standard toolbar and then point to Add or Remove Buttons on the Toolbar Options menu.**

The Toolbar Options menu and the Add or Remove Buttons submenu display (Figure D-1).

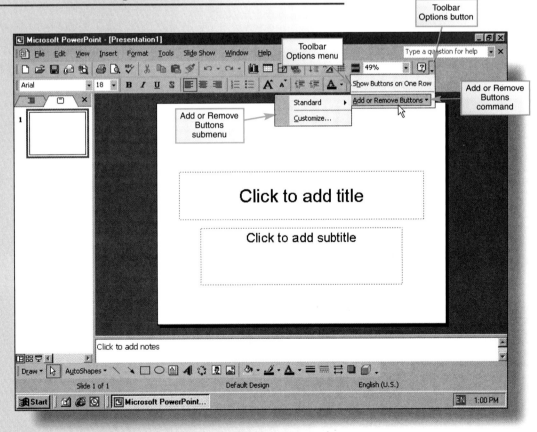

FIGURE D-1

2 **Point to Standard on the Add or Remove Buttons submenu. When the Standard submenu displays, scroll down and then point to Reset Toolbar.**

The Standard submenu displays indicating the buttons and boxes that display on the toolbar (Figure D-2). Clicking a button name with a check mark to the left of the name removes the check mark and then removes the button from the toolbar.

3 **Click Reset Toolbar.**

PowerPoint resets the Standard toolbar to its installation settings.

4 **Reset the Formatting toolbar by following Steps 1 through 3 and replacing any reference to the Standard toolbar with the Formatting toolbar.**

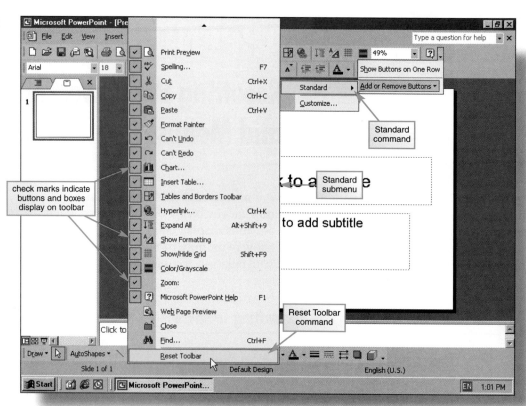

FIGURE D-2

1. On View menu point to Toolbars, click Customize on Toolbars submenu, click Toolbars tab, click toolbar name, click Reset button, click OK button, click Close button

2. Right-click toolbar, click Customize on shortcut menu, click Toolbars tab, click toolbar name, click Reset button, click OK button, click Close button

Steps **To Reset Menus**

1 **Click the Toolbar Options button on the Standard toolbar and then point to Add or Remove Buttons on the Toolbar Options menu. Point to Customize on the Add or Remove Buttons submenu.**

The Toolbar Options menu and the Add or Remove Buttons submenu display (Figure D-3).

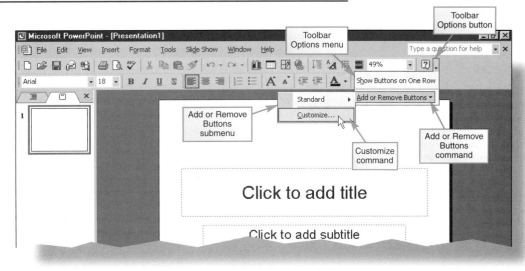

FIGURE D-3

2 **Click Customize. When the Customize dialog box displays, click the Options tab and then point to the Reset my usage data button.**

*The Customize dialog box displays (Figure D-4). The **Customize dialog box** contains three tabbed sheets used for customizing the PowerPoint toolbars and menus.*

3 **Click the Reset my usage data button. When the Microsoft PowerPoint dialog box displays, click the Yes button. Click the Close button in the Customize dialog box.**

PowerPoint resets the menus to the installation settings.

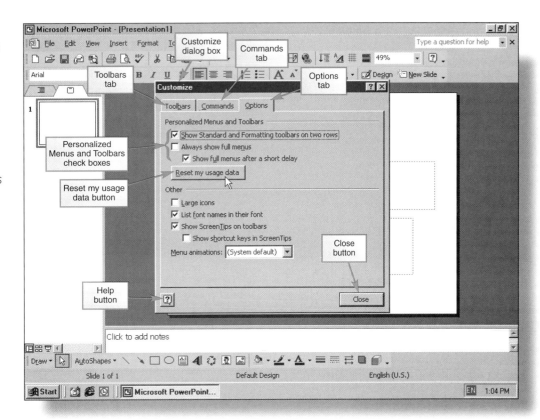

FIGURE D-4

Other **Ways**

1. On View menu point to Toolbars, click Customize on Toolbars submenu, click Options tab, click Reset my usage data button, click Yes button, click Close button

In the **Options sheet** in the Customize dialog box shown in Figure D-4 on the previous page, you can turn off toolbars displaying on two rows and turn off short menus by removing the check marks from the two top check boxes. Click the **Help button** in the lower-left corner of the Customize dialog box to display Help topics that will assist you in customizing toolbars and menus.

Using the **Commands sheet**, you can add buttons to toolbars and commands to menus. Recall that the menu bar at the top of the PowerPoint window is a special toolbar. To add buttons, click the Commands tab in the Customize dialog box. Click a category name in the Categories list and then drag the command name in the Commands list to a toolbar. To add commands to a menu, click a category name in the Categories list, drag the command name in the Commands list to the menu name on the menu bar, and then, when the menu displays, drag the command to the desired location in the menu list of commands.

In the **Toolbars sheet**, you can add new toolbars and reset existing toolbars. If you add commands to menus as described in the previous paragraph and want to reset the menus to their default settings, do the following: (1) Click View on the menu bar and then point to Toolbars; (2) click Customize on the Toolbars submenu; (3) click the Toolbars tab; (4) click Menu Bar in the Toolbars list; (5) click the Reset button; (6) click the OK button; and then (7) click the Close button.

APPENDIX E
Microsoft Office User Specialist
Certification Program

What Is MOUS Certification?

The Microsoft Office User Specialist (MOUS) Certification Program provides a framework for measuring your proficiency with the Microsoft Office XP applications, such as Word 2002, Excel 2002, Access 2002, PowerPoint 2002, Outlook 2002, and FrontPage 2002. The levels of certification are described in Table E-1.

Table E-1	Levels of MOUS Certification		
LEVEL	*DESCRIPTION*	*REQUIREMENTS*	*CREDENTIAL AWARDED*
Expert	Indicates that you have a comprehensive understanding of the advanced features in a specific Microsoft Office XP application	Pass any ONE of the Expert exams: Microsoft Word 2002 Expert, Microsoft Excel 2002 Expert, Microsoft Access 2002 Expert, Microsoft Outlook 2002 Expert, Microsoft FrontPage 2002 Expert	Candidates will be awarded one certificate for each of the Expert exams they have passed: Microsoft Office User Specialist: Microsoft Word 2002 Expert, Microsoft Office User Specialist: Microsoft Excel 2002 Expert, Microsoft Office User Specialist: Microsoft Access 2002 Expert, Microsoft Office User Specialist: Microsoft Outlook 2002 Expert, Microsoft Office User Specialist: Microsoft FrontPage 2002 Expert
Core	Indicates that you have a comprehensive understanding of the core features in a specific Microsoft Office 2002 application	Pass any ONE of the Core exams: Microsoft Word 2002 Core, Microsoft Excel 2002 Core, Microsoft Access 2002 Core, Microsoft Outlook 2002 Core, Microsoft FrontPage 2002 Core	Candidates will be awarded one certificate for each of the Core exams they have passed: Microsoft Office User Specialist: Microsoft Word 2002, Microsoft Office User Specialist: Microsoft Excel 2002, Microsoft Office User Specialist: Microsoft Access 2002, Microsoft Office User Specialist: Microsoft Outlook 2002, Microsoft Office User Specialist: Microsoft FrontPage 2002
Comprehensive	Indicates that you have a comprehensive understanding of the features in Microsoft PowerPoint 2002	Pass the Microsoft PowerPoint 2002 Comprehensive Exam	Candidates will be awarded one certificate for the Microsoft PowerPoint 2002 Comprehensive exam passed.

Why Should You Get Certified?

Being a Microsoft Office User Specialist provides a valuable industry credential — proof that you have the Office XP applications skills required by employers. By passing one or more MOUS certification exams, you demonstrate your proficiency in a given Office XP application to employers. With over 100 million copies of Office in use around the world, Microsoft is targeting Office XP certification to a wide variety of companies. These companies include temporary employment agencies that want to prove the expertise of their workers, large corporations looking for a way to measure the skill set of employees, and training companies and educational institutions seeking Microsoft Office XP teachers with appropriate credentials.

The MOUS Exams

You pay $50 to $100 each time you take an exam, whether you pass or fail. The fee varies among testing centers. The Expert exams, which you can take up to 60 minutes to complete, consists of between 40 and 60 tasks that you perform online. The tasks require you to use the application just as you would in doing your job. The Core exams contain fewer tasks, and you will have slightly less time to complete them. The tasks you will perform differ on the two types of exams.

How Can You Prepare for the MOUS Exams?

The Shelly Cashman Series® offers several Microsoft-approved textbooks that cover the required objectives on the MOUS exams. For a listing of the textbooks, visit the Shelly Cashman Series MOUS site at scsite.com/offxp/cert.htm and click the link Shelly Cashman Series Office XP Microsoft-Approved MOUS Textbooks (Figure E-1). After using any of the books listed in an instructor-led course, you will be prepared to take the MOUS exam indicated.

How to Find an Authorized Testing Center

You can locate a testing center by calling 1-800-933-4493 in North America or visiting the Shelly Cashman Series MOUS site at scsite.com/offxp/cert.htm and then clicking the link Locate an Authorized Testing Center Near You (Figure E-1). At this Web site, you can look for testing centers around the world.

Shelly Cashman Series MOUS Web Page

The Shelly Cashman Series MOUS Web page (Figure E-1) has more than fifteen Web sites you can visit to obtain additional information on the MOUS Certification Program. The Web page (scsite.com/offxp/cert.htm) includes links to general information on certification, choosing an application for certification, preparing for the certification exam, and taking and passing the certification exam.

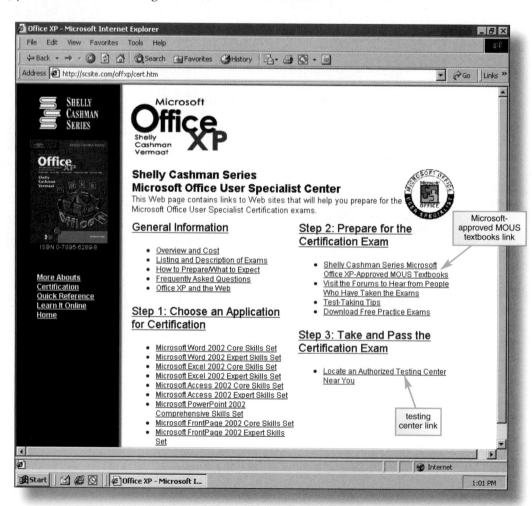

FIGURE E-1

Microsoft Powerpoint 2002 User Specialist Certification Comprehensive Map

This book has been approved by Microsoft as courseware for the Microsoft Office User Specialist (MOUS) program. After completing the first four projects and first two special features in this book, students will be prepared to take the Comprehensive-level Microsoft Office User Specialist Exam for Microsoft PowerPoint 2002. Table E-2 lists the Microsoft PowerPoint 2002 Comprehensive Exam skill sets, activities, page numbers where the activities are demonstrated, and page numbers where the activities can be practiced.

Table E-2 Microsoft PowerPoint 2002 MOUS Comprehensive Skill Sets, Activities, and Locations in Book			
SKILL SET	*ACTIVITY*	*ACTIVITY DEMONSTRATED IN BOOK*	*ACTIVITY EXERCISE IN BOOK*
I. Creating Presentations	A. Create presentations (manually and using automated tools)	PP 1.10-11, PP 1.19-44, PP 2.07-45, PP 3.05-52, PP 4.06-10	PP 1.68 (Apply Your Knowledge Steps 1-5), PP 1.69-71 (In the Lab 1 Steps 1-3), PP 1.72-73 (In the Lab 2 Steps 1-3), PP 1.74-75 (In the Lab 3 Steps 1-4), PP 1.76-79 (Cases & Places 1-7), PP 2.56 (Apply Your Knowledge Step 1), PP 2.57-58 (In the Lab 1 Steps 1-3), PP 2.59-60 (In the Lab 2 Steps 1-3), PP 2.61-62 (In the Lab 3 Step 1), PP 2.64-66 (Cases & Places 1-7), PP 3.57 (Apply Your Knowledge Step 1), PP 3.58 (In the Lab 1 Steps 1-7), PP 3.59-60 (In the Lab 2 Steps 1-5), PP 3.60 (In the Lab 3 Steps 1-7), PP 3.62-63 (Cases & Places 1-7), PP 4.74-75 (In the Lab 1 Steps 1-9), PP 4.76-77 (In the Lab 2 Steps 1-5), PP 4.78-79 (In the Lab 3 Step 1), PP 4.80-82 (Cases & Places 1-7), PPW 2.39 (In the Lab 3)
	B. Add slides to and delete slides from presentations	PP 1.32-33, PP 1.37, PP 1.41, PP 2.12, PP 2.14-15, PP 2.17, PP 3.07-11, PP 4.31	PP 1.69-71 (In the Lab 1 Steps 1-3), PP 1.72-73 (In the Lab 2 Steps 1-3), PP 1.74-75 (In the Lab 3 Steps 1-3), PP 1.76-79 (Cases & Places 1-7), PP 2.57-58 (In the Lab 1 Steps 1-3), PP 2.59-60 (In the Lab 2 Step 1), PP 2.61-62 (In the Lab 3 Step 1), PP 2.64-66 (Cases & Places 1-7), PP 3.57 (Apply Your Knowledge Step 2), PP 3.59 (In the Lab 2 Step 1), PP 3.60 (In the Lab 3 Steps 1, 3), PP 3.62-63 (Cases & Places 1-7), PP 4.74-75 (In the Lab 1 Steps 1, 7), PP 4.76 (In the Lab 2 Steps 1, 3-5), PP 4.78 (In the Lab 3 Step 4)
	C. Modify headers and footers in the Slide Master	PP 4.09, PP 4.13-14	PP 4.72-73 (Apply Your Knowledge Step 8), PP 4.76-77 (In the Lab 2 Step 8), PP 4.78-79 (In the Lab 3 Step 1)
II. Inserting and Modifying Text	A. Import text from Word	PP 3.07-09	PP 3.57, PP 3.59 (In the Lab 2 Step 1), PP 3.60-61 (In the Lab 3 Step 1), PP 3.62 (Cases & Places 3)
	B. Insert, format, and modify text	PP 1.22-24, PP 1.26-28, PP 1.34-43, PP 1.58, PP 2.10-11, PP 2.13-17, PP 3.33-34, PP 4.26, PP 4.33, PP 4.39, PP 4.44, PP 4.48, PP 4.51-53	PP 1.68 (Apply Your Knowledge Steps 2-5), PP 1.69-71 (In the Lab 1 Steps 2-3), PP 1.72-73 (In the Lab 2 Steps 2-3), PP 1.74-75 (In the Lab 3 Steps 2-3), PP 1.76-79 (Cases & Places 1-7), PP 2.56 (Apply Your Knowledge Step 2), PP 2.57-59 (In the Lab 1 Steps 2-3), PP 2.59-60 (In the Lab 2 Steps 1-2), PP 2.61-62 (In the Lab 3 Step 1), PP 2.64-66 (Cases & Places 1-7), PP 3.58 (In the Lab 1 Step 2), PP 3.59-60 (In the Lab 2 Steps 2-5), PP 3.60-61 (In the Lab 3 Steps 3, 7), PP 3.62-63 (Cases & Places 1-7), PP 4.72-73 (Apply Your Knowledge Step 3), PP 4.74-75 (In the Lab 1 Steps 2-3, 8), PP 4.76-77 (In the Lab 2 Steps 2-5), PP 4.78-79 (In the Lab 3 Steps 1-2, 5-7), PP 4.80-82 (Cases & Places 1-7)
III. Inserting and Modifying Visual Elements	A. Add tables, charts, clip art, and bitmap images to slides	PP 2.24-30, PP 3.14, PP 3.30-49, PP 4.32-37	PP 2.56-57 (Apply Your Knowledge Steps 2-5), PP 2.57-59 (In the Lab 1 Steps 2, 4-6), PP 2.59-60 (In the Lab 2 Steps 2-5), PP 2.61-63 (In the Lab 3 Steps 2-7), PP 2.64-66 (Cases & Places 1-7), PP 3.57 (Apply Your Knowledge Steps 3-4), PP 3.58 (In the Lab 1 Steps 3, 5), PP 3.59-60 (In the Lab 2 Step 5), PP 3.60-61 (In the Lab 3 Steps 5, 7-8), PP 3.62-63 (Cases & Places 1-6), PP 4.74-75 (In the Lab 1 Step 9), PP 4.80-82 (Cases & Places 1-7)

Table E-2 Microsoft PowerPoint 2002 MOUS Comprehensive Skill Sets, Activities, and Locations in Book *(continued)*

SKILL SET	ACTIVITY	ACTIVITY DEMONSTRATED IN BOOK	ACTIVITY EXERCISE IN BOOK
	B. Customize slide backgrounds	PP 4.15-18	PP 4.74 (In the Lab 1 Step 1), PP 4.76-77 (In the Lab 2 Step 1), PP 4.82 (Cases & Places 5, 7)
	C. Add OfficeArt elements to slides	PP 4.18-25	PP 4.72 (Apply Your Knowledge Step 4), PP 4.74-75 (In the Lab 2 Step 6), PP 4.76-77 (In the Lab 2 Step 6), PP 4.78-79 (In the Lab 3 Step 3), PP 4.80-82 (Cases & Places 1-3)
	D. Apply custom formats to tables	PP 3.33-38	PP 3.59-60 (In the Lab 2 Step 5), PP 3.60-61 (In the Lab 3 Step 7), PP 3.62-63 (Cases & Places 2, 4, 6)
IV. Modifying Presentation Formats	A. Apply formats to presentations	PP 1.19-21, PP 2.06-07, PP 2.21-23, PP 3.49-51, PP 4.33-34, PP 4.44-45, PP 4.61-64	PP 1.68 (Apply Your Knowledge Step 1), PP 1.69-71 (In the Lab 1 Step 1), PP 1.72-74 (In the Lab 2 Step 1), PP 1.74-75 (In the Lab 3 Step 1), PP 1.76-79 (Cases & Places 1-7), PP 2.56 (Apply Your Knowledge Step 1), PP 2.57-58 (In the Lab 1 Step 1), PP 2.59-60 (In the Lab 2 Step 1), PP 2.61-63 (In the Lab 3 Step 1), PP 2.64-66 (Cases & Places 1-7), PP 3.57 (Apply Your Knowledge Step 1), PP 3.58 (In the Lab 1 Step 1), PP 3.59 (In the Lab 2 Step 2), PP 3.60-61 (In the Lab 3 Steps 2-3), PP 4.74-75 (In the Lab 1 Steps 3-5, 7-8), PP 4.76-77 (In the Lab 2 Steps 1, 3-5), PP 4.78-79 (In the Lab 3 Steps 6, 9)
	B. Apply animation schemes	PP 2.39-41, PP 3.52-53	PP 2.57 (Apply Your Knowledge Step 6), PP 2.59 (In the Lab 1 Step 8), PP 2.61 (In the Lab 2 Step 7), PP 2.62 (In the Lab 3 Step 9), PP 2.64-66 (Cases & Places 1-7), PP 3.57 (Apply Your Knowledge Step 6), PP 3.58 (In the Lab 1 Step 8), PP 3.59-60 (In the Lab 2 Step 6), PP 3.60 (In the Lab 3 Step 9), PP 3.62-63 (Cases & Places 2-5), PP 4.76-77 (In the Lab 2 Step 7)
	C. Apply slide transitions	PP 4.56-58	PP 4.72 (Apply Your Knowledge Step 6), PP 4.74-75 (In the Lab 1 Step 10), PP 4.76-77 (In the Lab 2 Step 7), PP 4.78-79 (In the Lab 3 Step 10), PP 4.80-82 (Cases & Places 2-5, 7)
	D. Customize slide formats	PP 1.26-28, PP 2.44-45, PP 4.61-64	PP 1.68 (Apply Your Knowledge Steps 2-5), PP 1.69-71 (In the Lab 1 Step 2), PP 1.72-73 (In the Lab 2 Steps 2-3), PP 1.74 (In the Lab 3 Steps 2-3), PP 1.76-79 (Cases & Places 1-7), PP 2.56-57 (Apply Your Knowledge Steps 2-5), PP 2.57-59 (In the Lab 1 Steps 2, 4-6), PP 2.59-61 (In the Lab 2 Steps 2-4, 8), PP 2.63 (In the Lab 3 Steps 2-7), PP 2.64-66 (Cases & Places 1-7), PP 3.59 (In the Lab 2 Step 2), PP 3.60-61 (In the Lab 3 Step 3), PP 4.72 (Apply Your Knowledge Step 5), PP 4.74-75 (In the Lab 2 Step 7), PP 4.78 (In the Lab 3 Step 9)
	E. Customize slide templates	PP 4.10-18	PP 4.74 (In the Lab Step 1), PP 4.76-77 (In the Lab 2 Steps 1-4), PP 4.78 (In the Lab 3 Step 6)
	F. Manage a Slide Master	PP 3.21-29, PP 4.13-14	PP 3.57 (Apply Your Knowledge Step 5), PP 3.59 (In the Lab 2 Step 3), PP 3.60 (In the Lab 3 Step 4), PP 4.76 (In the Lab 2 Step 5)
	G. Rehearse timing	PP 4.58-61	PP 4.78-79 (In the Lab 3 Step 11), PP 4.82 (Cases & Places 7)
	H. Rearrange slides	PP 3.51-52	PP 3.59-60 (In the Lab 2 Step 4), PP 3.60-61 (In the Lab 3 Step 6)
	I. Modify slide layout	PP 1.19-21, PP 2.06-07, PP 2.2-23, PP 3.11, PP 3.14, PP 4.18-20, PP 4.33-34, PP 4.38-39, PP 4.44-45	PP 1.68 (Apply Your Knowledge Step 1), PP 1.71 (In the Lab 1 Step 1), PP 1.73 (In the Lab 2 Step 1), PP 1.74 (In the Lab 3 Step 1), PP 1.76-79 (Cases & Places 1-7), PP 2.56 (Apply Your Knowledge Step 1), PP 2.58 (In the Lab 1 Step 1), PP 2.59 (In the Lab 2 Step 1), PP 2.61-62 (In the Lab 3 Step 1), PP 2.64-66 (Cases & Places 1-7), PP 3.57 (Apply Your Knowledge Step 1), PP 3.58 (In the Lab 1 Step 1), PP 3.59 (In the Lab 2 Step 2), PP 3.60-61 (In the Lab 3 Step 3), PP 4.74-75 (In the Lab 1 Steps 4-5), PP 4.76 (In the Lab 2 Step 5)
	J. Add links to a presentation	PP 4.49-51	PP 4.78-79 (In the Lab 3 Step 8), PP 4.80-82 (Cases & Places 1, 5, 7)

Table E-2   Microsoft PowerPoint 2002 MOUS Comprehensive Skill Sets, Activities, and Locations in Book

SKILL SET	ACTIVITY	ACTIVITY DEMONSTRATED IN BOOK	ACTIVITY EXERCISE IN BOOK
V. Printing Presentations	A. Preview and print slides, outlines, handouts, and speaker notes	PP 1.60-61, PP 2.47-51, PP 3.53, PP 4.65-67, PPW 2.09-14	PP 1.68 (Apply Your Knowledge Steps 7-9), PP 1.71 (In the Lab 1 Steps 6-7), PP 1.74 (In the Lab 2 Step 6), PP 1.74 (In the Lab 3 Step 6), PP 1.76-79 (Cases & Places 1-7), PP 2.56-57 (Apply Your Knowledge Step 8), PP 2.57-59 (In the Lab 1 Step 10), PP 2.59-61 (In the Lab 2 Step 10), PP 2.61-63 (In the Lab 3 Step 12), PP 2.64-66 (Cases & Places 1-7), PP 3.57 (Apply Your Knowledge Step 8), PP 3.58 (In the Lab 1 Step 10), PP 3.59-60 (In the Lab 2 Step 8), PP 3.60 (In the Lab 3 Step 10), PP 4.72 (Apply Your Knowledge Step 11), PP 4.74-75 (In the Lab 1 Step 14), PP 4.76 (In the Lab 2 Step 11), PP 4.78-79 (In the Lab 3 Step 14), PP 4.82 (Cases & Places 5), PPW 2.33 (In the Lab 1 Step 2), PPW 2.36 (In the Lab 2 Step 2), PPW 2.39 (In the Lab 3 Step 4)
VI. Working with Data from Other Sources	A. Import Excel charts to slides	PP 4.37-42	PP 4.78-79 (In the Lab 3 Step 6)
	B. Add sound and video to slides	PP 4.27-29	PP 4.72 (Apply Your Knowledge Step 7), PP 4.76 (In the Lab 2 Step 5), PP 4.78 (In the Lab 3 Step 6), PP 4.80-81 (Cases & Places 2-3)
	C. Insert Word tables on slides	PP 4.44-46	PP 4.76-77 (In the Lab 2 Step 4), PP 4.81-82 (Cases & Places 3, 5)
	D. Export a presentation as an outline	PP 4.67-68	PP 4.76 (In the Lab 2 Step 9), PP 4.78-79 (In the Lab 3 Step 14)
VII. Managing and Delivering Presentations	A. Set up slide shows	PP 4.58-61	PP 4.78-79 (In the Lab 3 Step 11), PP 4.82 (Cases & Places 7)
	B. Deliver presentations	PP 1.47-51, PP 2.45-47, PP 4.58-61, PP 4.68-69	PP 1.72-74 (In the Lab 2 Step 5), PP 1.74 (In the Lab 3 Step 4), PP 2.62 (In the Lab 3 Step 11), PP 4.74-75 (In the Lab 1 Step 13), PP 4.76 (In the Lab 2 Step 10), PP 4.78-79 (In the Lab 3 Steps 11, 13), PP 4.82 (Cases & Places 7)
	C. Manage files and folders for presentations	PP 4.29-30	PP 4.72 (Apply Your Knowledge Step 1), PP 4.76 (In the Lab 2 Step 9)
	D. Work with embedded fonts	PP 4.53-55, PPW 2.29	PP 4.72 (Apply Your Knowledge Step 9), PP 4.74-75 (In the Lab 1 Step 12), PP 4.76 (In the Lab 2 Step 9), PP 4.78-79 (In the Lab 3 Step 14), PPW 2.36 (In the Lab 2 Step 4)
	E. Publish presentations to the Web	PPW 1.03-05, Appendix C	PPW 1.12 (In the Lab 1 Steps 2-3, 6), PPW 1.12-13 (In the Lab 2 Steps 2-3, 6)
	F. Use Pack and Go	PPW 2.27-31	PPW 2.33 (In the Lab Step 9), PPW 2.36 (In the Lab 1 Step 4)
VIII. Workgroup Collaboration	A. Set up a review cycle	PPW 2.02-09	PPW 2.39 (In the Lab 3 Step 2)
	B. Review presentation comments	PPW 2.14-23	PPW 2.33-36 (In the Lab 1 Steps 2-6), PPW 2.36-39 (In the Lab 2 Step 2), PPW 2.39 (In the Lab 3 Steps 3-4)
	C. Schedule and deliver presentation broadcasts	PPW 2.24-27	PPW 2.33 (In the Lab 1 Step 7), PPW 2.39 (In the Lab 3 Step 1)
	D. Publish presentations to the Web	PPW 1.03-05, Appendix C	PPW 1.12 (In the Lab 1 Steps 2-3, 6), PPW 1.12-13 (In the Lab 2 Steps 2-3, 6)

Index

Microsoft
POWERPOINT 2002
Quick Reference Summary

In Microsoft PowerPoint 2002, you can accomplish a task in a number of ways. The following table provides a quick reference to each task presented in this textbook. The first column identifies the task. The second column indicates the page number on which the task is discussed in the book. The subsequent four columns list the different ways the task in column one can be carried out. You can invoke the commands listed in the MOUSE, MENU BAR, and SHORTCUT MENU columns using Voice commands.

Microsoft PowerPoint 2002 Quick Reference Summary

TASK	PAGE NUMBER	MOUSE	MENU BAR	SHORTCUT MENU	KEYBOARD SHORTCUT
Action Button, Add	PP 6.18	AutoShapes button on Drawing toolbar | Action Buttons	Slide Show | Action Buttons		ALT+D | I
Action Button, Caption (Text Box)	PP 6.31	Text Box button on Drawing toolbar	Insert | Text Box		ALT+I | X
Action Button, Fill Color	PP 6.26	Fill Color button on Drawing toolbar	Format | AutoShape | Colors and Lines tab	Format AutoShape | Colors and	ALT+O | O | Colors and Lines tab
Action Button, Lines	PP 6.30	Line Style button on Drawing toolbar	Format | AutoShape | Colors and Lines tab Lines tab	Format | AutoShape | Colors and Lines tab	ALT+O | O | Colors and Lines tab
Action Button, Scale	PP 6.22	Drag sizing handle	Format | AutoShape | Size tab	Format AutoShape | Size tab	ALT+O | O | Size tab
Action Button, Shadow	PP 6.28	Shadow Style button on Drawing toolbar			
Animate Text	PP 2.40		Slide Show | Custom Animation | Add Effect button		ALT+D | M
Animation Scheme, Add to Selected Slides	PP 3.52		Slide Show | Animation Schemes	Slide Design | Animation Schemes	ALT+D | C
AutoContent Wizard	PP 4.07		View | Task Pane | From AutoContent Wizard		
AutoShape, Add Text	PP 6.46		Type desired text | Format | AutoShape | Text Box tab | Resize AutoShape to fit text	Type desired text | Format AutoShape | Text Box tab | Resize AutoShape to fit text	Type desired text | ALT+O | O | CTRL+TAB | TAB | SPACEBAR
AutoShape, Apply Animation Effect	PP 6.48, 6.49		Slide Show | Custom Animation | Add Effect button	Custom Animation | Add Effect button	ALT+D | M
AutoShape, Insert	PP 6.45	AutoShapes button on Drawing toolbar			ALT+U
Bullet Character, Change	PP 3.24		Format | Bullets and Numbering | Bulleted tab | Customize	Bullets and Numbering | Bulleted tab | Customize	ALT+O | B | ALT+U
Bullet Color, Change	PP 3.28		Format | Bullets and Numbering | Bulleted tab | Color box	Bullets and Numbering | Bulleted tab | Color box	
Chart, Insert	PP 4.35	Insert Chart button in content placeholder or on Standard toolbar	Insert | Chart		ALT+I | H
Chart, Insert Excel	PP 4.40		Insert | Object | Create from file		ALT+I | O | ALT+F
Chart, Scale	PP 4.43		Format | Object	Format Object	ALT+O | O

Microsoft PowerPoint 2002 Quick Reference Summary *(continued)*

TASK	PAGE NUMBER	MOUSE	MENU BAR	SHORTCUT MENU	KEYBOARD SHORTCUT
Check Spelling	PP 1.56	Spelling button on Standard toolbar	Tools | Spelling		F7
Clip Art, Add Animation Effects	PP 2.42		Slide Show | Custom Animation		ALT+D | M
Clip Art, Change Size	PP 2.34	Format Picture button on Picture toolbar | Size tab	Format | Picture | Size tab	Format Picture | Size tab	ALT+O | I | Size tab
Clip Art, Insert	PP 2.25	Insert Clip Art button on Drawing toolbar	Insert | Picture | Clip Art		ALT+I | P | C
Clip Art, Ungroup	PP 3.17	Draw button on Drawing toolbar | Ungroup		Grouping | Ungroup	SHIFT+F10 | G | U
Clip Art, Move	PP 2.33	Drag			
Color Scheme, Change	PP 4.11	Slide Design button on Formatting toolbar | Color Schemes	Format | Slide Design | Color Schemes	ALT+O | D | DOWN ARROW	
Comment, Accept	PPW 2.15	Apply button on Reviewing toolbar			
Comment, Insert	PPW 2.05	Insert Comment button on Reviewing toolbar	Insert | Comment		ALT+I | M
Comment, Reject	PPW 2.15	Delete Comment button on Reviewing toolbar			
Comment, Review	PPW 2.15	Next Item button on Reviewing toolbar			
Control, Add to Form	PP 5.34	Click Control in Toolbox			
Custom Background, Insert Picture	PP 4.15		Format | Background	Background	ALT+O | K
Delete an Object	PP 3.19	Select object | Cut button on Standard toolbar	Edit | Clear or Edit | Cut	Cut	ALT+E | A or DELETE or CTRL+X
Delete Slide	PP 3.10	Click slide icon | Cut button on Standard toolbar	Edit | Delete Slide	Delete Slide	ALT+E | D
Delete Text	PP 1.58	Cut button on Standard toolbar	Edit | Cut	Cut	CTRL+X or BACKSPACE or DELETE
Demote a Paragraph on Outline tab	PP 2.13	Demote button on Outlining toolbar	TAB or ALT+SHIFT+RIGHT ARROW		
Design Template	PP 1.19	Slide Design button on Formatting toolbar	Format | Slide Design	Slide Design	ALT+O | D
Design Template, Apply to Single Slide	PP 3.50	Slide Design button on Formatting toolbar | Arrow button on template | Apply to Selected Slides	Format | Slide Design | Arrow button on template | Apply to Selected Slides	Slide Design | Arrow button on template | Apply to Selected Slides	ALT+O | D Arrow button on template | S
Diagram, AutoFormat	PP 6.43	AutoFormat button on Diagram toolbar			
Diagram, Change Size	PP 6.39		Format | Diagram | Size tab	Format Diagram | Size tab	ALT+O | D | D | Size tab
Diagram, Insert	PP 6.36	Insert Diagram or Organization Chart button on Drawing toolbar	Insert | Diagram		ALT+I | G
Display a Presentation in Black and White	PP 1.58	Color/Grayscale button on Standard toolbar	View | Color/Grayscale | Pure Black and White		ALT+V | C | U
Edit Web Page through Browser	PPW 1.09	Edit button on Internet Explorer Standard Buttons toolbar	File on browser menu bar | Edit with Microsoft PowerPoint in browser window		ALT+F | D in browser window
E-Mail from PowerPoint	PP 2.52	E-mail button on Standard toolbar	File | Send To | Mail Recipient		ALT+F | D | A
Folder, Create	PP 4.30	Save button on Standard toolbar | Create New Folder button on Save As dialog box toolbar			

Microsoft PowerPoint 2002 Quick Reference Summary

TASK	PAGE NUMBER	MOUSE	MENU BAR	SHORTCUT MENU	KEYBOARD SHORTCUT
Font	PP 1.25 PP 4.52	Font box arrow on Formatting toolbar	Format | Font | Font tab	Font | Font tab	ALT+O | F; CTRL+SHIFT+F or ALT+O | F
Font Color	PP 1.25	Font Color button arrow on Formatting toolbar, desired color	Format | Font	Font | Color	ALT+O | F | ALT+C | DOWN ARROW
Font, Embed	PP 4.54		File | Save As | Tools | Save Options | Save tab | Embed TrueType fonts		ALT+F | A | ALT+L | S | E
Font Size, Decrease	PP 1.25	Decrease Font Size button on Formatting toolbar	Format | Font	Font | Size	CTRL+SHIFT+LEFT CARET (<)
Font Size, Increase	PP 1.27	Increase Font Size button on Formatting toolbar	Format | Font	Font | Size	CTRL+SHIFT+RIGHT CARET (>)
Footer, Modify on Title Master	PP 4.13	Normal View button + SHIFT | Footer Area | type text | Close Master View button on Slide Master View toolbar	View | Master | Slide Master		ALT+V | M | S | type text | ALT+C
Guides, Display	PP 6.23		View | Grid and Guides | Display drawing guides on screen	Grid and Guides | Display drawing guides on screen	ALT+V | I | I | I
Guides, Hide	PP 6.26		View | Grid and Guides | Display drawing guides on screen	Grid and Guides | Display drawing guides on screens	ALT+V | I | I | I
Header and Footer, Add to Outline Page	PP 2.37		View | Header and Footer | Notes and Handouts tab		ALT+V | H | Notes and Handouts tab
Help	PP 1.62 and Appendix A	Microsoft PowerPoint Help button on Standard toolbar	Help | Microsoft PowerPoint Help		F1
Hyperlink, Add	PP 4.49	Hyperlink button on Standard toolbar	Insert | Hyperlink		ALT+I | I or CTRL+K
Insert Slide from Another Presentation	PP 6.12		Insert | Slides from Files | Find Presentation tab | Browse | Open | Insert | Close		ALT+I | F | ALT+B | select desired file | ALT+O | select desired slide | I | ESC
Italicize	PP 1.26	Italic button on Formatting toolbar	Format | Font | Font style	Font | Font style	CTRL+I
Language Bar	PP 1.18	Language Indicator button in tray	Tools | Speech | Speech Recognition		ALT+T | H | H
Macro, Create by Using Macro Recorder	PP 5.19	Record Macro button on Visual Basic toolbar	Tools | Macro | Record New Macro		ALT+T | M | R
Macro, View VBA Code	PP 5.26	Visual Basic Editor button on Visual Basic toolbar	Tools | Macro | Macros | Edit		ALT+T | M | V
Menu, Customize by Adding a Command	PP 5.22	More Buttons button on Standard toolbar | Add or Remove Buttons | Customize | Commands tab	Tools | Customize | Commands tab	Customize | Commands tab	
Merge Slide Shows	PPW 2.09		Tools | Compare and Merge Presentations		ALT+T | P
Microsoft Design Gallery Web Site, Connect to	PPW 3.XX	Insert Clip Art button on Drawing toolbar | Clips Online in Insert ClipArt task pane	Insert | Picture | Clip Art | Clips Online in Insert ClipArt task pane		ALT + I | P | C | TAB
Microsoft Template Gallery Web Site, Connect to	PPW 3.XX		File | New | Templates on Microsoft.com		ALT+F | N | TAB
Move a Paragraph Down	PP 2.09	Move Down button on Outlining toolbar			ALT+SHIFT+DOWN ARROW
Move a Paragraph Up	PP 2.09	Move Up button on Outlining toolbar			ALT+SHIFT+UP ARROW
New Slide	PP 1.32	New Slide button on Formatting toolbar	Insert | New Slide		CTRL+M

Microsoft PowerPoint 2002 Quick Reference Summary *(continued)*

TASK	PAGE NUMBER	MOUSE	MENU BAR	SHORTCUT MENU	KEYBOARD SHORTCUT
Next Slide	PP 1.46	Next Slide button on vertical scroll bar			PAGE DOWN
Normal View	PP 2.19	Normal View button at lower-left PowerPoint window	View | Normal		ALT+V | N
Online Broadcast, Set Up and Schedule	PPW 2.24		Slide Show | Online Broadcast | Schedule a Live Broadcast		ALT+D | O | S
Open an Outline as a Presentation	PP 3.08		Insert | Slides from Outline		ALT+I | L
Open Presentation	PP 1.53	Open button on Standard toolbar	File | Open		CTRL+O
Open Presentation and Print by Executing Macro	PP 5.25	Run Macro button on Visual Basic toolbar	File | Open | double-click file name | Enable Macros | File | click macro command		ALT+F8, double-click macro name
Organization Chart, Add Subordinate and Coworker Shapes	PP 3.43	Insert Shape button on Organization Chart toolbar			ALT+SHIFT+N
Organization Chart Design Scheme, Change	PP 3.48	Autoformat button on Organization Chart toolbar			ALT+SHIFT+C | RIGHT ARROW
Organization Chart Diagram, Display	PP 3.39	Insert Diagram or Organization Chart button on Drawing toolbar	Insert | Picture | Organization Chart		ALT+I | P | O
Organization Chart Shape, Change	PP 3.46	Layout button on Organization Chart toolbar			ALT+SHIFT+L
Pack and Go Wizard	PPW 2.27		File | Pack and Go		ALT+F | K
Paragraph Indent, Decrease	PP 1.40	Decrease Indent button on Formatting toolbar			SHIFT+TAB or ALT+SHIFT+ LEFT ARROW
Paragraph Indent, Increase	PP 1.34	Increase Indent button on Formatting toolbar			TAB or ALT+SHIFT+RIGHT ARROW
Previous Slide	PP 1.46	Previous Slide button on vertical scroll bar			PAGE UP
Print a Presentation	PP 1.61	Print button on Standard toolbar	File | Print		CTRL+P
Print Comments	PPW 2.09		File | Print | Include comment pages		CTRL+P | TAB
Print Outline	PP 2.48		File | Print | Print what box arrow | Outline View		CTRL+P | TAB | TAB | DOWN ARROW | Outline View
Print Speaker Notes	PP 4.66		File | Print | Print what box arrow | Notes Pages		CTRL+P | ALT+W | DOWN ARROW
Promote a Paragraph on Outline tab	PP 2.14	Promote button on Outlining toolbar			SHIFT+TAB or ALT+SHIFT+LEFT ARROW
Quit PowerPoint	PP 1.52	Close button on title bar or double-click control icon on title bar	File | Exit		ALT+F4 or CTRL+Q
Rearrange Slides	PP 3.51	Drag slide thumbnail or slide icon to new location			
Redo Action	PP 1.23	Redo button on Standard toolbar	Edit | Redo		CTRL+Y or ALT+E | R
Regroup Objects	PP 3.20	Drag through objects | Draw button on Drawing toolbar | Regroup		Grouping | Regroup	SHIFT+F10 | G | O
Save a Presentation	PP 1.29	Save button on Standard toolbar	File | Save		CTRL+S
Save as Web Page	PPW 1.03		File | Save as Web Page		ALT+F | G
Save in Rich Text Format	PP 4.68		File | Save As | Save as type box arrow | Outline/RTF		ALT+F | A | ALT+T, DOWN ARROW
Self-Running Presentation, Create	PP 6.52		Slide Show | Set Up Show | Browsed at a kiosk (full screen)		ALT+D | S | ALT+K

Microsoft PowerPoint 2002 Quick Reference Summary

TASK	PAGE NUMBER	MOUSE	MENU BAR	SHORTCUT MENU	KEYBOARD SHORTCUT
Send Presentation for Review	PPW 2.08		File | Sent To | Mail Recipient (for Review)		ALT+F | D | C
Slide Background, Format	PP 4.62		Format | Background		ALT+O | K
Slide Layout	PP 2.22		Format | Slide Layout	Slide Layout	ALT+O | L
Slide Master, Display	PP 3.22		View | Master | Slide Master		SHIFT | Normal View
Slide Show Timings, Set Manually	PP 6.55		Slide Show | Slide Transition | Automatically after | Automatically after box up arrow	Slide Transition | Automatically after | Automatically after box up arrow	ALT+D | T | type desired time
Slide Show View	PP 1.48	Slide Show button at lower-left PowerPoint window	View | Slide Show		F5 or ALT+V | W
Slide Sorter View	PP 2.18	Slide Sorter View button at lower-left PowerPoint window	View | Slide Sorter		ALT+V | D
Slide Transition, Add	PP 4.57		Slide Show | Slide Transition	Slide Transition	ALT+D | T
Sound Effect, Add	PP 4.28		Insert | Movies and Sounds | Sound from File		ALT+I | V | N
Table, Format	PP 3.36	Table button on Tables and Borders toolbar | Select Table	Format | Table	Borders and Fill	ALT+O | T
Table, Format Cell	PP 3.33	Click cell			
Table, Insert	PP 3.30 PP 4.45	Insert Table button on Standard toolbar	Insert | Table Insert | Object | Create from file		ALT+I | B, ALT+I | O | ALT+F
Table, Scale	PP 4.46		Format | Object	Format Object	ALT+O | O
Task Pane	PP 1.11		View | Task Pane		ALT+V | K
Timings, Rehearse	PP 4.59		Slide Show | Rehearse Timings		ALT+D | R
Title Text Placeholder, Delete	PP 4.19	Cut button on Standard toolbar	Edit | Cut		CTRL+X or DELETE
Toolbar, Add Button	PP 5.12	Toolbar Options button on toolbar | Add or Remove Buttons | Customize | Commands tab	Tools | Customize | Commands tab	Customize | Commands tab	
Toolbar, Create	PP 5.10	More Buttons button on Standard toolbar | Add or Remove Buttons | Customize | Toolbars tab | New button	Tools | Customize | Toolbars tab | New button	Customize | Toolbars tab | New button	
Toolbar, Display Reviewing	PPW 2.05		View | Toolbars | Reviewing	Any toolbar | Reviewing	ALT+V | T
Toolbar, Reset	Appendix D	Toolbar Options button on toolbar, Add or Remove Buttons, Customize, Toolbars tab		Customize | Toolbars tab	ALT+V | T | C | B
Toolbar, Show Entire	PP 1.12	Double-click move handle			
Undo Action	PP 1.23	Undo button on Standard toolbar	Edit | Undo		CTRL+Z or ALT+E | U
Visual Basic Editor, Close and Return to Microsoft PowerPoint	PP 5.52	Save button on Standard toolbar | Close button on Visual Basic Editor title bar	File | Return to Microsoft PowerPoint		ALT+Q
Visual Basic IDE, Open	PP 5.29		Tools | Macro | Visual Basic Editor		ALT+F11
Web Session, Close	PPW 3.XX			Microsoft Internet Explorer button on taskbar | Close | Yes	
WordArt, Height and Width	PP 4.24	Format WordArt button on WordArt toolbar | Size tab	Format | WordArt | Size tab	Format WordArt | Size tab	ALT+O | O | ALT+E
WordArt, Style	PP 4.21	Insert WordArt button on Drawing toolbar	Insert | Picture | WordArt		ALT+I | P | W
Zoom Percentage, Increase	PP 1.45	Zoom Box arrow on Standard toolbar	View | Zoom		ALT+V | Z